Visit us at

www.syngress.com

Syngress is committed to publishing high-quality books for IT Professionals and delivering those books in media and formats that fit the demands of our customers. We are also committed to extending the utility of the book you purchase via additional materials available from our Web site.

SOLUTIONS WEB SITE

To register your book, visit www.syngress.com/solutions. Once registered, you can access our solutions@syngress.com Web pages. There you may find an assortment of valueadded features such as free e-books related to the topic of this book, URLs of related Web sites, FAQs from the book, corrections, and any updates from the author(s).

ULTIMATE CDs

Our Ultimate CD product line offers our readers budget-conscious compilations of some of our best-selling backlist titles in Adobe PDF form. These CDs are the perfect way to extend your reference library on key topics pertaining to your area of expertise, including Cisco Engineering, Microsoft Windows System Administration, CyberCrime Investigation, Open Source Security, and Firewall Configuration, to name a few.

DOWNLOADABLE E-BOOKS

For readers who can't wait for hard copy, we offer most of our titles in downloadable Adobe PDF form. These e-books are often available weeks before hard copies, and are priced affordably.

SYNGRESS OUTLET

Our outlet store at syngress.com features overstocked, out-of-print, or slightly hurt books at significant savings.

SITE LICENSING

Syngress has a well-established program for site licensing our e-books onto servers in corporations, educational institutions, and large organizations. Contact us at sales@syngress.com for more information.

CUSTOM PUBLISHING

Many organizations welcome the ability to combine parts of multiple Syngress books, as well as their own content, into a single volume for their own internal use. Contact us at sales@syngress.com for more information.use. Contact us at sales@syngress.com for more information.

SYNGRESS®

The Real MCTS/MCITP Exam 70-649 Upgrading Your MCSE on Windows Server 2003 to Windows Server 2008 Prep Kit

Brien Posey Technical Editor

Tariq Azad
Colin Bowern
Laura Hunter
John Karnay
Mohan Krishnamurthy
Jeffery Martin

Tony Piltzecker
Susan Snedaker
Arno Theron
Shawn Tooley
Gene Whitley

KEY	SERIAL NUMBER
001	HJIRTCV764
002	PO9873D5FG
003	829KM8NJH2
004	BPOQ48722D
005	CVPLQ6WQ23
006	VBP965T5T5
007	HJJJ863WD3E
008	2987GVTWMK
009	629MP5SDJT
010	IMWQ295T6T

PUBLISHED BY
Syngress Publishing, Inc. Elsevier, Inc.
30 Corporate Drive
Burlington, MA 01803

The Real MCTS/MCITP Exam 649 Preparation Kit

ISBN 13: 978-1-59749-234-8

Publisher: Andrew Williams
Acquisitions Editor: David George
Technical Editor: Brien Posey
Project Manager: Gary Byrne

Page Layout and Art: SPI
Copy Editors: Adrienne Rebello and Audrey Doyle
Indexers: Ed Rush and Nara Wood
Cover Designer: Michael Kavish

For information on rights, translations, and bulk sales, contact Matt Pedersen, Commercial Sales Director and Rights, at Syngress Publishing; email m.pedersen@elsevier.com.

Technical Editor

Brien Posey is a freelance technical writer who has received Microsoft's MVP award four times. Over the last 12 years, Brien has published over 4,000 articles and whitepapers, and has written or contributed to over 30 books. In addition to his technical writing, Brien is the cofounder of Relevant Technologies and also serves the IT community through his own Web site.

Prior to becoming a freelance author, Brien served as CIO for a nationwide chain of hospitals and healthcare facilities and as a network administrator for the Department of Defense at Fort Knox. He has also worked as a network administrator for some of the nation's largest insurance companies.

Brien wishes to thank his wife, Taz, for her love and support throughout his writing career.

Contributing Authors

Tariq Bin Azad is the principal consultant and founder of NetSoft Communications Inc., a consulting company located in Toronto, Canada. He is considered a top IT professional by his peers, coworkers, colleagues, and customers. He obtained this status by continuously learning and improving his knowledge and information in the field of information technology. Currently, he holds more than 100 certifications, including MCSA, MCSE, MCTS, MCITP (Vista, Mobile 5.0, Microsoft Communications Server 2007, Windows 2008, and Microsoft Exchange Server 2007), MCT, CIW-CI, CCA, CCSP, CCEA, CCI, VCP, CCNA, CCDA, CCNP, CCDP, CSE, and many more. Most recently, Tariq has been concentrating on Microsoft Windows 2000/2003/2008, Exchange 2000/2003/2007, Active Directory, and Citrix implementations. He is a professional speaker and has trained architects, consultants, and engineers on topics such as Windows 2008 Active Directory, Citrix Presentation Server, and Microsoft Exchange 2007. In addition to owning and operating an independent consulting company, Tariq works as a senior consultant and has utilized his training skills in numerous workshops, corporate trainings, and presentations. Tariq holds a Bachelor of Science in Information Technology from Capella University, USA, a bachelor's degree in Commerce from University of Karachi, Pakistan, and is working on his ALMIT (Masters of Liberal Arts in Information Technology) from Harvard University. Tariq has been a coauthor on multiple books, including the best-selling *MCITP: Microsoft Exchange Server 2007 Messaging Design and Deployment Study Guide: Exams 70-237 and 70-238* (ISBN: 047018146X) and *The Real MCTS/MCITP Exam 640 Preparation Kit* (ISBN: 978-1-59749-235-5). Tariq has worked on projects or trained for major companies and organizations, including Rogers Communications Inc. Flynn Canada, Cap Gemini, HP, Direct Energy, Toyota Motors, Comaq, IBM, Citrix Systems Inc., Unicom Technologies, and Amica Insurance Company. He lives in Toronto, Canada, and would like to thank his father, Azad Bin Haider, and his mother, Sitara Begum, for his lifetime of guidance for their understanding and support to give him the skills that have allowed him to excel in work and life.

Colin Bowern is the Vice President of Technology at official COMMUNITY in Toronto, Canada. Through his work with the clients, Colin and the team help recording artists build and manage an online community to connect with their fans. Colin came to official COMMUNITY from Microsoft where he was a Senior Consultant with the Microsoft Consulting Services unit working with enterprise customers on their adoption of Microsoft technology. During his time at Microsoft, Colin worked with several product groups to incorporate customer feedback into future product releases, as well as the MCSE certification exam development. Colin holds two Microsoft DeliverIt! awards for work done within the financial industry in Canada to drive the adoption of .NET as a development platform and developing an SMBIOS inventory tool that was incorporated into the Windows Pre-installation Environment. Colin has delivered a number of in-person and Microsoft Developer Network (MSDN) webcast sessions since the early part of the decade on topics ranging from .NET Development to infrastructure deployment with the Microsoft platform. In addition to technical talks, Colin participates in the community through active contributions on the MSDN and ASP.NET Forums, publishing code examples, sharing experiences through his blog, and attending local user group events. Colin has been a technical reviewer for Addison-Wesley's .NET development series, the Windows Server 2003 series from Microsoft Press, and has co-authored a Windows Server 2003 MCSE study guide for Syngress Publishing. In addition, he holds a Masters of Science degree from the University of Liverpool.

Laura E. Hunter (CISSP, MCSE, MCT, MCDBA, MCP, MCP+I, CCNA, A+, Network+, iNet+, Security+, CNE-4, CNE-5) is a senior IT specialist with the University of Pennsylvania, where she provides network planning, implementation, and troubleshooting services for various business units and schools within the university.

Her specialties include Microsoft Windows 2000/2003 design and implementation, troubleshooting, and security topics. As an "MCSE Early Achiever" on Windows 2000, Laura was one of the first in the country to renew her Microsoft credentials under the Windows 2000 certification structure. Laura's previous experience includes a position as the director of computer services for the Salvation Army and as the LAN administrator for a medical supply firm. She also operates as an independent consultant for small businesses in the Philadelphia metropolitan area and is a regular contributor to the TechTarget family of Web sites.

Laura has previously contributed to Syngress Publishing's *Configuring Symantec Antivirus, Corporate Edition* (ISBN 1-931836-81-7). She has also contributed to several other exam guides in the Syngress Windows Server 2003 MCSE/MCSA DVD Guide and Training System series as a DVD presenter, contributing author, and technical reviewer.

Laura holds a bachelor's degree from the University of Pennsylvania and is a member of the Network of Women in Computer Technology, the Information Systems Security Association, and InfraGard, a cooperative undertaking between the U.S. Government other participants dedicated to increasing the security of United States critical infrastructures.

John Karnay is a freelance writer, editor, and book author living in Queens, NY. John specializes in Windows server and desktop deployments utilizing Microsoft and Apple products and technology. John has been working with Microsoft products since Windows 95 and NT 4.0 and consults for many clients in New York City and Long Island, helping them plan migrations to XP/Vista and Windows Server 2003/2008. When not working and writing, John enjoys recording and writing music as well as spending quality time with his wife, Gloria, and daughter, Aurora.

Mohan Krishnamurthy Madwachar (MCSE, CCA) is the GM – Network Security at Almoayed Group in Bahrain. Mohan is a key contributor to Almoayed Group's projects division and plays an important role in the organization's network security initiatives. Mohan has a strong networking, security, and training background. His tenure with companies such as Schlumberger Omnes and Secure Network Solutions India adds to his experience and expertise in implementing large and complex network and security projects. Mohan holds leading IT industry-standard and vendor certifications in systems, networking, and security. He is a member of the IEEE and PMI.

Mohan would like to dedicate his contributions to this book to his friends: Pankaj Sehgal, V.P. Ajan, Anand Raghavendra Rao, Vijendran (Vijay) Rao, Neeti (D'lima) Rodrigues, Ali Khan, Vishnu Venkataraman, Azeem Usman Bharde, Hasan Qutbi, Dharminder Dargan, Sudhir Sanil, Venkataraman Mahadevan, Amitabh Tiwari, Aswinee Kumar Rath, Rajeev Saxena, Rangan Chakravarthy and Venkateswara Rao Yendapalli.

Mohan has co-authored five books published by Syngress: *Designing & Building Enterprise DMZs* (ISBN: 1597491004), *Configuring Juniper Networks NetScreen & SSG Firewalls* (ISBN: 1597491187), *How to Cheat at Securing Linux* (ISBN: 1597492078), *How to Cheat at Administering Office Communications Server 2007* (ISBN: 1597492126), and *Microsoft Forefront Security Administration Guide* (ISBN: 1597492447). He also writes in newspaper columns on various subjects and has contributed to leading content companies as a technical writer and a subject matter expert.

Jeffery A. Martin MS/IT, MS/M (MCSE, MCSE:Security, MCSE: Messaging, MCDBA, MCT, MCSA, MCSA:Security, MCSE:Messaging, MCP+I, MCNE, CNE, CNA, CCA, CTT, A+, Network+, I-Net+, Project+, Linux+, CIW, ADPM) has been working with computer networks for more than 20 years. He is an editor, coeditor, author, or coauthor of more than 15 books and enjoys training others in the use of technology.

Tony Piltzecker (CISSP, MCSE, CCNA, CCVP, Check Point CCSA, Citrix CCA), author and technical editor of Syngress Publishing's *MCSE Exam 70-296 Study Guide and DVD Training System* and *How to Cheat at Managing Microsoft Operations Manager 2005*, is an independent consultant based in Boston, MA. Tony's specialties include network security design, Microsoft operating system and applications architecture, and Cisco IP Telephony implementations. Tony's background includes positions as Systems Practice Manager for Presidio Networked Solutions, IT Manager for SynQor Inc, Network Architect for Planning Systems, Inc, and Senior Networking Consultant with Integrated Information Systems. Along with his various certifications, Tony holds a bachelor's degree in business administration. Tony currently resides in Leominster, MA, with his wife, Melanie, and his daughters, Kaitlyn and Noelle.

Susan Snedaker (MCSE, MCT), principal consultant for Virtual Team Consulting, LLC (www.virtualteam.com), is an accomplished business and technology consultant, speaker, and author. During her career, she has held executive and technical positions with companies such as Microsoft, Honeywell, Keane, and Apta Software. As a consultant, she has worked with small, medium-sized, and large companies, including Canyon Ranch, University of Arizona, National University, Sabino Investment Management, Pyron Solar, University of Phoenix, DDB Ventures, ShopOrganic.com, and the Southern Arizona AIDS Foundation.

Susan's latest book, *Business Continuity and Disaster Recovery for IT Professionals*, Syngress (978-1-59749-172-3) was released in the spring of 2007. Additionally, Susan has written four other books and contributed chapters to 11 books. She has also written numerous technical articles on a variety of technology, information security, and wireless technologies. Susan is an experienced trainer, facilitator, and speaker.

Susan holds a Master of Business Administration (MBA) and a Bachelor of Arts in Management (BAM) from the University of Phoenix. In 2006, she received an Executive Certificate in International Management from Thunderbird University's Garvin School of International Management. Susan also holds a certificate in Advanced Project Management from Stanford University and attained Microsoft Certified Systems Engineer (MCSE) and Microsoft Certified Trainer (MCT) certifications. Susan is a member of the Project Management Institute (PMI) and the Information Technology Association of Southern Arizona (ITASA).

Arno Theron (ITIL Service Foundation, MCSA, MCSE: Messaging, MCITP, MCTS, and MCT) is an independent information security professional with seven years' network/server administration experience and six years' IT training experience as a Microsoft Certified Trainer. He is dedicated to improving training policy and implementation with high-quality technical information. Arno has previously contributed to Syngress Publishing's *Microsoft Forefront Security Administration Guide* (ISBN 978-1-59749-244-7). Arno is currently involved with designing and improving large-scale solutions and adapting such solutions to comply with Microsoft Operation Framework.

Shawn Tooley owns a consulting firm, Tooley Consulting Group, LLC, that specializes in Microsoft and Citrix technologies, for which he is the principal consultant and trainer. Shawn also works as network administrator for a hospital in North Eastern Ohio. Shawn's certifications include Microsoft Certified Trainer (MCT), Microsoft Certified System Engineer (MCSE), Citrix Certified Enterprise Administrator, Citrix Certified Sales Professional, HP Accredited System Engineer, IBM XSeries Server Specialist, Comptia A+, and Comptia Certified Trainer. In his free time he enjoys playing golf.

Gene Whitley (MBA, MCSE, MCSA, MCTS, MCP, Six Sigma Green Belt) is a senior systems engineer with Nucentric Solutions (www.nucentric.com), a technology integration firm in Davidson, NC. Gene started his IT career in 1992 with Microsoft, earning his MCP in 1993 and MCSE in 1994. He has been the lead consultant and project manager on numerous Active Directory and Exchange migration projects for companies throughout the U.S. Gene has been a contributing author on such books as *How To Cheat At IIS 7 Server Administration*, *How To Cheat At Microsoft Vista Administration*, and *Microsoft Forefront Security Administration Guide*. When not working, he spends his time with his wife and best friend, Samantha. Gene holds an MBA from Winthrop University and a BSBA in Management Information Systems from The University of North Carolina at Charlotte.

Contents

Chapter 3 Configuring Certificate Services and PKI **153**

Foreword

This book's primary goal is to help you prepare to take and pass Microsoft's exam number 70-649, *Upgrading Your MCSE on Windows Server 2003 to Windows Server 2008*. Our secondary purpose in writing this book is to provide exam candidates with knowledge and skills that go beyond the minimum requirements for passing the exam and help to prepare them to work in the real world of Microsoft computer networking.

What Is MCTS Exam 70-649?

Microsoft Certified Technology Specialist (MCTS) Exam 70-649 is a requirement for those upgrading their Windows Server 2003 MCSE certification to the Microsoft Certified Information Technology Professional (MCITP) for Windows Server 2008. Microsoft's stated target audience consists of IT professionals with MCSE certification on Windows Server 2003 and experience on a medium-sized or large company network. This means a multisite network with at least three domain controllers, running typical network services such as file and print services, messaging, database, firewall services, proxy services, remote access services, an intranet, and Internet connectivity.

Exam 70-649 is composed of topics from three other MCTS exams: Exam 70-640 (Configuring Active Directory), Exam 70-642 (Configuring Network Infrastructure), and Exam 70-634 (Configuring Application Platform), and covers the basics of administering a Microsoft Windows Server 2008 network. The book includes the following task-oriented objectives:

- **Configuring Network Access** This includes configuring remote access, configuring Network Access Protection components, configuring network authentication, configuring data transmission protocols, configuring wireless access, configuring certificate services, configuring DHCP, configuring IPv4 and IPv6 addressing, and configuring routing.

- **Configuring Terminal Services** This includes configuring TS remote programs, TS gateway, and TS load balancing; configuring resource allocation for TS, and configuring TS licensing, client connections, and server options.

- **Configuring a Web Services Infrastructure** This includes configuring FTP Server, backups, web applications, application pools, and IIS components; publishing IIS web sites; migrating sites and web applications; configuring SMTP service; and configuring UDDI service.

- **Configuring Security for Web Services** This includes configuring handlers, .NET trust levels, authentication, rights, permissions, authorization, and certificates.

- **Deploying and Monitoring Servers** This includes configuring WDS, capturing and deploying WDS images, configuring Windows activation, creating virtual machines, configuring Virtual Server settings, installing Windows Server Enterprise, and installing server core.

- **Configuring Server Roles** This includes implementing server roles using Server Manager; and configuring ADLDS, ADRMS, server core, RODC, Certificate Services, and Federation Services.

- **Maintaining the Active Directory Environment** This includes configuring backup and recovery, performing offline maintenance, and configuring custom application directory partitions.

- **Configuring the Active Directory Infrastructure** This includes configuring communication security for Active Directory and configuring the global catalog.

Path to MCTS/MCITP/MS Certified Architect

Microsoft certification is recognized throughout the IT industry as a way to demonstrate mastery of basic concepts and skills required to perform the tasks involved in implementing and maintaining Windows-based networks. The certification program is constantly evaluated and improved, and the nature of information technology is changing rapidly. Consequently, requirements and specifications for certification can also change rapidly. This book is based on the exam objectives as stated by Microsoft at the time of writing; however, Microsoft reserves the right to make changes to the objectives and to the exam itself at any time. Exam candidates should regularly visit the Certification and Training Web site at www.microsoft.com/learning/mcp/default.mspx for the most updated information on each Microsoft exam.

Microsoft currently offers three basic levels of certification on the technology level, professional level, and architect level:

- **Technology Series** This level of certification is the most basic, and it includes the **Microsoft Certified Technology Specialist (MCTS)** certification. The MCTS certification is focused on one particular Microsoft technology. There are 19 MCTS exams at the time of this writing. Each MCTS certification consists of one to three exams, does not include job-role skills, and will be retired when the technology is retired. Microsoft Certified Technology Specialists will be proficient in implementing, building, troubleshooting, and debugging a specific Microsoft technology.

- **Professional Series** This is the second level of Microsoft certification, and it includes the **Microsoft Certified Information Technology Professional (MCITP)** and **Microsoft Certified Professional Developer (MCPD)** certifications. These certifications consist of one to three exams, have prerequisites from the Technology Series, focus on a specific job role, and require an exam refresh to remain current. The MCITP certification offers nine separate tracks as of the time of this writing. There are two Windows Server 2008 tracks, Server Administrator and Enterprise Administrator. To achieve the Server Administrator MCITP for Windows Server 2008, you must successfully complete one Technology Series exam and one Professional Series exam. To achieve the Enterprise Administrator MCITP for Windows Server 2008, you must successfully complete four Technology Series exams and one Professional Series exam.

- **Architect Series** This is the highest level of Microsoft certification, and it requires the candidate to have at least 10 years' industry experience. Candidates must pass a rigorous review by a review board of existing architects, and they must work with an architect mentor for a period of time before taking the exam.

Upgrading Your MCSE Certification

Those who already hold the MCSE Windows 2003 can upgrade their certifications to MCITP Server Administrator by passing:

- Exam 70-649

- Exam 70-646 *Windows Server 2008 Server Administrator*, a Professional Series exam

Those who already hold the MCSE in Windows 2003 can upgrade their certifications to MCITP Enterprise Administrator by passing:

- Exam 70-649

- Exam 70-620 *Configuring Windows Vista Client*, a Technology Series exam

- Exam 70-647 *Windows Server 2008 Enterprise Administrator*, a Professional Series exam

NOTE

Upon passing Exam 70-649, you have completed the requirements for Technology Specialist certification in Windows Server 2008 Active Directory Configuration (Exam 70-640), Windows Server 2008 Network Infrastructure Configuration (Exam 70-642), and Windows Server 2008 Applications Configuration.

Prerequisites and Preparation

Certification as an MCSE on Windows Server 2003 is a mandatory prerequisite for taking Exam 70-649.

Preparation for this exam should include the following:

- Visit the Web site at www.microsoft.com/learning/exams/70-649.mspx to review the updated exam objectives.

- Work your way through this book, studying the material thoroughly and marking any items you don't understand.

- Answer all practice exam questions at the end of each chapter.

- Complete all hands-on exercises in each chapter.

- Review any topics that you don't thoroughly understand

- Consult Microsoft online resources such as TechNet (www.microsoft. com/technet/), white papers on the Microsoft Web site, and so forth, for better understanding of difficult topics.

- Participate in Microsoft's product-specific and training and certification newsgroups if you have specific questions that you still need answered.

- Take one or more practice exams, such as the one included on the Syngress/Elsevier certification Web site at www.syngress.com/ certification.

Exam Day Experience

Taking the exam is a relatively straightforward process. Prometric testing centers administer the Microsoft 70-649 exam. You can register for, reschedule, or cancel an exam through the Prometric Web site at www.register.prometric.com. You'll find listings of testing center locations on these sites. Accommodations are made for those with disabilities; contact the individual testing center for more information.

Exam price varies depending on the country in which you take the exam.

Exam Format

Exams are timed. At the end of the exam, you will find out your score and whether you passed or failed. You will not be allowed to take any notes or other written materials with you into the exam room. You will be provided with a pencil and paper, however, for making notes during the exam or doing calculations.

In addition to the traditional multiple-choice questions and the select and drag, simulation, and case study questions, you might see some or all of the following types of questions:

- *Hot area* questions, in which you are asked to select an element or elements in a graphic to indicate the correct answer. You click an element to select or deselect it.

- *Active screen* questions, in which you change elements in a dialog box (for example, by dragging the appropriate text element into a text box or selecting an option button or checkbox in a dialog box).

- *Drag and drop* questions, in which you arrange various elements in a target area.

Test-Taking Tips

Different people work best using different methods. However, there are some common methods of preparation and approach to the exam that are helpful to many test-takers. In this section, we provide some tips that other exam candidates have found useful in preparing for and actually taking the exam.

- Exam preparation begins before exam day. Ensure that you know the concepts and terms well and feel confident about each of the exam objectives. Many test-takers find it helpful to make flash cards or review notes to study on the way to the testing center. A sheet listing acronyms and abbreviations can be helpful, as the number of acronyms (and the similarity of different acronyms) when studying IT topics can be overwhelming. The process of writing the material down, rather than just reading it, will help to reinforce your knowledge.

- Many test-takers find it especially helpful to take practice exams that are available on the Internet and with books such as this one. Taking the practice exams can help you become used to the computerized exam-taking experience, and the practice exams can also be used as a learning tool. The best practice tests include detailed explanations of why the correct answer is correct and why the incorrect answers are wrong.

- When preparing and studying, you should try to identify the main points of each objective section. Set aside enough time to focus on the material and lodge it into your memory. On the day of the exam, you be at the point where you don't have to learn any new facts or concepts, but need simply to review the information already learned.

- The value of hands-on experience cannot be stressed enough. Exam questions are based on test-writers' experiences in the field. Working with the products on a regular basis—whether in your job environment or in a test network that you've set up at home—will make you much more comfortable with these questions.

- Know your own learning style and use study methods that take advantage of it. If you're primarily a visual learner, reading, making diagrams, watching video files on CD, etc., may be your best study methods. If you're primarily auditory, classroom lectures, audiotapes you can play in the car as you drive, and repeating key concepts to yourself aloud may be more effective. If you're a kinesthetic learner, you'll need to actually *do* the exercises, implement the security measures on your own systems, and otherwise perform hands-on tasks to best absorb the information. Most of us can learn from all of these methods, but have a primary style that works best for us.

- Although it may seem obvious, many exam-takers ignore the physical aspects of exam preparation. You are likely to score better if you've had sufficient sleep the night before the exam and if you are not hungry, thirsty, hot/cold or otherwise distracted by physical discomfort. Eat prior to going to the testing center (but don't indulge in a huge meal that will leave you uncomfortable), stay away from alcohol for 24 hours prior to the test, and dress appropriately for the temperature in the testing center (if you don't know how hot/cold the testing environment tends to be, you may want to wear light clothes with a sweater or jacket that can be taken off).

- Before you go to the testing center to take the exam, be sure to allow time to arrive on time, take care of any physical needs, and step back to take a deep breath and relax. Try to arrive slightly early, but not so far in advance that you spend a lot of time worrying and getting nervous about the testing process. You may want to do a quick last-minute review of notes, but don't try to "cram" everything the morning of the exam. Many test-takers find it helpful to take a short walk or do a few calisthenics shortly before the exam to get oxygen flowing to the brain.

- Before beginning to answer questions, use the pencil and paper provided to you to write down terms, concepts and other items that you think you may have difficulty remembering as the exam goes on. Then you can refer back to these notes as you progress through the test. You won't have to worry about forgetting the concepts and terms you have trouble with later in the exam.

- Sometimes the information in a question will remind you of another concept or term that you might need in a later question. Use your pen and paper to make note of this in case it comes up later on the exam.

- It is often easier to discern the answer to scenario questions if you can visualize the situation. Use your pen and paper to draw a diagram of the network that is described to help you see the relationships between devices, IP addressing schemes, and so forth.

- When appropriate, review the answers you weren't sure of. However, you should change your answer only if you're sure that your original answer was incorrect. Experience has shown that more often than not, when test-takers start second-guessing their answers, they end up changing correct answers to the incorrect. Don't "read into" the question (that is, don't fill in or assume information that isn't there); this is a frequent cause of incorrect responses.

- As you go through this book, pay special attention to the Exam Warnings, as these highlight concepts that are likely to be tested. You may find it useful to go through and copy these into a notebook (remembering that writing something down reinforces your ability to remember it) and/or go through and review the Exam Warnings in each chapter just prior to taking the exam.

- Use as many little mnemonic tricks as possible to help you remember facts and concepts. For example, to remember which of the two IPsec protocols (AH and ESP) encrypts data for confidentiality, you can associate the "E" in encryption with the "E" in ESP.

Pedagogical Elements

In this book, you'll find a number of different types of sidebars and other elements designed to supplement the main text. These include the following:

- **Exam Warning** These sidebars focus on specific elements on which the reader needs to focus in order to pass the exam (for example, "Be sure you know the difference between symmetric and asymmetric encryption").

- **Test Day Tip** These sidebars are short tips that will help you in organizing and remembering information for the exam (for example, "When preparing for the exam on test day, it may be helpful to have a sheet with definitions of these abbreviations and acronyms handy for a quick last-minute review").

- **Configuring & Implementing** These sidebars contain background information that goes beyond what you need to know from the exam, but provide a "deep" foundation for understanding the concepts discussed in the text.

- **New & Noteworthy** These sidebars point out changes in Windows Server 2008 from Windows Server 2003, as they will apply to readers taking the exam. These may be elements that users of Windows Server 2003 would be very familiar with that have changed significantly in Windows Server 2008 or totally new features that they would not be familiar with at all.

- **Head of the Class** These sidebars are discussions of concepts and facts as they might be presented in the classroom, regarding issues and questions that most commonly are raised by students during study of a particular topic.

Each chapter of the book also includes hands-on exercises in planning and configuring the features discussed. It is essential that you read through and, if possible, perform the steps of these exercises to familiarize yourself with the processes they cover.

You will find a number of helpful elements at the end of each chapter. For example, each chapter contains a *Summary of Exam Objectives* that ties the topics discussed in that chapter to the published objectives. Each chapter also contains an *Exam Objectives Fast Track,* which boils all exam objectives down to manageable summaries that are perfect for last-minute review. *The Exam Objectives Frequently Asked Questions* section answers those questions that most often arise from readers and students regarding the topics covered in the chapter. Finally, in the *Self Test* section, you will find a set of practice questions written in a multiple-choice format that will assist you in your exam preparation These questions are designed to assess your mastery of the exam objectives and provide thorough remediation, as opposed to simulating the variety of question formats you may encounter in the actual exam. You can use the *Self Test Quick Answer Key* that follows the *Self Test* questions to quickly determine what information you need to review again. The *Self Test Appendix* at the end of the book provides detailed explanations of both the correct and incorrect answers.

Additional Resources

There are two other important exam preparation tools included with this study guide. One is the CD included in the back of this book. The other is the concept review test available from our Web site.

- **A CD that provides book content in multiple electronic formats for exam-day review** Review major concepts, test day tips, and exam warnings in PDF, PPT, MP3, and HTML formats. Here, you'll cut through all of the noise to prepare you for exactly what to expect when you take the exam for the first time. You will want to use this CD just before you head out to the testing center!

- **Web-based practice exams** Just visit us at **www.syngress.com/ certification** to access a complete Windows Server 2008 concept multiple-choice review. These remediation tools are written to test you on all of the published certification objectives. The exam runs in both "live" and "practice" mode. Use "live" mode first to get an accurate gauge of your knowledge and skills, and then use practice mode to launch an extensive review of the questions that gave you trouble.

Chapter 1

MCTS/MCITP
Exam 649

Deploying Servers

Exam objectives in this chapter:

- **Installing Windows Server 2008**
- **The Windows Deployment Service**
- **Configuring Storage**
- **Configuring High Availability**
- **Configuring Windows Activation**

Exam objectives review:

- ☑ **Summary of Exam Objectives**
- ☑ **Exam Objectives Fast Track**
- ☑ **Exam Objectives Frequently Asked Questions**
- ☑ **Self Test**

Introduction

After you learn that Microsoft has released a new server operating system, it is only natural to want to learn everything there is to know about this new product and its new technologies. The extensive lengths that were taken to integrate more security into a product already established in the market are evident. Gathering information about an operating system is relatively easy, and learning how to integrate such a technology into an existing or new organization has proven rather easy to achieve as well.

Computer and network security is of paramount importance for companies in the global marketplace, and a large percentage of these companies have Microsoft infrastructures in place, including domain controllers (DCs), Exchange servers, and Vista and XP workstations. A Windows server provides a number of useful functions in a company's network infrastructure.

This chapter covers how an individual or group can achieve the aptitude needed to implement and maintain the desired deployment required by the organization. With the new certification track Microsoft has implemented, individuals can prove their skills in much more detail in the marketplace.

Installing Windows Server 2008

For any computer to function, it needs an operating system, also known as the network operating system (NOS), which is used to describe a server operating system. To decide which software you will need as your NOS, you will need to examine and consider scalability, security, and stability. Windows Server 2008 meets all of these requirements on different levels.

Installing the server operating system on a new server might seem like a daunting task to any system administrator, especially if it's a newly released OS with many new features. Having the skill to install a server OS is sometimes not enough. The planning and preparation stage is vital to a successful rollout. Any experienced system administrator will know that spending enough time in the planning phase of a new OS rollout and making the installation procedure simplified and well laid out will not only standardize organization server OS configurations, but also make the task of rolling out a new server infrastructure much easier, even when it involves upgrading an existing infrastructure.

The overall IT life cycle (from the beginning to the end) of an OS or infrastructure solution may be large or small. Using Microsoft Solutions Framework (MSF) and Microsoft Operations Framework (MOF), here are the four steps required to create and operate the new solution (or change to an existing one) in a production environment:

■ **Plan** Understand the business requirements to create the right solution. This includes the features and settings due to be implemented.

 ■ **Build** Complete the features and components set out in the planning phase using the appropriate development tools and processes.

 ■ **Deploy** Deploy into the production environment using strong release management processes.

 ■ **Operate** Maintain operational excellence.

Understanding the need for documenting, assessing the impact of, and reviewing changes in an IT environment is at the heart of standardizing and communicating such a solution.

Changes in Functionality from Windows Server 2003 with SP1 to Windows Server 2008

Microsoft introduced many new features and technologies in the Windows Server 2008 operating system, as well as improved some existing features. These additions and changes will help to increase security and productivity and reduce administrative overhead. The following paragraphs describe some of these features and technologies.

Active Directory Certificate Services (AD CS) provides customizable services for creating and managing public key certificates when employing public key technologies. Security is enhanced by binding the identity of a person, device, or service to a corresponding private key. The following are improvements made in AD CS functionality:

- Online Certificate Status Protocol support (online responders and responder arrays)

- Network Device Enrollment Service (NDES is now part of the OS)

- Web enrollment (new enrollment control)

- Policy settings (new policy stores added)

- Restricted Enrollment Agent (limiting permissions for users enrolling smart card certificates on behalf of other users)

- Enterprise PKI (PKIView) (monitors the health of certificate authorities [CAs] in the public key infrastructure [PKI] and supports Unicode character encoding

Active Directory Domain Services (AD DS) stores information about users, computers, and other devices on the network. AD DS is required to install directory-enabled applications. The following are improvements made in AD DS functionality:

- Auditing (log value changes that are made to AD DS objects and their attributes)

- Fine-grained password policies (functionality to assign a special password and account lockout policies for different sets of users)

- Read-only DCs (hosts a read-only partition of the AD DS database)

- Restartable AD DS (can be stopped so that updates can be applied to a DC)

- Database mounting tool (compare different backups, eliminating multiple restores)

- User interface improvements (updated AD DS Installation Wizard)

Active Directory Federation Services (AD FS) is used to create extensible and scalable solutions that can operate across multiple platforms, including Windows and non-Windows environments, for secure identity access. Federation Services was first introduced with Windows Server 2003 R2 and is now included in Microsoft Windows Server 2008 as a server role. New functionality includes improved installation and improved application support.

Active Directory Lightweight Directory Services (AD LDS) is a Lightweight Directory Access Protocol (LDAP) directory service. It eliminates dependencies that are required for AD DS by providing data storage and retrieval for directory-enabled applications. AD LDS replaces Active Directory Application Mode (ADAM) for previous versions of Windows.

Active Directory Rights Management Services (AD RMS) includes features not available in Microsoft Windows RMS. Windows RMS was available for Windows Server 2003 and was used to restrict access to rights-protected content to files made by RMS-enabled applications. The added features were incorporated to ease administrative overhead of AD RMS and to extend use outside the organization. New features include:

- AD RMS is now a server role

- Microsoft Management Console (MMC) snap-in

- Integration with AD FS

- Self-enrollment of AD RMS servers

- The ability to delegate responsibility with new AD RMS administrative roles

Server Manager is a single source for managing identity and system information, managing server status, identifying problems with server role configuration, and managing all roles installed on the server. It replaces the "Manage Your Server, Configure Your Server, and add or Remove Windows Components" feature in Windows Server 2003.

The Server Core is a minimal environment. This option limits the roles that can be performed; however, it can improve security and reduce the management and installation footprint.

The Application Server Role is an expanded role and integrated environment for running custom, server-based business applications. Typically, deployed applications running on the Application Server take advantage of Internet Information Services (IIS), the Hypertext Transfer Protocol (HTTP), the .NET Framework, ASP.NET, COM+, message queuing, and Web services that are built with Windows Communication Foundation (WCF).

The Terminal Services Role enables users to access Windows-based programs that are installed on the terminal server.

Terminal Services Core Functionality offers users the following features:

- Remote Desktop Connection 6.1

- Plug and Play Device redirection for media players and digital cameras

- Microsoft Point of Service for .NET 1.11 device redirection

- Single sign-on

Terminal Services also includes the following enhancements and improvements:

- Terminal Services printing has been enhanced with the addition of the Terminal Services Easy Print printer.

- Terminal Services RemoteApp allows access to Windows-based programs from any location, provided that the new Remote Desktop Connection (RDC) client is installed.

- Terminal Services Web Access makes Terminal Services RemoteApp programs and provides users with the ability to connect from a Web browser to a remote desktop of any server or client.

- Terminal Services Licensing includes the ability to track Terminal Services per User CALs.

- Terminal Services Gateway allows remote users to connect to resources on an internal corporate network using the Remote Desktop Protocol (RDP) over HTTP.

- Terminal Services Session Broker runs session load balancing between terminal servers.

- Microsoft Windows System Resource Manager provides the functionality to set how CPU and memory resources are assigned to applications, services, and processes.

The Print Services Role Server manages integration with Print Services. The DNS Server Role has the following improvements:

- Background zone loading (the domain name system [DNS] server can respond to queries while the zone is loading)

- Support for IPv6 addresses (full support for IPv6 [128 bits long] and IPv4 [32 bits long])

- Read-only DC support (the read-only DC [RODC] has a full read-only copy of any DNS zones)

- GlobalNames zone (commonly used to map a canonical name [CNAME] resource record to a fully qualified domain name [FQDN])

- Global Query block list (prevents DNS name hijacking)

The Fax Server Role replaces the fax console. The File Services Role helps to manage storage and shared folders, as well as enable file replication and fast file searching. The following list describes changes in functionality:

- **Distributed File System** New functionality includes access-based enumeration, cluster support, replication improvements, and support for read-only DCs.

- **File Server Resource Manager** Enforces storage limits on folders and volumes, and offers the ability to prevent specific file types and to generate storage reports.

- **Windows Server Back-up** Offers improvements in backup technology, restoration, application recovery, scheduling, and remote administration.

- **Services for the Network File System** Offers the ability to share files between Windows and UNIX environments. New functionality includes Active Directory lookup, 64-bit support, enhanced server performance, special device support, and enhanced UNIX support.

- **Storage Manager for SANs** This is an optional feature in Windows Server 2008.

- New Transactional NTFS and the Transactional Registry

- **New Self-Healing NTFS** No requirement for offline Chkdsk.exe usage.

- **New Symbolic Linking** This is a file system object pointing to another file system object.

The Network Policy and Access Services (NPAS) provides deployment of virtual private network (VPN), dial-up networking, and 802.11-protected wireless access and is a new set of operating system components. NPAS includes the following functions:

- Network Access Protection (NAP) Used to ensure that computers on the private network meet requirements for system health

- Network Policy Server (NPS) Provides organization-wide network access policies for system health

- Routing and Remote Access Service Features the Secure Socket Tunneling Protocol (SSTP), a mechanism to encapsulate PPP traffic over the Secure Sockets Layer (SSL) channel

The Web Server (IIS) role delivers Web publishing that integrates IIS, ASP.NET, and Windows Communication Foundation. Improvements include the ability to enable distributed configuration, new administration tools, the ability to make single pipeline requests, and the ability to perform Web site diagnostics.

The Streaming Media Services Role includes new cache/proxy management and playlist attributes.

The Virtualization Role is technology that is a component of the Windows Server 2008 OS and enables you to create a virtualized server computing environment. This new feature is provided through Hyper-V.

The Windows Deployment Services (WDS) role is the redesigned version of Remote Installation Services (RIS). WDS components are organized into these three categories: Server Components, Client Components, and Management Components.

Windows BitLocker Drive Encryption (BitLocker) provides protection on the operating system volume. New functionality includes full-volume encryption, integrity checking, recovery options, remote management, and secure decommissioning.

User Account Control is a new security component that allows an administrator to enter credentials to perform an administrative task when needed in a nonadministrative logged-in session. This increases security as there is now no need to ever log in to a session as the local administrator.

Authorization Manager's new features include custom object pickers, business rule groups and stores. Authorization Manager can store authorization stores in SQL, AD, or XML.

New functionality in the Encrypting File System includes smart card key storage, increased configurability of EFS through Group Policy, and an Encrypting File System rekeying wizard.

Changes to the Security Configuration Wizard include installation, securing servers, Windows Firewall, and Advanced Security integration.

Installing Windows Server 2008 Enterprise Edition

Before you install the operating system, you first need to know the organization's requirements. Knowing this upfront will facilitate the installation procedure as well as consecutive configuration tasks, and help to ensure that they run smoothly. Second, verify the installation and configuration plan with the stakeholders before the project commences. Before you install Windows Server 2008, follow the steps in this section to prepare for the installation. Depending on the role the server will take, you will have to check the server for application compatibility. This is important whether the server will just have Windows Server 2008, or whether it will host any other Microsoft or third-party applications.

Microsoft Windows Server 2008 is available in multiple editions, based on the organization's needs, size, and operating systems, and providing support for different levels of hardware compatibility.

Windows Server 2008 Standard Edition provides key server functionality. It includes both full and Server Core installation options. It is designed to increase the flexibility and reliability of your server infrastructure, with built-in virtualization and enhanced Web capabilities. Enhanced security features and high dependability come with this edition. The Standard Edition includes the following:

- **32-bit and 64-bit** Support for up to four CPUs
- **32-bit** Support for up to 4 GB of RAM
- **64-bit** Support for up to 32 GB of RAM

Windows Server 2008 Enterprise Edition provides even greater scalability and availability and adds technologies such as failover clustering and AD FS. The enterprise-class platform improves security and lays down the foundation for a scalable IT infrastructure. The Enterprise Edition includes the following:

- **32-bit and 64-bit** Support for up to eight CPUs
- **32-bit** Support for up to 64 GB of RAM
- **64-bit** Support for up to 2 TB of RAM

Windows Server 2008 Datacenter Edition offers the same functionality as the Enterprise Edition, but with additional memory and processor capabilities from two to 64 processors. With its unlimited virtual image usage rights, the Datacenter Edition is the foundation on which to build large enterprise-class solutions. The Datacenter Edition includes the following:

- **32-bit** Support for up to 32 CPUs
- **64-bit** Support for up to 64 CPUs
- **32-bit** Support for up to 64 GB of RAM
- **64-bit** Support for up to 2 TB of RAM

Windows Web Server 2008 is designed to be used as a single-purpose Web server. Other server roles are not available in this edition. The Web edition delivers a solid Web infrastructure with newly redesigned tools. The Web Server Edition includes the following:

- **32-bit and 64-bit** Support for up to four CPUs
- **32-bit** Support for up to 4 GB of RAM
- **64-bit** Support for up to 32 GB of RAM

Windows Server 2008 for Itanium-based Systems is designed for use with Intel Itanium 64-bit processors. This is designed to provide high availability for large databases and line-of-business applications, and to provide high availability to meet the needs of mission-critical solutions. The Itanium-based edition includes the following:

- Support for up to 64 × 64-bit Itanium CPUs
- Support for up to 2 TB of RAM

When working with the Windows Server 2008 Enterprise Edition, you must complete a few preinstallation tasks. First, check the system hardware requirements. Table 1.1 lists the requirements for Windows Server 2008 Enterprise Edition.

Table 1.1 Hardware Requirements for Windows Server 2008 Enterprise Edition

Component	Requirement
Processor	Minimum: 1 GHz (x86 processor) or 1.4 GHz (x64 processor)
	Recommended: 2 GHz or faster
	Note: An Intel Itanium 2 processor is required for Windows Server 2008 for Itanium-based systems.
Memory	Minimum: 512 MB of RAM
	Recommended: 2 GB or more of RAM
	Maximum (32-bit systems): 4 GB (Standard) or 64 GB (Enterprise and Datacenter)
	Maximum (64-bit systems): 32 GB (Standard) or 2 TB (Enterprise, Datacenter, and Itanium-based systems)
Available disk space	Minimum: 10 GB
	Recommended: 40 GB or greater
	Note: Computers with more than 16 GB of RAM will require more disk space for paging, hibernation, and dump files.
Drive	DVD-ROM drive
Display and peripherals	Super VGA (800 × 600) or higher-resolution monitor
	Keyboard
	Microsoft mouse or compatible pointing device

Once you have determined that the hardware meets the minimum requirements and that the software that will run on the server meets the requirements of the hardware, it is time to decide whether you want to do a clean install of the operating system on the new or used server hardware or whether you want to upgrade an older version of Server 2008 or Server 2003. In an upgrade, you retain options such as the desktop, users and groups, and program groups. If you don't have an operating system you want to upgrade, you need to perform a clean install.

Table 1.2 shows which Windows operating systems can be upgraded to which editions of this release of Windows Server 2008.

Table 1.2 Upgrade Paths

If you are running:	You can upgrade to this version of:
Windows Server 2003 R2 Standard Edition	Full installation of Windows Server 2008 Standard
Windows Server 2003 Standard Edition with Service Pack 1 (SP1)	Full installation of Windows Server 2008 Enterprise
Windows Server 2003 Standard Edition with Service Pack 2 (SP2)	
Windows Server 2008 Standard RC0	
Windows Server 2008 Standard RC1	
Windows Server 2003 R2 Enterprise Edition	Full installation of Windows Server 2008 Enterprise
Windows Server 2003 Enterprise Edition with SP1	
Windows Server 2003 Enterprise Edition with SP2	
Windows Server 2008 Enterprise RC0	
Windows Server 2008 Enterprise RC1	
Windows Server 2003 R2 Datacenter Edition	Full installation of Windows Server 2008 Datacenter
Windows Server 2003 Datacenter Edition with SP1	
Windows Server 2003 Datacenter Edition with SP2	
Windows Server 2008 Datacenter RC0	
Windows Server 2008 Datacenter RC1	

Before you begin the upgrade, consider the following:

- You may want to back up and test the backup of the server before the upgrade starts.

- Upgrading from Server 2003 to the Server Core of Windows Server 2008 is not supported.

- An upgrade to Windows Server 2008 cannot be uninstalled; however, if the installation failed, you can roll back to the previous operating system.

- Be sure to do an application compatibility check before the upgrade is started. Microsoft made an application compatibility toolkit available for this reason.

TEST DAY TIP

To completely prepare for test day, perform an attended installation of Windows Server 2008.

EXERCISE 1.1

INSTALLING WINDOWS SERVER 2008

To install Windows Server 2008, follow these steps:

1. Insert the Windows Server 2008 Enterprise Edition DVD in the DVD-ROM drive.

2. Make the necessary selections in Figure 1.1 and click **Next**.

Figure 1.1 Installing Windows Server 2008

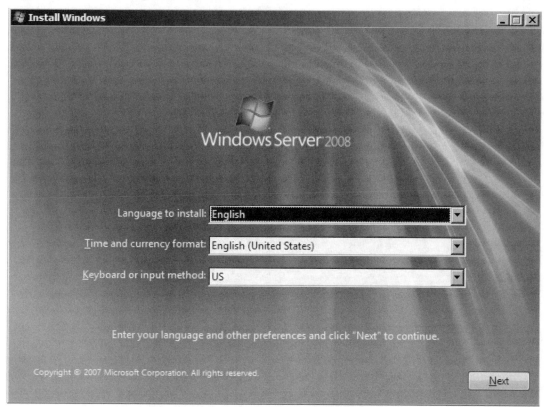

3. Click **Install now**, as shown in Figure 1.2.

Figure 1.2 Clicking Install Now

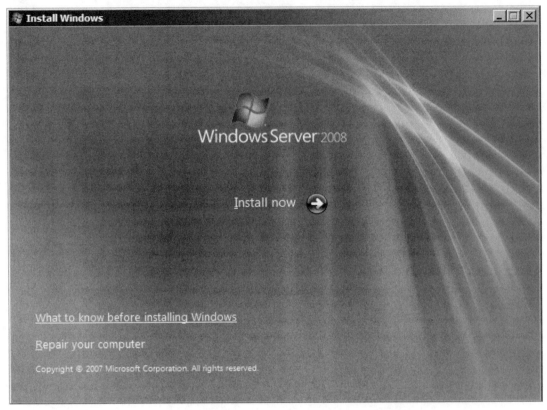

4. Figure 1.3 shows a list of the editions of the operating system available on the DVD. Make a selection and click **Next**.

Figure 1.3 Selecting the Operating System

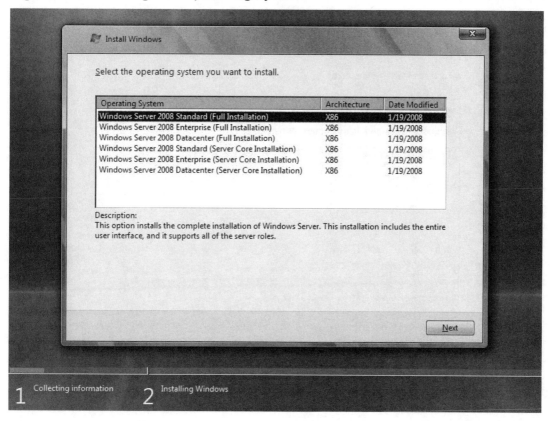

5. Accept the license terms as shown in Figure 1.4, and click **Next**.

Figure 1.4 Accepting the Terms and Conditions

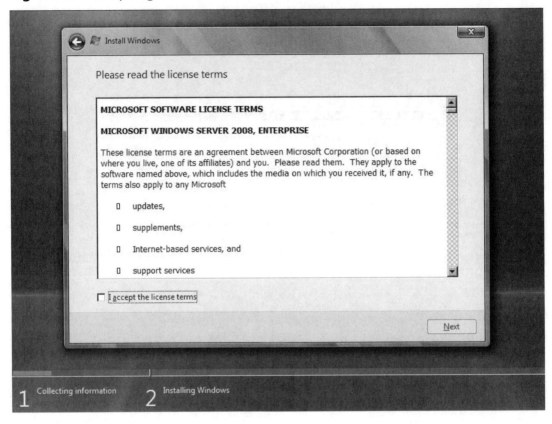

6. Select to perform either an **Upgrade** or a **Custom** (clean) install, as shown in Figure 1.5.

Figure 1.5 Selecting the Type of Installation

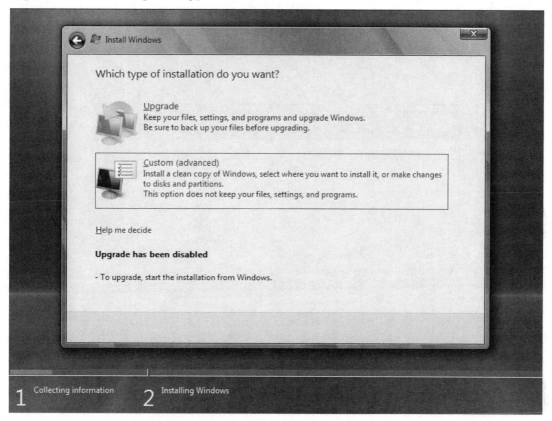

7. Click on **New**, as shown in Figure 1.6, to create a partition based on the unallocated disk space available on the server. You can also perform formats and extend volumes.

Figure 1.6 Creating a Partition

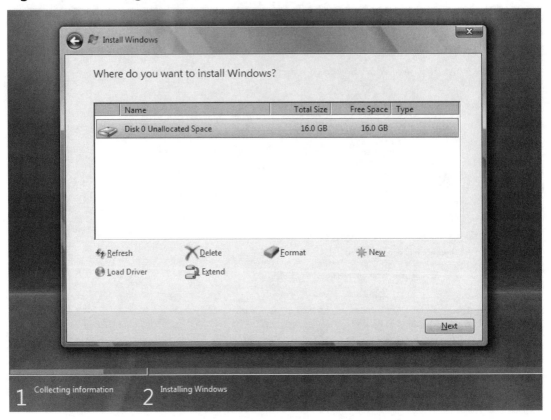

8. Figure 1.7 shows a successfully created 16 GB primary partition. Click **Next**.

Figure 1.7 The Newly Created Partition

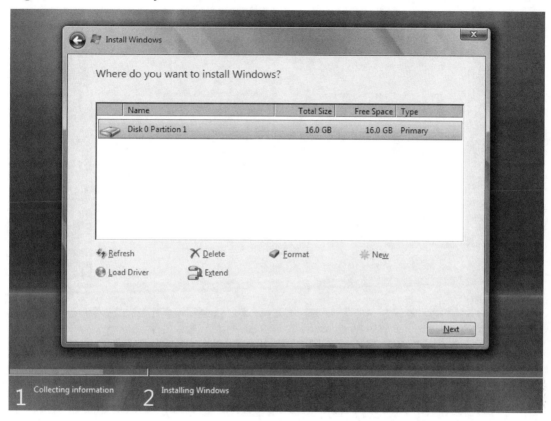

9. Figure 1.8 shows the Windows Installation going through all the install stages. Depending on your configuration, the server restarts between the Installing Updates stage and the Completing Installations stage.

Figure 1.8 Installing Windows

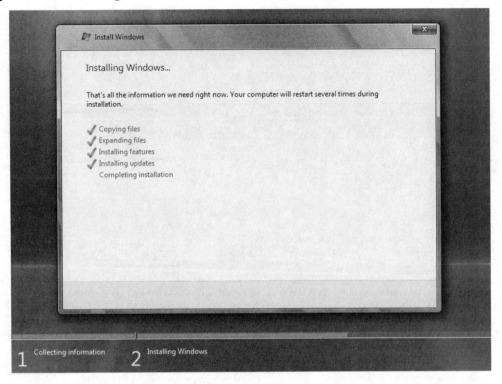

10. Once the installation is complete, the server will restart so that the changes can take effect.

New and Noteworthy...

Upgrading to Windows Server 2008

Upgrading from Windows Server 2003 to Windows Server 2008 requires additional free disk space. When running the upgrade process extra disk space is required for the new operating system, the setup process, and any other installed server roles. Additionally, for the DC role you also need to

Continued

consider disk space requirements. Please note the following: The volume containing the Active Directory database requires free space that is equal to, or at least 10% of, the current database size, or at least 250 MB, whichever is greater. In addition to this, the volume that hosts the log files also needs at least 50 MB of free space. The default installation of the Active Directory database and log file is under %WINDIR%\NTDS. The NTDS.DIT database file and log files are temporarily copied to the quarantine location, hence the requirement for free disk space.

When upgrading a 64-bit version of the Windows Server 2008 operating system, remember that Windows Server 2008 requires you to use updated and digitally signed drivers for the hardware attached to the server. In the case of Plug and Play or software installation without digitally signed drivers, you will receive an error and Windows Server 2008 will not load the unsigned driver. To digitally sign drivers means that the publisher of the driver has put an electronic security mark, "a digital signature," in the driver. This prevents someone from altering the contents of the original driver package. This means the driver has been signed and its identity can be verified by the CA that issued the certificate. This is to ensure that users are using the highest-quality drivers. If, for whatever reason, you are not sure whether the driver package you are using is digitally signed, or if you can no longer boot into your computer or server after the installation, use the following procedure to disable the driver signature prerequisite. This enables your computer or server to start correctly, and the unsigned driver will load successfully. To disable the signature requirement for the current boot process:

1. During startup, press **F8**.
2. Select **Advanced Boot Options**.
3. Select **Disable Driver Signature Enforcement**.
4. Reboot into Windows, then uninstall the unsigned driver and check with the hardware vendor for available 64-bit device drivers.

What Is New in the AD DS Installation?

AD DS has several new installation options in Windows Server 2008, including the following:

- RODC
- DNS
- Global Catalog (GC) servers

New OS installation options include Full Install and Core Server Install.

The first thing you must do when adding a Windows Server 2008 DC to a Windows 2003 forest is to prepare the forest for the Windows 2008 server by extending the schema to accommodate the new server:

- To prepare the forest for Windows Server 2008 run the following command: *adprep /forestprep.*

- To prepare the domain for Windows Server 2008 run the following command: *adprep /domainprep.*

It is recommended that you host the primary domain controller (PDC) emulator operations master role in the forest root domain on a DC that runs Windows Server 2008 and to make this server a GC server. The first Windows Server 2008 DC in the forest cannot be an RODC. Before installing the first RODC in the forest, run the following command: *adprep /rodcprep.*

Making sure the installation was successful; you can verify the AD DS installation by checking the following:

- Check the Directory Service log in Event Viewer for errors.

- Make sure the SYSVOL folder is accessible to clients.

- Verify DNS functionality.

- Verify replication.

To run *adprep /forestprep* you have to be a member of the Enterprise Admins and Schema Admins groups of Active Directory. You must run this command from the DC in the forest that has the Schema Master FSMO role. Only one Schema Master is needed per forest.

To run *adprep /domainprep* you have to be a member of the Domain Admins or Enterprise Admins group of Active Directory. You must run this command from each Infrastructure Master FSMO role in each domain after you have run *adprep /forestprep* in the forest. Only one Infrastructure Master is needed per domain.

To run *adprep /rodcprep* you have to be a member of the Enterprise Admins group of Active Directory. You can run this command on any DC in the forest. However, it is recommended that you run this command on the Schema Master.

EXERCISE 1.2

INSTALLING A NEW WINDOWS SERVER 2008 FOREST USING THE WINDOWS INTERFACE

Follow these steps to install a new Windows Server 2008 forest by using the Windows interface. To perform this procedure, you must be logged on as the local Administrator for the computer.

1. On the Select Server Roles page (Figure 1.9), click the **Active Directory Domain Services** checkbox, and then click **Next**.

Figure 1.9 Installing AD DS

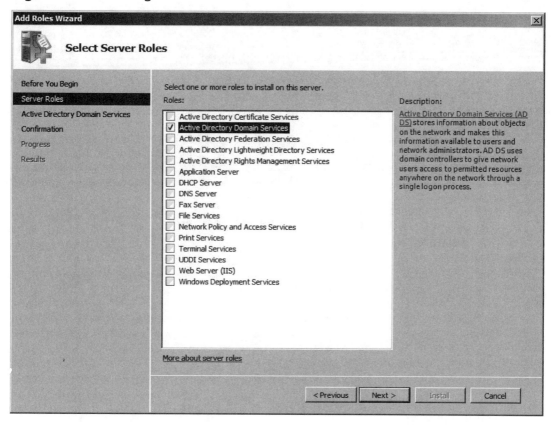

2. If necessary, review the information on the Active Directory Domain Services page (Figure 1.10) and then click **Next**.

Figure 1.10 AD DS Introduction

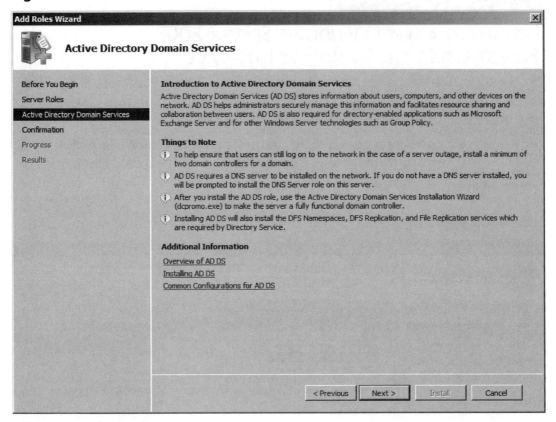

3. On the Confirm Installation Selections page (Figure 1.11), click **Install**.

Figure 1.11 Confirming the Installation

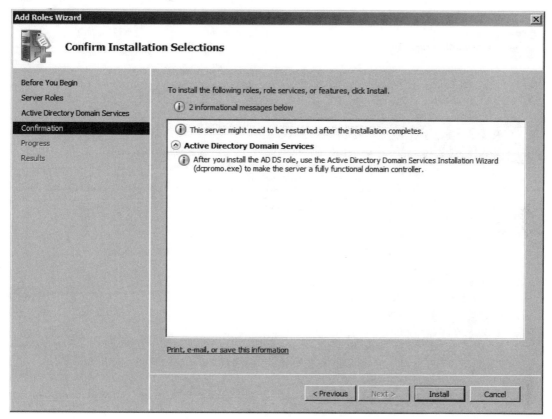

4. Figure 1.12 shows the result of the installation and gives you the option to run dcpromo.exe. Click **Next**.

Figure 1.12 Installation Result

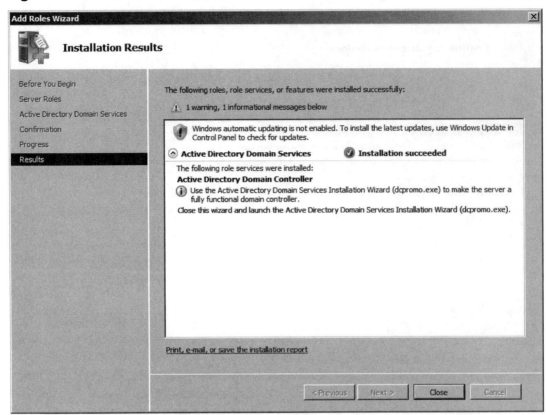

5.   On the Installation Results page (Figure 1.12), click **Close this wizard** and launch the Active Directory Domain Services Installation Wizard (dcpromo.exe). Alternatively, click **Start | Run**, type **dcpromo.exe**, and click **OK**. Figure 1.13 shows the Welcome Page to the AD DS Installation Wizard; click **Next**. You can select the **Use advanced mode installation** checkbox to get additional installation options.

Figure 1.13 The Welcome Page

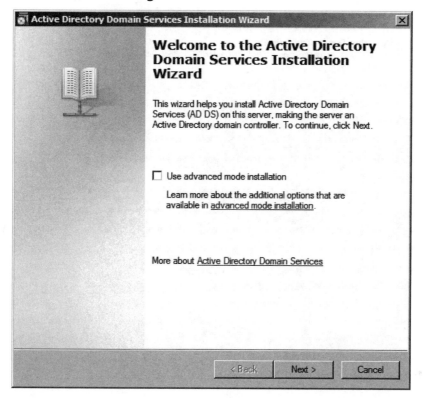

6. On the Operating System Compatibility page (Figure 1.14), review the warning about the default security settings for Windows Server 2008 DCs and then click **Next**.

Figure 1.14 Operating System Compatibility Page

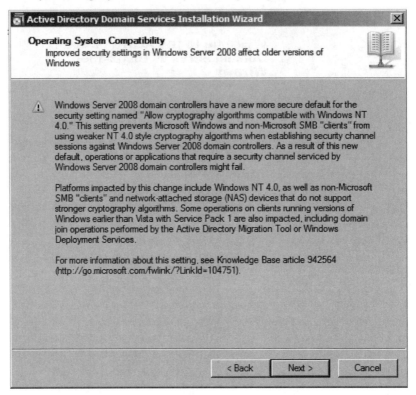

7. On the Choose a Deployment Configuration page (Figure 1.15), click **Create a new domain in a new forest**, and then click **Next**.

Figure 1.15 Choosing a Deployment Configuration

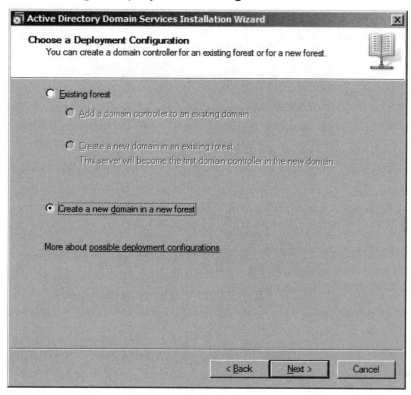

8. On the Name the Forest Root Domain page (Figure 1.16), type the full DNS name for the forest root domain, and then click **Next** (e.g., Syngress.com).

Figure 1.16 Naming the Forest Root Domain

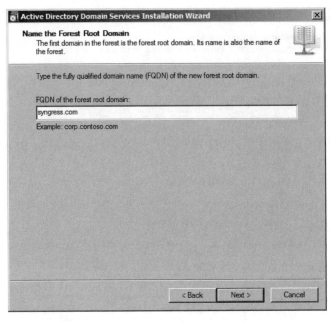

9. On the Set Forest Functional Level page (Figure 1.17), select the forest functional level that accommodates the DCs you plan to install anywhere in the forest, and then click **Next**.

Figure 1.17 Setting the Forest Functional Level

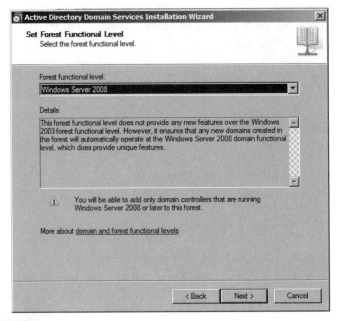

10. On the Additional Domain Controller Options page (Figure 1.18), **DNS server** is selected by default so that your forest DNS infrastructure can be created during AD DS installation. If you plan to use Active Directory-integrated DNS, click **Next**. If you have an existing DNS infrastructure and you do not want this DC to be a DNS server, clear the **DNS server** checkbox, and then click **Next**.

Figure 1.18 Additional DC Options

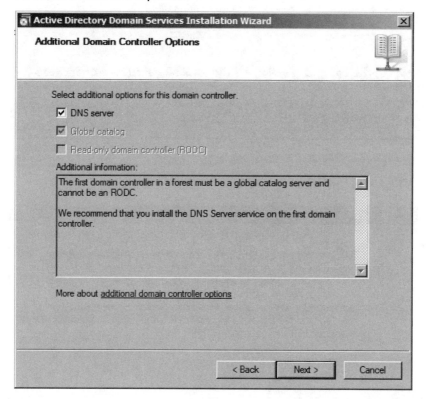

11. On the Static IP assignment page (Figure 1.19), it is picked up that the server does not have a static Internet Protocol (IP) address assigned to its network card. It is recommended that you assign a static IP to the network card and then continue with the installation. Click **No, I will assign static IP addresses to all physical network adapters**; this will display the screen shown in Figure 1.18 again. Assign a static IP to the network card and click **Next** (configure a static IPv4 and IPv6 IP address for this prompt to stop). If the wizard cannot create a delegation for the DNS server, it displays a message to indicate that you can create the delegation manually. To continue, click **Yes** (see Figure 1.20).

Figure 1.19 Assigning a Static IP Address

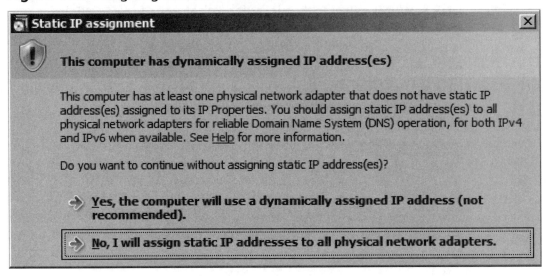

Figure 1.20 DNS Prompts

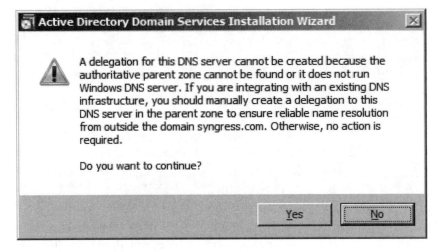

12. On the Location for Database, Log Files, and SYSVOL page (Figure 1.21), type or browse to the volume and folder locations for the database file, the directory service log files, and the SYSVOL files, and then click **Next**. Windows Server Back-up backs up the directory service by volume. For backup and recovery efficiency, store these files on separate volumes that do not contain applications or other nondirectory files.

Figure 1.21 The Location for the Database

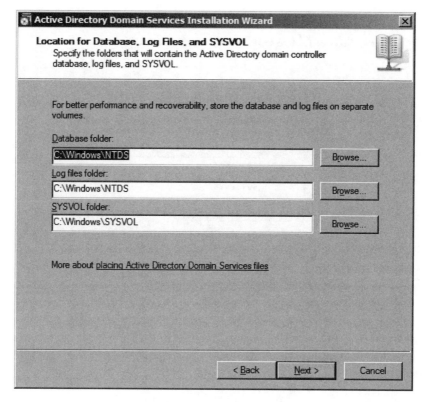

13. On the Directory Services Restore Mode Administrator Password page (Figure 1.22), type and confirm the restore mode password, and then click **Next**. This password must be used to start AD DS in Directory Service Restore Mode for tasks that must be performed offline. It is recommended that this password is *NOT* the same as the domain administrator password.

Figure 1.22 Directory Services Restore Mode Password

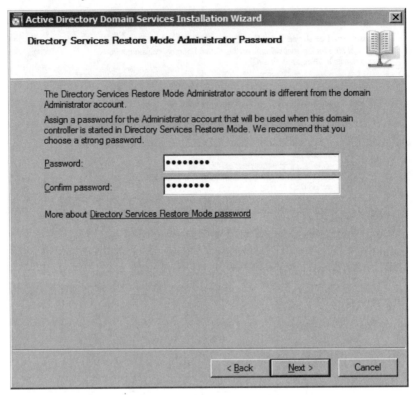

14. On the Summary page (Figure 1.23), review your selection. Click **Back** to change any selection, if necessary. To save the selected settings to an answer file that you can use to automate subsequent AD DS operations, click **Export settings**. Type the name for your answer file, and then click **Save**. When you are sure that your selections are accurate, click **Next** to install AD DS.

Figure 1.23 The Summary Page

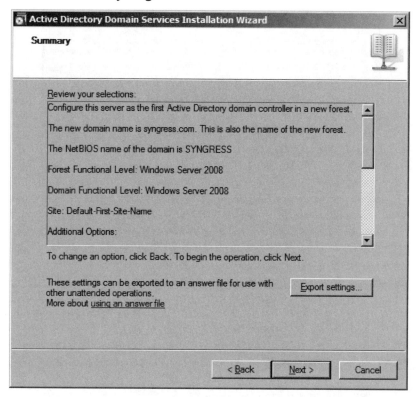

15. You can either select the **Reboot on completion** checkbox (Figure 1.24) to have the server restart automatically, or you can restart the server to complete the AD DS installation when you are prompted to do so.

Figure 1.24 The AD DS Installation Wizard

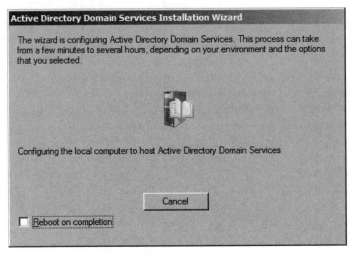

16. On the Completion page (Figure 1.25), you should see a message stating that the installation was successful and is complete. Click **Finish**.

Figure 1.25 The Completion Page

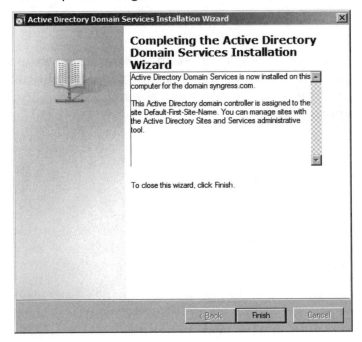

Installing from Media

Install from media (IFM) is a feature that was available with Windows 2000 SP3 and Windows Server 2003. Historically, it has been a problem rolling out new DC and GC servers at remote sites. Restoring or rolling out a DC in a remote site also had the disadvantage of large amounts of data being replicated between the newly restored DC and an active DC in the domain. IFM offers you the option to restore or build a new DC from a recently made backup. To take advantage of this feature, you must back up the DC's system state information (this contains Active Directory) and restore it to a media source such as a CD, DVD, tape, or even shared network drive. On a new server that is to be promoted, run the *dcpromo.exe /adv* command. This will give you the advanced Active Directory installation options.

The advanced option gives you the choice to specify the location of the restored backup file that contains the system state of a DC from which you sourced Active Directory. This will allow you to create a new DC from a recent backup instead of conducting a live replication from another active DC. Once the installation is complete, replication will commence with an active DC to replicate data changes that took place since the original backup used for IFM was created.

This solution provides you with the functionality to provide immediate disaster recovery of a DC or GC server by maintaining a current system state backup of any DC in the domain and restoring it to media such as a CD, DVD, tape, or shared network drive. It is, however, very important that you keep these backups as secure as possible, as you don't want a copy of the organization's Active Directory to fall into the wrong hands. There are a few IFM limitations. It works only for the same domain, and the system state backup must be current because the default value for the tombstone lifetime entry is 60 days for objects within Active Directory.

EXERCISE 1.3

PREPARING FOR DISASTER RECOVERY USING IFM

Follow these steps to prepare for disaster recovery using IFM. You will need at least one Windows 2003 DC in the domain and a Windows 2003 member server in that domain that is to be promoted. DNS must be installed and the SRV records for the first DC must be populated.

TEST DAY TIP

You cannot use the IFM feature to create a new domain.

1. Log on to one of the active DCs in the organization.
2. Create a directory called backup on the C drive.
3. Use Windows Backup to back up the system state to the newly created backup directory on the C drive.
4. Log on to the member server that is to become the new DC.
5. Create a directory called NTDSrestore on the C drive and share it as NTDSrestore. Make sure the permissions on the share are set to the Everyone group with Full Control privilege.
6. On the DC, map a drive to NTDSrestore (the share created in step 5).
7. On the DC, open the Windows Backup utility and use the Restore Wizard to restore the backup created in step 3 to the NTDSrestore share.
8. From the member server, log on as an administrator, click on **Start | Run**, and DCPromo /ADV. Go through the dialog as you normally would. elect the option **From These Restored Backup Files** and enter the path to the directory where you put the restored files (not the backup file, but the restored files).

   DCpromo.exe will continue as normal and will reboot the server. It will find a source DC and sync with it to get updated information to make up the gap from when the media was created.

Installing Server Core

One of the most notable new features of Windows Server 2008 is the new Server Core. Server Core is a considerably scaled down installation where no Windows Explorer shell is installed or available. However, some control panel applets, such as regional settings, are available. Features such as the .NET Framework, Internet Explorer, and many others not related to Server Core are not included. The Server Core installation option only installs the subset of the binary files that are required by the supported server roles. Configuration and maintenance is done entirely through the command-line interface in Windows, or by connecting to the Server

Core machine remotely using the MMC. You can configure a Server Core machine for several basic roles:

- DC/AD DS
- AD LDS
- DNS server
- Dynamic Host Configuration Protocol (DHCP) server
- File server
- Print server
- Windows Media Server
- TS Remote Programs TS Gateway
- IIS 7 Web Server (without .NET support)
- Windows Server Virtualization Role (Hyper-V)

Server Core features improvements for the branch office scenario. A combination of Server Core, RODC, and BitLocker in a branch office makes for a very secure and stable system.

Server Core provides the following benefits:

- Reduced maintenance and management on the overall install of the server operating system
- Reduced attack surface because there are fewer applications to attack
- Less disk space requirements, at 1 GB to install and 2 GB for operations

Table 1.3 lists the availability of Server Core roles on various versions of Windows Server 2008.

Table 1.3 Server Core Availability

Server Role	Enterprise	Datacenter	Standard	Web	Itanium
Web Services (IIS)	Yes	Yes	Yes	Yes	No
Print Services	Yes	Yes	Yes	No	No
Hyper-V	Yes	Yes	Yes	No	No

Continued

Table 1.3 Continued. Server Core Availability

Server Role	Enterprise	Datacenter	Standard	Web	Itanium
Active Directory Domain Services	Yes	Yes	Yes	No	No
Active Directory Lightweight	Yes	Yes	Yes	No	No
DHCP Server	Yes	Yes	Yes	No	No
DNS Server	Yes	Yes	Yes	No	No
File Services	Yes	Yes	Partial	No	No

EXERCISE 1.4

MANUALLY INSTALLING AND CONFIGURING A SERVER CORE INSTALLATION

To manually install and configure Server Core follow these steps:

1. Insert the appropriate Windows Server 2008 installation media into your DVD drive.

2. When the auto-run dialog box appears, click **Install Now**.

3. Follow the instructions on the screen to complete the setup.

4. After the setup completes, press **Ctrl + Alt + Delete**, click **Other User**, type **Administrator** with a blank password, and then press **ENTER**. You will be prompted to set a password for the Administrator account.

5. To set a static IP address to the new Server Core type the following at the command prompt: *netsh interface ipv4 show interfaces*. Note the Idx number next to the network adapter to which you want to set the static IP address.

6. At the command prompt, type **netsh interface ipv4 set address name= "<ID>" source=static address=<StaticIP> mask=<SubnetMask> gateway=<DefaultGateway>**.

7. At the command prompt type **netsh interface ipv4 add dnsserver name="ID>" address=<DNSIP>index=1**.

8. To rename the server, type **netdom renamecomputer <ComputerName> /NewName:<NewComputerName>**.

9. To join the server to a domain, at the command prompt type **netdom join <ComputerName> /domain:<DomainName> /userd: <UserName> /password:*** .

10. To restart the server, type **shutdown /r**.

The Windows Server 2008 Server Core supports the following optional features:

- Failover clustering
- Network load balancing
- Subsystem for UNIX-based applications
- Backup
- Multipath IO
- Removable storage
- BitLocker drive encryption
- Simple Network Management Protocol (SNMP)
- Windows Internet Name Service (WINS)
- Telnet client

The Windows Deployment Service

RIS has been updated and redesigned to become Windows Deployment Services (WDS) in Windows Server 2008; it has a number of changes relating to RIS features. This also applies to WDS installed on Windows Server 2003. WDS enables deployments of operating systems such as Windows Server 2008 and Windows Vista in small environments, to rollouts of up to hundreds of servers or client-operating systems. WDS allows you to set up operating systems on computers without physically being present at the computer with a DC or DVD by creating operating system images from the server and storing them on the server for later use, while deploying client or server operating systems. WDS can use it to set up new computers by using a network-based installation.

What Is WDS?

WDS consists of the following components:

- **Server components** Pre-Boot Execution Environment (PXE) server and Trivial File Transfer Protocol (TFTP) server

- **Client components** Windows Pre-Installation Environment (Windows PE)

- **Management components** Tools that can be used to manage the server, OS images, and client computer accounts

Table 1.4 shows the changes.

Table 1.4 Windows Deployment Modifications Made in WDS
for Windows Server 2008

Changes from RIS	Changes from WDS on Windows Server 2003
Ability to deploy Windows Vista and Windows 2008.	Ability to create multicast transmissions of data and images.
Windows PE is the boot operating system.	Ability to transmit data and images using multicasting on a stand-alone server (when you install Transport Server).
Image-based installation using Windows image (.wim) files.	
Ability to create multicast transmissions of data and images.	Does not support RISETUP images or OSChooser screens.
Ability to transmit data and images using multicasting on a stand-alone server (when you install Transport Server).	Enhanced TFTP server. Ability to network-boot x64-based computers with Extensible Firmware Interface (EFI).
An extensible and higher-performing PXE server.	Metric reporting for installations.

Continued

Table 1.4 Continued. Windows Deployment Modifications Made in WDS for Windows Server 2008

Changes from RIS	Changes from WDS on Windows Server 2003
A new boot menu format for selecting boot images.	
A new GUI that you can use to select and deploy images and to manage WDS servers and clients.	

The following are the requirements for installing WDS:

- AD DS (member server or DC)
- DHCP (WDS works with PXE, which works with DHCP)
- DNS.
- NTFS volume (required for storing images)
- Credentials (to install WDS, local administrator rights are needed)

NOTE

The Deployment Server requires that AD DS, DHCP, and DNS are available on your network. The Transport Server does not require any additional roles or services. Both of these services require an NTFS partition for the file store.

Before you begin, you need to configure WDS by running either the Windows Deployment Services Configuration Wizard or WDSUtil.exe. You will also need to add at least one boot image and one install image to the image store.

To install Windows operating systems from a WDS server, either the client computers must be PXE-enabled or you must use the Windows Server 2008 version of Windows PE.

Configuring WDS

Configuring and installing WDS on Windows Server 2003 is an update available in the Windows Automated Installation Kit (WAIK) and in SP2 for Server 2003.

However, installing WDS on a Windows Server 2008 computer is much easier because you can use the server manager to install the WDS Role. Together with the requirements, WDS is an easy-to-install and easy-to-use solution for deploying Vista and Server 2008 operating systems.

EXERCISE 1.5

CONFIGURING WDS ON WINDOWS SERVER 2008

1. On the Add Server Roles Wizard page (Figure 1.26), click the **Windows Deployment Services** checkbox, and then click **Next**.

Figure 1.26 Selecting Windows Deployment Services

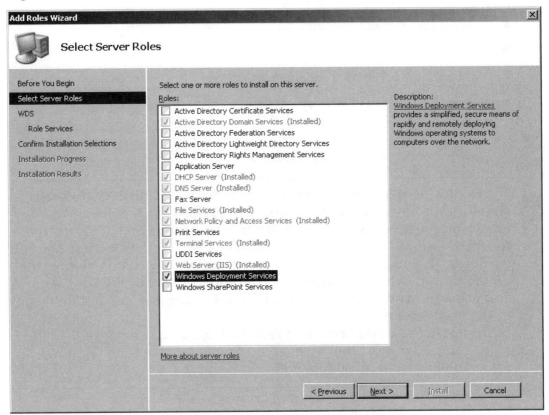

2. If necessary, review the information on the Windows Deployment Services page (Figure 1.27), and then click **Next**.

Figure 1.27 Reviewing WDS Information

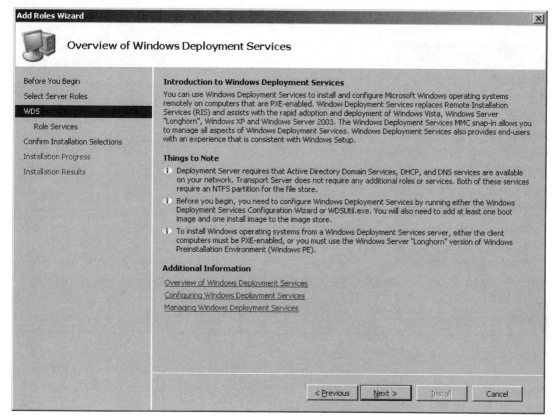

3. On the Select Role Services page (Figure 1.28), check the boxes required and then click **Next**.

Figure 1.28 Selecting the Role Services to Install

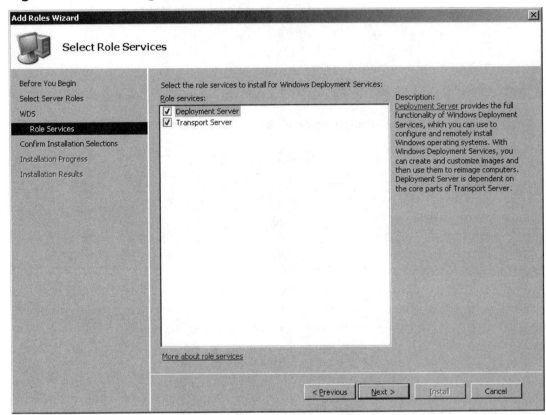

4. On the Confirm Installation Selections page (Figure 1.29), click **Install**.

Figure 1.29 Confirming the Installation Selections

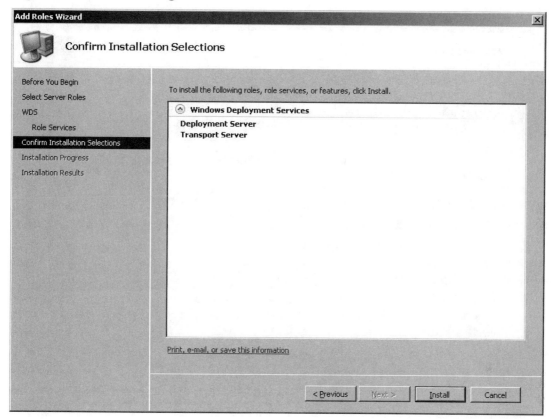

5. On the Welcome Page of the WDS installation page (Figure 1.30), click **Next**.

Figure 1.30 The Configuration Wizard Welcome Page

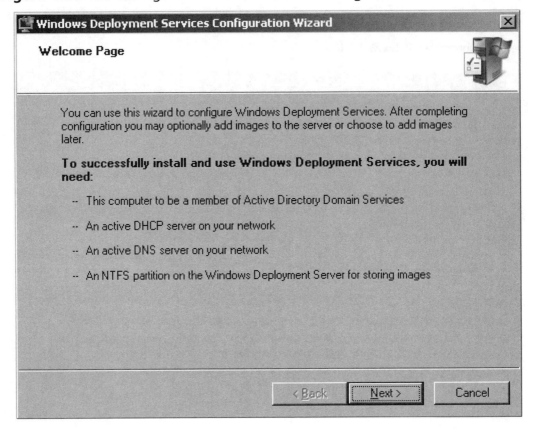

6. On the System Volume Warning page (Figure 1.31), click **Next**.

Figure 1.31 The System Volume Warning

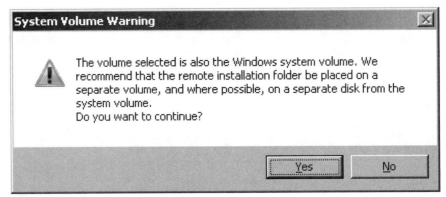

7. On the DHCP Option 60 page (Figure 1.32), select whether you want to configure the server to not listen on port 67 and to configure DHCP option 60 to PXE client, and then click **Next**.

Figure 1.32 DHCP Options

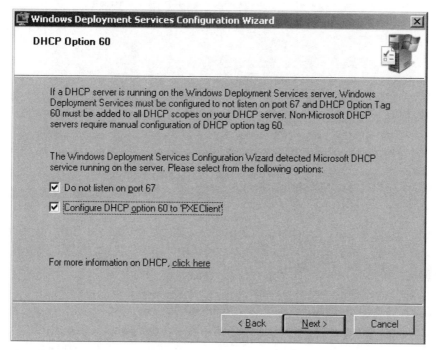

8. On the PXE Server Initial Settings page (Figure 1.33), specify how you would like the WDS server to respond to client computers, and then click **Finish**.

Figure 1.33 Configuring PXE Server Initial Settings

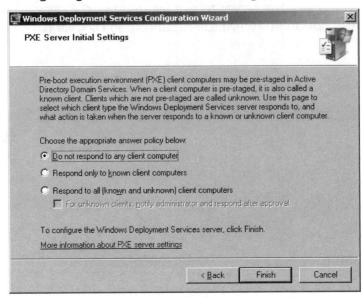

9. On the Configuration Complete page (Figure 1.34), choose whether you would like to add images to the WDS Server now and then click **Finish**.

Figure 1.34 The Configuration Complete Page

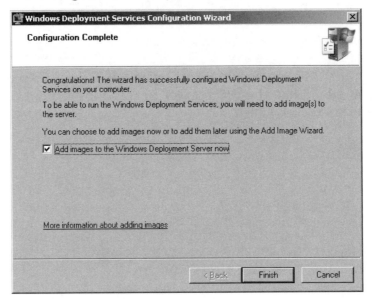

Capturing WDS Images

WDS allows you to capture the following kinds of images using the Windows Image (.wim) format:

- **Boot Image** Windows PE 2.0 is the new boot image format and it presents you with a boot menu that contains a list of images that users can install. The standard boot images included with Vista and Server 2008 are located on the installation media at \Sources\boot.wim.

- **Capture Image** This launches the WDS capture utility instead of Set-up. The reference computer previously prepared with Sysprep boots into a capture image and becomes the host from which an image is created, and then saves the image as a .wim file.

- **Discover Image** This forces the client computer to start in WDS mode to discover the WDS server. This is meant for computers that are not PXE-enabled.

- **Install Image** The standard install image included with Vista and Windows Server 2008 is located on the installation media at \Sources\ install.wim.

The following prerequisites are required for creating images:

- Sufficient disk space is needed when creating new images; also, images must be kept on an NTFS volume.

- A writable CD or DVD drive with writable media is required for creating bootable media.

- Local Administrator membership is required.

- The version of sysprep.exe that is running to prepare a client computer to be captured must match the version of sysprep.exe located on that operating system.

- Windows IAK is needed to create bootable .ISO images.

You can also associate an unattend file with an image. This means you will be able to deploy images with WDS to client computers and have the unattend.xml file answer all the questions needed by user input (such as entering credentials, choosing an install image, and configuring the disk), making the operating system rollout completely automatic. The unattend file is stored on the WDS server in the \WDSClientUnattend folder. This is called the WDS client unattend file.

A second unattend file is called the Image unattend file. It is used to automate the remaining phases of setup (e.g., offline servicing, Sysprep specialize, and Mini-Setup).

In addition to installing the Deployment Server you also have the choice of installing the Transport Server. The Transport Server will be used to enable multi-cast downloads of data. This is a subset of the functionality of WDS. The Transport Server can be a stand-alone server and does not need the AD DS, DHCP, or DNS server roles to function.

Creating multicast transmissions of images allows you to deploy a large number of client computers without putting a burden on the network. By default, this feature is disabled. The following two options are available for the multicast type:

- **Auto-Cast** As two clients request the same image at different timed intervals they are both joined to the same transmission.

- **Scheduled-Cast** Based on a schedule specified by date and or start time, the transmission will begin for a number of clients requesting images.

TEST DAY TIP

WDS is not included in Windows Server 2008 for Itanium-based systems or Windows Server 2008 Web Edition.

Deploying WDS Images

Working as a network administrator and having to deal with adding multiple computers to a network or constant reformatting is a familiar occurrence. WDS is a great way to easily deploy images across a network, and best of all, it is included with Windows Server 2008.

EXERCISE 1.6

USING WDS TO DEPLOY IMAGES FROM WINDOWS SERVER 2008

Follow these steps to use WDS to deploy images from Windows Server 2008:

1. Click on **Start | Administrative Tools | Windows Deployment Services**.

2. In the left pane of the Windows Deployment Services MMC snap-in, expand the server list.

3. Click the server that you want to manage.

4. Right-click the **Install Images** folder and select **Add Install Image**.

5. Create a new image group and click **Next**.

6. Browse to the install media of Vista or Server 2008; in the \source directory choose the install.wim file and click **Next**, as shown in Figure 1.35.

Figure 1.35 The Add Image Wizard

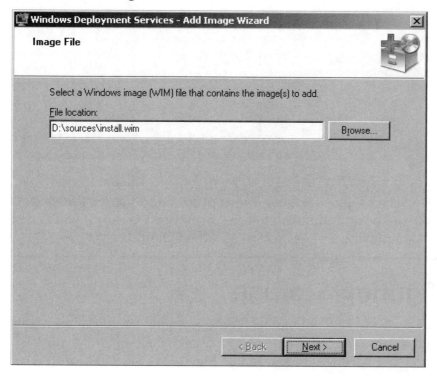

7. Name the capture image, as shown in Figure 1.36, and click **Next**.

Figure 1.36 Naming the Capture Image

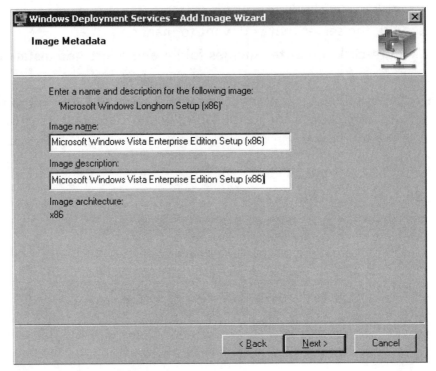

8. Select a place to save the capture image and click **Next**. Once the boot and install images have been created, you can start deploying images to PXE-enabled clients.

Configuring Storage

In the mid- to late 1990s, storage was not a real issue because most organizations didn't need to store large amounts of data or archives. This is not the case today, as there is a great need for storage and archiving. The demand for storage and archiving, coupled with the high availability of storage, has increased exponentially. Networked attached storage (NAS), storage area networks (SANs), and technologies such as Fibre Channels and others used to be available only in enterprise class storage devices; now you can get this functionality at the server level. Windows Server 2008 includes a massive number of improvements to its storage features, making storage decisions easier for the administrator and resulting in a more stable and more available infrastructure for users.

RAID Types

RAID (Redundant Array of Inexpensive Disks) provides higher levels of reliability, performance, and storage capacity, all at a lower cost. It compromises out of multiple disk drives (an array). These fault-tolerant arrays are classified into six different RAID levels, numbered 0 through 5. Each level uses a different set of storage algorithms to implement fault tolerance.

There are two types of RAID: hardware RAID and software RAID. Hardware RAID will always have a disk controller dedicated to the RAID to which you can cable up the disk drives. Software RIAD is more flexible and less expensive, but requires more CPU cycles and power to run. It also operates on a partition-by-partition grouping basis as opposed to hardware RAID systems, which group together entire disk drives.

RAID 0 is an array of disks implemented with disk striping. This means that if there are two disks in the array it will offer two times the speed of one disk, which offers no drive redundancy or fault tolerance. The only advantage it offers is speed.

RAID 1 is an array of disks implemented in a mirror; this means that one disk will be a copy of the other disk. Each time any data gets written to the disk, the system must write the same information to both disks. To increase system performance in RAID 1, you need to implement a duplex RAID 1 system. This means that each mirrored array of disks will have its own host adapter.

RAID 2 is an array of disks implemented with disk striping with added error correction code (ECC) disks. Each time any data is written to the array these codes are calculated and will be written alongside the data on the ECC disks to confirm that no errors have occurred from the time when the data was written.

RAID 3 is an array of disks implemented with disk striping and a dedicated disk for parity information. Because RAID 3 uses bit striping, its write and read performance is rather slow compared to RAID 4.

RAID 4 is an array of disks implemented with disk striping and a dedicated disk for parity information. It is similar to RAID 3, bit it performs block striping or sector striping instead of bit striping. Thus, with RAID 4 one entire sector is written to one drive and the next sector is written to the next drive.

RAID 5 is an array of disks implemented with disk striping and a disk for parity also striped across all disks. RAID 5 is handles small amounts of information efficiently. This is the preferred option when setting up fault tolerance.

RAID 6 is the same as RAID 5, with the added feature of calculating two sets of parity information and striping it across all drives. This allows for the failure of two disks but decreases performance slightly.

Nested RAID 01 and 10 combine the best features of both RAID technologies. RAID 01 is a mirror of two striped sets and RAID 10 is a stripe of mirrored sets.

RAID 3, RAID 4, and RAID 5 disk array designs allow for data recovery. When one of the drives in the array becomes faulty in any way, the parity disk is able to rebuild the faulty drive in the array.

Network Attached Storage

NAS is a technology that delivers storage over the network. An NAS will be attached directly to the organization's network and will reduce the shortcomings previously experienced in a normal LAN. These shortcomings were:

- The rise of storage capacity needs
- The rise of protection and security to the data stored
- Management complexity for the system administrator

The NAS could be seen as a solution to these challenges. With the added benefit of being attached directly to the organization's IP network, it becomes accessible to all computers that are part of the network. NAS devices or servers are designed for their simplicity of deployment, plugged into the network without interfering with other services. NAS devices are mostly maintenance free and managing them is minimal due to their scaled-down functionality on the software side. The scaled-down operating system and other software on the NAS unit offer data storage and access functionality and management. Configuring the NAS unit is mostly done through a Web interface, as opposed to being connected to it directly. A typical NAS unit will contain one or more hard disks normally configured into a logical RAID layout. NAS provides storage and a file system with a file-based protocol such as Network File System (NFS) or Server Message Block (SMB).

The benefits that come with a NAS are as follows:

- Extra networked storage capacity
- Its own CPU, motherboard, RAM, etc.
- Built-in RAID
- Expandability

Potential drawbacks of NAS include:

- Potentially too many input/output operations
- More difficult to upgrade than a server

You can include an NAS as part of a more comprehensive solution such as a SAN. In an NAS, file serving is much faster as the file I/O is not competing for server resources compared to a file server hosting other solutions. You also can use NAS as centralized storage for managing backups or other operating system data.

Storage Area Networks

A SAN is architecture connected to the organization's LAN. This architecture could consist of numerous types of vendor and/or sizes of disk arrays, or even tape libraries. Connecting disk arrays to the organization's LAN using a high-speed medium (Fibre Channel or Gigabit Ethernet) typically through SAN using Fibre Channel switches to servers benefits the organization by increasing storage capacity, as multiple servers can share the storage for common file sharing, e-mail servers, or database servers. Large enterprises have been benefiting from SAN technologies in which the storage is separate, from being physically connected to servers to being attached directly to the network, for many years. SANs are highly scalable and provide flexible storage allocation, better storage deployment, and higher efficiency backup solutions which can span over a WAN.

Traditionally, SANs have been difficult to deploy and maintain. Ensuring high data availability and optimal resource usage out of the storage array connected to switches in the middle, as well as monitoring the physical network, has become a full-time job and requires different skills than managing storage on a server. As a result, small to medium-size businesses have started to need SAN technology, and with the different set of skills required it has proven difficult to implement and manage. Fibre Channel, being the established storage technology during the past decade, made this almost impossible for smaller businesses. With this in mind, other well-known IP technologies are now becoming a viable option when using iSCSI. Simplifying a SAN does not mean removing the current SAN infrastructure. It means hiding the complexity of managing such a storage solution by implementing a technology such as iSCSI.

Figure 1.37 shows the differences between Direct Attached Storage (DAS), NAS, and SAN.

Figure 1.37 Differences Between DAS, NAS, and SAN

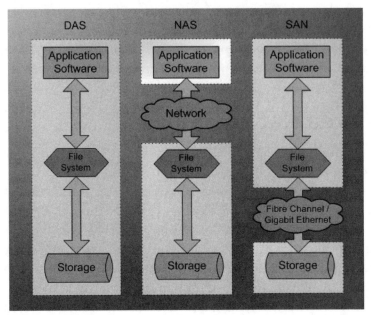

SAN benefits include the following:

- Simplified administration
- Storage flexibility
- Servers that boot from SAN
- Efficient data recovery
- Storage replication
- iSCSI protocols developed to allow SAN extension over IP networks, resulting in less costly remote backups

The core SAN Fibre Channel infrastructure uses a technology called *fabric technology*. This is designed to handle storage communications and it provides a reliable level of data storage compared to an NAS. In addition, it allows many-to-many communication in the SAN infrastructure. A typical fabric is made up of a number of Fibre Channel switches.

Fibre Channel

The Fibre Channel Protocol (FCP) is the interface protocol used to talk to SCSI on the Fibre Channel. The Fibre Channel has the following three topologies, just like in a network topology design. The topologies designate how ports are connected. In Fibre Channel terms, a port is a device connected to the network.

- **Point-to-Point (FC-P2P)** Two networked devices connected back to back.

- **Arbitral loop (FC-AL)** All networked devices connected in a loop. This is similar to the token ring network topology, and carries the same advantages and disadvantages.

- **Switched fabric (FC-SW)** All networked devices connected to Fibre Channel switches.

The line speed rates for Fibre Channel can be anything from 1 GB per second up to 10 GB per second, depending on the topology and hardware implemented. The Fibre Channel layers start with a Physical layer (FC0), which includes the cables, fiber optics, and connectors. The Data Link layer (FC1) implements encoding and decoding. The Network layer (FC2) is the core of the Fibre Channel and defines the protocols. The Common services layer (FC3) could include functions such as RAID encryption. The Protocol Mapping layer (FC4) is used for protocol encapsulation. The following ports are defined in the Fibre Channel:

- **N_port** The node port
- **NL_port** The node loop port
- **F_port** The fabric port
- **FL_port** The fabric loop port
- **E_port** An expansion port used to link two Fibre Channels
- **EX_port** A connection between the router and switch
- **TE_port** Provides trunking expansion, with e_ports trunked together
- **G_port** A generic port
- **L_port** The loop port
- **U_port** A universal port

The Fibre Channel Host Bus Adapter (HBA) has a unique World Wide Name (WWN); this is comparable to a network card's Media Access Control (MAC) address. The HBA installs into a server, like any other network card or SCSI host adapter.

iSCSI

Internet Small Computer System Interface (iSCSI) is a very popular SAN protocol, utilizing attached storage with the illusion of locally attached disks. It is unlike Fibre Channel, which requires special fibre cabling. You can use iSCSI to use storage located anywhere in the LAN as part of the SAN over an existing infrastructure VPN or Ethernet. In essence, iSCSI allows a server and a RAID array to communicate using SCSI commands over the IP network. iSCSI requires no additional cabling, and as a result, iSCSI is the low-cost alternative to Fibre Channel.

iSCSI Initiators and Targets

iSCSI uses both initiators and targets. The initiator acts as the traditional SCSI bus adapter, sending SCSI commands. There are two broad types of initiator: software initiator and hardware initiator.

The software initiator implements iSCSI, using an existing network stack and a network interface card (NIC) to emulate a SCSI device. The software initiator is available in the Windows 2008 operating system. Figure 1.38 shows the iSCSI Initiator Properties page.

The hardware initiator uses dedicated hardware to implement iSCSI. Run by firmware on the hardware, it alleviates the overhead placed on iSCSI and Transmission Control Protocol (TCP) processing. The HBA is a combination of a NIC and SCSI bus adapter within the hardware initiator. If a client requests data from a RAID array, the operating system does not have to generate the SCSI commands and data requests; the hardware initiator will.

Figure 1.38 The iSCSI Initiator Properties Page

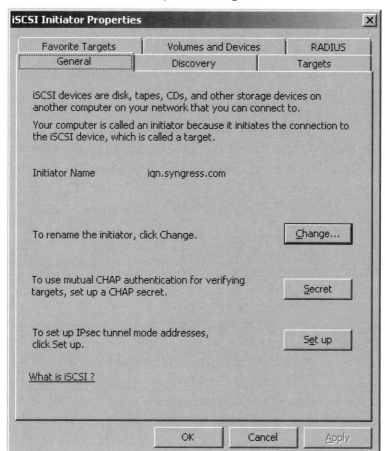

The iSCSI target represents hard disk storage and is available in the Windows Server 2008 operating system. A storage array is an example of an iSCSI target. A Logical Unit Number (LUN) symbolizes an individual SCSI device. The initiator will talk to the target to connect to a LUN, emulating a SCSI hard disk. The iSCSI system will actually have the functionality to format and manage a file system on the iSCSI LUN.

When iSCSI is used in a SAN it is referred to by special iSCSI names. iSCSI provides the following three name structures:

- iSCSI Qualified Name (IQN)
- Extended Unique Identifier (EUI)
- T11 Network Address Authority (NAA)

An iSCSI participant is usually defined by three or four fields:

- Hostname or IP address (e.g., iscsi.syngress.com)

- Port number (e.g., 3260)

- iSCSI name (e.g., the IQN iqn.2008–02.com.syngess:01.acd4ab21.fin256)

- Optional CHAP secret (e.g., chapsecret)

Now that the iSCSI initiators and targets have names, they have to prove their identity; they do this by using the Challenge-Handshake Authentication Protocol (CHAP). This prevents cleartext identity from taking place. In addition to using CHAP for securing identity handshaking, you can also use IPSec over the IP-based protocol. To ensure that traffic flowing between initiators and targets is as secure as possible, the SAN is run in a logically isolated network segment.

Additionally, as with all IP-based protocols, IPSec can be used at the network layer. The iSCSI negotiation protocol is designed to accommodate other authentication schemes, though interoperability issues limit their deployment. This eliminates most of the security concerns for important data traveling on the IP LAN. The other security concern is for servers to initiate to the storage array, without it being authorized. Regular audits and checks have to be put in place to ensure that initiators that are authenticated to an array are legitimately initiated to a LUN.

Targets can be much more than a RAID array. If a physical device with a SCSI parallel interface or a Fibre Channel interface gets bridged by using iSCSI target software, it can also become part of the SAN. Virtual Tape Libraries (VTLs) are used in a disk storage scenario for storing data to virtual tapes. Security surveillance with IP-enabled cameras can be the initiator targeting iSCSI RAID as a target to store hours of quality video for later processing.

Mount Points

One of the benefits of using NTFS is having the ability to use volume mount points. A volume mount point is essentially placed in a directory on a current volume (hard disk). For example, this means that a folder on the C: drive called "removable" can be made the mount point to the new hard drive you have added to the computer. The "removable" folder will be the gateway to store data on the newly added volume. The volume to be mounted can be formatted in a number of file systems, including NTFS, FAT16, FAT32, CDFS, or UDF.

To better understand volume mount points, consider this scenario. A user has installed the computer operating system on a relatively small C: drive and is concerned about unnecessarily using up storage space on the C: drive which will be needed by the Windows operating system itself. The user works with large motion graphics files. Knowing that these files can consume a lot of storage space, the user creates a volume mount point to the C: drive called "motion". The user then configures the motion graphics application to store the motion graphic files under c:/motion. This means that the files are not using up valuable storage space on the C: drive, but are actually using storage space on the new volume mount point.

EXERCISE 1.7

MOUNTING A NEW VOLUME TO THE C: DRIVE

1. Create an empty folder on the NTFS formatted C: drive, called "mount point" (this folder name can be whatever you want; it doesn't have to be mount point).

2. Open **Computer Management** and select **Disk Management**.

3. Right-click the new volume (e.g., the newly added 40 GB partition or physical drive) and select **Change Drive Letter and Path,** as shown in Figure 1.39.

Figure 1.39 Adding a Mount Point

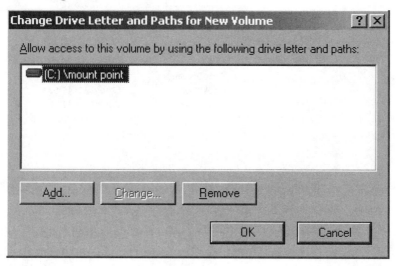

4. Click **Add,** and select **Mount into the following empty NTFS folder**.

5. Browse to the empty NTFS folder on the C: drive and select **OK**.

6. Figure 1.40 shows what the result will look like. The "mount point" folder in the C: drive with a drive icon is a mount point to the physical drive or partition that was selected in Disk Management. The result is that now you have an extra 40 GB of storage mounted to the C: drive that you can use.

Figure 1.40 The New Mount Point

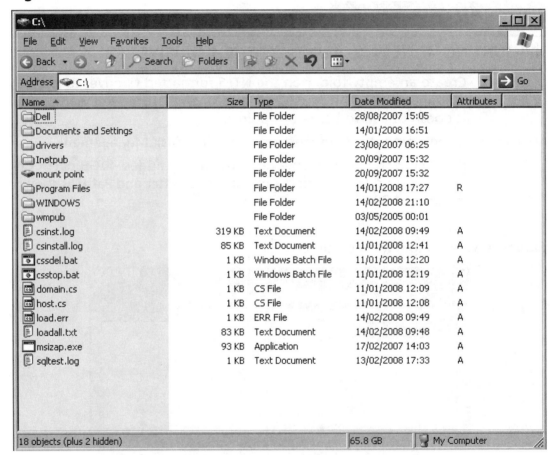

7. To remove the mount point from the selected folder, follow the same steps and choose **Remove** from the menu in step 4. Removing the mount point does not remove the folder originally created, nor does it remove the files stored in the physical disk. You can mount the drive again, or you can assign another drive letter to the drive to access the files on the drive.

Configuring High Availability

High availability is one of the main objectives of a successful IT department when it comes to business-critical systems, services, and applications. The business can result in considerable losses if services go down or fail. High availability can be described as implementing a design, which ensures a very high level of production continuity over a specific amount of time. High availability will mean something different to the individual or the organization as a whole, with either the entire picture in mind, or in a centric sense, concentrating on only one service or system. The goal is to minimize the time a service is down or unavailable.

Windows Server 2008 supports two already popular high-availability features to help prevent disastrous downtime on critical systems. Improvements to failover clustering and network load balancing (NLB) features have been made in Windows Server 2008, offering simplified management and even more robust functionality built into the operating system.

Failover Clusters

A failover cluster consists of two or more independent servers configured with software and connected to storage, working together as one system. This configuration provides high availability. During production hours, if a failure occurs on the failover cluster on one of the server nodes, the cluster will redirect resources to one of the other server nodes in the failover cluster. This ensures that server hardware failures are not the cause of lengthy downtime in a production environment.

The failover cluster feature is available only in the Windows Server 2008 Enterprise and Windows Server 2008 Datacenter editions of Windows Server 2008. Windows Server 2008 failover clusters aim to make the process of clustering more than one server together easy, secure, and stable. Setting up and managing clusters is now easier, cluster communication with storage has improved, and security and networking have also been improved.

A geographically dispersed cluster is a cluster setup which consists of nodes in different geographic locations. Windows Server 2008 failover clustering has enabled the cluster administrator to use a geographical cluster (geocluster) more readily. This type of cluster is built on a storage and networking infrastructure that is very different from the normal quorum device cluster. The storage infrastructure consists of data-replication software whereby the quorum disk is also replicated in real time. Before Windows Server 2008, the networking infrastructure had to be constructed out of a non-routed VLAN. With Windows Server 2008 the failover cluster in a geographically dispersed configuration no longer has to connect with VLANs and the limitation to a single subnet is now removed. The heartbeat timeout between the nodes is now configurable, which means that the geocluster can now be hosted over even greater distances.

Installing and Validating a Failover Cluster

The clustering hardware required includes disks shared between the nodes in the cluster. The shared disks must be on a SAN using Fibre Channel to utilize the improvements made for applications that use dynamic data, such as database servers or e-mail servers. Data must be stored on a SAN solution so that it will allow each node in the cluster to access the data in the event that one node has a failure. Hardware components that are part of the complete configuration (servers, network, and storage) must be marked as certified for Windows Server 2008. The complete configurations have to pass all the tests put on hardware when running the Cluster Validation Tool located in the Failover Cluster Management tool shown in Figure 1.39. A cluster depends on other technologies, including AD DS and name resolution services such as DNS and WINS,. Also, it is recommended that you use static IP addresses for all of the nodes in the cluster.

EXERCISE 1.8

INSTALLING FAILOVER CLUSTERING ON A WINDOWS SERVER 2008 OPERATING SYSTEM

Complete these steps to install failover clustering on a Windows Server 2008 operating system:

1. Open the **Server Manager**.
2. Click on **Add Features**.
3. Check the **Failover Clustering** checkbox and click **Next**. Figure 1.41 shows the Failover Cluster Management Console.

Figure 1.41 The Failover Cluster Management Console

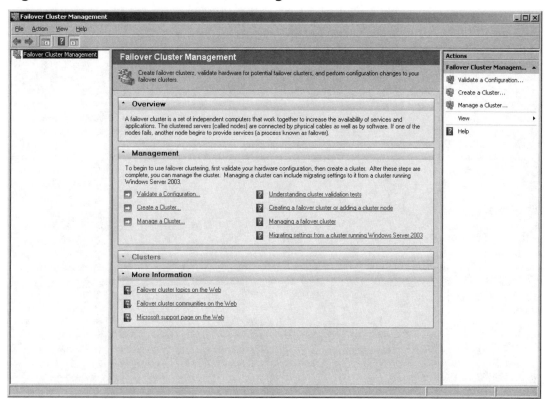

4. Click on **Install**.
5. When the installation is complete, click **Close**.

Figure 1.42 shows a typical two-node failover cluster. Node 1 and node 2 have each passed the hardware validation, and the Windows 2008 failover clustering feature is successfully installed. The storage shared by both nodes in the cluster also holds the witness disk. The witness disk holds the cluster log files and votes on which node to use in a failover scenario. Each node has a Resource Group consisting of applications and services; it also includes the elements needed by the resource, such as IP address and network name. If node 1 fails, the resource group needed to run the services and application on node 1 will start up on node 2; this means the failover has completed successfully and you can start troubleshooting why node 1 has failed.

Figure 1.42 The Failover Cluster

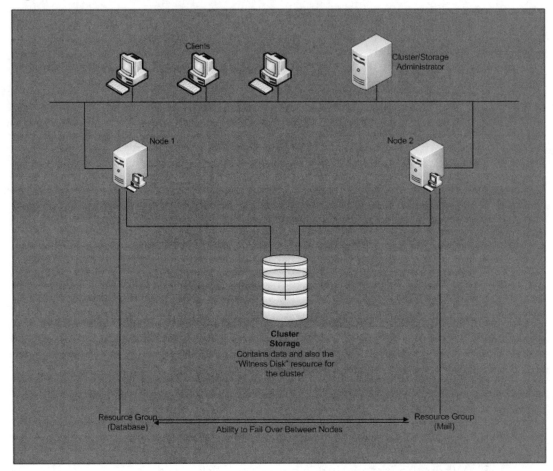

Once the hardware, network, and storage have been validated the setup can start. Setup has been improved in Windows Server 2008 to make it much easier for the administrator to script an installation and automate the cluster rollout. If the need is there to migrate a cluster from one environment to another, the cluster settings can be captured and then applied to another cluster.

Managing the Failover Cluster

When backing up a failover cluster, you can choose to back up the configuration or the data on the disks, or you can choose to back up both. To back up a cluster the cluster must be running and must have quorum. You can restore a node in a failover cluster in two different ways. Restoring the node only (a non-authoritative restore) restores the failed node to its previous state, whereas restoring the entire cluster configuration (an authoritative restore) restores the entire configuration of the cluster's previous state.

In Windows Server 2008, management operations have been improved for ease of use. For instance, you can use Windows Management Instrumentation (WMI) to manage a cluster, which means you can easily manage any cluster from any server by using PowerShell.

In addition, backing up and restoring the cluster configuration is now easier, thanks to the Volume Shadow Copy Service.

Improvements have also been made to the infrastructure of the cluster. For instance, you can now configure the witness disk (previously the quorum disk) to become unavailable and have the rest of the cluster stay available. The rule is that two of the three must be available: either one node and the witness disk, or two nodes and no witness disk. Also, greater stability has been accomplished by isolating dynamic link library (DLL) files that execute a false action.

New functionality in Windows Server 2008 failover cluster includes support for globally unique identifier (GUID) partition table (GPT) disks. This means that it is now possible to have partitions larger than 2 terabytes. GPT disks also have built-in redundancy in the way partition information is stored.

IPv6 and DNS improvements have been incorporated with the removal of the NetBIOS and WINS requirement.

Windows Server 2008 has limits on how many server computers can be in a failover cluster. Windows Server 2008 32-bit can support up to eight nodes. The Windows Server 2008 64-bit version can support up to 16 nodes. The Windows Server 2008 maximum node count can be limited by the application run on the nodes, or by a mixed server environment; for example, if the cluster has a mix of Windows Server 2000 and Server 2003 nodes, the limit will come down from eight nodes to four nodes, as the maximum number of nodes in a Server 2000 cluster is four nodes.

TEST DAY TIP

The failover cluster feature is not available in Windows Web Server 2008 or Windows Server 2008 standard.

Network Load Balancing

As the need is there for technology such as a failover cluster, the need is also there for server or service scalability. Network servers need to scale performance for handling huge numbers of network client requests. Because NLB does not need to comply with a list of system hardware requirements, it is easier to implement on any hardware, making it more scalable than other load balancing technologies that exist. NLB clusters can have up to 32 hosts, and all of the hosts must be on the same subnet.

EXERCISE 1.9

INSTALLING AND CONFIGURING NETWORK LOAD BALANCING

Complete these steps to install NLB on a Windows Server 2008 operating system:

1. Open the **Server Manager**.
2. Click on **Add Features**.
3. Check the **Network Load Balancing** checkbox and click **Next**.
4. Click on **Install**. Figure 1.43 shows a typical NLB configuration.

Figure 1.43 A Typical NLB Configuration

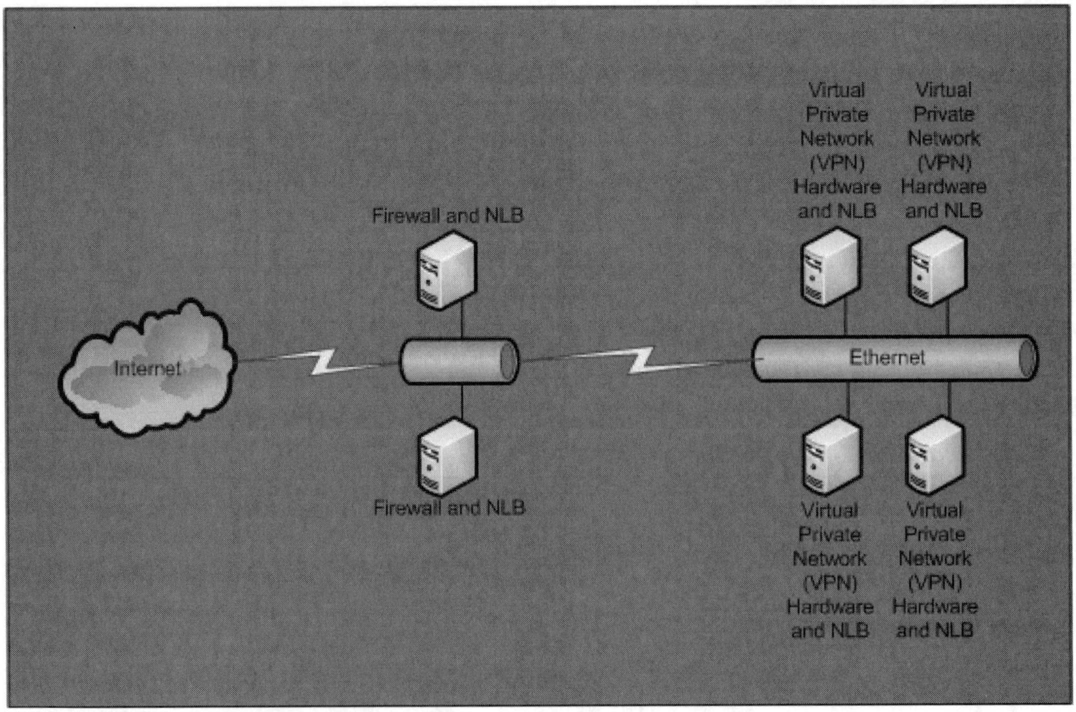

5. When the installation is complete, click **Close**.

Once the NLB feature has been installed you can start configuring the NLB cluster.

6. Open the **Network Load Balancing Manager**.

7. Right-click on **Network Load Balancing Clusters** and choose **New Cluster**.

8. Type the name of the first host that is going to be part of the NLB cluster and click **Connect** and then **Next**.

9. Use the **Dedicated IP Addresses** windows to add all the Transmission Control Protocol/Internet Protocol (TCP/IP) addresses of the servers in the NLB cluster, and then click **Next**. Add the second and consecutive servers that will be part of the cluster. Figure 1.44 shows the two servers added in this example. When you're done, click **Next**.

Figure 1.44 The New NLB Cluster Hosts

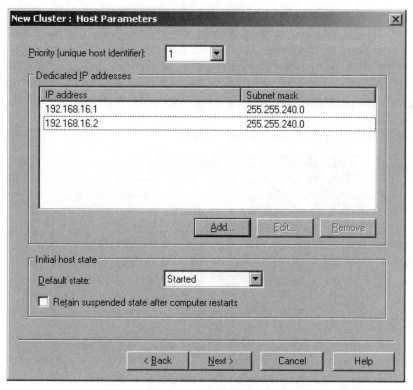

10. Use the **Cluster IP Addresses** window (Figure 1.45) to specify the virtual IP address that will be used to connect to the NLB cluster, and then click **Next**.

Figure 1.45 The Cluster IP Address Window

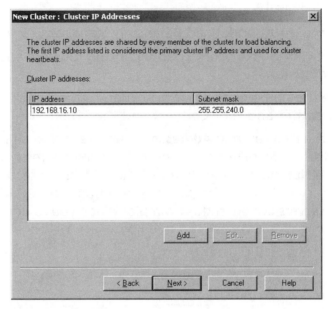

11. In the **Cluster Parameters** window (Figure 1.46), you can add the full Internet name for the cluster. You can also set the cluster operation mode. Click **Next** when you're done.

Figure 1.46 Setting the Cluster Parameters

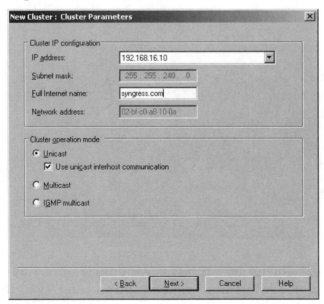

With NLB, when a client computer on the network makes a connection to the service or application hosted, it will make a connection to the virtual IP address (the cluster IP address) shown in Figure 1.45. The cluster will then decide which server in the NLB cluster will handle the request; all the other hosts on the NLB cluster will then drop the request.

NLB in Windows Server 2008 has been improved in various ways. For instance, IPv4 and IPv6 are both completely supported, including support for the IPv6 namespace in WMI. Plus, multiple IP addresses per node in the NLB cluster are now supported. In addition, Microsoft ISA server integration has also been improved with the new NLB, adding enhanced functionality by supporting clients with IPv4 and IPv6 traffic.

Configuring Windows Activation

With the release of Windows Vista and Windows Server 2008 a new approach to licensing has been taken to address counterfeit software within the computing ecosystem. The approach introduces activation across all editions of Windows Vista and Windows Server 2008, including volume licensing customers. The activation process ties together the product key, a copy of the software, and the device on which is it installed. This is done by establishing a unique hardware identification hash and associating it with the key. You can use several types of keys in this revised activation process:

- **Retail keys** Traditional single-machine keys that are activated via the Internet or telephone as part of installation

- **OEM keys** Used by system builders to activate the machine before shipping it to end-users

- **Multiple Activation Keys (MAKs)** One-time perpetual keys that can be activated via the Internet or telephone, up to a predetermined limit

- **Key Management Service (KMS) keys** Allow machines to activate through a locally hosted key management service which governs the number of activations allowed

The changes to the activation policies will require some additional planning for larger organizations; however, they have been accompanied by a set of services and guidance to minimize disruption to deployment processes. For users of retail keys the process has not changed from what has historically existed through previous versions of Windows. Both MAK and KMS keys, obtained through the volume license program, replace the volume license keys from previous releases, and introduce several new concepts in activation management.

Using Multiple Activation Keys

MAKs operate in a fashion that is similar to retail keys, but add a number of tools that ease administration by providing a set number of activated hosts on a single key and a proxy service that handles reactivation during rebuilds. In the most basic form, a MAK has a set number of activations that it can perform. This number does not necessarily align with your volume license agreement, but instead operates as though you were purchasing blocks of licenses. For each MAK you can activate a number of machines using an independent or proxied activation. Under the independent activation, each device will contact the Microsoft licensing clearinghouse as it would with a retail key to validate and activate the license. With proxy activation the computer will locate and activate through an instance of the Volume Activation Management Tool (VAMT), which is a stand-alone application residing on a computer in the network. Located using Active Directory, Workgroup membership, or a direct computer name/IP address, the VAMT processes the activation on behalf of the machine using the Installation ID (IID), storing the activation Confirmation ID (CID) and passing it on to the machine to activate. The advantage of the proxy method is that the machine can later be reactivated without having to contact the Microsoft clearinghouse. In addition, the MAK can handle disconnected activation through the transmission of an XML data file via a removable storage device. This can be useful for isolated and secure deployments that do not permit direct communication with Internet-based services.

Using Key Management Service Keys

For organizations with more than five servers or 25 clients, you can use the Key Management Service (KMS) to manage activation within the organization. The KMS provides a customer-hosted solution for managing activations among clients and servers within the domain, workgroup, and/or network (see Figure 1.47). When setting up a KMS on a Windows Server 2003 Service Pack 1 or later, or Windows Server 2008 system, you will automatically enable systems to find the KMS and register for authentication. To do this you need to first authorize the KMS by providing a KMS key that is validated with Microsoft. Once that process has been completed, clients can look to the KMS host to provide their activation license, which entitles them to 180 days of valid usage. After the initial activation, systems will attempt to reactivate the license every seven days to extend the 180-day window of their activation (similar to how DHCP works). The KMS host will also do its part to stay current by contacting Microsoft every 180 days to ensure that its key is valid.

Figure 1.47 KMS Communication

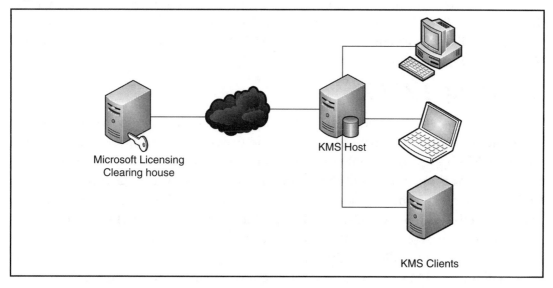

Microsoft Licensing
Clearing house

KMS Host

KMS Clients

License States

Regardless of the licensing method you choose, the state of your machine will fall into one of five license states:

- **Initial Grace (or Out-of-Box Grace) Period** The state that the system is in after the operating system has been installed, which is limited to 30 days and can be reset (rearmed) up to two additional times.

- **Non-Genuine Grace Period** When a computer is determined to be a non-genuine copy by the Windows Genuine Activation process it is put in this state, allowing you 30 days to reactivate it using a genuine copy and license key.

- **Out-of-Tolerance Grace** Begins when the hardware in the underlying system changes enough or when a system using a KMS key goes beyond 180 days without contact with a KMS host and lasts for 30 days.

- **Licensed** The state of the system when it has been properly activated.

- **Unlicensed** When any of the grace periods expire the system falls into a reduced functionality mode providing limited access to the system in one-hour increments.

Reporting

It should be noted that none of the license methods are tied to billing. It is still your responsibility to ensure that you have obtained the appropriate number of licenses for your organization. To assist you in this process you can retrieve statistical data through WMI, Systems Management Service 2003 Service Pack 3 or later, Systems Center Configuration Manager 2007, the KMS Operations Manager Pack, or the VAMT tool for MAK keys.

Installing a KMS

The KMS ships with volume license editions of Windows Server 2008. When you install the software it automatically bundles the necessary bits to make any particular server a KMS host. It is available on both standard and core installations of Windows Server 2008. You can also install the KMS on Windows Server 2003 with Service Pack 1 or later using the additional components located at http://go.microsoft.com/fwlink/?LinkID=82964 for 32-bit and http://go.microsoft.com/fwlink/?LinkId=83041 for 64-bit systems. Overall it uses very few resources and will easily coexist with other services installed on the server.

Installing the KMS host requires nothing more than a few commands. You can use this process for up to six KMS hosts per key. This gives you the flexibility to deploy KMS close to your clients and servers. Each host is autonomous in its operation. You will not need to deal with any information synchronization because the process of activation deals mainly with counterfeit software and less with enforcing limits based on the number of acquired licenses.

EXERCISE 1.10

INSTALLING A KMS HOST

1. Install a volume license edition of Windows Server 2008; do not provide a product key during the setup process.

2. When the installation is complete, open a command prompt and execute the following command to install the KMS key on the server:

   ```
   CSCRIPT %SYSTEMROOT%\SYSTEM32\SLMgr.vbs /ipk <KMS Key>
   ```

3. With the KMS key installed, you can activate the KMS host using either online or telephone activation. To activate the host using the Internet, open a command prompt and execute the following command:

   ```
   SCRIPT %SYSTEMROOT%\SYSTEM32\SLMgr.vbs /ato
   ```

4. To active the host using the telephone, open a command prompt and execute the following command:

```
%SYSTEMROOT%\SYSTEM32\SLUI.exe 4
```

Configuring & Implementing...

Choosing the Key to Use

Both MAK and KMS keys are broken into groups to simplify activation. Each group applies to a specific set of products. MAK keys will activate only products within the group, whereas KMS keys are hierarchical, meaning that they will activate products within the group and lower groups as well. The groups are listed in Table 1.5.

Since KMS keys are hierarchical, you should always use the KMS key that covers the highest product group your organization has licensed. This way, you can ensure that all KMS clients can be activated from the KMS host. Although each KMS key supports up to six KMS hosts, a single host can support an unlimited number of activations.

Table 1.5 KMS Product Groups

Product Group	Windows Editions
Vista	Windows Vista Business
	Windows Vista Enterprise
Server Group A	Windows Web Server 2008
Server Group B	Windows Server 2008 Standard
	Windows Server 2008 Enterprise
Server Group C	Windows Server 2008 Datacenter
	Windows Server 2008 for Itanium-based Systems

The KMS host is now ready to be used by KMS clients for activation. Once it is installed, make sure that TCP port 1688 is open and accessible to clients, as that is the port used for KMS communication. Additional configuration is optional and will usually not be required. If necessary, you can modify the various options using SLMgr.vbs and one of the following command-line parameters:

- **Change the TCP port** *SLMgr.vbs /SPrt <Port>*
- **Disable Automatic DNS Publishing** *SLMgr.vbs /CDNS*
- **Enable Automatic DNS Publishing** *SLMgr.vbs /SDNS*
- **Force the KMS Host to a Lower Process Priority** *SLMr.vbs /CPri*
- **Revert the KMS Host to a Normal Process Priority** *SLMgr.vgs /SPri*
- **Set the Client Activation Interval (default is 120 minutes)** *SLMgr. vbs /sai <Interval>*
- **Set the Client Activation Renewal Interval (default is 7 days)** *SLMgr.vbs /sri <Interval>*

After you change any of the preceding parameters, be sure to restart the Microsoft Software Licensing service using the following command:

```
NET STOP SLSVC && NET START SLSVC
```

Creating a DNS SRV Record

When the KMS host is activated it will automatically attempt to publish an SRV record in the local DNS zone to assist clients in locating the service. The SRV record, defined in RFC 2782, is supported by a number of DNS servers, including Microsoft's DNS Server. In addition, the KMS host will attempt to use Dynamic DNS to update the record to ensure that the information is up-to-date. When the KMS is installed, however, you will need to manually remove the SRV record.

EXERCISE 1.11

ADDING THE KMS DNS RECORDS MANUALLY

1. Open the **Control Panel**, and under **System and Maintenance | Administration Tools** double-click the **DNS** shortcut.

2. In the **DNS Manager** management console, expand the server and **Forward Lookup Zones** nodes in the left-hand pane.

3. Right-click the domain in which you wish to create the record, and select **Other New Records**.

4. In the **Resource Record Type** dialog, select **Service Location (SRV)** and click **Create Record**.

5. In the **New Resource Record** dialog, type in the following values and click **OK**, and then **_VL**.

   Service: **_VLMCS**
   Protocol: **_TCP**
   Port Number: **1688**
   Host Offering This Service: **mykmshost.contoso.com**

For larger organizations, you may need to have the SRV record published across several DNS zones. You can do this by adding each domain in the *DnsDomainPublishList* Registry value. You can easily add this value with the following code:

```
%SYSTEMROOT%\SYSTEM32\REG.EXE ADD "HKLM\SOFTWARE\Microsoft\Windows NT\
CurrentVersion\SL" /v DnsDomainPublishList /t REG_MULTI_SZ /d contoso.com\
0fabrikam.com
```

In addition to using Reg.exe, you can also modify the value using the Registry Editor. Once you have completed your modifications, restart the service for the changes to take effect.

Enabling Clients to Use KMS

When deploying clients and servers from volume license media, they will look for a KMS host to process their activation request. This is done through automatic service location using an SRV record in the primary domain or through a specified IP address. When the system is joined to the domain it will first look in the domain's DNS zone. If the system runs in workgroup mode it will search DNS based on the primary DNS suffix of the machine, or the one assigned via DHCP option 15. If neither of those options works for your environment you can also point the machine to use a specific hostname/IP address. To do this open a command prompt and run the following command:

```
CSCRIPT %SYSTEMROOT%\SYSTEM32\SLMgr.vbs /SKMS <Hostname or IP Address>[:Port]
```

After restarting the Microsoft Software Licensing Service the computer will use the specified address to locate the KMS host. The service supports fully qualified names, local NetBIOS names, and IPv4/IPv6 addresses.

Activating the System

After installing a machine, you may want to activate the system prior to distribution. This is useful when you are distributing mobile laptops or systems that will be disconnected for a period of time. To activate a machine, from a command prompt run the following command:

```
CSCRIPT %SYSTEMROOT%\SYSTEM32\SLMgr.vbs -ato
```

In addition to activation, a number of other options are available to help you determine the current license state and install/uninstall a license:

- **Install a Product Key** *SLMgr.vbs –ipk <Product Key>*
- **Activate Windows** *SLMgr.vbs -ato*
- **Display License Information** *SLMgr.vbs –dli [Activation ID|All]*
- **Display Detailed License Information** *SLMgr.vbs – dlv [Activation ID|All]*
- **Display Expiration Date for Current License** *SLMgr.vbs -xpr*
- **Clear Product Key from the Registry** *SLMgr.vbs -cpky*
- **Install License** *SLMgr.vbs –ilc <License File>*
- **Re-Install System License Files** *SLMgr.vbs –rilc*
- **Re-arm the License Status of the Machine** *SLMgr.vbs -rearm*
- **Uninstall the Product Key** *SLMgr.vbs -upk*
- **Display the Installation ID for Offline Activation** *SLMgr.vbs -dti*
- **Activate the Product with the Confirmation ID** *SLMgr –atp <Confirmation ID>*

Summary of Exam Objectives

In this chapter, we reviewed what is necessary to install a Microsoft Server 2008 operating system. The changes in functionality between Windows Server 2003 with SP1 to Windows Server 2008 are very important because understanding where changes are implemented and understanding where features have been improved will not only help in passing the exam, but will also make you understand why this technology acts the way it does. Knowing how to tell what hardware components are appropriate, and which operating systems are designed for which roles and functionalities, is critical when you are choosing a new server, or deciding whether an existing server is up to the new task.

We also looked at key new feature, including Server Core, read-only DCs, and BitLocker technology, and how most or all of these features incorporated into a central or branch office scenario can really improve the user experience, improve the system administrator experience, and improve organizational security. Windows deployment services, one of the key important products that Microsoft has improved throughout new releases of server operating systems, immensely improve client and server operating system rollout and management of boot and install images.

Configuring storage on Microsoft Windows Server 2008, changing the way these features and tools are used, and the added functionality in the way the server interacts with storage area networks and the way it utilizes iSCSI have all improved significantly. This enables ease of decision making and a more stable and more available infrastructure.

Configuring high availability is a major consideration in the organization, which the IT department has to consider for critical systems. With changes made to failover clustering and network load balancing, the system administrator will find it increasingly easy to install, configure, and run a configuration in a robust infrastructure.

When it comes to licensing, the approach has changed with the release of Windows Vista and Windows Server 2008. You must activate all editions to ensure that they are genuine copies of Windows. You activate retail and OEM copies of Windows Server 2008 in the same way you have activated past releases—by contacting Microsoft through the Internet or via telephone. For volume license customers, you will receive either a Multiple Activation Key (MAK) or a Key Management Service (KMS) key. Under the MAK scheme, each machine will contact Microsoft, either directly or via the Volume Activation Management Tool proxy, to obtain a confirmation ID for the installation. For organizations using the KMS, you will need to set up and activate a KMS host within your environment. KMS clients will then activate with the host. Both the clients and the hosts will need to reactivate every 180 days to remain valid.

Exam Objectives Fast Track

Installing Windows Server 2008

☑ Planning requirements for installing Microsoft Windows Server 2008 including server editions and detailed installation steps.

☑ Server and Domain Controller disaster recovery using Install From Media (IFM) reducing the amount of time spent recovering from a DC failure.

☑ New Server Core installation steps, main features and integration scenarios.

The Windows Deployment Service

☑ The improved Windows Deployment Services used to manage and roll out server and workstation operating systems.

☑ Installing and configuring WDS and looking at the deployment and transport roles of WDS and how WDS responds to clients.

☑ Preparing the boot and install images, making them ready for a customized deployment.

☑ Steps in deploying images within the organization to managed server and workstations.

Configuring Storage

☑ Revisit RAID and the different types of RAID to choose from.

☑ Reasons why network attached storage (NAS) can be beneficial to an organization.

☑ iSCSI implementation over a LAN or WAN for IP-based SCSI.

☑ Fibre Channel basics and implementation basics and standard.

☑ Storage Area Network advantages and implementation scenarios and comparisons between other storage types.

☑ Increasing hard drive space without changing partition sizes using mount points in Microsoft Windows.

Configuring High Availability

☑ Basics of a failover cluster and improvements made in the new Windows Server 2008 operating systems.

☑ Geographically dispersed failover cluster improvements made with Windows Server 2008.

☑ How to use network load balancing, increasing scalability on a number of organization platforms.

Configuring Windows Activation

☑ Windows Server 2008 ships with a new activation policy that requires all editions to be activated.

☑ For volume license customers, you will either have Multiple Activation Keys (MAKs) or Key Management Services (KMS) keys, depending on your license.

☑ MAK keys operate similar to retail keys, but can be used for multiple systems, whereas KMS keys use a locally hosted key management service which activates machines on behalf of the licensing clearinghouse.

☑ MAK keys can be validated through a proxy service known as the Volume Activation Management Tool (VAMT), which caches the validation for future system rebuilds.

☑ KMS hosts and clients will need to reactivate every 180 days. Hosts will need to contact Microsoft, and clients will need to contact their KMS host.

Exam Objectives
Frequently Asked Questions

Q: Are there any clustering enhancements in Windows Server 2008?

A: In Windows Server 2008, the improvements to failover clusters make clusters more secure, simplify clusters, and enhance cluster stability. In addition, geoclustering has been improved and there is now support for GUID partition tables on cluster storage.

Q: Can I add Windows Server 2008 to an existing Windows 2003 Active Directory environment?

A: Yes. Adding a Windows Server 2008 DC to a current Windows 2003 Active Directory domain will make no difference to the 2003 Active Directory domain. However, you must install a full installation. The first 2008 DC cannot be a 2008 RODC, as it will need a full installation of the 2008 DC from which to replicate data.

Q: I have closed the command prompt on the Server Core terminal, and now I only see a blue background and cannot get the command prompt window back up. How do I get the command prompt window back without restarting the server?

A: Press **Ctrl + Alt + Delete** on the keyboard, open the Task Manager, and from the File menu choose **Run**, then type **cmd.exe** and click **OK**. This will bring back the command prompt window.

Q: Is an upgrade from Windows 2000 Server to Windows Server 2008 supported?

A: No. Only an upgrade from Windows Server 2003 is possible.

Q: What is Network Access Protection?

A: Network Access Protection (NAP) deals with the problem of unhealthy computers accessing the organization's network. NAP ensures that any computer that makes a connection to the network meets the requirements set out by the organization's policies. This limits access to the network and provides remediation services.

Q: Can I use my MAK key to set up a KMS host?

A: No, the KMS key and MAK key are separate key types. You should talk with your local software reseller about obtaining a KMS key if you wish to deploy the KMS within your organization.

Q: Why was the KMS introduced?

A: In previous releases of Windows, several customer volume license keys were leaked to the public and there were no facilities to stop the spread of these keys. The KMS host contacts Microsoft every 180 days, allowing Microsoft to block keys that are leaked.

Q: My evaluation copy of Windows Server 2008 is going to expire soon. Can I extend it?

A: You can extend the 30-day grace period up to three times, for a total of 120 days. Use the SLMgr.vbs script with the *rearm* parameter to reset the counter for another 30 days. You will need to perform this step every 30 days, up to the 120 days.

Q: How do I set up replication among KMS hosts?

A: There is no need for replication, as each KMS host acts autonomously. The license data that it holds is not used for billing purposes, and as such, the data does not need to be reconciled among KMS hosts.

Q: What should I back up from the KMS host service?

A: Nothing. The KMS host can be reactivated if needed, and it will return to service as it was prior to the need for disaster recovery procedures.

Q: I am trying to install Windows Server 2008 in the forest as a new domain controller, but I am not able to start the installation for Active Directory Domain Services. How do I do this?

A: To do this, you need to prepare the Active Directory forest for the new Windows Server 2008 domain controller. You can do this by running *adprep /forestprep* on the Schema Master operations master role domain controller.

Q: I am trying to install a domain controller in a domain that is in a Windows 2003 functional level. Do I have to choose Windows 2008 functional level when I install Windows Server 2008?

A: No, the functional level can always be upgraded to Windows Server 2008 at a later date.

Q: I want to be able to assign different account lockout policies to different sets of objects within Active Directory. Is this possible?

A: Yes, AD DS has a new Fine-Grained Password Policy that can be applied.

Q: We have successfully deployed a WDS server and have created the appropriate images from source computers. However, now that we have started up the first bare configured computer it doesn't seem to be able to find the WDS server. What should I do?

A: Check to see whether the DHCP server has been configured correctly and has an active scope.

Q: I realized that after I deployed images to 10 new computers they all have the same computer name. What should I do?

A: You will have to prepare the source computer with Sysprep. Then capture the image again and redeploy the images to the computers.

Self Test

1. Your company has recently increased in size, after acquiring another company twice the size. You have been given the task to set up a cluster in the main datacenter. You have been given the scope of the project and decided that the cluster will have to consist of eight nodes for high availability. Which editions of Windows Server 2008 will not be suitable for the eight nodes in the cluster? (Choose all that apply.)

   A. Windows Server 2008 Standard Edition

   B. Windows Server 2008 Enterprise Edition

   C. Windows Server 2008 Datacenter Edition

   D. Windows Web Server 2008

2. You have been asked to install the first Windows Server 2008 server in the domain. This server will be for testing purposes, so you will use older hardware with minimum hardware requirements for Windows Server 2008. You have decided to install a 32-bit edition of Server 2008 Standard Edition. What is the minimum amount of disk space required to install the Standard Edition of Server 2008?

   A. 8 GB

   B. 10 GB

   C. 12 GB

   D. 40 GB

3. You have been running Windows Server 2003 Enterprise Edition with Service Pack 2 (SP2) on all five of the current Exchange Servers in the organization's datacenter, which serves e-mail for the company on a global basis. You have now been asked to upgrade all the Exchange Servers to Windows Server 2008. Which of the following options do you have as an upgrade path for the Exchange Servers?

   A. Full installation of Windows Server 2008 Standard Edition

   B. Full installation of Windows Server 2008 Standard Edition R2

   C. Full installation of Windows Server 2008 Enterprise Edition

   D. Full installation of Windows Server 2008 Datacenter Edition

   E. Full installation of Windows Server 2008 for Itanium-based systems

4. You have been running earlier releases of Windows Server 2008 on test servers to see whether your organization will be able to make good productive use of Server 2008. You have been running the RC0 release of Windows Server 2008 Standard Edition and have now been asked to upgrade the current RC0 release. Which of the following options do you have as an upgrade path? (Choose all that apply.)

   A. Full installation of Windows Server 2008 Standard Edition

   B. Full installation of Windows Server 2008 Standard Edition R2

   C. Full installation of Windows Server 2008 Enterprise Edition

   D. Full installation of Windows Server 2008 Datacenter Edition

   E. Full installation of Windows Server 2008 for Itanium-based systems

5. You have been asked to upgrade the 28 domain controllers in the organization to Windows Server 2008. Upgrading a server with Active Directory installed requires you to make provisions for the extra hard drive space needed when upgrading the operating system. What size requirements does Active Directory have during an OS upgrade?

   A. 5% of the current database size or 200 MB, whichever is greater

   B. 10% of the current database size or 250 MB, whichever is greater

   C. 25% of the current database size or 550 MB, whichever is greater

   D. 50% of the current database size or 1 GB, whichever is greater

6. Installing Active Directory Domain Services on a newly installed Windows Server 2008 computer gives you three new additional options to install during the installation of Active Directory. Which of the following is not one of them? (Choose all that apply.)

   A. DNS Server

   B. Global Catalog

   C. DHCP

   D. Server Core

   E. RODC

7. You have five member servers, each with its own role. Before you upgraded all five member servers to Windows Server 2008 Standard Edition, you had

Windows Server 2003 Standard Edition SP2 on all the member servers. The decision has now been made to create an Active Directory domain and have these five member servers all take the domain controller role. You need to install Active Directory on all five member servers. What should you do?

A. Install the Active Directory Federation Services role on one of the five member servers

B. Install the Active Directory Rights Management Services role on one of the five member servers

C. Install the Active Directory Lightweight Directory Services role on all five of the member servers

D. Run the Dcpromo utility on one of the five member servers

E. Run the Dcpromo utility on all five of the member servers

8. When installing the very first domain controller in a new forest, which one of the following must be installed during the Active Directory installation?

A. DHCP

B. DNS

C. WINS

D. Global Catalog

E. RODC

9. One of the domain controllers in one of the remote sites has crashed. You have instructed the local resource to install Server 2008 Standard Edition on a new server. You have created a recent backup of the Active Directory database and made this database available to the local resource as a restore database on DVD. What feature will you now use to restore Active Directory to the new server?

A. AD Recovery Tool

B. ADSI Edit

C. Install from Media

D. Server Core Installation from Media

E. Recover from Media

10. The new Server Core installation option for Windows Server 2008 has the benefit of reduced management and maintenance and a reduced attack surface.

Also, the Server Core has a smaller hardware requirement than a full installation of the operating system. What is the minimum amount of hard disk space required to install Server Core?

A. 1 GB

B. 4 GB

C. 8 GB

D. 10 GB

Self Test Quick Answer Key

1.	**A, D**	6.	**C, D**
2.	**B**	7.	**E**
3.	**C**	8.	**D**
4.	**A, C**	9.	**C**
5.	**B**	10.	**A**

Chapter 2

MCTS/MCITP Exam 649

Configuring Server Roles in Windows 2008

Exam objectives in this chapter:

- New Roles in 2008
- Read-Only Domain Controllers (RODCs)
- Active Directory Lightweight Directory Service (LDS)
- Active Directory Rights Management Service (RMS)
- Active Directory Federation Services (ADFS)

Exam objectives review:

- ☑ Summary of Exam Objectives
- ☑ Exam Objectives Fast Track
- ☑ Exam Objectives Frequently Asked Questions
- ☑ Self Test
- ☑ Self Test Quick Answer Key

Introduction

With the introduction of new revisions to Microsoft products—be it Windows, Exchange, Communications Server, or others—we have seen a trend toward "roles" within each product, as opposed to the various products being an all-in-one type of solution (as with Exchange 2007), or being additional features that work as a snap-in, such as DNS in Windows 2003.

With earlier versions of Windows Server 2000 or 2003, an Active Directory server was just that—an Active Directory server. What we are trying to say here is that it was more-or-less an "all-or-nothing" deal when creating a domain controller in Windows 2003. Very little flexibility existed in the way a domain controller could be installed, with the exception of whether a domain controller would also be a global catalog server or flexible single master operation (FSMO) server.

With the release of Windows Server 2008, we have several new ways to deploy an Active Directory domain controller. In this chapter, we will discuss the new roles available in Windows Server 2008, how to create a domain controller, and how to implement and manage server roles.

New Roles in 2008

Windows Server 2008 offers many new ways to "skin the Active Directory cat," if you will. With the introduction of these new roles is a new way to determine how they are implemented, configured, and managed within an Active Directory domain or forest. We will be discussing each of these Active Directory roles in depth later in this chapter, but the new roles (and the official Microsoft definitions) are as follows:

- **Read-only domain controller (RODC):** This new type of domain controller, as its name implies, hosts read-only partitions of the Active Directory database. An RODC makes it possible for organizations to easily deploy a domain controller in scenarios where physical security cannot be guaranteed, such as branch office locations, or in scenarios where local storage of all domain passwords is considered a primary threat, such as in an extranet or in an application-facing role.

- **Active Directory Lightweight Directory Service (ADLDS):** Formerly known as Windows Server 2003 Active Directory Application Mode (ADAM), ADLDS is a Lightweight Directory Access Protocol (LDAP) directory service that provides flexible support for directory-enabled applications, without the dependencies required for Active

Directory Domain Services (ADDS). ADLDS provides much of the same functionality as ADDS, but does not require the deployment of domains or domain controllers.

- **Active Directory Rights Management Service (ADRMS):** Active Directory Rights Management Services (ADRMS), a format and application-agnostic technology, provides services to enable the creation of information-protection solutions. ADRMS includes several new features that were available in Active Directory Rights Management Services (ADRMS). Essentially, ADRMS adds the ability to secure objects. For example, an e-mail can be restricted to read-only, meaning it cannot be printed, copied (using **Ctrl + C**, and so on), or forwarded.

- **Active Directory Federation Services (ADFS):** You can use Active Directory Federation Services (ADFS) to create a highly extensible, Internet-scalable, and secure identity access solution that can operate across multiple platforms, including both Windows and non-Windows environments. Essentially, this allows cross-forest authentication to external resources—such as another company's Active Directory. ADFS was originally introduced in Windows Server 2003 R2, but lacked much of its now-available functionality.

So, these are the roles themselves, but as also mentioned, they can be managed in a number of new ways:

- **Server Manager:** This is likely to be a familiar tool to engineers who have worked with earlier versions of Windows. It is a single-screen solution that helps manage a Windows server, but is much more advanced than the previous version.

- **Server Core:** Server Core brings not only a new way to manage roles, but an entirely new way to deploy a Windows Server. With Server Core, we can say goodbye to unnecessary GUIs, applications, services, and many more commonly attacked features.

Discussing Server Core is going to take considerably longer, so let's start with Server Manager.

Using Server Manager to Implement Roles

Although we will be discussing Server Manager (Figure 2.1) as an Active Directory Management tool, it's actually much more than just that.

Figure 2.1 Server Manager

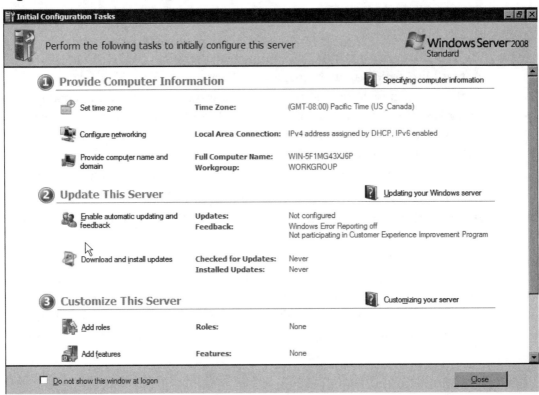

In fact, Server Manager is a single solution (technically, a Microsoft Management Console [MMC]) snap-in that is used as a single source for managing system identity (as well as other key system information), identifying problems with servers, displaying server status, enabled roles and features, and general options such as server updates and feedback.

Table 2.1 outlines some of the additional roles and features Server Manager can be used to control:

Table 2.1 Partial List of Additional Server Manager Features

Role/Feature	Description
Active Directory Certificate Services	Management of Public Key Infrastructure (PKI)
Dynamic Host Configuration Server	Dynamic assignment of IP addresses to clients
Domain Name Service	Provides name/IP address resolution
File Services	Storage management, replication, searching
Print Services	Management of printers and print servers
Terminal Services	Remote access to a Windows desktop or application
Internet Information Server	Web server services
Hyper-V	Server virtualization
BitLocker Drive Encryption	Whole-disk encryption security feature
Group Policy Management	Management of Group Policy Objects
SMTP Server	E-mail services
Failover Clustering	Teaming multiple servers to provide high availability
WINS Server	
Legacy NetBIOS name resolution	
Wireless LAN Service	Enumerates and manages wireless connections

Server Manager is enabled by default when a Windows 2008 server is installed (with the exception of Server Core). However, Server Manager can be shut off via the system Registry and can be re-opened at any time by selecting **Start | Administrative Tools | Server Manager**, or right-clicking **Computer** under the **Start** menu, and choosing **Manage** (Figure 2.2).

Figure 2.2 Opening Server Manager

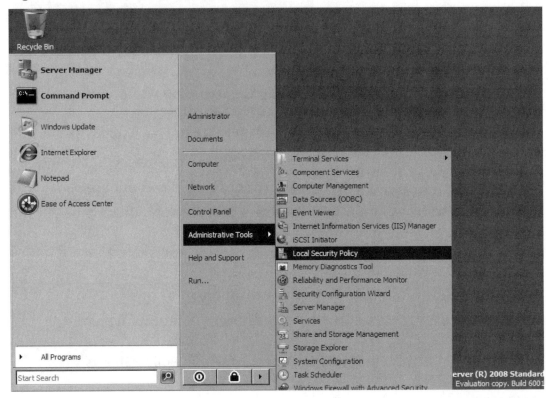

So, those are the basics of Server Manager. Now let's take a look at how we use Server Manager to implement a role. Since we will be discussing the four Active Directory roles in depth later in this chapter, let's take the IIS role and talk about using the Add Role Wizard to install Internet Information Services (IIS).

EXERCISE 2.1

USING THE ADD ROLE WIZARD

Notice in Figure 2.1 that the Server Manager window is broken into three different sections:

- Provide Computer Information
- Update This Server
- Customize This Server

Under the **Customize This Server** section, click the **Add Role** icon. When the wizard opens, complete the following steps to install IIS onto the server.

1. Click the **Add Roles** icon.

2. At the **Before You Begin** window, read the information provided, and then click **Next**.

3. From the list of server roles (Figure 2.3), click the check box next to **Web Server (IIS)** and then click **Next**.

Figure 2.3 List of Server Roles

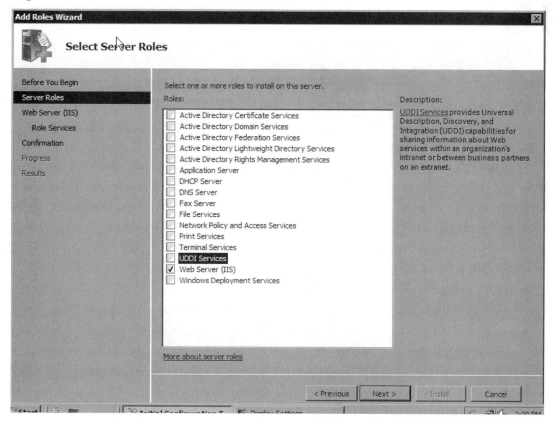

4. If you are prompted to add additional required features, read and understand the features, and then click **Add Required Features**.

5. When you return to the **Select Server Roles** screen, click **Next**.

6. Read the information listed in the **Introduction to Web Server (IIS)** window, and then click **Next**.

7. For purposes of this exercise, we will select all of the default Role Services, and then click **Next**.

8. Review the Installation Summary Confirmation screen (Figure 2.4), and then click **Install**.

Figure 2.4 The Installation Summary Confirmation Screen

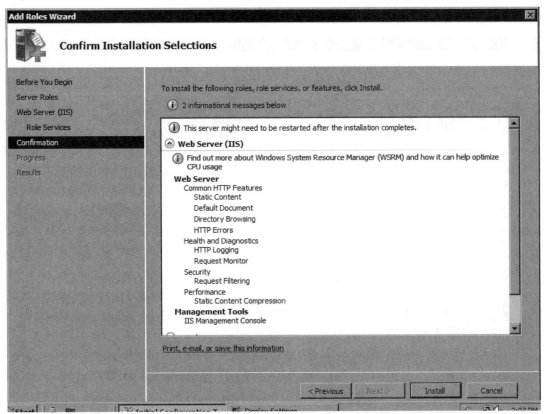

9. When installation is complete, click **Close**.

10. Notice that on the Server Manager screen, Web Server (IIS) is now listed as an installed role.

Configuring & Implementing...

Scripting vs. GUI

Sure, you can always use a wizard to implement a role, but you also have the option of using a script. Realistically speaking, it's generally not the most efficient way to deploy a role for a single server, however. Unless you are going to copy and paste the script, the chance of error is high in typing out the commands required. For example, take the following IIS script syntax:

start /w pkgmgr /iu:IIS-WebServerRole;IIS-WebServer;IIS-Common HttpFeatures;IIS-StaticContent;IIS-DefaultDocument;IIS-DirectoryBrowsing; IIS-HttpErrors;IIS-HttpRedirect;IIS-ApplicationDevelopment;IIS-ASPNET; IIS-NetFxExtensibility;IIS-ASP;IIS-CGI;IIS-ISAPIExtensions;IIS-ISAPIFilter; IIS-ServerSideIncludes;IIS-HealthAndDiagnostics;IIS-HttpLogging;IIS-LoggingLibraries;IIS-RequestMonitor;IIS-HttpTracing;IIS-CustomLogging;IIS-ODBCLogging;IIS-Security;IIS-BasicAuthentication;IIS-WindowsAuthentication;IIS-DigestAuthentication;IIS-ClientCertificateMappingAuthentication; IIS-IISCertificateMappingAuthentication;IIS-URLAuthorization;IIS-RequestFiltering;IIS-IPSecurity;IIS-Performance;IIS-HttpCompressionStatic; IIS-HttpCompressionDynamic;IIS-WebServerManagementTools;IIS-ManagementConsole;IIS-ManagementScriptingTools;IIS-Management-Service;IIS-IIS6ManagementCompatibility;IIS-Metabase;IIS-WMICompatibility;IIS-LegacyScripts;IIS-LegacySnapIn;IIS-FTP PublishingService;IIS-FTPServer;IIS-FTPManagement;WAS-Windows ActivationService;WAS-ProcessModel;WAS-NetFxEnvironment; WAS-ConfigurationAPI

This script installs ALL of the IIS features, which may not be the preferred installation for your environment, and within the time it took to type it out, you may have already completed the GUI install!

Using Server Core and Active Directory

For years, Microsoft engineers have been told that Windows would never stand up to Linux in terms of security simply because it was too darn "heavy" (too much) code, loaded too many modules (services, startup applications, and so on), and was generally too GUI heavy. With Windows Server 2008, Microsoft engineers can stand tall, thanks to the introduction of Server Core.

What Is Server Core?

What is Server Core, you ask? It's the "just the facts, ma'am" version of Windows 2008. Microsoft defines Server Core as "a minimal server installation option for Windows Server 2008 that contains a subset of executable files, and five server roles." Essentially, Server Core provides only the binaries needed to support the role and the base operating systems. By default, fewer processes are generally running.

Server Core is so drastically different from what we have come to know from Windows Server NT, Windows Server 2000, or even Windows Server 2003 over the past decade-plus, that it looks more like MS-DOS than anything else (Figure 2.5). With Server Core, you won't find Windows Explorer, Internet Explorer, a Start menu, or even a clock! Becoming familiar with Server Core will take some time. In fact, most administrators will likely need a cheat sheet for a while. To help with it all, you can find some very useful tools on Microsoft TechNet at http://technet2.microsoft .com/windowsserver2008/en/library/e7e522ac-b32f-42e1-b914-53ccc78d18161033 .mspx?mfr=true. This provides command and syntax lists that can be used with Server Core. The good news is, for those of you who want the security and features of Server Core with the ease-of-use of a GUI, you have the ability to manage a Server Core installation using remote administration tools.

Figure 2.5 The Server Core Console

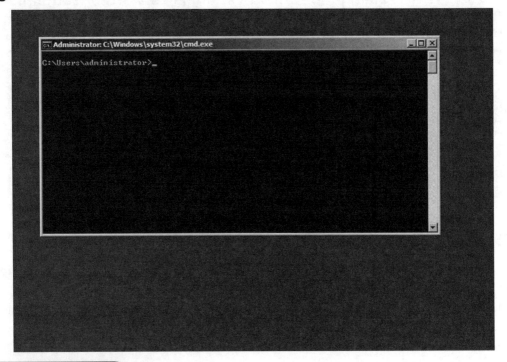

Before going any further, we should discuss exactly what will run on a Server Core installation. Server Core is capable of running the following server roles:

- Active Directory Domain Services Role
- Active Directory Lightweight Directory Services Role
- Dynamic Host Configuration Protocol (DHCP)
- Domain Name System (DNS) Services Role
- File Services Role
- Hyper-V (Virtualization) Role
- Print Services Role
- Streaming Media Services Role
- Web Services (IIS) Role

NOTE

Internet Information Server is Microsoft's brand of Web server software, utilizing Hypertext Transfer Protocol to deliver World Wide Web documents. It incorporates various functions for security, allows for CGI programs, and also provides for Gopher and FTP servers.

Although these are the roles Server Core supports, it can also support additional features, such as:

- Backup
- BitLocker
- Failover Clustering
- Multipath I/O
- Network Time Protocol (NTP)
- Removable Storage Management
- Simple Network Management Protocol (SNMP)
- Subsystem for Unix-based applications
- Telnet Client
- Windows Internet Naming Service (WINS)

> **NOTE**
>
> BitLocker Drive Encryption is an integral new security feature in Windows Server 2008 that protects servers at locations, such as branch offices, as well as mobile computers for all those roaming users out there. BitLocker provides offline data and operating system protection by ensuring that data stored on the computer is not revealed if the machine is tampered with when the installed operating system is offline.

The concept behind the design Server Core is to truly provide a minimal server installation. The belief is that rather than installing all the application, components, services, and features by default, it is up to the implementer to determine what will be turned on or off.

Installation of Windows 2008 Server Core is fairly simple. During the installation process, you have the option of performing a Standard Installation or a Server Core installation. Once you have selected the hard drive configuration, license key activation, and End User License Agreement (EULA), you simply let the automatic installation continue to take place. When installation is done and the system has rebooted, you will be prompted with the traditional Windows challenge/response screen, and the Server Core console will appear.

EXERCISE 2.2

CONFIGURING THE DIRECTORY SERVICES ROLE IN SERVER CORE

So let's put Server Core into action and use it to install Active Directory Domain Services. To install the Active Directory Domain Services Role, perform the following steps:

1. The first thing we need to do is set the IP information for the server. To do this, we first need to identify the network adapter. In the console window, type **netsh interface ipv4 show interfaces** and record the number shown under the **Idx** column.

2. Set the IP address, Subnet Mask, and Default Gateway for the server. To do this, type **netsh interface ipv4 set address name= "<ID>" source=static address=<StaticIP> mask=<SubnetMask>**

gateway=<**DefaultGateway**>. ID represents the number from step 1, <StaticIP> represents the IP address we will assign, <SubnetMask> represents the subnet mask, and <Default Gateway> represents the IP address of the server's default gateway. See Figure 2.6 for our sample configuration.

Figure 2.6 Setting an IP Address in Server Core

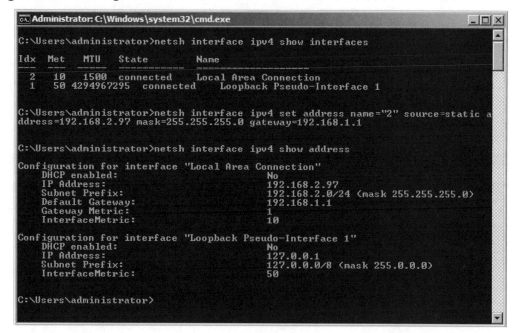

3. Assign the IP address of the DNS server. Since this will be an Active Directory Domain Controller, we will set the DNS settings to point to the DNS server. From the console, type **netsh interface ipv4 add dnsserver name="<ID>" address=<DNSIP> index=1. >**. ID represents the number from step 1, and <StaticIP> represents the IP address of the DNS server (in this case, the same IP address from step 2).

So, here is where things get a little tricky. When installing the Directory Services role in a full server installation, we would simply open up a **Run** window (or a command line) and type in **DCPromo**. Then, we would follow the prompts for configuration (domain name, file location, level of forest/domain security), and then restart the system. Installing the role in

Server Core isn't so simple, yet it's not exactly rocket science. In order to make this installation happen, we are going to need to configure an *unattended installation file*. An unattended installation file (see Figure 2.7) s nothing more than a text file that answers the questions that would have been answered during the DCPromo installation. So, let's assume you have created the unattended file and placed it on a floppy disk, CD, or other medium, and then inserted it into the Server Core server. Let's go ahead and install Directory Services:

1. Sign in to the server.

2. In the console, change drives to the removable media. In our example, we will be using drive E:, our DVD drive.

3. Once you have changed drives, type **dcpromo answer:\answer.txt**. Answer.txt is the name of our unattended file (see Figure 2.7).

Figure 2.7 Installing Directory Services in Server Core

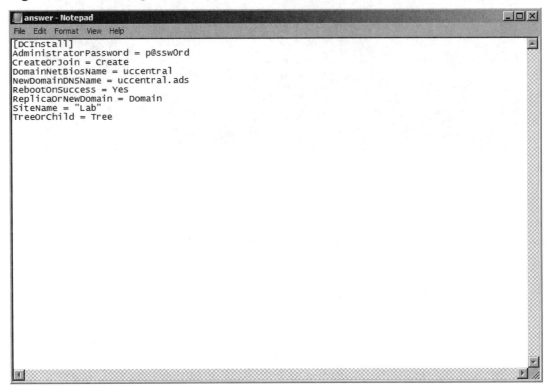

4. Follow the installation process as it configures directory services. Once the server has completed the installation process, it will reboot automatically.

When the server reboots, you will have a fully functional Active Directory implementation!

Read-Only Domain Controllers (RODCs)

One of the biggest mistakes IT organizations make is underestimating the security risk presented by remote offices. As a consultant, I have seen many organizations (big and small) make major investments in their corporate IT security strategy, and then turn around and place a domain controller on top of a desk in a small/remote office—right next to an exit. Several times during the course of the day, employees, delivery people, solicitors, and more walk by this door—and often the server itself. Typically, little exists to stop these people from walking out the door and selling their newly found (stolen) hardware on eBay. And this is probably a best-case scenario. What would happen if the information on this server actually ended up in the *wrong* hands?

Introduction to RODC

Read-only domain controllers were designed to combat this very problem. Let's take a scenario where a corporation has a remote office with ten employees. On a daily basis, these ten people are always in the office, while another five to ten "float" in and out and sometimes aren't there for weeks at a time. Overall, the company has about 1,000 employees. In a Windows 2000 Server or Windows Server 2003 Active Directory environment (or, pity you, a Windows NT 4.0 domain), if you have placed a domain controller in this remote office, *all information for every user account in the organization is copied to this server.* Right now, there's probably a light bulb going off above your head (we can see it all the way from here) as to why this is a problem just waiting to happen.

Its Purpose in Life

The purpose of the read-only domain controller (RODC) is to deal directly with this type of issue, and many issues like it. RODCs are one component in the Microsoft initiative to secure a branch office. Along with RODCs, you may also want to consider implementing BitLocker (whole-disk encryption), Server Core, as well as

Role Distribution—the ability to assign local administrator rights to an RODC without granting a user full domain administrator rights.

Its Features

A number of features come with a RODC, which focus on providing heightened security without limiting functionality to the remote office users. Some of the key points here are:

- **Read-only replicas of the domain database:** Clients are not allowed to write changes directly to an RODC (much like a Windows NT BDC). RODC holds all the Active Directory Domain Services (AD DS) objects and attributes that a writable domain controller holds, with the exception of account passwords. Clients, however, are not able to write changes directly to the RODC.

- **Filtered Attribute Sets:** The ability to prevent certain AD attributes from being replicated to RODCs.

- **Unidirectional Replication:** Since clients cannot write changes to an RODC, there is no need to replicate *from* an RODC *to* a full domain controller. This prevents potentially corrupt (or hijacked) data from being disbursed, and also reduces unnecessary bandwidth usage.

- **Read-only DNS:** Allows one-way replication of application directory partitions, including ForestDNSZones and DomainDNSZones.

- **Cached accounts:** By caching accounts, if the RODC were ever compromised, only the accounts that have been compromised need to be reset. The full DCs are aware of which accounts are cached, and a report can be generated for auditing purposes.

So these are the key features of a read-only domain controller. Now let's step through the installation process.

Configuring RODC

Configuring an RODC isn't all that different from adding a traditional domain controller. The most important thing to remember about an RODC is that a writable domain controller *must* exist somewhere in the domain. Once this prerequisite is met, we can go ahead and configure our RODC. Let's assume that our writable DC is in place, using the domain information from the previous exercise.

Head of the class...

Adding an RODC to an Existing Forest

A read-only domain controller can be added to a preexisting forest, but this will require that schema changes be made to the forest for this to work properly. The process is fairly simple. Using the *adprep* tool with the */rodcprep* switch (the actual syntax would be **adprep /rodcprep**), we can add the necessary schema changes to support our RODC.

EXERCISE 2.3

CONFIGURING A READ-ONLY DOMAIN CONTROLLER

Let's begin configuring our RODC:

1. Click **Start | Administrative Tools | Server Manager**.

2. Scroll down to **Role Summary**, click **Add roles**.

3. When the **Before You Begin** page opens, click **Next**.

4. On the **Select Server Roles** page, choose **Active Directory Domain Services**, and then click **Next**.

5. Click **Next** again on the **Active Directory Domain Services** page.

6. On the **Confirm Installation Selections** page (Figure 2.8), click **Install**.

Figure 2.8 Confirming Installation Selections

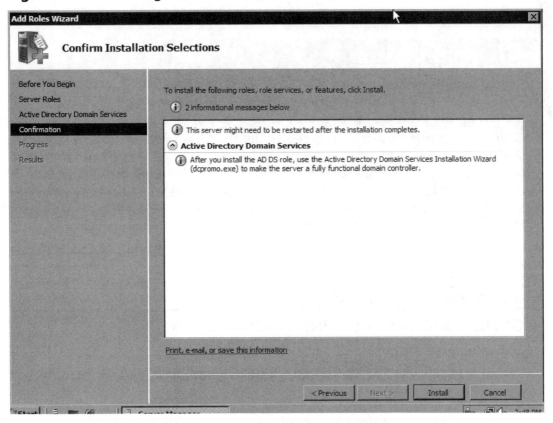

7. When installation is complete, click **Close**.

8. If the Server Manager window has closed, re-open it.

9. Expand **Roles,** and then click **Active Directory Domain Services**.

10. Under Summary (Figure 2.9), click the link to **Run The Active Directory Domain Services Installation Wizard**.

Figure 2.9 The Summary Page

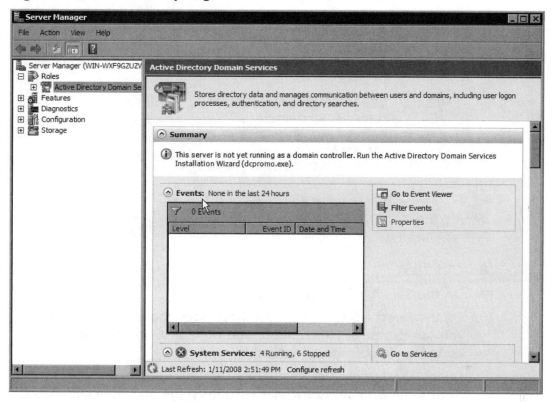

11. Click **Next** on the **Welcome To The Active Directory Domain Services Installation Wizard** page.

12. On the **Operating System Compatibility** page, click **Next**.

13. On the **Choose A Deployment Configuration** page, click **Existing Forest**.

14. Ensure **Add A Domain Controller To An Existing Domain** is selected, and then click **Next**.

15. On the **Network Credentials** page, verify that your domain is listed, and click **Set**.

16. In the **User Name** field, type **<domain>\administrator**.

17. In the **Password** field, type your administrator password, and then click **OK** (see Figure 2.10).

Figure 2.10 Setting Account Credentials

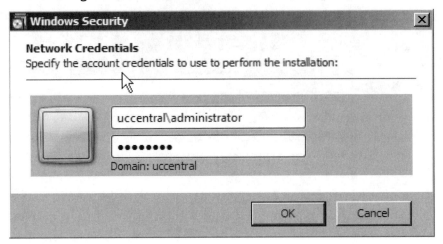

18. Click **Next**.

19. On the **Select a Domain** page, click **Next**.

20. On the **Select a Site** page (if you have Sites and Services configured), you can choose to which site to add this RODC. In this case, we are using the default site, click **Next**.

    Select **DNS Server** and **Read-Only Domain Controller** on the **Additional Domain Controller Options** page and then click **Next**.

21. In the **Group Or User** field, type **<domain>\administrator**, and then click **Next**.

22. Verify the file locations, and click **Next**.

23. On the **Active Directory Domain Services Restore Mode Administrator Password** page, type and confirm a restore mode password, and then click **Next**.

24. On the **Summary** page, click **Next**.

25. The Active Directory Domain Services Installation Wizard dialog box appears. After installation, reboot the server.

EXAM TIP

It is possible to "stage" an RODC and delegate rights to complete an RODC installation to a user or group. In order to do this, you must first create an account in Active Directory for the RODC in Active Directory

Users and Computers. Once inside of ADU&C, you must right-click the **Domain Controllers** OU container, and select **Pre-create Read-Only Domain Controller Account**. From here, you can set the alternate credential for a user who can then finish the installation. On the server itself, the user must type **dcpromo /UseExistingAccount:Attach** in order to complete the process.

Removing an RODC

There may come a time when you need to remove an RODC from your forest or domain. Like anything in this world, there is a right way and a wrong way to go about doing this. For the exam, you'll want to make sure you know the right way. Removing a read-only domain controller is almost as simple as adding an RODC. One important thing to remember with an RODC is that it cannot be the first—or the last—domain controller in a domain. Therefore, all RODCs must be detached before removing a final writable domain controller. Fewer steps make up the removal process. Let's take a look at how this is done.

1. Choose **Start | Run**.
2. In the **Run** window, type **dcpromo.exe**.
3. At the **Welcome To Active Directory Domain Services Installation Wizard** screen, click **Next**.
4. On the **Delete The Domain** window, make sure the check box is not checked, and then click **Next**.
5. Enter your administrator password, and then click **Next**.
6. Click **Next** in the **Summary** window, and then click **Next** again.
7. When removal is complete, reboot the server.
8. When the server reboots, sign back in.
9. Select **Start | Administrative Tools | Server Manager**.
10. Scroll down to **Role Summary**.
11. Expand **Roles**, and then click **Remove Roles**.

12. On the **Before You Begin** page, click **Next**.

13. Remove the checkmark from **Active Directory Domain Services** and **DNS Server** and click **Next**.

14. Review the confirmation details, and then click **Remove**.

15. Review the results page, and click **Close**.

16. Restart the server if necessary.

Active Directory Lightweight Directory Service (LDS)

As mentioned earlier, Active Directory Lightweight Directory Service is a slimmed-down version of AD. The concept of LDS is not new. In fact, it has been around for several years. However, to date it is probably not as widely known or recognized as the full ADS installation. Now that AD LDS is a part of the Windows Server 2008 media, you can expect to see many more deployments of the product.

When to Use AD LDS

So, when should you use AD LDS? Well, there are many situations when this is a more viable option. Typically, LDS is used when *directory-aware applications need directory services, but there is no need for the overhead of a complete forest or domain structure.* Demilitarized Zones (DMZs) are a great example of this. If you are not familiar with DMZs, Wikipedia defines a DMZ as a physical or logical subnetwork that contains an organization's external services to a larger untrusted network, usually the Internet. The purpose of a DMZ is to add an additional layer of security to an organization's local area network (LAN). You may be hosting an application or Web site in a DMZ where you want to have the added security of challenge/response using a directory services model. Since this is in a DMZ, you probably have no need for organizational units, Group Policy, and so on. By using LDS, you can eliminate these unnecessary functions and focus on what really is important: authentication and access control.

The other popular option for using LDS is in a situation where you want to provide authentication services in a DMZ or extranet for internal corporate users. In this scenario, account credentials can be synchronized between the full internal domain controller and the LDS instances within the DMZ. This option provides a single sign-on solution, as opposed to the end user being required to remember multiple usernames and passwords.

Changes from Active Directory Application Mode (ADAM)

As mentioned earlier, the LDS concept has been around since Windows Server 2003 R2, but many improvements and new features have been introduced since the previous release. Some of the key changes between ADAM and LDS are listed next:

- **Auditing:** Directory Service changes can now be audited for when changes are made to objects and their attributes. In this situation, both old and new values are logged.

- **Server Core Support:** AD LDS is now a supported role for installation in a Server Core implementation of Windows Server 2008. This makes it ideal for DMZ-type situations.

- **Support for Active Directory Sites and Services:** This makes it possible for management of LDS instance replication using the more-familiar ADS&S tool.

- **Database Mounting Tool:** Provides a means to compare data as it exists in database backups that are taken at different times to help the process of deciding which backup instance to restore.

These are the "key" improvements from ADAM in Windows Server 2003 R2 to AD LDS in Windows Server 2008, but the fact that the product has had more time to be "baked in" will greatly improve the functionality and usage of this technology.

Configuring AD LDS

By now, you're probably beginning to see a trend in how things are accomplished in Windows Server 2008. Everything is done with the use of server roles. Active Directory Lightweight Directory Services are no different. In our example, we are going to walk through the process of installing a clean LDS implementation.

EXERCISE 2.4

CONFIGURING LDS

1. Choose **Start | Administrative Tools | Server Manager**.
2. Scroll down to **Role Summary**, and then click **Add Roles**.
3. When the **Before You Begin** page opens, click **Next**.

4. On the **Select Server Roles** page, select the **Active Directory Lightweight Directory Services** option, and then click **Next**.

5. The installation steps for the role are very straightforward, follow the prompts and then click **Install**. After the role installation is complete, move on to creating an LDS instance.

6. Select **Start | Administrative Tools | Active Directory Lightweight Directory Services Setup Wizard**.

7. On the **Welcome** page, click **Next**.

8. On the page, select **A Unique Instance**, and then click **Next**.

9. On the **Instance Name** page (Figure 2.11), provide a name for the AD LDS instance and click **Next**.

Figure 2.11 The Instance Name Page

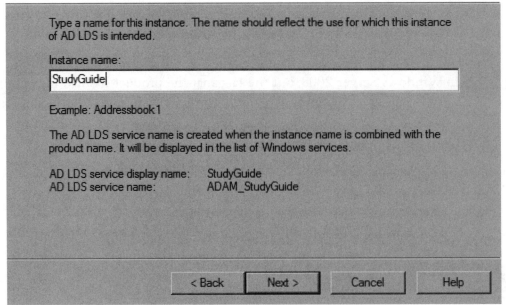

10. On the **Ports** page, we can specify the ports the AD LDS instance uses to communicate. Accept the default values of 389 and 636, and then click **Next**.

11. On the **Application Directory Partition** (Figure 2.12) page, we will create an application directory partition by clicking **Yes**.

Figure 2.12 The Application Directory Partition Page

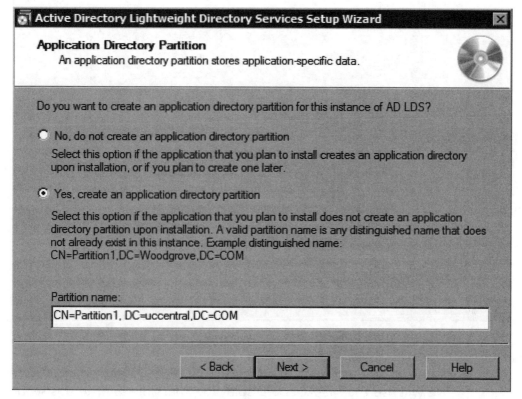

12. On this page, we will also need to specify the distinguished name of our partition. Follow the format in Figure 2.12, and then click **Next**.

13. On the **File Locations** page, review the file locations and click **Next** to accept the default locations.

14. On the **Service Account Selection** page, select an account to be used as the service account. By default, the Network Service account is used. Click **Next** to accept the default option.

15. On the **AD LDS Administrators** page (Figure 2.13), select a user (or group to) that will be used as the default administrator for this instance. Click the default value (**Currently Logged On User**) and then click **Next**.

Figure 2.13 The AD LDS Administrators Page

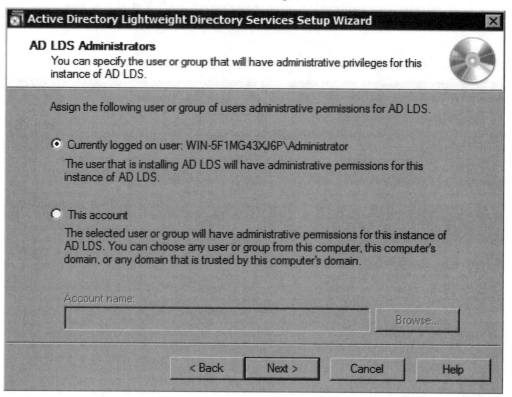

16. Select particular LDIF files to work with our LDS implementation. We will use the MS-ADLDS-DisplaySpecifiers file later in this section, so check this option off, and then click **Next**.

17. Review the **Ready To Install** page and click **Next** to begin the installation process. When setup is complete, click **Finish**.

Working with AD LDS

Several tools can be used to manage an LDS instance. In this book, we will work with two of these tools. The first is the ADSI Edit tool. ADSI stands for Active Directory Service Interfaces, and is used to access the features of directory services from different network providers. ADSI can also be used to automate tasks such as adding users and groups and setting permissions on network resources. While making changes to LDS (or Active Directory) is outside the scope of this book, we will show you how to use ADSI Edit to connect to an LDS instance.

1. Choose **Start | Administrative Tools | ADSI Edit**.

2. In the console tree, click **ADSI Edit**.

3. On the **Action** menu, click **Connect to**.

4. In the **Name** field, type a recognizable name for this connection. This name will appear in the console tree of ADSI Edit.

5. In **Select Or Type A Domain Or Server**, enter the fully qualified domain name (or IP address) of the computer running the AD LDS instance, followed by a colon and 389—representing the port of the LDS instance.

6. Under **Connection point**, click **Select** and choose your distinguished name, then click **OK**.

7. In the console tree of the ADSI Edit snap-in, double-click the name you created in step 4, and then double-click the distinguished name of your LDS instance.

8. Navigate around the containers to view the partition configuration.

The second tool we will discuss is the Active Directory Sites and Services snap-in. As mentioned earlier in this section, you can use the ADS&S snap-in to manage replication of directory information between sites in an LDS implementation. This is useful when LDS may be implemented in a geographically disbursed environment. For example, a server farm that may be collocated in a company datacenter and a disaster recovery location may require replication, and the easiest way to perform this is via this snap-in. However, it's important to note that we *must* import the MS-ADLDS-DisplaySpecifiers.ldf file during the instance configuration (earlier in this section) in order to use ADS&S. Let's review how to use ADS&S to connect to an LDS instance.

1. Choose **Start | Administrative Tools | Active Directory Sites & Services**.

2. Right-click **Active Directory Sites and Services**, and then click **Change Domain Controller**.

3. In the **Change Directory Server** window, type the FQDN or IP address of the server running the LDS instance, followed by **:389**.

4. Navigate the containers to view information about the LDS instance.

Active Directory Rights Management Service (RMS)

If you were to poll 100 corporations, you would probably find out that 99 out of 100 companies have probably had a confidential e-mail or document leave their environment and fall into the hands of someone it was not originally intended. Microsoft recognized this issue several years back and began working on a product named Rights Management Server (RMS). RMS is a great product and is in use at many companies, but the price of the product often put it out of reach for many companies. With Windows Server 2008, Microsoft has rebranded and incorporated the product in the operating system itself. As industry and governmental restrictions continue to increase, as well as the penalties for mishandling information, providing a technology such as RMS (or AD RMS in 2008) essentially became a demand on the part of customers. Although Microsoft is including the server portion in Windows Server 2008, don't be fooled—there is still a Client Access License (CAL) for Rights management. The three main functions of AD RMS are:

- **Creating rights-protected files and templates:** Trusted users can create and manage protection-enhanced files using common authoring tools (including Office products such as Word, Excel, and Outlook), as well as templates from AD RMS-enabled applications.

- **Licensing rights-protected information:** Certainly, the key component of RMS. Issues a special certificate, known as a *rights account certificate*, used to identify trusted objects, such as users and groups, which have the authority to generate rights-protected content.

- **Acquiring licenses to decrypt rights-protected content and applying usage policies:** As the name implies, RMS works with Active Directory to determine if users have a required rights account certificate in order to access rights-protected content.

As stated earlier, RMS has been around for some time, but there have been a number of advancements since the product was released. Let's take a look at some of these features.

What's New in RMS

We mentioned early on that probably the most substantial change from earlier versions of RMS is the fact that it is no longer a separate product from Windows Server. Besides the fact that this significantly reduces the barrier to entry to use such a technology, it has also improved the installation and management of the product. At this stage, you should be familiar with how we install roles. In fact, the RMS installation also takes care of the prerequisites—such as IIS, Message Queuing—during the installation process. Isn't it exciting to know that installing the RMS role is just as simple? We will get to the installation and configuration of RMS later in this section. First though, let's look at three other areas where improvements have been made over the older product:

- **Self-Enrollment:** In previous versions of RMS, an RMS server was forced to connect (via the Internet) to the Microsoft Enrollment Service in order to receive a server licensor certificate (SLC), which gives RMS the rights to issue licenses (and its own certificates). In Windows Server 2008, Microsoft has eliminated this need by bundling a self-enrollment certificate into Windows Server 2008, which signs the SLC itself.

- **Delegation of Roles:** AD RMS now gives you the flexibility to delegate certain RMS roles out to other users/administrators. There are four RMS roles: *AD RMS Service Group, AD RMS Enterprise Administrators, AD RMS Template Administrators*, and *AD RMS Auditors*. The RMS Service Group essentially holds the service account used by RMS. Enterprise Administrators has full control of all settings and policies—much like an Active Directory Enterprise Administrator. As the name implies, a Template Administrator has rights to create, modify, read, and export templates. Auditors have rights to only view RMS information, as well as logs and report generation.

- **Integration with Federation Services:** We will be covering AD FS in the next section, but this allows for the ability to share rights-protected documents with external entities.

RMS vs. DRMS in Vista

Digital Rights Management (DRM) is a tricky topic, particularly when couched in the common terms of the movie makers versus the general public. Since that discussion is intensely personal and very controversial, I want to steer clear of making any statements that endorse or condemn DRM—it is your decision whether or not to use it. The key differentiator between RMS and DRM is that DRM is generally used by content manufacturers (music companies, movie companies, and so on), whereas RMS is intended more for corporations that want to protect company-sensitive data.

With DRM, content consumers intend to make sure their wishes are met when producing and distributing content—and it's hard to argue with that goal. If you write the next Great American Novel, or you've painted "What the Mona Lisa Did Next," you're justified in releasing it only for what you consider to be appropriate recompense, or withholding it from the public until you are satisfied with your remuneration.

The objection to DRM (except from those who insist that all information, all art, and all content "wants to be free") comes from putative content consumers who are concerned that their own ability to consume the content is unnecessarily restricted—they may want to view the movie they purchased on a different screen, or add subtitles to it so that they can watch it with a deaf relative.

Too much DRM protection on content means that the content is no longer acceptably usable by your targeted consumers—if your goal is to sell content to those consumers, clearly this is a losing proposition. You don't make money by killing piracy, unless you make money by selling more products as a result.

For publicly available content, however, some protection may remind otherwise-honest consumers that the content they are viewing is not completely licensed to them, distribution rights have not been granted, and the content is only intended to be accessed through the method or media purchased. Disappointing for the consumer who bought a DVD, intending to watch it on a remote device, but not totally unsurprising. (If there is a market for watching movies on remote devices, maybe a smart company will come along and exploit it by licensing content for distribution in that way.)

Configuring RMS

Another day, another role. As you can imagine, we're going to be using Server Manager to deploy Rights Management Server. In order to make this work, a number of things will be in play. During the installation process, we will need to configure a certificate (via IIS), and install and complete the configuration of the RMS server role. Let's begin by configuring the certificate.

NOTE

Exercise 2.5 will require the use of a certificate authority. You may want to wait on this exercise until you review Chapter 3, which covers CAs. We can understand how you may be too excited to wait, but rather than making you go through the CA process twice, bookmark this section and come back to it once you have completed that chapter.

EXERCISE 2.5

CONFIGURING RIGHTS MANAGEMENT SERVER

1. Select **Start | Administrative Tools | Internet Information Services (IIS) Manager**. We installed the IIS role earlier in this chapter.
2. Double-click the server name.
3. In the details pane, double-click **Server Certificates**.
4. Click **Create Domain Certificate**.
5. In the **Common name** field, type the **FQDN** name of your server (Figure 2.14).

Figure 2.14 Creating a Domain Certificate

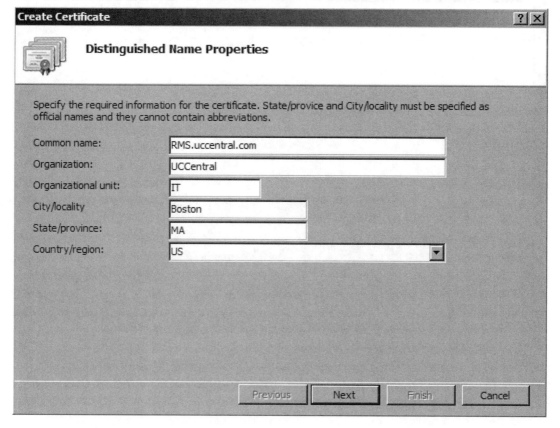

6. In the **Organization** field, enter a company name.
7. In the **Organization Unit** field, enter a division.

8. In the **City/locality** field, enter your city.

9. In the **State/province** field, enter your state, and then click **Next**.

10. Review the **Online Certification Authority** page, and click **Select**.

11. Select your Certificate Authority (Figure 2.15), and then click **OK**.

Figure 2.15 Selecting a Certificate Authority

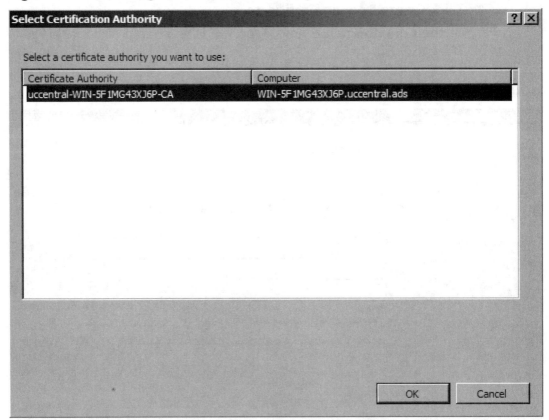

12. In the **Friendly name** field, enter the NetBIOS name of this server (Figure 2.16), and click **Finish**.

Figure 2.16 Entering a Friendly Name

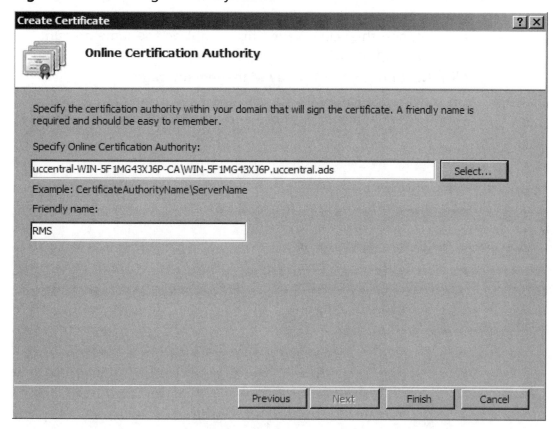

Now, let's install the role.

1. Choose **Start | Administrative Tools | Server Manager**.

2. Scroll down to **Role Summary**, click **Add Roles**.

3. When the **Before You Begin** page opens, click **Next**.

4. On the **Select Server Roles** page, click **Active Directory Rights Management Services**.

5. In the **Add Roles Wizard**, click **Add Required Role Services**, and then click **Next**.

6. Click **Next** on the **Active Directory Rights Management Services** page.

7. Click **Next** on the **Select Role Services** page.

8. Click **Next** on the **Create Or Join An AD RMS Cluster** page.

9. Click **Next** on the **Set Up Configuration Database** page.

10. On the **Specify Service Account** page, click **Specify** to choose an account, and then click **Next**. This cannot be the same account you are using to install RMS.

11. Click **Next** on the **Set Up Key Management** page.

12. On the **Specify Password for AD RMS Encryption** page (Figure 2.17), enter a password and then click **Next**.

Figure 2.17 The AD RMS Encryption Page

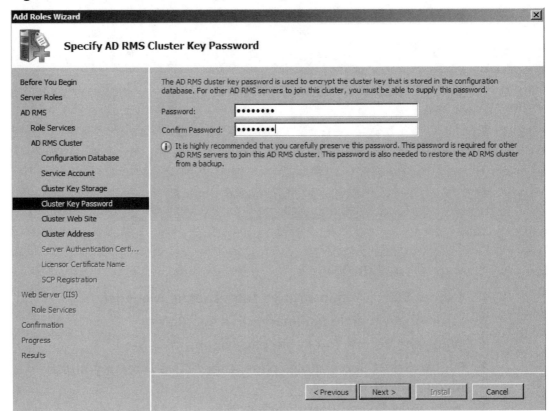

13. Click **Next** on the **Select Web Site** page.

14. Review the information on the **Specify Cluster Address** page (Figure 2.18), click **Validate**, and then click **Next**.

Figure 2.18 Specifying a Cluster Address

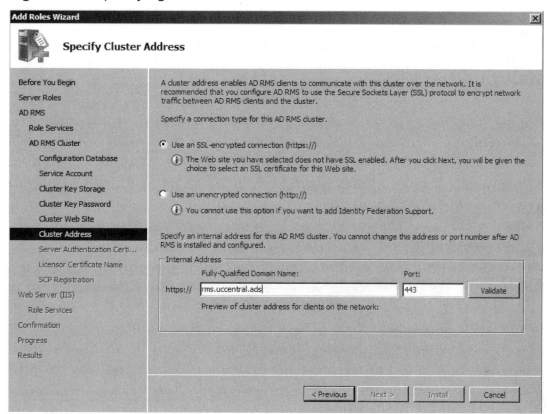

15. Verify that **Choose An Existing Certificate For Secure Socket Layer (SSL) Encryption** is selected on the **Choose A Server Authentication Certificate For SSL Encryption** page (Figure 2.19), choose your server name, and then click **Next**. SSL provides secure communications on the Internet for such things as Web browsing, e-mail, Internet faxing, instant messaging, and other data transfers.

Figure 2.19 Setting SSL Encryption

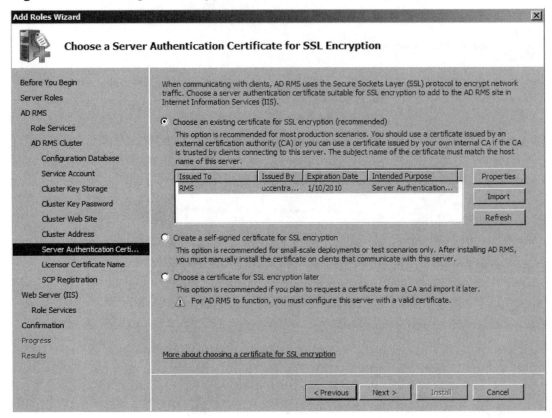

16. Click **Next** on the **Specify a Friendly Name for the Licensor Certificate**.

17. Click **Next** on the **Set up Revocation** page.

18. Click **Next** on the **Register This AD RMS Server In Active Directory** page.

19. Click **Next** on the **Web Server** page.

20. Click **Next** on the **Select Role Services** page.

21. Review the confirmation page, and then click **Install**.

22. When the installation is complete, click **Close**.

Next, we need to set up the RMS cluster settings. In this case, clusters are used as a single server—or set of servers—that share AD RMS publishing and licensing requests. Let's walk through configuring the cluster settings.

1. Choose **Start | Administrative Tools | Active Directory Rights Management Services**.

2. Select your server.

3. Right-click the server and choose **Properties**.

4. Move to the **SCP** tab and select **Change SCP**. Click **OK**. The SCP is the service connection point that identifies the connection URL for the service to the clients.

5. Click **Yes** in the **Active Directory Rights Management Services** dialog.

6. Right-click the server name, and then click **Refresh**.

7. Close the window.

At this stage, the server setup is complete. If you wanted to test the RMS functionality, you could create a document in Word or Excel 2007 and set the permissions by clicking the Office ribbon and preparing access restrictions.

Active Directory Federation Services (ADFS)

Federation Services were originally introduced in Windows Server 2003 R2. F provides an identity access solution, and AD Federation Services provides authenticated access to users inside (and outside) an organization to publicly (via the Internet) accessible applications. Federation Services provides an identity management solution that interoperates with WS-* Web Services Architecture–enabled security products. WS-Federation Passive Requestor Profile (WS-F PRP) also makes it possible for federation to work with solutions that do not use the Microsoft standard of identity management. The WS-Federation specification defines an integrated model for federating identity, authentication, and authorization across different trust realms and protocols. This specification defines how the WS-Federation model is applied to passive requestors such as Web browsers that support the HTTP protocol. WS-Federation Passive Requestor Profile was created in conjunction with some pretty large companies, including IBM, BEA Systems, Microsoft, VeriSign, and RSA Security.

What Is Federation?

As we described earlier in this chapter, federation is a technology solution that makes it possible for two entities to collaborate in a variety of ways. When servers are deployed in multiple organizations for federation, it is possible for corporations to share resources and account management in a trusted manner. Earlier in this chapter, we were discussing Active Directory Rights Management Server. This is just one way companies can take advantage of FS. With ADFS, partners can include external third parties, other departments, or subsidiaries in the same organization.

Why and When to Use Federation

Federation can be used in multiple ways. One product that has been using federation for quite some time is Microsoft Communication Server (previously, Live Communication Server 2005, now rebranded as Office Communication Server 2007). Federation is slightly different in this model, where two companies can federate their environments for the purposes of sharing presence information. This makes it possible for two companies to securely communicate via IM, Live Meeting, Voice, and Video. It also makes it possible to add "presence awareness" to many applications, including the Office suite, as well as Office SharePoint Server. If you want to know more about OCS and how federation works for presence, we recommend *How to Cheat at Administering Office Communication Server 2007*, also by Elsevier.

A little closer to home, Federation Services can also be used in a variety of ways. Let's take an extranet solution where a company in the financial service business shares information with its partners. The company hosts a Windows SharePoint Services (WSS) site in their DMZ for the purposes of sharing revenue information with investment companies that sell their products. Prior to Active Directory Federation Services, these partners would be required to use a customer ID and password in order to access this data. For years, technology companies have been touting the ability to provide and use single sign-on (SSO) solutions. These worked great inside an organization, where you may have several different systems (Active Directory, IBM Tivoli, and Solaris), but tend to fail once you get outside the enterprise walls.

With AD FS, this company can federate their DMZ domain (or, their internal AD) with their partner Active Directory infrastructures. Now, rather than creating a username and password for employees at these partners, they can simply add the users (or groups) to the appropriate security groups in their own Active Directory (see Figure 2.20). It is also important to note that AD FS requires either Windows Server 2008 Enterprise edition or Datacenter edition.

Figure 2.20 The Active Directory Federation Services Structure

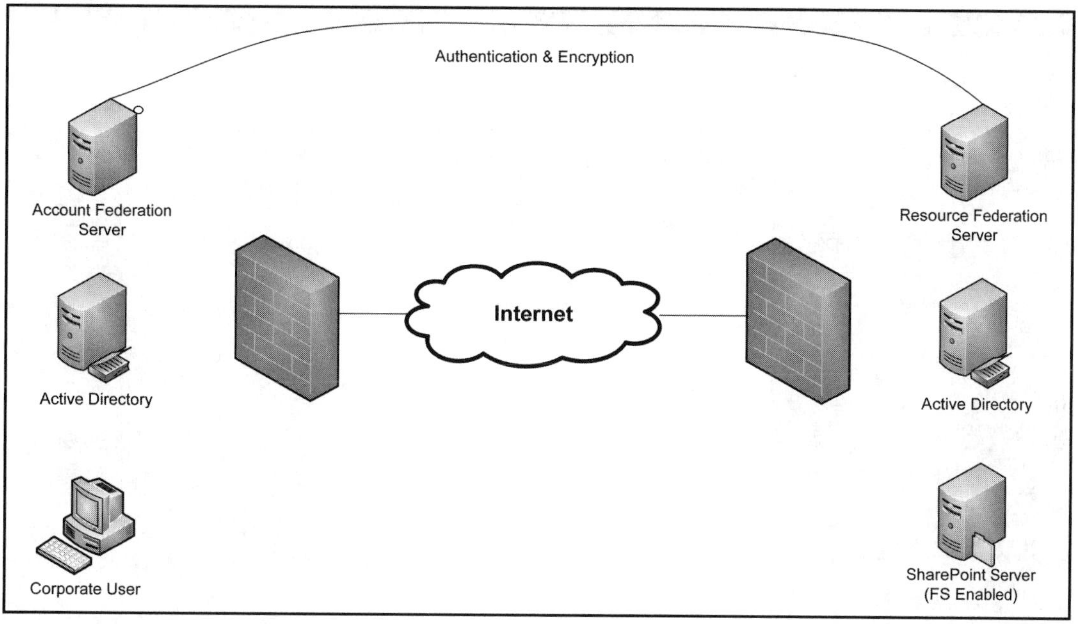

Configuring ADFS

In this exercise, we are going to create the account side of the ADFS structure. The resource is the other half of the ADFS configuration, which is the provider of the service that will be provided to an account domain. To put it in real-world terms, the resource would provide the extranet application to the partner company (the account domain).

EXERCISE 2.6

CONFIGURING FEDERATION SERVICES

1. Click **Start | Administrative Tools | Server Manager**.
2. Scroll down to **Role Summary**, and then click **Add Roles**.
3. When the **Before You Begin** page opens, click **Next**.
4. On the **Select Server Roles** page, select **Active Directory Federation Services** (see Figure 2.21) from the list and click **Next**.

Figure 2.21 Selecting the Role

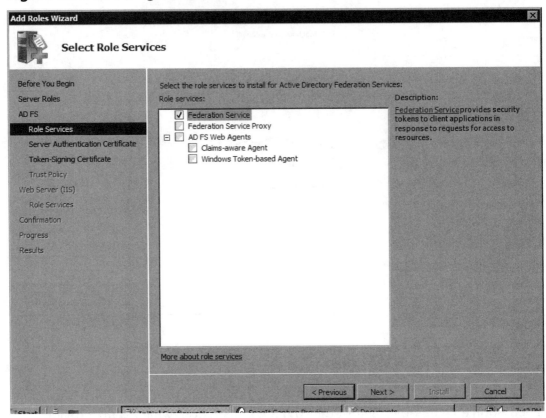

5. Click **Next** on the **Active Directory Federation Services** page.

6. In the **Select Role Services** window, select **Federation Service**, and then click **Next**. If prompted, add the additional prerequisite applications.

7. Click **Create A Self-Signed Certificate For SSL Encryption** (Figure 2.22), and then click **Next**.

Figure 2.22 Creating a Self-Signed Token-Signing Certificate

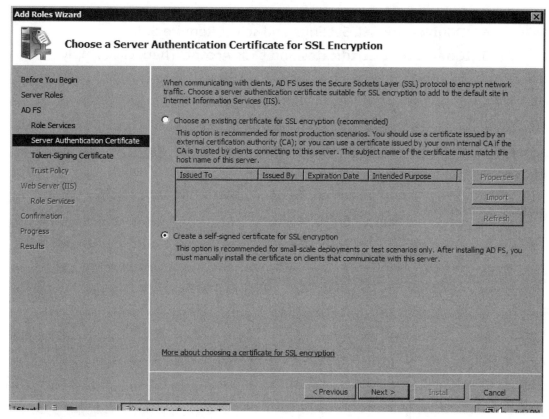

8. Click **Create A Self-Signed Token-Signing Certificate**, and then click **Next**.

9. Click **Next** on the **Select Trust Policy** page.

10. If prompted, click **Next** on the **Web Server (IIS)** page.

11. If prompted, click **Next** on the **Select Role Services** page.

12. On the **Confirm Installation Selections** page, click **Install**.

13. When the installation is complete, click **Close**.

The next step in configuring AD FS is to configure IIS to require SSL certificates on the Federation server:

1. Choose **Start | Administrative Tools | Internet Information Services (IIS) Manager**.

2. Double-click the server name.

3. Drill down the left pane to the Default Web Site and double-click it.

4. Double-click **SSL Settings** and select **Require SSL**.

5. Go to **Client Certificates** and click **Accept**. Then, click Apply (Figure 2.23).

Figure 2.23 Requiring Client Certificates

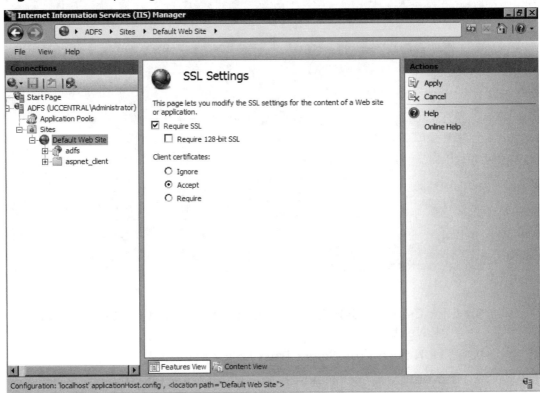

6. Click **Application Pools**.

7. Right-click **AD FS AppPool**, and click **Set Application Pool Defaults**.

8. In the **Identity** pane (Figure 2.24), click **LocalSystem**, and then click **OK**.

Figure 2.24 Setting Application Pool Defaults

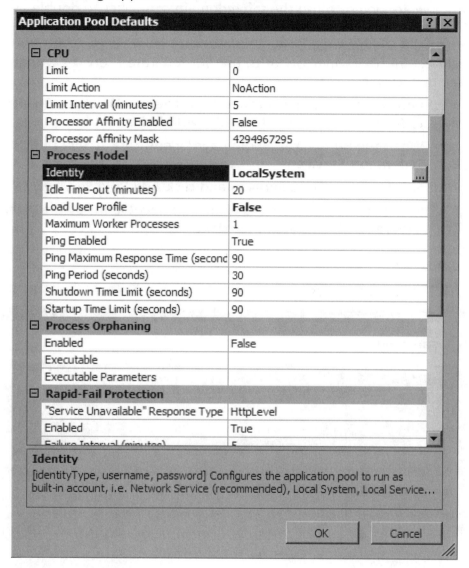

9. Click **OK** again.

10. Before we close IIS, we need to create a self-signed certificate. Double-click the server name again.

11. Double-click **Server Certificates**.

12. Click **Create Self-Signed Certificate**.

13. In the **Specify Friendly Name** field, enter the NetBIOS name of the server and click **OK**.

Next, we need to configure a resource for use with AD FS. In this case, we are going to use the same domain controller to double as a Web server. What we will be doing is installing the AD FS Web Agent, essentially adding an additional role to the server, as part of the AD FS architecture. This will allow us to use our federated services within a Web application.

1. Choose **Start | Administrative Tools | Server Manager**. Scroll down to **Role Summary**, and then click **Add Roles**.

2. When the **Before You Begin** page opens, click **Active Directory Federation Services**.

3. Scroll down to **Role Services** and click **Add Role Services**.

4. In the **Select Role Services** window, select **Claims-aware Agent** (Figure 2.25), and then click **Next**.

Figure 2.25 Setting Services

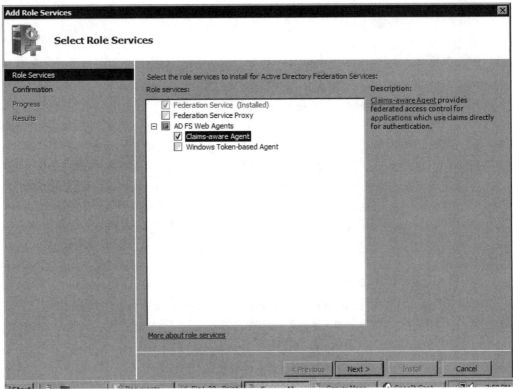

5. Confirm the installation selections (Figure 2.26), and then click **Install**.

Figure 2.26 Confirming the Installation

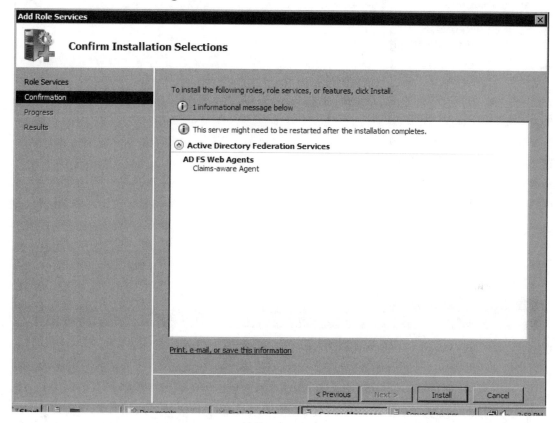

6. When installation is complete, click **Close**.

Now we need to configure the trust policy which would be responsible for federation with the resource domain.

1. Choose **Start | Administrative Tools | Active Directory Federation Services**.

2. Expand Federation Service by clicking the + symbol (see Figure 2.27).

Figure 2.27 AD FS MMC

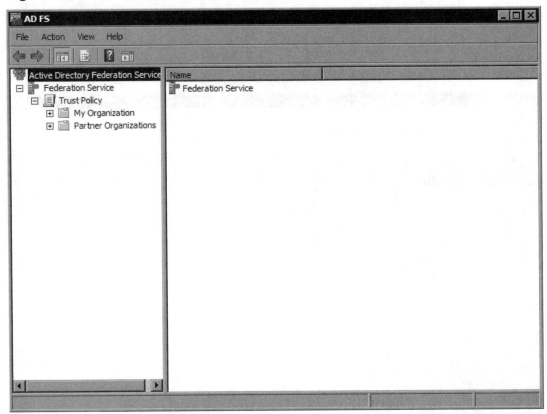

3. Right-click **Trust Policy**, and then choose **Properties**.

4. Verify the information in Figure 2.28 matches your configuration (with the exception of the FQDN server name), and then click **OK**.

Figure 2.28 Trust Policies

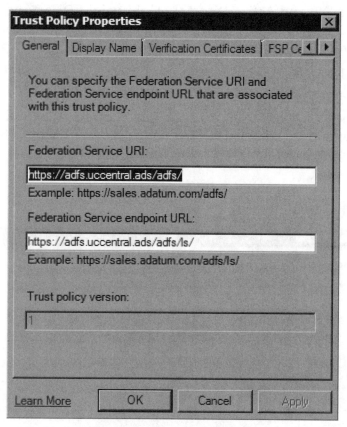

5. When you return to the AD FS MMC, expand **Trust Policy** and open **My Organization**.

6. Right-click **Organization Claims**, and then click **New | Organization Claim**.

7. This is where you enter the information about the resource domain. A claim is a statement made by both partners and is used for authentication within applications. We will be using a Group Claim, which indicates membership in a group or role. Groups would generally follow business groups, such as accounting and IT.

8. Enter a claim name (we will use **PrepGuide Claim**). Verify that Group Claim is checked as well before clicking **OK**.

9. Create a new account store. Account stores are used by AD FS to log on users and extract claims for those users. AD FS supports

two types of account stores: Active Directory Domain Services (AD DS) and Active Directory Lightweight Directory Services (AD LDS). This makes it possible to provide AD FS for full Active Directory Domains and AD LDS domains.

10. Right-click **Account Store** and choose **New | Account Store**.

11. When the **Welcome** window opens, click **Next**.

12. Since we have a full AD DS in place, select **Active Directory Domain Services (AD DS)** from the **Account Store Type** window (Figure 2.29), and then click **Next**.

Figure 2.29 The Account Store Type Window

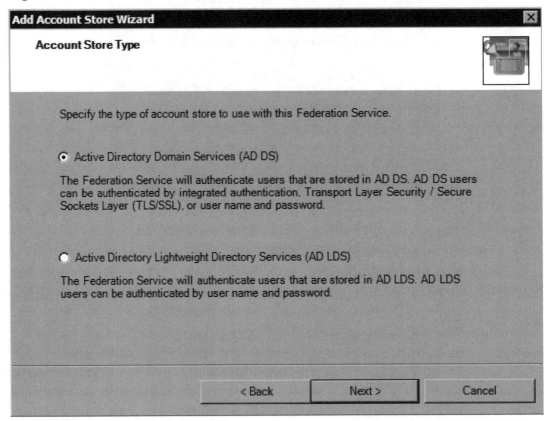

13. Click **Next** on the **Enable This Account Store** window.

14. Click **Finish** on the completion page.

Now, we need to add Active Directory groups into the Account Store.

1. Expand **Account Stores**.

2. Right-click **Active Directory**, and then click **New | Group Claim Extraction**.

3. In the **Create A New Group Claim Extraction** window (Figure 2.30), click **Add** and click **Advanced**.

Figure 2.30 The Create A New Group Claim Extraction Window

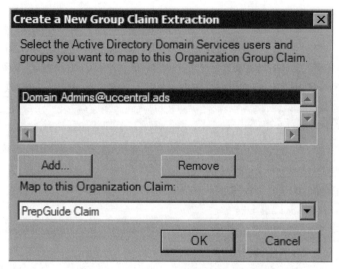

4. Click **Object Types**, remove the checkmarks from everything except Groups, and then click **OK**.

5. Click **Find Now**.

6. Select **Domain Admins** from the list of groups by double-clicking.

7. Click **OK**.

8. The Map To This Organization Claim field should show the claim we created earlier. Click **OK** to close the window.

Finally, we will work to create the partner information of our resource partner, which is prepguides.ads.

1. Expand **Partner Organizations**.

2. Right-click **Resource Partners**, and then select **New | Resource Partner**.

3. Click **Next** on the **Welcome** window.

4. We will not be importing a policy file, so click **Next**.

5. In the **Resource Partner Details** window (Figure 2.31), enter a friendly name for the partner, and the URI and URL information of the partner. Note it is identical to what we entered earlier in Figure 2.28. When the information is complete, click **Next**.

Figure 2.31 Resource Partner Details

Resource Partner Details

Type the display name, Federation Service Uniform Resource Identifier (URI), and Federation Service endpoint Uniform Resource Locator (URL) that you want to assign to this resource partner.

Display name:

PrepGuides.ads

Federation Service URI: (Example: https://sales.adatum.com/adfs/)

https://adfs.prepguides.ads/adfs

Federation Service endpoint URL:

https://adfs.prepguides.ads/adfs/ls

(Example: https://sales.adatum.com/adfs/ls/)

To successfully create a federation trust relationship between both partners, the Federation Service URI value must match the URI value that is specified by the partner.

< Back   Next >   Cancel

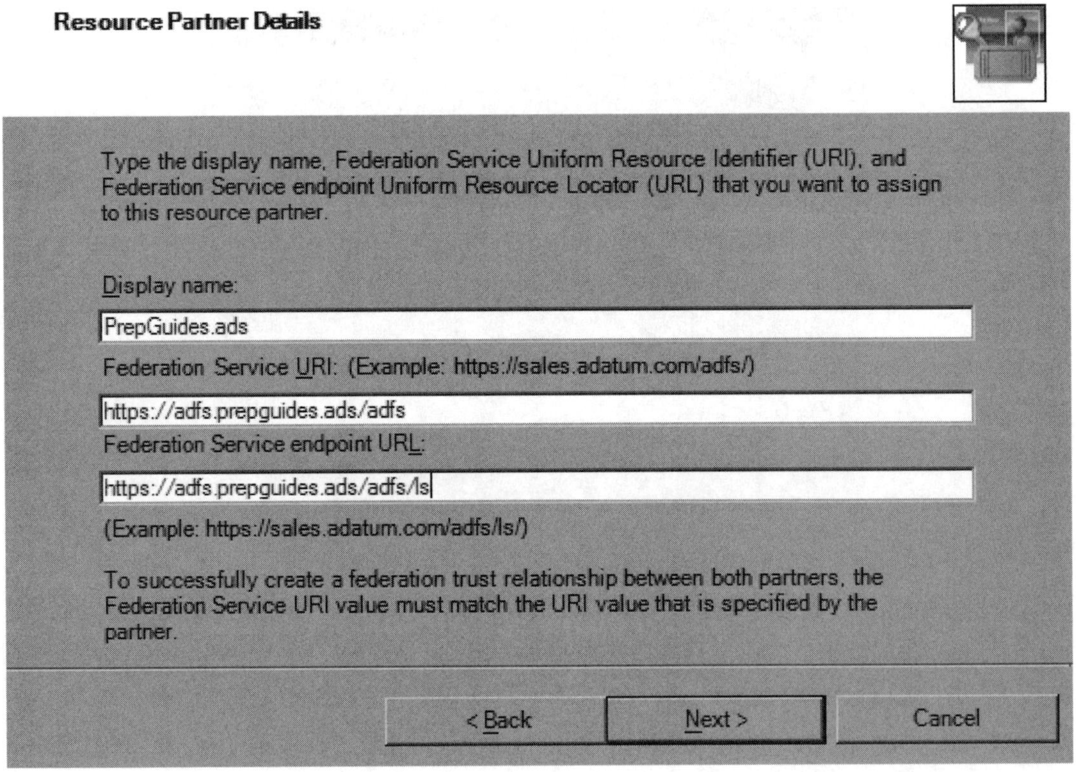

6. Click **Next** on the **Federation Scenario** page. This is the default selection, which is used for two partners from different organizations when there's no forest trust.

7. On the **Resource Partner Identity Claims** page, check **UPN Claim** and click **Next**. A UPN Claim is based on the domain name of your Active Directory structure. In our case, the UPN is uccentral.ads.

8. Set the UPN suffix. Verify that Replace All UPN Suffixes With The Following: is selected and then enter your server's domain name. This is how all suffixes will be sent to the resource partner. Click **Next**.

9. Click **Next** to enable the partner.

10. Click **Finish** to close the wizard.

We're almost at the end of our account partner configuration. The last thing we need to do is create an outgoing claim mapping. This is part of a claim set. On the resource side, we would create an identical incoming claim mapping.

1. Expand **Resource Partners**.

2. Right-click your resource partner, and then choose **New | Outgoing Group Claim Mapping**.

3. Select the claim we created earlier, enter **PrepGuide Mapping**, and then click **OK**.

As you can imagine, this process would be duplicated on the resource domain, with the exception that the outgoing claim mapping would be replaced with an incoming mapping.

Summary of Exam Objectives

As you can see, Windows 2008 includes a number of amazing advancements in Windows 2008, in particular those concerning Active Directory services. Each of these roles provides new layers of features, functions, and security options that were either not available in previous versions of the product or were not quite "baked in" enough, often being included in Version 1.0 of the solution.

When you factor in the additional security of the Server Core installation, Active Directory has come a long way from its original release in Windows 2000. As you will find throughout the rest of this book, you can apply Active Directory roles, and Server Core, in many ways.

Exam Objectives Fast Track

New Roles in 2008

- ☑ With the release of Windows Server 2008, an Active Directory domain controller can be deployed in several new ways.

- ☑ Server Manager is a single solution that is used as a single source for managing identity and system information.

- ☑ Server Manager is enabled by default when a Windows 2008 server is installed.

- ☑ Server Core is a minimal server installation option for Windows Server 2008 that contains a subset of executable files, as well as five server roles.

Read–Only Domain Controllers

- ☑ RODC holds all of the Active Directory Domain Services (AD DS) objects and attributes that a writable domain controller holds, with the exception of account passwords.

- ☑ Unidirectional replication prevents RODCs from replicating information to a writable domain controller.

- ☑ The installation of read–only domain controllers can be delegated to other users.

Active Directory Lightweight Directory Service

☑ Active Directory Lightweight Director Service is a slimmed-down version of AD.

☑ LDS is used when directory-aware applications need directory services, but there is no need for the overhead of a complete forest or domain structure.

☑ LDS has many new features over ADAM, including Auditing, Server Core Support, Support for Active Directory Sites and Services, and a Database Mounting Tool.

Active Directory Rights Management Services

☑ RMS does require a Client Access License.

☑ The three main functions of AD RMS are creating rights-protected files and templates, licensing rights-protected information, and acquiring licenses to decrypt rights-protected content and apply usage policies.

☑ The three new features of AD RMS are delegation of roles, integration with Federation Services, and self-enrollment.

Active Directory Federation Services

☑ Federation Services were first available in Windows Server 2003 R2.

☑ Federation Services provides an identity management solution that interoperates with WS-* Web Services Architecture-enabled security products.

☑ WS-Federation Passive Requestor Profile (WS-F PRP) also makes it possible for federation to work with solutions that do not use the Microsoft standard of identity management.

☑ The WS-Federation specification defines an integrated model for federating identity, authentication, and authorization across different trust realms and protocols.

☑ WS-Federation Passive Requestor Profile was created in conjunction between IBM, BEA Systems, Microsoft, VeriSign, and RSA Security.

Exam Objectives
Frequently Asked Questions

Q: Can an RODC replicate to another RODC?

A: No. RODCs can only replicate with full domain controllers. This is a feature of the RODC, which is meant to be—as the name implies—a read-only server. Since neither RODC would have write capabilities in this example, it would be pointless to have them replicate to one another.

Q: Can I federate with a Windows Server 2003 R2 forest?

A: Yes, you can, but keep in mind that they will not have all of the same functionality. Federation was introduced in Windows Server 2003 R2 to allow IT organizations to take advantage of the basics of federation. However, features such as integration with other applications like AD RMS and Office Sharepoint Server 2007 are not available.

Q: Can an RODC exist in a mixed-mode (Windows 2003 and Windows 2008) domain?

A: Yes, but you must run *adprep* with the proper switches in order for it to succeed. If the domain is not prepped for this new Windows Server 2008 role, the RODC installation will fail almost immediately. *adprep* is required to add the appropriate schema modifications for RODC.

Q: LDS sounds pretty cool. Can I just run that for my AD environment?

A: The short answer is yes, but if you are running AD internally, you would probably want the full functionality of Domain Services. LDS is meant for smaller environments, such as a DMZ, where additional functionality—in particular, management—is not a requirement.

Q: Does Rights Management work with mobile devices?

A: Yes, there is a mobile module for Rights Management Services. However, only Windows Mobile devices are supported with Rights Management. Check with your wireless vendor or mobile manufacturer for support and availability on particular models.

Q: I've heard that Server Core is only supported in 64-bit edition. Is that true?

A: No. Server Core works in both 32-bit and 64-bit editions, Hyper-V (virtualization) only runs on 64-bit. It should be noted that as of the writing of this book, Windows Server 2008 is expected to be the final 32-bit server operating system released by Microsoft.

Q: Do I have to use Server Manager for role deployment?

A: No. You can also use scripting tools to deploy roles. Also, depending on the role, role "bits" (the actual files that make up the role) can sometimes be added automatically. For example, if you forget to add the Directory Services role prior to running dcpromo.exe, dcpromo will add the role for you. However, this is not the case with all roles.

Self Test

1. You are the administrator for a nationwide company with over 5,000 employees. Your main office has approximately 4,500 employees, while the company's ten remote offices have 50 users residing in each. You are often unaware of the physical security in place at these offices. However, since there is a fairly sizable amount of users at each office, you must provide them with directory services. What is the BEST option to use for directory services when security is often an unknown?

   A. Lightweight Directory Services

   B. Read-only domain controllers

   C. Active Directory Federation Services

   D. Active Director Rights Management Services

2. _____ is a format and application-agnostic technology, which provides services to enable the creation of information-protection solutions.

   A. Lightweight Directory Services

   B. Read-only domain controllers

   C. Active Directory Federation Services

   D. Active Director Rights Management Services

3. You are the administrator for a nationwide company with over 5,000 employees. Your director tells you your company has just signed into a partnership with another organization, and that you will be responsible for ensuring that authentication can occur between both organizations without the need for additional sign-on accounts. Your boss mentions that the partner has a variety of Directory Services installed throughout their organizations. Which of the following can Active Directory Federation Services NOT connect to?

   A. Lightweight Directory Services

   B. Windows Server 2003 Directory Services

   C. Windows Server 2003 R2 Directory Services

   D. All of the above

4. You are the administrator for a nationwide company with over 5,000 employees. Your main office has approximately 4,500 employees, while your company's ten remote offices have 50 users each residing in them. You are often unaware of the physical security in place at these offices. However, since

there is a fairly sizable amount of users at each office, you need to provide them with directory services. What is the BEST option to use for directory services when security is often an unknown?

A. Lightweight Directory Services

B. Read-only domain controllers

C. Active Directory Federation Services

D. Active Director Rights Management Services

5. The Web development team has requested that you implement a new Web server in a DMZ that will be used for presenting Web sites to customers. Which of the following is NOT a reason for using Windows Server 2008 Core Server?

A. A Core installation does not require a Windows Server 2008 license.

B. A Core installation does not provide GUIs, which limits console access.

C. Core Server installs fewer services than a full installation of Windows Server 2008.

D. Core Server uses fewer resources than a full installation of Windows Server 2008.

6. You have a Windows Server 2003 R2 domain currently running in your organization. You would like to install a read-only domain controller into your Directory Services structure, but you do not want to completely upgrade your domain to Windows Server 2008 Directory Services just yet. What do you need to do in order to add an RODC?

A. Change the domain functional level to Windows Server 2008 mixed mode.

B. Change the forest functional level to Windows Server 2008 mixed mode.

C. Run *adprep* on a Windows Server 2003 R2 domain controller.

D. An RODC cannot be added until the entire domain is a Windows Server 2008 Directory Services domain.

7. You are looking to upgrade your environment to Windows Server 2008, and you are explaining the new Server Manager console to your boss. Which *three* of the following answers correctly describe ways that Server Manager can be used?

A. Server Manager can be used to add new server roles.

B. Server Manager can be used to add new server features.

C. Server Manager can be used to configure server failover.

D. Server Manager can be used for scripting commands.

8. You are attempting to install Directory Services on a Windows Server 2008 Server Core installation. You type *dcpromo* at the command prompt, but the server fails to install Directory Services. What is the MOST LIKELY reason for this?

   A. Directory Services are not supported on a Server Core installation, only read-only domain controllers.

   B. You must use an unattended file to complete the Directory Services installation.

   C. You must use the Server Manager from another Windows Server 2008 system to complete the installation.

   D. Your server's chipset does not support Directory Services in a Server Core installation.

9. Which of the following Directory Services administration tools can be used in a Windows Server 2008 Lightweight Directory Services installation?

   A. Active Directory Users and Computers

   B. Active Directory Sites and Services

   C. Active Directory Domains and Trusts

   D. Active Directory Licensing Manager

10. BitLocker is a new technology that is available in Windows Server 2008 as well as Windows Vista. Which is NOT an advantage of using BitLocker?

    A. BitLocker can be used to prevent a hacker from detecting my password.

    B. BitLocker prevents someone from removing a hard drive from a system and reading it by installing it on another system.

    C. BitLocker prevents someone from loading another operating system onto the server and reading the contents of the disk using this additional operating system.

    D. All of the above selections are an advantage of using BitLocker.

Self Test Quick Answer Key

1. **B**

2. **D**

3. **B**

4. **B**

5. **A**

6. **C**

7. **A, B, and C**

8. **B**

9. **B**

10. **A**

Chapter 3

MCTS/MCITP
Exam 649

Configuring Certificate Services and PKI

Exam objectives in this chapter:

- **What Is PKI?**
- **Analyzing Certificate Needs within the Organization**
- **Working with Certificate Services**
- **Working with Templates**

Exam objectives review:

- ☑ **Summary of Exam Objectives**
- ☑ **Exam Objectives Fast Track**
- ☑ **Exam Objectives Frequently Asked Questions**
- ☑ **Self Test**
- ☑ **Self Test Quick Answer Key**

Introduction

Computer networks have evolved in recent years to allow an unprecedented sharing of information between individuals, corporations, and even national governments. The need to protect this information has also evolved, and network security has consequently become an essential concern of most system administrators. Even in smaller organizations, the basic goal of preventing unauthorized access while still allowing legitimate information to flow smoothly requires the use of more and more advanced technology.

That being stated, all organizations today rely on networks to access information. These sources of information can range from internal networks to the Internet. Access to information is needed, and this access must be configured to provide information to other organizations that may request it. When we need to make a purchase, for example, we can quickly check out vendors' prices through their Web pages. In order not to allow the competition to get ahead of our organization, we must establish our own Web page for the advertising and ordering of our products. Within any organization, many sites may exist across the country or around the globe. If corporate data is available immediately to employees, much time is saved. In the corporate world, any time saved is also money saved.

In the mid 1990s, Microsoft began developing what was to become a comprehensive security system of authentication protocols and technology based on already developed cryptography standards known as public key infrastructure (PKI). In Windows 2000, Microsoft used various standards to create the first Windows-proprietary PKI—one that could be implemented completely without using third-party companies. Windows Server 2008 expands and improves on that original design in several significant ways, which we'll discuss later in this chapter.

PKI is the method of choice for handling authentication issues in large enterprise-level organizations today. Windows Server 2008 includes the tools you need to create a PKI for your company and issue digital certificates to users, computers, and applications. This chapter addresses the complex issues involved in planning a certificate-based PKI. We'll provide an overview of the basic terminology and concepts relating to the public key infrastructure, and you'll learn about public key cryptography and how it is used to authenticate the identity of users, computers, and applications/services. We'll discuss different components of PKI, including private key, public key, and a trusted third party (TTP) along with PKI enhancements in Windows Server 2008. We'll discuss the role of digital certificates and the different types of certificates (user, machine, and application certificates).

You'll learn about certification authorities (CAs), the servers that issue certificates, including both public CAs and private CAs, such as the ones you can implement on your own network using Server 2008's certificate services. Next, we'll discuss the CA hierarchy and how root CAs and subordinate CAs act together to provide for your organization's certificate needs. You'll find out how the Microsoft certificate services work, and we'll walk you through the steps involved in implementing one or more certification authorities based on the needs of the organization. You'll learn to determine the appropriate CA type—enterprise or stand-alone CA—for a given situation and how to plan the CA hierarchy and provide for security of your CAs. We'll show you how to plan for enrollment and distribution of certificates, including the use of certificate requests, role-based administration, and autoenrollment deployment.

Next, we'll discuss how to implement certificate templates, different types of templates that you can use in your environment. Finally, we'll discuss the role of key recovery agent and how it works in a Windows Server 2008 environment.

What Is PKI?

The rapid growth of Internet use has given rise to new security concerns. Any company that does not configure a strong security infrastructure is literally putting the company at risk. An unscrupulous person could, if security were lax, steal information or modify business information in a way that could result in major financial disaster. To protect the organization's information, the middleman must be eliminated. Cryptographic technologies such as public key infrastructure (PKI) provide a way to identify both users and servers during network use.

PKI is the underlying cryptography system that enables users or computers that have never been in trusted communication before to validate themselves by referencing an association to a trusted third party (TTP). Once this verification is complete, the users and computers can now securely send messages, receive messages, and engage in transactions that include the interchange of data.

PKI is used in both private networks (intranets) and on the World Wide Web (the Internet). It is actually the latter, the Internet, that has driven the need for better methods for verifying credentials and authenticating users. Consider the vast number of transactions that take place every day over the internet—from banking to shopping to accessing databases and sending messages or files. Each of these transactions involves at least two parties. The problem lies in the verification of who those parties are and the choice of whether to trust them with your credentials and information.

The PKI verification process is based on the use of *keys*, unique bits of data that serve one purpose: identifying the owner of the key. Every user of PKI actually generates or receives two types of keys: a *public key* and a *private key*. The two are actually connected and are referred to as a *key pair*. As the name suggests, the public key is made openly available to the public while the private key is limited to the actual owner of the key pair. Through the use of these keys, messages can be *encrypted* and *decrypted*, allowing data to be exchanged securely (this process will be covered in a few sections later in this chapter).

The use of PKI on the World Wide Web is so pervasive that it is likely that every Internet user has used it without even being aware of it. However, PKI is not simply limited to the Web; applications such as Pretty Good Privacy (PGP) also leverage the basis of PKI technology for e-mail protection; FTP over SSL/TLS uses PKI, and many other protocols have the ability to manage the verification of identities through the use of key-based technology. Companies such as VeriSign and Entrust exist as trusted third-party vendors, enabling a world of online users who are strangers to find a common point of reference for establishing confidentiality, message integrity, and user authentication. Literally millions of secured online transactions take place every day leveraging their services within a public key infrastructure.

Technology uses aside, PKI fundamentally addresses relational matters within communications. Specifically, PKI seeks to provide solutions for the following:

- Proper authentication
- Trust
- Confidentiality
- Integrity
- Nonrepudiation

By using the core PKI elements of public key cryptography, digital signatures, and certificates, you can ensure that all these equally important goals can be met successfully. The good news is that the majority of the work involved in implementing these elements under Windows Server 2008 is taken care of automatically by the operating system and is done behind the scenes.

The first goal, proper *authentication*, means that you can be highly certain that an entity such as a user or a computer is indeed the entity he, she, or it is claiming to be. Think of a bank. If you wanted to cash a large check, the teller will more than likely ask for some identification. If you present the teller with a driver's license and the picture on it matches your face, the teller can then be highly certain that you are that person—that is, if the teller trusts the validity of the license itself. Because the driver's license is issued by a government agency—a trusted third party—the teller is more likely to accept it as valid proof of your identity than if you presented an employee ID card issued by a small company that the teller has never heard of. As you can see, trust and authentication work hand in hand.

When transferring data across a network, *confidentiality* ensures that the data cannot be viewed and understood by any third party. The data might be anything from an e-mail message to a database of social security numbers. In the last 20 years, more effort has been spent trying to achieve this goal (data confidentiality) than perhaps all the others combined. In fact, the entire scientific field of cryptology is devoted to ensuring confidentiality (as well as all the other PKI goals).

NOTE

Cryptography refers to the process of encrypting data; *cryptanalysis* is the process of decrypting, or "cracking" cryptographic code. Together, the two make up the science of *cryptology*.

As important as confidentiality is, however, the importance of network data *integrity* should not be underestimated. Consider the extreme implications of a patient's medical records being intercepted during transmission and then maliciously or accidentally altered before being sent on to their destination. Integrity gives confidence to a recipient that data has arrived in its original form and hasn't been changed or edited.

Finally we come to *nonrepudiation*. A bit more obscure than the other goals, nonrepudiation allows you to prove that a particular entity sent a particular piece of data. It is impossible for the entity to deny having sent it. It then becomes extremely difficult for an attacker to masquerade as a legitimate user and then send malevolent data across the network. Nonrepudiation is related to, but separate from authentication.

The Function of the PKI

The primary function of the PKI is to address the need for privacy throughout a network. For the administrator, there are many areas that need to be secured. Internal and external authentication, encryption of stored and transmitted files, and e-mail privacy are just a few examples. The infrastructure that Windows Server 2008 provides links many different public key technologies in order to give the IT administrator the power necessary to maintain a secure network.

Most of the functionality of a Windows Server 2008-based PKI comes from a few crucial components, which are described in this chapter. Although there are several third-party vendors such as VeriSign (www.verisign.com) that offer similar technologies and components, using Windows Server 2008 can be a less costly and easier to implement option—especially for small and medium-sized companies.

Components of PKI

In today's network environments, key pairs are used in a variety of different functions. This series will likely cover topics such as virtual private networks (VPNs), digital signatures, access control (SSH), secure e-mail (PGP—mentioned already—and S/MIME), and secure Web access (Secure Sockets Layer, or SSL). Although these technologies are varied in purpose and use, each includes an implementation of PKI for managing trusted communications between a host and a client.

While PKI exists at some level within the innards of several types of communications technologies, its form can change from implementation to implementation. As such, the components necessary for a successful implementation can vary depending on the requirements, but in public key cryptography there is always:

- A private key
- A public key
- A trusted third party (TTP)

Since a public key must be associated with the name of its owner, a data structure known as a public key certificate is used. The certificate typically contains the owner's name, their public key and e-mail address, validity dates for the certificate, the location of revocation information, the location of the issuer's policies, and possibly other affiliate information that identifies the certificate issuer with an organization such as an employer or other institution.

In most cases, the private and public keys are simply referred to as the private and public key certificates, and the trusted third party is commonly known as the certificate authority (CA). The certificate authority is the resource that must be available to both the holder of the private key and the holder of the public key. Entire hierarchies can exist within a public key infrastructure to support the use of multiple certificate authorities.

In addition to certificate authorities and the public and private key certificates they publish, there are a collection of components and functions associated with the management of the infrastructure. As such, a list of typical components required for a functional public key infrastructure would include but not be limited to the following:

- Digital certificates

- Certification authorities

- Certificate enrollment

- Certificate revocation

- Encryption/cryptography services

Although we have already covered digital certificates and certificate authorities at a high level, it will be well worth our time to revisit these topics. In the sections to follow, we will explore each of the aforementioned topics in greater detail.

New & Noteworthy...

PKI Enhancements in Windows Server 2008

Windows Server 2008 introduces many new enhancements that allow for a more easily implemented PKI solution and, believe it or not, the development of such solutions. Some of these improvements extend to the clients, such as the Windows Vista operating system. Overall, these improvements have increased the manageability throughout Windows PKI. For example, the revocations services have been redesigned, and the attack surface for enrollment has decreased. The following list items include the major highlights:

- **Enterprise PKI (PKIView)** PKIView is a Microsoft Management Console (MMC) snap-in for Windows Server 2008. It can be used to monitor and analyze the health of the certificate authorities and to view details for each certificate authority certificate published in Active Directory Certificate Servers.

- **Web Enrollment** Introduced in Windows Server 2000, the new Web enrollment control is more secure and makes the use of

Continued

scripts much easier. It is also easier to update than previous versions.

- **Network Device Enrollment Service (NDES)** In Windows Server 2008, this service represents Microsoft's implementation of the Simple Certificate Enrollment Protocol (SCEP), a communication protocol that makes it possible for software running on network devices, such as routers and switches that cannot otherwise be authenticated on the network, to enroll for X.509 certificates from a certificate authority.

- **Online Certificate Status Protocol (OCSP)** In cases where conventional CRLs (Certificate Revocation Lists) are not an optimal solution, Online Responders can be configured on a single computer or in an Online Responder Array to manage and distribute revocation status information.

- **Group Policy and PKI** New certificate settings in Group Policy now enable administrators to manage certificate settings from a central location for all the computers in the domain.

- **Cryptography Next Generation** Leveraging the U.S. government's Suite B cryptographic algorithms, which include algorithms for encryption, digital signatures, key exchange, and hashing, Cryptography Next Generation (CNG) offers a flexible development platform that allows IT professionals to create, update, and use custom cryptography algorithms in cryptography-related applications such as Active Directory Certificate Services (AD CS), Secure Sockets Layer (SSL), and Internet Protocol Security (IPsec).

How PKI Works

Before we discuss how PKI works today, it is perhaps helpful to understand the term encryption and how PKI has evolved. The history of general cryptography almost certainly dates back to almost 2000 B.C. when Roman and Greek statesmen used simple alphabet-shifting algorithms to keep government communication private. Through time and civilizations, ciphering text played an important role in wars and politics. As modern times provided new communication methods, scrambling information became increasingly more important. World War II brought about the first use of the computer in the cracking of Germany's Enigma code. In 1952,

President Truman created the National Security Agency at Fort Meade, Maryland. This agency, which is the center of U.S. cryptographic activity, fulfills two important national functions: It protects all military and executive communication from being intercepted, and it intercepts and unscrambles messages sent by other countries.

Although complexity increased, not much changed until the 1970s, when the National Security Agency (NSA) worked with Dr. Horst Feistel to establish the Data Encryption Standard (DES) and Whitfield Diffie and Martin Hellman introduced the first public key cryptography standard. Windows Server 2008 still uses Diffie-Hellman (DH) algorithms for SSL, Transport Layer Security (TLS), and IPsec. Another major force in modern cryptography came about in the late 1970s. RSA Labs, founded by Ronald Rivest, Adi Shamir, and Leonard Adleman, furthered the concept of key cryptography by developing a technology of key pairs, where plaintext that is encrypted by one key can be decrypted only by the other matching key.

There are three types of cryptographic functions. The hash function does not involve the use of a key at all, but it uses a mathematical algorithm on the data in order to scramble it. The secret key method of encryption, which involves the use of a single key, is used to encrypt and decrypt the information and is sometimes referred to as symmetric key cryptography. An excellent example of secret key encryption is the decoder ring you may have had as a child. Any person who obtained your decoder ring could read your "secret" information.

There are basically two types of symmetric algorithms. Block symmetric algorithms work by taking a given length of bits known as blocks. Stream symmetric algorithms operate on a single bit at a time. One well-known block algorithm is DES. Windows 2000 uses a modified DES and performs that operation on 64-bit blocks using every eighth bit for parity. The resulting ciphertext is the same length as the original cleartext. For export purposes the DES is also available with a 40-bit key.

One advantage of secret key encryption is the efficiency with which it takes a large amount of data and encrypts it quite rapidly. Symmetric algorithms can also be easily implemented at the hardware level. The major disadvantage of secret key encryption is that a single key is used for both encryption and decryption. There must be a secure way for the two parties to exchange the one secret key.

In the 1970s this disadvantage of secret key encryption was eliminated through the mathematical implementation of public key encryption. Public key encryption, also referred to as asymmetric cryptography, replaced the one shared key with each user's own pair of keys. One key is a public key, which is made available to everyone and is used for the encryption process only. The other key in the pair, the private key, is available only to the owner. The private key cannot be created as a result of the public key's being available. Any data that is encrypted by a public key can be decrypted only by using the private key of the pair. It is also possible for the owner to use a private key to encrypt sensitive information. If the data is encrypted by using the private key, then the public key in the pair of keys is needed to decrypt the data.

DH algorithms are known collectively as *shared secret key* cryptographies, also known as symmetric key encryption. Let's say we have two users, Greg and Matt, who want to communicate privately. With DH, Greg and Matt each generate a random number. Each of these numbers is known only to the person who generated it. Part one of the DH function changes each secret number into a nonsecret, or public, number. Greg and Matt now exchange the public numbers and then enter them into part two of the DH function. This results in a private key—one that is identical to both users. Using advanced mathematics, this shared secret key can be decrypted only by someone with access to one of the original random numbers. As long as Greg and Matt keep the original numbers hidden, the shared secret key cannot be reversed.

It should be apparent from the many and varied contributing sources to PKI technology that the need for management of this invaluable set of tools would become paramount. If PKI, like any other technology set, continued to develop without standards of any kind, then differing forms and evolutions of the technology would be implemented ad hoc throughout the world. Eventually, the theory holds that some iteration would render communication or operability between different forms impossible. At that point, the cost of standardization would be significant, and the amount of time lost in productivity and reconstruction of PKI systems would be immeasurable.

Thus, a set of standards was developed for PKI. The Public-Key Cryptography Standards (PKCS) are a set of standard protocols sued for securing the exchange of information through PKI. The list of these standards was actually established by RSA laboratories—the same organization that developed the original RSA encryption standard—along with a group of participating technology leaders that included Microsoft, Sun, and Apple.

PKCS Standards

Here is a list of active PKCS standards. You will notice that there are gaps in the numbered sequence of these standards, and that is due to the retiring of standards over time since they were first introduced.

- **PKCS #1: RSA Cryptography Standard** Outlines the encryption of data using the RSA algorithm. The purpose of the RSA Cryptography Standard is in the development of digital signatures and digital envelopes. PKCS#1 also describes a syntax for RSA public keys and private keys.

The public-key syntax is used for certificates, while the private-key syntax is used for encrypting private keys.

- **PKCS #3: Diffie-Hellman Key Agreement Standard** Outlines the use of the Diffie-Hellman Key Agreement, a method of sharing a secret key between two parties. The secret key used to encrypt ongoing data transfer between the two parties. Whitefield Diffie and martin Hellman developed the Diffie-Hellman algorithm in the 1970s as the first public asymmetric cryptographic system (asymmetric cryptography was invented in the United Kingdom earlier in the same decade, but was classified as a military secret). Diffie-Hellman overcomes the issue of symmetric key system, because management of the keys is less difficult.

- **PKCS #5: Password-based Cryptography Standard** A method for encrypting a string with a secret key that is derived from a password. The result of the method is an octet string (a sequence of 8-bit values). PKCS #8 is primarily used for encrypting private keys when they are being transmitted between computers.

- **PKCS #6: Extended-certificate Syntax Standard** Deals with extended certificates. Extended certificates are made up of the X.509 certificate plus additional attributes. The additional attributes and the X.509 certificate can be verified using a single public-key operation. The issuer that signs the extended certificate is the same as the one that signs the X.509 certificate.

- **PKCS #7: Cryptographic Message Syntax Standard** The foundation for Secure/Multipurpose Internet Mail Extensions (S/MIME) standard. It is also compatible with Privacy-Enhanced Mail (PEM) and can be used in several different architectures of key management.

- **PKCS #8: Private-key Information Syntax Standard** Describes a method of communication for private-key information that includes the use of public-key algorithm and additional attributes (similar to PKCS #6). In this case, the attributes can be a DN or a root CA's public key.

- **PKCS #9: Selected Attribute Types** Defines the types of attributes for use in extended certificates (PKCS #6), digitally signed messages (PKCS #7), and private-key information (PKCS #8).

- **PKCS #10: Certification Request Syntax Standard** Describes a syntax for certification request. A certification request consists of a DN, a public key, and additional attributes. Certification requests are sent to a CA, which then issues the certificate.

- **PKCS #11: Cryptographic Token Interface Standard** Specifies an application program interface (API) for token devices that hold encrypted information and perform cryptographic functions, such as smart cards and Universal Serial Bus (USB) pigtails.

- **PKCS #12: Personal Information Exchange Syntax Standard** Specifies a portable format for storing or transporting a user's private keys and certificates. Ties into both PKCS #8 (communication of private-key information) and PKCS #11 (Cryptographic Token Interface Standard). Portable formats include diskettes, smart cards, and Personal Computer Memory Card International Association (PCMCIA) cards. On Microsoft Windows platforms, PKCS #12 format files are generally given the extension *.pfx*. PKCS #12 is the best standard format to use when exchanging private keys and certificates between systems.

TEST DAY TIP

On the day of the test, do not concern yourself too much with what the different standard numbers are. It is important to understand why they are in place and what PKCS stands for.

RSA-derived technology in its various forms is used extensively by Windows Server 2008 for such things as Kerberos authentication and S/MIME. In practice, the use of the PKI technology goes something like this: Two users, Dave and Dixine, wish to communicate privately. Dave and Dixine each own a key pair consisting of a public key and a private key. If Dave wants Dixine to send him an encrypted message, he first transmits his public key to Dixine. She then uses Dave's public key to encrypt the message. Fundamentally, since Dave's public key was used to encrypt, only Dave's private key can be used to decrypt. When he receives the message, only he is able to read it. Security is maintained because only public keys are transmitted—the private keys are kept secret and are known only to their owners. Figure 3.1 illustrates the process.

Figure 3.1 Public/Private Key Data Exchange

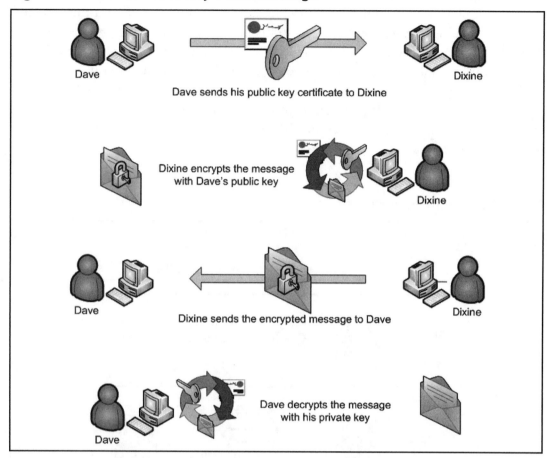

Dave

Dave sends his public key certificate to Dixine

Dixine

Dixine encrypts the message with Dave's public key

Dixine

Dave

Dixine sends the encrypted message to Dave

Dixine

Dave decrypts the message with his private key

Dave

EXAM WARNING

In a Windows Server 2008 PKI, a user's public and private keys are stored under the user's profile. For the administrator, the public keys would be under *Documents and Settings\Administrator\System Certificates\ My\Certificates* and the private keys would be under *Documents and Settings\Administrator\Crypto\RSA* (where they are double encrypted by Microsoft's Data Protection API, or DPAPI). Although a copy of the public keys is kept in the registry, and can even be kept in Active Directory, the private keys are vulnerable to deletion. If you delete a user profile, the private keys will be lost!

RSA can also be used to create "digital signatures" (see Figure 3.2). In the communication illustrated in Figure 3.1, a public key was used to encrypt a message and the corresponding private key was used to decrypt. If we invert the process, a private key can be used to encrypt and the matching public key to decrypt. This is useful, for example, if you want people to know that a document you wrote is really yours. If you encrypt the document using your private key, then only your public key can decrypt it. If people use your public key to read the document and they are successful, they can be certain that it was "signed" by your private key and is therefore authentic.

Figure 3.2 Digital Signatures

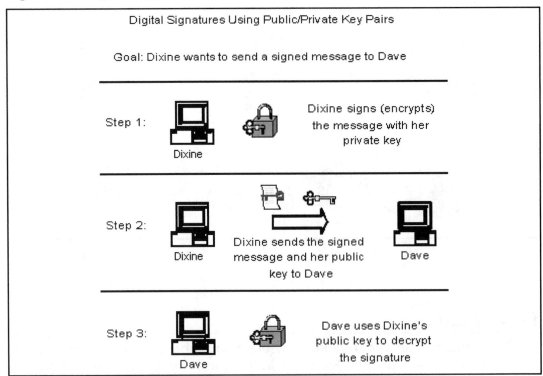

Head of the Class...

Modern Cryptography 101

Thanks to two mathematical concepts, prime number theory and modulo algebra, most of today's cryptography encryption standards are considered intractable—that is, they are unbreakable with current technology in a reasonable amount of time. For example, it might take 300 linked computers over 1,000 years to decrypt a message. Of course, quantum computing is expected to some day change all that, making calculations exponentially faster and rendering all current cryptographic algorithms useless—but we won't worry about that for now.

First, an explanation of the *modulo* operator. Let's go back to elementary school where you first learned to do division. You learned that 19/5 equals 3 with a remainder of 4. You also probably concentrated on the 3 as the important number. Now, however, we get to look at the remainder. When we take the modulus of two numbers, the result is the remainder—therefore 19 mod 5 equals 4. Similarly, 24 mod 5 also equals 4 (can you see why?). Finally, we can conclude that 19 and 24 are congruent in modulo 4. So how does this relate to cryptography and prime numbers?

The idea is to take a message and represent it by using a sequence of numbers. We'll call the sequence x_i. What we need to do is find three numbers that make the following modulo equation possible: $(x^e)^d \bmod y = x$.

The first two numbers, e and d, are a pair and are completely interchangeable. The third number, y, is a product of two very large prime numbers (the larger the primes, the more secure the encryption). Prime number theory is too complex for an in-depth discussion here, but in a nutshell, remember that a prime number is only divisible by the number 1 and itself. This gives each prime number a "uniqueness."

Once we have found these numbers (although we won't go into how because this is the really deep mathematical part), the encryption key becomes the pair (e, y) and the decryption key becomes the pair (d, y). Now it doesn't matter which key we decide to make public and which key we make private because they're interchangeable. It's a good thing that Windows Server 2008 does all of the difficult work for us!

How Certificates Work

Before we delve into the inner workings of a certificate, let's discuss what a certificate actually is in layman's terms. In PKI, a digital certificate is a tool used for binding a public key with a particular owner. A great comparison is a driver's license. Consider the information listed on a driver's license:

- Name
- Address
- Date of birth
- Photograph
- Signature
- Social security number (or another unique number such as a state issued license number)
- Expiration date
- Signature/certification by an authority (typically from within the issuing state's government body)

The information on a state license photo is significant because it provides crucial information about the owner of that particular item. The signature from the state official serves as a trusted authority for the state, certifying that the owner has been verified and is legitimate to be behind the wheel of a car. Anyone, like an officer, who wishes to verify a driver's identity and right to commute from one place to another by way of automobile need only ask for and review the driver's license. In some cases, the officer might even call or reference that license number just to ensure it is still valid and has not been revoked.

A digital certificate in PKI serves the same function as a driver's license. Various systems and checkpoints may require verification of the owner's identity and status and will reference the trusted third party for validation. It is the certificate that enables this quick hand-off of key information between the parties involved.

The information contained in the certificate is actually part or the X.509 certificate standard. X.509 is actually an evolution of the X.500 directory standard. Initially intended to provide a means of developing easy-to-use electronic directories of people that would be available to all Internet users, it became a directory and mail standard for a very commonly known mail application: Microsoft Exchange 5.5. The X.500 directory standard specifies a common root of a hierarchical tree although the "tree" is inverted: the root of the tree is depicted at the "top" level while the other branches—called "containers"—are below it. Several of these types of containers exist with a specific naming convention. In this naming convention, each portion of a name is specified by the abbreviation of the object type or a container it represents. For example, a *CN=* before a username represents it is a "*common name*", a *C=* precedes a "*country*," and an *O=* precedes "*organization*". These elements are worth remembering as they will appear not only in discussions about X.500 and X.509, but they are ultimately the basis for the scheme of Microsoft's premier directory service, Active Directory.

X.509 is the standard used to define what makes up a digital certificate. Within this standard, a description is given for a certificate as allowing an association between a user's *distinguished name (DN)* and the user's public key. The DN is specified by a *naming authority (NA)* and used as a unique name by the *certificate authority (CA)* who will create the certificate. A common X.509 certificate includes the following information (see Table 3.1 and Figures 3.3 and 3.4):

Table 3.1 X.509 Certificate Data

Item	Definition
Serial Number	A unique identifier.
Subject	The name of the person or company that is being identified, sometimes listed as "Issued To".
Signature Algorithm	The algorithm used to create the signature.
Issuer	The trusted authority that verified the information and generated the certificate, sometimes listed as "Issued By".
Valid From	The date the certificate was activated.
Valid To	The last day the certificate can be used.
Public Key	The public key that corresponds to the private key.
Thumbprint Algorithm	The algorithm used to create the unique value of a certificate.
Thumbprint	The unique value of every certificate, which positively identifies the certificate. If there is ever a question about the authenticity of a certificate, check this value with the issuer.

Figure 3.3 A Windows Server 2008 Certificate Field and Values

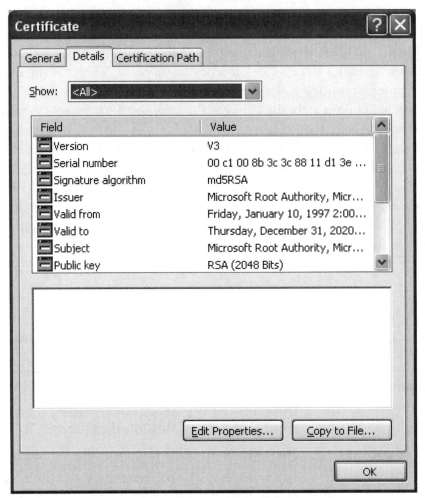

Figure 3.4 A Windows Server 2008 Certificate Field and Values

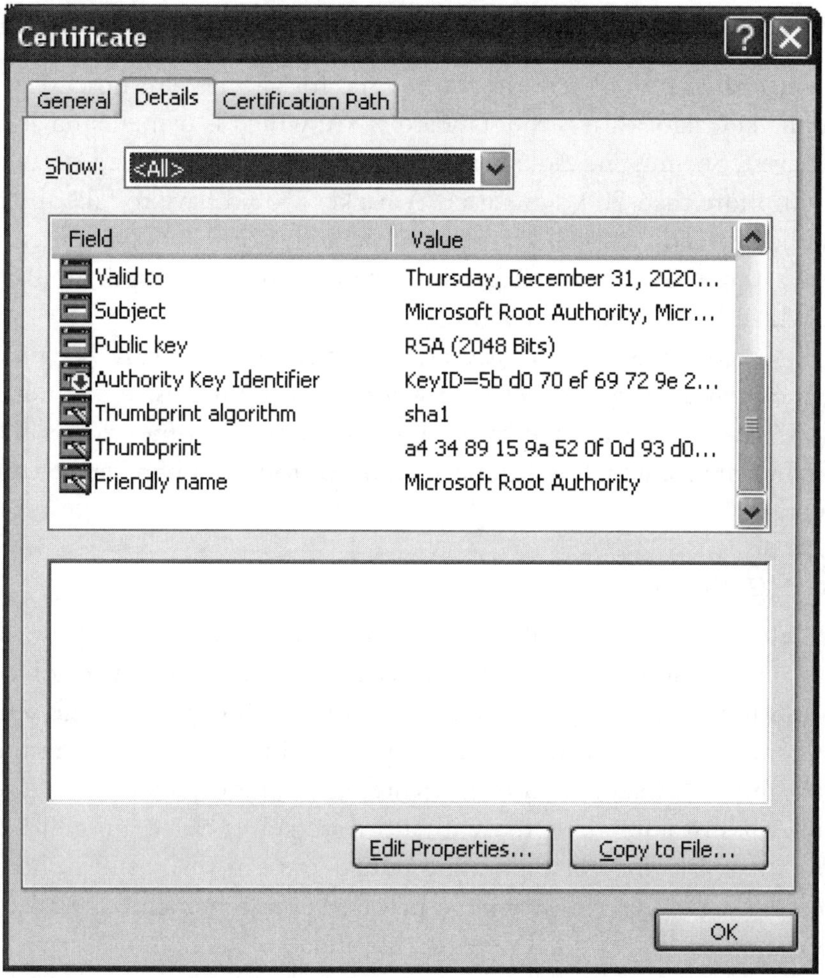

Public Key Functionality

Public key cryptography brings major security technologies to the desktop in the Windows 2000 environment. The network now is provided with the ability to allow users to safely:

- Transmit over insecure channels

- Store sensitive information on any commonly used media

- Verify a person's identity for authentication

- Prove that a message was generated by a particular person

- Prove that the received message was not tampered with in transit

Algorithms based on public keys can be used for all these purposes. The most popular public key algorithm is the standard RSA, which is named after its three inventors: Rivest, Shamir, and Adleman. The RSA algorithm is based on two prime numbers with more than 200 digits each. A hacker would have to take the ciphertext and the public key and factor the product of the two primes. As computer processing time increases, the RSA remains secure by increasing the key length, unlike the DES algorithm, which has a fixed key length.

Public key algorithms provide privacy, authentication, and easy key management, but they encrypt and decrypt data slowly because of the intensive computation required. RSA has been evaluated to be from 10 to 10,000 times slower than DES in some environments, which is a good reason not to use public key algorithms for bulk encryption.

Digital Signatures

Document letterhead can be easily created on a computer, so forgery is a security issue. When information is sent electronically, no human contact is involved. The receiver wants to know that the person listed as the sender is really the sender and that the information received has not been modified in any way during transit. A hash algorithm is implemented to guarantee the Windows 2000 user that the data is authentic. A hash value encrypted with a private key is called a digital signature. Anyone with access to the corresponding public key can verify the authenticity of a digital signature. Only a person having a private key can generate digital signatures. Any modification makes a digital signature invalid.

The purpose of a digital signature is to prevent changes within a document from going unnoticed and also to claim the person to be the original author. The document itself is not encrypted. The digital signature is just data sent along with the data guaranteed to be untampered with. A change of any size invalidates the digital signature.

When King Henry II had to send a message to his troops in a remote location, the letter would be sealed with wax, and while the wax was still soft the king would use his ring to make an impression in it. No modification occurred to the original message if the seal was never broken during transit. There was no doubt that King Henry II had initiated the message, because he was the only person possessing a ring that matched the waxed imprint. Digital signatures work in a similar fashion in that only the sender's public key can authenticate both the original sender and the content of the document.

The digital signature is generated by a message digest, which is a number generated by taking the message and using a hash algorithm. A message digest is regarded as a fingerprint and can range from a 128-bit number to a 256-bit number. A hash function takes variable-length input and produces a fixed-length output. The message is first processed with a hash function to produce a message digest. This value is then signed by the sender's private key, which produces the actual digital signature. The digital signature is then added to the end of the document and sent to the receiver along with the document.

Since the mere presence of a digital signature proves nothing, verification must be mathematically proven. In the verification process, the first step is to use the corresponding public key to decrypt the digital signature. The result will produce a 128-bit number. The original message will be processed with the same hash function used earlier and will result in a message digest. The two resulting 128-bit numbers will then be compared, and if they are equal, you will receive notification of a good signature. If a single character has been altered, the two 128-bit numbers will be different, indicating that a change has been made to the document, which was never scrambled.

Authentication

Public key cryptography can provide authentication instead of privacy. In Windows 2000, a challenge is sent by the receiver of the information. The challenge can be implemented one of two ways. The information is authenticated because only the corresponding private key could have encrypted the information that the public key is successfully decrypting.

In the first authentication method, a challenge to authenticate involves sending an encrypted challenge to the sender. The challenge is encrypted by the receiver, using the sender's public key. Only the corresponding private key can successfully decode the challenge. When the challenge is decoded, the sender sends the plaintext back to the receiver. This is the proof for the receiver that the sender is truly the sender.

For example, when Alice receives a document from Bob, she wants to authenticate that the sender is really Bob. She sends an encrypted challenge to Bob, using his public key. When he receives the challenge, Bob uses his private key to decrypt the information. The decrypted challenge is then sent back to Alice. When Alice receives the decrypted challenge, she is convinced that the document she received is truly from Bob.

The second authentication method uses a challenge that is sent in plaintext. The receiver, after receiving the document, sends a challenge in plaintext to the sender. The sender receives the plaintext challenge and adds some information before adding a digital signature.

The challenge and digital signature now head back to the sender. The digital signature is generated by using a hash function and then encrypting the result with a private key, so the receiver must use the sender's public key to verify the digital signature. If the signature is good, the original document and sender have at this point been verified mathematically.

Secret Key Agreement via Public Key

The PKI of Windows 2000 permits two parties to agreed on a secret key while they use nonsecure communication channels. Each party generates half the shared secret key by generating a random number, which is sent to the other party after being encrypted with the other party's public key. Each receiving side then decrypts the ciphertext using a private key, which will result in the missing half of the secret key.

By adding both random numbers together, each party will have an agreed-upon shared secret key, which can then be used for secure communication even though the secret key was first obtained through a nonsecure communication channel.

Bulk Data Encryption without Prior Shared Secrets

The final major feature of public key technology is that it can encrypt bulk data without generating a shared secret key first. The biggest disadvantage of using asymmetric algorithms for encryption is the slowness of the overall process, which results from the necessary intense computations; the largest disadvantage of using symmetric algorithms for encryption of bulk data is the need for a secure communication channel for exchanging the secret key. The Windows 2000 operating system combines symmetric and asymmetric algorithms to get the best of both worlds at just the right moment.

For a large document that must be kept secret, because secret key encryption is the quickest method to use for bulk data, a session key is used to scramble the document. To protect the session key, which is the secret key needed to decrypt the protected data, the sender encrypts this small item quickly by using the receiver's public key. This encryption of the session key is handled by asymmetric algorithms, which use intense computation, but do not require much time due to the small size of the session key. The document, along with the encrypted session key, is then sent to the receiver. Only the intended receiver will possess the correct private key to decode the session key, which is needed to decode the actual document. When the session key is in plaintext, it can be applied to the ciphertext of the bulk data and then transform the bulk data back to plaintext.

EXERCISE 3.1

REVIEWING A DIGITAL CERTIFICATE

Let's take a moment to go on the Internet and look at a digital certificate.

1. Open up your Web browser, and go to www.syngress.com.

2. Select a book and add it to your cart.

3. Proceed to the checkout.

4. Once you are at the checkout screen, you will see a padlock in your browser. In Internet Explorer 7, this will be to the right of the address box; older browsers place the padlock in the bottom right of the window frame. Open the certificate properties. In Internet Explorer 7, you do this by clicking on the padlock and selecting "View Certificates" from the prompt; older browsers generally let you double-click the padlock.

5. Move around the tabs of the Properties screen to look at the different information contained within that certificate.

The Windows Server 2008 PKI does many things behind the scenes. Thanks in part to auto enrollment (discussed later in this chapter) and certificate stores (places where certificates are kept after their creation), some PKI-enabled features such as EFS work with no user intervention at all. Others, such as IPsec, require significantly less work than would be required without an advanced operating system.

Even though a majority of the PKI is handled by Server, it is still instructive to have an overview of how certificate services work.

1. First, a system or user generates a public/private key pair and then a certificate request.

2. The certificate request, which contains the public key and other identifying information such as user name, is forwarded on to a CA.

3. The CA verifies the validity of the public key. If it is verified, the CA issues the certificate.

4. Once issued, the certificate is ready for use and is kept in the certificate store, which can reside in Active Directory. Applications that require a certificate use this central repository when necessary.

In practice, it isn't terribly difficult to implement certificate services, as Exercise 3.2 shows. Configuring the CA requires a bit more effort, as does planning the structure and hierarchy of the PKI—especially if you are designing an enterprise-wide solution. We'll cover these topics later in this chapter.

EXERCISE 3.2

INSTALLING CERTIFICATE SERVICES

1. After logging on with administrative privileges, click **Start**, click **All Programs,** click **Administrative Tools**, and then click **Server Manager**.

2. In the **Roles Summary** section, click **Add Roles.**

3. On the **Before You Begin** page, click **Next** (see Figure 3.5).

Figure 3.5 Before You Begin Page

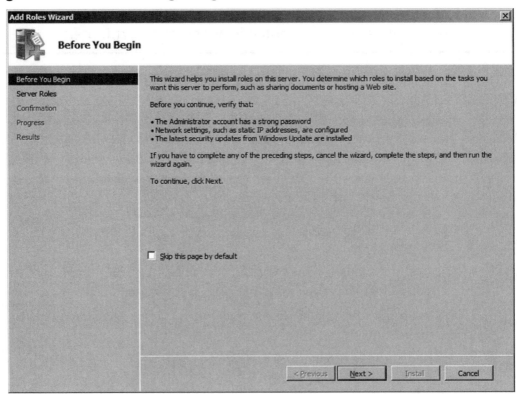

4. On the **Select Server Roles** page, click the **Active Directory Certificate Services** (see Figure 3.6). Click **Next**.

Figure 3.6 Select Server Roles Page

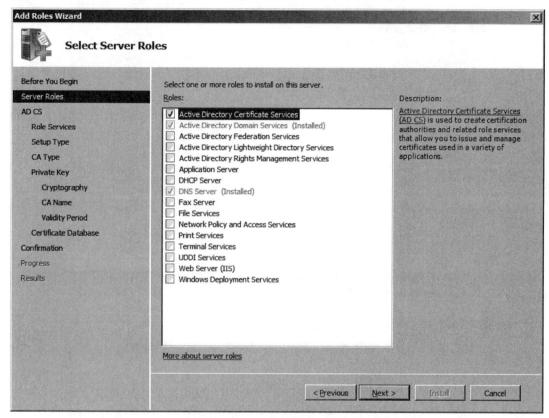

5. On the **Introduction to Active Directory Certificate Services** page, click **Next**.

6. On the **Select Role Services** page, click the **Certification Authority** check box, as shown in Figure 3.7. Click **Next**.

Figure 3.7 Select Role Services Page

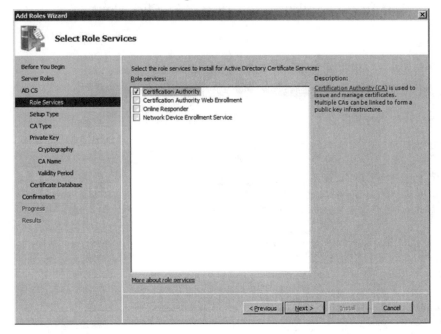

7. On the **Specify Setup Type** page, click **Enterprise**, as shown in Figure 3.8. Click **Next**.

Figure 3.8 Specify Setup Type Page

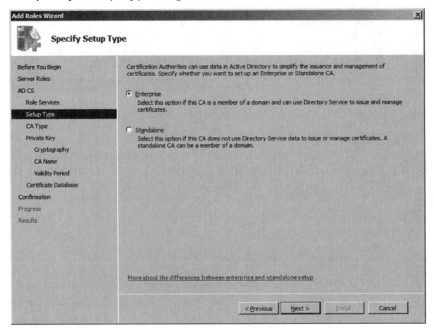

8. On the **Specify CA Type** page, click **Root CA**, as shown in Figure 3.9. Click **Next**.

Figure 3.9 Specify CA Type Page

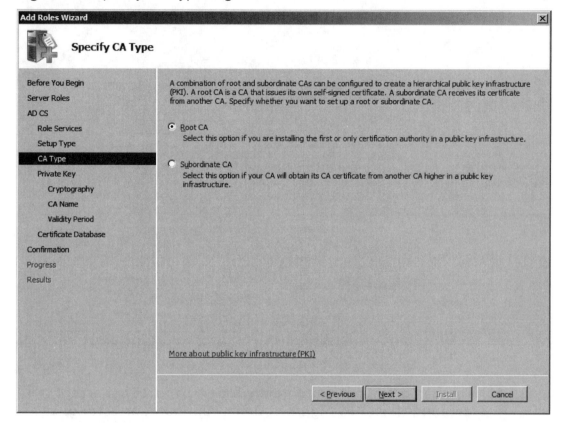

9. On the **Set Up Private Key** page, either accept the default value or configure optional configuration settings. For this exercise, choose the default settings as shown in Figure 3.10. Click **Next**.

Figure 3.10 Set Up Private Key Page

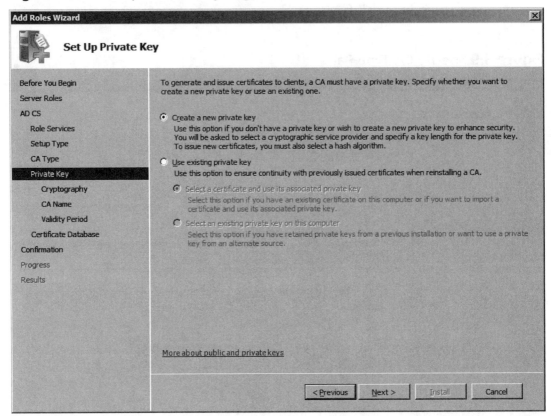

10. On the **Configure Cryptography for CA** page, either accept the default value or configure optional configuration settings as per project requirements. For this exercise, choose the default settings as shown in Figure 3.11. Click **Next**.

Figure 3.11 Configure Cryptography for CA Page

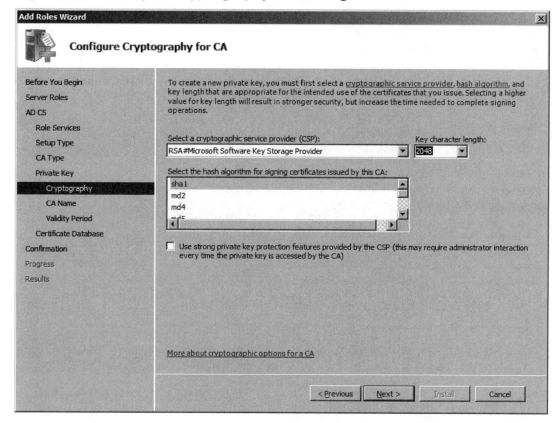

11. In the **Common name for this CA** box, type the common name of the CA. For this exercise, type **MyRootCA** as shown in Figure 3.12. Click **Next**.

Figure 3.12 Configure CA Name Page

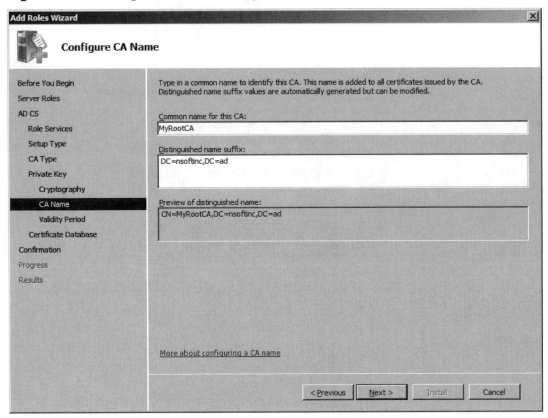

12. On the **Set the Certificate Validity Period** page, you can change the default five-year validity period of the CA. You can set the validity period as a number of days, weeks, months or years. Accept the default validity duration for the root CA as shown in Figure 3.13, and then click **Next**.

Figure 3.13 Set Validity Period Page

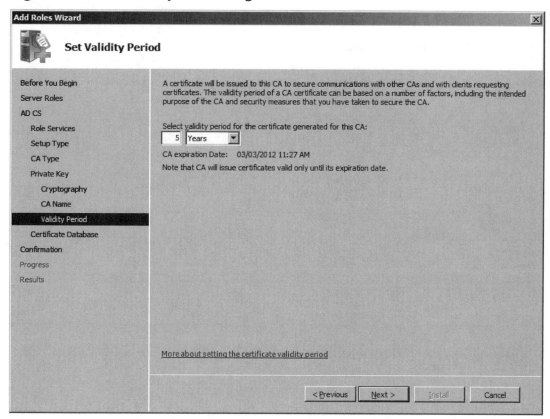

14. On the **Configure Certificate Database** page, for this exercise, accept the default values or specify other storage locations for the certificate database and the certificate database log (see Figure 3.14). Click **Next**.

Figure 3.14 Configure Certificate Database Page

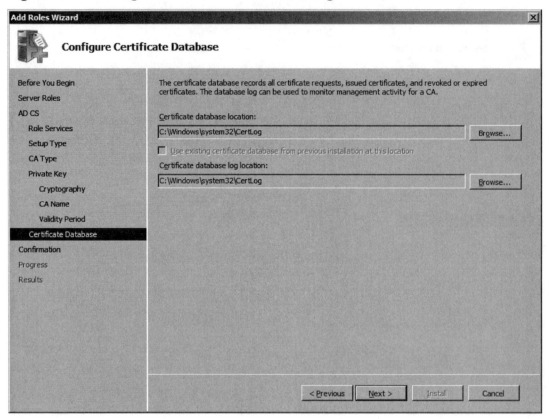

15. On the **Confirm Installation Selections** page, click **Install** (see Figure 3.15).

Figure 3.15 Confirm Installation Selections Page

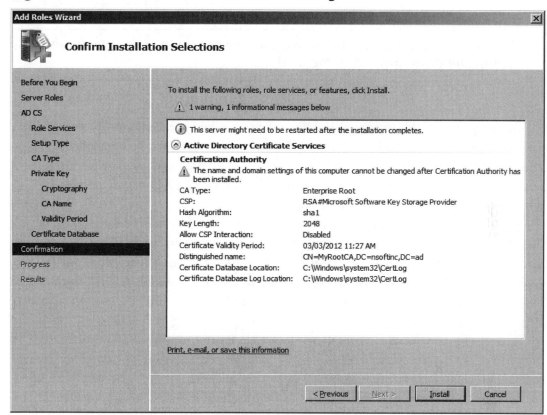

16. On the Installation Results page, review the information and make sure it read **Installation succeeded.**

17. Click **Close** to close the **Add Roles Wizard**.

TEST DAY TIP

Pay special attention to the above exercise as you may be asked questions about the distinguished name of the CA.

In our previous discussion of public and private key pairs, two users wanted to exchange confidential information and did so by having one user encrypt the data with the other user's public key. We then discussed digital signatures, where the sending user "signs" the data by using his or her private key. Did you notice the security vulnerability in these methods?

In this type of scenario, there is nothing to prevent an attacker from intercepting the data mid-stream, and replacing the original signature with his or her own, using of course his or her own private key. The attacker would then forward the replacement public key to the unsuspecting party. In other words, even though the data is signed, how can you be sure of who signed it? The answer in the Windows PKI is the certificate.

Think of a certificate as a small and portable combination safe. The primary purpose of the safe is to hold a public key (although quite a bit of other information is also held there). The combination to the safe must be held by someone you trust—that trust is the basis for the entire PKI system. If I am a user and want to send you my public key so that you can encrypt some data to send back to me, I can just sign the data myself, but I am then vulnerable to the attack mentioned above. However if I allow a trusted third party entity to take my public key (which I don't mind because they're trustworthy), lock it away in the safe and then send the safe to you, you can ask the trusted party for the combination. When you open the safe, you can be certain that the public key and all other information inside really belongs to me, because the safe came from a trustworthy source. The "safe" is really nothing more than a digital signature, except that the signature comes from a universally trusted third party and not from me. The main purpose of certificates, then, is to facilitate the secure transfer of keys across an insecure network. Figure 3.16 shows the properties of a Windows certificate—notice that the highlighted public key is only part of the certificate.

Figure 3.16 A Windows Server 2008 Certificate

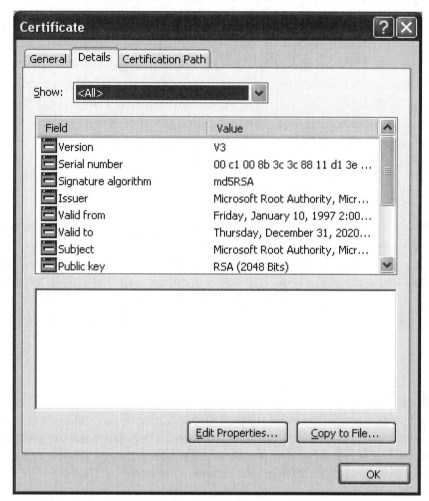

User Certificates

Of the three general types of certificates found in a Windows PKI, the *user certificate* is perhaps the most common. User certificates are certificates that enable the user to do something that would not be otherwise allowed. The Enrollment Agent certificate is one example. Without it, even an administrator is not able to enroll smart cards and configure them properly at an enrollment station. Under Windows Server 2008, required user certificates can be requested automatically by the client and subsequently issued by a certification authority (discussed below) with no user intervention necessary.

Machine Certificates

Also known as computer certificates, *machine certificates* (as the name implies) give the system—instead of the user—the ability to do something out of the ordinary. The main purpose for machine certificates is authentication, both client-side and server-side. As stated earlier, certificates are the main vehicle by which public keys are exchanged in a PKI. Machine certificates are mainly involved with these behind-the-scenes exchanges, and are normally overseen by the operating system. Machine certificates have been able to take advantage of Windows' autoenrollment feature since 2000 Server was introduced. We will discuss auto-enrollment later in this chapter.

Application Certificates

The term *application certificate* refers to any certificate that is used with a specific PKI-enabled application. Examples include IPsec and S/MIME encryption for e-mail. Applications that need certificates are generally configured to automatically request them, and are then placed in a waiting status until the required certificate arrives. Depending upon the application, the network administrator or even the user might have the ability to change or even delete certificate requests issued by the application.

TEST DAY TIP

Certificates are at the very core of the Windows PKI. Make certain that you understand what certificates are, and why they are needed when using public keys. Also, be familiar with the types of certificates listed in this section and the differences between them.

Analyzing Certificate Needs within the Organization

We've just concluded a tour of most of the properties associated with a CA, but knowing what you *can* do does not mean that we know what you *should* do. To find out more about what you should do, you need to analyze the certificate needs of your organization, and then move on to create an appropriate CA structure.

According to Microsoft's TechNet, the analysis of certificate needs springs primarily from "the analysis of business requirements and the analysis of applications that benefit from PKI-based security". In other words, when designing a PKI/CA structure, you will need to understand the different uses for certificates and whether your organization needs to use certificates for each of these purposes. Examples include SSL for a secure Web server, EFS for encryption of files, and S/MIME for encryption of e-mail messages. The use of S/MIME might dictate that your CA hierarchy have a trust relationship with external CAs, and the use of SSL might lead you to implement a stand-alone CA instead of an enterprise CA. Thus, analyzing these needs *before* you implement your PKI can save you a lot of time and trouble.

Working with Certificate Services

Certificate Services in Windows Server 2008 is an easier venture than ever before. As we look at what is entailed in the components involved in establishing and supporting a PKI in Windows Server 2008 we need to quickly discuss what Certificate Services do for us.

In Active Directory and Windows Server 2008, Certificate Services allow administrators to establish and manage the PKI environment. More generally, they allow for a trust model to be established within a given organization. The trust model is the framework that will hold all the pieces and components of the PKI in place. Typically, there are two options for a trust model within PKI: a *single CA model* and a *hierarchical model*. The certificate services within Windows Server 2008 provide the interfaces and underlying technology to setup and manage both of these type of deployments.

Configuring a Certificate Authority

By definition, a certificate authority is an entity (computer or system) that issues digital certificates of authenticity for use by other parties. With the ever increasing demand for effective and efficient methods to verify and secure communications, our technology market has seen the rise of many trusted third parties into the market. If you have been in the technology field for any length of time, you are likely familiar with many such vendors by name: VeriSign, Entrust, Thawte, GeoTrust, DigiCert and GoDaddy are just a few.

While these companies provide an excellent and useful resource for both the IT administrator and the consumer, companies and organizations desired a way to establish their own certificate authorities. In a third-party, or external PKI, it is up to the third-party CA to positively verify the identity of anyone requesting a certificate from it. Beginning with Windows 2000, Microsoft has allowed the creation of a trusted *internal* CA—possibly eliminating the need for an external third party. With a Windows Server 2008 CA, the CA verifies the identity of the user requesting a certificate by checking that user's authentication credentials (using Kerberos or NTLM). If the credentials of the requesting user check out, a certificate is issued to the user. When the user needs to transmit his or her public key to another user or application, the certificate is then used to prove to the receiver that the public key inside can be used safely.

Certificate Authorities

Certificates are a way to transfer keys securely across an insecure network. If any arbitrary user were allowed to issue certificates, it would be no different than that user simply signing the data. In order for a certificate to be of any use, it must be issued by a trusted entity—an entity that both the sender and receiver trust. Such a trusted entity is known as a *Certification Authority* (CA). Third-party CAs such as VeriSign or Entrust can be trusted because they are highly visible, and their public keys are well known to the IT community. When you are confident that you hold a true public key for a CA, and that public key properly decrypts a certificate, you are then certain that the certificate was digitally signed by the CA and no one else. Only then can you be positive that the public key contained inside the certificate is valid and safe.

In the analogy we used earlier, the state driver's licensing agency is trusted because it is known that the agency requires proof of identity before issuing a driver's license. In the same way, users can trust the certification authority because they know it verifies the authentication credentials before issuing a certificate. Within an organization leveraging Windows Server 2008, several options exist for building this trust relationship. Each of these begins with the decisions made around selecting and implementing certificate authorities. With regard to the Microsoft implementation of PKI, there are at least four major roles or types of certificate authorities to be aware of:

- Enterprise CA
- Standard CA
- Root CA
- Subordinate CA

Believe it or not, beyond this list at least two variations exist: intermediate CAs and leaf CAs, each of which is a type of subordinate CA implementation.

Standard vs. Enterprise

An enterprise CA is tied into Active Directory and is required to use it. In fact, a copy of its own CA certificate is stored in Active Directory. Perhaps the biggest difference between an enterprise CA and a stand-alone CA is that enterprise CAs use Kerberos or NTLM authentication to validate users and computers before certificates are issued. This provides additional security to the PKI because the validation process relies on the strength of the Kerberos protocol, and not a human administrator. Enterprise CAs also use templates, which are described later in this chapter, and they can issue every type of certificate.

There are also several downsides to an enterprise CA. In comparison to a stand-alone CA, enterprise CAs are more difficult to maintain and require a much more in-depth knowledge about Active Directory and authentication. Also, because an enterprise CA requires Active Directory, it is nearly impossible to remove it from the network. If you were to do so, the Directory itself would quickly become outdated—making it difficult to resynchronize with the rest of the network when brought back online. Such a situation would force an enterprise CA to remain attached to the network, leaving it vulnerable to attackers.

Root vs. Subordinate Certificate Authorities

As discussed earlier, there are two ways to view PKI trust models: single CA and hierarchical. In a single CA model PKIs are very simplistic; only one CA is used within the infrastructure. Anyone who needs to trust parties vouched for by the CA is given the public key for the CA. That single CA is responsible for the interactions that ensue when parties request and seek to verify the information for a given certificate.

In a hierarchical model, a root CA functions as a top-level authority over one or more levels of CAs beneath it. The CAs below the root CA are called subordinate CAs. Root CAs serve as a *trust anchor* to all the CA's beneath it and to the users who trust the root CA. A trust anchor is an entity known to be trusted without requiring that it be trusted by going to another party, and therefore can be used as a base for trusting other parties. Since there is nothing above the root CA, no one can vouch for its identity; it must create a *self-signed* certificate to vouch for itself. With a self-signed certificate, both the certificate issuer and the certificate subject are exactly the same. Being the trust anchor, the root CA must make its own certificate available to all of the users (including subordinate CAs) that will ultimately be using that particular root CA.

Hierarchical models work well in larger hierarchical environments, such as large government organizations or corporate environments. Often, a large organization also deploys a Registration Authority (RA, covered later in this chapter), Directory Services and optionally Timestamping Services in an organization leveraging a hierarchical approach to PKI. In situations where different organization are trying to develop a hierarchical model together (such as post acquisition or merger companies or those that are partnered for collaboration), a hierarchical model can be very difficult to establish as both parties must ultimately agree upon a single trust anchor.

When you first set up an internal PKI, no CA exists. The first CA created is known as the root CA, and it can be used to issue certificates to users or to other CAs. As mentioned above, in a large organization there usually is a hierarchy where the root CA is not the only certification authority. In this case, the sole purpose of the root CA is to issue certificates to other CAs in order to establish their authority.

Any certification authority that is established after the root CA is a subordinate CA. Subordinate CAs gain their authority by requesting a certificate from either the root CA or a higher level subordinate CA. Once the subordinate CA receives the certificate, it can control CA policies and/or issue certificates itself, depending on your PKI structure and policies.

Sometimes, subordinate CAs also issue certificates to other CAs below them on the tree. These CAs are called *intermediate CAs*. Is most hierarchies, there is more than one intermediate CA. Subordinate CAs that issue certificates to end users, server, and other entities but do not issue certificates to other CAs are called *leaf CAs*.

Certificate Requests

In order to receive a certificate from a valid issuing CA, a client—computer or user—must request a certificate from a CA.

There are three ways that this request can be made:

- Autoenrollment
- Use of the Certificates snap-in
- Via a web browser

It is very likely that the most common method for requesting a certificate is autoenrollment, and we'll discuss its deployment shortly. A client can also request a certificate by use of the **Certificates** snap-in. The snap-in, shown in Figure 3.17, can be launched by clicking **Start | Run**, and then typing in **certmgr.msc** and pressing **Enter**. Note that the **Certificates** snap-in does *not* appear in the **Administrative Tools** folder as the **Certification Authority** snap-in does after installing certificate services. Once you open the Certificate Snap-in, expand the **Personal** container, and then right-clicking the **Certificates** container beneath it. You can start the **Certificate Request Wizard** by choosing **All Tasks | Request New Certificate...**, as shown in the following figure:

Figure 3.17 Certificates Snap-in

Next, you will receive the **Before You Begin** welcome screen, as shown in Figure 3.18. Click **Next**.

Figure 3.18 Before You Begin

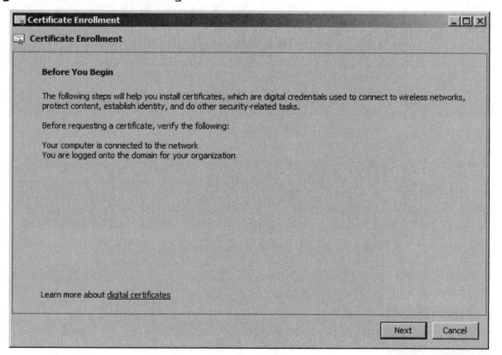

Next to Welcome screen, the wizard prompts you to choose the certificate enrollment type. Figure 3.19 shows you the available options. You can choose only a type for which the receiving CA has a template. Once you choose an appropriate template, click **Enroll**.

Figure 3.19 Request Certificates

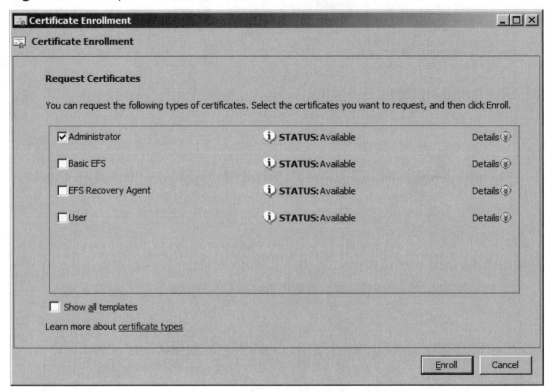

Next to Certificate Enrollment screen, verify it reads, STATUS: Succeeded, as shown in Figure 3.20. Click **Finish** to complete the request.

Figure 3.20 Certificate Installation Results

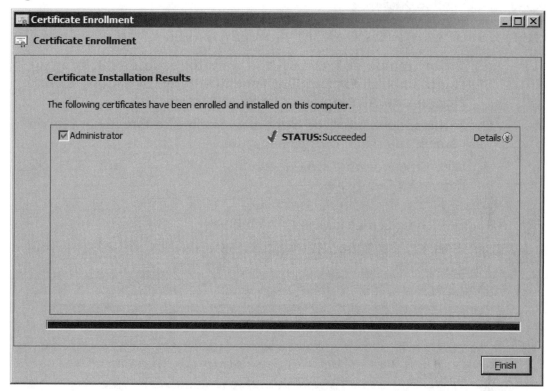

The last method for requesting a certificate is to use a Web browser on the client machine. Note that if you use this option, IIS must be installed on the CA. Exercise 3.3 shows the steps for requesting a certificate using a client machine in this manner.

Test Day Tip

The order of component installation can be important when dealing with CAs. If you install certificate services *before* you install IIS, a client will *not* be able to connect as in the exercise below until you run the following from the command line: **certutil –vroot**. This establishes the virtual root directories necessary for Web enrollment. Note also that you must have selected the Web enrollment support option during the certificate services installation procedure that we completed in Exercise 3.1.

EXERCISE 3.3

REQUEST A CERTIFICATE FROM A WEB SERVER

1. On any computer for which you want to request a certificate, launch Internet Explorer (version 5.0 or later) by clicking **Start | Programs** or **All Programs | Internet Explorer**.

2. In the address bar, type **http://servername/certsrv**, where servername is the name of the issuing CA.

3. When the welcome screen appears, as shown in Figure 3.21, click **Request a Certificate**.

Figure 3.21 Welcome Screen of the CA's Web Site

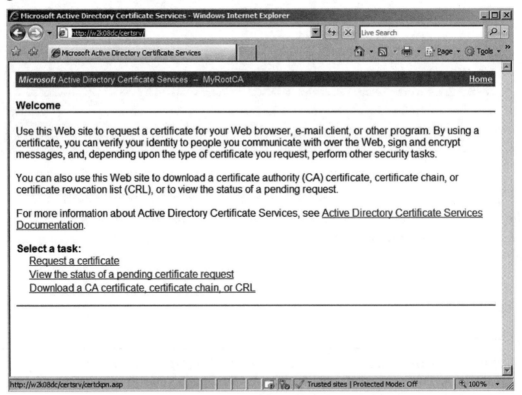

4. Click **User Certificate**, then **Submit** when the next screen appears.

5. When the **Certificate Issued** page appears, click **Install This Certificate**. Close the browser.

Certificate Practice Statement

As the use of X.509-based certificates continues to grow it becomes increasingly important that the management an organization of certificates be as diligent as possible. We know what a digital certificate is and what its critical components are, but a CA can issue a certificate for a number of different reasons. The certificate, then, must indicate exactly what the certificate will be used for. The set of rules that indicates exactly how a certificate may be used (what purpose it can e trusted for, or perhaps the community for which it can be trusted) is called a certificate policy. The X.509 standard defines certificate policies as "a named set of rules that indicates the applicability of a certificate to a particular community and/or class of application with common security requirements."

Different entities have different security requirements. For example, users want a digital certificate for securing e-mail (either encrypting the incoming messages signing outgoing mail), Syngress (as other Web vendors do) wants a digital certificate for their online store, etc. Every user will want to secure their information, and a certificate owner will use the policy information to determine if they want to accept a certificate.

It is important to have a policy in place to state what the appropriate protocol is for use of certificates—how they are requested, how and when they may be used, etc.—but it is equally as important to explain exactly how to implement those policies. This is where the Certificate Practice Statement (CPS) comes in. A CPS describes how the CA plans to manage the certificates it issues.

Key Recovery

Key recovery is compatible with the CryptoAPI architecture of Windows 2008, but it is not a necessary requirement. For key recovery, an entity's private key must be stored permanently. The storage of private keys guarantees that critical information will always be accessible, even if the information should get corrupted or deleted. On the other hand, there is a security issue in the backup of the private keys. The archived private key should be used to impersonate the private key owner only if corruption occurs on your system.

Backup and Restore

Microsoft recommends that you back up your entire CA server. By backing up the system state data on your CA, you will automatically get a backup of the certificate store, the registry, system files, and Active Directory (if your CA is a domain controller). Sometimes, you may want to just back up the certificate services portion of your computer without doing a full backup of everything else.

Exercise 3.4 walks you through backing up Certificate Services. Your backups are only useful if you can restore them—Exercise 3.5 walks you through restoring Certificate Services.

EXERCISE 3.4

BACKING UP CERTIFICATE SERVICES

1. On any computer for which you want to take a backup, Log on with administrative privileges.

2. Click **Start**, click **All Programs,** click **Administrative Tools,** and then click **Certification Authority**.

3. Right-click the name of your CA, and choose **All Tasks | Back up CA...** from the pop-up menu, as shown in Figure 3.22.

Figure 3.22 Certificate Authority Page

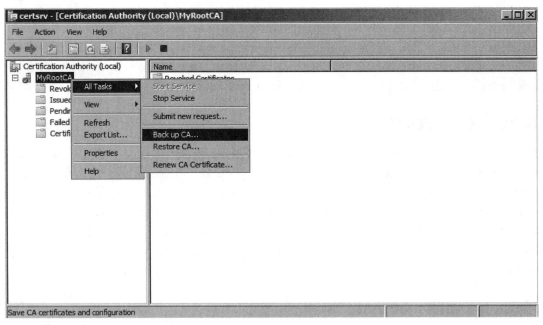

4. On the **Welcome to the Certification Authority Backup Wizard** page, click **Next** to continue.

5. **On Items to Back Up page**, click **Private key and CA certificate** and **Certificate database and certificate database log**. Type in the path of back up location, and then click **Next** (see Figure 3.23).

Figure 3.23 Items to Back Up

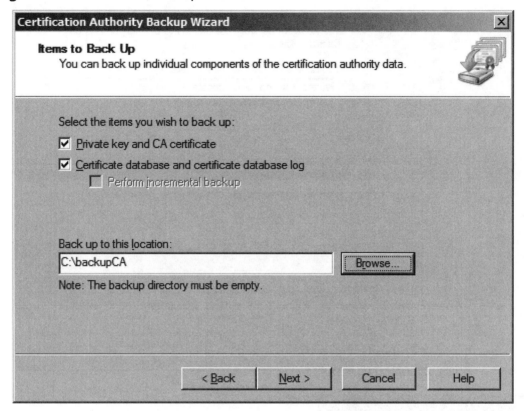

6. Type in the backup password twice and click **Next**.

7. On **Completing the Certification Authority Backup Wizard** page, verify it reads as follows: You have successfully completed the **Certification Authority Backup Wizard**, as shown in Figure 3.24.

Figure 3.24 Completing the CA Backup Wizard

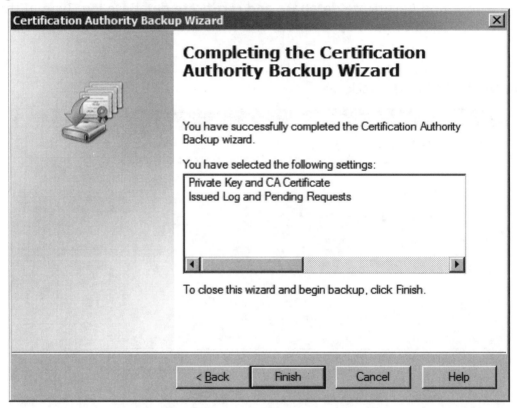

8. Click **Finish** to close the wizard.

EXERCISE 3.5

RESTORING CERTIFICATE SERVICES

1. On any computer for which you want to take a restore, Log on with administrative privileges.

2. Click **Start**, click **All Programs,** click **Administrative Tools**, and then click **Certification Authority**.

3. Right-click the name of your CA, and choose **All Tasks | Restore CA...** from the pop-up menu, as shown in Figure 3.25.

Figure 3.25 Certificate Authority page

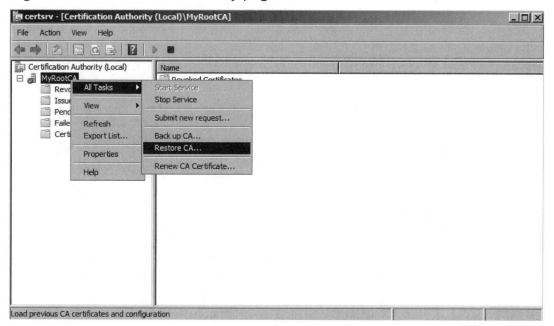

4. Click **OK** to stop Certificate Services from running and start the wizard.

5. On the **Welcome to the Certification Authority Restore Wizard** page, click **Next** to continue.

6. On **Items to Restore** page, click **Private key and CA certificate** and **Certificate database and certificate database log** to restore the backup of **Private key, CA certificate, Certificate database** and **database log** file (see Figure 3.26). Alternatively, you can choose only few components as per your requirements. Type in the path of back up location, and then click **Next**.

Figure 3.26 Items to Restore

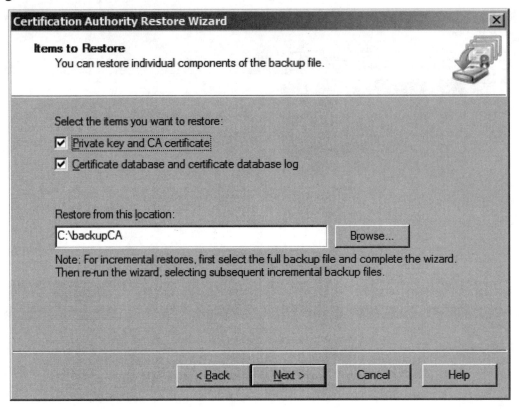

7. On the **Provide Password** page, type in the restore password, and then click **Next**.

8. On **Completing the Certification Authority Restore Wizard** page, verify it reads as You have successfully completed the **Certification Authority Restore Wizard**, as shown in Figure 3.27.

Figure 3.27 Completing the CA Restore Wizard

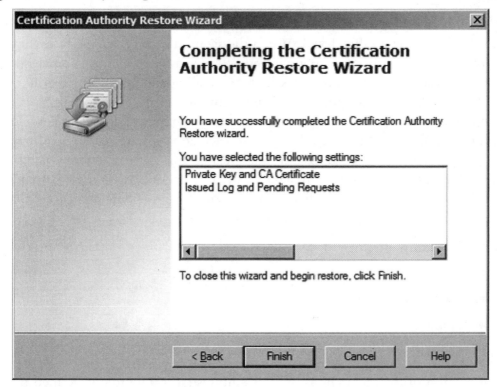

9. Click **Finish** to complete the wizard.

10. You will now be prompted to restart the certificate services, as shown in Figure 3.28. Click **Yes** to restart the services.

Figure 3.28 Certification Authority Restore Wizard

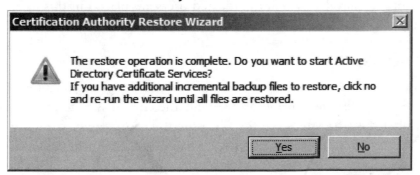

Assigning Roles

In a small network of one or two servers and just a handful of clients, administration is generally not a difficult task. When the size of the network increases, however, the complexity of administration seems to increase exponentially. Microsoft's recommendations for a large network include dividing administrative tasks among the different administrative personnel. One administrator may be in charge of backups and restores, whereas another administrator may have complete control over a certain domain and so on. The role of each administrator is defined by the tasks that he or she is assigned to, and individual permissions are granted based on those tasks. PKI administration, which can be as daunting as general network administration, can be similarly divided. Microsoft defines five different roles that can be used within a PKI to facilitate administration:

- CA Administrator
- Certificate Manager
- Backup Operator
- Auditor
- Enrollee

At the top of the hierarchy is the CA administrator. The role is defined by the *Manage CA* permission and has the authority to assign other CA roles and to renew the CA's certificate. Underneath the CA administrator is the certificate manager. The certificate manager role is defined by the *Issue and Manage Certificates* permission and has the authority to approve enrollment and revocation requests.

The Backup Operator and the Auditor roles are actually operating system roles, and not CA specific. The Backup Operator has the authority to backup the CA and the Auditor has the authority to configure and view audit logs of the CA. The final role is that of the Enrollees. All authenticated users are placed in this role, and are able to request certificates from the CA.

Enrollments

In order for a PKI client to use a certificate, two basic things must happen. First, a CA has to make the certificate available and second, the client has to request the certificate. Only after these first steps can the CA issue the certificate or deny the request.

Making the certificate available is done through the use of certificate templates and is a topic that we discuss in detail below.

Like Windows Server 2003, Windows Server 2008 PKI also supports autoen-rollment for user certificates as well as for computer certificates. The request and issuance of these certificates may proceed without user intervention. Group policies are used in Active Directory to configure autoenrollment. In **Computer Configuration | Windows Settings | Security Settings | Public Key Policies**, there is a group policy entitled **Automatic Certificate Request Settings**. The Property sheet for this policy allows you to choose to either **Enroll certificates automatically** or not. Also, you will need to ensure that **Enroll subject without requiring any user input** option is selected on the **Request Handling** tab of the certificate template Property sheet. Finally, be aware that doing either of the following will cause autoenrollment to fail:

- Setting the **This number of authorized signatures** option on the **Issuance Requirements** tab to higher than one.

- Selecting the **Supply in the request** option on the **Subject Name** tab.

Test Day Tip

Remember that autoenrollment is only available for user certificates if the client is Windows XP, Windows Server 2003, or Windows Server 2008.

Revocation

A CA's primary duty is to issue certificates, either to subordinate CAs, or to PKI clients. However, each CA also has the ability to revoke those certificates when necessary. Certificates are revoked when the information contained in the certificate is no longer considered valid or trusted. This can happen when a company changes ISPs (Internet Service Providers), moves to a new physical address or when the contact listed on the certificate has changed. Essentially, a certificate should be revoked whenever there is a change that makes the certificate's information "stale" and no longer reliable from that point forward.

NOTE

Information that has already been encrypted using the public key in a certificate that is later revoked is not necessarily invalid. Maintaining the example of a driver's license, checks that are written and authenticated by a cashier using your driver's license one week are not automatically voided if you lose your license or move states the next.

In addition to the changes in circumstance that can cause a certification revocation, certain owners may have their certificate revoked upon terminating employment. The most important reason to revoke a certificate is if the private key as been compromised in any way. If a key has been compromised, it should be revoked immediately.

EXAM WARNING

Certificate expiration is different from certificate revocation. A certificate is considered revoked if it is terminated prior to the end date of the certificate.

Along with notifying the CA of the need to revoke a certificate, it is equally important to notify all certificate users of the date that the certificate will no longer be valid. After notifying users and the CA, the CA is responsible for changing the status of the certificate and notifying users that it has been revoked.

When a certificate revocation request is sent to a CA, the CA must be able to authenticate the request with the certificate owner. Once the CA has authenticated the request, the certificate is revoked and notification is sent out. CAs are not the only ones who can revoke a certificate. A PKI administrator can revoke a certificate, but without authenticating the request with the certificate owner. This allows for the revocation of certificates in cases where the owner is no longer accessible or available as in the case of termination.

The X.509 standard requires that CA's publish certificate revocation lists (CRLs). In their simplest form, a CRL is a published form listing the revocation status of certification that the CA manages. There are several forms that revocation lists may take, but the two most noteworthy are *simple CRLs* and *delta CRLs*.

A simple CRL is a container that holds a list of revoked certificates with the name of the CA, the time the CRL was published, and when the next CRL will be published. It is a single file that continues to grow over time. The fact that only information about the certificates is included and not the certificate itself helps to manage the size of a simple CRL.

Delta CRLs can handle the issues that simple CRLs cannot- size and distribution. While simple CRLs contain only certain information about a revoked certificate, it can still become a large file. How, then, do you continually distribute a large file to all parties that need to see the CRL? The solution is in Delta CRLs. In an environment leveraging delta CRLs, a base CRL is sent to all end parties to initialize their copies of the CRL. Afterwards, updates know as deltas are sent out on a periodic basis to inform the end parties of any changes.

In practice within Windows Server 2008, the tool that the CA uses for revocation is the *certificate revocation list*, or CRL. The act of revoking a certificate is simple: from the **Certification Authority** console, simply highlight the **Issued Certificates** container, right-click the certificate and choose **All | Revoke Certificate.** The certificate will then be located in the **Revoked Certificates** container.

When a PKI entity verifies a certificate's validity, that entity checks the CRL before giving approval. The question is: how does a client know where to check for the list? The answer is the CDPs, or CRL Distribution Points. CDPs are locations on the network to which a CA publishes the CRL; in the case of an enterprise CA under Windows Server 2008, Active Directory holds the CRL, and for a standalone, the CRL is located in the *certsrv\certenroll* directory. Each certificate has a location listed for the CDP, and when the client views the certificate, it then understands where to go for the latest CRL. Figure 3.29 shows the Extensions tab of the CA property sheet, where you can modify the location of the CDP.

Figure 3.29 Extensions Tab of the CA Property Sheet

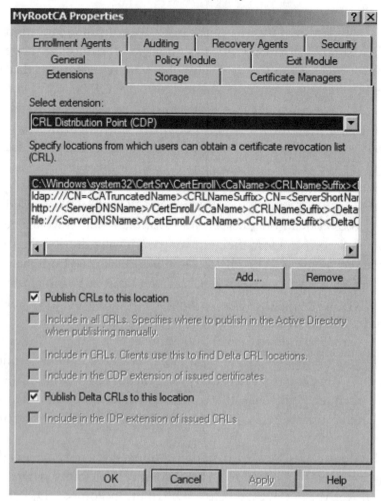

In order for a CA to publish a CRL, use the **Certificate Authority** console to right-click the **Revoked Certificates** container and choose **All Tasks | Publish**. From there, you can choose to publish either a complete CRL, or a Delta CRL.

TEST DAY TIP

On the day of the test, be clear as to which types of CRLs are consistently made available to users in Windows Server 2008. Since Server 203, Delta CRLs have been used to publish only the changes made to an original CRL for the purposes of conserving network traffic.

Whether you select a New CRL or a Delta CRL, you are next prompted to enter a publication interval (the most frequent intervals chosen are one week for full CRLs and one day for Delta CRLs). Clients cache the CRL for this period of time, and then check the CDP again when the period expires. If an updated CDP does not exist or cannot be located, the client automatically assumes that all certificates are invalid.

Working with Templates

A *certificate template* defines the policies and rules that a CA uses when a request for a certificate is received. Often when someone refers to building and managing a PKI for their enterprise, they are usually only thinking of the Certificate Authority and the associated infrastructure needed to support the authentication and authorization required to support the function of the CA. While this is certainly important for the proper function of the PKI, it is only half of the picture—the certificates themselves must be carefully planned to support the business goals that are driving the need to install and configure the PKI.

When you consider that certificates are flexible and can be used in scores of different scenarios, the true power of the certificate becomes apparent. While these different uses can all coexist within a single PKI, the types and functions of the certificates can be very different. Certificates that are used to support two-factor authentication on smart cards can be very different than those used to establish SSL connections to web servers, sign IPsec traffic between servers, support 802.1x wireless access through NAP, or even certificates used to sign e-mail communication.

In all of these cases, the CA and the PKI it supports are the same, but it is the certificate itself that is changing. For each of these different uses, it is important for the certificate to contain appropriate data to facilitate in the function that the designer of the PKI has intended and no more. While additional data could be provided in the certificate, the fact that these are intended to mediate security exchanges makes it inappropriate to include any more information than is necessary to complete the certificate's objective. It is the Certificate Template that specifies the data that must be included in a certificate for it to function as well as to ensure that all of the needed data are provided to ensure the certificate's validity.

EXAM WARNING

Many different types of certificates can be used together within a single Public Key Infrastructure. It is the Certificate Templates that allow the certificates to differentiate themselves for different purposes ensuring that the appropriate information is stored in the cert.

For an individual certificate, there are a number of properties and settings that go into the certificate template specification. Each of these combine to build the final template that will determine the settings for the resulting Certificate.

There are many built-in templates that can be viewed using the **Certificate Templates** snap-in (see Figure 3.30). The snap-in can be run by right-clicking the **Certificate Templates** container located in the **Certification Authority** console and clicking **Manage**. You can use one of the built-in templates or create your own.

Figure 3.30 Certificate Templates Snap-in

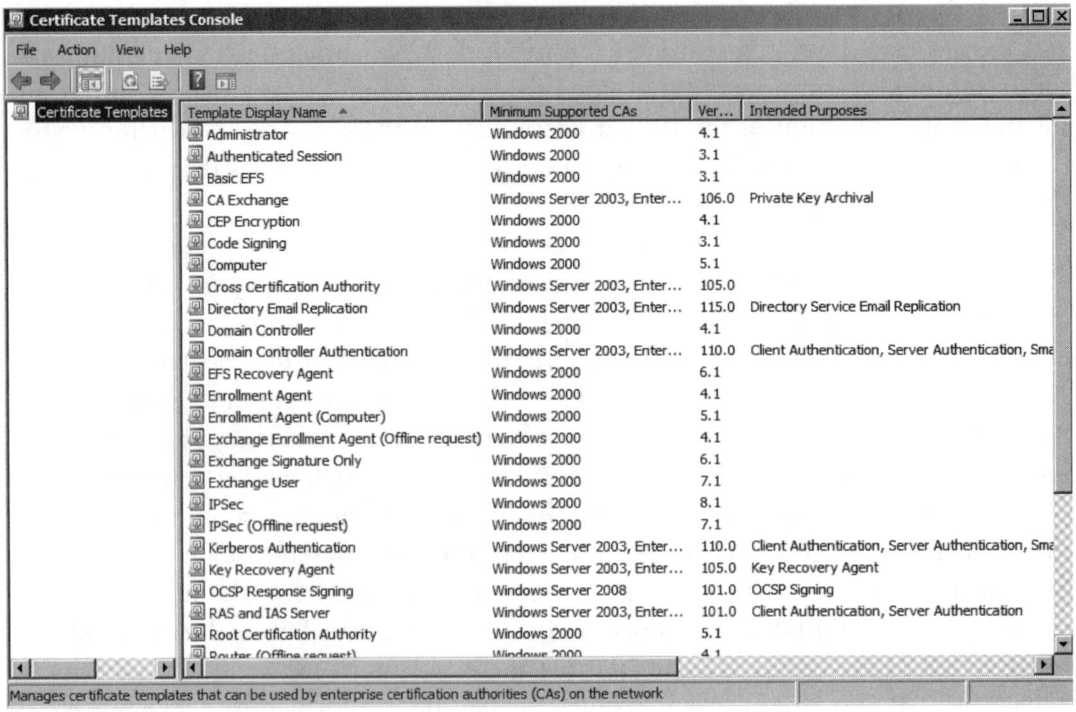

When creating your own template, you have multiple options that will guide the CA in how to handle incoming requests. The first step in the creation process is to duplicate an existing template. You do this by using the **Certificate Templates** snap-in, then right-clicking the template you wish to copy and selecting *Duplicate Template*. On the **General** tab that appears by default (seen in Figure 3.31), there are time-sensitive options such as validity period and renewal period. Note the default validity period of one year, and the default renewal period of six weeks. There are also general options such as the template display name and a checkbox for publishing the certificate in Active Directory.

Figure 3.31 General Tab of the New Template Property Sheet

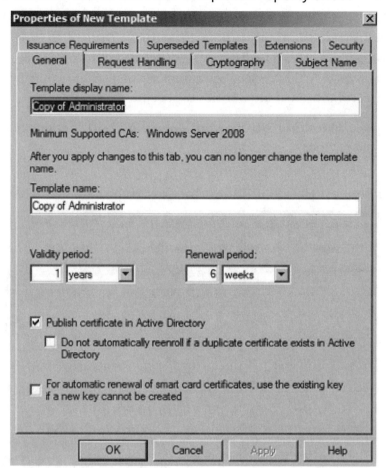

General Properties

Now we'll describe the following settings under the General tab of the new certificate template:

- **Template Display Name** It is important that the certificate that you are creating has a descriptive name accurately describes the function of the certificate. This name cannot be changed once it is assigned, but you can always recreate the certificate from another template later.

- **Validity Period** This is the period for which the derived certificates are valid. This time should be long enough so as not to create a burden on the end user, but not so long as to create a security problem.

- **Renewal Period** This is the period in which the certificate is notified of its expiration and that it will attempt to renew if this is an option for the certificate.

- **Publish in Active Directory** Some certificates can be stored in the active directory tied to security principals there. This generally applies to User certificates that are not ties to specific hardware.

The **Request Handling** tab, shown in Figure 3.32, has options to enroll without user interaction.

Figure 3.32 Request Handling Tab of the New Template Property Sheet

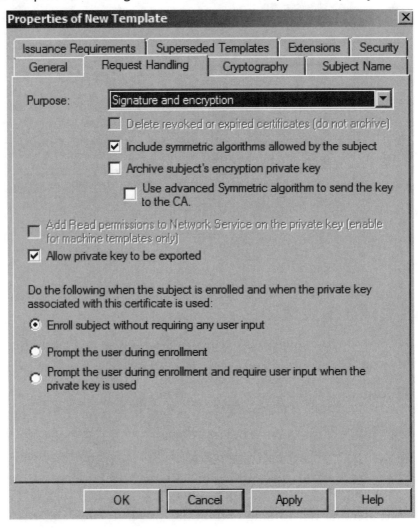

Request Handling

The Request Handling tab includes the following settings:

- **Purpose** It is important to consider the activities for which this new certificate will be responsible. Some keys can be used just to validate identity while others can also provide signing for encryption.

  - The private key can also be archived or shared with the CA so that it may be recovered in the event of loss. Otherwise, the certificate must be recreated.

- **Enrollment Actions** Different notification actions can be specified when the private key for this certificate is used. This can range from transparent usage of the key to full notification prompting the certificate owner for permission.

The **Cryptography** tab seen in Figure 3.33, gives you the choice of algorithms that can be used.

Figure 3.33 Cryptography Tab

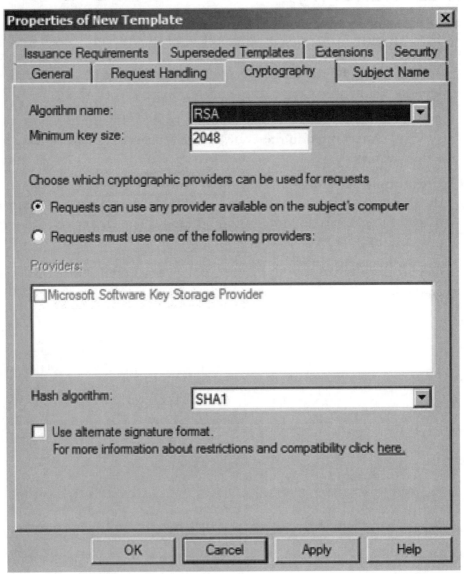

Cryptography

The Cryptography tab includes the following settings:

- **Algorithm Name** There are a number of cryptographic Algorithms that can be used to provide encryption for the keys. Valid methods under server 2008 are RSA, ECDH_P256, ECDH_P384, ECDH_P521.

- Note: If the Purpose is changed to Signature, additional algorithms become available: ECDSA_P256, ECDSA_P384, ECDSA_P521.

- **Hash Algorithm** To provide one-way hashes for key exchanges, a number of algorithms are available. These include: MD2, MD4, MD5, SHA1, SHA256, SHA384, SHA512.

The **Subject Name** tab seen in Figure 3.34, gives you the choice of obtaining subject name information from Active Directory or from the certificate request itself. In the latter case, autoenrollment (which we'll discuss later in the chapter) is not available.

Figure 3.34 Subject Name Tab of the New Template Property Sheet

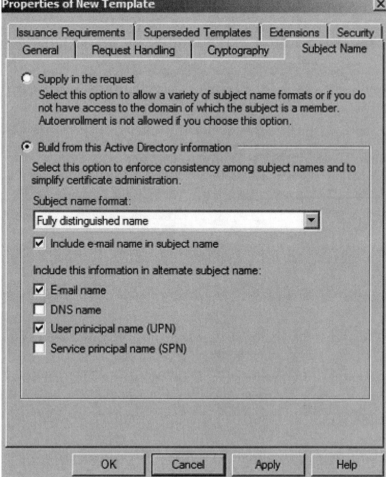

Subject Name

The Subject Name tab includes the following settings:

- **Supply in the Request** Under this option, the CA will expect to get additional subject information in the certificate request. As noted, this will not permit autoenrollment, requiring intervention to issue the certificate.

- **Build from this AD Information** Under this option, the Active Directory will be queried and the certificate will be built based on the AD files you specify.

Usually the default of the Distinguished Name is adequate for most purposes, but the common name will sometime be preferable.

The **Issuance Requirements** tab seen in Figure 3.35 allows you to suspend automatic certificate issuance by selecting the CA certificate manager approval checkbox.

Figure 3.35 Issuance Requirements Tab of the New Template Property Sheet

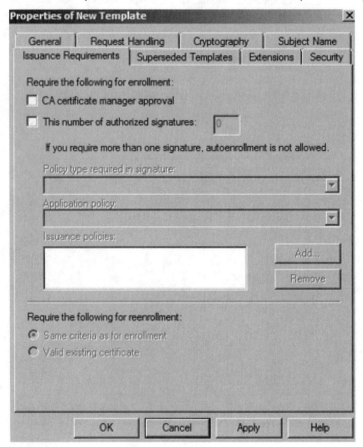

Issuance Requirements

These settings can be used to manage the approval requirements in order for a certificate to be issued. These settings allow for a workflow or approval chain to be applied to the certificate type.

- **CA Certificate Manager Approval** Using this setting will require that the CA Manager assigned in the CA approve of the certificate before it is released to the end-user of the certificate.

- **Number of Authorized Signatures** Under these settings, additional approvals steps may be required to release the certificate. In these scenarios, two or more approval authorities will have to consent before the certificate is generated.

- **Require the Following for Reenrollment** These settings specify the approval and prerequisites that are in place for renewal of the certificate. This gives the network administrator to allow subjects with valid certificates to renew without having to go through the approval chain.

The **Superseded Templates** tab, as shown in Figure 3.36, is used to define which certificates are superseded by the current template. Usually, this tab is used to configure a template that serves several functions, e.g. IPsec and EFS. In this case, a template used *only* for IPsec or a template used *only* for EFS would be placed on the superseded templates list. This section allows the network administrator to specify other templates that are superseded by the new template type. This allows control of both versioning and wholesale template replacement.

As templates evolve, it may be useful to replace templates that are already deployed in the wild with a new template.

Figure 3.36 Superseded Templates Tab of the New Template
Property Sheet

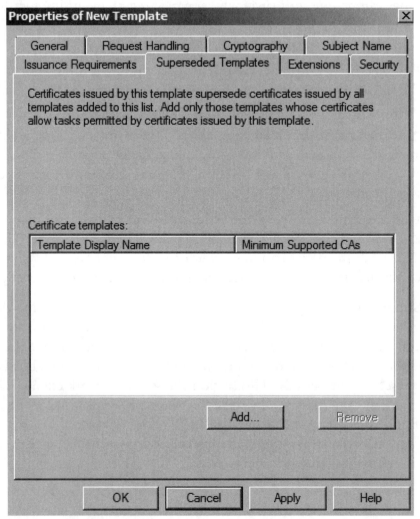

In addition to the standard usage patterns that are inherited from the parent certificate, it is sometimes important to specify new circumstances and roles that a certificate will fill. In this case, additional extensions to the certificate will be applied to provide this new functionality.

Under these settings, a new ability such as code signing can be applied to all derivative certificates to allow these new subjects the ability to complete multiple tasks.

The **Extensions** tab as seen in Figure 3.37 can be used to add such things as the Application Policies extension, which defines the purposes for which a generated certificate can be used. The Issuance Policies extension is also worth mentioning, because it defines when a certificate may be issued.

Figure 3.37 Extensions Tab of the New Template Property Sheet

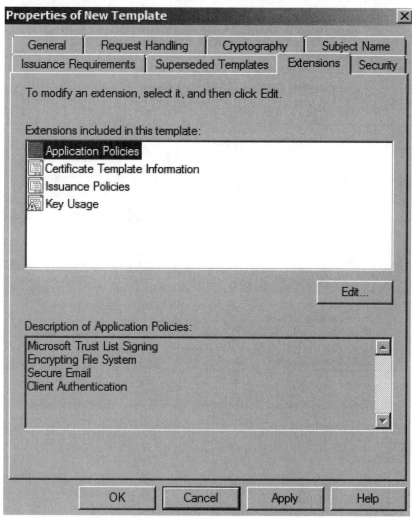

The **Security** tab is similar to the **Security** tab that we saw in Figure 3.38, except that this tab is used to control who may edit the template and who may request certificates using the template. Figure 3.38 shows the default permission level for the **Authenticated Users** group. In order for a user to request a certificate, however, the user must have at least the **Enroll** permission assigned to them for manual requests, and the **Autoenroll** permission for automatic requests.

Figure 3.38 Security Tab of the New Template Property Sheet

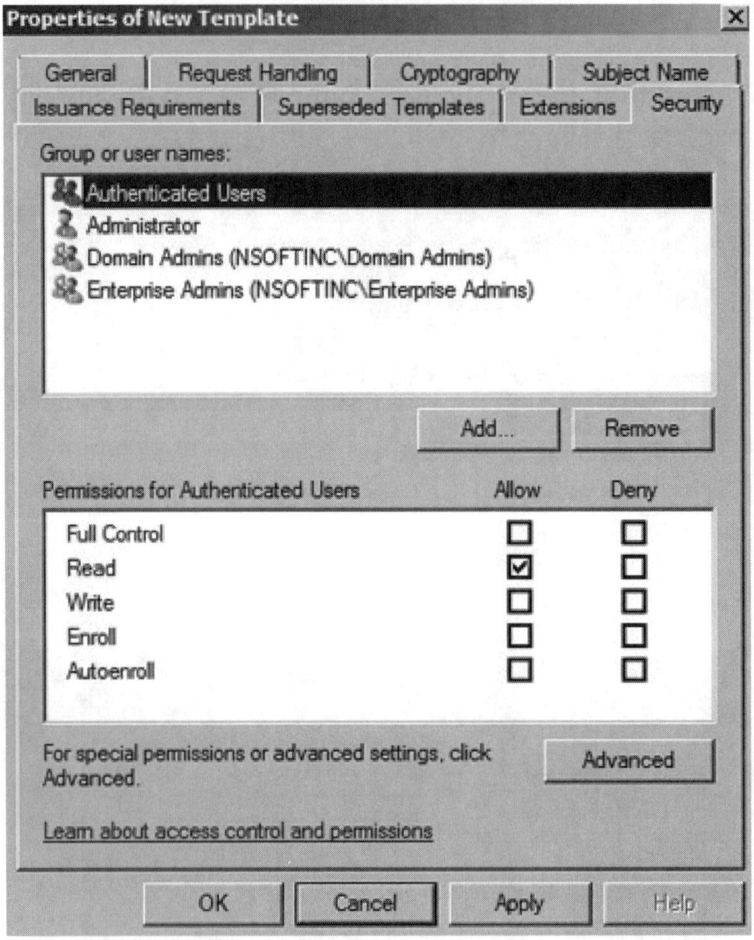

Security

The security settings control the actions that different types of users are able to perfume on a certificate template.

- **Enroll** These subjects are able to request that a certificate be created from this template and assigned to them. This enrollment process will abide by the constraints listed under the Issuance Requirements tab.

- **Autoenroll** These subjects are able to make a request to the CA and will be automatically issued the certificate if the subject meets the Issuance Requirements. In this case, the certificate will be applied without administrator intervention or assistance.

After you have configured a particular template, it still cannot be used by the CA to issue certificates until it is made *available*. To enable a template, you use the **Certification Authority** console and right-click the **Certificate Templates** container. Selecting **New | Certificate Template to Issue** completes the process.

Types of Templates

There are a number of different templates that are included with Windows Server 2008 that provide basic signing and encryption services in the Enterprise Windows PKI role. In addition to these pre-built templates, the network administrator also has the option to build custom templates to address needs that might not be covered by the standard templates or to provide interoperation with other systems.

The Subject Field of the Certificate templates determines the scope of action and the types of objects to which the resulting certificates can be bound.

User Certificate Types

User Certificate Templates are intended to be bound to a single user to provide identity and/or encryption services for that single entity.

- **Administrator** This certificate template provides signature and encryption services for administrator accounts providing account identification and trust list (CTL) management within the domain. Certificates based on the Administrator Template are stored in the Active Directory.

- **Authenticated Session** This certificate template allows users to authenticate to a web server to provide user credentials for site logon. This is often deployed for remote users as a way to validate identity without storing formation insecurely in a cookie while avoiding the need for a user to log on to the site each time.

- **Basic EFS** Certificates derived from this template are stored in Active Directory with the associated user account and are used to encrypt data using the Encrypting File System (EFS).

- **Code Signing** These certificate templates allow developers to create certificates that can be used to sign application code. This provides a check on the origin of software so that code management systems and end-users can be sure that the origin of the software is trusted.

- **EFS Recovery Agent** Certificates of this type allow files that have been encrypted with the EFS to be decrypted so that the files can be used again.

EFS Recovery Agent certificates should be a part of any disaster recovery plan when designing an EFS implementation.

- **Enrollment Agent** Certificates derived from this template are used to request and issue other certificates from the enterprise CA on behalf of another entity. For example, the web enrollment application uses these certificates to manage the certificate requests with the CA.

- **Exchange Enrollment Agent** These certificates are used to manage enrollment services form within exchange to provide certificates to other entities within the exchange infrastructure.

- **Exchange Signature** Certificates derived from the Exchange Signature template are user certificates used to sign e-mail messages sent from within the Exchange system.

- **Exchange User** Certificates based on the Exchange User template are user certificates that are stored in the Active Directory used to encrypt e-mail messages sent from within the Exchange system.

- **Smartcard Logon** These certificates allow the holder of the smart card to authenticate to the active directory and provides identity and encryption abilities. This is usually deployed as a part of a two-factor security schema using smart cards as the physical token.

- **Smartcard User** Unlike the Smartcard Logon certificate template, these types of certificates are stored in the Active Directory and limit the scope of identity and encryption to e-mail systems.

- **Trust List Signing** These certificates allow the signing of a trust list to help manage certificate security and to provide affirmative identity to the signer.

- **User** This template is used to create general User Certificates—the kind that are usually thought of when talking about user certificates. These are stored in the Active Directory and are responsible for user activities in the AD such as authentication, EFS encryption, and interaction with Exchange.

- **User Signature Only** These certificates allow users to sign data and provide identification of the origin of the signed data.

Computer Certificate Types

Computer Certificate Templates are intended to be bound to a single computer entity to provide identity and/or encryption services for that computer. These are often the cornerstone of workstation authentication systems like NAP and 802.1x which might require computer certificates for EAP authentication.

- **CA Exchange** These certificates are bound to Certificate Authorities to mediate key exchange between CAs allowing for PK sharing and archival.

- **CEP Encryption** Certificates of this type are bound to servers that are able to respond to key requests through the Simple Certificate Enrollment Protocol (SCEP).

- **Computer** This template is used to generate standard Computer certificates that allow a physical machine to assert its identity on the network. These certificates are extensively used in EAP authentication in identifying endpoints in secured communication tunnels.

- **Domain Controller Authentication** Certificates of this type are used to authenticate users and computers in the active directory. This allows a Domain Controller to access the directory itself and provide authentication services to other entities.

- **Enrollment Agent (Computer)** These certificates allow a computer to act as an enrollment agent against the PKI so that they can offer computer certificates to physical machines.

- **IPsec** Certificates based on this template allow a computer to participate in IPsec communications. These computers are able to assert their identity as well as encrypt traffic on the network. This is used in IPsec VPN tunnels as well as in Domain and Server Isolation strategies.

- **Kerberos Authentication** These certificates are used by local computers to authenticate with the Active Directory using the Kerberos v5 protocol.

- **OCSP Response Signing** This is a unique certificate type to Windows Server 2008 allowing a workstation to act as an Online Responder in the validation of certificate request queries.

- **RAS and IAS Server** These certificates are used to identify and provide encryption for Routing and Remote Access Server (RRAS) as well as Internet Authorization Servers (IAS) to identify themselves in VPN and RADIUS communications with RADIUS Clients.

- **Router** This is also a new role to Windows Server 2008 providing services to provide credentials to routers making requests through SCEP to a CA.

- **Web Server** These certificates are commonly used by servers acting as web servers to provide end=point identification and traffic encryption to their customers. These kinds of certificates are used to provide Secure Socket Layer (SSL) encryption enabling clients to connect to the web server using the HTTPS protocol.

- **Workstation Authentication** Like general computer certificates, the workstation certificate allows computers that are domain members the ability to assert their identity on the network and encrypt traffic that they send across the network.

Other Certificate Types

There are a number of other certificate types that are not directly tied to either user or computer entities. These are usually infrastructure-based certificate types that are used to manage the domain or the Certificate Authorities themselves.

- **Cross-Certification Authority** These certificates are used within the Certificate Authority Infrastructure to cross -certify CAs to validate the hierarchy that makes up the PKI.

- **Directory E-mail Replication** Certificates that are derived from this type are used within the larger Exchange infrastructure to allow for the replication of e-mail across the directory service.

- **Domain Controller** This kind of certificate is only held by the Domain Controllers in the domain. These differentiate from the Domain Controller Authentication certificates as they identify the individual DC rather than facilitate authorization of inbound authentication requests.

- **Root CA** These certificates are only issued to Root Certificate Authorities to assert its identity in the Public Key Infrastructure.

- **Subordinate CA** This certificate type is used to assert the identity of Subordinate Certificate Authorities in the PKI. This type of certificate can only be issued by a computer holding the Root CA certificate or another Subordinate CA that is the direct parent of the on to which the new certificate is being issued.

Custom Certificate Templates

In some circumstances, it might be necessary to create a custom certification type that can be used to support a specific business need. If you are using a version of

Windows Server 2008 that is not either the WEB or Standard edition, you can create your own templates.

EXERCISE 3.6

CREATING A CUSTOM TEMPLATE

In this exercise, we will create a new User Template based on the existing default user template. This new template will be valid for 10 years rather than the default 1-year expiration date.

1. Log in to your domain with an account that is a member of the Domain Admins group.

2. Navigate to **Start | Administrative Tools | Certificate Authority.**

3. Right-click the **Certificate Templates** folder on the left pane. Choose **Manage** to open the Certificate Templates Console (see Figure 3.39).

Figure 3.39 Creating a Custom Template

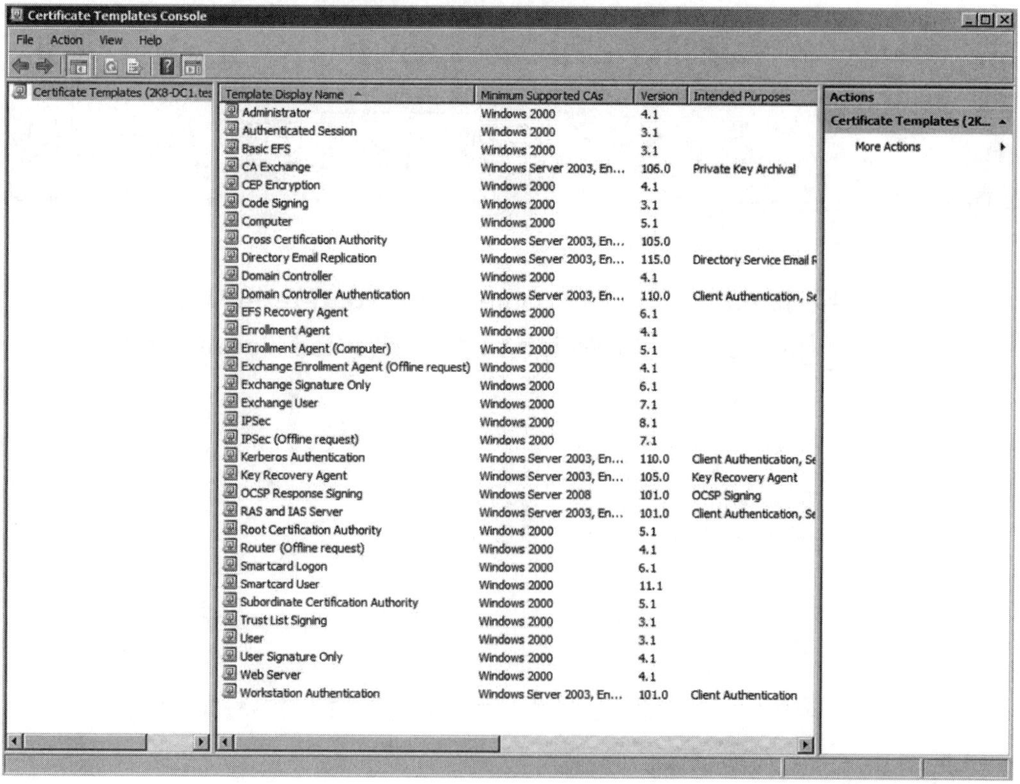

4. Right-click the **User Template**. Choose **Duplicate Template**.

5. On the Duplicate Template page, choose **Server 2008** versioning as all of our CAs are running Server 2008 (see Figure 3.40). Click **OK**.

Figure 3.40 Creating a Custom Template

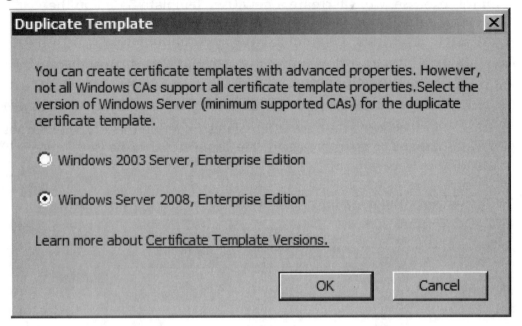

6. In the **Template display name**, enter **Long-term User**.

7. Change the **Validity Period** to 10 Years (see Figure 3.41).

Figure 3.41 Creating a Custom Template

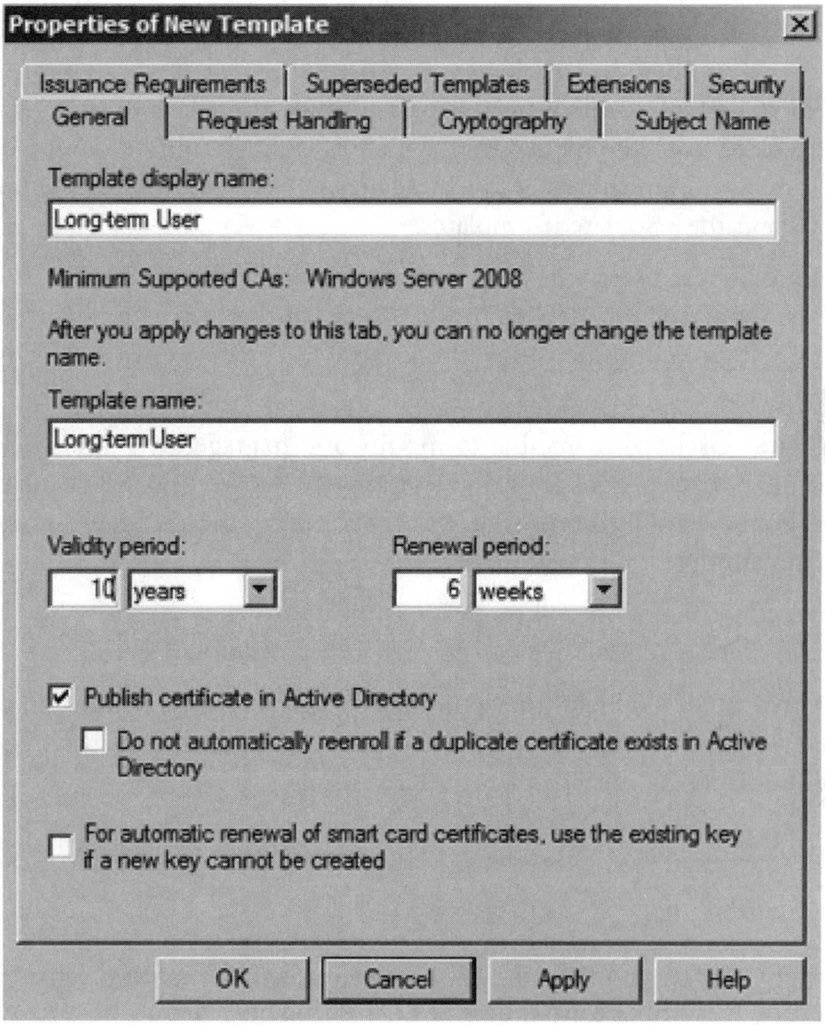

8. Click **OK**.

___

The new Long-term User certificate template has now been created on this CA and is ready to be used to create new derivative certificates.

Securing Permissions

With the wide set of configuration options that are available when creating a new Certificate Template, it might come as a surprise that the permissions model is relatively simple. All of the more complicated security controlling the approval process and revocation is already built into the Certificate Template itself, so there is little left to control through the more traditional Access Control Entries on the template's Access Control List.

- **Full Control** Users with this permission have access to do anything with the Certificate Template. Users with this right should be confined to the Domain Administrators and CA Managers who will be maintaining the CA and the associated Templates.

- **Read** These users will be able to read the template and view its contents. It is important for users to be able to Read the template if they are to apply it and continue to use the associated certificates issued from the template.

- **Write** Users who are able to modify and manage the template will need to have write permissions on the template. Again, this should be confined to Domain Administrators and CA Managers who will be responsible for maintaining the Templates.

- **Enroll** Users who will request certificates of this type or who already have these certs will need to have Enroll privileges.

- **AutoEnroll** Subjects that will request new certificates through the autoenrollment process will need to have autoenrollment privileges in addition to the enroll and read permissions.

NOTE

In order to keep the Certificate Authority communicating with the Active Directory, it is important that the Cert Publishers group be protected. Make sure that this group is not inadvertently destroyed or changed.

Versioning

Certificates are all tagged with version information allowing them to evolve over time. Without this feature, when a Certificate Template would get updated, all of the certificates based on the old template would have to be revoked forcing the end-users to apply for new certificates again. This is disruptive to business and introduces a large amount of risk to business continuity as the certificates are brought into compliance again.

With versioning, a new version of the Certificate Template can be issued into the production environment. Then using the autoenrollment process, these certificates can be superseded bring all of the certificate holding subjects into compliance quickly and with a minimum of both disruption to the business and administrative intervention.

EXAM WARNING

In an environment that has been upgraded from a previous version of Windows Server into the Server 2008 platform, an update to the certificate templates may be required to bring the templates into compliance. This should be done before the domain is upgraded to ensure continuity with the active directory.

Key Recovery Agent

Sometimes it is necessary to recover a key from storage. One of the problems that often arise regarding PKI is the fear that documents will become lost forever—irrecoverable because someone loses or forget their private key. Let's say that employees use Smart Cards to hold their private keys. If a user were to leave his smart card in his wallet which was left in the pants that he accidentally threw into the washing machine, then that user might be without his private key and therefore incapable of accessing any documents or e-mails that used his existing private key.

Many corporate environments implement a key recovery server solely for the purpose of backing up and recovering keys. Within an organization, there is at least one *key recovery agent*. A key recovery agent is an employee who has the authority to retrieve a user's private key. Some key recover servers require that two key recovery agents retrieve private user keys together for added security. Some key recovery servers also have the ability to function as a key escrow server, thereby adding the ability to split the keys onto two separate recovery servers, further increasing security.

Luckily, Windows Server 2008 provides a locksmith of sorts (called a Registration Authority, or RA) that earlier versions of Windows did not have. A key recovery solution, however, is not easy to implement and requires several steps. The basic method follows:

1. Create an account to be used for key recovery.
2. Create a new template to issue to that account.
3. Request a key recovery certificate from the CA.

4. Have the CA issue the certificate.

5. Configure the CA to archive certificates by using the **Recovery Agents** tab of the CA property sheet (shown in Figure 3.42).

6. Create an archive template for the CA.

Figure 3.42 Recovery Agents Tab of the CA Property Sheet

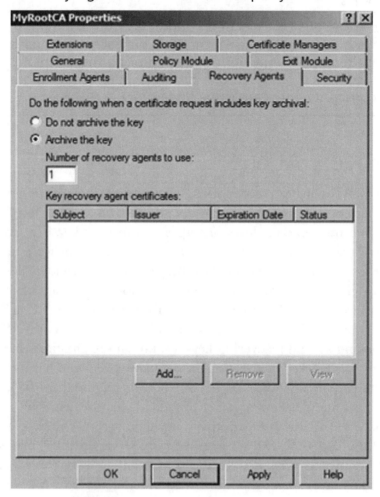

Each of these steps requires many substeps, but can be well worth the time and effort. It is worth noting again that key recovery is not possible on a stand-alone CA, because a stand-alone cannot use templates. It is also worth noting that only encryption keys can be recovered—private keys used for digital signatures cannot.

Summary of Exam Objectives

The purpose of a PKI is to facilitate the sharing of sensitive information such as authentication traffic across an insecure network. This is done with public and private key cryptography. In public key cryptography, keys are generated in pairs so that every public key is matched to a private key and vice versa. If data is encrypted with a particular public key, then only the corresponding private key can decrypt it. A digital signature means that an already encrypted piece of data is further encrypted by someone's private key. When the recipient wants to decrypt the data, he or she must first "unlock" the digital signature by using the signer's public key, remembering that only the *signer's* public key will work. This might seem secure, but because anyone at all can sign the data, how does the recipient know for certain the identity of the person who actually signed it?

The answer is that digital signatures need to be issued by an authoritative entity, one whom everyone trusts. This entity is known as a certification authority. An administrator can use Windows Server 2008, a third-party company such as VeriSign, or a combination of the two to create a structure of CAs. Certification authorities, as the name implies, issue certificates. In a nutshell, certificates are digitally signed public keys. Certificates work something like this: party A wants to send a private message to party B, and wants to use party B's public key to do it. Party A realizes that if B's public key is used to encrypt the message, then only B's private key can be used to decrypt it and since B and no one else has B's private key, everything works out well. However, A needs to be sure that he's really using B's public key and not an imposter's, so instead of just asking B for B's public key, he asks B for a certificate. B has previously asked the CA for a certificate for just such an occasion (B will present the certificate to anyone who wants to verify B's identity). The CA has independently verified B's identity, and has then taken B's public key and signed it with its own private key, creating a certificate. A trusts the CA, and is comfortable using the CA's well-known public key. When A uses the CA's public key to unlock the digital signature, he can be sure that the public key inside really belongs to B, and he can take that public key and encrypt the message.

The "I" in PKI refers to the infrastructure, which is a system of public key cryptography, certificates, and certification authorities. CAs are usually set up in a hierarchy, with one system acting as a root and all the others as subordinates at one or more levels deep. By analyzing the certificate requirements for your company, you can design your CA structure to fit your needs. Most organizations use a three-tier model, with a root CA at the top, an intermediate level of subordinates who control CA policy, and a bottom level of subordinates who actually issue certificates to users, computers, and applications. In addition to choosing root and subordinate structure for the CA hierarchy, each CA during installation needs to be designated as either an enterprise or a stand-alone. Each of these choices has distinct advantages and disadvantages. Most CA configuration after installation is done through the Certification Authority snap-in. In addition to issuing certificates, CAs are also responsible for revoking them when necessary. Revoked certificates are published to a CRL that clients can download before accepting a certificate as valid.

Enterprise CAs use templates to know what to do when a certificate request is received and how to issue a certificate if approved. There are several built-in templates included in Server 2008, or you can configure new ones. Once a CA is ready to issue certificates, clients need to request them. Autoenrollment, Web enrollment, or manual enrollment through the Certificates snap-in are the three ways by which a client can request a certificate. Autoenrollment is available for computer certificates, and in Windows Server 2008, for user certificates as well.

Exam Objectives Fast Track

Planning a Windows Server 2008 Certificate-Based PKI

☑ A PKI combines public key cryptography with digital certificates to create a secure environment where network traffic such as authentication packets can travel safely.

☑ Public keys and private keys always come in pairs. If the public key is used to encrypt data, only the matching private key can decrypt it.

☑ When public key-encrypted data is encrypted again by a private key, that private key encryption is called a digital signature.

☑ Digital signatures provided by ordinary users aren't very trustworthy, so a trusted authority is needed to provide them. The authority (which can be Windows-based) issues certificates, which are basically digitally signed containers for public keys and other information.

☑ Certificates are used to safely exchange public keys, and provide the basis for applications such as IPsec, EFS, and smart card authentication.

Implementing Certification Authorities

☑ Certificate needs are based on which applications and communications an organization uses and how secure they need to be. Based on these needs, CAs are created by installing certificate services and are managed using the Certification Authority snap-in.

☑ A CA hierarchy is structured with a root and one or more level of subordinates—three levels are common. The bottom level of subordinates issues certificates. The intermediate level controls policies.

☑ Enterprise CAs require and use Active Directory to issue certificates, often automatically. Stand-alone CAs can be more secure, and need an administrator to manually issue or deny certificate requests.

☑ CAs need to be backed up consistently and protected against attacks. Keys can be archived and later retrieved if they are lost. This is a new feature for Windows Server 2008.

☑ CAs can revoke as well as issue certificates. Once a certificate is revoked, it needs to be published to a CRL distribution point. Clients check the CRL periodically before they can trust a certificate.

Planning Enrollment and Distribution of Certificates

☑ Templates control how a CA acts when handed a request, and how to issue certificates. There are a quite a few built-in templates, or you can create your own using the Certificate Template snap-in. Templates must be enabled before a CA can use them.

☑ Certificates can be requested with the Certificates snap-in or by using Internet Explorer and pointing to *http://servername/certsrv* on the CA.

☑ Machine and user certificates can be requested with no user intervention requirement by using autoenrollment. Autoenrollment for user certificates is new to Windows Server 2008.

☑ Role-based administration is recommended for larger organizations. Different users can be assigned permissions relative to their positions, such as certificate manager.

Exam Objectives
Frequently Asked Questions

Q: In what format do CAs issue certificates?

A: Microsoft certificate services use the standard X.509 specifications for issued certificates and the Public Key Cryptography Standard (PKCS) #10 standard for certificate requests. The PKCS #7 certificate renewal standard is also supported. Windows Server 2003 also supports other formats, such as PKCS #12, DER encoded binary X.509, and Base64 Encoded X.509, for exporting certificates to computers running non-Windows operating systems.

Q: If certificates are so important in a PKI, why don't I see more of them?

A: Many portions of a Windows PKI are hidden to the end user. Thanks to features such as autoenrollment, some PKI transactions can be completely done by the operating system. Most of the work in implementing a PKI comes in the planning and design phase. Operations such as encrypting data via EFS use certificates, but the user does not "see" or manually handle the certificates.

Q: I've heard that I can't take my laptop overseas because it uses EFS. Is this true?

A: Maybe. The backbone of any PKI-enabled application such as EFS is encryption. Although the U.S. government now permits the exporting of "high encryption" standards, some countries still do not allow their import. The Windows Server 2008 PKI can use high encryption, and so the actual answer depends on the country in question. For information on the cryptographic import and export policies of a number of countries, see http://www.rsasecurity.com/rsalabs/faq/6-5-1.html.

Q: Can I create my own personal digital signature and use it instead of a CA?

A: Not if you need security. The purposes behind digital signatures are privacy and security, and a digital signature at first glance seems to fit the bill. The problem, however, is not the signature itself, but the lack of trust in a recipient. Impersonations become a looming security risk if you can't guarantee that the digital signatures you receive came from the people with whom they were supposed to have originated. For this reason, a certificate issued by a trusted third party provides the most secure authentication.

Q: Can I have a CA hierarchy that is five levels deep?

A: Yes, but that's probably overkill for most networks. Microsoft's three-tier model of root, intermediate, and issuing CAs will more than likely meet your requirements. Remember that your hierarchy can be wide instead of deep.

Q: Do I have to have more than one CA?

A: No. Root CAs have the ability to issue all types of certificates and can assume responsibility for your entire network. In a small organization, a single CA might be sufficient for your purposes. For a larger organization, however, this structure would not be suitable.

Q: How can I change the publishing interval of a CRL?

A: From the **Certification Authority** console, right-click the **Revoked Certificates** container and choose **Properties.** The **CRL Publishing Parameters** tab allows you to change the default interval for full and Delta CRLs.

Q: Why can't I seem to get autoenrollment for user certificates to work?

A: Remember that autoenrollment for machines is a feature that has been around since Windows 2000, but autoenrollment for user certificates is new to Windows Server 2003. In order to use this feature, you need to be running either a Windows Server 2003 or XP client and you must log on to a Windows Server 2003 domain. Finally, autoenrollment must be enabled through Active Directory's group policy. Also, you won't be able to autoenroll a user unless the user account has been assigned an e-mail address.

Q: What is the default validity period for a new certificate?

A: The default, which can be changed on the **General** tab of a new template's **Property** sheet, is one year. Other important settings, such as minimum key size and purpose of the certificate, can be found on the sheet's other tabs.

Q: If my smart card is lost or stolen, can I be reissued one?

A: Yes. The enrollment agent can enroll a new card for you at the enrollment station. Although most smart card providers allow cards to be reused (such as when they are found), a highly secure company may require old cards to be destroyed. For similar security reasons, PINs should not be reused on a newly issued card although it is possible. Remember that a card is only good to a thief if the corresponding PIN is obtained as well.

Q: When setting up smart cards for my company, can I use the MS-CHAP or MS-CHAP v2 protocols for authentication?

A: No. EAP is the only authentication method you can use with smart cards. It is considered the pinnacle of the authentication protocols under Windows Server 2003. MS-CHAP v2 is probably the most secure of the password-based protocols, but still does not provide the level of protection that smart cards using EAP do. This is because EAP is not really an authentication protocol by itself. It interfaces with other protocols such as MD5-CHAP, and is therefore extremely flexible. As a result it has been widely implemented by many different vendors. MS-CHAP and MS-CHAP v2 are Microsoft proprietary, and do not enjoy the same popularity or scrutiny applied to EAP. It is this scrutiny over the last several years that gives EAP the reputation of a highly secure protocol.

Q: How can I determine the length of time for which a certificate should be valid?

A: It is important to plan out your PKI implementation before it goes into production. In the case of certificate validity, you'll want to choose a time period that will cover the majority of your needs without being so long as to open your environment up to compromise.

If you are planning a certificate to support a traveling workforce that only connects to the corporate infrastructure once a quarter, it would be detrimental to expire certificates once a month. At the same time, specifying a certificate to be valid for 20 years might open your business up to compromise by an ex-employee long after his employment has been terminated.

Finally, you will want to ensure that your certificate lifetime is less than the lifetime for the lifetime of the CA's own cert. If the issuing CA will only be valid for a year, having a subordinate cert that is good for 5 years will lead to problems when the parent authority is revoked.

Q: My domain has been active for some time, but I have only recently implemented a Certificate Authority in my domain. I am now getting messages that my Domain Controllers do not have appropriate certificates. What should I do?

A: Make sure that you have enabled auto enrollment on your Domain Controller certificate templates. This step is often missed and can lead to a number of secondary problems, the least of which is annoying messages in the Event Logs.

Self Test

1. You have been asked to provide an additional security system for your company's internet activity. This system should act as an underlying cryptography system. It should enable users or computers that have never been in trusted communication before to validate themselves by referencing an association to a trusted third party (TTP). The method of security the above example is referencing is?

   A. Certificate Authority (CA)

   B. Nonrepudiation

   C. Cryptanalysis

   D. Public Key Infrastructure (PKI)

2. You are engaged in an exercise that is meant to demonstrate the Public-Key Cryptography Standards (PKCS). You arrive at a portion of the exercise dealing with encrypting a string with a secret key based on a password. Which of the following PKCS does this exercise address?

   A. PKCS #5

   B. PKCS #1

   C. PKCS #8

   D. PKCS #9

3. You are working in a Windows Server 2008 PKI and going over various user profiles that are subject to deletion due to company policy. The public keys for these users are stored under Documents and Settings\Administrator\System Certificates\My\Certificates and the private keys would be under Documents and Settings\Administrator\Crypto\RSA. You possess copies of the public keys in the registry, and in Active Directory. What effect will the deletion of the user profile have on the private key?

   A. It will have no effect.

   B. It will be replaced by the public key that is stored.

   C. The Private Key will be lost.

   D. None of the above.

4. Two users, Dave and Dixine, wish to communicate privately. Dave and Dixine each own a key pair consisting of a public key and a private key. If Dave wants

Dixine to send him an encrypted message, which of the following security measures occurs first?

A. Dave transmits his public key to Dixine.

B. Dixine uses Dave's public key to encrypt the message.

C. Nothing occurs the message is simply sent.

D. Dixine requests a access to Dave's private key.

5. You are browsing your company's e-commerce site using Internet Explorer 7 and have added a number of products to the shopping cart. You notice that there is a padlock symbol in the browser. By right clicking this symbol you will be able to view information concerning the site's:

A. Private Key.

B. Public Key.

C. Information Architecture.

D. Certificates.

6. You are engaged in an exercise that is meant to demonstrate the Public-Key Cryptography Standards (PKCS) used in modern encryption. You arrive at a portion of the exercise which outlines the encryption of data using the RSA algorithm. Which of the following PKCS does this exercise address?

A. PKCS #5

B. PKCS #1

C. PKCS #8

D. PKCS #9

7. You are the administrator of your company's Windows Server 2008-based network and are attempting to enroll a smart card and configure it at an enrollment station. Which of the following certificates must be requested in order to accomplish this action?

A. A machine certificate.

B. An application certificate.

C. A user certificate.

D. All of the above.

8. Dave and Dixine each own a key pair consisting of a public and private key. A public key was used to encrypt a message and the corresponding private

key was used to decrypt. Dave wants Dixine to know that a document he is responding with was really written by him. How is this possible using the given scenario?

A. Dave's private key can encrypt the document and the matching public key can be used to decrypt it.

B. Dave can send Dixine his private key as proof.

C. Dixine can allow Dave access to her private key to encrypt the document.

D. None of the above.

9. You are administrating a large hierarchal government environment in which a trust model needs to be established. The company does not want external CA's involved in the verification process. Which of the following is the best trust model deployment for this scenario?

A. A hierarchal first party trust model.

B. A third party single CA trust model.

C. A first party single CA trust Model.

D. None of these will meet the needs of the company.

10. Two users, Dave and Dixine, wish to communicate privately. Dave and Dixine each own a key pair consisting of a public key and a private key. A public key was used to encrypt a message and the corresponding private key was used to decrypt. What is the major security issue with this scenario?

A. Private keys are revealed during the initial transaction.

B. Information encrypted with a public key can be decrypted too easily with out the private key.

C. An attacker can intercept the data mid-stream, and replace the original signature with his or her own, using his private key.

D. None of the Above.

Self Test Quick Answer Key

1. **D**

2. **A**

3. **C**

4. **A**

5. **C**

6. **B**

7. **C**

8. **A**

9. **A**

10. **C**

Chapter 4

MCTS/MCITP
Exam 649

Maintaining an Active Directory Environment

Exam objectives in this chapter:

- **Backup and Recovery**
- **Offline Maintenance**
- **Monitoring Active Directory**

Exam objectives review:

- ☑ **Summary of Exam Objectives**
- ☑ **Exam Objectives Fast Track**
- ☑ **Exam Objectives Frequently Asked Questions**
- ☑ **Self Test**
- ☑ **Self Test Quick Answer Key**

Introduction

Being able to implement a Windows Server 2008 Active Directory environment is only half the battle. You must also be able to maintain the environment to provide minimum downtime and optimum performance of your enterprise. Various solutions and strategies come into play as part of maintenance. Some can be seen as larger "disaster recovery" components, whereas others may simply be "tweaking" the environment to improve user experience.

In some situations, "maintenance" may fall somewhere in between—a user account is accidentally deleted, a file is accidentally deleted, or replication is under-performing or not performing at all! In this chapter, you will learn about the many maintenance and management tools offered as a part of Windows Server 2008, as well as some solutions to better improve your Windows Active Directory environment. These topics will be critical not only to your exam success, but also to your success as an IT professional. We will begin this section with a discussion of Windows Server Backup and how it has changed drastically from earlier versions of the Windows server product.

Backup and Recovery

Most people never think about backup and recovery until they need it. Microsoft has been shipping a simple backup solution with Windows since Windows NT 3.1 back in 1993. The technology used today has changed since then, but the needs are still the same. Administrators need the ability to effectively back up servers, data, and the system state while also having an easy way to restore when needed.

Windows Server 2008 does not support the old NTBackup.exe tool or its backup format. It now uses a backup feature called Windows Server Backup. This feature cannot read the old .bkf files. Therefore, it cannot restore any backups from NTBackup.exe. Windows Server Backup is primarily intended for use by small businesses and companies that do not have full-time or a highly technical IT staff.

Windows Server Backup uses the same backup technology found in Windows Vista, which is a block-level image. It uses .vhd image files just like those found in Microsoft Virtual Server. After the first full backup is complete, Windows Server Backup can be configured to automatically run incremental backups, therefore saving only the data that has changed and not the entire object over and over again. Restoration is also simplified in that an administrator no longer has to manually restore from multiple backups if an item was stored on an incremental backup. They can now restore items by choosing a backup to recover from and then select the item(s) to restore. One thing that you cannot do in Windows Server Backup, however, is back up to tape. Tape is not a supported medium for Windows Server Backup. You can back up to disks, DVDs, and network shares.

New and Noteworthy...

Windows Server Backup

Although you cannot use Windows Server Backup to recover files from a .bkf format, you can download a version of Windows Backup for Windows Server 2008. It is for use by administrators who need to recover data from backups taken using NTBackup. The downloadable version cannot be used to create additional backups on Windows Server 2008. To download NTBackup for Windows Server 2008 go to http://go.microsoft.com/fwlink/?LinkId=82917.

Using Windows Server Backup

Before using Windows Server Backup, you must install the feature. Just like many of the features within Windows Server 2008, Windows Server Backup is installed via a wizard through Server Manager. Installing the Windows Server Backup feature is easy and simple; just follow the steps in Exercise 4.1.

EXERCISE 4.1

INSTALLING WINDOWS SERVER BACKUP

1. Log on to Windows Server 2008 as an administrator (domain admin or local admin).

2. Click Start | Administrative Tools | Server Manager. Server Manager should come up.

3. In Server Manager, on the left window pane also known as the Console Tree, click on the top icon where it reads Server Manager <server name>. In our case, it reads Server Manager (SIGMA).

4. You'll now see a list of different options. Go to **Features** and click on it. Server Manager will show the different features installed on that particular server in the Details pane to the right of the console tree. Figure 4.1 is an example of what an administrator would see after doing this.

Figure 4.1 The List of Features Installed

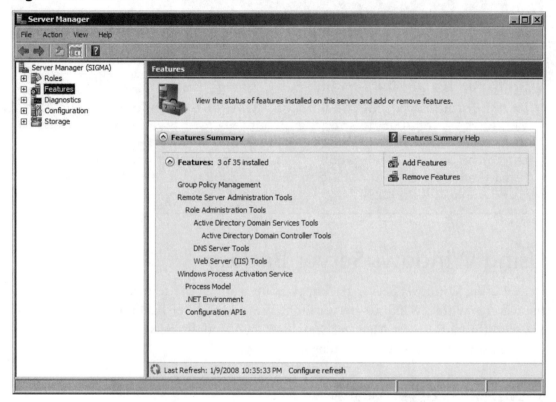

5. In the console tree, right-click **Features** and choose **Add Features**. You will now come to the **Select Features** window via the **Add Features Wizard**. Scroll down the list to where you see **Windows Server Backup Features** and put a check beside it and click **Next**. In Figure 4.2, you'll notice that you are installing the **Windows Server Backup** and the **Command-line Tools**.

Head of the Class...

Command-Line Tools

If you want to install the **Command-line Tools** with the **Windows Server Backup Features**, you must also install the **Windows PowerShell**. The Windows PowerShell is a command-line and scripting language that allows IT professionals to better control system administration and automation. It is built on top of the .NET Framework and uses cmdlet's (command lets), which is a single-function command-line tool built into the shell.

Figure 4.2 Selecting Windows Server Backup Features

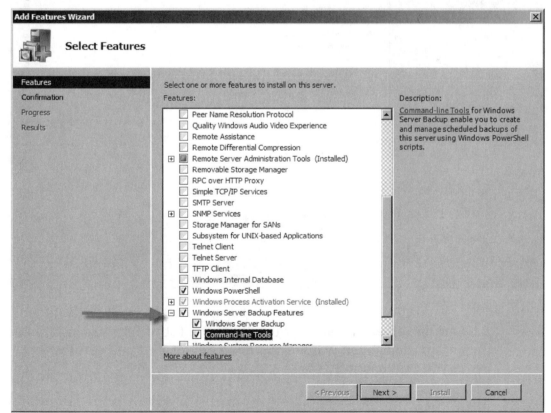

6. Now you will come to the **Confirm Installation Selections** screen. Once you've verified that the feature(s) you plan to install are shown in the confirmation list, click **Install**.

7. Once the installation has completed, you will come to the **Installation Results** screen, as shown in Figure 4.3. Notice that we installed the **Windows PowerShell** and the **Windows Server Backup Features** successfully. Once the installation is complete, click on **Close**.

Figure 4.3 Installation Results

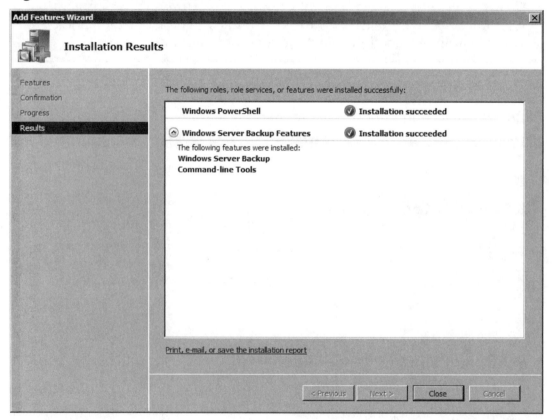

8. Back in Server Manager, you will see the list of features installed, and in the list you will see Windows Server Backup Features, just as you see in Figure 4.4.

Figure 4.4 The List of Features Installed

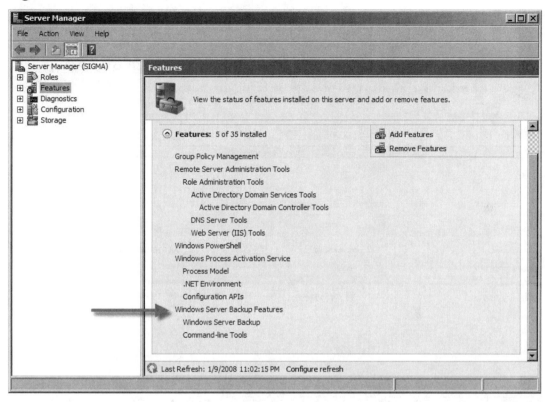

To use the newly installed Windows Server Backup, simply click **Start |
Administrative Tools | Windows Server Backup**. As you can see in Figure 4.5,
Windows Server Backup's interface is pretty straightforward. Information about
backups and messages is shown in the left pane, and options such as the following
are shown in the right pane:

- Backup Schedule
- Backup Once
- Recover
- Configure Performance Settings
- Connect To Another Computer

Figure 4.5 Windows Server Backup

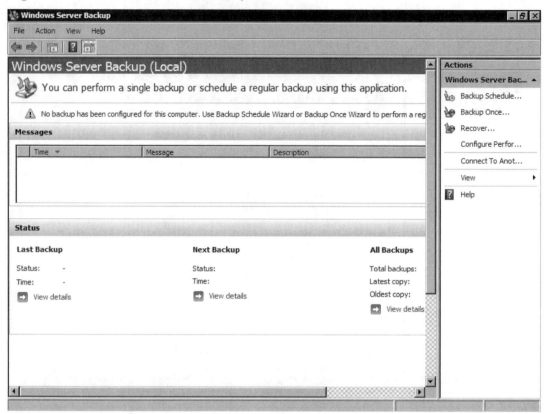

Scheduling a Backup

Windows Server Backup allows administrators and operators with sufficient rights to schedule backups to take place at certain times on a regular basis. In scheduling a backup, you need to decide what you want to back up, how often and when the backup(s) are to take place, and where to store the backup(s). To schedule a backup, follow the steps in Exercise 4.2.

EXERCISE 4.2

SCHEDULING A BACKUP

1. In **Windows Server Backup** go to the **Actions** pane and select **Backup Schedule**. This will kick off the **Backup Schedule Wizard** which you see in Figure 4.6.

Figure 4.6 The Backup Schedule Wizard's Getting Started Screen

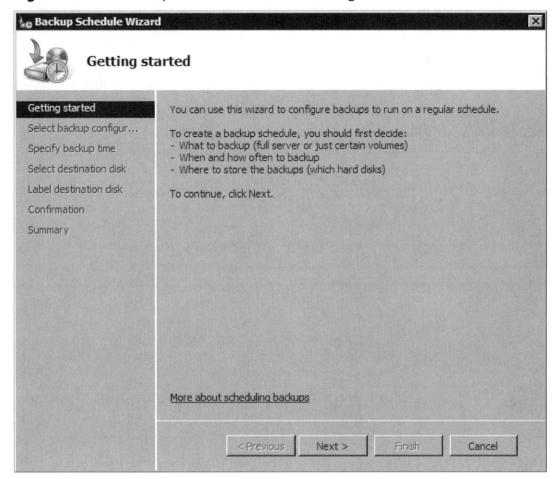

2. Next you're asked what type of configuration you want to schedule. You can select **Full Server** or you can select **Custom**, as shown in Figure 4.7. The full server configuration will back up all data, applications, and system state. Selecting Custom, though, allows you to select which items you would prefer to back up. For our example, we will choose to conduct a **Full Server** backup. After you have made your decision just click **Next**.

Figure 4.7 Selecting Backup Configuration

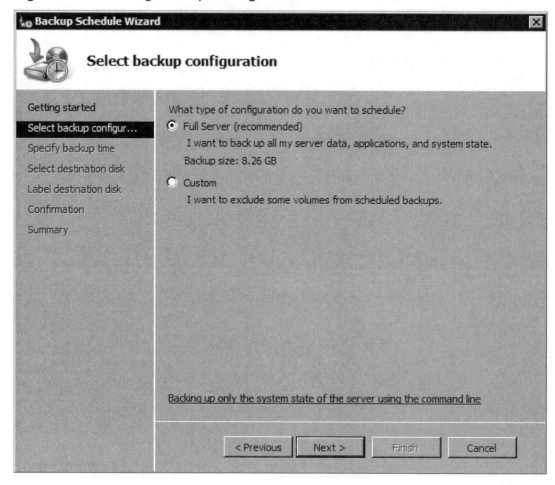

3. The next thing we need to do in scheduling our backup is decide how often we want to conduct a backup and what time(s) to run it. In Figure 4.8, you see we have decided to kick off our backup once a day at midnight. After deciding when and how often backups are to take place, click **Next** to continue.

Figure 4.8 Specifying the Backup Time

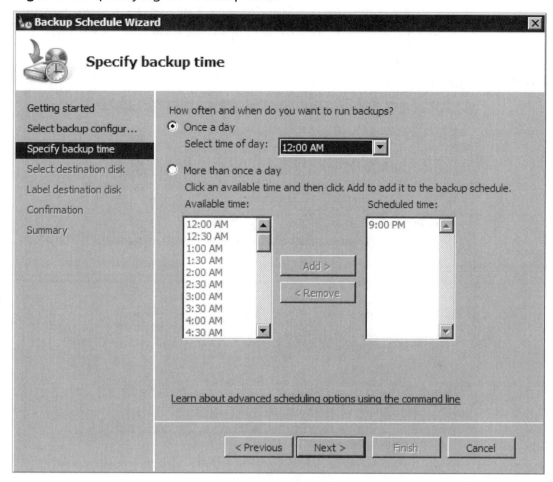

4. Now we need to tell Windows Server Backup where we want to store the backup. For scheduled backups, we have to use a locally attached drive. This can be a DVD drive, a USB flash drive, or even an externally attached drive. It cannot be a network drive. Although Windows Server Backup does allow you to back up to a network drive, you are not allowed to schedule a job that does. On our system, we have a second drive listed as volume E. We will have our scheduled backup job use this as the destination; to continue we just click **Next**. You'll notice a pop-up from Windows Server Backup, letting you know that it will reformat the destination drive you selected and that it will only be dedicated to backing up files and will not show up in Windows Explorer.

To continue, just click **Yes**. Figure 4.9 shows that we have chosen the E drive as our destination disk and Figure 4.10 informs us that the destination drive will be reformatted, among other things.

Figure 4.9 Selecting the Destination Disk

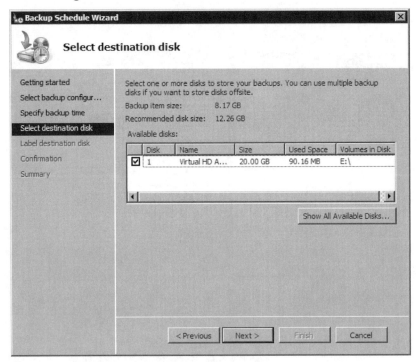

Figure 4.10 The Destination Drive Will Be Reformatted

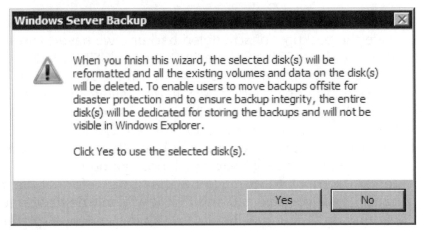

5. Windows Server Backup will now label the destination disk. The default name will be in the form of *<server name> year_month_ date <military time>*. As you see in Figure 4.11, our label will be **SIGMA 2008_01_10 14:08**. After confirming this, you can click **Next**.

Figure 4.11 Labeling the Destination Disk

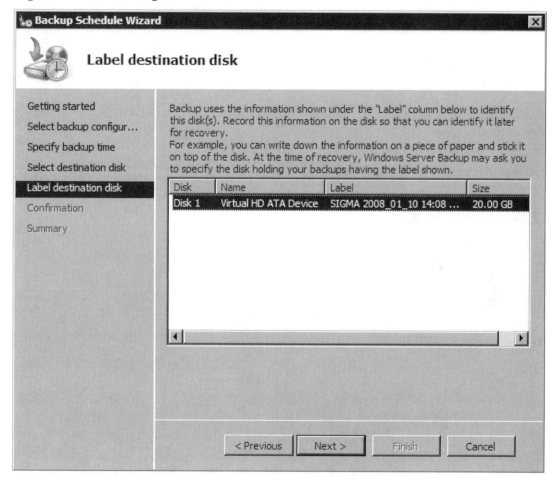

EXAM WARNING

It is highly recommended that administrators and backup operators alike write the label name on the destination drive. During recovery Windows Server Backup may specify a disk holding backups with a specific label name.

6. The final step in scheduling a backup is to confirm your selections. The **Confirmation** screen will show you what you have chosen at the backup items, times, and the destination, as you see in Figure 4.12. After you've confirmed your choices, click **Finish**.

Figure 4.12 The Backup Schedule Confirmation

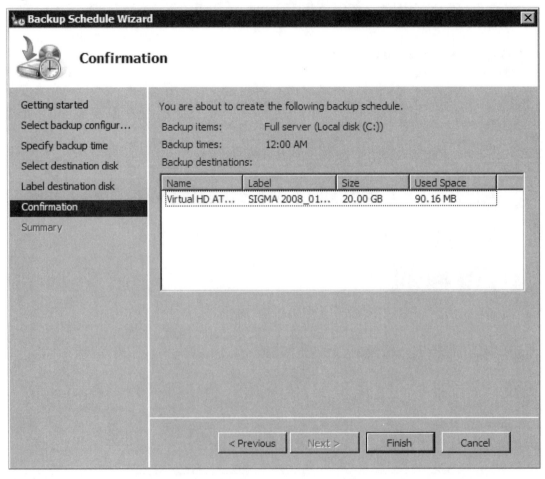

Now that we have a scheduled backup, we can just wait for it to kick off at midnight. In Figure 4.13, you'll notice in Windows Server Backup we went ahead and ran a full backup. You'll see under **Messages** and **Status** that we have conducted a successful backup. We did this by going into the **Actions** pane and selecting **Backup Once**. This gave us a chance to test the backup configuration.

Figure 4.13 A Successful Backup

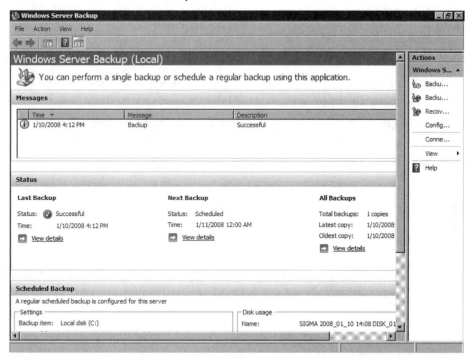

As you've seen, we've gone through installing Windows Server Backup, and gone over the media it supports, how to schedule a backup, and how to immediately start one. What we have not covered, which you will be tested on, is how to use the *wbadmin* command.

Wbadmin.exe is the command-line utility that comes with Windows Server Backup. It can be used to perform backups and restores from the command line or via batch files and scripts. Table 4.1 is a list of the commands supported by wbadmin.exe.

Table 4.1 The wbadmin.exe Command

Command	Description
wbadmin enable backup	Enables or configures scheduled daily backups
wbadmin disable backup	Disables running scheduled daily backups
wbadmin start backup	Runs a backup job

Continued

Table 4.1 Continued. The wbadmin.exe Command

Command	Description
wbadmin stop job	Stops a running backup or recovery job
wbadmin get versions	Reports information about the available backups
wbadmin get items	Lists the items included in a backup based on parameters you specify
wbadmin start recovery	Runs a recovery of the volumes, applications, or files and folders specified
wbadmin get status	Gives the status of a backup or recovery job
wbadmin get disks	Lists disks that are currently online
wbadmin start systemstaterecovery	Recovers the system state from a backup
wbadmin start systemrecovery	Runs a full system recovery. Available only if you are using the Windows Recovery environment.
wbadmin start recovery	Runs a recovery
wbadmin restore catalog	Recovers a catalog that has been corrupted. Helpful in times if the recovery from the backup catalog has been corrupted.
wbadmin delete catalog	Deletes a catalog that has been corrupted
wbadmin start systemstatebackup	Runs a system state backup
wbadmin delete systemstatebackup	Deletes a system state backup(s)

Backing Up to Removable Media

Windows Server 2008, WBS can back up to removable media such as DVD and USB-based flash drives. Although the wizard-driven GUI interface cannot back up to removable media, wbadmin.exe can. One of the big advantages of being able to back up to removable media is that you can easily take it offsite. One disadvantage to using removable media with WBS is that recovery can be done only at the volume level. It cannot be done by recovering individual files or folders that can be done only via the GUI which does not support removable media. So, how do we back up to removable media? That's a good question. In Exercise 4.3, we will back up a server to DVDs.

EXERCISE 4.3

BACKING UP TO DVD

1. Make sure your system has a DVD burner either attached to it or internal to the server.

2. Log on as either the Administrator or a member of the Backup Operators.

3. Put a blank DVD in the DVD burner.

4. Open a command prompt (**Start | Command Prompt**); at the prompt type **wbadmin start backup –backupTarget:E: -include:C:** and then press **Enter**. You should see a screen similar to that shown in Figure 4.14 (if your DVD drive is another drive letter instead of E, use that drive letter for the *backupTarget* argument).

Figure 4.14 Backing Up the Server to DVD

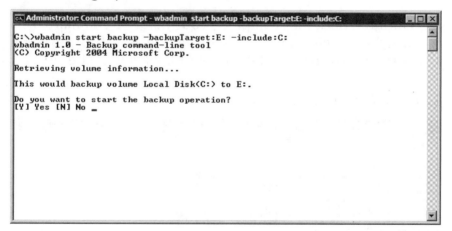

5. At the **Do you want to start the backup operation?** prompt, type **Y** for yes and press **Enter**.

6. Now you are told to insert new media, which in this case is a DVD, which we will label as **SIPOC 2008_01_14 23:19 DVD_01**, as shown in Figure 4.15. The naming standard is *<server name>*

<year_month_date> <time (in military time)> <type of media_ number of media just used>. So, take the first DVD out, write down the proper label, and put in a newly blank DVD and type **C** to continue. For our example, we are also asked to submit a third DVD. The second DVD will have the name **SIPOC 2008_01_14 23:19 DVD_02** and any additional DVDs will have the same name except for the DVD_##.

Figure 4.15 Labeling the First DVD and Continuing

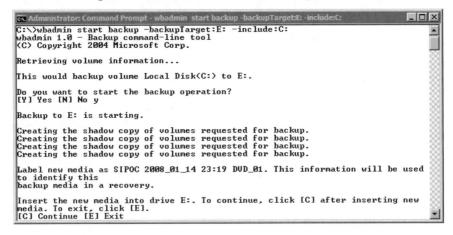

7. Once the backup is complete, you will get a summary by wbadmin similar to the one in Figure 4.16. After you're finished with the backup, just take the last DVD out of the DVD burner.

Figure 4.16 The Completed Backup

```
Administrator: Command Prompt                                          _ □ ×
media. To exit, click [E].
[C] Continue [E] Exit c

Formatting media...
Formatting media...
Running backup of volume Local Disk(C:), copied (98%).
Running backup of volume Local Disk(C:), copied (98%).
Running backup of volume Local Disk(C:), copied (99%).
Running backup of volume Local Disk(C:), copied (99%).
Running backup of volume Local Disk(C:), copied (99%).
Running backup of volume Local Disk(C:), copied (99%).
Running backup of volume Local Disk(C:), copied (100%).
Verification 4% complete...
Verification 21% complete...
Verification 42% complete...
Verification 76% complete...
Verification 100% complete...
Backup completed successfully.

Summary of backup:
------------------

Backup of volume Local Disk(C:) completed successfully.

C:\>
```

Head of the Class...

Unformatted DVDs

If a DVD is unformatted, Windows Server 2008 will automatically format it during the backup.

Backing Up System State Data

The components that make up the system state in Windows Server 2008 depend on the role(s) that are installed on a server and which volumes host the critical files that the operating system and the installed roles use. The system state for all servers at a minimum includes the Registry, the COM+ Class Registration database, system files, boot files, and files under Windows Resource Protection (WRP). WRP is the new name for what was known as Windows File Protection under Windows Server 2003 and earlier. Servers that are domain controllers (DCs) also include the Active Directory Domain Services database and the System Volume (SYSVOL) directory. Other servers, depending on their roles, may also include the Active Directory Certificate Services database, cluster service information, and the Internet Information Server (IIS) metadirectory.

Backing up the System State in Windows Server 2008 creates a point-in-time snapshot that you can use to restore a server to a previous working state. It does this using the Volume Shadow Copy Service (VSS). VSS helps to prevent inadvertent data loss. It creates "shadow" copies of files and/or folders stored on network file shares set up at predetermined time intervals. It is essentially a previous version of the file or folder at a specific point in time.

Without a copy of the System State, recovery of a crashed server would be impossible. The System State is always backed up when full backups are invoked, whether through the WBS Wizard or wbadmin. To back up the System State by itself you must use the *wbadmin* command, though, and it cannot be scheduled unless you create a script that forces it to. In Exercise 4.4, we will back up the system state to our E drive.

EXERCISE 4.4

PERFORMING A SYSTEM STATE BACKUP

1. Log on to a Windows Server 2008 server and open a command prompt (**Start | Command Prompt**).

2. In the command prompt, type wbadmin.exe Start SystemStateBackup –backuptarget:E:.

3. We are told that This would backup the system state from volume(s) Local Disk (C:) to E:. Do you want to start the backup operation? Type Y for yes.

   Next, wbadmin creates the shadow copy of the C drive. After it does this it identifies the system state files to back up. Once it has completed its search for system state files, it begins the backup. Figure 4.17 shows that we have finished performing a system state backup.

Figure 4.17 The System State Backup Is Complete

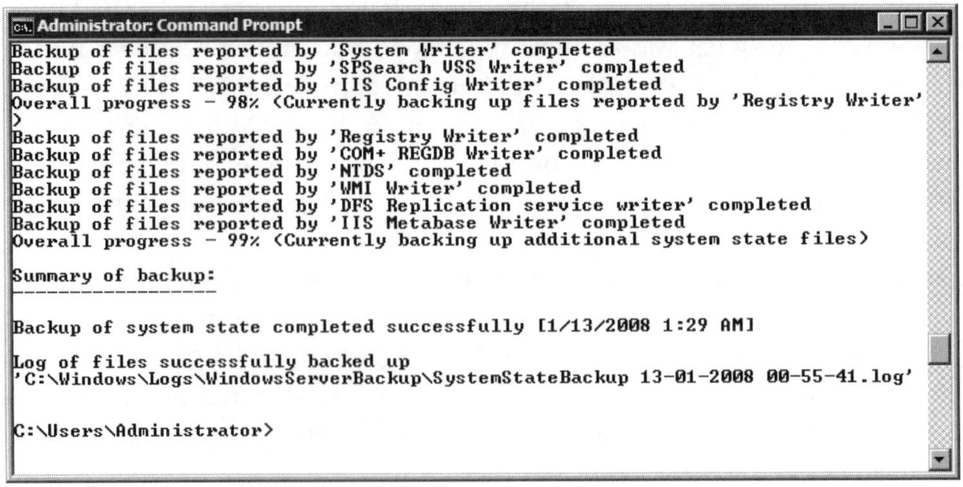

```
Administrator: Command Prompt                                      _ □ ×

Backup of files reported by 'System Writer' completed
Backup of files reported by 'SPSearch VSS Writer' completed
Backup of files reported by 'IIS Config Writer' completed
Overall progress - 98% (Currently backing up files reported by 'Registry Writer'
)
Backup of files reported by 'Registry Writer' completed
Backup of files reported by 'COM+ REGDB Writer' completed
Backup of files reported by 'NTDS' completed
Backup of files reported by 'WMI Writer' completed
Backup of files reported by 'DFS Replication service writer' completed
Backup of files reported by 'IIS Metabase Writer' completed
Overall progress - 99% (Currently backing up additional system state files)

Summary of backup:
-------------------

Backup of system state completed successfully [1/13/2008 1:29 AM]

Log of files successfully backed up
'C:\Windows\Logs\WindowsServerBackup\SystemStateBackup 13-01-2008 00-55-41.log'

C:\Users\Administrator>
```

As you can see, once the backup is complete, wbadmin creates a log with a naming convention of **SystemStateBackup 13-01-2008 00-55-41.log**. Opening the log you see the different files that were backed up. Figure 4.18 is a view of our log.

Figure 4.18 A SystemStateBackup Log

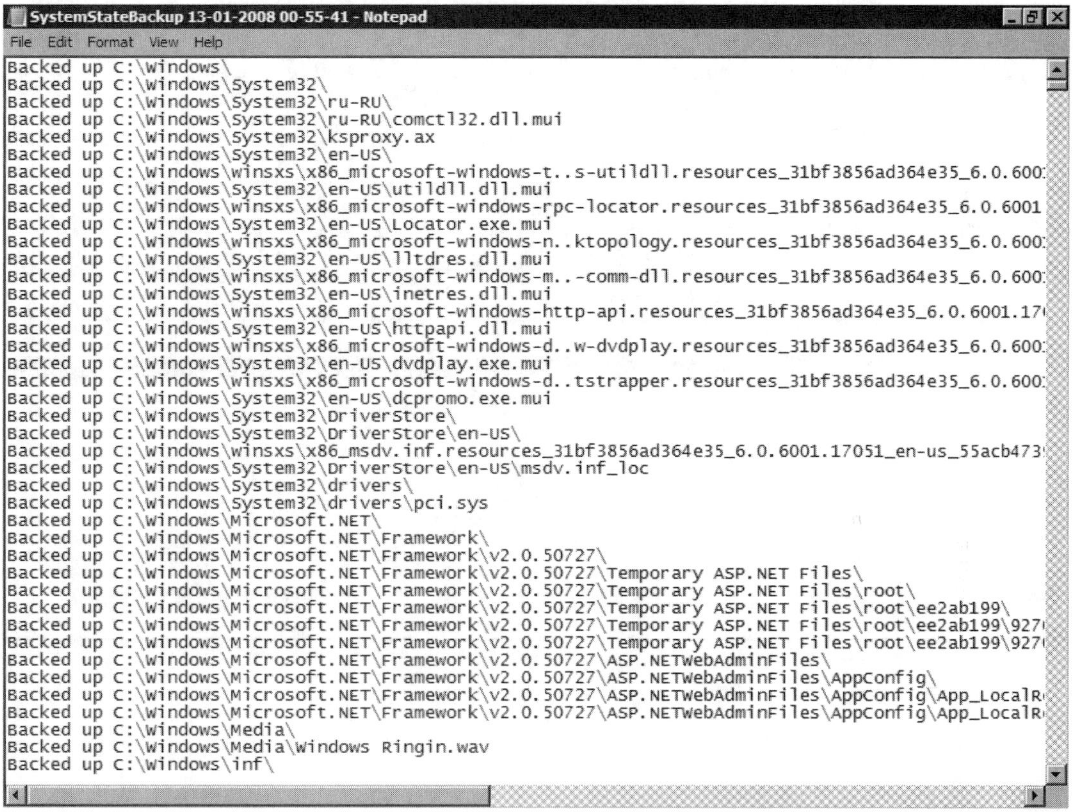

```
SystemStateBackup 13-01-2008 00-55-41 - Notepad
File Edit Format View Help
Backed up C:\Windows\
Backed up C:\Windows\System32\
Backed up C:\Windows\System32\ru-RU\
Backed up C:\Windows\System32\ru-RU\comctl32.dll.mui
Backed up C:\Windows\System32\ksproxy.ax
Backed up C:\Windows\System32\en-US\
Backed up C:\Windows\winsxs\x86_microsoft-windows-t..s-utildll.resources_31bf3856ad364e35_6.0.600
Backed up C:\Windows\System32\en-US\utildll.dll.mui
Backed up C:\Windows\winsxs\x86_microsoft-windows-rpc-locator.resources_31bf3856ad364e35_6.0.6001
Backed up C:\Windows\System32\en-US\Locator.exe.mui
Backed up C:\Windows\winsxs\x86_microsoft-windows-n..ktopology.resources_31bf3856ad364e35_6.0.600
Backed up C:\Windows\System32\en-US\lltdres.dll.mui
Backed up C:\Windows\winsxs\x86_microsoft-windows-m..-comm-dll.resources_31bf3856ad364e35_6.0.600
Backed up C:\Windows\System32\en-US\inetres.dll.mui
Backed up C:\Windows\winsxs\x86_microsoft-windows-http-api.resources_31bf3856ad364e35_6.0.6001.17
Backed up C:\Windows\System32\en-US\httpapi.dll.mui
Backed up C:\Windows\winsxs\x86_microsoft-windows-d..w-dvdplay.resources_31bf3856ad364e35_6.0.600
Backed up C:\Windows\System32\en-US\dvdplay.exe.mui
Backed up C:\Windows\winsxs\x86_microsoft-windows-d..tstrapper.resources_31bf3856ad364e35_6.0.600
Backed up C:\Windows\System32\en-US\dcpromo.exe.mui
Backed up C:\Windows\System32\DriverStore\
Backed up C:\Windows\System32\DriverStore\en-US\
Backed up C:\Windows\winsxs\x86_msdv.inf.resources_31bf3856ad364e35_6.0.6001.17051_en-us_55acb473
Backed up C:\Windows\System32\DriverStore\en-US\msdv.inf_loc
Backed up C:\Windows\System32\drivers\
Backed up C:\Windows\System32\drivers\pci.sys
Backed up C:\Windows\Microsoft.NET\
Backed up C:\Windows\Microsoft.NET\Framework\
Backed up C:\Windows\Microsoft.NET\Framework\v2.0.50727\
Backed up C:\Windows\Microsoft.NET\Framework\v2.0.50727\Temporary ASP.NET Files\
Backed up C:\Windows\Microsoft.NET\Framework\v2.0.50727\Temporary ASP.NET Files\root\
Backed up C:\Windows\Microsoft.NET\Framework\v2.0.50727\Temporary ASP.NET Files\root\ee2ab199\
Backed up C:\Windows\Microsoft.NET\Framework\v2.0.50727\Temporary ASP.NET Files\root\ee2ab199\927
Backed up C:\Windows\Microsoft.NET\Framework\v2.0.50727\Temporary ASP.NET Files\root\ee2ab199\927
Backed up C:\Windows\Microsoft.NET\Framework\v2.0.50727\ASP.NETWebAdminFiles\
Backed up C:\Windows\Microsoft.NET\Framework\v2.0.50727\ASP.NETWebAdminFiles\AppConfig\
Backed up C:\Windows\Microsoft.NET\Framework\v2.0.50727\ASP.NETWebAdminFiles\AppConfig\App_LocalR
Backed up C:\Windows\Microsoft.NET\Framework\v2.0.50727\ASP.NETWebAdminFiles\AppConfig\App_LocalR
Backed up C:\Windows\Media\
Backed up C:\Windows\Media\Windows Ringin.wav
Backed up C:\Windows\inf\
```

Our system state backup resides at **E:\WindowsImageBackup\SIGMA\SystemStateBackup\Backup 2008-01-13 055541**. The E drive here is another fixed disk within our local server. Figure 4.19 shows the files in this directory. Notice that the system state backup alone is around 6GB and that it is a .vhd file, the new format for Windows Backup Server, and no longer a .bkf file.

Figure 4.19 The System State VHD File

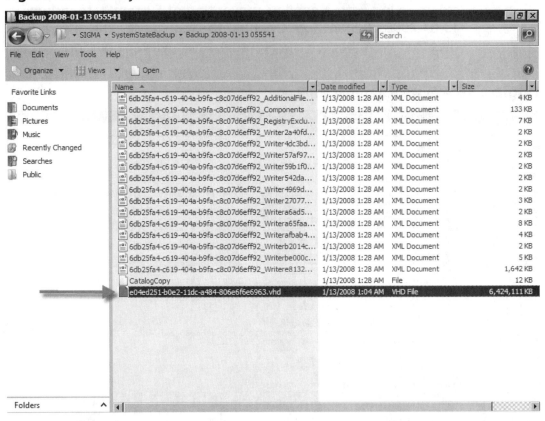

> ! **EXAM WARNING**
>
> System state backups must have local drives as targets. They are not supported on DVDs, removable media, or remote/network drives. You can back up to a local drive and then copy the **SystemStateBackup** directory to another drive or device once the system state backup has been completed.

Backing Up Key Files

Windows Server Backup does not allow you to back up specific files or directories. In other words, you must specify the volume you plan to back up. For example, if I wanted to back up the Users directory on a server, I would need to back up that entire volume so that any other files and folders are automatically backed up. So, if the Users directory resides on the C drive of the server, performing a backup on that volume will back up that directory and the files within it. On our server, in Figure 4.20, you see that the user swhitley has numerous files in the Users\swhitley\lab results directory. To back this up we can do a full backup of the server or a backup of the volume where this user's data resides. As we showed earlier, to manually back up the server, just open **Windows Server Backup**, go to the **Actions** pane and select **Backup Once**.

After the backup, we'll run through a scenario where we will need to restore this data. Let's walk through backing up the drive to DVD using wbadmin.exe.

Figure 4.20 swhitley's User Directory

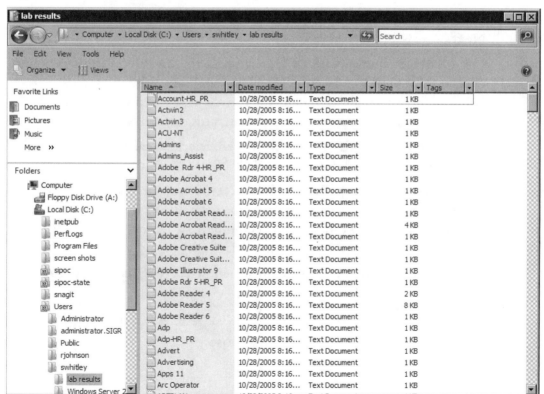

Backing Up Critical Volumes

Disks and volumes in a Windows Server 2008 system are divided into two categories: critical and noncritical. Critical volumes are those containing system state or operating system components. They include the boot and system volumes. A volume containing the Active Directory database (ntds.dit) on a DC is also an example of a critical volume. Critical disks are those that contain critical volumes. Here are two ways to back up critical volumes; the first uses the Windows Server Backup utility and the second uses wbadmin.

To back up critical volumes with the GUI:

1. Click **Start | Administrative Tools | Windows Server Backup**.

2. In the **Action** pane, select **Backup Once**.

3. In the wizard, at the **Backup options** screen, select **Different options** and then click **Next**.

4. If this is the first backup of the DC, select **Yes** to confirm that this is the first backup.

5. On the **Select backup configuration** screen, select **Custom** and then **Next**.

6. On the **Select backup items** screen, select the **Enable system recovery** checkbox, or you can clear that checkbox and select the individual volumes that you want to include. If you do this, you must select the volume(s) that store the operating system, ntds.dit, and SYSVOL.

7. On the **Specify destination type** screen, select **Local drives** or **Remote shared folder** and then click **Next**.

8. On the **Select backup destination** screen, select the backup location. If you are backing up to a local drive, in the **Backup destination** select a drive and click **Next**. If you're backing up to a remote shared folder, type the path using the UNC name and click **Next**.

9. On the **Specify advanced option** screen, select **VSS copy backup** (default) then click **Next**.

10. At the **Summary** screen, review your selections and click **Backup**.

11. After the backup is complete choose **Close**.

To back up critical volumes using wbadmin.exe do the following:

1.   Click Start | Command Prompt.

2.   At the command prompt type **wbadmin start backup –allCritical –backuptarget:** *targetdrive:* *–quiet*.

      The *–quiet* switch allows you to bypass having to type **Y** when asked to proceed with the backup operation.

Recovering System State Data

Sometimes the operating system may become corrupt or unstable. Maybe a role or service needs to be rolled back to a previously backed up state. The fastest and easiest method to do this is to perform a system state recovery. As we already know, the only way to back up system state independently is to use wbadmin.exe. This is the same for recovery. You must use wbadmin to independently restore the system state. In our example in backing up the system state, we saved the system state on another local hard drive on the server (the E drive). The .vhd file, which is the actual backup file, resides in E:\WindowsImageBackup\SIGMA\ SystemStateBackup\Backup 2008-01-13 055541. Exercise 4.5 walks you through the steps in recovering the system state for a member server.

EXERCISE 4.5

RECOVERING SYSTEM STATE FOR MEMBER SERVER

1.   To recover a system state we must log on to the server as the administrator.

2.   Pull up the command prompt (**Start | Command Prompt**).

3.   In the command prompt type **wbadmin get versions**. You'll see a list of the backups you've made on that server. They will be arranged by date and time. You'll also see what you can recover with each backup. At the bottom of the list in Figure 4.21, notice that the last backup's time of backup, its target, the version identifier, and what it can recover match our example earlier in the chapter. That is the backup we will recover.

Figure 4.21 The Command Prompt

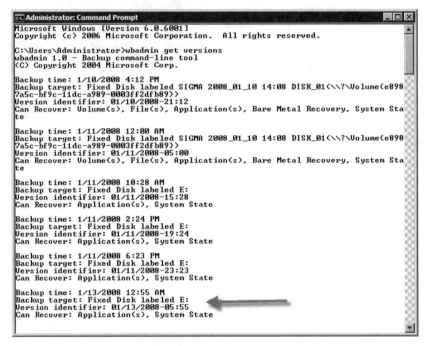

4. In the command prompt, select your desired backup by highlighting the version identifier, which in our case is **01/13/2008-05:55**, and pressing **Enter**. This stores it in the Clipboard.

5. At the prompt, type **wbadmin Start SystemStateRecovery -version: 01/13/2008-05:55** and press **Enter** (remember that you can paste the version identifier by clicking on the upper-left corner of the command prompt and selecting **Edit | Paste**).

6. Next, wbadmin will prompt you with **Do you want to start the system state recovery operation?** Type **Y** for yes and press **Enter**.

7. The system state recovery takes a few minutes to complete. After it's finished, reboot the server and that's it. You've recovered the system state.

EXAM WARNING

To recover the system state for a DC, you must be in Directory Services Restore Mode (DSRM).

Recovering Key Files

With WSB, we can recover individual files and folders as long as the backup resides on a local drive with the system. In other words, if a full backup was made to a network drive, DVD, or any other remote/removable media we would have to restore the entire volume. In the "Backing Up Key Files" section earlier in this chapter, we showed that the user swhitley had a directory called lab results within her Users directory (refer back to Figure 4.20). As we all know, sometimes files and, worse, directories are deleted accidentally. Well, one day swhitley gets to work and notices her lab results directory is gone, as shown in Figure 4.22. She needs this directory ASAP. One option with Windows Server 2008 is to use WSB to individually recover directories and/or files. Exercise 4.6 shows how to do this.

EXERCISE 4.6

RECOVERING FILES AND DIRECTORIES

Figure 4.22 An Accidentally Deleted Directory

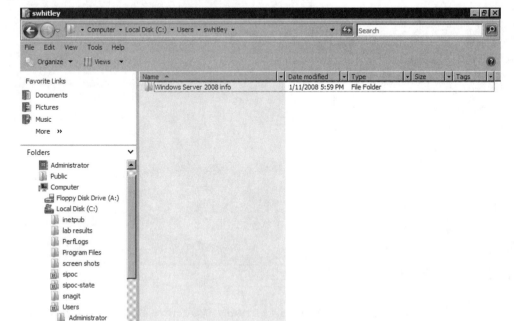

1. Pull up WSB (**Start | Administrative Tools | Windows Server Backup**).

2. In the **Actions** pane select **Recover**.

3. At the **Getting Started** screen, you're asked **Which server do you want to recover data from?** For our scenario, we will select **This server (SIGMA)**. Click **Next**.

4. In Figure 4.23, you see that we must select the date of a backup we want to use for the recovery. We will select a backup done on 01/14/2008 at 6:45 P.M. located on the E drive. Click **Next**.

Figure 4.23 Selecting the Backup Date

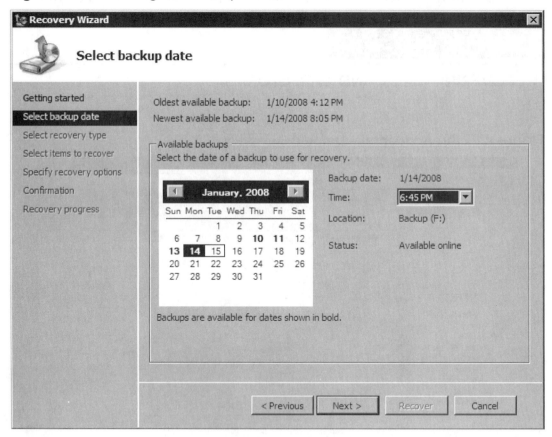

5. We now need to select a recovery type. We have three options: **File and Folders**, **Applications** (grayed out), and **Volumes**. If we select **Volumes**, we can restore the entire volume, such as drive C, but we will not be able to individually select files or folders to

recover. **Applications** are available when an application's plug-ins are registered. Currently we do not have any; therefore, this option is grayed out. **Files and Folders** will allow us to individually select what files or folders we want to recover. Because we want to recover swhitley's lab results folder, we will choose this option, as shown in Figure 4.24. Click **Next**.

Figure 4.24 Selecting the Recovery Type

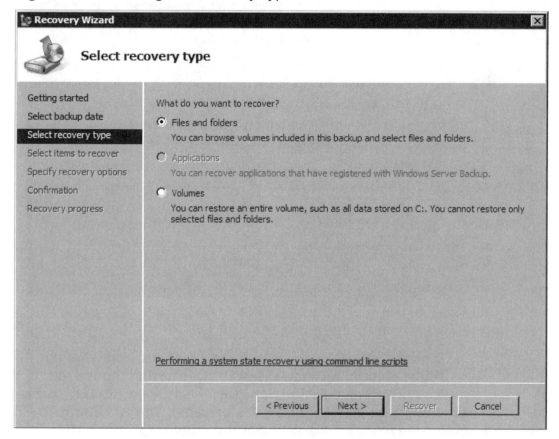

6. We must now choose what items we want to recover. We need to get to swhitley's Users directory and choose **Lab Results**, as shown in Figure 4.25, and then click **Next**.

Figure 4.25 Selecting Items to Recover

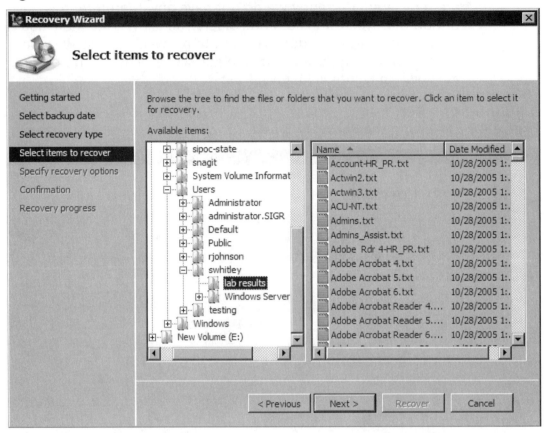

7. Figure 4.26 shows that we have to specify recovery options such as recovery destination, how to handle conflicts, and whether to restore security settings. We will be recovering the lab results folder in its original destination. We will also select **Create copies so I have both versions of the file or folder**. This is the safest option we have. Finally, we want the original security settings that were there before the folder was deleted in place. Once we've done that we can click **Next**.

Figure 4.26 Specifying Recovery Options

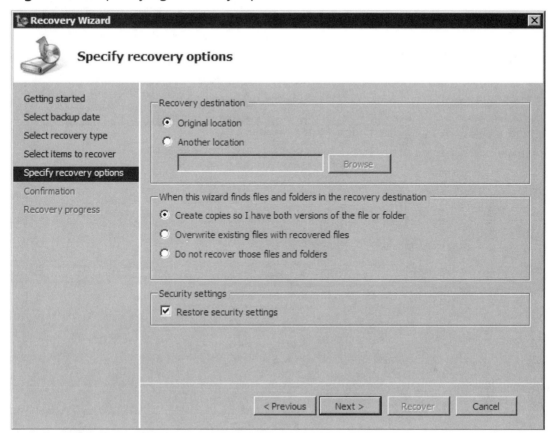

8. WSB will now ask us to confirm what we want to recover, as shown in Figure 4.27. Once we've done that we can click **Recover**.

Figure 4.27 Confirming What We Want to Recover

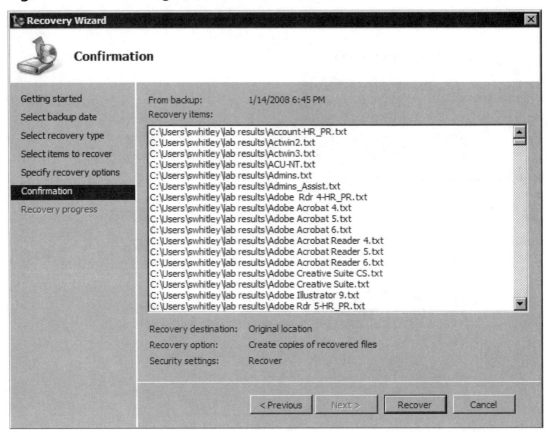

9. After the recovery process is over, just click **Close**.

We can now check swhitley's Users directory to see whether the lab results directory was recovered and whether the files that resided there are restored as well. Figure 4.28 shows that we have a successful recovery of her directory and the files that reside there.

Figure 4.28 Verifying That the Directory and Files Have Been Restored

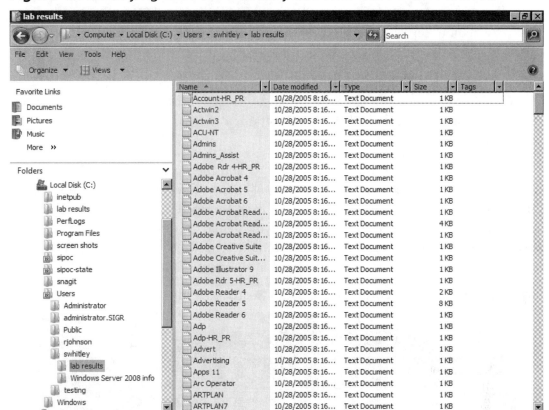

Directory Services Restore Mode

Directory Services Restore Mode (DSRM) is a special boot mode in Windows Server 2008. You use it to log on to a DC when either Active Directory has failed or an object needs to be restored. During setup, you were asked to provide a password for the DSRM administrator. This administrator account (Administrator) is separate from the domain administrator account. This account is used once you boot into DSRM.

If you have forgotten the DSRM password, you can reset it by doing the following:

1. Click Start | Command Prompt.

2. In the command prompt, type **ntdsutil** then press **Enter**.

3. At the ntdsutil prompt, type **set dsrm password** and press **Enter**.

4. At the **Reset DSRM Administrative Password** prompt, type **reset password on server null** (if you are resetting the DSRM password on a remote server, type **reset password on server <*servername*>**).

5. Type in the new password, press **Enter**, and then retype the password for verification and press **Enter** again.

6. After you receive the Password has been set successfully message, type quit at both the Reset DSRM Administrator Password prompt and the ntdsutil prompt.

To access DSRM, you must restart the DC and then press **F8** immediately after the BIOS POST screen and before the Windows Server 2008 logo appears. Once you've done this, you will see the **Advanced Boot Options** screen shown in Figure 4.29. To restore Active Directory you would choose **Directory Services Restore Mode** and then perform either an authoritative or a nonauthoritative restore, which we will cover in more detail in the next section.

Figure 4.29 Choosing Directory Services Restore Mode

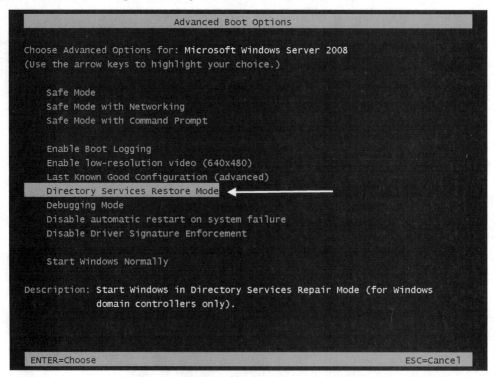

So, what if you don't remember the password for the DSRM administrator? No problem; Microsoft anticipated this. Just follow the steps in Exercise 4.7.

EXERCISE 4.7

RESETTING THE DSRM ADMINISTRATOR PASSWORD

1. Open a command prompt (**Start | Command Prompt**).
2. At the C prompt, type **ntdsutil** and press **Enter**.
3. At the **ntdsutil** prompt, type **set dsrm password** and press **Enter**.
4. You will now come to the **Reset DSRM Administrator Password** prompt. Type **reset password on server null** and press **Enter**.

Configuring and Implementing...

Resetting DSRM Administrator Passwords

You can reset the DSRM Administrator password on another server by typing **reset password on server** *<servername's FQDN>* at the **Reset DSRM Administrator Password** prompt.

5. At the **Please type password for DS Restore Mode Administrator Account** type the new password. You will notice that you will not see the characters that you are typing. After you do this, press **Enter**.
6. You will now be prompted to confirm the password; do so and press **Enter**.
7. After you have done this correctly, ntdsutil will confirm that the password has been reset.
8. Now type **q** and press **Enter** at the **Reset DSRM Administrator Password** prompt.
9. At the ntdsutil prompt, type **q** and press **Enter**. You have now reset the DSRM Administrator's password, which you can see in Figure 4.30.

Figure 4.30 Successfully Resetting the DSRM Administrator's Password

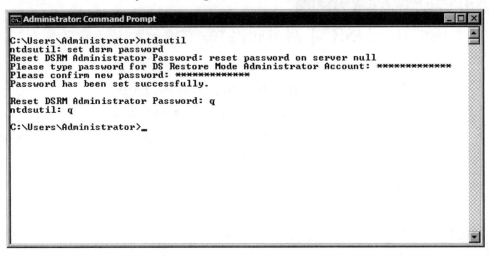

Performing Authoritative and Nonauthoritative Restores

One day you may find yourself with a DC that has a corrupted copy of ntds.dit. To resolve issues such as this you would need to perform a nonauthoritative restore, which we will cover soon. Other times you may have accidentally deleted an object (user, computer, printer, etc.) from Active Directory and you have no way to restore it within Active Directory. This is usually because after the object is deleted, the change has already been replicated to the other DCs in the domain. To fix this you need to perform an authoritative restore, which we will discuss in the next section.

Authoritative Restore

As just mentioned, one of the reasons to perform an authoritative restore is when an object is accidentally deleted in Active Directory and the deletion has already replicated to the remaining DCs. If you simply did a nonauthoritative restore, the object would restore but would be deleted after the other DCs replicated with the recovered system. Exercise 4.8 provides the steps for conducting an authoritative restore.

EXERCISE 4.8

PERFORMING AN AUTHORITATIVE RESTORE

In this example, we are going to "accidentally" delete the user Alan T. Jackson. As you see in Figure 4.31, you Alan's user account is in the Users organizational unit (OU). We will now "accidentally" delete it.

Figure 4.31 User Alan T. Jackson before Deletion

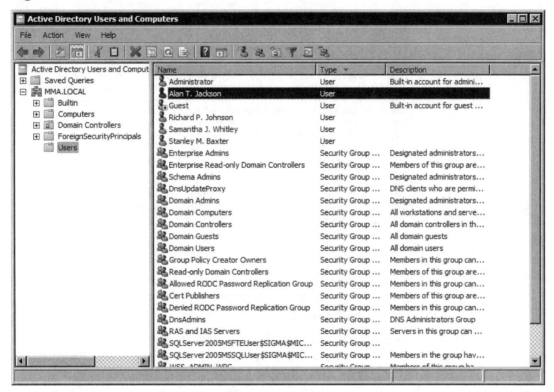

In Figure 4.32, you can see that Alan's user account has been deleted.

Figure 4.32 User Alan T. Jackson Deleted

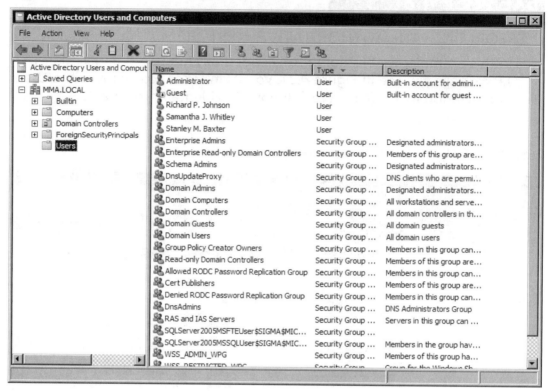

Here are the steps to follow to perform an authoritative restore so that we can restore Alan's user account:

1. First we need to get the version identifier for the most recent backup. Go into a command prompt (**Start | Command Prompt**) and type **wbadmin Get Versions** and press **Enter**. You should see a list of the backups that have been performed on that server. At the bottom is the backup about which we need to get the information. The **Version identifier** for the backup we want is **01/15/2008-01:05**. Also notice that it is stored on the server's E drive in Figure 4.33.

Figure 4.33 Getting Backup Information

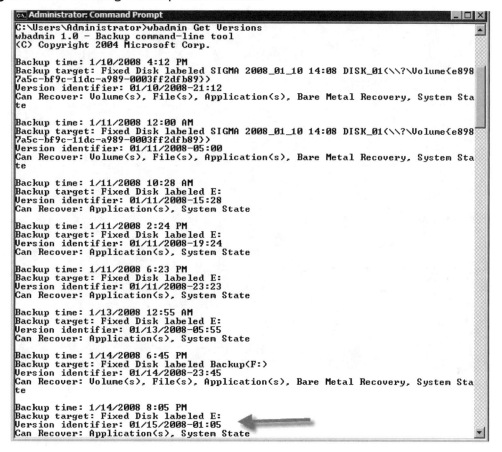

2. Restart the server and press **F8** to open the **Advanced Boot Options**. However, in the **Advanced Boot Options**, select **Directory Services Restore Mode** and press **Enter**.

3. DSRM will boot up into safe mode and will check the file system on all locally attached drives (except for DVDs). Press **Ctrl + Alt + Del** when asked. At the logon screen, click on **Switch User** so that you don't try to log on as the domain administrator, and then click on **Other User**, as shown in Figure 4.34.

Figure 4.34 Selecting Other User

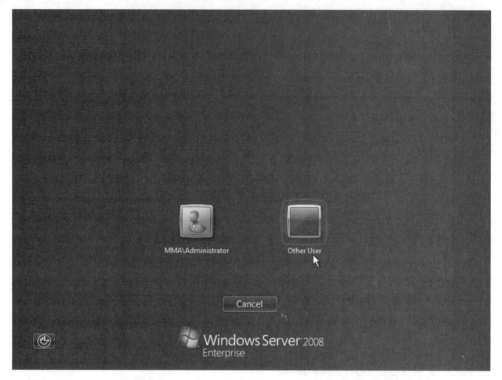

4. For the username, type in the DSRM's administrator account and its password. Notice in Figure 4.35 that we have typed it as **sigma\administrator**. Click on the **blue button with the white arrow** next to where the password is typed to continue.

Figure 4.35 Logging On As the DSRM Administrator

5. Once in safe mode, open the command prompt. Because all we need to do is restore the system state, we can type **wbadmin start SystemStateRecovery –version:01/15/2008-01:05**. This is the same format we covered earlier in recovering the system state.

6. You are then asked whether you want to start the system state recovery. Type **Y** for yes and press **Enter**. Recovery may take a few minutes or longer.

7. Once recovery is finished, you are asked to restart your computer, as shown in Figure 4.36. For an authoritative restore you do not restart the system.

Figure 4.36 The System State Recovery Is Complete

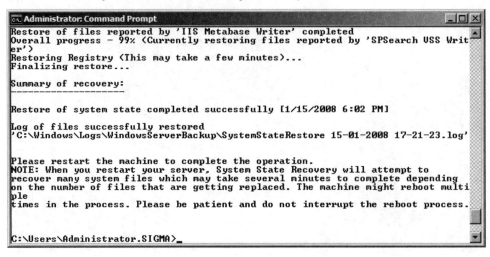

8. As this is an authoritative restore, we must pull up ntdsutil to restore the user ajackson. At the command prompt, type **ntdsutil** and press **Enter**.

9. At the ntdsutil prompt, type **activate instance ntds** and press **Enter**.

10. The ntdsutil prompt will return. At the prompt, type **authoritative restore** and press **Enter**.

11. This will bring up an **authoritative restore** prompt. At the prompt, type **restore subtree CN=ajackson,CN=Users,DC=MMA, DC=LOCAL** and press **Enter**. Note there are *no* spaces between the commas and the next entry.

12. You will now be asked whether you are sure you want to perform the authoritative restore. Click **Yes**.

13. One record will be found and will be successfully updated. You will see the message **Authoritative Restore completed successfully**. At the **authoritative restore** prompt just type **q** for quit and do the same at the ntdsutil prompt. You can now restart the computer and let it come to the normal logon screen.

14. Log on as the domain administrator and let the system state recovery finish. Once it's done, you can examine **Active Directory Users and Computers (ADUC)** and go to the Users OU and see that the user Alan T. Jackson has been restored.

Nonauthoritative Restore

Nonauthoritative restores are used to bring back Active Directory Domain Services to a working state on a DC. The prerequisite for a nonauthoritative restore is that a critical-volume backup exists. A nonauthoritative restore is in order for situations such as lost data that can include updates to passwords for user accounts, computer accounts, and even trusts. Updates to group memberships, policies, the replication topology, and its schedules to name a few. To conduct a nonauthoritative restore follow the same procedures we outlined for the authoritative restore. After the system state is restored, you can go ahead and restart the server when prompted instead of loading ntdsutil. Once a nonauthoritative restore is complete, any changes to Active Directory objects are replicated to the server from ….. that has just gone through a nonauthoritative restore.

Linked Value Replication

When the forest level is at Windows Server 2003 or above, linked value replication (LVR) is available. Previously in Active Directory, primarily with Windows 2000, when an attribute changed the entire attribute was replicated to all other DCs on the network. Now, with LVR, changes in group membership to store and replicate values for individual members instead of replicating the entire membership as a single unit. LVR lowers the amount of bandwidth used in replication and the amount of processor power used during replication.

Backing Up and Restoring GPOs

Backing up a Group Policy Object (GPO) consists of making a copy of the GPO data to the file system. The backup consists of the following data:

- Domain where the GPO resides
- Owner of the GPO
- Date created
- Date modified
- User revisions
- Computer revisions
- Globally unique identifier (GUID)
- GPO status

Exercise 4.9 takes you through the steps of backing up a GPO.

EXERCISE 4.9

BACKING UP THE GPO

You must back up GPOs from the Group Policy Management Console (GPMC). You can get to it by clicking on **Start | Administrative Tools | Group Policy Management**. Let's walk through the process of backing up GPOs:

1. Open the GPMC.

2. In the console tree, click on the plus sign (**+**) next to the forest. In our case, we click on the plus sign next to **Forest:MMA.LOCAL**.

3. Scroll down the tree **Domains | <*Domain Name*> | Group Policy Objects**. In Figure 4.37, you see that we have four GPOs. In reality, you would probably have significantly more, but for demonstration purposes we'll keep it simple.

Figure 4.37 The GPMC

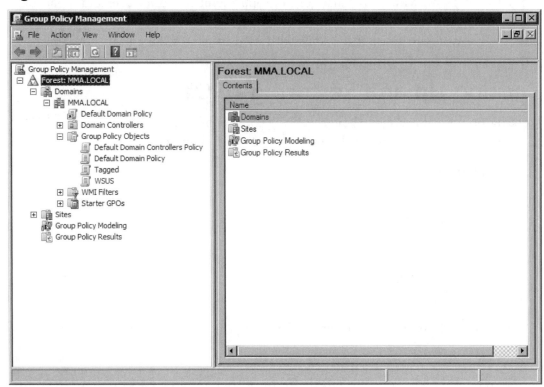

4. Highlight **Group Policy Objects** and right-click it. Select **Back Up All**, as shown in Figure 4.38.

Figure 4.38 Selecting Back Up All

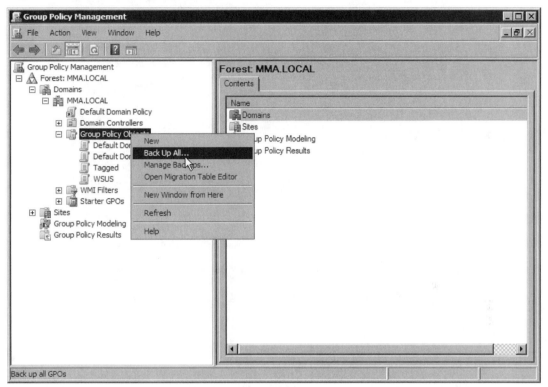

5. When the **Back Up Group Policy Object** screen comes up, as shown in Figure 4.39, set the location to a directory either on a local drive or on a mapped drive on a remote server. In our case, we are backing up our GPOs to the directory C:\GPO Backups. As for a description, you can type anything you want that will remind you what this certain backup pertains to. After you've done this, you can click on **Back Up**.

Figure 4.39 Location to Store Backups

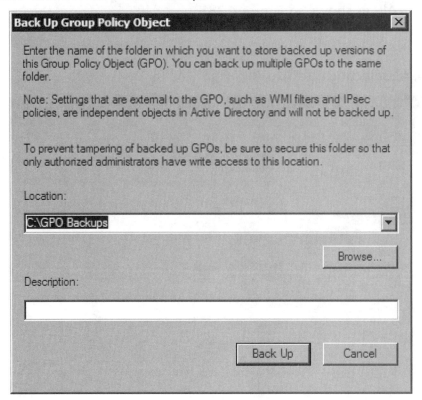

6. Next you'll see the backup progress take place. Once it's finished, it will provide you with the status of the backup for each GPO. As you can see in Figure 4.40, our four GPOs were successfully backed up. Once your GPOs have backed up successfully, just click **OK** to finish.

Figure 4.40 Backup Status

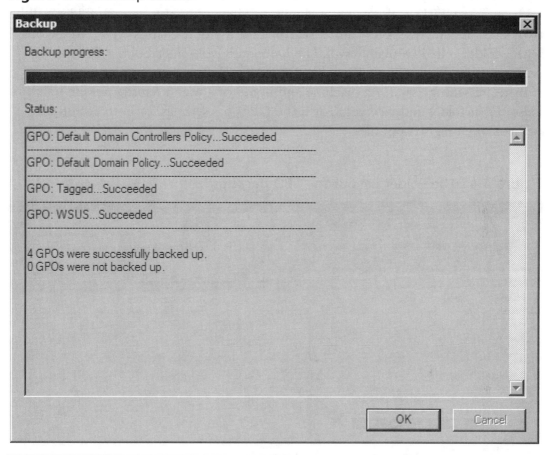

![Exam Warning]

EXAM WARNING

With Windows Server 2008 comes a new type of GPO called Starter GPOs. Starter GPOs are not included in the backup of GPOs; you have to back them up separately. To do so, highlight the **Starter GPOs** folder, right-click it, select **Backup Up All**, and follow the same procedure we went through in Exercise 4.9.

In the directory where we backed up our GPOs, you see that each GPO has a folder with a GUID as the name, as shown in Figure 4.41. Inside each folder will be two XML documents—one named Backup and the other named gpreport—along with a folder called DomainSysvol. The DomainSysvol folder holds a GPO folder with two subfolders—one for machine settings and the other for user settings. If there are settings, say, for a machine and none for a user a registry.pol file will exist in that folder and vice versa, or if the GPO has settings for both each folder will contain a registry.pol file.

Figure 4.41 The Folder Layout for GPO Backups

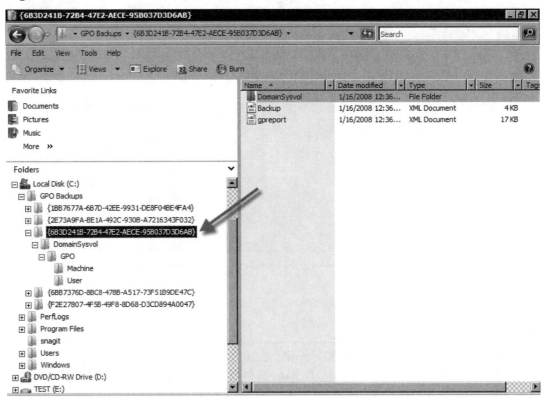

In Figure 4.38, you can see that we have a GPO named **Tagged**. How would we restore that GPO if it were accidentally deleted? The process is quite simple; let's walk through it in Exercise 4.10.

EXERCISE 4.10

RESTORING A GPO

1. Open the GPMC (**Start | Administrative Tools | Group Policy Management**).

2. In the GPMC, go to **Forest:MMA.LOCAL | Domains | MMA.LOCAL | Group Policy Objects** and verify that the GPO has been deleted. In Figure 4.42, you see that the Tagged GPO is no longer there.

Figure 4.42 The Tagged GPO Deleted

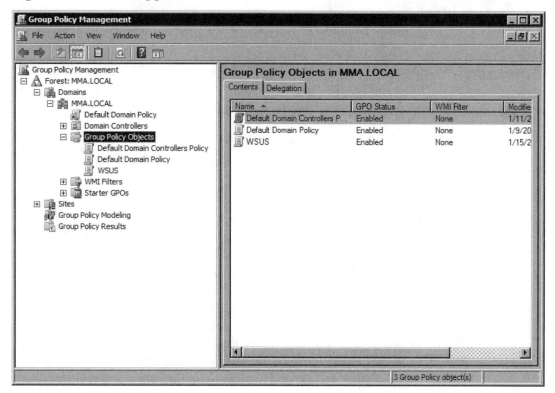

3. In the GPMC, right-click **Group Policy Objects** and select **Manage Backups**, as shown in Figure 4.43.

Figure 4.43 Selecting Manage Backups

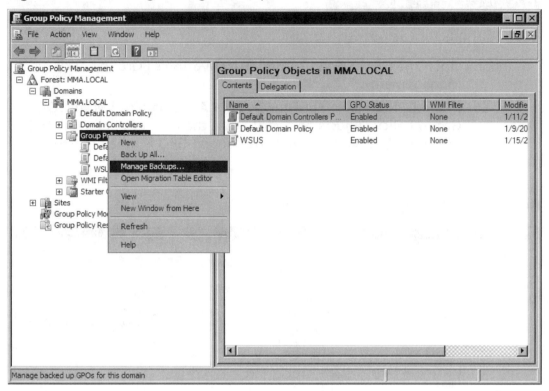

4. In the **Manage Backups** screen shown in Figure 4.44, select the **Tagged** GPO and click **Restore**. You will be asked whether you want to restore the selected backup; choose **OK**. As you'll notice here, we could show only the most up-to-date backups if we wanted to, or we could have all backups come up. We can delete the backup of the GPO(s) and we can view settings from the GPO itself. In the settings you will see items such as the GPO's GUID, whether it is enabled, any links, Security Filtering, WMI Filtering, delegation, and computer and user configuration. The settings will come up as an .htm file and will be shown in Internet Explorer.

Figure 4.44 The Manage Backups Screen

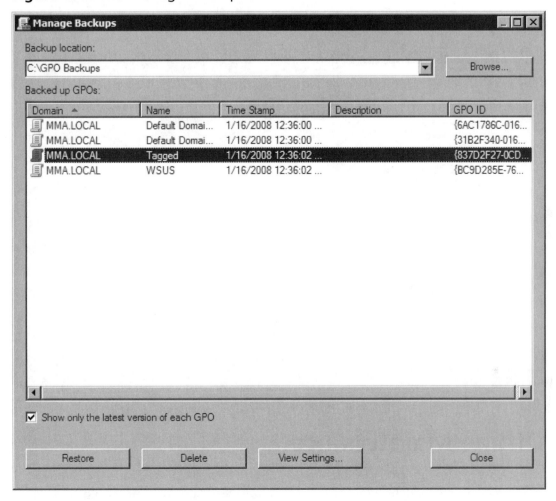

5. Once the restore is complete, the status window should read **Tagged ... Succeeded**. If so, just click **OK**. Then click **Close** in the **Manage Backups** screen.

6. Now looking at the GPOs via the GPMC, you should see that the Tagged GPO has been restored, as shown in Figure 4.45.

Figure 4.45 The Tagged GPO Restored

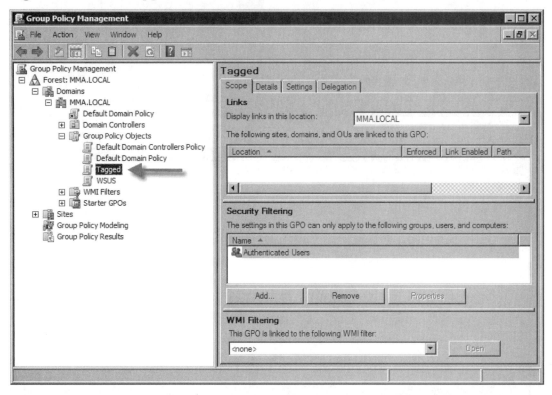

Offline Maintenance

In the past, with Windows 2000 and Windows Server 2003, to do any offline maintenance such as defragging the Active Directory database you would have to reboot and go into the DSRM. If users relied on services such as file and print, the Dynamic Host Configuration Protocol (DHCP), and others they were out of luck until the server was back online. That has now changed under Windows Server 2008. Windows Server 2008 now supports the use of restartable Active Directory Domain Services which brings offline maintenance to a whole new level.

Restartable Active Directory

Restartable Active Directory Domain Services is a new feature in Windows Server 2008. It allows administrators to perform routine maintenance tasks on a DC far quicker and with less interruption than ever before. The key is that Active Directory

Domain Services can be stopped without affecting other services on a DC, such as DHCP and file/print. With the advent of restartable Active Directory Domain Services, DCs running Windows Server 2008 now have three possible states to run in, as shown in Table 4.2.

Table 4.2 Three States of Server 2008 DCs

State	Description
Active Directory Domain Services Started	Active Directory Domain Services is running. Services provided by a DC are running.
Active Directory Domain Services Stopped	Active Directory Domain Services has been stopped. From an administrator's point of view, this provides the ability to perform offline maintenance just like running in DSRM. Maintenance is much faster than having to use DSRM. This primarily will act as a member server while the service is stopped.
Directory Services Restore Mode	This is unchanged from Windows Server 2003, except that an administrator can run *dcpromo /forceremoval* to remove Active Directory Domain Services from that particular DC.

There are some things to keep in mind regarding restartable Active Directory Domain Services. A DC cannot start up with Active Directory Domain Services stopped. If you set the **startup type** to **Disabled** and reboot the server, it will come back with Active Directory Domain Services started and set back to **automatic**. Stopping Active Directory Domain Services also stops the File Replication Service (FRS), Kerberos Key Distribution Center (KDC), intersite messaging, the domain name system (DNS) server (if installed), and Distributed File System (DFS) replication. Restarting Active Directory Domain Services, though, will automatically restart those services as well.

You can stop and start restartable Active Directory Domain Services using the Microsoft Management Console (MMC) via Services or by using the *net.exe* command. Exercise 4.11 runs through stopping and starting Active Directory Domain Services in Windows Server 2008.

EXERCISE 4.11

STOPPING AND STARTING RESTARTABLE ACTIVE DIRECTORY DOMAIN SERVICES

1. Log on to a DC as an administrator.

2. Click **Start | Administrative Tools | Services**.

3. In the list of services, highlight and right-click on **Active Directory Domain Services** and click **Properties**.

4. The service status should read **Started**; just click **Stop**.

5. After you click **Stop**, a window will pop up titled **Stop Other Services**, which you can see in Figure 4.46. This window will inform you of the other services that will also be stopped. Click **Yes** and then **OK**.

Figure 4.46 Services That Stop with Active Directory Domain Services

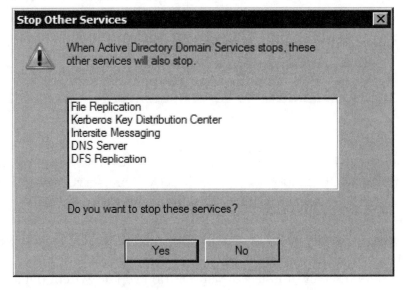

6. Now you will see that Active Directory Domain Services has stopped (see Figure 4.47).

Figure 4.47 Active Directory Domain Services Stopped

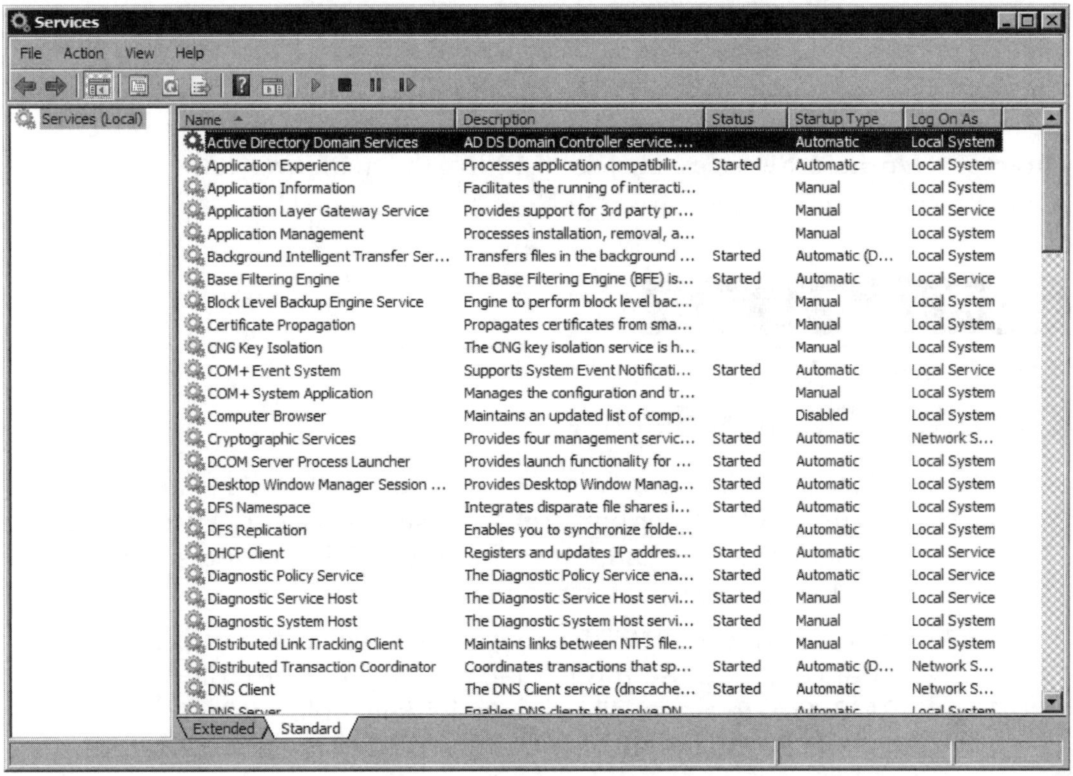

EXAM TIP

In step 3 of Exercise 4.11, you could simply right-click on the Active Directory Domain Services service and select **Stop**. This will stop the service just as well.

Offline Defrag and Compaction

Active Directory's database file is ntds.dit, and it is based on the Extensible Storage Engine (ESE) and is located in C:\Windows\NTDS. One of the biggest reasons, if not the only reason, to defrag/compact the ntds.dit file is if you are running low on disk space. Depending on the size of your environment, the ntds.dit file can grow to more than 6 GB in size, even though the database within it may only be 1 GB. Back in the days of Windows 2000 and Windows Server 2003, we had to perform offline defrags in the DSRM because there was no way to easily shut down Active Directory and perform the defrag. As you've already seen, that has changed, and for the better, in Windows Server 2008. We simply go into **Services** and stop **Active Directory Domain Services**. Exercise 4.12 lists the steps involved in defragging Active Directory in Windows Server 2008.

EXERCISE 4.12

DEFRAGGING ACTIVE DIRECTORY DOMAIN SERVICES

1. Before performing a defrag of ntds.dit, perform a system state backup of the DC or perform a full server backup. Even though we can move or rename the old ntds.dit file, having a backup is essential in case of catastrophe.

2. Go to **C:\Windows\NTDS** and note the size of the ntds.dit file. In our case, because this is a lab machine our ntds.dit file is only 12 MB. Create a new directory to initially hold the new ntds.dit file that will be created during the defragging process. Our directory is C:\Windows\NTDS\defragged.

3. Log on to the server as an administrator and stop the **Active Directory Domain Services** service, as discussed in the preceding section.

4. After Active Directory Domain Services has stopped, open a command prompt (**Start | Command Prompt**), type **ntdsutil**, and press **Enter**.

5. At the ntdsutil prompt, type **Activate Instance ntds** and press **Enter**. You will get a message stating **Active instance set to "ntds"**.

6. At the ntdsutil prompt, type **files** and press **Enter**. This will pull up the **file maintenance** prompt.

7. At the file maintenance prompt, type **info** and press **Enter**. This provides you with information about the location of the ntds.dit file, the backup directory, the working directory, and the log directory. Figure 4.48 shows an example.

Figure 4.48 The Drive and DS Path Information

```
Administrator: Command Prompt - ntdsutil                          _ □ ×

C:\Users\Administrator>ntdsutil
ntdsutil: activate instance ntds
Active instance set to "ntds".
ntdsutil: files
file maintenance: info

Drive Information:

        C:\ NTFS (Fixed Drive  ) free(2.7 Gb) total(24.9 Gb)
        E:\ NTFS (Fixed Drive  ) free(13.7 Gb) total(19.9 Gb)
        F:\ NTFS (Fixed Drive  ) free(14.5 Gb) total(34.9 Gb)
        Z:\ NTFS (Network Drive) free(25.7 Gb) total(74.5 Gb)

DS Path Information:

        Database   : C:\Windows\NTDS\ntds.dit - 12.1 Mb
        Backup dir : C:\Windows\NTDS\dsadata.bak
        Working dir: C:\Windows\NTDS
        Log dir    : C:\Windows\NTDS - 30.0 Mb total
                     edbres00002.jrs - 10.0 Mb
                     edbres00001.jrs - 10.0 Mb
                     edb.log - 10.0 Mb
file maintenance: _
```

8. At the file maintenance prompt, type **compact to c:\windows\ ntds\defragged** and press **Enter**. The defrag process will run. The larger your ntds.dit file is, the longer the defrag process will take. Figure 4.49 shown an example of a successful defrag.

Figure 4.49 A Successful Defrag

```
Administrator: Command Prompt                                     _ □ ×

Initiating DEFRAGMENTATION mode...
     Source Database: C:\Windows\NTDS\ntds.dit
     Target Database: c:\windows\ntds\defragged\ntds.dit

            Defragmentation  Status (% complete)

     0   10   20   30   40   50   60   70   80   90  100
     !----!----!----!----!----!----!----!----!----!----!
     ..................................................

It is recommended that you immediately perform a full backup
of this database. If you restore a backup made before the
defragmentation, the database will be rolled back to the state
it was in at the time of that backup.

Compaction is successful. You need to:
   copy "c:\windows\ntds\defragged\ntds.dit" "C:\Windows\NTDS\ntds.dit"
and delete the old log files:
   del C:\Windows\NTDS\*.log

file maintenance: q
ntdsutil: q

C:\Users\Administrator>
```

9. After the defrag has completed, type **q** at the file maintenance prompt and do the same at the ntdsutil prompt. This should bring you back to a normal C prompt; you can close the command prompt at this time.

10. Go to the **C:\Windows\NTDS** folder and either rename the ntds.dit file there or delete it.

11. Go to the **defragged** directory and move the ntds.dit file from there to the **C:\Windows\NTDS** directory.

12. In the **C:\Windows\NTDS** directory, rename or delete the **edb.log** file.

13. Go back to **Services** and **restart** Active Directory Domain Services. After it restarts, you're finished.

Active Directory Storage Allocation

As you've learned, the ntds.dit file can get quite large. With this comes concern regarding available drive space. To conserve drive space, we've already walked through defragging and compacting the ntds.dit file. Sometimes that's not enough, and you have to move it and its log files to another drive or partition. Before doing this, you have to confirm the size of the files in the C:\Windows\NTDS folder. You need to check the amount of drive space used by the files in the directory when Active Directory Domain Services is online and offline, because the files that are offline are what you will actually move, but when Active Directory Domain Services is back online the amount of drive space increases.

So, why is there a difference in the amount of space used in C:\Windows\NTDS when Active Directory Domain Services is offline versus online? The answer is quite simple: Active Directory will create a temp.edb file and you have to consider that when determining the amount of space to allocate to Active Directory. Here are some scenarios in which you would determine storage allocation for Active Directory:

- **NTDS.DIT only** The size of the file plus an additional 20% of the current file size or 500 MB, whichever is greater

- **Log files only** The combined size of the log files plus 20% of the combined logs or 500 MB, whichever is greater

- **NTDS.DIT and log files** If the database file and the logs are located on the same partition, the free space should be at least 20% of the combined NTDS.DIT and log files, or 1 GB, whichever is greater

Monitoring Active Directory

Monitoring Active Directory is a key in making sure that objects and attributes are up-to-date and consistent among DCs, whether they are local to each other or located at different sites. One area to monitor is replication between the DCs. To do this we use tools such as Network Monitor, the Event Viewer, replmon, and repadmin. We also need to ensure the performance of the DCs so that they are able to authenticate and replicate in a timely manner by using tools such as the Task Manager, systems resource manager, reliability and performance monitor, and the Event Viewer. Let's examine each of these tools.

The Network Monitor

It's important for administrators to keep tabs on network traffic that's flowing across the network. Monitoring the network has allowed administrators to have a better understanding of how the bandwidth on their networks is being utilized. Network Monitor from Microsoft is such a tool. It is a protocol analyzer that allows administrators to capture network traffic, and then view and analyze it. Administrators can see things such as DHCP requests, DNS name resolutions, Hypertext Transfer Protocol (HTTP), and so on. As of this writing, Network Monitor Version 3.1 runs on Windows Server 2008. It does not ship with Active Directory, but you can download it from www.microsoft.com/downloads/details.aspx?FamilyID=18b1d59d-f4d8-4213-8d17-2f6dde7d7aac&displaylang=en.

To start Network Monitor just click **Start | Microsoft Network Monitor 3.1 | Microsoft Network Monitor 3.1**. You will see the **Start Page** shown in Figure 4.50. Here you can create a new capture or open an existing one. You will also notice the Welcome screen to the right, which will mention all the changes in Network Monitor. In addition to the Start Page tab, you will see the Parsers tab, which allows you to parse packs. Network Monitor applies knowledge of the structure of the various protocols to the hex data contained in the packets and displays the resultant interpretation.

Figure 4.50 The Network Monitor

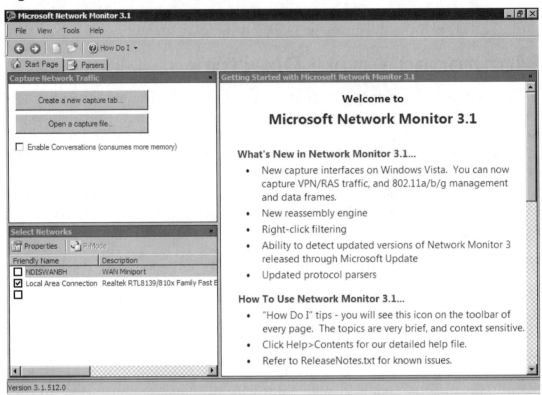

Although we can't actually see the information transmitted across the wire for Active Directory replication, we can see things such as when a new DC comes up and queries DNS for an existing Lightweight Directory Access Protocol (LDAP) server at the **Default-First-Site-Name** sight. Figure 4.51 shows this in the **Display Filter**.

Figure 4.51 The Display Filter in Network Monitor 3.1

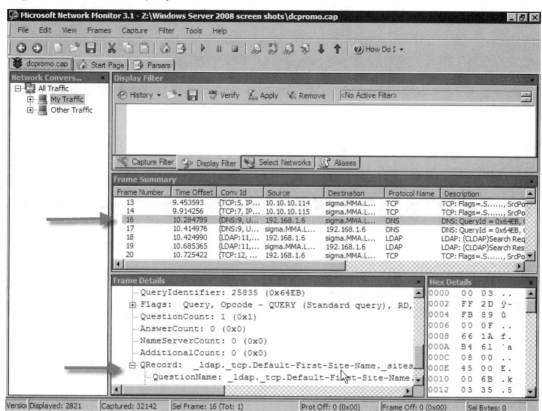

Figure 4.51 represents a snapshot of what was happening when a member server was running DCPROMO and was being promoted to a DC. In the figure, the new DC (192.168.1.6) performs a DNS query to SIGMA.MMA.LOCAL, wanting the information about the LDAP server at that site. The DNS server, in this case SIGMA.MMA.LOCAL, responds with the A record and a type SRV of _ldap._tcp.Default-First-Site-Name. As you can see in Figure 4.52, it informs the new DC (192.168.1.6) that the resource name is SIGMA.MMA.LOCAL and that the Internet Protocol (IP) address is 10.10.10.8. In this example, it just so happens that the LDAP server at this site is also the DNS server. In some instances it may not be, depending on the environment.

Figure 4.52 The Response to the DNS Query

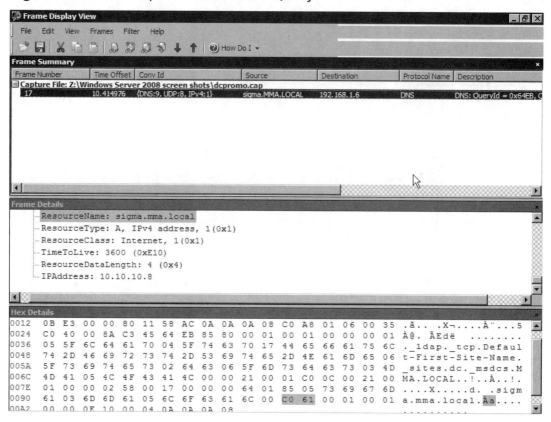

To get the view in Figure 4.52, we highlighted the **Frame Number** in the **Frame Summary** and right-clicked on it, and then chose **View Selected Frame(s) in a New Window**. This made it easier for us to read the DNS server's response. Alternatively, we could have right-clicked the Frame Number and selected **Copy**, **Copy Cell Value**, **Copy Cell as Filter**, **Add Cell to Display Filter**, **Parse Frame as XML**, **View Selected Frame(s) in a New Window**, or **Add Selected Frame(s) To**.

As you can see, a tool such as Network Monitor can be valuable in determining what is actually happening on the wire and where problems may arise.

The Task Manager

You can monitor the load and performance of DCs through the Task Manager, which hasn't changed much since Windows Server 2003. The Task Manager shown in Figure 4.53 can show administrators what may be causing slow logons for users, along with what processes and executables are using resources, causing strain on a DC. You can pull up the Task Manager in quite a few ways. The easiest way is to just click **Start | Run** and type **taskmgr.exe** and press **Enter**. Other ways to launch the Task Manager include right-clicking the **task bar** and selecting **Task Manager**, pressing **Ctrl + Shift + Esc**, and pressing **Ctrl + Alt + Delete** and selecting **Start Task Manager**.

Figure 4.53 The Task Manager

The Task Manager is very useful for administrators looking for an immediate view of resources such as processor activity, process activity, network activity, memory usage, resource consumption, and even user information. A Services tab has been added to the Task Manager, along with a Services button that allows administrators to pull up the Services Management Console. Another big change is the Resource Monitor button within the Performance tab. Let's briefly go over each tab in the Task Manager.

The Applications Tab

The first tab in the Task Manager is the Applications tab, which lists all the tasks and programs currently running on the server and their status. The status of programs will be either **Running** or **Not Responding**. However, when an application's status is at Not Responding, it may be waiting for a process to respond, in which case it could return to a Running state. If an application remains at a Not Responding state for some time, an administrator can simply right-click the application in the list and choose **End Task**, as shown in Figure 4.54.

Figure 4.54 Ending a Task

Figure 4.54 shows other options as well. By selecting **Switch To** you can switch to a different running task. Selecting **Bring To Front** will bring that application/task to the front of the desktop. You can use **Create Dump File** for a point-in-time snapshot of whatever process you need to examine for more advanced troubleshooting.

The Processes Tab

The Processes tab provides a list of processes that are currently running on the server. These processes are measured by performance by such things as **CPU**, **User Name** (or the context under which the image is running), and **Memory** (Private Working Set), among others. Administrators can sort out what processes are using the most or least CPU cycles by clicking on CPU and Memory column headers. You can shut down a process by right-clicking the process name and selecting **End Process**. You also can add other columns; for instance, you can add a PID column by clicking on **View | Select Columns** and choosing **PID (Process Identifier)**, and then clicking **OK**. Figure 4.55 shows the results.

Figure 4.55 Adding a PID Column

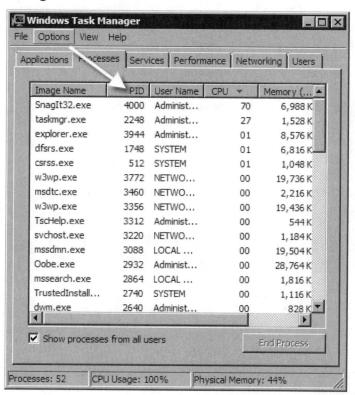

The Services Tab

The newest tab in the Task Manager—but one that's been overdue—is the Services tab. With this tab, administrators can quickly assess and troubleshoot a specific service by viewing its status. By default, it shows the service's name, PID, description, status, and group. As mentioned earlier, you can even launch the Services Console by clicking on the **Services** button in the bottom-right corner, as shown in Figure 4.56.

Figure 4.56 The Services Tab

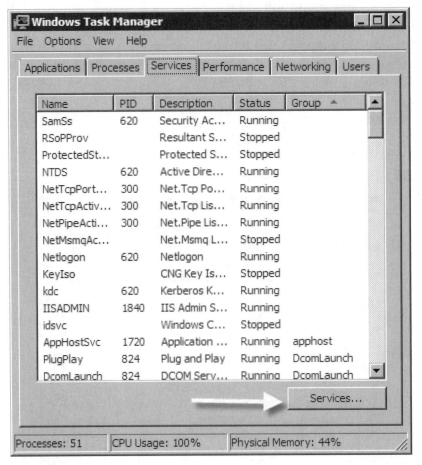

The Performance Tab

The Performance tab allows administrators to view CPU and physical memory usage in an easier-to-understand/graphical manner. It is very useful when an administrator needs a quick analysis of how the system is running. The Performance tab shows CPU usage in a real-time manner, while also showing a brief usage history.

It does the same for memory usage as well. By default, the Performance tab shows usage by User Mode processes and threads. If you want to see Kernel Mode usage as well, all you have to do is click on **View | Show Kernel Times**. You will then see kernel mode operations in red in the CPU Usage area. If your server has multiple processors, you will be able to view each individual processor and its corresponding graph. Notice in Figure 4.57 a button in the bottom right labeled Resource Monitor. By clicking on this, you can perform even more analysis. We will cover the System Resource Monitor a little later.

Figure 4.57 The Performance Tab

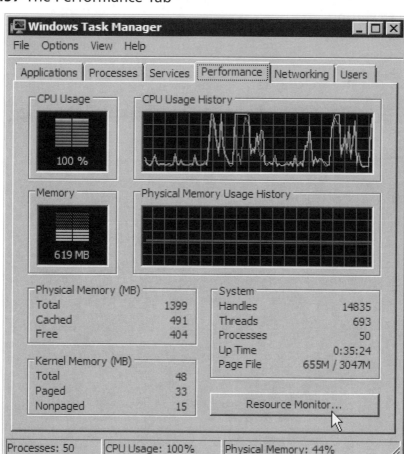

The Networking Tab

The Networking tab provides information about network traffic for each adapter in a particular server. Multiple adapters and adapter types are supported. For instance, you could have a LAN connection, a virtual private network (VPN) connection, and a dial-up connection all showing up as separate adapters. The Networking tab will show a graphical comparison of the traffic for any connection a server has. Administrators are able to get information about network utilization, link speed, and even the state of the connection. You can examine network traffic in the graph in terms of bytes sent, bytes received, and the total number of bytes simply by clicking **View | Network Adapter History** and selecting what you want. As with many of the other tabs in the Task Manager, you can add more columns to widen your analysis. Simply click **View | Select Columns** and select the column(s) you need. In Figure 4.58, you see that we have added the column **Adapter Description**.

Figure 4.58 The Networking Tab

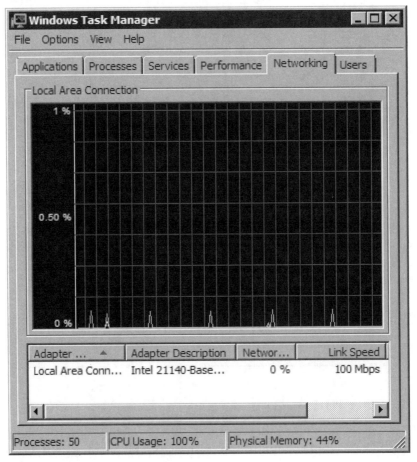

The Users Tab

The last tab in the Task Manager is the Users tab. It displays the users who are connected to or logged on to the server. It provides user, ID, status, client name, and session information by default. Although there are no additional columns to add, you can remove any you feel are unnecessary. Figure 4.59 shows that the only user connected to this server is the administrator and that he is at the console.

Figure 4.59 The Users Tab

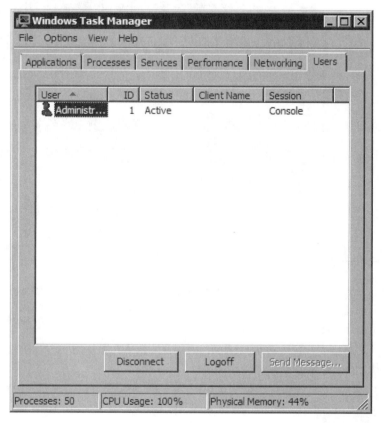

The Event Viewer

The Event Viewer is traditionally the first place to look when troubleshooting anything in Windows (see Figure 4.52). You can access the Event Viewer by clicking on **Start | Administrative Tools | Event Viewer**. This tool which has stood the test of time since the days of NT 3.1 has been completely rewritten and is based on XML. Many new features, functionality, and even a new interface have been added to the Event Viewer in Windows Server 2008. Figure 4.60 shows the new interface for the Event Viewer, taken from MMC Version 3.0.

Figure 4.60 The Event Viewer

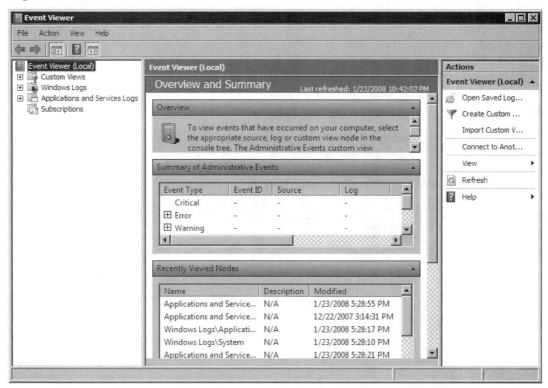

Looking at Figure 4.60, you'll notice that the Event Viewer consists of Custom Views, Windows Logs, Applications and Services Logs, and Subscriptions. Let's examine each of these more closely.

Custom Views

Custom Views in the Event Viewer are filters created by either Windows Server 2008 or an administrator to the system. Custom views created by Windows

Server 2008 can happen when a server takes on a new role such as a DC running Active Directory Domain Services or installs a feature such as DNS. Administrators are able to create filters that target only the events they are interested in viewing. In Exercise 4.13, we'll create a custom view in the Event Viewer. To create a custom view in the Event Viewer, right-click **Custom Views** and select **Create Custom View**.

EXERCISE 4.13

CREATING A CUSTOM VIEW

1. Open the Event Viewer by clicking **Start | Administrative Tools | Event Viewer**.

2. In the Event Viewer, right-click **Custom Views** and select **Create Custom View**.

3. Next, the **Create Custom View** form comes up. In the **Logged** drop-down list choose when you want events logged. For instance, you can choose to do **Any time**, **Last hour**, **Last 12 hours**, **Last 24 hours**, **Last 7 days**, **Last 30 days**, or a **Custom range**. When choosing **Custom range** you decide the date and time from the first event to the date and time of the last event. You can even choose the actual time. For our example, we chose **Last 30 days** for this exercise.

4. Next, choose the **Event level** you want to include. These are the same old standbys we've seen in previous versions of Windows: **Critical**, **Warning**, **Verbose**, **Error**, and **Information**. For our example, we'll select only **Warning**.

5. After you have decided on the **Event level**, you need to choose the event log(s) or the specific event sources to filter by. We'll simply choose **By log** and select **System** found beneath **Windows Logs**.

6. If you know exactly what event IDs you want to filter you can do that by simply typing the event ID(s). Because we don't, we'll leave it at *<All Event IDs>*. For **Keywords**, we can click on the pull-down menu and see a list of keywords from which to choose. We can enter any particular user or computer we like. For our example, we will only specify the server SIGMA in the **Computer(s)** line. Your **Create Custom View** should appear like the one in Figure 4.61. When you're done, click **OK**.

Figure 4.61 Creating a Custom View

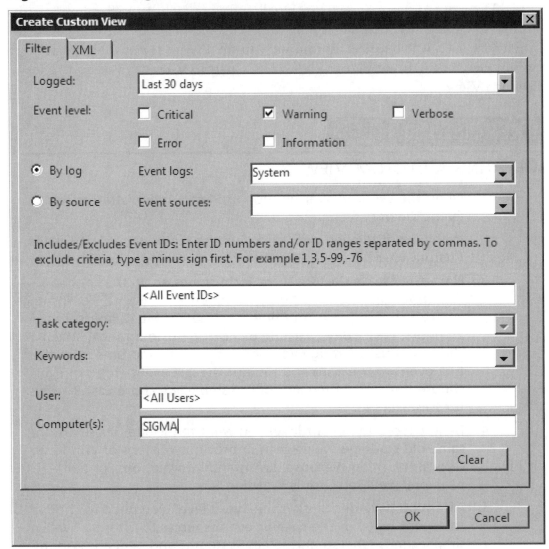

7. Next, you come to **Save Filter to Custom View**. You can choose a name to call your filter and provide a description if you like. You also get to choose where you want your custom view saved. For our example, the name will be SIGMA SysLog Warn and we'll allow it to be saved in the default location.

In Figure 4.62, you see we have created our custom view SIGMA SysLog Warn and that there are five events in it. Your server will probably have different warnings than the one shown in the figure.

Figure 4.62 A Newly Created Custom View

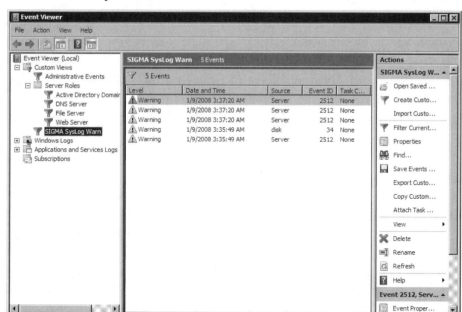

Windows Logs

Underneath the Windows Logs folder are the traditional logs we've seen before, with two new ones added. Table 4.3 provides a brief description of each log.

Table 4.3 Windows Logs

Log	Description
Application	Contains events from applications residing on the system
Security	Captures authentication and object access events that are audited
Setup	New log that captures events tailored around the installation of applications, server roles, and features
System	Events built around Windows system components are logged here
Forwarded Events	Consolidates and stores events that were captured from remote systems and sent to a single log to facilitate the identification, isolation, and solving of problems

Applications and Services Logs

There is a new category of event logs in Windows Server 2008: the Applications and Services logs. In Figure 4.62, you can see them just below the Windows Logs folder. These logs store events from a single application or component rather events like the logs underneath Windows Logs. You can find four subtypes of logs here: Admin, Operational, Analytic, and Debug. Admin logs are tailored more for users and administrators looking to troubleshoot problems. The events in the Admin log will provide administrators with information and guidance regarding how to respond. Events found in the Operational log are more likely to require more interpretation but can be helpful as well.

The Analytic and Debug logs are not user-friendly. You can use Analytic logs to trace an issue, and therefore a high number of events are logged. Developers use the Debug logs when debugging applications. The Analytic and Debug logs are hidden and disabled by default in Windows Server 2008. To show these logs select **Event Viewer | View | Show Analytic and Debug Logs**. Remember that this only shows the logs; it does not enable them. To enable the Analytic and Debug logs, make sure they are not hidden and then highlight the Analytic or Debug log you want to enable. Click on **Action | Properties** and in the **Log Properties** screen, shown in Figure 4.63, select **Enable logging** and click **OK**. You can also enable these logs via the command line by typing **wevutil sl *<logname>* /e:true**.

Figure 4.63 Enabling an Analytic Log

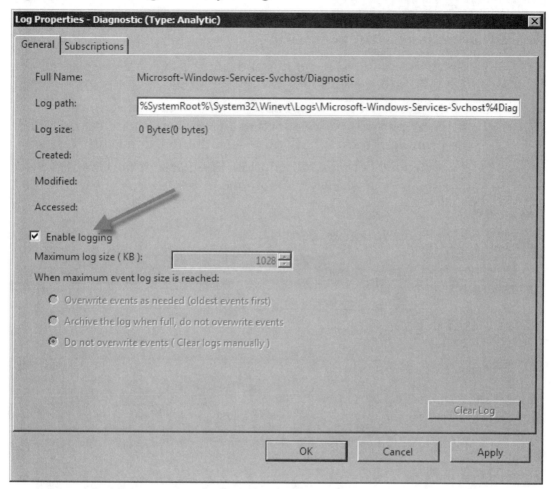

Subscriptions

The last folder shown in the Event Viewer is also a new feature in Windows Server 2008, called Subscriptions. The Subscriptions folder allows remote servers to forward events so that they can be locally viewed at a central station. A subscription specifies exactly what events will be collected and to which log they will be stored. Once collected, data from a subscription can be viewed and manipulated just as though it came directly from the server from which you're examining them. To use subscriptions, you must configure both the forwarding and collecting servers. Both the Windows Remote Management (WinRM) and Windows Event Collector (Wecsvc) services are required. Exercise 4.14 teaches how to create a new subscription.

EXERCISE 4.14

CREATING A NEW SUBSCRIPTION

1. Go to the collector computer and run the **Event Viewer** as an administrator.

2. In the Event Viewer click **Subscriptions** in the console tree. If the **Windows Event Collector** service is not running, you will be prompted to run it; if you receive this message click **Yes**.

3. Click **Actions | Create Subscription**. The **Subscription Properties** box appears, as shown in Figure 4.64.

Figure 4.64 The Subscription Properties Box

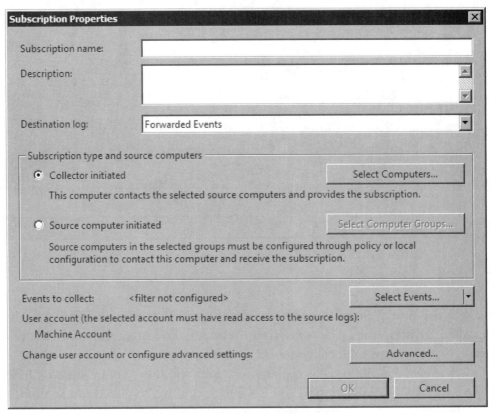

4. In the **Subscription name** box, type a name for the subscription. For our example, we chose **Test** as the name.

5. In the **Description** box, type an optional description for the subscription. We typed **Test subscription** for ours.

6. At the **Destination log** drop-down list, select the log file where the collected events are to be stored. The default, as you see in Figure 4.64, is **Forwarded Events**. For our example, we will accept the default.

7. Under **Subscription type and source computers**, choose the default of **Collector initiated** and click **Select Computers**.

8. In the **Computers** screen, click **Add Domain Computers**. You will now be asked to type the name of the computer(s) from which you would like to collect information. For our scenario, we typed **FMEA**. Click **Check Names** to verify and then click **OK** to continue.

9. Now the **Computers** screen will look like Figure 4.65, and you will see the computer we just selected. If it is correct click **OK** then **OK** again at the **Subscription Properties** screen.

Figure 4.65 The Computer Selected for Subscription

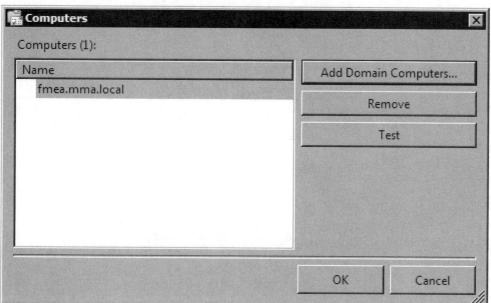

10. Now click **Select Events** and you should see the Query Filter. The Query Filter will be exactly like the Create Custom View you saw in Figure 4.61. For our example, we will choose **Any time** for

Logged, and **Critical, Warning,** and **Error** for **Event Level**. We will choose **By log** and the **Application** for **Event logs**. Everything else will remain the same, as shown in Figure 4.66. Now click **OK**.

Figure 4.66 The Query Filter

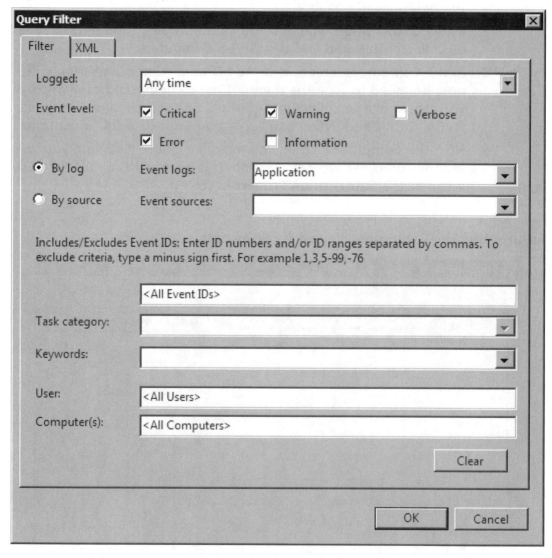

11. Now just go to the source server (the one that will forward events) and open a command prompt. In the command prompt, type **winrm quickconfig** and press **Enter**. On the collector server, at a command prompt type **wecutil qc** and press **Enter**.

12. Now add the collector server to the Administrators local group of the computer, and that's it!

Replmon

Replication Monitor, better known as Replmon, is a GUI tool that you can install with the Support Tools found on the Windows Server 2008 DVD. This tool enables administrators to view the detailed status of Active Directory replication. It also allows administrators to force synchronization between DCs, view the topology in an easier-to-understand graphical format, and monitor the status and performance of DC replication. Replmon is useful but not limited to the following:

- Noticing when a replication partner fails

- Viewing the history of both failed and successful replication

- Viewing the properties of directory replication partners

- Generating status reports including direct and transitive replication partners along with detailing a record of changes

- Displaying replication topology

- Forcing replication

- Triggering the Knowledge Consistency Checker (KCC) to recalculate the replication topology

- Displaying a list of trust relationships maintained by a DC that is being monitored

- Monitoring the replication status of DCs from multiple forests

Using Replmon

To use replmon you must be logged on to a DC. Once logged on, select **Start | Run** and type **replmon.exe** and press **Enter**. Replmon will then come up with a fairly blank page, as shown in Figure 4.67.

Figure 4.67 Replmon's Default Screen

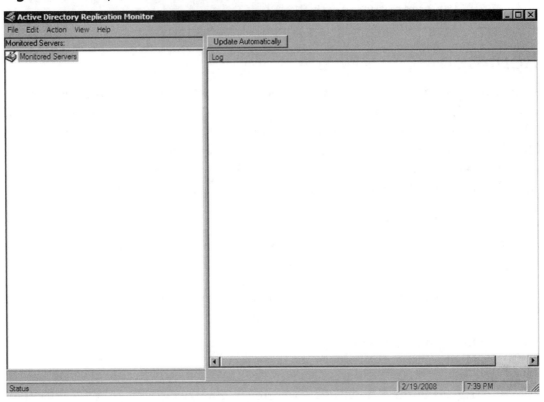

Right-click on the **Monitored Servers** icon in the upper left. You now have the option to **Add Monitored Server**. In the **Add Monitored Server Wizard** you have the choice to explicitly type in the name of the DC you want to add or enter a name of a domain within the forest from which to read site data. Figure 4.68 shows that we have decided to search the directory for a server and that our domain is MMA.LOCAL. Once you've done this select **Next**.

Figure 4.68 The Add Monitored Server Wizard

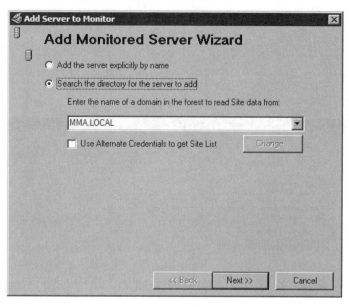

At the next screen, you see a list of sites that are available from Active Directory. You can expand a site and select any particular server located there. In Figure 4.69, you see that we have chosen to monitor a DC out of the South-Region called FMEA. Once you've done this you can click **Finish**.

Figure 4.69 Selecting a DC to Monitor

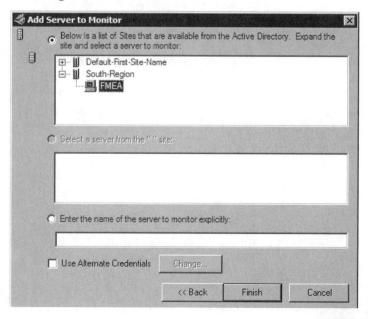

In Figure 4.70, you see that the DC we're monitoring has five directory partitions displayed. Underneath each partition you see this DC's replication partner. In this case, it is a DC called SIGMA. Normally, if there are any replication issues you will see a red *X* underneath the partition(s) where the problem exists. In Figure 4.71, we show the replication status of the Schema and the Update Sequence Number (USN).

Figure 4.70 Directory Partitions

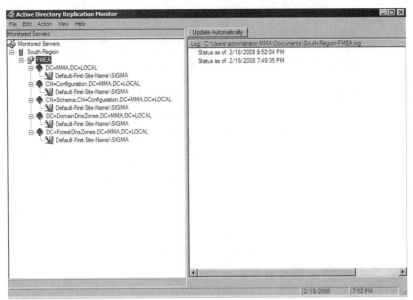

Figure 4.71 Viewing the Logs Pane in Replmon

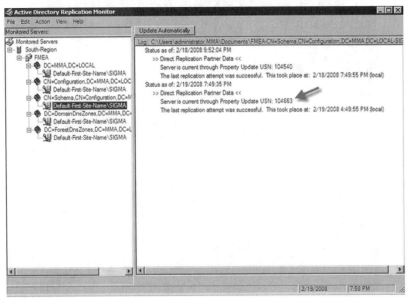

If you right-click the server, you will see a list of options you have in replmon, as shown in Figure 4.72.

Figure 4.72 Replmon Options

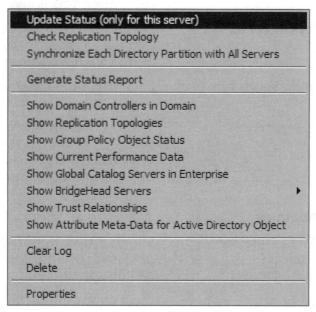

Table 4.4 lists the options and their descriptions.

Table 4.4 Replmon Options Described

Option	Description
Update Status (only for this server)	Rechecks the replication status of the server. The time of the updated status is logged and displayed.
Check Replication Topology	Causes the KCC to recalculate the replication topology for the server
Synchronize Each Directory Partition with All Servers	Starts an immediate replication for all of the server's directory partitions with each replication partner
Show Domain Controllers in Domain	Lists all known DCs

Continued

Table 4.4 Continued. Replmon Options Described

Option	Description
Show Replication Topologies	Shows a graphical view of the replication topology
Show Group Policy Object Status	Lists all the Domain's Group Policies and their respective Active Directory and SYSVOL version numbers
Show Global Catalog Servers in Enterprise	Lists all Global Catalog servers
Show Bridgehead Servers	Two options are available: In This Server's Site and In the Enterprise. Will show bridgehead servers based on information provided by the monitored DC.
Show Trust Relationships	Will show all trusts with this domain
Show Attribute Meta-Data for Active Directory Object	Shows attribute data for a particular object specified using that object's distinguished name (DN)
Clear Log	Clears the *<site-dcname>*.log file
Delete	Deletes the DC from the monitored servers list
Properties	Shows server properties of the monitored DC. Provides information such as Flexible Single Manager Operation (FSMO) roles for the domain (shown in Figure 4.73), inbound replication connections, Transmission Control Protocol/Internet Protocol (TCP/IP) configuration, server flags, and other general information.

Figure 4.73 The FSMO Roles Tab in Server Properties

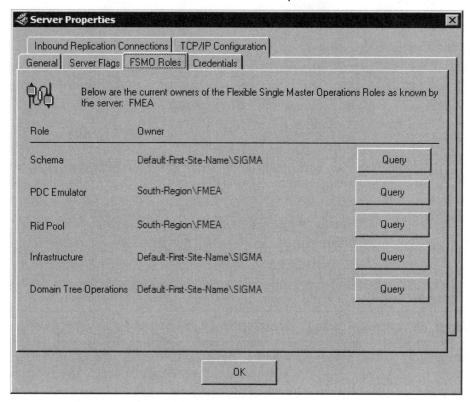

Replmon is a very useful and powerful tool in troubleshooting replication issues and for just finding information about a domain.

Head of the Class...

Support Tools

After installing Windows Server 2008, it is highly recommended that you install the support tools that reside on the installation media, allowing you immediate access to tools such as replmon.

RepAdmin

Another tool that comes with the installation of Windows Server 2008 is the command-line tool **RepAdmin**. Administrators can use RepAdmin to view replication topology, create replication topology, and force replication, whether it is for the entire directory or for specific portions of it. You also can use RepAdmin for monitoring an Active Directory forest. You must run the RepAdmin command in an elevated prompt, either by right-clicking the **Command Prompt** and then clicking **Run as administrator** or simply by logging on as an administrator and running it. You must also have administrative rights on every DC that RepAdmin targets. For instance, Domain Admins can run RepAdmin on any DC in the domain. Enterprise Admins can run RepAdmin on any DC in the forest. Here is the syntax for RepAdmin; Table 4.5 lists the commands:

*Repadmin <cmd> <args> [/u: {domain\user}] [/pw:{password | *}] [/retry [:<retries>] [:<delay>]] [/csv]*

Table 4.5 RepAdmin Commands

Command/Parameters	Description
Repadmin /kcc	Forces the KCC to immediately recalculate the inbound replication topology from the targeted DCs.
	Example: *repadmin /kcc site:south*
	The preceding command triggers the KCC to run on each DC in the south site.
Repadmin /prp	Specifies the Password Replication Policy (PRP) for read-only DCs (RODCs).
	Example: *repadmin /prp view SIGMA reveal*
	The preceding command lists the users whose passwords are currently cached on the DC named SIGMA.
Repadmin /queue	Shows the inbound replication requests that the DC must issue to become consistent with its source replication partners.
	Example: *repadmin /queue FMEA*
	The preceding command returns the queue of inbound replication requests that a bridgehead server named FMEA has yet to process.

Continued

Table 4.5 Continued. RepAdmin Commands

Command/Parameters	Description
Repadmin /replicate	Triggers immediate replication of the specified directory partition to a target DC from a source DC. Example: *repadmin /replicate SIGMA FMEA DC=MMA, DC=com* The preceding command replicates the MMA naming context from the SIGMA DC to the FMEA DC.
Repadmin /replsingleobj	Replicates a single object between two DCs that share common directory partitions. Example: *repadmin /replsingleobj SIGMA FMEA cn=swhitley, ou=sales, dc=MMA, dc=com* The preceding command triggers replication of the *swhitley* object from the SIGMA DC to the FMEA DC.
Repadmin /replsummary	Identifies DCs that are failing inbound replication or outbound replication and summarizes the results in a report. Example: *repadmin /replsum * /bysrc /bydest /sort:delta* The preceding command targets all DCs in the forest to retrieve summary replication status from each.
Repadmin /rodcpwdrepl	Triggers the replication of passwords for the specified users from the source DC to one or more RODCs. Example: *repadmin /rodcpwdrepl dest-rodc* source-dc cn=swhitley, ou=sales, dc=MMA, dc=com* The preceding command triggers replication of the passwords for the user swhitley from the source DC named source-dc to all RODCs that have the name prefix dest-rodc.
Repadmin /showattr	Displays the attributes of an object Example: *repadmin /showattr SIGMA "cn=accountants, cn=users, dc=MMA, dc=com"*

Continued

Table 4.5 Continued. RepAdmin Commands

Command/Parameters	Description
	The preceding command queries the SIGMA DC and shows all attributes for the above object using its DN.
Repadmin /showobjmeta	Displays the replication metadata for a specified object in Active Directory Domain Services. It can be an attribute ID, version number, originating and local USNs, the GUID of the originating server, and even a date and timestamp
	Example: *repadmin /showobjmeta SIGMA "<GUID=6f3427ba-g25c-5e85-c129-125bbc897d23>"*
	The preceding command targets the SIGMA DC and requests the replication metadata for an object by specifying its GUID.
Repadmin /showrepl	Displays the replication status when the specified DC last attempted to perform inbound replication on Active Directory partitions.
	Example: *repadmin /showrepl * /errorsonly*
	The preceding command reports inbound replication status for all DCs in the forest that are experiencing a replication error.
Repadmin /showutdvec	Displays the highest committed USN that Active Directory Domain Services, on the targeted DC, shows as committed for itself and its transitive partners.
	Example: *repadmin /showutdvec dc=MMA, dc=com*
	The preceding command shows the highest committed USN on the local DC for the MMA.com directory partition.
Repadmin /syncall	Synchronizes a specified DC with all replication partners.

Continued

Table 4.5 Continued. RepAdmin Commands

Command/Parameters	Description
	Example: *repadmin /syncall FMEA dc=MMA, dc=com /d /e /a*
	The preceding command synchronizes the target DC with all its partners, including DCs at other sites.

Windows System Resource Manager

Sometimes an application, process, or service will take up a majority of the CPU cycles to the point that it affects everything else running on the server. To combat that Microsoft has provided a feature in Windows Server 2008 called Windows System Resource Manager (WSRM). WSRM provides an interface where administrators can configure how both processor and memory resources are allocated among applications, services, and processes. The ability to do this allows administrators to ensure server stability. To install WSRM do the following:

1. Log on to a Windows Server 2008 system and launch **Server Manager**.

2. In **Server Manager**, click **Features** in the console pane on the left side and choose **Add Features** in the **Details** pane.

3. Next, the **Select Features** box opens. Scroll down to **Windows System Resource Manager** and select it. Then click **Next**.

4. At the **Confirm Installation Selections** screen, verify the feature you are installing and then click **Install**.

5. After the installation is finished, just click **Close** and you're done.

WSRM uses resource allocation policies to allocate CPU time and memory usage among applications, services, processes, and even users. These resource allocation policies can be in effect all the time or you can run them on a scheduled basis. WSRM policies, though, are enforced only when CPU usage goes above 70% and are never active on processes owned by the operating system or items in the exclusion list.

If and when certain events take place or the system behaves differently, WSRM can switch to a different policy and ensure system stability. If accounting is enabled in WSRM, administrators of the servers can examine the data collected and determine when and why resource allocation policies were either too restrictive or too lax. Administrators can adjust resource allocation policies using the information obtained by accounting.

There are four predefined resource allocation policies with WSRM in Windows Server 2008. These predefined policies make it easy for administrators to quickly allocate resources. Table 4.6 shows the predefined resource allocation policies.

Table 4.6 WSRM Predefined Policies

Policy	Description
Equal per Process	Resources are equally allocated among all running processes, thus preventing one process from monopolizing all available CPU and memory resources.
Equal per User	Resources are equally allocated among all users, thus preventing one user from monopolizing all available CPU and memory resources.
Equal per Session	Resources are equally allocated among all Terminal Services sessions, thus preventing one session from monopolizing all available CPU and memory resources.
Equal per IIS Application Pool	Resources are allocated equally among all IIS application pools, thus preventing one application pool from monopolizing all available CPU and memory resources.

Matching criteria is a common task performed with WSRM. Administrators use these rules to include or exclude processes, services, or applications that WSRM needs to monitor. These rules are used later in the WSRM management process.

Custom resource allocation policies are similar to matching criteria rules in that they look for specific processes, services, and application criteria. The custom resource allocation policy provides an administrator with the ability to define how much of a resource should be allocated to a specific process, service, or application. For instance, if only 15% of the system processing should be reserved to the sqlwriter.exe process, the resource allocation would be defined to limit the allocation of resources to that process.

The calendar in WSRM is used to schedule policy enforcement on a set basis by one time event or recurring event(s). It's possible, for instance, that policy enforcement may be necessary only during business hours.

Administrators can allocate system resources to sessions or users who are active on Terminal Services. Configuring a policy can ensure that the sessions will behave correctly and that system availability will be stable for all users of Terminal Services. You can do this using the Equal per User or Equal per Session policy within WSRM.

The Windows Reliability and Performance Monitor

The Windows Reliability and Performance Monitor allows administrators to monitor application and hardware performance in real time and customize data they want to collect in logs, predefined thresholds for alerts, and automatic actions. Administrators can generate reports and view past performance data in a variety of ways. The Windows Reliability and Performance Monitor is a combination of pervious tools such as Performance Logs and Alerts, Server Performance Advisor, and System Monitor. It provides a graphical interface for the customization of Data Collector Sets and Event Trace Sessions. The Windows Reliability and Performance Monitor consists of three monitoring tools:

- Resource Overview
- Performance Monitor
- Reliability Monitor

There are two ways to start the Windows Reliability and Performance Monitor. One way is to click **Start | Administrative Tools | Reliability and Performance Monitor**; the other is to simply click **Start | Run**, type **perfmon**, and then press **Enter**. Figure 4.74 is a view of the Windows Reliability and Performance Monitor console.

Figure 4.74 The Windows Reliability and Performance Monitor

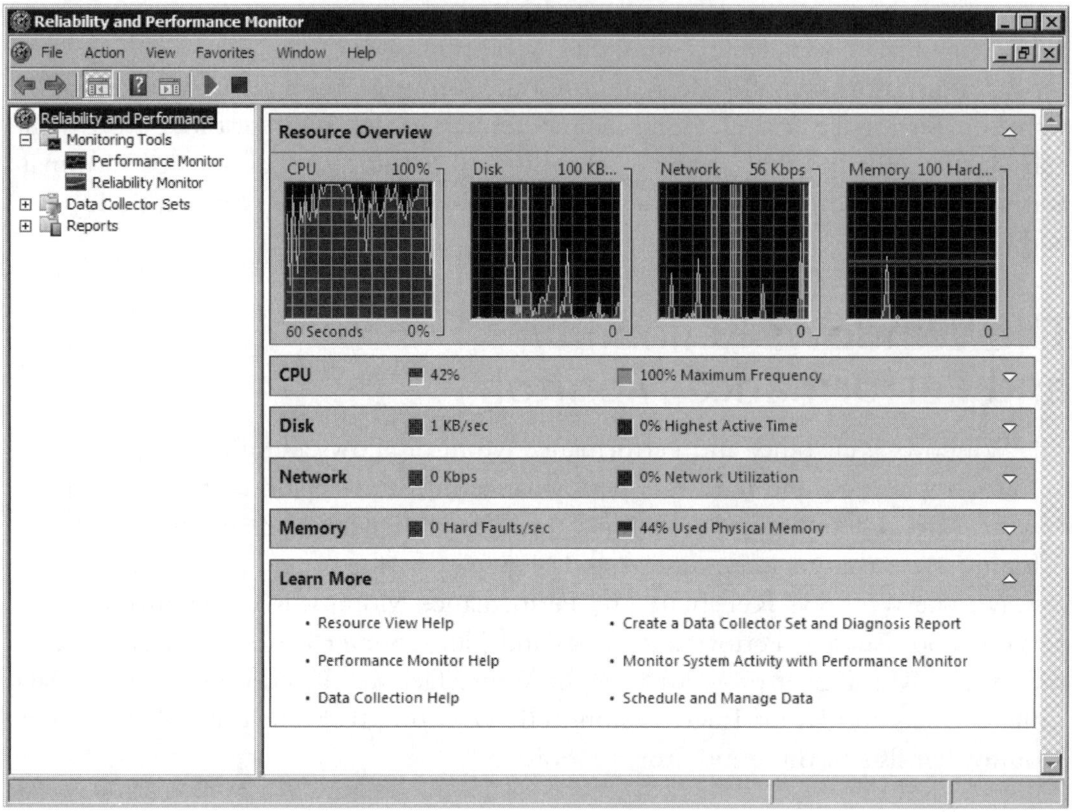

Resource Overview

The Resource Overview screen is also known as the Home Page in the Details pane. The Resource Overview screen presents data about the system in a real-time graphical manner. You see similar categories as those you saw in the Task Manager: CPU, Network, Memory, and Disk (the latter which is not shown in the Task Manager).

You can expand the subsections by clicking on the white down arrow to the far right of the bar. When you do you will see additional, more detailed information. For instance, if you expand CPU, you will see information such as the image, PID, description, threads, CPU, and average CPU. Table 4.7 lists the subsections and their associated headings.

Table 4.7 Subsections and Headings

Subsection	Headings
CPU	Image, PID, Description, Threads, CPU, Average CPU
Disk	Image, PID, File, Read, Write, IO Priority, Response Time
Network	Image, PID, Address, Send, Receive, Total
Memory	Image, PID, Hard Faults, Commit, Working Set, Shareable, Private

The Performance Monitor

Under Monitoring Tools is the Performance Monitor, which provides a display of built-in performance counters, in real time or viewed as historical data. The Performance Monitor allows administrators the ability to analyze system data, research performance, and bottlenecks. To open the Performance Monitor you can click on it underneath Monitoring Tools. The Performance Monitor is just like the System Monitor before it. The System Monitor in Windows Server 2003 allowed you to measure the performance of your own system or that of other Windows systems on the network. It allowed you to collect and view real-time performance data. With the Performance Monitor in Windows Server 2008, you have objects, counters, and instances. Table 4.8 provides a quick description of each.

Table 4.8 Components of the Performance Monitor

Component	Description
Object	System components are grouped into objects. They are grouped according to system functionality. Depending on the configuration, the number of objects depends on the system.
Counter	Provides a subset of objects. Also provides more detailed information about an object. Examples are queue length, session % used, and pages converted.
Instances	If more than one similar object is on a server, each one is considered an instance. Servers with multiple processors have an instance for each.

Exercise 4.15 takes you through the steps of counters in the Performance Monitor.

EXERCISE 4.15

ADDING COUNTERS IN THE PERFORMANCE MONITOR

1. Open **Reliability and Performance Monitor** either by clicking **Start | Administrative Tools | Reliability and Performance Monitor** or **Start | Run**. Type **perfmon** and press **Enter**.

2. In the console tree, click **Monitoring Tools | Performance Monitor**. This will open the Performance Monitor.

3. Click the green plus sign in the Details pane and the **Add Counters** screen should come up and start loading a list of counters.

4. Now it's time to select the counters. We will be setting up counters to help us set up a baseline for the system. To do that the counters we need are Memory-Pages/sec, Physical Disk-Avg. Disk Queue Length, and Processor-%Processor Time.

5. To add Memory-Pages/sec, go down the list of counters and click on **Memory**. Now go down its list and select **Pages/sec** and then click **Add**. Do the same for Physical Disk-Avg. Disk Queue Length and Processor-%Processor Time. Once you're done adding your counters, click on **OK**. You may get a message letting you know that one of the counters is already present. That is the %Processor Time. Just click **OK**.

6. Now you should see the Performance Monitor with the counters you just added, similar to Figure 4.75. Notice that if you highlight any one of the lines on the chart you get the value at that point in time.

Figure 4.75 The Performance Monitor with Baseline Counters

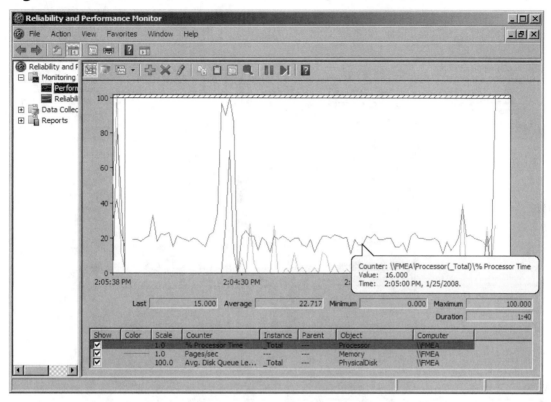

The Reliability Monitor

The Reliability Monitor provides a system stability overview and information about events that impact reliability. It is great for troubleshooting the root cause associated with any reduced reliability of the system. For instance, we may have a server that is slow to perform read and write requests. By using the Reliability Monitor, we can examine the server's trend over a period of time and examine failure types with details. The Reliability Monitor calculates the Stability Index which is shown in the System Stability Chart, and helps in diagnosing items that might be impacting the system. An index of 1 means the system is in its least stable stage, whereas an index rating of 10 indicates the system is at its most stable state. The index number is derived from the number of specified failures seen over a historical period. Figure 4.76 shows the System Stability Chart of the server called SIGMA.

Figure 4.76 The System Stability Chart

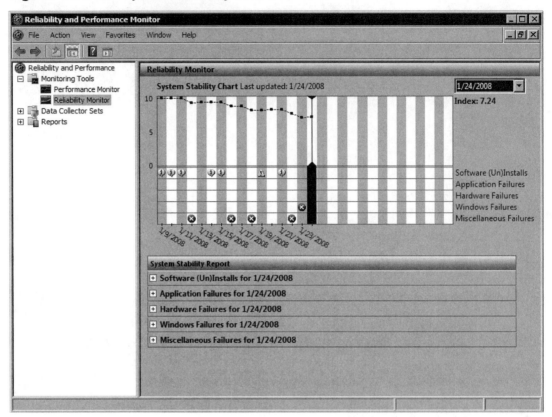

Notice that this server's Index seems to have headed toward a downward slope. The current index is 7.24; although it is not the worst it could be, there are obviously some problems that need to be addressed. When you examine any of the System Stability Reports below the chart, you see information such as Failure Type, Version, Failure Detail, and Date. In Figure 4.77, we have opened the latest error that took place; the failure type is "OS Stopped working" and the failure detail is a group of hex values.

Figure 4.77 A Windows Failure in the System Stability Report

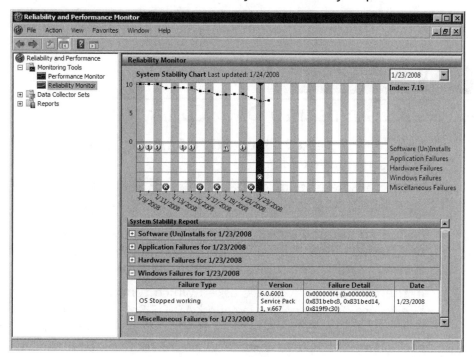

The failure detail here is one that is shown in a "blue screen" crash. The next thing this administrator should do is look for a file named memory.dmp and then contact Microsoft Product Support Services to have the file examined.

Data Collector Sets

A Data Collector Set organizes multiple data collection points into a single component that you can use to review or log performance. It can be created and then recorded separately, grouped with other sets, and incorporated into logs. Data Collector Sets can contain the following types of data collectors: performance counters, event trace data, and system configuration information. There are two types of Data Collector Sets: User Defined and System. User Defined are customized by the user/administrator whereas System Collector Data Sets are predefined and are broken down into Active Directory Diagnostics, LAN Diagnostics, System Diagnostics, and System Performance.

Data Collector Sets can be created from templates, existing sets of data collectors in a Performance Monitor view, or by selecting individual Data

Collectors and setting each individual option in the Data Collector Set properties. Exercise 4.16 walks you through the process of creating a User Defined Data Collector Set.

EXERCISE 4.16

CREATING A USER-DEFINED DATA COLLECTOR SET

1. First go into the **Reliability and Performance Monitor** as you did in the previous exercise.

2. In the console tree, go to **Data Collector Sets | User Defined**.

3. Right-click on **User Defined** and select **New | Data Collector Set**.

4. At the first **Create a new Data Collector Set** screen type in a descriptive name. For our example, we called ours **AD DS Set**. Select **Create from a template** and press **Next**.

5. In the next screen, you are asked which template you would like to use. Because ours is called AD DS Set, we obviously want to select **Active Directory Diagnostics**, so we'll select that and click **Next**. The Active Directory Diagnostics will collect data on this local server that includes Registry keys, performance counters, and trace events that are helpful in troubleshooting Active Directory Domain Services performance issues.

6. Next we are asked where we would like the data to be saved. Accept the default, which in this case is **%systemdrive%\Perflogs\ Admin\AD DS Set**, and then click **Next**.

7. Now we are asked whether we want to create the data collector set. Select the default of **Save and Close** and click **Finish**.

8. Now under **User Defined** beneath **Data Collector Sets**, you should see the newly created Data Collector Set AD DS Set, as shown in Figure 4.78.

Figure 4.78 Newly Created User-Defined Data Collector Set

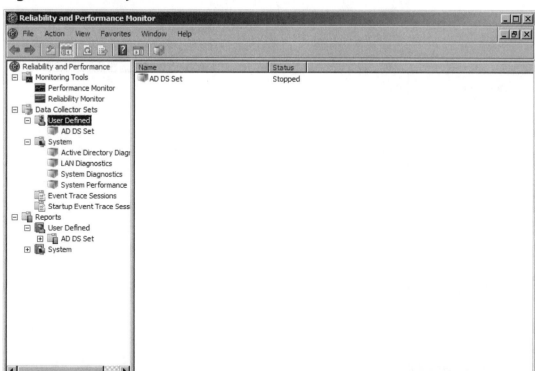

Reports

The last folder in the Windows Reliability and Performance Monitor is Reports. Reports support administrators who need to troubleshoot and analyze system performance and issues. Reports are based on Data Collector Sets and are also broken down into User Defined and System. Once you've created the Data Collector Set, its corresponding reports folder is available, as shown in Figure 4.79.

Figure 4.79 A User-Defined Report Automatically Created

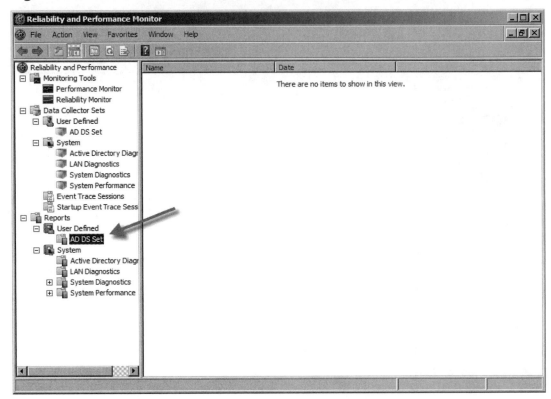

Summary of Exam Objectives

Maintaining an Active Directory environment constitutes 13% of the total exam for 70–640. It covers areas concerning backup and recovery, offline maintenance, and monitoring Active Directory. With the release of Windows Vista, backup and recovery have changed since Windows 2003 and those changes are further evident in Windows Server 2008. No longer is backup performed using ntbackup.exe, but rather through the Windows Server Backup interface or by using the wbadmin command-line tool. One of the changes in the new backup is DVD support. Also, after the first full backup all future jobs automatically run incremental backups by default. You can back up to removable media such as DVD only via the command prompt and not through the GUI. Restoration is also simplified in that administrators no longer have to restore from a multitude of media if the backup was done via an incremental backup. One thing that is no longer supported is the ability to back up to tape. Microsoft has removed this capability.

You install Windows Backup in Server 2008 via Server Manager and adding it as a feature. The command-line tools are not installed by default, so you must select them and they must be accompanied by the installation of the Windows PowerShell. Windows Server Backup is more conducive for personnel not heavily savvy in Windows or IT as a whole. The interface is easy to navigate and creating jobs is wizard-based. Specific backups such as only including the system state must be done via the *wbadmin* command. Full backups scheduled through the GUI do include the system state, but restoring just the system state is only done via the command line, and on a DC the administrator must be in DSRM.

DSRM is a special boot mode in Windows Server 2008. If the Active Directory database file (ntds.dit) becomes corrupt, for instance, it is through DSRM that an administrator can restore an uncorrupted version. You can access DSRM via the boot process before loading Windows and just after the BIOS POST. To enter DSRM, you must press F8 during the boot-up procedure and choose Directory Services Restore Mode from the list of options. It is in DSRM that authoritative and nonauthoritative restores are done.

Just as in previous versions of Windows Server, both authoritative and nonauthoritative restores are supported. In the case mentioned earlier regarding a corruption in ntds.dit, an administrator would perform a nonauthoritative restore of ntds.dit and any discrepancies between the restored copy and those residing on the other DCs in the domain would be updated or removed via the replication process. In some situations, though—for instance, accidentally removing an object such as a user account in Active Directory—performing a nonauthoritative restore will do nothing to bring back the previously deleted object. This is where performing an authoritative restore is required. An authoritative restore is performed in DSRM and the object being restored is restored at the authoritative restore prompt. After an authoritative restore, the object is then replicated back to all the DCs in the domain.

Linked Value Replication is performed when the forest level is at a Windows Server 2003 level or above. LVR replicates individual values of an object—not the entire object or an entire attribute, but just the value that has changed—thus reducing the amount of bandwidth consumed during replication.

Backing up a Group Policy Object consists of making a copy of the GPO data to the file system. Backups and restores are performed within the Group Policy Management Console. Another type of GPO that can be backed up is the Starter GPO. These GPOs are not included in the backup of regular GPOs and must be specifically backed up within the GPMC.

Offline maintenance has changed under Windows Server 2008. No longer do tasks such as defragging and compacting require booting into DSRM; with the advent of Restartable Active Directory end-user productivity is less affected than before. Restartable Active Directory runs as a service known as Active Directory Domain Service and is seen in the Services console in Windows Server 2008. Services such as DHCP and file/print are unaffected by stopping the Active Directory Domain Service. Stopping the Active Directory Domain Service, though, will stop services such as the Kerberos Key Distribution Center (KDC), intersite messaging, DNS server, and DFS replication. Restarting the Active Directory Domain Service does restart those services as well. To defrag the ntds.dit file just stop the Active Directory Domain Service and run the *ntdsutil* command, activate the *ntds* instance, pull up the File Maintenance prompt, and then type the *compact* command. Once finished, there is no need to reboot the server; just restart the Active Directory Domain Service.

Making sure that objects and attributes are up-to-date and consistent among DCs is a key in monitoring Active Directory. Tools such as the Network Monitor (netmon), Event Viewer, Replication Monitor (replmon), and Replication Administrator (repadmin) are key. Performance of DCs is also of concern and tools such as the Task Manager, Windows System Resource Manager, Windows Reliability and Performance Monitor, and Event Viewer are used to monitor them.

Exam Objectives Fast Track

Backup and Recovery

- ☑ Windows Server 2008 backup uses block-level images and .vhd files.

- ☑ Tape is no longer supported.

- ☑ Windows Server Backup is the new GUI for backup in Windows Server 2008.

- ☑ Backups can be scheduled more than once a day and at specific times.

- ☑ Wbadmin.exe is the new command-line interface for backup.

- ☑ Backup and restore of just the system state must be done using wbadmin.exe.

- ☑ Directory Services Restore Mode (DSRM) is used to perform authoritative and nonauthoritative restores.

- ☑ Authoritative restores should be performed after an object in Active Directory has been accidentally deleted and replication to the other DCs has taken place.

- ☑ Nonauthoritative restores are good for lost updates such as a password for a user account and corruption found in the ntds.dit file.

- ☑ Linked Value Replication (LVR) is used when changes in group membership occur and only the individual member(s) is replicated and not the entire membership group as a whole.

- ☑ GPOs and Startup GPOs are backed up separately.

Offline Maintenance

- ☑ Active Directory Domain Services runs as a service under Windows Server 2008 and can be started and stopped at will but can never be paused.

- ☑ Because of restartable Active Directory Domain Services routine tasks can be performed without affecting other services such as DHCP and file/print services.

- ☑ The three states that a Windows Server 2008 DC runs in are AD DS Started, AD DS Stopped, and Domain Services Restore Mode (DSRM).

- ☑ Offline defrag and compaction shrink the size of ntds.dit, thus saving disk space.

☑ If ntds.dit and its logs are located on the same partition, free space should be at least 20% of the combined database file and logs or 1 GB, whichever is greater.

Monitoring Active Directory

☑ Tools used to monitor Active Directory are the Network Monitor, Event Viewer, replmon, and repadmin.

☑ DC performance and stability are monitored using the Task Manager, Windows System Resource Manager (WSRM), Windows Reliability and Performance Monitor, and Event Viewer.

☑ Network Monitor (netmon) Version 3.0 and later are supported on Windows Server 2008 and must be downloaded to install.

☑ Netmon is very useful in verifying that traffic is flowing as it's supposed to along with making sure name resolution is occurring correctly.

☑ The Task Manager is ideal for immediate viewing of resources being used on a server.

☑ The Event Viewer is typically the first place to start troubleshooting anything that has to do with the server or Active Directory.

☑ The Event Viewer is now based on XML.

☑ Replmon (Replication Monitor) is a GUI tool used to examine replication among DCs and view the replication topology.

☑ RepAdmin (Replication Administrator) is a command-line version of Replmon.

☑ The Windows System Resource Manager (WSRM) allows an administrator to configure how processor and memory resources are allocated among applications.

☑ The Windows Reliability and Performance Monitor allows administrators to monitor application and hardware performance in real time.

Exam Objectives
Frequently Asked Questions

Q: Since Windows Server Backup doesn't read .bkf files, is there any way to restore any information from one in Windows Server 2008?

A: Yes. You can download a version of ntbackup for Windows Server 2008 for the sole purpose of restoring items that were backed up with the old software, but you cannot back up with it. You can download the ntbackup for Windows Server 2008 from http://go.microsoft.com/fwlink/?LinkId=82917.

Q: Does Windows Server Backup support tape?

A: No. It supports backing up to disk, removable media such as DVD, and network drives.

Q: Does Windows Server Backup come preinstalled with Windows Server 2008?

A: No. You must add it as a feature.

Q: Can you back up just the system state with Windows Server Backup?

A: No. Windows Server Backup backs up at the volume level and does not include an option for choosing just the system state or a particular directory or file. You can use wbadmin.exe via a command prompt to back up just the system state.

Q: Since Windows Server 2008 supports backing up to DVD, can you also back up to USB-based flash drives as well?

A: Yes. To back up to any removable media such as DVD or USB flash drives, you must do so using the wbadmin.exe command-line tool.

Q: If I forget the Directory Services Restore Mode (DSRM) administrator's password, can I still get in DSRM?

A: No, but if you change the DSRM Administrator's password at the ntdsutil prompt in Windows Server 2008, you can.

Q: What is the difference between an authoritative restore and a nonauthoritative restore?

A: An authoritative restore restores a directory object, such as a user account that may have been deleted accidentally, and flags it so that its restoration is replicated among the other DCs. A nonauthoritative restore is useful for when the Active Directory database file (ntds.dit) has become corrupt and you need to restore it. After restoration, directory replication brings it up-to-date with all the other DCs.

Q: Does Windows Server Backup back up GPOs?

A: No. You must back up GPOs and Starter GPOs via the Group Policy Management Console (GPMC).

Q: Do you still have to boot into DSRM to perform offline defragging?

A: No. You can simply stop Active Directory Domain Services in the Services console and perform it without going into the DSRM. Functions such as DHCP and file/print are unaffected and are still operational.

Q: Can I monitor Active Directory replication using the Network Monitor (netmon)?

A: You cannot see the actual replication itself, but you can verify that the DCs are talking to each other. A better alternative would be to use either the Replication Monitor (replmon) or Replication Administrator (repadmin).

Q: What are some of the new benefits of the Event Viewer?

A: The Event Viewer is now XML-based, so it's even easier to import information from it into different applications. You can create subscriptions, which allows remote servers to forward events to a centrally located server so that they can be examined in one place.

Q: What does the Windows Reliability and Performance Monitor actually do?

A: It allows administrators to monitor application and hardware performance in real time as well as customize the data they collect in logs. It's made up of three primary monitoring tools: the Resource Overview, Performance Monitor, and Reliability Monitor. You can customize the data you log by creating Data Collector Sets which you can examine via Reports in the tool.

Self Test

1. You've just finished installing a new Windows Server 2008 DC. It is the policy of the IT department to perform a full backup of newly installed DCs. You click on **Start | Administrative Tools | Windows Server Backup**. When Windows Server Backup loads you see the following screen.

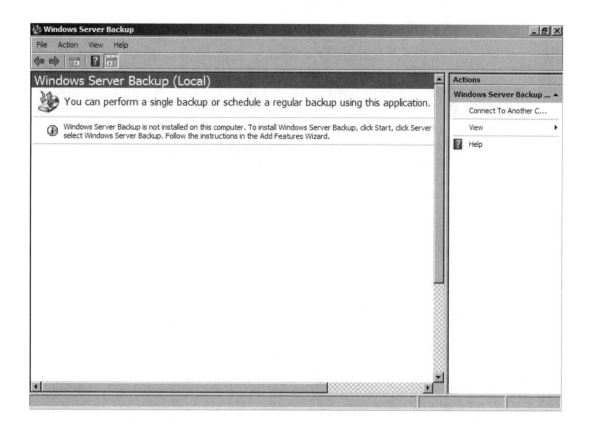

What do you need to do to ensure that the backup takes place?

A. Run DCPROMO

B. Install the Windows Server Backup feature

C. Go to a command prompt and run wbadmin.exe

D. Boot into DSRM and conduct the backup from there

2. You are responsible for performing backups on the DCs on your network. Your boss has requested that you conduct system state backups to DVD. How do you accomplish this?

    A. Run the **Windows Server Backup Wizard**, select **System State Backup**, and set your target to the DVD drive

    B. Run the **Windows Server Backup Wizard**, select a local drive as the target, and then copy the system state backup to the DVD drive

    C. Run the *wbadmin.exe* command with the *start systemstatebackup* command and target it to the DVD drive

    D. Run the *wbadmin.exe* command with the *start systemstatebackup* command, set the target to a local fixed drive, and then copy the system state backup to a DVD

3. You are the network administrator for your company. Last night you successfully performed a system state backup of one of your DCs. Do to an unforeseen issue, you now need to perform a system state restore. What do you need to do to conduct a system state restore on a DC?

    A. Reboot the DC, go into DSRM, and run wbadmin.exe to perform the system state restore

    B. Log on to the DC as usual and run wbadmin.exe to restore the system state

    C. Stop Active Directory Domain Services and then run the *wbadmin.exe* command to restore the system state

    D. Just restore the system state via the Windows Server Backup Wizard

4. You are the network administrator for your company. You have a scheduled backup job run three times a day: 10:00 A.M., 4:00 P.M., and 11:00 P.M. At 4:50 P.M., you get a call that user Janet Harrell has deleted the company budget on the server. There are no previous versions available. What should you do to restore the company budget?

    A. Run **ntbackup**, select the company budget from the list of files backed up, and choose **Restore**

    B. Run **Windows Server Backup**, select **Recover** from the **Actions** pane, choose **Files and Folders** as the recovery type. Select the company budget from the **Available items** list. Choose **Original location** for recovery destination, create copies so that you have both versions of the file or folder under **When the wizard find files and folders in the recovery destination**, and choose **Restore security settings**.

C. Go into **DSRM**, run **wbadmin.exe**, and conduct a system state recovery

D. Stop Active Directory Domain Services, load ntbackup, select the company budget, and choose Restore

5. You are the network administrator at your company. The Active Directory database file on one of your DCs is corrupt. You decide to perform a non-authoritative restore on the DC. You reboot the server into DSRM and try to log on as the domain administrator but you cannot. You need to get this DC back up and functioning as soon as possible. What can you do to achieve this?

A. Log on to the server with another domain administrator's account

B. Log on to the server using the local administrator's account

C. Change the domain administrator's password from another DC and then log on using the account with the new password

D. Log on using the DSRM administrator's account and password

6. You are the domain admin for your company. You have tasked Susan, a member of the Account Operators group, to delete Amber Chambers' user account because she quit yesterday. Susan accidentally deletes Andy Chambers' account. Before she realizes what's happened the change is replicated to the other DCs. What can you do to bring back Andy Chambers' user account?

A. Reboot the DC into DSRM, restore the system state, and conduct a nonauthoritative restore on Andy Chambers' user account from the most recent backup using wbadmin.exe

B. Reboot the DC into DSRM, restore the system state, and conduct an authoritative restore on Andy Chambers' user account from the most recent backup using wbadmin.exe

C. Log on to the DC in normal mode, stop Active Directory Domain Services, load Windows Server Backup, restore the system state, and perform an authoritative restore of Andy Chambers' user account

D. Log on to the DC in normal mode, stop Active Directory Domain Services, load Windows Server Backup, restore the system state, and perform a non-authoritative restore of Andy Chambers' user account

7. You are the domain administrator for your company. Examining one of the DCs, you notice that the file ntds.dit is almost 6 GB in size. You decide that

to save disk space and increase performance you will defrag Active Directory Domain Services. How would you accomplish this?

A. Log on to the server as an administrator. Perform a system state backup of the DC. Create a new directory on the system drive called C:\defrag. Stop Active Directory Domain Services. Start an instance of ntdsutil and activate Instance ntds. At the ntdsutil prompt pull up the file maintenance prompt and type **compact to c:\defrag**. Go to the %systemdrive%\Windows\ NTDS directory and delete the old ntds.dit file as well as any .log files. Copy the ntds.dit file in the C:\defrag folder to %systemroot%\Windows\ NTDS, and then restart Active Directory Domain Services.

B. Log on to the server as an administrator. Perform a system state backup of the DC. Create a new directory on the system drive called C:\defrag. Start an instance of ntdsutil and activate Instance ntds. At the ntdsutil prompt, pull up the file maintenance prompt and type **compact to c:\defrag**. Go to the %systemdrive%\Windows\NTDS directory and delete the old ntds.dit file as well as any .log files. Copy the ntds.dit file in the C:\defrag folder to the %systemroot%\Windows\NTDS.

C. Log on to the server as an administrator in DSRM. Perform a system state backup of the DC. Create a new directory on the system drive called C:\defrag. Stop Active Directory Domain Services. Start an instance of ntdsutil and activate Instance ntds. At the ntdsutil prompt, pull up the file maintenance prompt and type **compact to c:\defrag**. Go to the %systemdrive%\Windows\NTDS directory and delete the old ntds.dit file as well as any .log files. Copy the ntds.dit file in the C:\defrag folder to the %systemroot%\Windows\NTDS, and then restart Active Directory Domain Services.

D. Log on to the server as an administrator. Perform a system state backup of the DC. Create a new directory on the system drive called C:\defrag. Stop Active Directory Domain Services. Start an instance of ntdsutil and activate Instance ntds. At the ntdsutil prompt, pull up the file maintenance prompt and type **compact to c:\defrag**. Go to the %systemdrive%\ Windows\NTDS directory and delete the old ntds.dit file as well as any .log files. Copy the ntds.dit file in the C:\defrag folder to %systemdrive%\ Windows\NTDS.

8. You are the domain administrator for your company. Your network consists of three DCs, each running Windows Server 2008. Two are at site A, and the third

is located at site B. There seems to be a replication problem between the DCs at site A and the DC at site B. What is the best tool to use in troubleshooting directory replication?

A. Network Monitor

B. Task Manager

C. RepAdmin

D. Event Viewer

9. You are the domain administrator for your company. Your network consists of multiple DCs at multiple sites. A DC at your local site is having problems with replicating. You need to know when this DC last attempted to perform an inbound replication on the Active Directory partitions. How would you accomplish this?

A. Open a command prompt on the DC and run *ntdsutil*

B. Open a command prompt on the DC and run *repadmin /replicate*

C. Open a command prompt on the DC and run *repadmin /rodcpwdrepl*

D. Open a command prompt on the DC and run *repadmin /showrepl*

10. You are the domain administrator for your company. At your site you have a single DC that also acts as an application server. From 10:00 A.M. to 4:00 P.M., users complain about slow logons to the network and that accessing resources from this DC is incredibly slow during most of the workday. You log on to the DC, pull up the Task Manager, and notice that a process called CustApp.exe is using just more than 90% of the CPU cycles. The application must remain running during the day, but you also need to resolve the slow logon issues. There is no money in the budget for additional hardware. What is the best way to handle this situation?

A. Go into the Windows System Resource Manager on the DC, and create a new recurring calendar event to start at 8:00 A.M. and end at 5:00 P.M. daily. Associate the event with the Equal_Per_Process policy.

B. Go into the Task Manager and into the Processes tab. Find CustApp.exe and set the priority to Below Normal.

C. Go into the Task Manager and into the Process tab. Find CustApp.exe and end the process.

D. Purchase a second server to run only the CustApp.exe application

Self Test Quick Answer Key

1. **B**

2. **D**

3. **A**

4. **B**

5. **D**

6. **B**

7. **A**

8. **C**

9. **D**

10. **A**

Chapter 5

MCTS/MCITP
Exam 649

Configuring the Active Directory Infrastructure

Exam objectives in this chapter:

- **Working with Forests and Domains**
- **Working with Sites**
- **Working with Trusts**

Exam objectives review:

- ☑ **Summary of Exam Objectives**
- ☑ **Exam Objectives Fast Track**
- ☑ **Exam Objectives Frequently Asked Questions**
- ☑ **Self Test**
- ☑ **Self Test Quick Answer Key**

Introduction

A Microsoft Active Directory network has both a physical and a logical structure. Forests and domains define the logical structure of the network, with domains organized into domain trees in which subdomains (called child domains) can be created under parent domains in a branching structure. Domains are logical units that hold users, groups, computers, and organizational units (OUs, which in turn can contain users, groups, computers, and other OUs). Forests are collections of domain trees that have trust relationships with one another, but each domain tree has its own separate namespace.

In order to allow Active Directory to support the physical structure of your network, we will also discuss the configuration of Active Directory sites, site links, and subnet objects. Active Directory sites and subnets define the physical structure of an Active Directory network. Sites are important in an enterprise-level multiple location network, for creating a topology that optimizes the process of replicating Active Directory information between domain controllers (DCs). Sites are used for replication and for optimizing the authentication process by reducing authentication traffic across slow, high-cost WAN links. Site and subnet information is also used by Active Directory-enabled services to help clients find the nearest service providers.

In this chapter, you will learn all about the functions of forests and domains in the Windows Server 2008 Active Directory infrastructure, and we will walk you through the steps of creating a forest and domain structure for a network. You'll learn to create the forest root domain and a child domain, as well as the importance of Flexible Single Manager Operation (FSMO) roles within an Active Directory domain and forest. We will also discuss the role of sites in the Active Directory infrastructure, and how replication, authentication, and distribution of services information work within and across sites. We will explain the relationship of sites with domains and subnets, and how to create sites and site links. You'll also learn about site replication and how to plan, create, and manage a replication topology. We'll walk you through the steps of configuring replication between sites, and discuss how to troubleshoot replication failures.

In addition to these concepts, we will also discuss Active Directory trust relationships. Trust relationships define the ways in which users can access network resources across domains and forests. Without a trust between the domain to which a user belongs and the domain in which a resource resides, the user won't be able to access that file, folder, printer, or other resource. Hence, it is important for network administrators to understand how the built-in (implicit) trusts in the Active Directory network function, and how to create explicit trusts to provide access (or faster access) between domains.

Working with Forests and Domains

Active Directory is composed of a number of components, each associated with a different type of Active Directory functionality; you should understand each component before making any changes to the network. Active Directory Domain Services is a distributed database, which means it can be spread across multiple computers within a domain or a forest. Among the major logical components that you need to be familiar with are:

- Forests
- Trees
- Domains
- The domain namespace

Administrative boundaries, network and directory performance, security, resource management, and basic functionality are all dependent on the proper design and placement of these elements.

Figure 5.1 shows the logical view of a Windows Server 2008 Active Directory. Note that the differentiation between forests and trees is most obvious in the namespace. By its nature, a tree is one or more domains with a contiguous namespace. Each tree consists of one or more domains, and each forest consists of one or more trees. Because a forest can be composed of discrete multiple trees, a forest's namespace can be discontiguous. By discontiguous, we mean that the namespaces anchor to different forest-root domain name system (DNS) domains, such as cats.com and dogs.com. Both are top-level domains and are considered two trees in a forest when combined into a single directory, as shown in Figure 5.1.

Figure 5.1 The Logical View of a Windows Server 2008 Active Directory

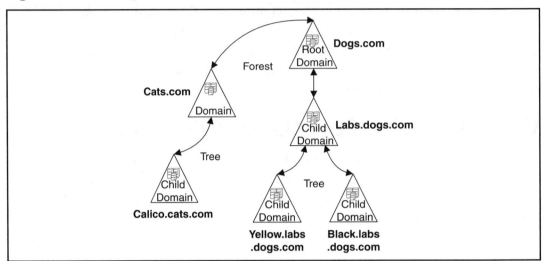

Understanding Forests

An Active Directory always begins with a *forest root domain*, which is automatically the first domain you install. This root domain becomes the foundation for additional directory components. As the cornerstone of your enterprise-computing environment, you should protect it well. Fault tolerance and good backups are not optional—they are essential. If an administrative error or hardware failure results in the unrecoverable loss of this root structure, the entire forest becomes inoperable. Certain forest objects and services are present only at the root (e.g., the Enterprise Administrators and Schema Administrators groups, and the Schema Master and Domain Naming Master FSMO roles which we will discuss later in this chapter).

Understanding Domains

The *domain* serves as the administrative boundary of Active Directory. It is the most basic component that can functionally host the directory. Simply put, Active Directory uses the domain as a container of computers, users, groups, and other object containers. Objects within the domain share a common directory database partition, replication boundaries and characteristics, security policies, and security relationships with other domains.

Typically, administrative rights granted in one domain are valid only within that domain. This also applies to Group Policy Objects (GPOs), but not necessarily to trust relationships, which you will learn more about later in the book. Security policies such as the password policy, account lockout policy, and Kerberos ticket policy are defined on a per-domain basis. The domain is also the primary boundary defining your DNS and NetBIOS namespaces. The DNS infrastructure is a requirement for an Active Directory domain, and should be defined before you create the domain.

There are several good reasons for a multiple-domain model, although a significant number of Active Directory implementations rely on a single-domain forest model. In the early days of Windows 2000, the most common recommendation was for a so-called "empty forest root" model, in which the forest root domain contains only built-in objects, and all manually created objects reside in one or more child domains. Whatever the design decision reached by your organization, it is a good practice to avoid installing additional domains unless you have a specific reason for them, as each additional domain in a forest incurs additional administrative overhead in the form of managing additional DCs and replication traffic. Some of the more common reasons to create additional domains include:

- Groups of users with different security policy requirements, such as strong authentication and strict access controls.

- Groups of users requiring additional autonomy, or administrative separation for security reasons.

- A requirement for decentralized administration due to political, budgetary, time zone, or policy pressures.

- A requirement for unique namespaces.

- Controlling excessive directory replication traffic by breaking the domain into smaller, more manageable pieces. This often occurs in an extremely large domain, or due to a combination of geographical separation and unreliable WAN links.

- Maintaining a preexisting NT domain structure.

You can think of a domain tree as a DNS namespace composed of one or more domains. If you plan to create a forest with discontiguous namespaces, you must create more than one tree. Referring back to Figure 5.1, you see two trees in that forest, Cats.com and Dogs.com. Each has a *contiguous namespace* because each domain in the hierarchy is directly related to the domains above and below it in each tree. The forest has a *discontiguous namespace* because it contains two unrelated top-level domains.

The primary Active Directory partitions, also called *naming contexts*, are replicated among all DCs within a domain. These three partitions are the schema partition, the configuration partition, and the domain partition.

- The **schema partition** contains the *classSchema* and the *attributeSchema* objects that make up the directory schema. These classes and attributes define all possible types of objects and object properties within the forest. Every DC in the entire forest has a replica of the schema partition.

- The **configuration partition**, replicated identically on all DCs throughout the forest, contains Active Directory's replication topology and other configuration data.

- The **domain partition** contains the local domain objects, such as computers, users, and groups, which all share the same security policies and security relationships with other domains. If multiple DCs exist within a domain, they contain a replica of the same domain partition. If multiple domains exist within a forest, each domain contains a unique domain partition.

Because each domain contains unique principles and resources, there must be some way for other domains to locate them. Active Directory contains objects that adhere to a naming convention called the DN, or *distinguished name*. The DN contains enough detail to locate a replica of the partition that holds the object in question. Unfortunately, most users and applications do not know the DN, or what partition might contain it. To fulfill that role, Active Directory uses the *Global Catalog (GC)*, which can locate DNs based on one or more specific attributes of the needed object. (We will discuss the GC later in this chapter).

Forest and Domain Functional Levels

Forest functional levels and *domain functional levels* are a mechanism that Microsoft uses to support backward compatibility with previous versions of Active Directory, and to expose more advanced functionality as functional levels are raised. Functional levels are a feature that helps improve performance and security. In Windows 2000, each domain had two functional levels (which were called "modes"), native mode and mixed mode, and the forest had only one functional level. Windows Server 2003 introduced two more functional levels to consider in both domains and forests. Windows Server 2008 drops support for two legacy functional levels that were designed to support Windows NT Backup Domain Controllers, and adds another forest and domain functional level to support pure Windows Server 2008 environments. To enable the Windows Server 2008 forest and domain-wide features, all DCs must be running Windows Server 2008 and the functional levels must be set to Windows Server 2008. Table 5.1 summarizes the levels, DCs supported in each level, and each level's primary purpose.

Table 5.1 Domain and Forest Functional Levels

Type	Functional Level	Supported DCs	Purpose
Domain Default	Windows 2000	2000, 2003, 2008	Supports upgrades from 2000 to 2008; no support for NT backup domain controllers (BDCs).
Domain	Windows Server 2003	2003, 2008	Supports upgrades from 2003 to 2008; all Windows Server 2003 domain-wide Active Directory features are enabled.
Domain	Windows Server 2008	2008	Provides support for all features of Windows Server 2008 Active Directory
Forest Default	Windows 2000	2000, 2003, 2008	Supports mixed environments during upgrade; lower security, high compatibility
Forest	Windows Server 2003	2003, 2008	Supports upgrades from 2003 to 2008; all Windows Server 2008 Active Directory features are enabled.
Forest	Windows Server 2008	2008	Provides support for all features of Windows Server 2008 Active Directory

Using Domain Functional Levels

Active Directory technology debuted with Windows 2000. Now, with Windows Server 2008, it has been refined and enhanced. Active Directory is now easier to deploy, is more efficient at replication, has improved administration, and poses a better end-user experience. Some features are enabled right away, whereas others require a complete migration of DCs to the new release before they become available. There are countless new features, the most significant of which we will discuss next.

Using the Windows 2000 Domain Functional Level

The Windows 2000 domain functional level is the default domain functional level in Windows Server 2008, and is primarily intended to support an upgrade from Windows 2000 to Windows Server 2008. This domain functional level offers full compatibility with all down-level operating systems for Active Directory DCs, and is characterized by the following features:

Microsoft Windows NT 4.0 DCs are not supported.

The following Active Directory features are supported in this mode:

- Universal Security Groups
- Group nesting
- Converting groups between distribution and security groups
- SIDHistory

The following Active Directory features are *not* supported in this mode:

- DC rename
- Logon timestamp attribute updated and replicated
- User password support on the *InetOrgPerson objectClass*
- Constrained delegation
- Users and Computers container redirection
- Can be raised to the Windows Server 2003 or Windows Server 2008 domain functional level

Windows Server 2003 Domain Functional Level

The Windows Server 2003 domain functional level supports both Windows Server 2003 and Windows Server 2008 DCs. This level does not allow for the presence of Windows NT or Windows 2000 DCs, and is designed to support an upgrade from 2003 to 2008. All 2003 Active Directory domain features are enabled at this level, providing a good balance between security and backward compatibility.

DCs *not* supported at this level:

- Windows NT 4.0 DCs
- Windows 2000 DCs

The following Active Directory domain-wide functions are supported at both this level and the Windows 2000 domain functional level:

- Universal Security Groups
- Group nesting
- Converting groups between distribution and security groups
- SIDHistory

The following upgraded Active Directory domain-wide functionality is supported at this domain functional level:

- DC rename
- Logon timestamp attribute updated and replicated
- User password support on the *InetOrgPerson objectClass*
- Constrained delegation
- Users and Computers container redirection
- Can be raised to the Windows Server 2008 domain functional level
- Can never be lowered to the Windows 2000 domain functional level

In the Windows Server 2003 domain functional level, only Windows Server 2003 and Windows Server 2008 DCs can exist.

Windows Server 2008 Domain Functional Level

The Windows Server 2008 domain functional level supports only Windows Server 2008 DCs. This level does not allow for the presence of Windows NT, Windows 2000, or Windows Server 2003, and is designed to support the most advanced Active Directory feature set possible. All 2008 Active Directory domain features are enabled at this level, providing the highest level of security and functionality and the lowest level of backward compatibility.

The following Windows Server 2008 domain-wide functions are supported only at this level:

- Distributed File System (DFS) replication support for the Windows Server 2008 System Volume (SYSVOL) share, providing more robust and fault-tolerant replication of SYSVOL and its contents
- Advanced Encryption Standard (AES 128 and AES 256) encryption support for the Kerberos protocol

- Logging of Last Interactive Logon Information, including:

    - The time of the last successful interactive logon for a user

    - The name of the workstation from which the used logged on

    - The number of failed logon attempts since the last logon

- Fine-grained password policies, which allow you to specify password and account lockout policies for individual users and groups within an Active Directory domain

- Cannot be raised to any higher domain functional level, because no higher level exists at this time

- Can never be lowered to the Windows 2000 or Windows Server 2003 domain functional level

In the Windows Server 2008 domain functional level, only Windows Server 2008 DCs can exist.

Configuring Forest Functional Levels

The Windows Server 2008 forest functional levels are named similarly to the domain functional levels, and serve a similar purpose. Table 5.1 summarizes the levels, the DCs supported in each level, and each level's primary purpose.

As with domain functional levels, each forest functional level carries over the features from lower levels, and activates new features as well. These new features apply across every domain in your forest. After you raise the forest functional level, earlier OSs cannot be promoted to DCs. For example, Windows NT 4.0 BDCs are not supported by any forest functional level, and Windows 2000 DCs cannot be part of the forest except through external or forest trusts once the forest level has been raised to Windows Server 2003.

Windows 2000 Forest Functional Level (default)

The Windows 2000 forest functional level is primarily designed to support mixed environments during the course of an upgrade. Typically, this applies to a transition from Windows 2000 to Windows Server 2003 or Windows Server 2008. It is also the default mode for a newly created Windows Server 2008 domain. It is characterized by relatively lower-security features and reduced efficiency, but maintains the highest compatibility level possible for Active Directory. In the Windows 2000 forest functional level:

- Windows 2000, Windows Server 2003, and Windows Server 2008 DCs are supported

- Windows NT 4.0 BDCs are *not* supported

A Windows Server 2008 forest at the Windows 2000 forest functional level can be raised to either the Windows 2003 or the Windows Server 2008 forest functional level.

Windows Server 2003 Forest Functional Level

The Windows Server 2003 forest functional level enables a number of forest-wide features that were not available at the Windows 2000 forest functional level, and is designed to allow for a 2003 to 2008 upgrade process. This level does not allow for the presence of Windows NT or Windows 2000 DCs anywhere in the forest. All Windows Server 2003 Active Directory forest features are enabled at this level, as follows:

- DCs *not* supported at this level:
  - Windows NT 4.0 DCs
  - Windows 2000 DCs
- All new Active Directory forest features are supported at this level.

The following forest-wide improvements are available at this forest functional level:

- Efficient group member replication using linked value replication
- Improved Knowledge Consistency Checker (KCC) intersite replication topology generator algorithms
- ISTG aliveness no longer replicated
- Attributes added to the GC, such as ms-DS-Entry-Time-To-Die, Message Queuing-Secured-Source, Message Queuing-Multicast-Address, Print-Memory, Print-Rate, and Print-Rate-Unit
- Defunct schema objects
- Cross-forest trust
- Domain rename
- Dynamic auxiliary classes

- InetOrgPerson objectClass change

- Application groups

- Reduced NTDS.DIT size

- Improvements in intersite replication topology management

- Can be raised to the Windows Server 2008 forest functional level

- Cannot be downgraded to the Windows 2000 forest functional level without performing a full forest recovery

In the Windows Server 2003 forest functional level, both Windows Server 2003 and Windows Server 2008 DCs can exist.

Windows Server 2008 Forest Functional Level

The Windows Server 2008 forest functional level is the highest forest functional level available in Windows Server 2008, and supports only Windows Server 2008 DCs in each domain within a forest. At present, this forest functional level does not expose any new functionality over and above the 2003 forest functional level. The primary advantage of the 2008 forest functional level at present is that, once you have raised the functional level to 2008, any domains that are subsequently added to the forest will be automatically created at the Windows Server 2008 domain functional level.

Raising Forest and Domain Functional Levels

Before increasing a functional level, you should prepare for it by performing the following steps:

1. Inventory your domain or forest for DCs that are running any earlier versions of the Windows Server operating system.

2. *Physically* locate any down-level DCs in the domain or forest as needed, and either upgrade or remove them.

3. Verify that end-to-end replication is working in the forest using repadmin. exe and/or dcdiag.exe.

4. Verify the compatibility of your applications and services with the version of Windows that your DCs will be running, and specifically their compatibility with the target functional level. Use a lab environment to test for compatibility issues, and contact the appropriate vendors for compatibility information.

When you are considering raising the domain functionality level, remember that the new features will directly affect only the domain being raised. The two domain functional levels available to raise are:

- Windows Server 2003
- Windows Server 2008

Once the functional level of a particular domain has been raised, no prior version DCs can be added to the domain. In the case of the Windows Server 2003 domain functional level, no Windows 2000 servers can be promoted to DC status after the functionality has been raised. In the case of the Windows Server 2008 domain functional level, no Windows Server 2003 DCs can be added to the domain after the functional level has been raised to Windows Server 2008.

Raising the Domain Functional Level

Before raising the functional level of a domain, all DCs must be upgraded to the minimum OS level as shown in Table 5.1. Remember that when you raise the domain functional level to Windows Server 2003 or Windows Server 2008, it can never be changed back to a previous domain functional level. Exercise 5.1 takes you systematically through the process of verifying the current domain functional level. Exercise 5.2 takes you through the process of raising the domain functional level. To raise the domain functional level, you must be a Domain Admin in the domain in question.

EXERCISE 5.1

VERIFYING THE DOMAIN FUNCTIONAL LEVEL

1. Log on as a Domain Admin of the domain you are checking.
2. Click on **Start | Control Panel | Performance and Maintenance | Administrative Tools | Active Directory Users and Computers**, or use the Microsoft Management Console (MMC) preconfigured with the Active Directory Users and Computers snap-in.
3. Locate the domain in the console tree that you are going to raise in functional level. Right-click the domain and select **Raise Domain Functional Level**.
4. In the Raise Domain Functional Level dialog box, the current domain functional level appears under **Current domain functional level**.

EXERCISE 5.2

RAISING THE DOMAIN FUNCTIONAL LEVEL

1. Log on locally as a Domain Admin to the PDC or the PDC Emulator FSMO of the domain you are raising.

2. Click on **Start | Administrative Tools | Active Directory Domains and Trusts**, or use the MMC preconfigured with the Active Directory Domain and Trusts snap-in.

3. Locate the domain in the console tree that you are going to raise in functional level. Right-click the domain and select **Raise Domain Functional Level**.

4. A dialog box will appear titled **Select an available domain functional level**. There are only two possible choices, although both might not be available:

   ▪ Select **Windows Server 2003**, and then click the **Raise** button to raise the domain functional level to Windows Server 2003.

   ▪ Select **Windows Server 2008**, and then click the **Raise** button to raise the domain functional level to Windows Server 2008.

Understanding the Global Catalog

Active Directory uses the Global Catalog (GC), which is a copy of all the Active Directory objects in the forest, to let users search for directory information across all the domains in the forest. The GC is also used to resolve user principal names (UPNs) when the DC that is authenticating logon isn't aware of the account (because that account resides in a different domain). When the DC can't find the user's account in its own domain database, it then looks in the GC. The GC also stores information about membership in Universal Groups.

The GC contains a portion of every naming context in the directory, including the schema and configuration partitions. To be able to find everything, the GC must contain a replica of every object in the Active Directory. Fortunately, it maintains only a small number of attributes for each object. These attributes are those most commonly used to search for objects, such as a user's first, last, and logon names. The GC extends an umbrella of awareness throughout the discontiguous namespace of the enterprise.

Although the GC can be modified and optimized, it typically requires infrequent attention. The Active Directory replication system automatically builds and maintains the GC, generates its replication topology, and determines which attributes to include in its index.

The GC is a vital part of Active Directory functionality. Given the size of enterprise-level organizations, on many networks, there will be multiple domains and, at times, multiple forests. The GC helps in keeping a list of every object without holding all the details of those objects; this optimizes network traffic while still providing maximum accessibility.

NOTE

The first DC in a domain becomes the GC server by default.

Whenever a user is searching for an object in the directory, the GC server is used in the querying process for multiple reasons. The GC server holds partial replicas of all the domains in a forest, other than its own (for which it holds a full replica). Thus, the GC server stores the following:

- Copies of all the objects in the domain in which it resides
- Partial copies of objects from other domains in the forest

NOTE

When we say that the GC server holds a partial copy of an object, we mean that it includes only some of the object's attributes in its database. Attributes are object properties, and each object has a number of attributes. For example, one attribute of a *User Account* object would be the username. You can customize the attributes of a particular object type by editing the *schema*, which we will discuss later in this chapter.

The key point is that the GC is designed to have the details that are most commonly used for searching for information. This allows for efficient response from a GC server. There is no need to try to find one item out of millions of attributes, because the GC has the important search-related items only. This makes for quick turnaround on queries.

The scope of Directory Services has changed from the days of Windows NT 4.0 Directory Services. With Active Directory, a user record holds more than just a username for an individual. The person's telephone number, e-mail address, office location, and so forth can be stored in Active Directory. With this type of information available, users will search the directory on a regular basis. This is especially true when Microsoft Exchange is in the environment.

Whether a person is looking for details on another user, looking for a printer, or simply trying to locate another resource, the GC will be involved in the final resolution of the object. As mentioned previously, the GC server holds a copy of every object in its own domain and a partial copy of objects in other domains in the forest. Therefore, users can search outside their own domains as well as within, something that could not be done with the old Windows NT Directory Services model.

UPN Authentication

The UPN is meant to make logon and e-mail usage easier, because the two (your user account and your e-mail address) are the same. An example of a UPN is Brian@ syngress.com. The GC provides assistance when a user from a domain logs on and the DC doesn't know about the account. When the DC doesn't know the account, it generally means that the account exists in another domain. The GC will help in finding the user's account in Active Directory. The GC server will help to resolve the user account so that the authenticating DC can finalize logon for the user.

EXAM WARNING

With Windows Server 2008 and beyond, you will see more and more references to UPN use in single or multiple domain environments. Be sure to understand how the UPN works in relation to logon, and how the GC keeps this information available efficiently.

Directory Information Search

With Active Directory, users have the ability to search for objects such as other users or printers. To help a user who is searching the database for an object, the GC answers requests for the entire forest. Because the complete copy of every object available is listed in the GC, searches can be completed quickly and with little use of network bandwidth.

When you search the entire directory, the request is directed to the default GC port 3268. The GC server is also known to other computers on the network because of SRV records in the DNS. That is how a node on the network can query for a GC server. There are SRV records specifically for GC services. These records are created when you create the domain.

When users search for information in Active Directory, their queries can cross WAN links, depending on the network layout. Each organization is different. Figure 5.2 shows an example layout with GC servers in the corporate office in Chicago and a branch office in Seattle. The other two sites do not have GC servers. When queries are initiated at the Chicago branch office, the queries use the corporate office GC server. With a high-speed fiber connection, bandwidth isn't an issue.

Figure 5.2 Example GC Search Query

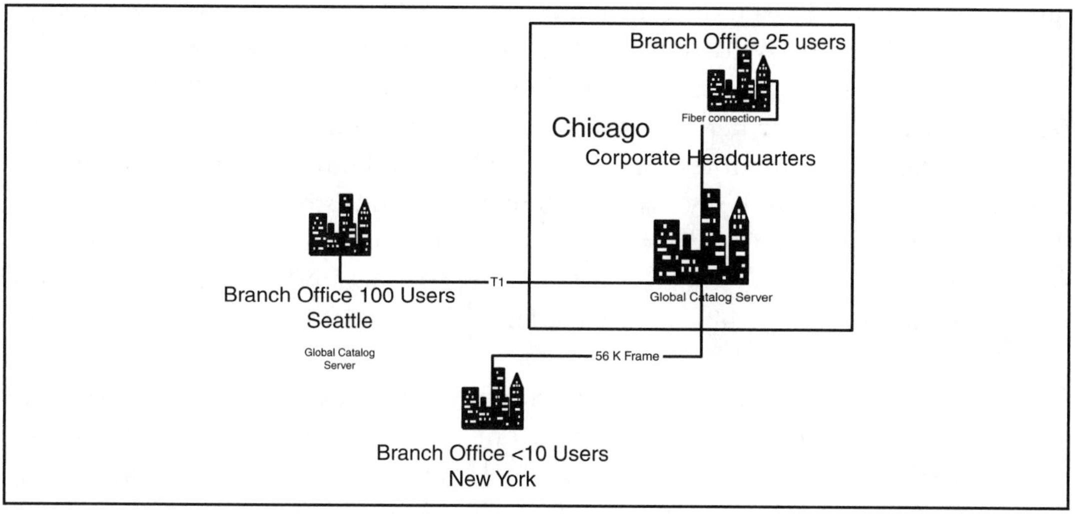

The branch office in New York has a slow link but less than 10 users. These users will use the GC in Chicago as well. Even though the pipe between these locations is only 56K, the minimal number of users doesn't warrant having a GC server in New York. The Seattle office has a T1, which is decent connectivity, but there are more than 100 users in this location. Considering that, searches will be more efficient with a GC server locally. We will look at sites later in the chapter, but Figure 5.2 will help you get a basic understanding of how the query process works.

EXAM WARNING

Be prepared to see diagrams similar to Figure 5.2 that show network lay-outs and the various GC servers you have on your network. Part of being a successful network administrator is being able to determine whether the design is good. Because many Active Directory-integrated applications, such as Microsoft Exchange, need access to a GC for authentication, GCs should be placed in sites that support these applications, as well as sites that are connected over lower-speed WAN links.

Universal Group Membership Information

When setting up your network, certain features will be available based on the forest functional level and domain functional level. Universal Groups is one of these features that will or will not be available depending on your functional level. If your domain functional level is set to at least Windows 2000 Native or later, you will have Universal Groups available on your network. Universal Groups can have members belonging to various domains in the forest. Without a GC server, Universal Groups could not exist. That is because Universal Group membership is stored in the GC only. This means that every DC will not have a copy of Universal Group membership; only the DCs serving as GC servers have this information. When a user logs on, his Universal Group membership is checked. The GC provides this information to the authenticating DC.

Universal Group membership information is stored in all GC servers, so you need to consider the design of your GC server layout when adding to or changing the GC server configuration. The number of users at a location will help to determine when you need a GC server. A large number of queries of the GC information over slow links aren't recommended; placing a GC at each site is a better design. With sites with a small number of users, you can get away with not having a GC server at each site. We discuss this in more detail later in this chapter, in the section "Placing GC Servers within Sites."

Understanding GC Replication

You know now that GC servers hold information for all of the objects in their own domains and a partial copy of the objects from other domains in the forest. For this to be possible, some type of replication has to happen between the GC servers.

The default attributes included in the GC make up the most commonly searched for items. These items are part of normal Active Directory replication.

The Knowledge Consistency Checker (KCC) generates the GC replication topology. The GC is only replicated between DCs that are GC servers; the information is not replicated to other DCs. A few things can affect replication; for example, Universal Group membership, and the number of attributes included in the GC.

Universal Group Membership

The GC holds the sole responsibility of maintaining Universal Group membership. The names of the Global Groups and Domain Local Groups are also in the GC, but their membership lists are not. This helps to keep the size of the database small enough to efficiently answer queries.

For replication purposes, it is best to keep Universal Group membership relatively static. Every change made to a Universal Group is replicated to every GC server. Keeping these changes to a minimum will keep the GC replication traffic to a minimum.

Test Day Tip

Universal Groups can exist only if the functional level of your network is Windows 2000 native or later. Universal Group information is replicated between GC servers. Replication traffic can consume bandwidth, which is why site topology is important; putting a GC at each site keeps replication traffic to a minimum.

Attributes in the Global Catalog

When you first set up Active Directory, a series of default attributes from Active Directory are in the GC. Sometimes the default set of attributes is missing an item you would like to see. For example, perhaps you want to have a coworker's department number as part of his user record; you can accomplish this by adding an attribute. You can use the Active Directory Schema snap-in to include additional attributes in the GC by placing a checkmark next to the **Index this attribute** checkbox, as shown in Figure 5.3. To get to this option, open the **Schema** snap-in, and expand the **Attributes** section. Right-click any attribute, and select **Properties**.

Figure 5.3 Adding Attributes to the GC

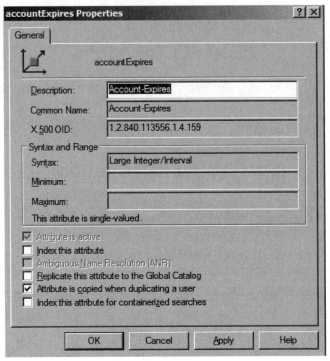

Prior to Windows Server 2003, each time the GC attribute set was extended, a full synchronization of all attributes stored in the GC was completed. In a large network, this often caused a serious amount of network traffic. With Windows Server 2003 and Windows Server 2008, only the additional attribute or attributes are replicated to other GC servers. This makes for more efficient use of network bandwidth.

Placing GC Servers within Sites

Another consideration when it comes to replication is placement of your GC servers. In a small network with one physical location, GC server placement is easy. Your first DC that is configured will hold the GC role. If you have one site, but more than one DC, you can move the role to another DC if you want to or configure additional DCs as GCs. Most networks today consist of multiple physical locations, whether in the same city or across the country. If you have high-speed links connecting your branch offices you might be okay, but many branch office links use limited bandwidth connections. If the connection between locations is less than a T1, you might have limited bandwidth depending on what traffic is crossing the wire. As a network administrator, you will have to work with your provider to gauge how much utilization there is across your WAN links.

Another factor is reliability. If your WAN links are unreliable, replication traffic and synchronization traffic might not successfully cross the link. The less reliable the link, the more the need for setting up sites and site links between the locations.

Without proper planning, replication traffic can cause problems in a large network. Sites help to control replication traffic. Making the most of available bandwidth is an important factor in having a network that allows your users to be productive. Logon and searching Active Directory are both affected by GC server placement. If users cannot find the information they need from Active Directory, they might not be able to log on or find the information or data they need.

Configuring & Implementing…

GC in an Exchange Server Environment

Now that Active Directory is the single directory used in Windows 2000, Windows Server 2003, and Windows Server 2008 networks, there is very tight integration with Microsoft Exchange. Prior to Exchange 2000, Exchange had its own directory and the domain had its own directory service. There were links between the two, but they were still technically separate directories.

Because all user information (first name, last name, and contact information) is kept in Active Directory, users will be searching more and more throughout the directory. In previous versions of Exchange, there was a Global Address List that you could search to locate people within your organization. Information such as telephone numbers, fax numbers, and office locations can be part of your GC strategy with Windows Server 2003. It is important for administrators to ensure that users can reach the data for which they are searching as quickly and easily as possible. Proper planning and location of your GC information is important to successful queries of your directory information.

Bandwidth and Network Traffic Considerations

Active Directory replication works differently depending on whether it is *intersite* or *intrasite* replication. DCs that are part of the same site (intrasite) replicate with one another more often than DCs in different sites (intersite). If you have sites that are geographically dispersed, you need to be careful how you handle your GC server placement. The bandwidth between geographically dispersed offices is often minimal. The rule of thumb is to have GC servers in selected sites. In most cases, you do not want to have a GC server in every site because of the vast amount of replication that would occur. The following examples describe situations in which you should have a GC server within a site:

- If you have a slow WAN link between geographic locations. If you have a DC at each location, a good rule is to also have a GC server at each location. If the WAN link supports traffic for normal DC traffic, it should also handle GC traffic.

- If you have an application that relies heavily on GC queries across port 3268, you'll want to have a GC server in the site in which the application runs. An example of this is Exchange 2000, which relies heavily on GC information.

- You'll want to have GCs in as many sites as possible to support Universal Group membership authentication. We look at caching of Universal Groups, which can reduce traffic related to this, in the next section.

TEST DAY TIP

Microsoft's documentation recommends that if you have 50 or more users at a given location, you should give that location a DC serving as a GC server. This will help to reduce the number of queries crossing the WAN for Active Directory object searches.

Data replicated between sites is compressed, which makes better use of available bandwidth. Because the data is compressed, more can be sent over a limited amount of bandwidth. This is how site placement and design can be critical to efficient network operation.

Universal Group Membership Caching

The Windows Server 2003 Active Directory introduced *Universal Group caching* as a new feature, and this feature is also available in Windows Server 2008. When a user logs on to the network, his membership in Universal Groups is verified. For this to happen, the authenticating DC has to query the GC. If the GC is across a WAN link, the logon process will be slow every time. To alleviate this, the DC that queries the GC can cache this information, which cuts down on the amount of data traveling across the WAN link for Universal Group information.

The cache is loaded at the first user logon. Every eight hours by default, the DC will refresh the cache from the nearest GC server. Caching functionality is administered in Active Directory Sites and Services as shown in Figure 5.4, and can be turned off if desired. You can also designate the GC server from which you want the cache to refresh, giving you more control over traffic distribution on the network.

> ### NOTE
>
> The NTDS Site Settings Properties box is not the same NTDS Settings Properties box you accessed to make a DC act as a GC. Instead of accessing the properties of NTDS settings under the DC node in the Servers container, you must access the properties of NTDS Site Settings in the right console pane when you select a site name (e.g., Default-First-Site-Name). The similarity of these two settings can be confusing if you haven't worked with the console much.

Figure 5.4 Configuring Universal Group Caching

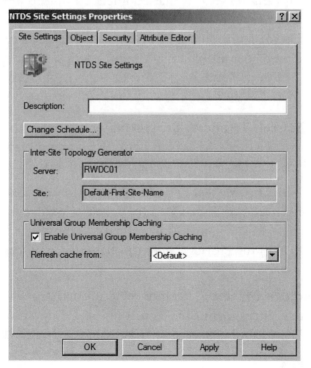

Prior to Windows Server 2003, Active Directory logon would immediately fail if a GC could not be located to check Universal Group membership. With Universal Group caching in Windows Server 2003 and Windows Server 2008, DCs cache complete group membership information, so even if a GC server cannot be reached, logon will still happen based on cached Universal Group information.

Working with Flexible Single Master Operation (FSMO) Roles

In Windows NT 4.0, the domain had only one authoritative source for domain-related information, the primary domain controller or PDC. With the implementation of Active Directory came the multimaster replication model, where objects and their properties can be modified on any DC and become authoritative through replication conflict resolution measures. This scalability effort came with a price in complexity, however, and Active Directory FSMO roles were introduced to control certain domain and forest-wide operations that are not well suited for a multimaster environment. Some operations such as modifying the Active Directory schema or adding or removing a domain or domain tree are sufficiently critical or sensitive that their functions need to reside on a single DC within the domain or forest.

The advantage of using FSMOs is that conflicts cannot be introduced while a particular Operations Master is offline; the alternative would involve resolving conflicts later, possibly to significantly negative result. The disadvantage is that all Operations Masters must be available at all times to support all dependent activities within the domain or forest. Windows Server 2008 Active Directory requires five operational master roles:

- **Schema Master** To update the schema of a forest, you must have access to the Schema Master DC, which controls all schema updates and modifications. There can be only one Schema Master in the forest.

- **Domain Naming Master** The Domain Naming Master DC controls the addition or removal of domains in the forest as well as adding and removing any cross-references to domains in external Lightweight Directory Access Protocol (LDAP) directories. There can be only one Domain Naming Master in the forest.

- **Infrastructure Master** The Infrastructure Master is responsible for updating references from objects in the local domain to objects in other domains. There can be only one Infrastructure Master DC in each domain.

- **Relative ID (RID) Master** The RID Master processes RID pool requests from all DCs in the local domain. These relative identifiers are the unique part of the SID, which is a Security Identifier used to uniquely identify objects and group memberships. There can be only one RID Master DC in each domain.

- **PDC Emulator** The PDC Emulator is a DC that advertises itself as the PDC to workstations, member servers, and BDCs running Windows NT. It is also the Domain Master Browser, and handles Active Directory password changes, maintenance of trust relationships, as well as time synchronization for servers and clients within a domain. There can be only one PDC Emulator in each domain.

Two of these operate at the forest level only, you will have a single Schema Master and Domain Naming Master within each Active Directory forest regardless of how many domains exist within the forest. Conversely, the RID Master, PDC Emulator, and Infrastructure Master operate at the domain level. To examine this role relationship between master roles and the required authorization for administering them in the forest and domains, refer to Table 5.2.

Table 5.2 Valid Authorization Levels for Viewing, Transferring, and Seizing Operations Master Roles

Role	Task	Domain Administrator on the Local Domain	Domain Administrator on the Forest-Root Domain	Enterprise Administrator
Schema Master	Viewing, transferring, or seizing		X (Plus *Schema Admins* membership)	X
Domain Naming Master Viewing, transferring, or seizing	X		X	

Continued

Table 5.2 Continued. Valid Authorization Levels for Viewing, Transferring, and Seizing Operations Master Roles

Role	Task	Domain Administrator on the Local Domain	Domain Administrator on the Forest-Root Domain	Enterprise Administrator
Infrastructure Master	Viewing, transferring, or seizing	X		X
RID Master	Viewing, transferring, or seizing	X		X
PDC Emulator	Viewing, transferring, or seizing	X		X

To illustrate, if you have a single Active Directory forest containing a parent domain and a child domain, you will have one each of the Schema Master and Domain Naming Master FSMO roles, and two each of the Infrastructure Master, RID Master, and PDC Emulator, with one of each domain-wide FSMO configured in each of the two domains. A single-domain forest, therefore, has five roles—one of each. Each domain added after the forest root domain has three additional masters. With that information, we can determine the number of operations master servers required in a given forest with the following formula:

((*Number of domains* * 3) + 2)

Given the formula, we can determine that the forest depicted in Figure 5.5, with three domains, needs a maximum of 11 server platforms to support the 11 FSMO roles (3 * 3 = 9, and 9 + 2 = 11), unless you assign multiple roles to a single DC. Often, small domains, empty root domains, or best practices will make combining several of these roles onto a single DC desirable. In the example shown in Figure 5.5, the following roles exist:

- One Schema Master in Dogs.com

- One Domain Naming Master in Dogs.com

- Three PDC Emulators (one each in Dogs.com, Fish.com, and Cat.fish.com)

- Three RID Masters (one each in Dogs.com, Fish.com, and Cat.fish.com)

- Three Infrastructure Masters (one each in Dogs.com, Fish.com, and Cat.fish.com)

Figure 5.5 Creating a New Child Domain in an Existing Domain

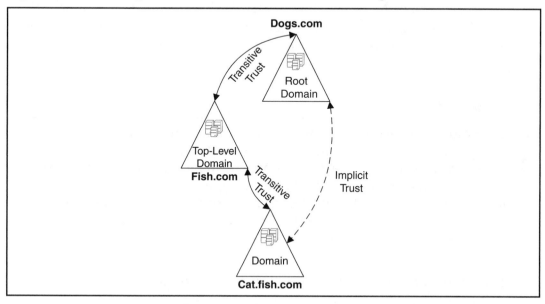

Placing, Transferring, and Seizing FSMO Role Holders

The first DC that you install in the forest root will automatically host all five roles. The first DC that you install in any additional domains will automatically host the three roles of PDC Emulator, RID Master, and Infrastructure Master.

You can use the ntdsutil.exe command-line utility to transfer FSMO roles, or you can use an MMC snap-in tool. Depending on which role you want to transfer, you can use one of the following three MMC snap-in tools:

- Active Directory Schema snap-in (Schema Master role)

- Active Directory Domains and Trusts snap-in (Domain Naming Master role)

- Active Directory Users and Computers snap-in (RID Master, Infrastructure Master, and PDC Emulator roles)

To forcibly seize a role, you must use the ntdsutil utility. If a computer cannot be contacted due to a hardware malfunction or long-term network failure, the role must be seized. If the PDC Emulator role holder fails, you can seize the PDC Emulator FSMO role to another DC and then return the role to the original role holder when it comes back online. In the case of other FSMO role holders, particularly the RID Master and Schema Master FSMO role holders, you must take significantly greater care if you need to seize the FSMO role due to a hardware or network failure. If you seize the Schema Master or RID Master FSMO role holder to another DC, the original role holder must never be returned to Active Directory; the original role holder must be reformatted before being returned to your production environment.

EXAM WARNING

Remember this distinction between the GC and the Schema Master: The *GC* contains a limited set of attributes of all objects in the Active Directory. The *Schema Master* contains formal definitions of every object class that can exist in the forest and every object attribute that can exist within an object. In other words, the GC contains every *object*, whereas the schema contains every *definition* of every type of object.

Locating and Transferring the Schema Master Role

The DC that hosts the Schema Master role controls each update or modification to the schema. You must have access to the Schema Master to update the schema of a forest.

NOTE

You must be a member of the Schema Admins group to perform this operation. The built-in Administrator account in the forest root domain is automatically configured as a member of this group when the Active Directory forest is created.

Refer to Exercise 5.3 for instructions on how to identify the DC that is performing the Schema Master operations role for your forest using the command line or the GUI. Refer to Exercise 5.4 for instructions on how to transfer the Schema Master operations role for your forest to a different DC, and Exercise 5.9, later in this chapter, for steps to seize the role to another DC in case of a failure.

Temporary loss of the Schema Master is not noticeable to domain users. Enterprise and domain administrators will not notice the loss either, unless they are trying to install an application that modifies the schema during installation or trying to modify the schema themselves. You should seize the schema FSMO role to the standby operations master only if your old Schema master will be permanently offline.

EXERCISE 5.3

LOCATING THE SCHEMA OPERATIONS MASTER

1. Log on as an Enterprise Administrator in the forest you are checking.

2. Click **Start | Run**.

3. Type **regsvr32 schmmgmt.dll** in the **Open** box, and click **OK**. This registers the Schmmgmt.dll.

4. Click **OK** in the dialog box showing that the operation succeeded.

5. Click **Start | Run**, type **mmc**, and then click **OK**.

6. On the menu bar, click **File | Add/Remove Snap-in**, click **Add**, double-click **Active Directory Schema**, click **Close**, and then click **OK**.

7. Expand and then right-click **Active Directory Schema** in the top-left pane, and then select **Operations Masters** to view the server holding the Schema Master role, as shown in Figure 5.6.

Figure 5.6 The Server Holding the Schema Master Role

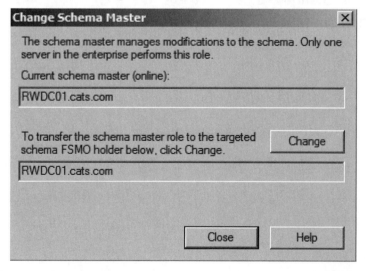

EXERCISE 5.4

TRANSFERRING THE SCHEMA OPERATIONS MASTER ROLE

1. Log on as an Enterprise Administrator in the forest where you want to transfer the Schema Master role.

2. Click **Start | Run**.

3. Type **regsvr32 schmmgmt.dll** in the **Open** box, and then click **OK**. This registers the Schmmgmt.dll.

4. Click **OK** in the dialog box showing that the operation succeeded.

5. Click **Start | Run**, type **mmc**, and then click **OK**.

6. On the menu bar, click **File | Add/Remove Snap-in**, click **Add**, double-click **Active Directory Schema**, click **Close**, and then click **OK**.

7. Right-click **Active Directory Schema** in the top-left pane, and then click **Change Active Directory Domain Controller**.

8. As shown in Figure 5.7, select the **This Domain Controller or AD LDS instance**, enter the name of the DC that will be the new role holder, and then click **OK**.

9. Right-click **Active Directory Schema** again, and then click **Operations Master**.

10. Click **Change**.

11. Click **OK** to confirm that you want to transfer the role, and then click **Close**.

Figure 5.7 Changing an Active Directory Domain Controller

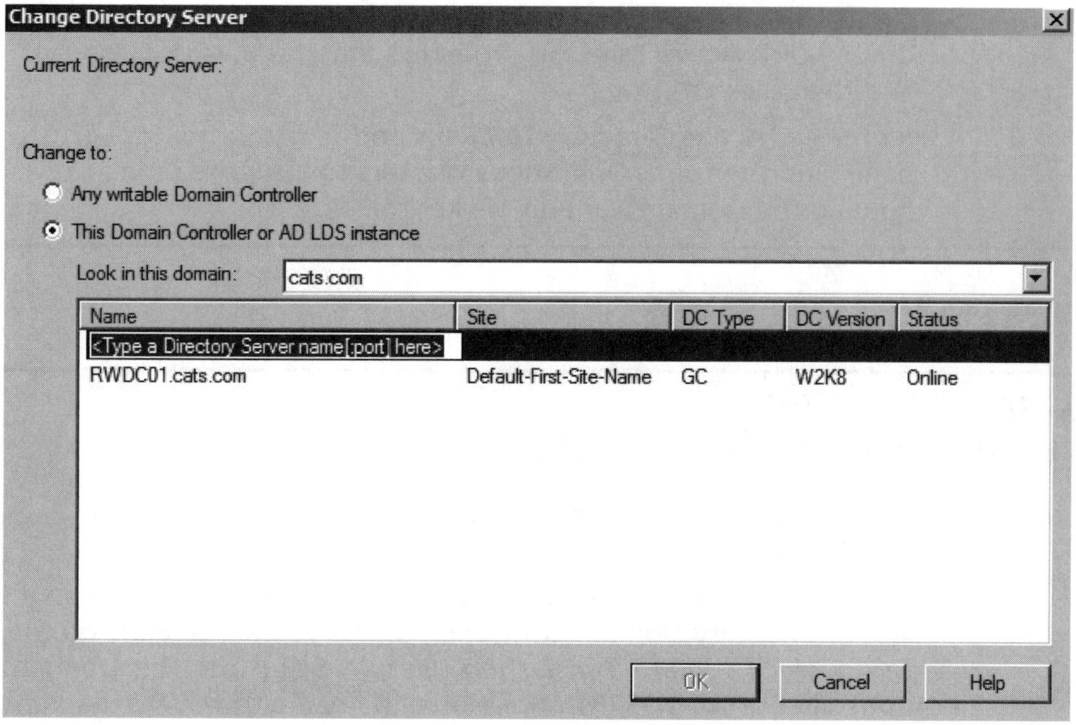

Locating and Transferring the Domain Naming Master Role

The Domain Naming Master DC controls the addition or removal of domains in the forest, *and* adding and removing any cross-references to domains in external LDAP directories. There can be only one Domain Naming Master in the forest.

Refer to Exercise 5.5 for instructions on how to identify the DC that is performing the Domain Naming Master operation role for your forest. Refer to Exercise 5.6 for instructions on how to transfer the Domain Naming Master operations role for your forest to a different DC.

EXERCISE 5.5

LOCATING THE DOMAIN NAMING OPERATIONS MASTER

1. Log on as an Enterprise Administrator in the forest you are checking.

2. Click **Start | Run**, type **mmc**, and then click **OK**.

3. On the menu bar, click **File | Add/Remove Snap-in**, click **Add**, double-click **Active Directory Domains and Trusts**, click **Close**, and then click **OK**.

4. Right-click **Active Directory Domains and Trusts** in the top-left pane, and then click **Operations Masters** to view the server holding the Domain Naming Master role.

EXERCISE 5.6

TRANSFERRING THE DOMAIN NAMING MASTER ROLE

1. Click **Start | Administrative Tools | Active Directory Domains and Trusts**.

2. Right-click **Active Directory Domains and Trusts**, and click **Change Active Directory Domain Controller**, *unless you are already on the DC to which you are transferring the role*. Select the **This Domain Controller or AD LDS instance**, enter the name of the DC that will be the new role holder, and then click **OK**.

3. In the console tree, right-click **Active Directory Domains and Trusts**, and then select **Operations Master**. Click **Change**.

4. Click **OK** for confirmation, and click **Close**.

Locating and Transferring the Infrastructure, RID, and PDC Operations Master Roles

The Infrastructure Master is responsible for updating references from objects in the local domain to objects in other domains. There can be only one Infrastructure Master DC in each domain. The RID Master processes RID pool requests from all DCs in the local domain. There can be only one RID Master DC in each domain. The PDC Emulator is a DC that advertises itself as the PDC to workstations, member servers, and BDCs running Windows NT. It is also the Domain Master Browser, and handles Active Directory password collisions, or discrepancies. There can be only one PDC Emulator in each domain.

Refer to Exercise 5.7 for instructions on how to identify the DCs that are performing the FSMO roles for your forest using the Active Directory Users and

Computers GUI interface. Refer to Exercise 5.8 for instructions on how to transfer the Infrastructure, RID, and PDC Master operations roles for your domain to different DCs, and to Exercise 5.9 for instructions on how to seize the FSMO Master roles.

EXERCISE 5.7

LOCATING THE INFRASTRUCTURE, RID, AND PDC OPERATIONS MASTERS

1. Log on as an Enterprise Administrator in the forest you are checking.

2. Click **Start | Run**, type **dsa.msc**, and click **OK**. This is an alternative method for opening the **Active Directory Users and Computers** administrative tool.

3. Right-click the selected Domain Object in the top-left pane, and then click **Operations Masters**.

4. Click the **Infrastructure** tab to view the server holding the Infrastructure Master role.

5. Click the **RID** tab to view the server holding the RID Master role.

6. Click the **PDC** tab to view the server holding the PDC Master role.

EXERCISE 5.8

TRANSFERRING THE INFRASTRUCTURE, RID, AND PDC MASTER ROLES

1. Click **Start | Administrative Tools | Active Directory Users and Computers**.

2. Right-click **Active Directory Users and Computers**, and click **Connect to Domain Controller** *unless you are already on the DC you are transferring to*. Select the **This Domain Controller or AD LDS instance**, enter the name of the DC that will be the new role holder, and then click **OK**.

3. In the console tree, right-click **Active Directory Users and Computers**, and click **All Tasks | Operations Master**.

4. Take the appropriate action for the role you want to transfer:
   - Click the **Infrastructure** tab, and click **Change**.
   - Click the **RID** tab, and click **Change**.
   - Click the **PDC** tab, and click **Change**.
5. Click **OK** for confirmation, and click **Close**.

EXERCISE 5.9

SEIZING THE FSMO MASTER ROLES

1. Log on to any working DC.
2. Click **Start | Run**, type **ntdsutil** in the Open box, and then click **OK**.
3. Type **activate instance ntds** and press **Enter**.
3. Type **roles**, and press **Enter**.
4. In ntdsutil, type **?** at any prompt to see a list of available commands, and press **Enter**.
5. Type **connections**, and press **Enter**.
6. Type **connect to server** *servername*, where *servername* is the name of the server that will receive the role, and press **Enter**.
7. At the **Server connections:** prompt, type **q**, and press **Enter**.
8. Type the appropriate seizing command, as shown next. See the example in Figure 5.8. If the FSMO role is available, ntdsutil.exe will perform a transfer instead. Respond to the Role Seizure Confirmation Dialog box, as shown in Figure 5.9.

```
seize Sfrastructure master
seize RID master
seize PDC
```

Figure 5.8 Seizing the PDC Master Role

```
D:\WINDOWS\system32\ntdsutil.exe: activate instance ntds
Active instance set to "ntds".
ntdsutil: roles
fsmo maintenance: connections
server connections: connect to server DC4
```

```
Binding to DC4 ...

Connected to DC4 using credentials of locally logged on user.

server connections: q

fsmo maintenance: seize PDC

Attempting safe transfer of PDC FSMO before seizure.

FSMO transferred successfully - seizure not required.

Server "DC4" knows about 5 roles

Schema - CN=NTDS Settings,CN=DC3,CN=Servers,CN=Default-First-Site-
    Name,CN=Sites,

CN=Configuration,DC=Dogs,DC=com

Domain - CN=NTDS Settings,CN=DC3,CN=Servers,CN=Default-First-Site-
    Name,CN=Sites,

CN=Configuration,DC=Dogs,DC=com

PDC - CN=NTDS Settings,CN=DC4,CN=Servers,CN=Default-First-Site-
    Name,CN=Sites,CN=

Configuration,DC=Dogs,DC=com

RID - CN=NTDS Settings,CN=DC4,CN=Servers,CN=Default-First-Site-
    Name,CN=Sites,CN=

Configuration,DC=Dogs,DC=com

Infrastructure - CN=NTDS Settings,CN=DC4,CN=Servers,CN=Default-First-
Site-
    Name,C

N=Sites,CN=Configuration,DC=Dogs,DC=com

fsmo maintenance:q
```

Figure 5.9 Seizing the Schema Operations Master Role

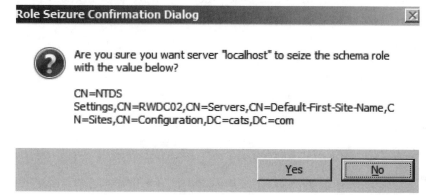

9. After you seize the role, type **q**, and then press **Enter** repeatedly until you quit the Ntdsutil tool.

Placing the FSMO Roles within an Active Directory Environment

It is a good idea to place the RID and PDC Emulator roles on the same DC. Down-level clients and applications target the PDC, making it a large consumer of RIDs. Good communication between these two roles is important. If performance demands it, place the RID and PDC Emulator roles on separate DCs, but make sure they stay in the same site and that they are direct replication partners with each other.

As a general rule, you should place the Infrastructure Master on a DC that is not a GC server to maintain proper replication. There are two exceptions to this rule:

- **Single domain forest** If your forest contains only one Active Directory domain, there can be no phantoms. The Infrastructure Master has no functionality in a single domain forest. In that case, you can place the Infrastructure Master on any DC.

- **Multidomain forest where every DC holds the GC** Again, there can be no phantoms if every DC in the domain hosts a GC. There is no work for the Infrastructure Master to perform. In that case, you can place the Infrastructure Master on any DC.

Additionally, ensure that the Infrastructure Master has a direct connection object to a GC server somewhere in the forest, preferably in the same site.

Considering the forest-wide FSMOs, the Schema Master and Domain Naming Master roles are rarely used and should be tightly controlled. For that reason, you can place them on the same DC. Another Microsoft-recommended practice is to place the Domain Naming Master FSMO on a GC server. Taking all of these practices together, a Microsoft-recommended best-practice empty root domain design might consist of two DCs with the following FSMO/GC placement:

- DC 1:
    - Schema Master
    - Domain Naming Master
    - GC
- DC 2:
    - RID Master
    - PDC Emulator
    - Infrastructure Master

Working with Sites

In today's distributed network environment, the communication must always be rapid and reliable. Geographical and other restrictions resulted in the need to create smaller networks, known as *subnets*. These subnets provide rapid and reliable communication between locations, which can also be attained in larger networks by using Microsoft Windows Server 2008 Active Directory Sites. They ensure rapid and reliable communication by using the methods offered by Microsoft Windows Server 2008 Active Directory Sites to regulate inter-subnet traffic.

A *site* defines the network structure of a Windows Server 2008 Active Directory. A site consists of multiple Internet Protocol (IP) subnets linked together by rapid and reliable connections. The primary role of sites is to increase the performance of a network by economic and rapid transmission of data. The other roles of sites are replication and authentication. The Active Directory physical structure manages when and how the authentication and replication must take place. The Active Directory physical structure allows the management of Active Directory replication scheduling between sites. The performance of a network is also based on the location of objects and *logon authentication* as users log on to the network.

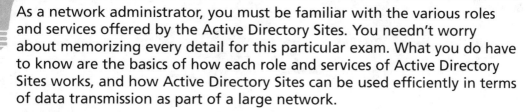

Test Day Tip

As a network administrator, you must be familiar with the various roles and services offered by the Active Directory Sites. You needn't worry about memorizing every detail for this particular exam. What you do have to know are the basics of how each role and services of Active Directory Sites works, and how Active Directory Sites can be used efficiently in terms of data transmission as part of a large network.

Understanding Sites

A site is as a collection of interconnected computers that operate over IP subnets. A site is also a place on a network having high-bandwidth connectivity. The relationship of sites to Active Directory components is based on the following network operations performed by sites:

- Control of replication occurrences
- Changes made with the sites
- How efficiently DCs within a domain can communicate

A site can contain one or more domains, and a domain can be part of one or more sites. Sites and domains do not have to maintain the same *namespace*. Sites and domains are interrelated because sites control replication of the domain information.

Head of the Class...

The Relationship between Sites and Domains

Domains are also defined as *units of replication.* All the DCs present in a particular domain can receive changes and replicate those changes to all other DCs present in the domain of a network. A DNS server recognizes each domain that is present in a particular site. If your network requires more than one domain, you can easily create multiple domains. Figure 5.10 illustrates the relationship between sites and domains in a network, and helps us to understand that a site can have one or more domains, and a domain can have one or more sites.

Figure 5.10 The Relationship between the Sites and Domains Present in a Network

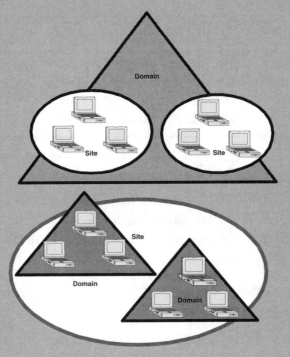

In Figure 5.10, we see how multiple sites reside in a single domain, and how a single site can consist of multiple domains. A domain provides the following benefits:

- It organizes domain objects.

- It publishes resources and information about domain objects.

- It applies GPOs to the domain to perform resource and security management.

- It delegates authority to eliminate the need for administrators with broad administrative authority.

- Security policies and settings such as user rights and password policies do not change from one domain to another.

- Each domain stores only the information about the objects located in that domain.

Exam Warning

Make sure you are familiar with the benefits provided by a domain, and how a domain works to provide them for you.

The sites present in an Active Directory denote the *physical structure* of a network. The physical structure information is available as site and site link objects in the directory. This information is used to build the most efficient replication topology. Generally, Active Directory Sites and Services are used to define sites and site links.

Whereas sites represent the physical structure of the network, domains represent the *logical structure* of the organization. This partitioning of physical and logical structures offers the following advantages:

- You can develop and manage the logical and physical structures of your network independently.

- You do not have to base domain namespaces on your physical network.

- You can deploy DCs for multiple domains within the same site.

- You can deploy DCs for the same domain in multiple sites.

TEST DAY TIP

Make sure you know and understand the differences between the physical and logical structures of the network. Be aware of how each is used to build the most efficient replication topology.

Subnets

In Active Directory, a site consists of a set of computers that are interconnected in a LAN. Computers within the same site typically exist in the same building, or on the same campus network. A single site consists of one or more IP subnets. These subnets are a section of an IP network, with each subnet having a unique network address.

A subnet address consists of a cluster of neighboring computers in much the same way as the postal codes group neighboring postal addresses. Figure 5.11 shows one or more clients residing within a subnet that defines an Active Directory site.

Figure 5.11 The Active Directory Site with One or More Client Computers within a Subnet

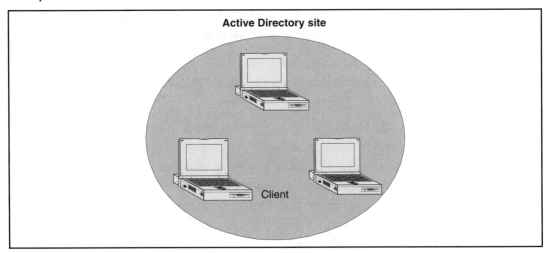

The subnet created through Active Directory Sites and Services are sections of an IP network, with each subnet having a unique network address. In Figure 5.11, 231.01.01.0/19 is a unique network address of the Active Directory site.

Sites and subnets are represented in Active Directory by site and subnet objects, which we create through the Active Directory Sites and Services administrative tool. Each site object is associated with one or more subnet objects.

Site Planning

You should plan thoroughly before creating and deploying an Active Directory. Site planning enables you to optimize the efficiency of the network and reduce administrative overhead. High-performance sites are developed based on the proper planning of the physical design of your network. Site planning enables you to determine exactly which sites you should create and how they can be linked using *site links* and *site link bridges*. Site information is stored in the *configuration partition*, which enables you to create sites and related information at any point in your deployment of Active Directory.

NOTE

A configuration partition is a portion of a basic disk that can contain logical drives. A configuration partition is used if you want to have more than four volumes on your basic disk. A DC always stores the partitions for the schema and configuration. The schema and configuration are replicated to every DC in the domain tree or forest.

Site planning enables you to publish site information in the directory for use by applications and services. Generally, the Active Directory consumes the site information. You'll see how replication impacts site planning later in this chapter.

Criteria for Establishing Separate Sites

When you initially create a domain, a single default Active Directory site called *Default-Site-First-Name* is created. This site represents your entire network. A domain or forest consisting of a separate site can be highly efficient for a LAN connected by high-speed bandwidth.

NOTE

A forest is defined as multiple Active Directory domains that share the same class, site, attribute definitions, and replication information (but not necessarily the same namespace). The domains present in the same forest are linked with two-way transitive trust relationships.

If a single LAN consists of a separate subnet or if a network consists of multiple subnets connected by a high-speed connection, establishing a separate site topology offers the following advantages:

- Simplified replication management

- Regular directory updates between all DCs

Establishing separate site topology enables all replication to occur as intrasite replication, which requires no manual replication configuration. A separate site design enables DCs to receive updates with respect to directory changes.

NOTE

Intrasite replication refers to replication among DCs within the same site. *Intersite* replication refers to replication among DCs located at different sites.

Creating a Site

Sites are created using the Active Directory Sites and Services tool of Windows Server 2008. Exercise 5.10 walks you through the steps involved in creating a site.

Active Directory Sites and Services is an MMC that you can use to administer the replication of directory data. You can also use this tool to create new sites, site links, subnets, and so forth.

EXERCISE 5.10

CREATING A NEW SITE

1. To open the **Active Directory Sites and Services** tool, click **Start | Control Panel | Administrative Tools | Active Directory Sites and Services**. The Active Directory Sites and Services console appears, as shown in Figure 5.12.

Figure 5.12 The Active Directory Sites and Services Tool

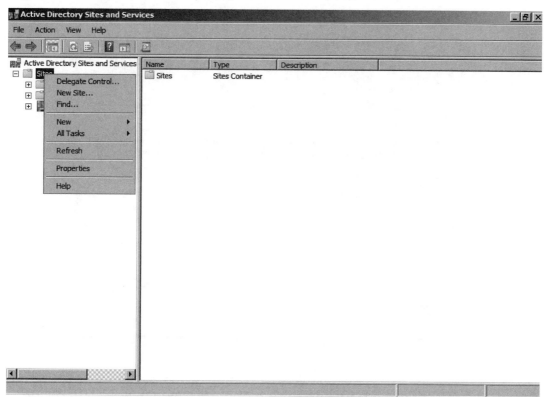

2. Highlight the **Sites** folder in the left-hand tree pane of the **Active Directory Sites and Services** console. Right-click and select the **Sites** folder's **New Site** option from the context menu, as shown in Figure 5.13.

Figure 5.13 The New Site Option

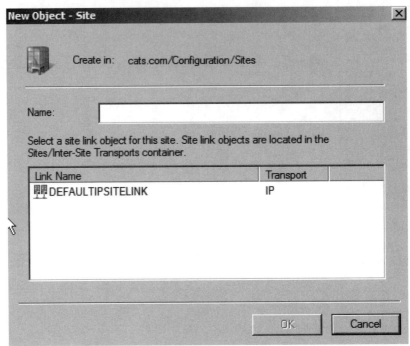

3. Selecting the **New Site** option opens a **New Object – Site** dialog box, as shown in Figure 5.14.

Figure 5.14 The New Object – Site Dialog Box

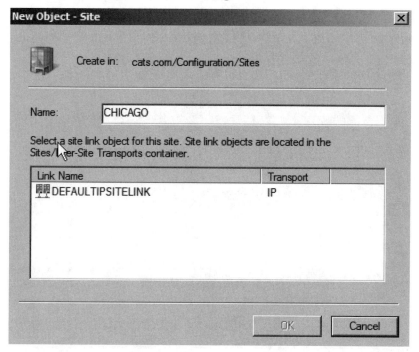

4. Type the name of the site in the **Name** box present in the **New Object – Site** dialog box, as shown in Figure 5.15.

Figure 5.15 The Name of the Site

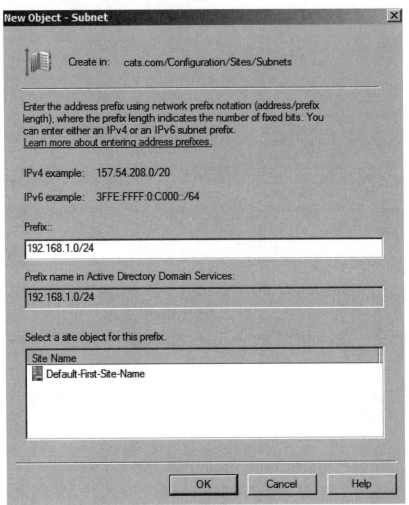

5. Select an initial site link object for the site from the **New Object – Site** dialog box.

6. Click **OK**. You will be presented with a pop-up box indicating the next steps that you should follow once the new site is created. Read this informational message and then click **OK**. This completes the process of creating a site using the **Active Directory Sites and Services** tool.

Renaming a Site

Renaming a site is one of the first tasks you should perform when administering a site structure. When you create a site initially, it is created with the default name Default-First-Site-Name. You can change this name based on the purpose of the site, such as the name of the physical location.

A site is also renamed when a network of an organization is expanded by one or more sites. Even if an organization is located in a single location, it makes sense to rename the Default-First-Site-Name, because you never know when the network will expand. Renaming a site enables administrators to differentiate sites present in a network easily and perform administration tasks efficiently.

When a DC becomes aware that its site has been renamed, it will update its DNS records appropriately. Because of issues with cached DNS lookups and client caching of site names that will lead to temporary delays in connectivity directly after a rename, it's best to name and rename sites as early as possible in the deployment. After renaming a site, it's advisable to manually force replication with other DCs in the same site.

You rename a site using the Active Directory Sites and Services tool of Windows Server 2008. Exercise 5.11 walks you through the steps involved in renaming a new site.

EXERCISE 5.11

RENAMING A NEW SITE

1. To open the **Active Directory Sites and Services** tool, click **Start | Control Panel | Administrative Tools**. Double-click **Active Directory Sites and Services**. The Active Directory Sites and Services dialog box appears.

2. Expand the **Sites** folder in the left-hand tree pane of the **Active Directory Sites and Services** console.

3. Right-click the site you want to rename and select the **Rename** option from the context menu.

4. Type the new name of the site in the **Name** box in the left console pane.

5. Click **OK**. This completes the process of renaming a site using the Active Directory Sites and Services tool.

> **NOTE**
>
> The Windows Server 2008 Active Directory consists of the default site link, named DEFAULTIPSITELINK, which is created automatically when the first domain in the network is created. This link is assigned to the Default-First-Site-Name site. These are the names assigned automatically when you create the first site. You should change the default names to something more descriptive.

Creating Subnets

Subnets are associated with the Active Directory sites to match client computers. The subnets are denoted by a range of IP addresses. The Active Directory Sites and Services user interface prevents you from having to provide the subnet names manually; instead, you are prompted for a network address. An example of a subnet name for an IP Version 4 network is 10.14.208.0/20. This IP address consists of two portions: The network address appears before the slash, and a representation of the subnet mask appears after the slash. Table 5.3 shows some common subnet masks and the corresponding slash notations. The number following the slash indicates the number of binary digits (bits) that make up the network partition of the IP address. The number 255 in decimal translates to 11111111 in binary (8 bits); thus, you can see how the subnet masks in Table 5.3 translate to the corresponding slash notations.

Table 5.3 Subnet Masks and Slash Notation

Subnet Mask	Slash Notation
255.0.0.0	/8
255.255.0.0	/16
255.255.255.0	/24
255.255.255.128	/25
255.255.255.192	/26
255.255.255.224	/27
255.255.255.240	/28

Continued

Table 5.3 Continued. Subnet Masks and Slash Notation

Subnet Mask	Slash Notation
255.255.255.248	/29
255.255.255.252	/30
255.255.255.254	/31

IP Version 6 (IPv6) is a new implementation of the Transmission Control Protocol/Internet Protocol (TCP/IP) that is increasing in prevalence, as it addresses a number of shortcomings that have appeared in IPv4 over time. Windows Server 2008 is the first version of the Windows operating system that has included support for IPv6 out of the box; IPv6 is one of the default protocols included in a fresh installation of the Windows Server 2008 operating system. IPv6 was developed to address a number of limitations of IPv4, the most notable being the limitations of the IPv4 address space, that is, the list of usable TCP/IP addresses provided by IPv4. When TCP/IP was developed in the 1960s, no one foresaw the Internet explosion of the 1990s that would threaten to exhaust the 4-billion-plus IP addresses available through IPv4. The useful lifespan of IPv4 has been extended through the use of private IP networks and the network address translator (NAT), but a long-term solution is still required. To this end, IPv6, the next generation of TCP/IP, was developed to provide a significantly larger address space for current and future implementations of TCP/IP networks.

IPv6 uses 128 bits, or 16 bytes, for its addressing scheme, which provides 2^{128} (about 340 billion) IP addresses. IPv6 address notation is noticeably different from the dotted-decimal of IPv4, using eight groups of four hexadecimal digits, separated by colons. For example, 192.168.1.243 is an example of an IPv4 IP address, and 5ab1:0c12:63d7:0237:9175:bade:0370:7334 is an example of an IPv6 IP address. If an IPv6 address contains a series of sequential zeros, the address can be shortened to use a single zero in each group, or else the entire grouping can be represented using a double colon (::). So, the following three strings all represent the same IPv6 address:

- 5925:0000:0000:0000:0000:0000:0000:2742
- 5925:0:0:0:0:0:0:2742
- 5925::2742

NOTE

The loopback address in IPv6 is expressed as ::1.

IPv6 includes a few other enhancements for performance and security. Notably, IP security through the use of IPSec is an integral part of IPv6, whereas it was an optional feature under IPv4.

You create subnets using the Active Directory Sites and Services tool of Windows Server 2008. Exercise 5.12 shows the steps involved in creating subnets.

EXERCISE 5.12

CREATING SUBNETS

1. To open the **Active Directory Sites and Services** tool, click **Start | Control Panel | Administrative Tools**, and then double-click **Active Directory Sites and Services**. The Active Directory Sites and Services console appears.

2. Highlight the **Sites** folder in the left-hand tree pane of the **Active Directory Sites and Services** console. Expand the **Sites** folder.

3. Right-click **Subnets** and select **New Subnet** from the context menu, as shown in Figure 5.16.

Figure 5.16 The New Subnet Option

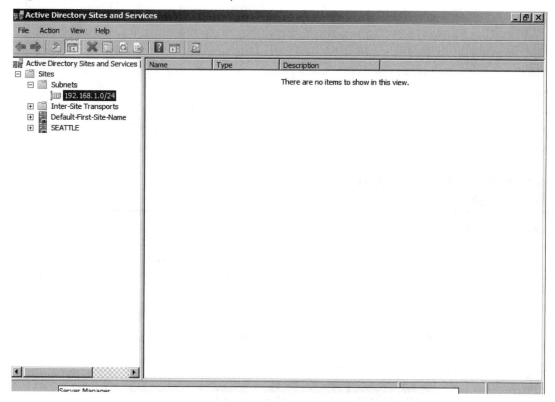

4. Selecting the New Subnet option opens a **New Object – Subnet** dialog box. Type the network address and subnet mask in the form of dotted-decimal notation in the text boxes present in the **New Object – Subnet** dialog box.

6. Select a site object for this subnet from the list provided in the **New Object – Subnet** dialog box.

7. Click **OK**. This completes the process of creating a subnet using the Active Directory Sites and Servi ces tool.

Associating Subnets with Sites

After creating sites and subnets, the next step is to associate your subnets with sites. Computers on Active Directory networks communicate with each other using the TCP/IP assigned to sites based on their locations in a subnet. Remember that a site consists of one or more IP subnets. You specify the subnets associated with each site on your network by creating subnet objects in the Active Directory Sites and Services console. The association of subnets with sites enables the computers on the Active Directory network to use the subnet information to find a DC in the same site so that authentication traffic will not cross over WAN links. Active Directory also uses subnets during the replication process to determine the best routes between DCs.

You associate subnets with sites using the Active Directory Sites and Services tool of Windows Server 2008. Exercise 5.13 walks you through the steps involved in associating subnets with sites.

EXERCISE 5.13

ASSOCIATING SUBNETS WITH SITES

1. To open the **Active Directory Sites and Services** tool, click **Start | Administrative Tools**, and then click **Active Directory Sites and Services**.

2. Highlight the **Subnet** folder present in the left-hand tree pane of the **Active Directory Sites and Services** console (see Figure 5.17).

Figure 5.17 The Subnet Folder

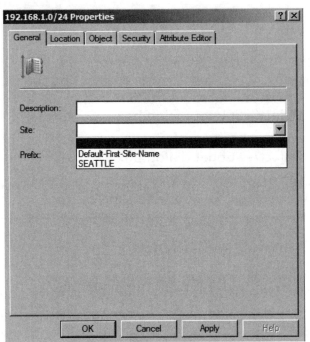

3. Right-click the newly created subnet and select the **Properties** option; this will open a Properties dialog box, as shown in Figure 5.18.

Figure 5.18 Subnet Dialog Box for Associating/Changing the Site

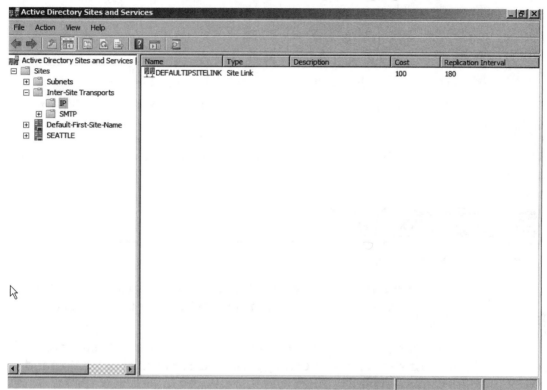

4. Associate any site with this subnet by selecting the available site from the site drop-down menu, and click **OK**. This completes the process of associating a subnet with a site using the Active Directory Sites and Services tool.

Creating Site Links

After creating and defining the scope of each site, the next step in the site configuration process is to establish connections between the sites. The physical connectivity between the sites is established between the Active Directory databases by site link objects. A *site link object* is an Active Directory object that embodies a set of sites that can communicate at uniform cost. A *site link* connects only two sites and corresponds to a WAN link for an IP transport. A site link connecting more than two sites corresponds to Asynchronous Transfer Mode (ATM) and metropolitan area network (MAN) through leased lines and IP routers. Each site link is based these four components:

- **Transport** The networking technology to move the replication traffic

- **Sites** The sites that the site link connects

- **Cost** The value to calculate the site links by comparing to others, in terms of speed and reliability charges

- **Schedule** The times and frequency at which the replication will occur

You create site links using the Active Directory Sites and Services tool of Windows Server 2008. Exercise 5.14 walks you through the steps involved in creating sitae links.

EXERCISE 5.14

CREATING SITE LINKS

1. To open the **Active Directory Sites and Services** tool, click **Start | Administrative Tools,** and then click **Active Directory Sites and Services**.

2. Highlight the **Inter-Site Transports** folder in the left-hand tree pane of the **Active Directory Sites and Services** console. Expand the **Inter-Site Transports** folder, as shown in Figure 5.19.

Figure 5.19 The Inter-Site Transports Folder

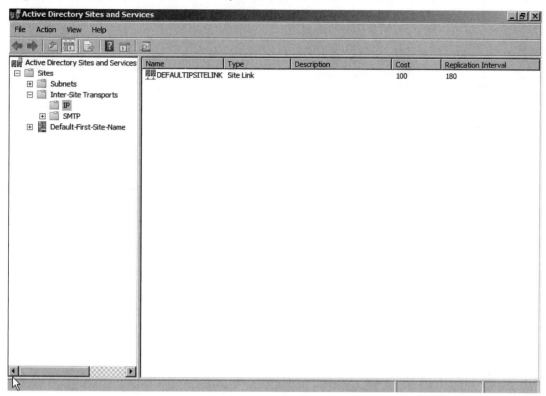

3. Right-click either the **IP** or the **SMTP** folder (depending on what protocol the network is based on) in the left-hand tree pane of the **Active Directory Sites and Services** console. Select **New Site Link** from the context menu, as shown in Figure 5.20.

Figure 5.20 The New Site Link Option

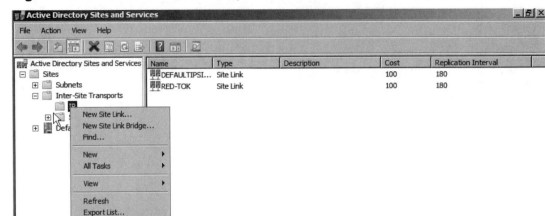

4. Selecting the **New Site Link** option opens a **New Object – Site Link** dialog box.

5. Type the name of the new site link object in the **Name** box in the **New Object – Site Link** dialog box.

6. Select two or more sites for establishing connection from the **Sites not in this site link** box, and click **Add**.

7. Click **OK**. This completes the process of creating a new site link object using the Active Directory Sites and Services tool.

Configuring Site Link Cost

Site link costs are calculated to determine how expensive an organization considers the network connection between two sites that the site link is connecting.

Higher costs represent more expensive connections. If two site links are available between two sites, the lowest-cost site link will be chosen. Each site link is assigned an IP or Simple Mail Transfer Protocol (SMTP) transport protocol, a cost, a replication frequency, and an availability schedule. All these parameters reflect the characteristics of the physical network connection.

The cost assigned to a site link is a number on an arbitrary scale that should reflect, in some sense, the expense of transmitting traffic using that link. Cost can be in the range of 1 to 32,767, and lower costs are preferred. The cost of a link should be inversely proportional to the effective bandwidth of a network connection between sites. For example, if you assign a cost of 32,000 to a 64 kbps line, you should assign 16,000 to a 128 kbps line and 1,000 to a 2 Mbps line. It makes sense to use a high number for the slowest link in your organization. As technology improves and communication becomes cheaper, it's likely that future WAN lines will be faster than today's, so there's little sense in assigning a cost of 2 for your current 128 kbps line and a cost of 1 for your 256 kbps line, because quicker links can't be priced more cheaply.

You configure site link costs using the Active Directory Sites and Services tool of Windows Server 2008. Exercise 5.15 illustrates the steps involved in creating site link costs.

EXERCISE 5.15

CONFIGURING SITE LINK COSTS

1. To open the **Active Directory Sites and Services** tool, click **Start | Administrative Tools**, and then click **Active Directory Sites and Services**.

2. Highlight the **Sites** folder in the left-hand tree pane of the **Active Directory Sites and Services** console and expand the **Sites** folder.

3. Highlight the **Inter-Site Transports** folder in the left-hand tree pane of the **Active Directory Sites and Services** console and expand the **Inter-Site Transports** folder.

4. Right-click the site link whose cost you want to configure in the left-hand tree pane of the **Active Directory Sites and Services** console, and select **Properties**. Selecting **Properties** opens a dialog box, as shown in Figure 5.21.

Figure 5.21 The Properties Option

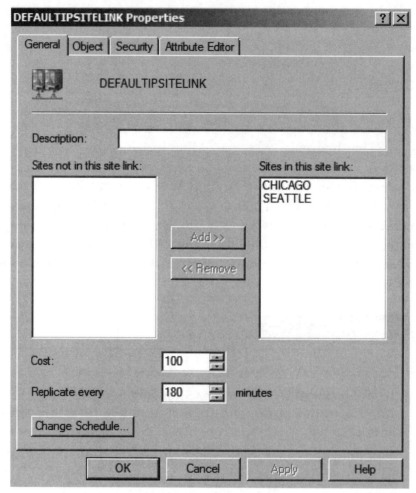

5. Type the value for the cost of replication of the site link object in the **Cost** box in the dialog box.

6. Click **OK**. This completes the process of configuring site link costs using the Active Directory Sites and Services tool.

Understanding Replication

Replication is defined as the practice of transferring data from a data store present on a source computer to an identical data store present on a destination computer to *synchronize* the data. In a network, the directory data must live in one or more places on the network to be equally available to all users. The Active Directory directory service manages a replica of directory data on one or more DCs, ensuring the availability of directory data to all users. The Active Directory works on the concept of sites to perform replication efficiently, and it uses the KCC to choose the best replication topology for the network automatically.

NOTE

The KCC is a process that runs on a DC, and identifies the most efficient replication topology for the network automatically, based on the data provided by the network in Active Directory Sites and Services.

Replication is an essential process for any domain that has multiple DCs. Replication ensures that each copy of the domain data is up-to-date, and is done by sending information regarding changes from one DC to another. Earlier versions of NT were configured in a single-master environment where the PDC was used to maintain and manage the master copy of the domain database, and was also in charge of replicating changes to the BDCs. In a *single-master environment*, if for some reason the PDC is unavailable, no changes can be made to the database.

In Windows Server 2008 domains, every writable DC has a complete copy of the Active Directory of its own domain. This is similar to the NT model, but the difference is that each Windows Server 2008 DC first accepts and makes changes to the database and then replicates those changes to other DCs. An environment in which multiple computers are used for managing changes is known as a *multimaster environment*.

A multimaster environment has many advantages over the single-master configuration, including the following:

- There are no single points of failure, as every DC can accept changes to the database.

- DCs that accept changes to the database are distributed throughout the network. This allows administrators to make changes on local DCs and let the replication ensure that these changes are updated to all other DCs in an efficient manner.

Replication in a Windows Server 2008 environment is one of two types:

- **Intrasite replication** Replication that occurs between DCs within a site

- **Intersite replication** Replication that occurs between DCs in different sites

It is important to understand the differences between these methods when planning the site structure and replication.

Intrasite Replication

Intrasite replication occurs between DCs within a site. The system implementing such replication uses high-speed, synchronous Remote Procedure Calls (RPCs).

Within a site, a ring topology is created by the KCC between the DCs for replication (see Figure 5.22). The KCC is a built-in process that runs on all DCs and helps in creating replication topology. It runs every 15 minute by default and delegates the replication path between DCs based on the connection available. The KCC automatically creates replication connections between DCs within the site. The ring topology created by the KCC defines the path through which changes flow within the site. All the changes follow the ring until every DC receives them.

Figure 5.22 Ring Topology for Replication

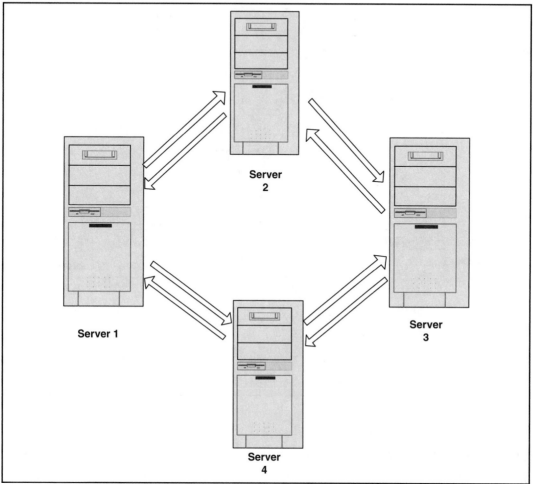

The KCC analyzes the replication topology within a site to ensure efficiency. If a DC is added or removed, it reconfigures the ring for maximum efficiency. It also configures the ring so that there will be no more than three hops between any two DCs within the site, which sometimes results in the creation of multiple rings (see Figure 5.23).

Figure 5.23 The Three-Hop Rule of Intrasite Replication

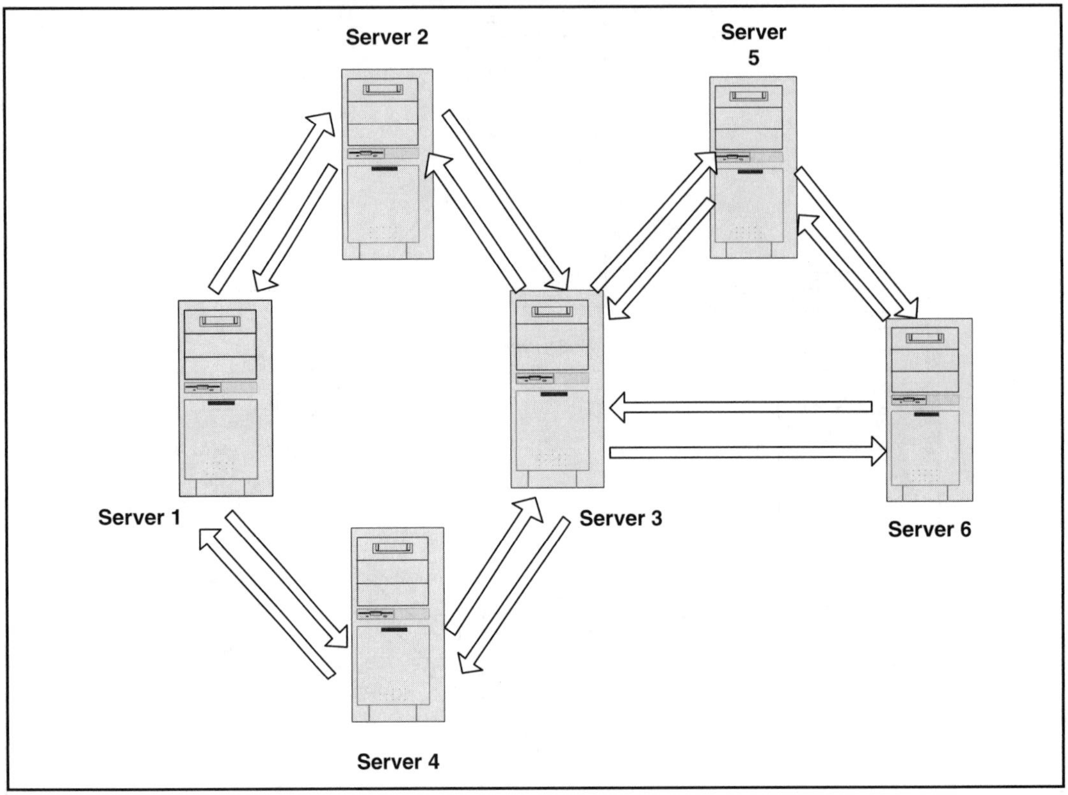

Intersite Replication

Intersite replication takes place between DCs in different sites. The drawback of inter-site communication is that you have to configure it manually. Active Directory builds an efficient intersite replication topology with the information provided by the user. The directory saves this information as site link objects. A DC running the ISTG service is used to build the topology. An Inter-site Topology Generator is an Active Directory process that runs on one DC in a site and considers the cost of intersite connections. It ensures that the previous DCs are no longer available, and checks to determine whether new DCs have been added. The KCC process updates the intersite replication topology. A least-cost spanning-tree algorithm is used to eliminate superfluous replication paths between sites. An intersite replication topology is updated regularly to respond to any changes that occur in the network. It would be useful if the traffic needs to cross a slower Internet link.

Intersite replication across site links occurs every 180 minutes; you can change this if necessary. In addition, you can schedule the availability of the site links for use. By default, a site link is accessible to carry replication 24 hours a day, seven days a week, and you can also change this if necessary. You also can configure a site link to use low-speed synchronous RPCs over TCP/IP or asynchronous SMTP transport. That is, replication within a site always uses RPC over IP, whereas replication between sites can use either RPC over IP or SMTP over IP. Replication between sites over SMTP is supported for only DCs of different domains. DCs of the same domain must replicate by using the RPC over IP transport. Hence, you can configure a site link to point-to-point, low-speed synchronous RPC over IP between sites, and low-speed asynchronous SMTP between sites.

Bridgehead Servers

A *bridgehead server* is a server that is mainly used for intersite replication. You can configure a bridgehead server for every site that is created for each intersite replication protocol. This helps to control the server that is used to replicate information to other servers.

To configure a server as a bridgehead server, follow these steps:

1. Choose **Start | Administrative Tools | Active Directory Sites and Services**.
2. Expand the **Sites** folder.
3. Expand the site in which a bridgehead server has to be created, and then expand the **Servers** folder.
4. Right-click on the server and choose **Properties**.
5. In the **Transports available for inter-site transfer** area, select the protocol for which this server should be a bridgehead and click **Add**.
6. Click **OK** to set the properties, and then close **Active Directory Sites and Services**.

The ability to configure a server as a bridgehead server gives you greater control over the resources used for replication between intersites.

Site Link Bridges

Often, there is no need to deal with site link bridges separately, as all the links are automatically bridged by a property known as a *transitive site link*. Sometimes when you need to control through which sites the data can flow, you need to create site link bridges. By default, all the site links created are bridged together.

The bridging enables the sites to communicate with each other. If this is not enabled by the automatic bridging due to the network structure, disable the same and create an appropriate site link bridge. In some cases, it is necessary to control the data flow through the sites. In these cases, it is necessary to create site link bridges. To disable transitive site links (automatic bridging), follow these steps:

1. Choose **Start | Administrative Tools | Active Directory Sites and Services**.

2. Expand the **Sites** folder and then expand the **Inter-Site Transports** folder.

3. Right-click on the transport for which the automatic bridging should be turned off, and choose **Properties**.

4. On the **General** tab, clear the **Bridge all site links** checkbox and click **OK**.

To create a site link bridge, follow these steps:

1. Choose **Start | Administrative Tools | Active Directory Sites and Services**.

2. Expand the **Sites** folder and then the **Inter-Site Transports** folder.

3. Right-click on the transport that needs to be used, and choose **New Site Link Bridge**.

4. In the **Name** box, enter a name for the site link bridge.

5. From the list of **Site links not in this bridge**, select the site link to be added.

6. Remove any extra site links in the **Site links in this bridge** box and click **OK**.

Scheduling

You can configure replication frequency by providing an integer value that informs the Active Directory as to how many minutes it should wait before it can use a connection to check replication updates. The interval of time must be not less than 15 minutes and not more than 10,080 minutes. For any replication to happen, a site link is essential. Follow these steps to configure site link replication frequency:

1. Choose **Start | Administrative Tools | Active Directory Sites and Services**.

2. Expand the **Inter-Site Transports** folder; select either the **IP** or the **SMTP** folder and right-click the site link for which the site replication frequency is to be set.

3. Click **Properties**, and in the Properties dialog box for the site link, enter in the **Replicate Every** box the number of minutes between replications. The default value is 180.

4. Click **OK**.

Forcing Replication

Data is usually replicated based on a change notification within sites. It's up to the administrator to force immediate replication. To do so for all data on a given connection in a single direction, perform the following steps:

1. Choose **Start | Administrative Tools | Active Directory Sites and Services**. Expand **Sites** in the left-hand tree pane.

2. Expand the name of the site that has to replicate to.

3. Expand the name of the server for replicating.

4. Select the server's **NTDS Settings** object. The right console pane will be populated with the server's inbound connection objects.

5. In the right pane, right-click the name of the server from which you want to replicate, and select **Replicate Now**.

You also can force replication from the command line by using the repadmin. exe utility from the Support Tools.

Replication Protocols

When creating site links, you have the option of using either IP or SMTP as the transport protocol:

- **SMTP replication** You can use SMTP only for replication over site links. It is asynchronous; that is, the destination DC does not wait for the reply, so the reply is not received in a short amount of time. SMTP replication also neglects Replication Available and Replication Not Available settings on the site link schedule, and uses the replication interval to indicate how often the server requests changes When choosing SMTP, you must install and configure an enterprise certificate authority (CA), as it signs the SMTP messages that are exchanged between DCs. SMTP replication is designed for use over slow or unreliable WAN links, in situations where IP connectivity between sites is too unreliable to be used for Active Directory replication.

- **IP replication** All replication within a site occurs over synchronous RPC over IP transport. The replication within a site is fast and has uncompressed delivery of updates. Replication events occur more frequently within a site than between sites, and the overhead of compression would be inefficient over fast connections.

Planning, Creating, and Managing the Replication Topology

An important job when implementing replication topology is planning, creating, and managing the replication topology, as discussed next.

Planning Replication Topology

Let's now discuss how to plan a replication topology:

- Before starting a replication planning process, we need to first finish the forest, domain, and DNS.

- It is essential to have an understanding of Active Directory replication, the File Replication Service (FRS), and SYSVOL replication used to replicate group policy changes.

- For Active Directory replication, a rule of thumb is that a given DC that acts as a bridgehead server should not have more than 50 active simultaneous replication connections at any given time.

Creating Replication Topology

The next step is to create the replication topology. Let's discuss how to create a replication topology:

- Active Directory replication is a one-way *pull* replication whereby the DC that needs updates (the target DC) gets in touch with the replication partner (the source DC). Then, the source DC selects the updates that the target DC needs, and copies them to the target DC. Because Active

Directory uses a multimaster replication model, each DC functions as both source and target for its replication partners. From the view of a DC, it has both inbound and outbound replication traffic, depending on whether it is the source or the destination of a replication sequence.

- Inbound replication is the incoming data transfer from a replication partner to a DC, and outbound replication is the data transfer from a DC to its replication partner.

- System policies and logon scripts that are stored in SYSVOL use FRS to replicate. Each DC keeps a copy of SYSVOL for network clients to access. FRS is also used for DFS.

- Components of the replication topology such as the KCC, connection objects, site links, and site link bridges are to be checked by the administrator.

There are two methods for creating a replication topology:

- Use the KCC to create connection objects. This method is recommended if there are 100 or fewer sites.

- Use a scripted or third-party tool for the creation of connection objects. This method is recommended if there are more than 100 sites.

Configuring Replication between Sites

To ensure that users can log on within a given span of time, it is necessary to locate DCs near them, which sometimes involves moving the DCs between sites. The purpose of a site is to help manage the replication between DCs and across slow network links. In addition to creating the site and adding subnets to that site, we also need to move DCs into the site, as replication happens between DCs. The DC has to be added to a site to which it belongs so that clients within a site can look for the DCs in the site and can log on to it.

To move DCs, follow these steps:

1. Select **Click Active Directory Sites and Services**.

2. Choose the **Sites** folder and then select the site where the server is located.

3. In the site, expand the **Servers** folder.

4. Right-click on the DC you want to move, and choose **Move**.

5. Select the destination subnet from the dialog box and click **OK**.

Troubleshooting Replication Failure

DCs usually handle the process involved with replication automatically. Unsuccessful network links and wrong configurations prevent the synchronization of information between DCs.

There are many ways to monitor the behavior of Active Directory replication and correct problems if they occur.

Troubleshooting Replication

A common symptom of replication problems is that the information is not updated on some or all DCs. There are several steps that you can take to troubleshoot Active Directory replication, including:

- **Check the network connectivity** The basic requirement for any type of replication to work properly in a distributed environment is network connectivity. The ideal situation is that all the DCs are connected by high-speed LAN links. In the real world, either a dial-up connection or a slow connection is common. Check to see whether the replication topology is set up properly. In addition, confirm whether the servers are communicating. Failed dial-up connection attempts can prevent important Active Directory information from being replicated.

- **Examine the replication topology** The Active Directory Sites and Services tool helps to verify whether a replication topology is logically consistent. You do this by right-clicking the **NTDS Settings** within a Server object and selecting **All Tasks | Check Replication Topology**. If there are any errors, a dialog box will alert you to the problem.

- **Validate the event logs** Whenever an error in the replication configuration occurs, events are written to the Directory Service event log. The Event Viewer administrative tool can provide the details associated with any problems in replication.

- **Verify whether the information is synchronized** Many administrators forget to execute manual checks regarding the replication of Active Directory information. One of the reasons for this is that Active Directory DCs have their own read/write copies of the Active Directory database. Therefore, no failures are encountered while creating new objects if connectivity does not exist. It is important to regularly check whether the objects have been synchronized between DCs. The manual check, although tedious, can prevent inconsistencies in the information stored on DCs.

- **Check router and firewall configurations** Firewalls are used to restrict the types of traffic transferred between networks. They increase security by preventing unauthorized users from transferring information. In some cases, company firewalls might block the types of network access that should be available for Active Directory replication to occur.

- **Verify site links** Before any DCs in different sites can communicate, the sites must be connected by site links. If replication between sites doesn't occur properly, verify whether the site links are in the proper positions.

Using Event Viewer

You use the Event Viewer for configuring Active Directory event logging. To configure Active Directory event logging, follow these steps:

1. Select **Start | Run**. In the **Open** box, type **regedit**, and click **OK**.

2. Locate and click the following Registry key: **HKEY_LOCAL_ MACHINE\SYSTEM\CurrentControlSet\Services\NTDS\ Diagnostics**.

3. Each entry in the right-hand pane of the Registry Editor window represents a type of event that Active Directory can log. All entries are set to the default value of 0 (None).

To configure event logging for the appropriate component, follow these steps:

1. In the right-hand pane of the Registry Editor, double-click the entry that represents the type of event that is to be logged; for example, **Security Events**.

2. Type the logging level that's needed in the **Value data** box, and click **OK**.

3. Repeat step 2 for each component that you want to be logged. Then, on the **Registry** menu, click **Exit** to quit the Registry Editor.

Some of the events that you can write to the event log include:

- KCC
- MAPI events
- Security events
- Replication events
- Directory access

- Internal configuration
- Internal processing
- Intersite messaging
- Service control setup

Each entry is assigned a value of 0 through 5, which determines the level of details of the events that are logged:

- **0** (None) Only critical events and error events are logged at this level. This is the default setting for all entries.

- **1** (Minimal) Very high-level events are recorded in the event log at this setting. Events can include one message for each major task that the service performs. You can use this when the location to start an investigation is not known.

- **2** (Basic) This level adds additional information beyond what is logged at the minimal level, without significantly impacting the system resources required to capture these log events

- **3** (Extensive) This level records more detailed information than the lower levels, such as steps that are performed to complete a task.

- **4** (Verbose) This level records significant details, but excludes the debug strings that are recorded at the highest logging level.

- **5** (Internal) This level logs all events, including debug strings and configuration changes. A complete log of the service is recorded.

NOTE

Logging levels should always be set to the default value of 0 (None) unless there is an investigation at issue. If the Registry Editor is used incorrectly, it can cause serious problems that will require reinstalling the operating system.

Working with Trusts

One of the many issues that need to be dealt with in any computer organization is how to protect resources. The main difficulty that administrators face is the dilemma of how to ensure that the company's resources are not accessible by those who do not need access. The other side of that coin, and something that is equally important, is how to ensure that people who do need access are granted access with the least amount of hassle. In small companies, the issues are simpler, because multiple domains rarely exist. In today's larger corporations and conglomerates, the issues of security are compounded. What administrators need is an easy tool to manage access across multiple domains and, often, across forests.

The tool is Active Directory Domains and Trusts. With Active Directory Domains and Trusts, an administrator can establish relationships between domains that will allow users in one domain to access the resources in another. This way, the administrator can ensure that all users who need access can have it without the hassles involved in having user accounts in multiple domains.

As the name implies, trusts are all about sharing information. For security purposes, you should carefully consider your reasons before creating a new trust relationship, as well as knowing which type of trust to implement. In Active Directory, a *shortcut* trust doesn't add more trust; rather, it can make the trusts you already have more efficient. *External* trusts are a concept left over from Windows NT, but are still necessary for sharing resources with a Windows NT domain or any other Windows domain outside your forest. Finally, you should consider the Windows Server 2008 *forest trust* to provide a transitive trust relationship between two Active Directory forests that are running Windows Server 2003 or Windows Server 2008 on all installed DCs. As you can see, trusts are varied in properties and purposes. The most important concepts to understand about trusts before you create them are *direction* and *transitivity*. Always be aware of the extent of any internal access that you grant to external users.

Trusts are predetermined avenues of access to forest resources. It is like giving someone a key to your house and hoping that he or she won't misuse your trust. DCs do the authenticating, but not all DCs necessarily trust each other. That's where you come in, setting the relationships between domains that govern the flow of information.

Two primary attributes of trusts are direction and transitivity. The *direction of trust* flows from the trusting domain to the trusted domain, as shown by the arrow in Figure 5.24. Cats.com *trusts* Dogs.com. The *direction of access* is always in the opposite direction; Dogs.com *accesses* resources in Cats.com. This is a one-way trust. Likewise, Dogs.com trusts Fish.com, but does not trust Cats.com. Two one-way trusts can combine to simulate a single two-way trust.

Figure 5.24 The Nontransitive Trust

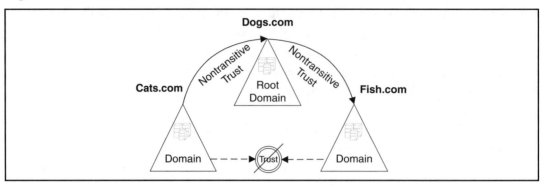

The second attribute of the trust is *transitivity*, or a measure of how far the trust extends. A nontransitive trust has limits. The trusted domain, *and only the trusted domain*, can access resources through the trust to the trusting domain. As shown in Figure 5.24, if the Dogs.com domain has trusts to other domains such as Fish.com, those other domains are barred from access to Cats.com unless they have a nontransitive trust of their own. The absence of the third leg of the trust breaks the circle of access. This is the behavior of all trusts in Windows NT.

Conversely, transitive trusts, such as the ones shown in Figure 5.25, are the skeleton keys of access. Anyone on the trusted side of the trust relationship can enter, including anyone trusted by the trusted domain. When a user or process requests access to a resource in another domain, a series of hand-offs occurs within the authentication process down the *trust path*, as shown in Figure 5.25. When Cats.com trusts Dogs.com, they must trust all Dogs.com child domains equally at the level of the trust. There are two types of trusts in Figure 5.25, *parent and child* and *tree-root*. All trusts shown are bidirectional and transitive, as they are by default in Windows Server 2008. Calico.cats.com has a trust relationship with Yellow.labs.dogs.com because of the trust path that extends through all three intervening domains. If Calico.cats.com has no reason to trust Yellow.labs.dogs.com, the cats must apply permissions to limit or block the access.

TEST DAY TIP

Remember that default Windows Server 2008 trust relationships are friendly. The default and most common trusts in Active Directory, which are *parent and child* and *tree-root* trusts, are both *bidirectional* and *transitive*, meaning that the *trust path* extends throughout the entire forest.

You can remember this type of transitive trust with the old saying, "Any friend of yours is a friend of mine."

Other types of Windows Server 2008 trusts exist, such as *forest, shortcut,* and *external,* each of which can be bidirectional or unidirectional and have different transitivity properties. One of the first things you should do when you sit down at the testing station is to write down the trusts and their properties on your scratch paper. Do this before starting the test so as not to waste valuable time.

Figure 5.25 The Transitive Trust

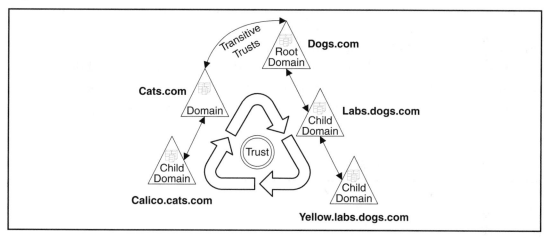

A *trust* is a logical authentication path between two domains. A *trust path* is the number of trusts that must be traversed between the source and destination of a resource request. Two trusts, *tree-root* and *parent and child,* are created by default when running the Active Directory Installation Wizard. You can create the other four trusts—*shortcut, external, realm,* and *forest*—as needed with the New Trust Wizard or the Netdom.exe command-line tool.

When creating those four trusts, you have the option of creating two one-way relationships, simulating bidirectional capabilities. As with any use of passwords, it is a security best practice to use long, random, and complex passwords in the establishment of trusts. The best option is to use the New Trust Wizard to create both sides simultaneously, in which case the wizard generates a strong password for you. Naturally, you must have the appropriate administrative credentials in both domains for this to work.

We've been talking about two-way (bidirectional) trusts; but a trust can also be one-way (unidirectional). One-way trusts are created to allow more restrictive control over which users are allowed access to resources. For example, in Figure 5.26, a one-way trust is created between Domain X and Domain Y. Users in Domain X have access to resources in Domain Y. However, users in Domain Y do not have access to resources in Domain X. In this definition, Domain X is referred to as the trusted domain, and Domain Y is the trusting domain. A two-way trust allows users in either domain to have access to resources in the other domain.

One-way trusts must specify the *direction* of the trust. One-way trusts can be either *incoming* or *outgoing,* depending on whether the trust is created from the trusting or the trusted domain. Incoming trusts permit the users in the domain where the trust is created (the *trusted* domain) to access resources in the specified domain (the *trusting* domain). Users in the trusting domain do not have access, through this trust, to the resources in the trusted domain. (You can, however, create a second trust that goes the other way, to accomplish the same effect as a two-way trust).

Outgoing trusts allow the users in the specified domain (the trusted domain) to have access to resources in the originating domain (the trusting domain). Users in the originating domain do not have access to resources in the specified domain.

Figure 5.26 One-Way Trust

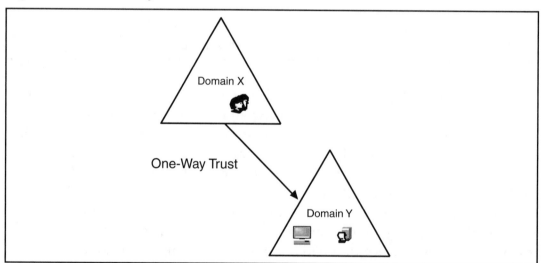

Another concept and set of terms to understand in regard to trusts is:

- Implicit
- Explicit

Implicit trusts are trusts that are created automatically by the nature of the built-in relationships between domains within a forest. These implicit trusts are two-way and transitive. Implicit trusts automatically exist between each domain that is created and its child domain(s). An implicit trust also exists between the root domain of each domain tree and the root domains of every other domain tree in the forest.

An *explicit* trust is one that is created by an administrator; it does not exist automatically, but has to be explicitly created. For example, an administrator can create an explicit trust (in this case, called a *shortcut trust*) between any two child domains in different domain trees to provide for a direct trust (and faster authentication) between them.

Explicit trusts are also used to enable authentication across forests. When a forest trust is created, a transitive trust is created between the forest root domains in both forests. This allows all the members in the forest to exchange authentication information with the other forest. The forest trust is also called an explicit trust between the two forests. If an additional forest trust is created between one of the original forests and a third forest, an implicit trust with the other original forest is not established to the third forest. For the third forest to have a trust relationship with the other forest, an explicit forest trust must be created between the two (see Figure 5.27).

Figure 5.27 Implicit Trust

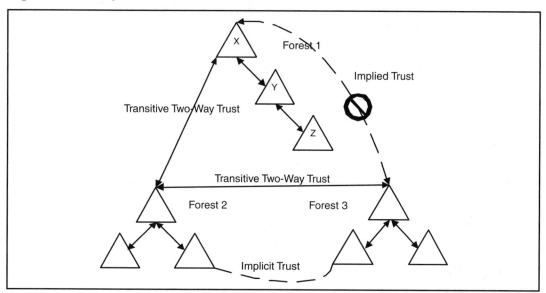

TEST DAY TIP

On the day of the test, you will want to review the types of trusts as well as when to use them. On the exam, you might be given a scenario that will require you to determine the type of trust that will best meet the requirements in the scenario.

The primary advantage of Active Directory trust relationships is that administrators no longer need to create multiple user accounts for each user who needs access to resources within each domain. Administrators can now add the users of the other domains to their access control lists (ACLs) to control access to a resource. To take full advantage of these relationships, the administrator must know about the various types of trust that exist, and when to use them.

Default Trusts

When the Active Directory Installation Wizard is used to create a new domain within an existing forest, two default trusts are created: a parent and child trust, and the tree-root trust. Four additional types of trusts can be created using the New Trust Wizard or the command-line utility netdom. The default trust relationships inside a Windows 2000, Windows Server 2003, and Windows Server 2008 forest are transitive, two-way trusts.

A parent and child trust is a transitive, two-way trust relationship. It allows authentication requests made in the child domain to be validated in the parent domain. Because the trusts are transitive, these requests pass upward from child to parent until they reach the root of the domain namespace. This relationship will allow any user in the domain to have access to any resource in the domain if the user has the proper permissions granted.

An additional transitive, two-way trust is created to simplify the navigation: the tree-root trust. This is especially needed in large organizations that might have multiple levels of child domains. The tree-root trust is a trust that is created between any child domain and the root domain. This provides a shortcut to the root. This trust relationship is also automatically created when a new domain is created.

Forest Trusts

A forest trust can only be created between the root domains in two forests. Both forests must be Windows Server 2003 or Windows Server 2008 forests. These trusts can be one- or two-way trusts. They are considered transitive trusts because the child domains inside the forest can authenticate themselves across the forest to access resources in the other forest.

> ## Exam Warning
>
> Although the trust relationship is considered transitive, this applies only to the child domains within forests. The transitive nature of the trust exists only within the two forests explicitly joined by a forest trust. The transitivity does not extend to a third forest unless you create another explicit trust (see Figure 5.27).

Forest trusts help to manage the Active Directory infrastructure. They do this by simplifying the management of resources between two forests by reducing the required number of external trusts. Instead of needing multiple external trusts, a two-way forest trust between the two root domains will allow full access between all the affected domains. Additionally, the administrator can take advantage of both the Kerberos and NTLM authentication protocols to transfer authorization data between forests.

Forest trusts can provide complete two-way trusts with every domain within the two forests. This is useful if you have created multiple forests to secure data within the forest or to help isolate directory replication within each forest.

External Trusts

You use an external trust when you need to create a trust between domains outside of your forest. These trusts can be one- or two-way trusts. They are always non-transitive in nature. This means you have created an explicit trust between the two domains, and domains outside this trust are not affected. You can create an external trust to access resources in a domain in a different forest that is not already covered by a forest trust (see Figure 5.28).

> ## Exam Warning
>
> You will always need to create an external trust when connecting to a Windows NT 4.0 or earlier domain. These domains are not eligible to participate in Active Directory. These trusts must be one-way trusts. If you have worked with Windows NT 4.0, you will remember that the only trusts allowed were nontransitive one-way trusts.

Figure 5.28 External Trust

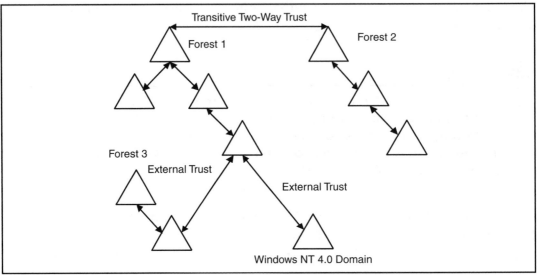

After the trust has been established between a domain in a forest and a domain outside the forest, the security principals from the domain outside the forests will be able to access the resources in the domain inside the forest. Security principals can be the users, groups, computers, or services from the external domain. They are account holders that are each assigned a SID automatically to control access to the resources in the domain.

The Active Directory in the domain inside the forest will then create foreign security principal objects representing each security principal from the trusted external domain. You can use these foreign security principals in the domain local groups. This means that the domain local groups can have members from the trusted external domain. You use these groups to control access to the resources of the domain.

The foreign security principals are seen in Active Directory Users and Computers. Because the Active Directory automatically creates them, you should not attempt to modify them.

Shortcut Trusts

Shortcut trusts are transitive in nature and can be either one-way or two-way. These are explicit trusts that you create when the need exists to optimize ("shortcut") the authentication process. Without shortcut trusts in place, authentication travels up

and down the domain tree using the default parent and child trusts, or by using the tree-root trusts. In large, complex organizations that use multiple trees, this path can become a bottleneck when authenticating users. To optimize access, the network administrator can create an explicit shortcut trust directly to the target domain (see Figure 5.29).

Figure 5.29 Shortcut Trust

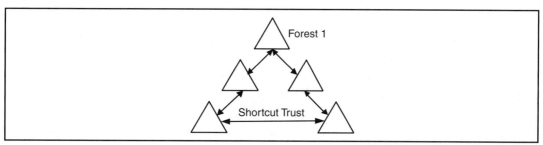

You use these trusts when user accounts in one domain need regular access to the resources in another domain. Shortcut trusts can be either one- or two-way. You should establish one-way shortcut trusts when the users in one domain need access to resources in the other domain, but those in the second domain do not need access to resources in the first domain. You should create two-way trusts when the users in both domains need access to the resources in the other domain. The shortcut trust will effectively shorten the authentication path, especially if the domains belong to two separate trees in the forest.

SID Filtering

One security concern when using trusts is a malicious user who has administrative credentials in the trusted domain sniffing the trusting domain to obtain the credentials of an administrator account. With the credentials of the trusting domain administrator, the malicious user could add his SID to allow full access to the trusting domain's resources. This type of threat is called an *elevation of privilege attack*.

The security mechanism used by Windows Server 2003 and Windows Server 2008 to counter an elevation of privilege attack is *SID filtering*. SID filtering is used to verify that an authentication request coming in from the trusted domain only contains the domain SIDs of the trusted domain. It does this by using the *SIDHistory* attribute on a security principal.

> **NOTE**
>
> *Security principal* is a term used to describe any account that has a SID automatically assigned. Examples of security principals are users, groups, services, and computers. Part of each security principal is the domain SID to identify the domain in which the account was created.

SID filtering uses the domain SID to verify each security principal. If a security principal includes a domain SID other than one from trusted domains, the SID filtering process removes the SID in question. This is done to protect the integrity of the trusting domain. This will prevent the malicious user from being able to elevate his or her privileges or those of other users.

There are some potential problems associated with SID filtering. It is possible for a user whose SID contains SID information from a domain that is not trusted to be denied access to the resources in the trusting domain. This is can be a problem when universal groups are used. Universal groups should be verified to contain only users that belong to the trusted domain.

You can disable SID filtering if there is a high level of trust for all administrators in the affected domains, there are strict requirements to verify all universal group memberships, and any migrated users have their *SIDHistories* preserved. To disable SID filtering, use the *netdom* command.

Summary of Exam Objectives

The logical structure of the network is defined by forests and domains, with domains organized into domain trees in which subdomains (called child domains) can be created under parent domains in a branching structure. Domains are logical units that hold users, groups, computers, and OUs (which in turn can contain users, groups, computers, and other OUs). Forests are collections of domain trees that have trust relationships with one another, but each domain tree has its own separate namespace. Aspects of the physical structure include sites, servers, roles, and links.

An Active Directory always begins with a forest root domain, which is automatically the first domain that you install. This root domain becomes the foundation for additional directory components. The domain is the starting point of Active Directory. It is the most basic component that can functionally host the directory. Simply put, Active Directory uses the domain as a container of computers, users, groups, and other object containers. Objects within the domain share a common directory database partition, replication boundaries and characteristics, security policies, and security relationships with other domains. The process of creating the forest and domain structure is centered on the use of the Active Directory Installation Wizard, which is also known as the dcpromo utility.

In Windows NT 4.0, the domain had only one authoritative source for domain-related information: the primary DC, or PDC. The implementation of Active Directory brought the multimaster model, where objects and their properties could be modified on any DC and become authoritative through replication conflict resolution measures. The problem with the multimaster architecture is that some domain and enterprise-wide operations are not well suited for it. The best design placed those functions on a single DC within the domain or forest, and Microsoft created the Active Directory FSMO roles. The Active Directory supports five operational master roles: the Schema Master, Domain Master, RID Master, PDC Emulator, and Infrastructure Master. Two of these operate at the forest level only: the Schema Master and the Domain Naming Master. Conversely, the RID Master, PDC Emulator, and Infrastructure Master operate at the domain level. You can use the ntdsutil.exe command-line utility to transfer FSMO roles, or you can use an MMC snap-in tool. Depending on which role you want to transfer, you need to use one of the following three MMC snap-in tools: Active Directory Schema, Active Directory Domains and Trusts, or Active Directory Users and Computers. To seize a role, you must use the ntdsutil utility. If a computer cannot be contacted due to a hardware malfunction or long-term network failure, the role must be seized. After you seize a Master role, the old DC that hosted it should never be brought back online.

This is especially true of the Schema Master, Domain Naming Master, and RID Master roles.

The GC server is one of the most important roles played by one or more DCs in your network. It might not appear to do much on the surface, but the GC is responsible for helping to resolve names for objects throughout your forest. The GC server holds a copy of all the objects in the domain in which the server is located. That same GC server holds a partial replica of other domains in the forest. The information that the GC holds from other domains includes common search items. This limited but frequently accessed information makes queries very efficient.

GC servers are responsible for UPN authentication. When a user logs on using the UPN, the GC is queried to locate the user account and a DC in the appropriate domain. GC servers are also responsible for answering queries against Active Directory. If a user wants to locate another person within the organization, that user could use his workstation to search Active Directory. The queries are sent to IP port 3268, which is used for GC communication.

You must consider placement of GC servers early in the design process for your network. If you don't determine where you do and do not need a GC server and plan accordingly, you could have communication problems and users could be adversely affected. A good rule of thumb is to remember that if a location has more than 50 users, a DC is needed at that location. Dividing the network into *sites* makes a difference in how replication traffic is handled in regard to GC information. Replication within a site (intrasite replication) is handled differently than replication between different sites (intersite replication). Placement of GC servers within every site might not be necessary, but you should keep track of how much bandwidth computers are using. GC queries in large quantities can tie up significant bandwidth.

Active Directory trust relationships come in many flavors to meet the needs of the situation where users in one domain need access to the resources in another domain. First, there are the default trusts created between parent and child domains. These trusts are automatically created to simplify usage of resources in a tree. The network administrator can create additional types of trusts, such as external, shortcut, realm, and forest trusts. External trusts link two external domains. Shortcut trusts simplify the authentication paths needed to authenticate users. Realm trusts are created to connect a non-Windows network to a Windows Server 2003 or Windows Server 2008 domain. Forest trusts link forests together in the enterprise.

As you create these additional trust types, you can determine whether the trust will work in one direction only, or in both directions. When the trust works in both directions, it is called a two-way or bidirectional trust, and users in both domains have access to resources in both domains.

Another issue is whether the trust is transitive. A transitive trust "passes" through one trusted domain to another. A transitive trust implies a trust relationship when more than two domains are involved. If Domain A trusts Domain B and Domain B trusts Domain C, Domain A trusts Domain C. This is sometimes not the effect you want when creating trusts. The administrator has control over the transitive nature of the trust. As a further protection, SID filtering prevents users from an untrusted domain from being able to access resources in your domain.

Finally, this chapter also explained the role of sites, and discussed the relationship of sites to other Active Directory components. We showed you how to create sites and site links, and explained site replication. This chapter enables you to become familiar with exam objectives covering such topics as the various roles and services offered by Active Directory sites.

Exam Objectives Fast Track

Working with Forests and Domains

- ☑ You should know what type of domain you want to install before you begin, and the namespace it will use.

- ☑ To improve a domain's reliability, you should always create at least two DCs in each domain.

- ☑ The first DC that you install in the forest is the root DC. It is responsible for the GC and for all five FSMO roles. Some roles can later be transferred to other DCs for performance and diversification.

Working with Sites

- ☑ Sites are used for optimizing the authentication process, by reducing authentication traffic across slow, high-cost WAN links.

- ☑ Subnets provide rapid and reliable communication between locations.

- ☑ The primary role of sites is to increase the performance of a network, which is achieved by economic and rapid transmission of data.

- ☑ Replication enables transferring data from a data store present on a source computer to an identical data store present on a destination computer.

- ☑ The KCC is a process that runs on a DC.

☑ The process of associating a subnet with a site notifies Active Directory sites about the physical networks that are represented by the site.

☑ Cost is the value used to calculate site links by comparing one to others, in terms of speed and reliability charges.

Working with Trusts

☑ Active Directory trust relationships allow users in one domain to access resources in another domain without having to create additional accounts in the domain with the resources.

☑ Whenever a child domain is created, two-way transitive trusts are automatically created between the parent and the child.

☑ Forest trusts are created between the root domains of two forests to allow users in one forest to access resources in the other forest.

☑ SID filtering is a security device that uses the domain SID to verify each security principal.

Exam Objectives
Frequently Asked Questions

Q: What is the big deal about raising the functional levels of my domains and forests? Shouldn't I raise the levels as soon as they meet the prerequisites?

A: No. Remember that functional levels, once raised, cannot be lowered again. In addition, some situations are better suited to skipping a level, rather than raising to one level and then the other. In this case, known future restructuring and upgrade activities should be considered before raising functional levels.

Q: How much of the Active Directory design stage should be complete before I install my first DC?

A: Primarily, the DNS design should be complete, and the decision should be made about how the forest-root domain will be used. Additional DCs and domains can be added later. FSMO roles and GCs can be shifted as needed, and trusts with other forests and external domains can be added later. Essentially, the first DC that you install should be in a lab environment. From that perspective, you should install your first DC for testing and training purposes as soon as possible.

Q: If every FSMO role can be seized by another DC upon failure, why would I want to spread the roles out among different machines?

A: There are several reasons. Chief among these are the associated risks of seizing roles. Lost or corrupted directory data can result from FSMO failures, especially if the malfunctioning machine ever comes back online. Seizing roles should not be considered a routine operation. Another consideration is performance. Each role exacts a certain amount of CPU and memory overhead, and your servers might perform better if roles are spread among multiple systems. If that weren't enough, some roles and functions should not coexist on the same DC, such as the Infrastructure Master and the GC. FSMO placement should not be ignored, and this knowledge will be important on the test.

Q: What are the differences between external, realm, and shortcut trusts?

A: An external trust is created to establish a relationship with a domain outside your tree or forest. A realm trust is created to establish a relationship with a non-Microsoft network using Kerberos authentication. A shortcut trust is used to optimize the authentication process.

Q: What type of trust needs to be created between the root domain and a domain that is several layers deep inside the same tree?

A: None. Transitive two-way trusts are automatically created between the layers of the tree structure. A root trust is also created automatically so that any child domain has a shortcut to the root domain.

Q: What is the difference between implied, implicit, and explicit trusts?

A: An implicit trust is one that is automatically created by the system. An example is the trusts created between parent and child domains. An explicit trust is one that is manually created. An example is a forest trust between two trees. An implied trust is one that is implied because of the transitive nature of trusts. An example is the trust between two child domains that are in different trees, and a forest trust was created between the roots of the tress.

Q: What exactly does SID filtering accomplish?

A: SID filtering is used to secure a trust relationship where the possibility exists that someone in the trusted domain might try to elevate his or her own or someone else's privileges.

Q: How do you change the time the KCC runs?

A: The KCC, which manages connection objects for inter- and intrasite replication, runs every 15 minutes by default. To change this, start **regedit** and go to the **HKEY_LOCAL_MACHINE\SYSTEM\CurrentControlSet\Services\ NTDS\Parameters** Registry entry. Then, from the **Edit** menu, select **New, DWORD Value**.

Q: How do I move a server to a different site?

A: If the sites and subnets are configured, new servers are automatically added to the site that owns the subnet. However, a server can be manually moved to a different site. To perform this task, start the **Active Directory Sites and Services**. Expand the site that currently contains the server, and expand the Servers container. Right-click the server and select **Move** from the context menu. There will be a list of all the sites. Select the new target site, and click **OK**.

Q: How can a server belong to more than one site?

A: By default, a server belongs to only one site. However, you can configure a server to belong to multiple sites. Because sites are necessary for replication, for clients to find resources, and to decrease traffic on intersite connections, simply modifying a site's membership might cause performance problems. To configure a server for multiple site membership, log on to the server you want to join multiple sites. Start **regedit** or **regedt32**. Go to the **HKEY_ LOCAL_MACHINE\SYSTEM\CurrentControlSet\ServicesNetlogon\ Parameters** Registry entry, select **Add Value** from the **Edit** menu, enter the name **Site Coverage** and a **REG_MULTI_SZ** value, and click **OK**. Next, enter the names of the sites to join, each on a new line. (Press **Shift + Enter** to move to the next line.) Click **OK**. Close the Registry Editor.

Q: How do I disable site link transitivity?

A: Site links are bridged together to make them transitive so that the KCC can create connection objects between DCs. We can disable site link transitivity manually by bridging specific site links. Start the **Active Directory Sites and Services** snap-in. (Select **Administrative Tools | Active Directory Sites and Services** from the **Start** menu.) Expand the **Sites** folder and expand the **Inter-Site Transports** folder. Right-click the protocol for which you want to disable transitivity (IP or SMTP), and select **Properties**. Clear the **Bridge all site links** checkbox, and click **Apply**.

Q: How do you rename a site?

A: When you install your first DC, the DC creates the default site, Default-First-Site-Name. This name isn't very descriptive, so you might want to rename it. Start the **Active Directory Sites and Services** snap-in. (Select **Administrative Tools | Active Directory Sites and Services** from the **Start** menu.) Expand the **Sites** folder. Right-click the site that is to be renamed (e.g., Default-First-Site-Name), and select **Rename**. Enter the new name, and press **Enter**.

Q: I want to enable GC functionality on a DC. Where do I do that?

A: In the **NTDS Settings Properties** window on the **General** tab. You simply check the box next to **Global Catalog** and click **OK**.

Q: I have an office with only 10 users. Should I put a GC server at this location?

A: Probably not; Microsoft recommends that 50 or more users at a location constitutes the necessity for a local DC at that office.

Q: I am noticing a large amount of traffic between my corporate office and branch office. I recently added a GC server/DC at my branch office. Why all the extra traffic?

A: More than likely, you didn't set up a site for each location. Having GC servers located in sites helps to control replication and should cut down on bandwidth usage. Data is compressed before being sent between sites, which keeps bandwidth usage down.

Self Test

1. A large company has just merged with yours. This organization has recently converted its internal network from IPv4 addressing to IPv6 to support a number of new network applications that required it. You must now begin to plan for IPv6 support on your own internal network. You are creating training materials for your junior networking staff. Which of the following features is built into IPv6 that was not required in IPv4?

   A. Classless Inter-Domain Routing (CIDR)

   B. IP Security through the use of IPSec

   C. Network address translator (NAT)

   D. Loopback IP addressing

2. Your IT manager wants you to link four divisions of the company through a ring of eight unidirectional cross-forest trusts. He uses this reasoning: If multiple forest trusts are established, authentication requests made in any domain of any forest can pass through multiple forest trusts, hence multiple Kerberos domains, on their way to their destination. Why is he wrong?

   A. Although each cross-forest trust is transitive at the forest level, where all domains in both forests can authenticate, they are not transitive at the federated forest level as he suggests. The trust path cannot include more than one cross-forest trust.

   B. Cross-forest trusts are not transitive, and will not allow pass-through authentication.

   C. To create a mesh trust relationship between four forests, you need only four cross-forest trusts.

   D. Cross-forest trusts are bidirectional, so only three trusts are needed to link all four forests. Completing the "ring" is not necessary.

3. What FSMO roles should exist in a child domain in a Windows Server 2008 forest? (Choose all that apply).

   A. Schema Master

   B. Domain Naming Master

   C. PDC Emulator

   D. RID Master

E. GC

F. Infrastructure Master

4. Your network operations center has identified excessive bandwidth utilization caused by authentication traffic in the root domain subnet, especially between Calico.cats.com and Labs.dogs.com. Your logical network is set up as shown in the diagram. What type of trust or trusts would you set up to alleviate the situation?

Question #4 Diagram

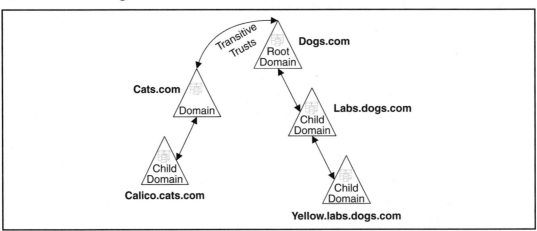

A. Set up a bidirectional transitive parent and child trust between Calico.cats. com and Labs.dogs.com.

B. Set up a shortcut trust between Calico.cats.com and the forest root, and set up a second shortcut trust between Labs.dogs.com and the forest root.

   C. Set up a shortcut trust between Calico.cats.com and Labs.dogs.com.

   D. Set up two shortcut trusts between Calico.cats.com and Labs.dogs.com.

   E. Set up a realm trust between Calico.cats.com and Labs.dogs.com.

5. Your company, mycompany.com, is merging with the yourcompany.com company. The details of the merger are not yet complete. You need to gain access to the resources in the yourcompany.com company before the merger is completed. What type of trust relationship should you create?

   A. Forest trust

   B. Shortcut trust

   C. External trust

   D. Tree Root trust

6. Your boss just informed you that your company will be participating in a joint venture with a partner company. He is very concerned about the fact that a trust relationship needs to be established with the partner company. He fears that an administrator in the other company might be able to masquerade as one of your administrators and grant himself privileges to resources. You assure him that your network and its resources can be protected from an elevated privilege attack. Along with the other security precautions that you will take, what will you tell your boss that will help him rest easy about the upcoming scenario?

   A. The permissions set on the Security Account Manager (SAM) database will prevent the other administrators from being able to make changes.

   B. The *SIDHistory* attribute tracks all access from other domains. Their activities can be tracked in the System Monitor.

   C. The *SIDHistory* attribute from the partner's domain attaches the domain SID for identification. If an account from the other domain tries to elevate its own or another user's privilege, the SID filtering removes the SID in question.

   D. SID filtering tracks the domain of every user who accesses resources. The *SIDHistory* records this information and reports the attempts to the Security log in the Event Viewer.

7. You recently completed a merger with yourcompany.com. Corporate decisions have been made to keep the integrity of both of the original companies; however, management has decided to centralize the IT departments. You are now responsible for ensuring that users in both companies have access to the resources in the other company. What type of trust should you create to solve the requirements?

    A. Forest trust

    B. Shortcut trust

    C. External trust

    D. Tree root trust

8. Robin is managing an Active Directory environment of a medium-size company. He is troubleshooting a problem with the Active Directory. One of the administrators made an update to a user object and another reported that he had not seen the changes appear on another DC. It was more than a week since the change was made. Robin checks the problem by making a change to another Active Directory object. Within a few hours, the change appears on a few DCs, but not on all of them. Which of the following is a possible cause for this problem?

    A. Connection objects are not properly configured.

    B. Robin has configured one of the DCs for manual updates.

    C. There might be different DCs for different domains.

    D. Creation of multiple site links between the sites.

9. James is a systems administrator for an Active Directory environment that consists of two dozen sites. The physical network environment is not fully routed, and James has disabled automatic site link transitivity. He now wants to set up three site links to be transitive, as they are physically connected to one another. Which of the following Active Directory objects is responsible for representing a transitive relationship between sites?

    A. Additional sites

    B. Additional site links

    C. Bridgehead servers

    D. Site link bridges

10. Steffi is an administrator of a medium-size organization responsible for managing Active Directory replication traffic. She finds an error in the replication configuration. How can she look for specific error messages related to replication?

    A. Use the Active Directory Sites and Services administrative tool

    B. Use the Disk Management tool

    C. View the System log option in the Event Viewer

    D. View the Directory Service log option in the Event Viewer

Self Test Quick Answer Key

1.	**B**	6.	**C**
2.	**A**	7.	**A**
3.	**C, D, and F**	8.	**A**
4.	**C**	9.	**D**
5.	**C**	10.	**D**

Chapter 6

MCTS/MCITP
Exam 649

Configuring Web Application Services

Exam objectives in this chapter:

- **Installing and Configuring Internet Information Services**
- **Securing Your Web Sites and Applications**
- **Managing Internet Information Services**

Exam objectives review:

- ☑ **Summary of Exam Objectives**
- ☑ **Exam Objectives Fast Track**
- ☑ **Exam Objectives Frequently Asked Questions**
- ☑ **Self Test**
- ☑ **Self Test Quick Answer Key**

Introduction

In the last three releases it would be hard to dismiss the incredible growth and maturing of the Windows Server Web application services offerings. From what was an add-on option pack item to a key component that businesses have come to rely on, you can bet that this release is nothing short of impressive. While carrying on the mandate to ship a secure, scalable solution for Web applications and services, the product group has managed to deliver an impressive foundation for Web-based solutions. This release focuses on seven themes that will be covered in this chapter as we discuss and discover the installation, provisioning, and key service features that will help you to maintain your Web farm, whether a single server or a global network of Web services.

Installing and Configuring Internet Information Services

It is hard today to be exposed to technology without being exposed to the Internet. By far one of the most popular applications on the Internet is the Web browser. Responding to the requests of your Web browser is the job of a Web server. For the Windows Server environment, the native Web server is Internet Information Services (IIS). Microsoft shipped the first release of IIS as a free add-on for Windows NT 3.51. Much has changed since that first release, and this evolution of IIS brings the momentum a giant leap forward with a scalable, pluggable, secure Web application server. IIS 7.0 first debuted with the release of Windows Vista. This move was to encourage developers and IT professionals to get an early look at what was being developed for Windows Server 2008 to gather feedback and promote application compatibility. Table 6.1 is an overview of features available across Windows Server 2008, both Full and Server Core installations, and the various editions of Windows Vista.

Table 6.1 Features Available for Windows Server 2008

Feature	Windows Server 2008		Windows Vista		
	Full Install	Server Core Install	Ultimate, Business, Enterprise	Home Premium	Home Basic, Starter
Common HTTP Features					
Static Content	●	●	●	●	○
Default Document	●	●	●	●	○
Directory Browsing	●	●	●	●	○
HTTP Errors	●	●	●	●	●
HTTP Redirection	●	●	●	●	●
Application Development Features					
ASP.NET	●	○	●	●	○
.NET Extensibility	●	○	●	●	●
Active Server Pages (ASP)	●	●	●	●	○
Common Gateway Interface (CGI)	●	●	●	●	○
ISAPI Extensions	●	●	●	●	○
ISAPI Filters	●	●	●	●	○
Server-Side Includes	●	●	●	●	○
Health and Diagnostics Features					
HTTP Logging	●	●	●	●	●
Logging Tools	●	●	●	●	●
Request Monitor	●	●	●	●	●
HTTP Tracing	●	●	●	●	●
Custom Logging	●	●	●	●	○
ODBC Logging	●	●	●	○	○

Continued

Table 6.1 Continued. Features Available for Windows Server 2008

Feature	Windows Server 2008		Windows Vista		
	Full Install	Server Core Install	Ultimate, Business, Enterprise	Home Premium	Home Basic, Starter
Security Features					
Basic Authentication	•	•	•	•	○
Windows Authentication	•	•	•	○	○
Digest Authentication	•	•	•	○	○
Client Certificate Mapping Authentication	•	•	•	○	○
IIS Client Certificate Mapping Authentication	•	•	•	○	○
Uniform Resource Location (URL) Authorization	•	•	•	•	•
Request Filtering	•	•	•	•	•
IP Address and Domain Name Restrictions	•	•	•	•	•
Performance Features					
Static Content Compression	•	•	•	•	•
Dynamic Content Compression	•	•	•	•	•
Management Features					
Management Console	•	○	•	•	○
Management Scripts and Tools	•	•	•	•	•
Management Service	•	○	•	•	○
IIS 6.0 Management Compatibility	•	•	•	•	•
IIS 6.0 Metabase Compatibility	•	•	•	•	•

Continued

Table 6.1 Continued. Features Available for Windows Server 2008

Feature	Windows Server 2008		Windows Vista		
	Full Install	Server Core Install	Ultimate, Business, Enterprise	Home Premium	Home Basic, Starter
IIS 6.0 Windows Management Instrumentation (WMI) Compatibility	●	●	●	●	○
IIS 6.0 Management Console	●	○	●	●	○
IIS 6.0 Management Scripts and Tools	●	●	●	●	○
Windows Process Activation Services (WAS) Features					
Process Model	●	●	●	●	●
.NET Environment	●	○	●	●	●
Configuration Programming Interface	●	○	●	●	●
File Transfer Protocol (FTP) Publishing Service Features					
FTP Publishing Service	●	●	●	○	○
Management Console	●	○	●	○	○
Connection Limits					
Simultaneous Connections	Unlimited	Unlimited	10	3	3

With the release of Windows Server 2008, IIS 7.0 has been further tuned to handle the full operational requirements that you and many others will need in a live production environment (see Figure 6.1). Whether you are new or come from the experience of having worked with previous releases of IIS, you will undoubtedly find an array of new features and functionality that will be both useful and empowering. Behind this release were seven core design goals:

- **Componentized** Splitting up IIS into a set of modules gives you a light-weight, simple server environment for your Web applications. This results in more secure server that efficiently uses the system resources. The trend in componentization can also be seen in other Microsoft server products including Windows, Exchange, and SQL Server.

Figure 6.1 IIS 7.0 Modular Architecture

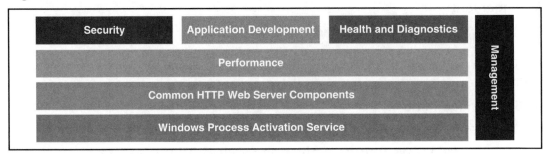

Test Day Tip

Instead of memorizing the names of every module, you should make an effort to understand how all the pieces fit together. Learning the concepts of how the pieces fit together will help you understand how to best address the scenarios presented to you in the exam and on the job.

- **Integrated** Simple, consistent, and enhanced server administration, configuration, and operations through an integrated management toolset. IT professionals have the ability to manage the server from a number of locations including:

  1. **Graphical Tools** IIS Manager, which ships with Windows Server 2008 can also be installed on Windows XP, Vista, and Server 2003.

  2. **Command-line Tools** AppCmd.exe replaces several VBScripts that shipped in previous releases with a robust, easy-to-use command-line tool.

  3. **Windows Management Instrumentation** A new WMI provider exposes a number of management methods for use through scripting,

programming languages, Windows PowerShell, Windows Remote Management (WinRM), and Windows Remote Shell (WinRS).

4. **Native Windows and .NET Programming Interfaces** In addition to native APIs the Microsoft.Web.Administration .NET assembly enables PowerShell scripts and .NET applications to take full advantage of IIS management through strongly typed objects.

- **Extensible** Building on a componentized architecture gives you the ability to add new modules or replace standard modules. This release introduces the ability to develop these modules in a managed .NET environment in addition to native Windows API development.

- **Supportable** New and enhanced tools for monitoring and troubleshooting give you greater insight into what is happening within your Web applications. A new programming interface to exposing real time request information, triggered error logging tool, and detailed client error messages assist developers and IT professionals in getting applications back online quickly.

- **Compatible** With the large number of changes in this release there was an effort to ensure that they were done in a way to ensure a high degree of backward compatibility with previous releases of IIS. The focus was to ensure at minimum a smooth migration for IIS 6 applications through features like the classic ASP.NET pipeline.

- **Delegation** –For growing Web farms, having the ability to delegate administration for various facets of the system is extremely useful. This release delivers an HTTP-based administration protocol, a configuration file hierarchy, a rich set of permissions, and the ability to replace authentication and authorization providers.

- **Secure** It is no secret that security is a necessary focus for all software vendors. The previous IIS release had a strong focus on this and delivered a core that withstood the test of time with no critical security patches required. IIS 7 continues through shipping a componentized architecture that enables you to install only what you need along with the ability to delegate a granular set of tasks.

Differences in Windows Editions

IIS is available in all editions and installations of Windows Server 2008. With Windows Server 2008 you can install IIS on a Server Core installation. There are some role services, however, that will not be available on Server Core:

- ASP.NET

- .NET Extensibility

- IIS Management Console

- IIS Management Service

- IIS 6 Management Console

Although these differences exist in this release, this still leaves you the ability to serve static, classic Active Server Pages (ASP), and Common Gateway Interface-based dynamic content (e.g., PHP, Perl, and Python).

Typical Deployment Scenarios

Depending on your business needs there are a number of scenarios in which IIS can be deployed.

Simple Web Server

Delivering one or more Web applications to a small number of users is the least complex scenario (see Figure 6.2). With this release of IIS the number of concurrent users that can be served continues to grow. IIS takes full advantage of 32-bit and 64-bit hardware to allow you to do more with less hardware.

Figure 6.2 Simple Web Server

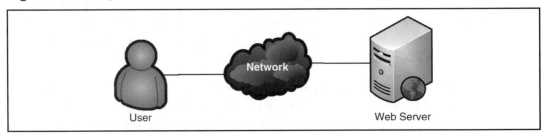

Small Web Farms

As you grow you can scale out to add additional Web servers to a farm using software-based load balancing. In this configuration you will split any database components off to a dedicated database server (see Figure 6.3).

Figure 6.3 Small Web Farm

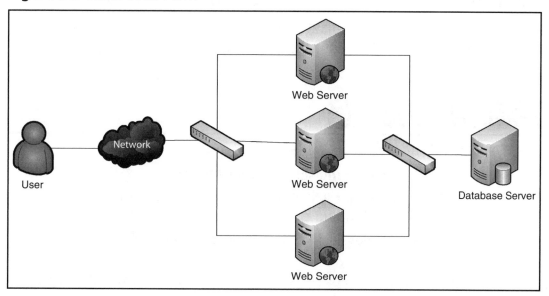

Large Web Farms

At a point in your growth it will be advantageous to use dedicated devices to provide load balancing, offloaded transport security, centralized storage, and application optimization. These devices are tuned to the specific tasks and can execute it more efficiently leaving your Web servers to focus on dynamic content assembly and delivery (see Figure 6.4).

Figure 6.4 Large Web Farm

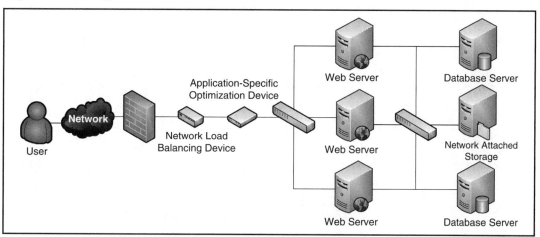

Installing Internet Information Services

The installation process for IIS follows the same process as most other Windows roles. The IIS features are found under the Web Server role alongside file transfer services. In this chapter we are focused on the Web functionality.

EXERCISE 6.1

INSTALLING THE WEB SERVER ROLE

1. From the **Start Menu** select **Server Manager**.

2. In **Server Manager,** scroll the right-hand pane to the **Roles Summary** section and click **Add Roles**.

3. In the **Add Roles Wizard** on the **Before You Begin** page, click **Next**.

4. On the **Server Roles** page (see Figure 6.5), select the **Web Server (IIS)** role and click **Next**.

Figure 6.5 Select Server Roles Page

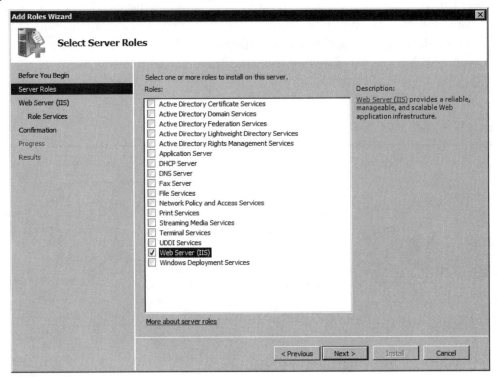

5. The **Web Server (IIS)** page gives you a brief description of the role along with some important notes and links to more information on the role (see Figure 6.6). Click **Next**.

   ■ If this is your first time setting up the Web Server (IIS) role you should read these notes as you speak to cover common issues that you will encounter.

Figure 6.6 Select Web Server (IIS) Role Services Page

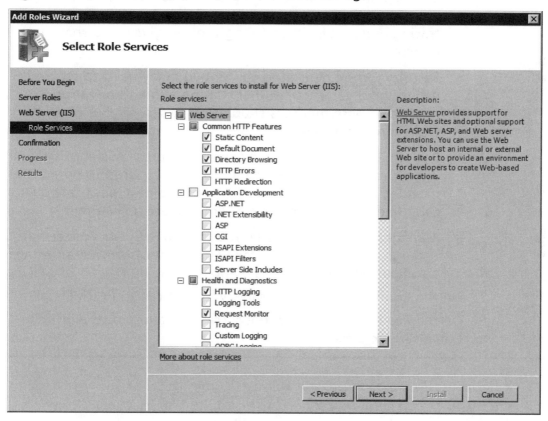

6. On the **Role Services** page you are prompted to install several groups of services to the role. To prepare for the exercises in this chapter select all of the services and click **Next**.

   ■ **Common HTTP Features** Services that are common to most Web server installations such as serving static content, returning rich HTTP error descriptions, basic HTTP redirection, and directory browsing. Note that even though they are considered common you have the ability to install IIS without these services.

- **Application Development** To deliver dynamic content to users or extend IIS you will need the appropriate runtime environments. In this section be sure to choose only the options that you need.

- **Health and Diagnostics** Tools to give you insight into what is happening on your Web server. You can choose basic logging through custom or database-driven logging along with tracing and request monitoring tools to give you a snapshot of activity.

- **Security** When delivering content you may need to secure it through a variety of authentication and authorization methods. These modules enable you to secure your content from anonymous users.

- **Performance** To reduce the overall resource consumption you can compress the content that is being delivered to users. The modules focus on two separate compression types that you can use depending on the content you are delivering.

- **Management Tools** Enables you to manage your Web server through a number of different types of tools as well as install a compatibility layer for IIS 6 applications.

7. On the **Confirmation** page review your choices and click **Install**.

8. On the **Results** page review the success or failure of the installation and click **Close**.

With the installation complete you will see the role appear in Server Manager. From here you can get an overview of related event log entries, Windows services, and the Role Services you have chosen to install. In addition the Resources and Support section gives you at-your-fingertips access to resources that go in-depth on common issues and best practices to consider (see Figure 6.7).

Figure 6.7 Server Manager after Installation of the Web Server (IIS) Role

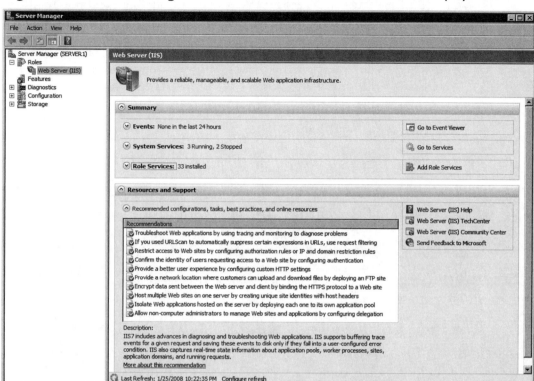

For Server Core the installation process involved a call to the package manager and optionally adding Windows Firewall exceptions to allow for remote administration.

EXERCISE 6.2

INSTALLING THE WEB SERVER ROLE ON SERVER CORE

1. Execute the following command to install the Web Server (IIS) role and all the role services available on a Server Core installation:

```
Start /W PkgMgr /IU:IIS-WebServerRole;IIS-WebServer;
IIS-CommonHttpFeatures;IIS-StaticContent;IIS-DefaultDocument;
IIS-DirectoryBrowsing;IIS-HttpErrors;IIS-HttpRedirect;
IIS-ApplicationDevelopment;IIS-ASP;IIS-CGI;IIS-ISAPIExtensions;
IIS-ISAPIFilter;IIS-ServerSideIncludes;IIS-HealthAndDiagnostics;
IIS-HttpLogging;IIS-LoggingLibraries;IIS-RequestMonitor;
```

```
IIS-HttpTracing;IIS-CustomLogging;IIS-ODBCLogging;
IIS-Security;IIS-BasicAuthentication;IIS-WindowsAuthentication;
IIS-DigestAuthentication;IIS-ClientCertificateMappingAuthentication;
IIS-IISCertificateMappingAuthentication;IIS-URLAuthorization;IIS-
RequestFiltering;IIS-IPSecurity;IIS-Performance;IIS-HttpCompressi
onStatic;IIS-HttpCompressionDynamic;IIS-WebServerManagementTools;
IIS-ManagementScriptingTools;IIS-IIS6ManagementCompatibility;IIS-
Metabase;IIS-WMICompatibility;IIS-LegacyScripts;WAS-WindowsActivati
onService;WAS-ProcessModel
```

Head of the Class...

Role Service Dependencies on Server Core

When you are installing any role and the corresponding set of features on Server Core you will need to be aware of dependencies. In the full installation you are notified of dependencies when you are selecting roles and role services. In Server Core the dependencies are not quite as clear. For example, classic ASP depends on the ISAPI Extensions and Request Filtering role services along with the Windows Activation Service role and its Process Model role service to be installed.

One of the easiest ways to identify the dependencies is through the OCLIST command, which is available on Server Core installations. Simply executing the command without parameters will show you the list dependencies underneath a particular role or role service as well as their current installation status. For example, Listing 6.1 shows you that the IIS-ISAPIExtensions role service is required to use IIS-ASP by listing it as a child of the IIS-ISAPIExtensions entry.

Listing 6.1 Role Service Dependencies Example

```
Not Installed:IIS-WebServerRole
    |─── Not Installed:IIS-WebServer
    |       |─── Not Installed:IIS-ApplicationDevelopment
    |       |       |─── Not Installed:IIS-ASP
    |       |       |─── Not Installed:IIS-ISAPIExtensions
    |       |       |       |─── Not Installed:IIS-ASP
```

2. If you have enabled Windows Firewall on your server you will need to add the following exceptions:

- **Remote Administration Service Exception:**

```
NetSh Firewall Set Service Type=RemoteAdmin Mode=Enable
```

- **Windows Management Instrumentation Exception:**

```
NetSh AdvFirewall Firewall Set Rule Group="Windows Management
Instrumentation (WMI)" New Enable=Yes
```

- **Lockdown the AHAdmin DCOM Endpoint to Port 49494:**

```
Reg Add "HKCR\AppId\{9FA5C497-F46D-447F-8011-05D03D7D7DDC}" /v
Endpoints /t REG_MULTI_SZ /d "ncacn_ip_tcp,0,49494"
```

- **Remote Web Server Management Exception:**

```
NetSh AdvFirewall Firewall Add Rule Name="Remote Web Server
Management (RPC)" Dir=In Action=Allow Program="C:\WINDOWS\
SYSTEM32\dllhost.exe" Protocol=TCP LocalPort=49494
```

```
NetSh AdvFirewall Firewall Add Rule Name="Remote Web Server
Management (RPC-EPMap)" Dir=In Action=Allow Program="C:\Windows\
system32\svchost.exe" Service=RPCSS Protocol=TCP LocalPort=RPC-
EPMap
```

- **If your security policy requires a more strict security setting you can use port exceptions on all or specific interfaces.**

3. If you want to use Windows Remote Shell you will need to enable it:

```
WinRM QuickConfig
```

Depending on your environment, you may not be able to directly administer your servers via the console. To aid in the management of our servers, especially Server Core installations that lack an administrative interface and command line tools, the product group has delivered a package of Remote Server Administration Tools. On Windows Vista the IIS Remote Server Administration Tool supplements the IIS Management Console to enable it to communicate with remote servers and sites.

EXERCISE 6.3

INSTALLING THE REMOTE SERVER ADMINISTRATION TOOLS

If you are running Windows Vista or Windows Server 2008 follow these steps:

1. From the **Control Panel** choose **Programs** and click the **Turn Windows Features On or Off** link.

2. In the Windows Features dialog expand Internet Information Services, Web Management Tools, and choose **IIS Management Console**.

If you are running Windows XP or Windows Server 2003 follow the next steps. For Windows Vista you will also need to follow these steps to allow you to remotely administer an IIS server since the out-of-the-box tools provide support for only the local IIS installation.

1. Double-click the **IIS Manager installation** package, follow the prompts for the update process to acknowledge the package, and accept the license agreement.

2. On the **Destination Folder** page accept the default value and click **Next**.

3. On the **Ready to Install** page click **Install**.

4. On the final page click **Finish**.

To access the administration tools you can find them in the Control Panel under System and Maintenance, Administration Tools, Internet Information Services Manager. Figure 6.8 shows the start page for Internet Information Services Manager.

Figure 6.8 Internet Information Services Manager

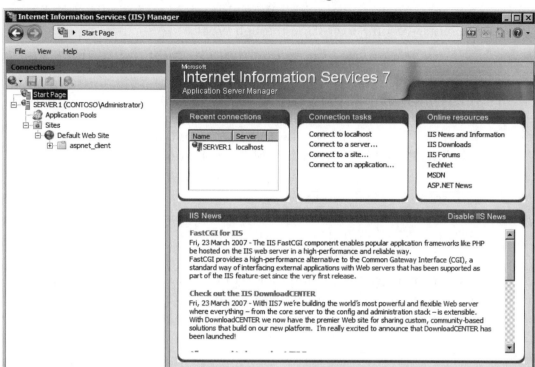

A word of warning—the graphical tools cannot connect to a Server Core installation. There are a few ways to remotely administer IIS on Server Core:

- **Command-line Tools** Using WinRS you can make calls to AppCmd. exe. Note that WinRM does not allow for interact sessions, instead outputting the results of your command.

```
WinRS.exe -Remote:WEBSERVER %SYSTEMROOT%\SYSTEM32\INETSRV\AppCmd.exe
LIST SITE
```

TEST DAY TIP

AppCmd uses a verb–noun combination. Open **Command Prompt**, type **AppCmd /?** and get to know the list of objects upon which you can take an action. The verb list will generally follow a common sense approach (e.g., you Create Backup, not Add Backup).

- **Windows Management Instrumentation** Scripting, programming languages, Windows PowerShell, WMIC, WinRM, and WinRS can all administer IIS on Server Core through WMI.

```
WMIC.exe /Output:Sites.txt /Node:WEBSERVER /Namespace:\root\
WebAdministration Path Site Get
```

- **COM and .NET Programming Interfaces** In addition to WMI you can use the Microsoft.ApplicationHost.AdminManager DCOM object in VBScript/JScript or the Microsoft.Web.Administration assembly through Windows PowerShell scripts and .NET applications.

```
[Reflection.Assembly]::LoadFrom("C:\WINDOWS\SYSTEM32\inetsrv\
Microsoft.Web. Administration.dll");

$WebServer = [Microsoft.Web.Administration.ServerManager]::
OpenRemote("WEBSERVER");

$WebServer.Sites | Format-Table Id, Name;
```

With our server and administration tools setup, you can now configure your server's features to fit your deployment scenario's needs. The following sections will take you through basic configuration steps for each of the functional areas.

EXAM WARNING

Know the differences between Server Core and full installations of Windows Server 2008 with Internet Information Services. There is a small subset of features that are not available on Server Core and they happen to be fairly important in the Microsoft Web application eco-system.

Provisioning Web Sites

With IIS installed the next step is to provision a Web site. The Web site is the top level container for content. It defines the entry point into the server and common set of properties that determines how your content is accessed. As part of the default IIS installation a Web site is created called "Default Web Site." You can choose to use this or remove it and create your own. If you choose to use it you should review the settings to ensure they meet your requirements and do not inadvertently expose your content.

You can create a site through the IIS Manager, AppCmd command-line tool, or through the various automation interfaces (e.g., WMI, Microsoft.Web. Administration assembly, Microsoft.ApplicationHost.AdminManager COM object). Under the covers each of these tools is modifying the applicationHost.config file, which is an XML-based configuration file located in the C:\WINDOWS\ SYSTEM32\inetsrv\Config folder. Listing 6.2 shows you an example of what an entry looks like inside this file.

Listing 6.2 Site element excerpt from applicationHost.config

```
<configuration>
  ...
  <system.applicationHost>
    ...
    <sites>
      ...
      <site name="Default Web Site" id="1">
        <application path="/">
          <virtualDirectory path="/" physicalPath="%SystemDrive%\inetpub\
          wwwroot" />
        </application>
        <bindings>
          <binding protocol="http" bindingInformation="*:80:" />
        </bindings>
      </site>
      ...
    </sites>
    ...
  </system.applicationHost>
  ...
</configuration>
```

More advanced users will find the flexibility of tools invaluable. The application-Host.config makes it easy to compare configurations across different environments using merge and differencing tools. For novice users and for everyday use the GUI and command-line tools will meet your needs.

EXERCISE 6.4

CREATING A WEB SITE

1. Open **Control Panel** and under **System and Maintenance | Administration Tools** double-click the **Internet Information Services (IIS) Manager** shortcut.

2. In the **Internet Information Services (IIS) Manager** management console, expand the server node in the left-hand pane, right-click **Sites**, and select **Add Web Site**.

3. In the **Add Web Site dialog** provide a descriptive **Site Name** and a **Physical Path** to the content if desired. Select an **IP Address** for the site and click **OK** (see Figure 6.9).

   ■ Host Headers enable you to share an IP address among multiple sites. Starting with HTTP 1.1 the HTTP protocol defined a header value that passes the host name being requested. For example, a call to www.contoso.com will result in "Host: www.contoso.com:80" being passed in the header of the request. This allows the HTTP protocol handler to hand the request off to the appropriate Web site. Because of this parsing if you make a request to the IP address of the Web site directly you will be passed to whichever site does not have a host header value defined.

Figure 6.9 Add Web Site Dialog

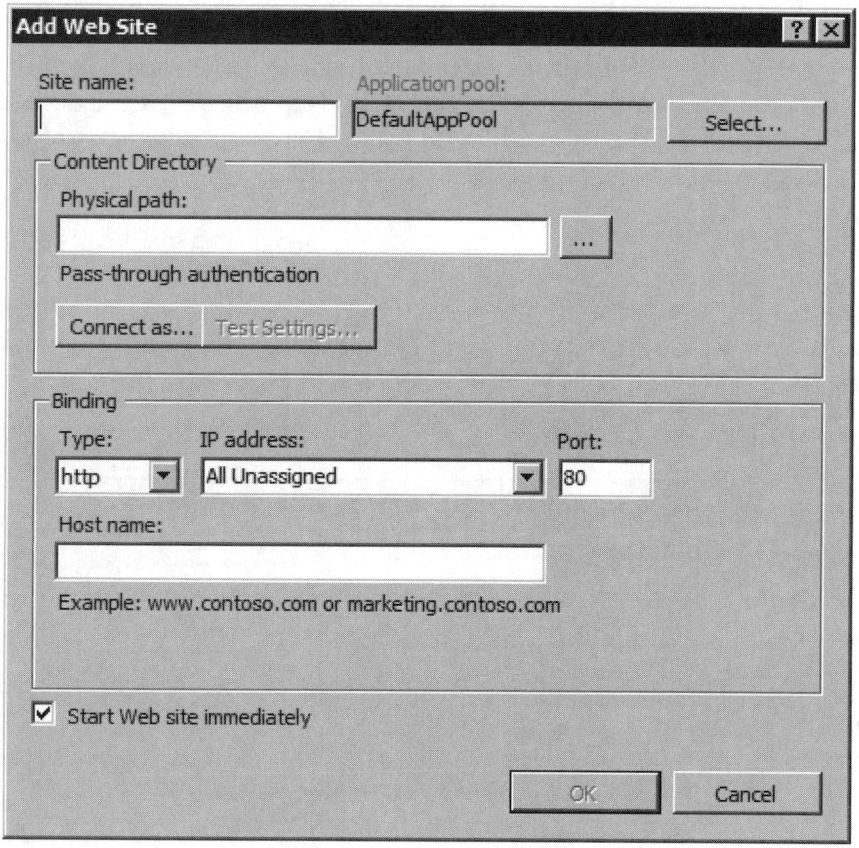

Configuring & Implementing…

Using Network Storage for Your Web Site Content

As your environment grows you will probably look to store your Web content on a remote storage device that will allow several Web servers to access the content. This can be implemented using Distribution File System, Network Attached Storage, or Storage Attached Networks. Using any of these technologies saves you from having to publish your Web content to multiple nodes in your Web farm.

Continued

When a user browses the site, IIS will need to determine which user's identity it will use to access the content on the remote storage device. If authentication for the content is set to allow anonymous users then IIS will use the anonymous account, which is the built-in IUSR account by default. For protected content IIS will use the credentials provided by the user through one of the authentication modules as the security content for accessing the content.

You can modify this default behavior by providing a set of credentials for IIS to use when accessing content on network-based storage. When creating a new Web site this shows up as the Contact As button in the Add Web Site dialog. When you click the button, IIS Manager will prompt you for a set of credentials to use as shown in Figure 6.10.

Figure 6.10 Connect As Dialog

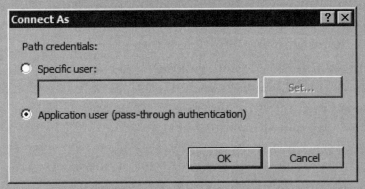

With this option set IIS will use this account to access the content. With this configuration you will need to ensure NTFS permissions are set appropriately to allow this account access to the content. Note that if you rely on NTFS auditing you will also lose the ability to record actions of specific authenticated users since this account will be used for both anonymous and authenticated connections.

If you have created a site and another one exists with the same IP address, port, and host header (or no host header) assigned (known as a binding) then your site will not start automatically. You must resolve the conflict first and then start your Web site. With the Web site started you are ready to add content. Like any folder hierarchy you can simply copy content into the folder structure.

Adding a Virtual Directory

There are times where you might need to reference content stored in another location. You could copy the content, but there is an easier method using Virtual Directories. A virtual directory works by creating a reference in the site configuration to where the content resides. As the request is being processed IIS will parse the request path and locate the content in the appropriate folder based on this configuration.

EXERCISE 6.5

CREATING A VIRTUAL DIRECTORY

1. Open **Control Panel** and under **System and Maintenance | Administration Tools,** double-click the **Internet Information Services (IIS) Manager** shortcut.

2. In the **Internet Information Services (IIS) Manager** management console expand the server and sites nodes in the left-hand pane, right-click your Web site, and select **Add Virtual Directory**.

3. In the **Add Virtual Directory** dialog provide the name of the virtual directory to be used by requests and a **Physical Path** to the content, and click **OK**.

Configuring the Default Document

A default document is the file that IIS will look for if one has not been specified by the user. For example browsing to http://www.contoso.com/foo will result in the following operations:

1. The server will send the client an HTTP redirect to http://www.contoso.com/foo/.

   - The trailing slash indicates that foo is a folder and that the default document should be served to the user. If foo were a file or one of the IIS modules was able to handle the request it would not have been redirected and the process would have delivered whatever the foo document contained.

2. The server will look in the physical folder for Default.htm.

3. If that is not found it will look for Default.asp.

4. If that is not found it will look for index.htm.

5.   If that is not found it will look for index.html.

6.   If that is not found it will look for iisstart.htm.

7.   If that is not found it will look for default.aspx.

If your configuration will not use any of these documents, or uses a particular file more frequently, you should adjust the order to save extra disk I/O operations. Likewise if you use a different name for a default document (e.g., Default.html), then you should add it. This can easily be done in the Default Document section of the configuration using the Add, Remove, Move Up, and Move Down options in the Actions pane as shown in Figure 6.11.

Figure 6.11 Default Document Module Configuration

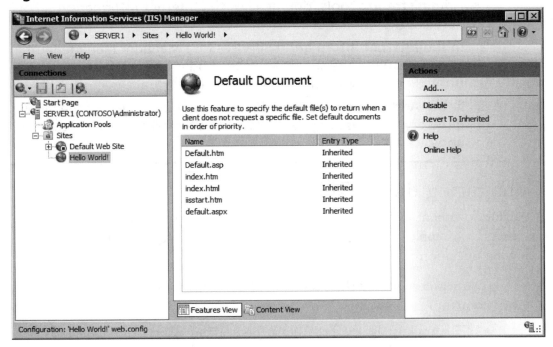

If you do not want the default document to be served you can disable the module. If you do not intend to use the default document module at all on the server you can remove it through Server Manager in the Web Server (IIS) role under Role Services.

Enabling Directory Browsing

Although not frequently used today, IIS provides the ability for users to browse the Web site using a directory listing (see Figure 6.12).

Figure 6.12 Directory Browsing Module Output

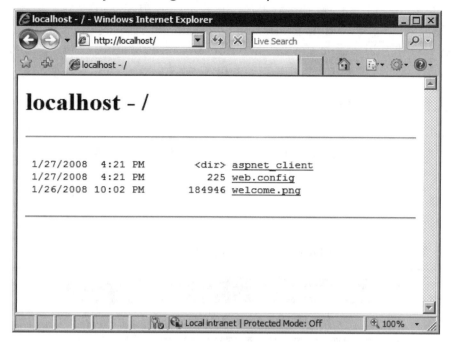

This can be useful if you are using the Web server as a file repository. The default Directory Browsing module allows you to control what file properties are returned with a directory listing (see Figure 6.13).

Figure 6.13 Directory Browsing Module Configuration

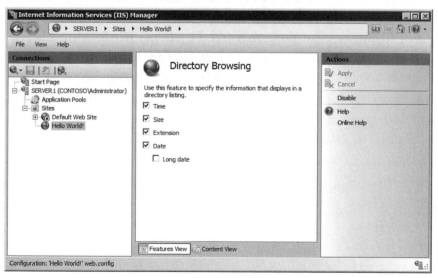

When you enable this module on a site or folder it will return a directory listing only if there is no existing default document in the container (assuming that the default document module is installed and enabled). As part of good security measures you should enable this module only if you have a need for it, otherwise leave it disabled or do not install it in the first place.

Customizing Error Pages

The default error pages that ship with a Web server are often very technical in nature. The default error pages in IIS 7 have been simplified, but are still very cold and technical (see Figure 6.14). If you want to have some fun with users or provide a more user-friendly explanation you can customize your error page.

Figure 6.14 Default File Not Found (404) Error Page for Users

For each HTTP error code you can configure the Web server to deliver a specific piece of static content; you can also redirect the request to another URL on the server or to another site altogether (see Figure 6.15). New for this release is the ability to send static content that is language-specific based on the HTTP request language header, which is set by the user's browser.

Figure 6.15 Add Custom Error Page Dialog

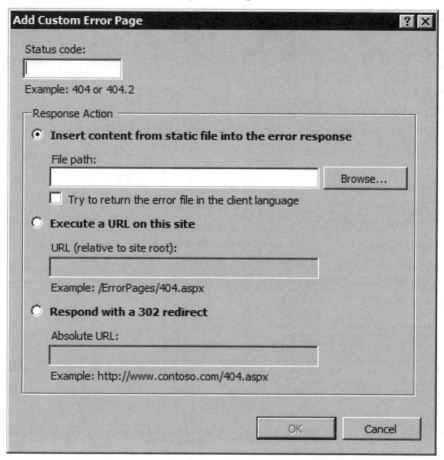

When you are making requests to your Web application from the server, by default, you will receive a detailed error message with more information about the particular request and state. This information will help you quickly understand the conditions under which the problem has occurred and enable you to take the necessary actions to resolve it (see Figure 6.16).

Figure 6.16 Default File Not Found (404) Error Page on the Server

The HTTP Errors module enables you to configure the behavior of this through the Edit Feature Settings link in the action pane. You can choose to send only the custom error pages, only the detailed error messages, or the custom error pages for remote requests and detail error pages for local requests. In most cases the default value will be suitable for your needs. One of the few scenarios you might choose to turn on detailed errors is in a development environment where people are testing a Web application and need the detailed information to help understand what is going on (see Figure 6.17).

Figure 6.17 Edit Error Pages Settings Dialog

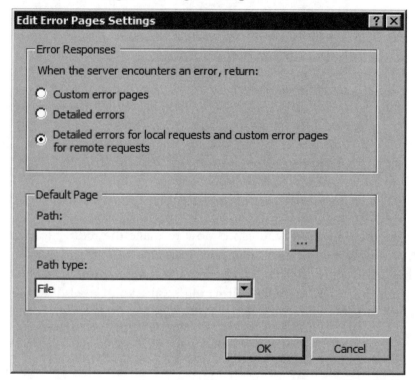

Redirecting Requests

The HTTP Redirect module enables you to redirect requests to a site, folder, or file to another URL (see Figure 6.18). This can be useful if you have moved content but wish to continue to maintain the URL (e.g., www.contoso.com/products/widget redirects to www.newvendor.com) or give users an easy way to navigate to a specific point (e.g., www.contoso.com/support redirects to support.contoso.com).

Figure 6.18 HTTP Redirect Module Configuration

Depending on your needs you can choose to make the redirection permanent, temporary, or simply redirect the client. These choices will affect how search engines interpret the direction. In the case of a permanent redirection they will favor the new URL over the older one when returning results. You can also set the redirect to ignore any additional entries in the path. For example a redirect on www.contoso.com/product/widget can redirect a request of www.contoso.com/products/widget/datasheet.xps to www.newvendor.com or www.newvendor.com/datasheet.xps. If you need to implement more elaborate HTTP redirection rules you can use one of several third-party HTTP modules found through www.iis.net/downloads.

Adding Custom Response Headers

Response Headers are included with the data being sent back to the client to instruct the browser to do something or for informational purposes. Most actionable response headers are generated by the Web server itself. These include instructions for the client to cache the content (or not), content language, and the HTTTP request status code among others. The custom response headers (see Figure 6.19) may be useful for scenarios where you want to identify a particular server in a load balanced scenario (e.g., send a response header of Web Farm Node: www1.contoso.com).

Figure 6.19 Custom Response Headers Module Configuration

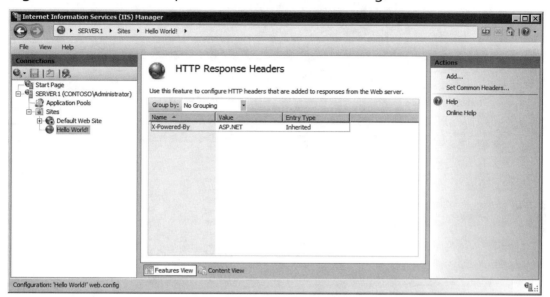

Unlike other modules you cannot uninstall this module. It is integrated into the HTTP protocol handler and exposes the ability to customize response headers. Adding a custom response header is as easy as coming up with a name/vale pair and assigning it to the site, folder, or file level by selecting the element, switching to Features View, and selecting the HTTP Response Headers icon. Be sure not to use a name that could be used by the server as defined in the HTTP protocol specification in RFC 2616. Doing so could cause issues with the client/server communication. The complete list of headers is located in Section 14 of RFC 2616, which can be found at www.w3.org/Protocols/rfc2616/rfc2616.html.

Adding MIME Types

MIME types are used by the HTTP to identify the type of data being sent to the browser. The browser will interpret the MIME type instead of trying to parse out the file extension of the request. This allows you to customize requests to use any extension you want. The reason for this additional measure is that the file extension does not necessarily dictate the content being sent. For example, a page ending in ASPX will typically serve XHTML content, but it can also be used to transmit binary files like images or files. The MIME type is the definitive way for Web browsers to know the format of a file so it can decide how to handle it (see Figure 6.20).

Figure 6.20 MIME Types Module Configuration

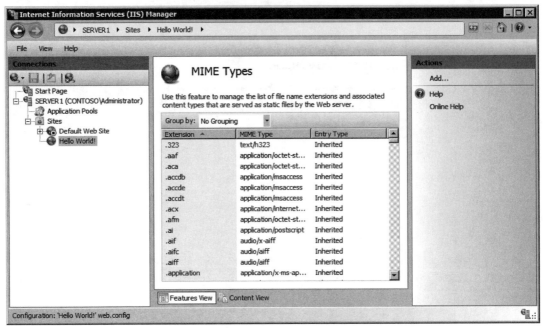

When IIS serves up static content it needs to append a MIME type to the response header. It determines which value to use based on the table of MIME types listed in IIS. It will cross reference the file type and send the corresponding value. For the most part you will not need to edit this section, but it can be useful when new static content types become available. MIME types, as with any configuration options, can be set at the site, folder, and file level. Select the relevant element using the left-hand content tree, switch to Features View, and double-click the MIME Types icon in the middle pane.

Configuring Web Applications

For most Web sites you will likely want to serve up more than static content. Dynamic content is the focus of Web applications. Under IIS there are specific features for Web applications focused on reliability, security, and extensibility. These features include Web applications, modules, and handlers.

The key component of a Web application under IIS is the application pool (see Figure 6.21). An application pool is a container in which one or more Web applications are executed. This change, introduced in IIS 6, isolates Web applications from each other to allow for greater overall system stability. If your application crashes, the IIS administrative process, inetinfo.exe, will start another instance to allow your application to continue to process requests. If you have separated your Web applications or sites using application pools this will limit the effects of the problem to the applications/sites belonging to the application pool. Application pools also give you a container to which you can apply resource constraints (see Windows Server Resource Manager for more information on resource constraints) and maintain a defined security context for application execution. The application pool is useful in a number of scenarios, for example when deploying a Web site that has commerce functionality. You can separate out the commerce section of the site from the rest of the site and apply a different security identity to the commerce functions. If the site itself were to be compromised in any fashion it would minimize the risk to the commerce components. For people hosting applications for multiple customers or lines-of-business you can give them their own execution context without having to invest in a large number of physical servers.

Figure 6.21 Application Pools

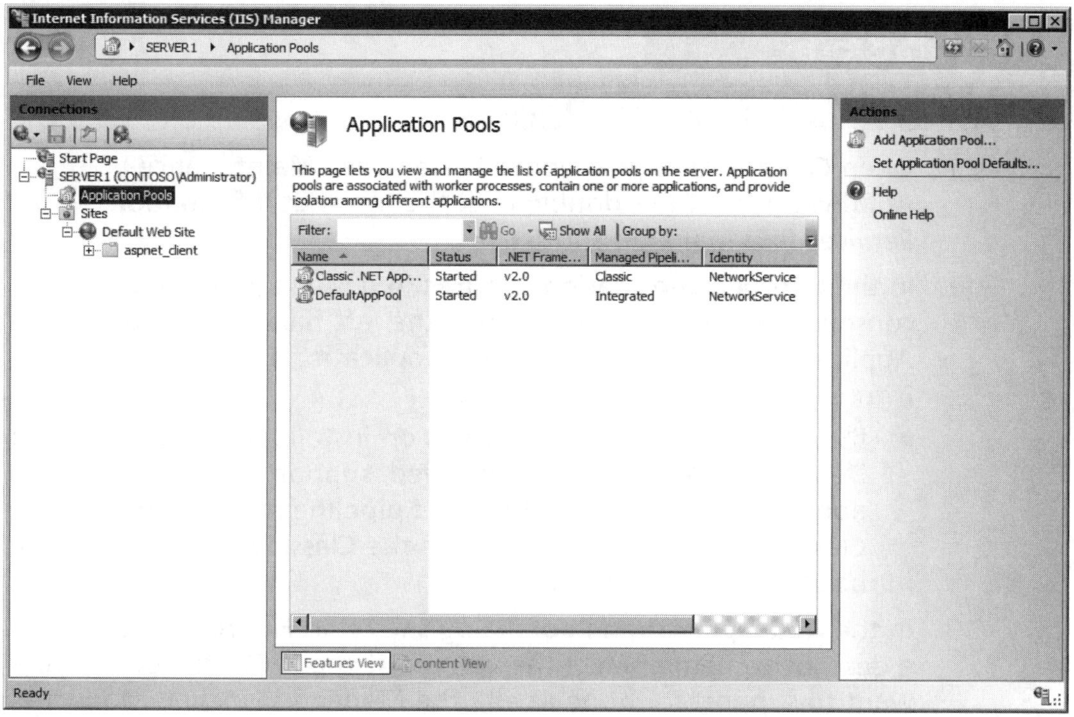

Configuring & Implementing…

Changes to ApplicationHost.config Result in Recycling

With the change to the XML-based configuration system, IIS 7 brought with it a characteristic of ASP.NET behavior that is less than desirable in change detection. As you make changes to your IIS configuration you will need to be aware as to what level of change you are making. If you make, for instance, a change at the server level to the modules list, it will cause all application pools to be stopped and restarted (recycled). For any requests in progress it means they will need to restart their request. When you make the change to a specific application pool setting then all instances of that pool are recycled.

EXERCISE 6.6

CREATING AN APPLICATION POOL

1. Open **Control Panel** and under **System and Maintenance | Administration Tools** double-click the **Internet Information Services (IIS) Manager** shortcut.

2. In the **Internet Information Services (IIS) Manager** management console expand the server node in the left-hand pane, right-click **Application Pools**, and select **Add Application Pool**, as shown in Figure 6.21.

   - IIS creates two application pools on installation—the DefaultAppPool, which, if installed, supports .NET Framework applications using the Integrated pipeline mode; and the Classic .NET AppPool, which uses the Classic pipeline mode for backward compatibility.

3. In the **Add Application Pool** dialog shown in Figure 6.22 provide a descriptive name, select the version of the .NET Framework you want to support (or none at all), the Managed Pipeline Mode, and click **OK**.

- **Integrated Pipeline Mode** ASP.NET-based applications partici-pate in the overall IIS request processing.

- **Classic Pipeline Mode** ASP.NET-based applications maintain a separate request processing stream from IIS, mainly used for backward compatibility with some older ASP.NET applications.

Figure 6.22 Add Application Pool Dialog

With the application pool created you can now create new applications or convert existing folders to a Web application. Starting with IIS 7 all Web sites are considered Web applications. This is a change from IIS 6 where you could create a Web site and remove all application execution properties. Under the covers this Web site would still be considered an application as it would be assigned to the DefaultAppPool, however it would not be able to execute dynamic content pages because it would not have any rights to do so. The change in IIS 7 makes this process more explicit as opposed to falling back to a default application pool.

EXERCISE 6.7

CONVERTING A FOLDER TO WEB APPLICATION

1. Open **Control Panel** and under **System and Maintenance | Administration Tools,** double-click the **Internet Information Services (IIS) Manager** shortcut.

2. In the **Internet Information Services (IIS) Manager** management console expand the server and sites nodes in the left-hand pane, right-click a folder within a Web site, and select **Convert to Application**.

3. In the **Add Application** dialog, select the application pool you want your application to run under, if desired set a content access identity, and click **OK** (see Figure 6.23).

Figure 6.23 Add Application Dialog

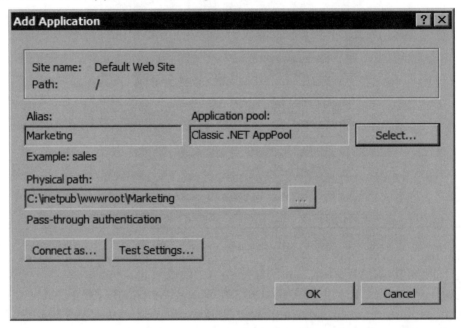

One other option you will see along the way is the ability to add a new Web application within a Web site. This process is the combination of creating a virtual directory and converting it to a Web application.

Head of the Class…

Correlating W3WP.EXE Instances with Web Applications

When you are using Task Manager, at first glance it may be difficult to determine which applications are being executed in which worker processes. One way of determining which application is running is the process identity. If you have assigned a unique identity to each application pool then it will show up beside the instance of w3wp.exe. If you are using the same identity across several pools it is a little more difficult to identify the separation at a glance. IIS Manager exposes the list of active worker processes at the server node level when you double-click the **Worker Processes** icon in the Features View. This view lists each active worker process, its process identifier, and high-level resource consumption information for the processor and memory (see Figure 6.24). The Private Bytes column shows the amount of memory allocated that cannot be shared with other processes. This is typically runtime data or libraries that have been loaded in a special manner just for use by the application (known as rebased libraries). The Virtual Bytes column shows the amount of virtual memory allocated to the worker process. This is a combination of physical memory and the system page file(s).

The AppCmd command-line tool will also help you determine what pool represents what application. In Listing 6.3, which shows the output from AppCmd.exe List WP, you can clearly see that the worker process using the Process Id of 3480 is the Marketing application pool while 4032 is the Finance application pool.

Continued

Figure 6.24 Worker Processes

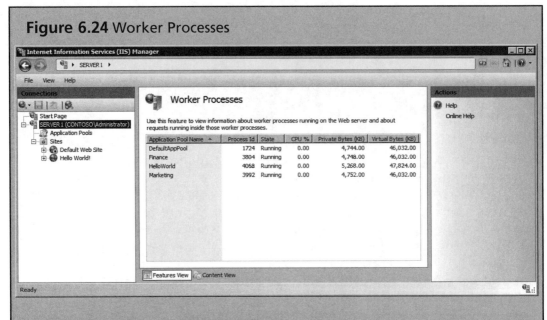

Listing 6.3 Application Pool Process Identities via AppCmd.exe

```
WP "3480" (applicationPool:Marketing)
WP "4032" (applicationPool:Finance)
WP "2128" (applicationPool:HelloWorld)
```

If you can't recall what applications are running inside that application pool then you can open up IIS Manager and use the View Applications action link after selecting the application pool, or as shown in Listing 6.4, use the AppCmd. exe List Apps command-line tool to display a list of applications along with their associated pools.

Listing 6.4 Applications and Their Pools via AppCmd.exe

```
APP "Default Web Site/" (applicationPool:DefaultAppPool)
APP "Hello World!/" (applicationPool:HelloWorld)
APP "Hello World!/finance" (applicationPool:Finance)
APP "Hello World!/finance/accounting" (applicationPool:Finance)
APP "Hello World!/finance/payroll" (applicationPool:Finance)
APP "Hello World!/marketing" (applicationPool:Marketing)
```

Application Pool Settings

Each application pool has number of settings that can be tuned to optimize how it behaves for your Web application. These settings are available through the Advanced Settings action available in the Application Pools section (see Figure 6.25).

Figure 6.25 Application Pool Advanced Settings Dialog

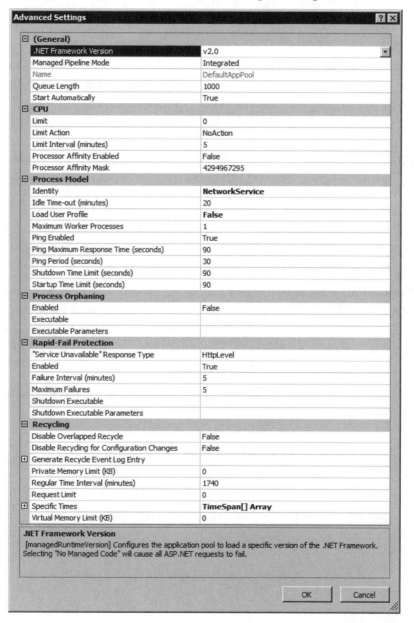

Outside of the application pool process identity most settings in their default state will service a majority of applications. Briefly we will take a look at each section, and highlight some of the features that are new to IIS 7:

- **General Settings** The ability to change pipeline modes, as discussed earlier, is exposed in this section.

- **CPU** The Processor Affinity settings, which enable you to configure your application to favor specific processors, is now exposed through the graphical user interface.

- **Process Model** In previous releases of IIS each application pool would run under a shared user profile, thereby accessing the same temporary folder when performing various file system operations. This introduced the potential for cross-pool information disclosure. In IIS 7 this option was added to allow you to take advantage of a more secure configuration where each individual worker process would maintain their own user profile on the server and thereby isolate activities such as temporary file storage.

- **Process Orphaning** The options in this section are new and exciting for developers as it allows you to attach a debugger to processes to capture their state upon failure. In previous releases you needed to use the tools that shipped as part of the IIS Resource Kit to perform similar actions.

- **Rapid-Fail Protection** The ability to modify the response type when services fail is powerful for scenarios that leverage load balancing. The option to fail to TCP as opposed to a 503 Service Unavailable message allows network load balancers to respond faster as they have less processing overhead to detect server failure.

- **Recycling** Exposes a number of options that were previously hidden in the metabase.

Application Development Settings

Depending on the runtime environment used by your Web application, ASP, ASP.NET, or another CGI-based environment (e.g., PHP, Perl, Python), the settings listed in the Application Development category in IIS Manager expose a number of runtime environment configuration values that you can tune to the needs of your application. A majority of the listed sections, with the exception of ASP and CGI, are specific to ASP.NET Web applications. After time has passed with the introduction of IIS 7 you may see other runtime environments expose their settings through this section as well. Most of these settings will be changed with guidance from your Web application developer. Their settings will largely depend on how the application was developed.

Enabling Third-Party Runtime Environments

One of the more common runtime environments that people add to a Web server is PHP. This processing language is similar in many ways to ASP. Other environments include Ruby on Rails, Perl, and Python. To enable a new runtime environment you will need to add a script map that points IIS to the appropriate executable that will handle the request and allow that executable to run.

EXERCISE 6.8

ENABLING PHP ON YOUR WEB SERVER

Before you begin you will need to obtain the latest PHP Installation Package from www.php.net/downloads.php.

1. Double-click the **PHP Installation Package**, follow the prompts for the update process to acknowledge the package, read and accept the license agreement.

2. On the **Destination Folder** page, click **Next**.

3. On the **Web Server Setup** page, choose **IIS ISAPI** and click **Next** (see Figure 6.26).

   - **ISAPI** Interfaces with IIS using native methods, thereby delivering the greatest performance. This choice may not be possible depending on your application as ISAPI-based applications have specific requirements around multithreaded handling. Consult your application vendor as to whether or not they support ISAPI installations.

   - **FastCGI** A revised version of the Common Gateway Interface (CGI) standard that has existed on Web servers for many years that deals with performance and security issues that exist in the original CGI specification.

   - **CGI** The original standard used by Web servers to call out to external runtime environments to process incoming requests.

Figure 6.26 Web Server Setup Page

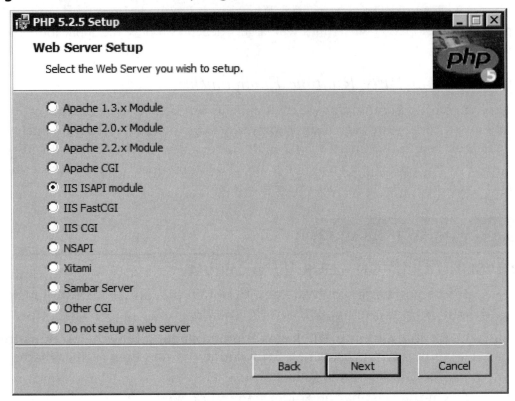

4. On the **Choose Items to Install** page choose the appropriate items needed by your application and click **Next**.

5. On the **Ready to Install** page click **Install**.

6. When the installation is finished open **Control Panel** and under **System and Maintenance | Administration Tools** double-click the **Internet Information Services (IIS) Manager** shortcut.

7. In the **Internet Information Services (IIS) Manager** management console select the server node.

8. In the middle pane double-click **Handler Mappings**.

9. On the **Handler Mappings** page in the right-hand **Actions** pane click **Add Script Map**.

10. In the **Add Script Map** dialog type *.php* in the **Request Path** text box, provide the **Executable** path to the php5isapi.dll (located in C:\Program Files\PHP by default), provide a descriptive **Name**, and click **OK**.

11. In the **Add Script Map** dialog asking you if you want to allow the extension click **Yes**.

12. Open a Web browser and browse to a PHP page on your site.

Migrating from Previous Releases

If you are migrating from a previous version of Internet Information Services then you may need the compatibility features offered by IIS. The following examples are some of the applications that will need this layer to function properly under IIS 7:

- ASP.NET 1.1-based applications

- Microsoft Office FrontPage server extensions

- Windows SharePoint Services 3.0

- IIS 6.0-based scripts

- Third-party applications that rely on custom metabase data

- IIS 7.0 SMTP service

Compatibility was a focus with this release and the optional role services around compatibility enable you to deploy Windows Server 2008 and continue to support your existing applications. For metabase calls IIS uses a layer called the Admin Base Object (ABO) Mapper. This layer provides translation between older metabase calls and the new ApplicationHost.config sections, elements, and attributes. As Windows Server 2008 deployments expand, expect to find additional guidance around migration available on the Tech Center for the Web Server role located at http://technet2.microsoft.com/windowsserver2008/en/servermanager/webserver.mspx.

Securing Your Web Sites and Applications

Protecting your Web application may require one or more tactics to ensure that the application is accessed only by authorized users:

- **Transport Security** Focused on privacy of data being transmitted between the user and the server

- **Authentication** Provides a method for determining the user's identity

- **Authorization** Evaluates a set of rules to determine if the user is allowed to make the request

This section will take you further into each tactic and the details behind them. There have been few key changes that support more secure communication, authentication, and authorization:

- **IIS_IUSRS Group** Replaces the IIS_WPG group from previous releases to service as a security group to which permissions are assigned that will be required by all the application pool identities.

- **Built-in IUSR Account** Replaces the IUSR_MachineName from previous releases with a built-in account that uses a constant security identifier (SID) across servers that helps to maintain consistent access control lists (ACL). Use of the built-in account eliminates the need to have a password assigned to this account as well. For IIS installations on domain controllers it will prevent the IUSR account from becoming a user-accessible domain account.

- **Inheritance and Merging of IP Restriction Rules** Allows more flexible ways to apply authorization rules based on a single computer, group of computers, a domain, all IP addresses, and/or any unlisted entries.

- **Request Filtering** The URLScan tool, which previously shipped as an add-on tool, is now incorporated in the HTTP protocol handler.

- **Native URL Authorization** A more efficient, globally accessible way to secure specific files and paths without having to rely on third-party tools or ASP.NET.

Transport Security

Protecting the privacy of the data being transmitted is the primary focus of transport security. There are a number of options within the Windows Server 2008 infrastructure to protect the privacy. You may want to wrap all data being transmitted, for example, through a virtual private network or IPSec tunnel. With this as the extreme at one end, IIS provides a more moderate and widely used method for protecting data using Secure Socket Layers (SSL) and Transport Layer Security (TLS). TLS is the more commonly deployed standard today and provides the ability to fall back to SSL 3.0 if the client does not support TLS. SSL/TLS uses digital certificates to encrypt the communication. At a high level the process works as follows:

1. The client makes a request to the Web server for a secure connection.

2. The server sends back its public encryption key.

3. The client checks the key to ensure:

- The name of the host being requested matches the key.

- The key is within the valid date range.

- The key's issuer is trusted by the client.

4. If the client determines that it can trust the server's public key it will send its public key to the server.

5. The server will generate a password and encrypt it using both the client's public key and the server's private key, and send it back to the client.

6. The client will decrypt the password as evidence that the server is the one who sent the password, thereby establishing that only the server and the client will be the only other party capable of reading the encrypted information.

7. The client will send the request to the server encrypted with the password that the server sent to it.

This process has been well established for quite some time and works with all major browsers. IIS fully supports using SSL/TLS certificates to encrypt communication between the server and users. Under the covers, IIS 7 now handles SSL/TLS requests in the kernel by default (it was available in IIS 6, but not enabled by default). This provides a big boost to the performance of secure requests.

New & Noteworthy...

Host Headers and SSL

As mentioned earlier in the chapter, host headers enable you to share an IP address among multiple sites. A call to www.contoso.com will result in Host: www.contoso.com:80 being passed in the header of the request. This allows the HTTP protocol handler to hand the request off to the appropriate Web site. For connections that use secure socket layer (SSL) the ability to use host headers was first introduced in Windows Server 2003 Service Pack 1.

Before you get too excited there are some restrictions that you will need to take into account. The first is that the SSL certificate must

Continued

contain all the common names of the sites. For example, if you are binding www.contoso.com and store.contoso.com to the same IP address, your SSL certificate will need to contain both host names in the common name field. The most secure approach is to use multiple common names using the subjectAltName property, but it is also the most difficult to obtain as it is not commonly available through certificate authorities (CA). Most certificate authorities promote the use of wildcard certificates instead. A wildcard certificate enables you to use the certificate for all subdomains (e.g., *. contoso.com would work for www.contoso.com, store.contoso.com, foo. contoso.com, bar.contoso.com, foo.bar.contoso.com). Consult your preferred certificate authority on the cost of a wildcard or subjectAltName certificate as they are not usually supported by the typical offering.

With your new certificate in hand you need to bind the certificate to a Web site. Under the covers IIS does not bind it to the Web site, but the IP address being used. The reason for this is simple; the HTTP header value that contains the host name is encrypted at the time that the HTTP protocol handler needs to make the decision of which certificate to use. This means that you can have only one SSL certificate per IP address and that explains why you need a wildcard certificate or one with the subjectAltName properties included. To see a list of certificates and their corresponding IP address bindings use the following NetSh command:

```
NetSh.exe HTTP Show SSLCert
```

Adding an SSL binding with host header support currently is not supported through the graphical user interface. You will need to use the AppCmd tool, programmatically, or edit the ApplicationHost.config to add the binding. Here is the AppCmd syntax for adding the binding:

```
AppCmd.exe Set Site /Site.Name:"Contoso Store" /+Bindings.[Protocol=
'HTTPS',BindingInformation='*:443:store.contoso.com']
```

With that in place you can now access both of your sites using SSL.

IIS 7 also introduces a new management interface for security certificates. This new interface gives you a single point to review all the certificates installed on your server along with exposing the ability to generate a self-signed certificate from within the interface. Previously self-signed certificates were available only through the command-line SelfSSL tool that shipped with the IIS 6.0 Resource Kit tools (see Figure 6.27).

Figure 6.27 Server Certificates Module Configuration

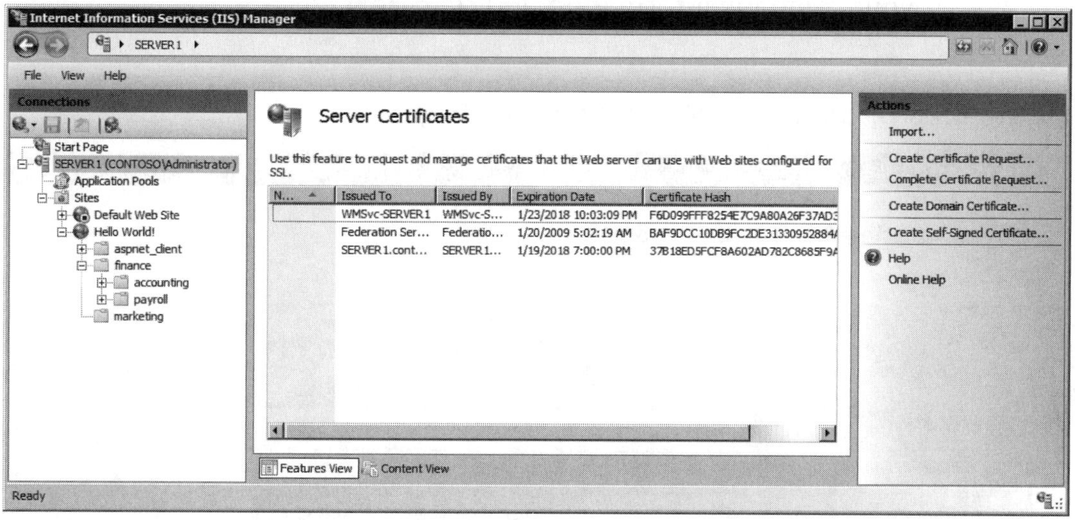

The first step to enabling a secure site is to import or create a new certificate into the server. When creating a certificate you can create one from an online connected certificate authority (CA) like the Certificate Services role that ships with Windows Server 2008, a third-party CA (e.g., Comodo, Thwarte, Verisign), or generate a self-signed certificate. Whichever path you choose the one thing to remember is that the client will need to trust the certificate's issuer in order to trust the certificate. When using a self-signed certificate no one will trust it unless they take steps to specifically add it to their trusted certificates list.

EXERCISE 6.9

ADDING A NEW SECURITY CERTIFICATE

1. Open **Control Panel** and under **System and Maintenance | Administration Tools**, double-click the **Internet Information Services (IIS) Manager** shortcut.

2. In the **Internet Information Services (IIS) Manager** management console click the server node, in the middle pane click **Server Certificates**.

3. In the right-hand **Actions** pane click **Create Certificate Request**.

4. In the **Request Certificate** dialog on the **Distinguished Name Properties** page (see Figure 6.28) provide the host name that will

be used to access your site (e.g., www.contoso.com) along with your company information and click **Next**.

Figure 6.28 Distinguished Name Properties Page

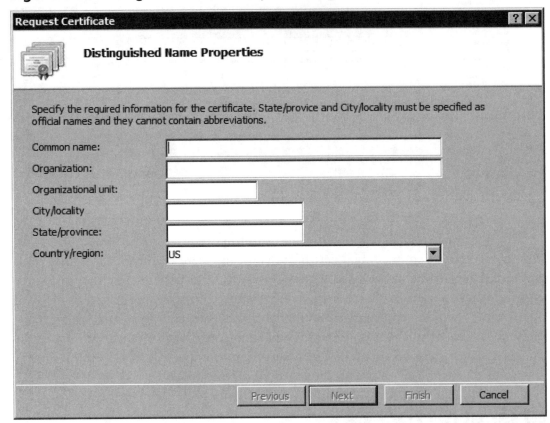

5. On the **Cryptographic Service Provider Properties** page choose a **Cryptographic Server Provider**, a minimum of 1,024 **Bit Length** for the key, and click **Next** (see Figure 6.29).

   ▪ **RSA SChannel Cryptographic Provider** Uses an MD5 hash with an SHA hash, signed with an RSA private key. It supports SSL2, PCT1, SSL3, and TLS1 protocols.

   ▪ **DH SChannel Cryptographic Provider** Uses the Diffie-Hellman algorithm and supports SSL3 and TLS1 protocols. Use this algorithm when you must exchange a secret key over an insecure network without prior communication with the client.

- **Bit Length** The default length supported by most browsers and certificate authorities is 1,024 bits. With processors becoming more powerful, expect to see a move toward 2,048 bit length certificates past the year 2010. Be sure to check with your chosen certificate authority to ensure they will support bit lengths larger than 1,024 before increasing this value.

Figure 6.29 Cryptographic Service Provider Page

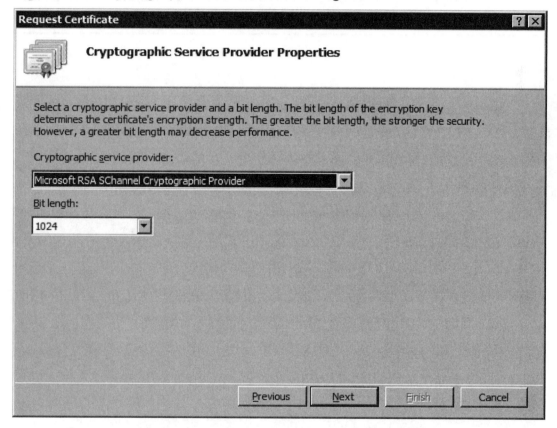

6. On the **File Name** page provide a path and name of a file where to sort the certificate request and click **Next**.

7. Contact your preferred certificate authority to obtain the response file for your request.

- If you are looking to test out the SSL functionality there are a number of providers that will give you a free trial SSL certificate that lasts for anywhere from 15 to 60 days. This is handy because they have all the trust features of regular certificates with no cost.

8. When you obtain the response file, open **IIS Manager** and return to the **Server Certificates** section.

9. In the right-hand actions pane click **Complete Certificate Request**.

10. In the **Complete Certificate Request** dialog on the **Specify Certificate Authority Response** page, locate the **Certificate Authority's Response** file, provide a **Friendly Name** for the certificate, and click **Next** to complete the process.

Configuring & Implementing...

The Real Differences between SSL Certificates

When you are out shopping for an SSL certificate it can get quite confusing as to what the differences are between the various offerings. For the most part you are buying trust in that the certificate you will be issued is trusted by the client. Under the covers the technical differences boil down to these:

- **Standard Certificate** A basic security certificate that will suit most users and will work for 40-bit encryption up to 256-bit encryption in most modern browsers

- **Server Gated Certificate** Before the United States dropped its cryptography export laws in January of 2000 these certificates added a step in the security handshake to see whether the client could support stronger cryptographic algorithms (ciphers). This allowed older browsers an opportunity to step-up their level of encryption if they did not use 128-bit or higher encryption by default.

- **Extended Validation Certificate** From a technical perspective these certificates are no different than a standard certificate with the exception that they have some additional metadata attached to the certificate. This metadata is used by browsers that are capable of reading it to determine if they should

Continued

identify for the user (e.g., turn the address bar green) that the site has gone through extra validation steps. The validation steps and data included are available in the extended validation certificate guidelines at www.cabforum.org. With the data in hand modern browsers will signal to the user through actions like turning the address bar green as shown in Figure 6.30. This feature of popular browsers like Internet Explorer 7 is meant to help users identify the site authenticity.

Figure 6.30 Internet Explorer Address Bar of a Site Using Extended Validation Certificate

- **Wildcard Certificate** One of the three preceding certificates, but using an asterisk (∗) somewhere in the domain name to signify a wildcard value. This is generally considered a premium service and commercial providers reflect this fact in their pricing model.

When choosing certificates remember that the level of encryption used in most cases is decided on as a mutual agreement between the client and the server. Both parties can choose to use a minimum level of encryption. With IIS this value is represented by a single check box to force clients to use a minimum of 128-bit encryption or have IIS refuse the connection request. Other advertised features have no impact on the security provided by the SSL-enabled session.

With the certificate in place you can now bind the certificate to your Web site. Under the covers the security certificate is bound to an IP address since the request header information is encrypted when the server needs to determine which certificate to use. Once the certificate is bound you can choose to force the use of SSL on all or part of the site.

EXERCISE 6.10

ENABLING SECURE COMMUNICATION ON YOUR WEB SITE

1. Open **Control Panel** and under **System and Maintenance | Administration Tools**, double-click the **Internet Information Services (IIS) Manager** shortcut.

2. In the **Internet Information Services (IIS) Manager** management console expand the server node, right-click your site, and select **Edit Bindings**.

3. In the **Site Bindings** dialog click **Add**.

4. In the **Add Site Binding** dialog set the Type to **HTTPS**. From the **SSL Certificate** list choose your certificate and click **OK** (see Figure 6.31).

Figure 6.31 Add Site Binding Dialog

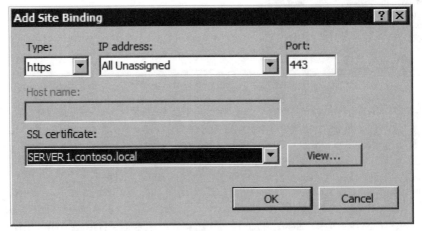

5. In the **Site Bindings** dialog click **Close**.

6. Expand your site node, locate and click a folder (or select the site to enforce SSL on the site as a whole) that you wish to secure.

7. In the middle pane under **Features View**, double-click **SSL Settings**.

8. In the **SSL Settings** module check **Require SSL, Require 128-bit SSL**, and in the right-hand Actions pane click **Apply** (see Figure 6.32).

- Most modern Web browsers support 128-bit SSL. This option was put in place because up until 2000 the United State government restricted the export of certain cryptographic algorithms, which left a good portion of the world stuck with 40- or 56-bit sessions, which provided a lesser degree of security.

Figure 6.32 SSL Settings Module Configuration

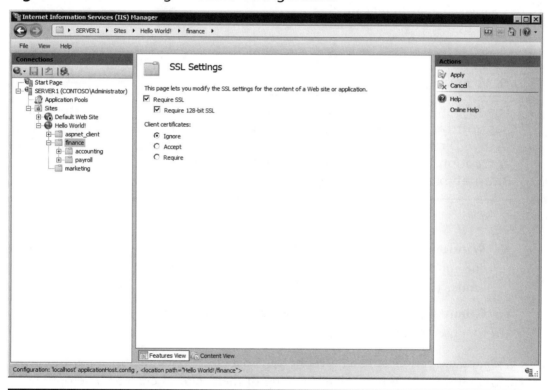

Authentication

Authentication is the process of asserting the identity of the user making a request to the Web server. With this identity we can track who is doing what and evaluate rules to determine if they are authorized to perform specific actions. IIS ships with several types of authentication modules that can be used to determine a user's identity:

- **Anonymous** Enabled by default to allow any user to access public content with a username and password.

- **Basic** Requires the user to provide a username and password. This authentication protocol is a standard across all platforms. It does not perform any sort of encryption with the information provided by the user. As such you should use it with SSL to ensure that the credentials are sent over a secure connection.

- **Digest** Similar to basic authentication but instead of sending the password in clear text it sends an MD5 hash across the wire, which is verified by the server. One of the disadvantages to this method is that it requires that the password be stored using reversible encryption. It is also vulnerable to man–in–the–middle attacks.

EXAM WARNING

The RFC-standard Digest authentication requires HTTP 1.1 and that the password is stored in reversible encryption within the security data store (Active Directory, local SAM). Advanced Digest gets around the reversible encryption by storing the hash in Active Directory, but it only works on Internet Explorer 5.0 or later.

- **Windows** Used mainly in intranet scenarios, it allows browsers to use the current user's Windows domain credentials to authenticate the connection. Under the covers it uses NTLM or Kerberos to handle the authentication.

- **Client Certificates** Users provide a digital certificate that is mapped to a user account.

With the exception of client certificates, enabling these authentication modules usually requires nothing more than toggling of their state to enabled. The options for most of the modules are limited to either identity impersonation options or default realms for authentication.

EXERCISE 6.11

ENABLING BASIC AUTHENTICATION ON A FOLDER

1. Open **Control Panel** and under **System and Maintenance | Administration Tools**, double-click the **Internet Information Services (IIS) Manager** shortcut.

2. In the **Internet Information Services (IIS) Manager** management console expand the server, site node, and locate a folder to secure (or choose the site as a whole) and click your selection.

3. In the middle pane under **Features View** double-click **Authentication**.

4. Right-click the **Basic Authentication** module and select **Enable** (see Figure 6.33).

Figure 6.33 Authentication Module Configuration

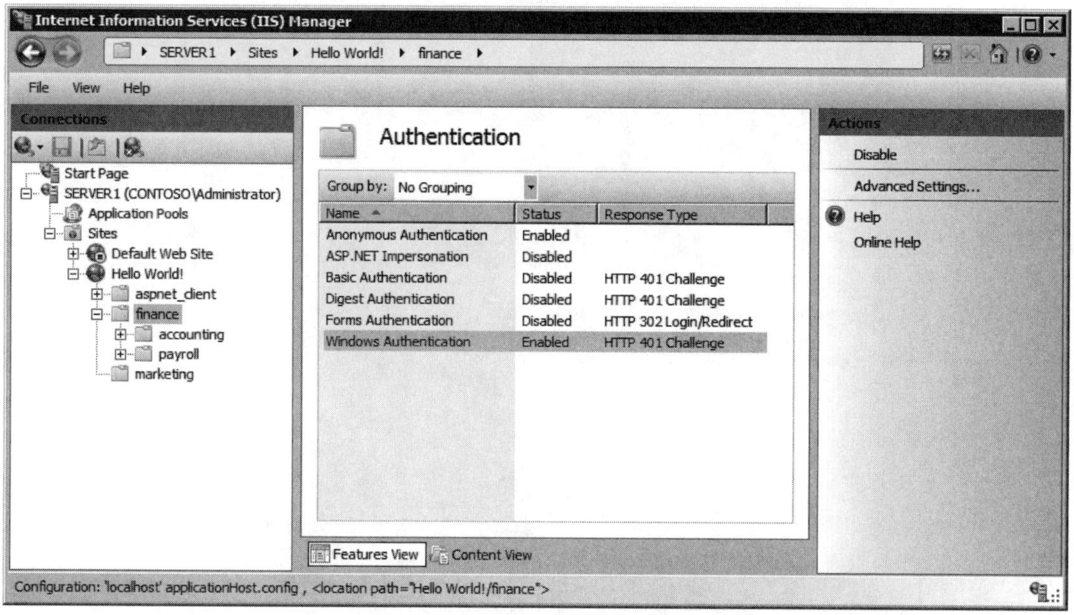

If you are using an ASP.NET runtime environment you have two other authentication modules that are specific to ASP.NET-based Web applications:

■ **Forms** Enables you to provide a rich Web-based authentication and user registration experience.

■ **ASP.NET Impersonation** Enables you to use a specific account, or the account specified by another IIS authentication module, to execute the application as opposed to the application pool identity.

These authentication modules have been available in ASP.NET since the 1.1 release of the .NET Framework. The IIS Manager exposes a number of the configuration options that traditionally have been managed through the ASP.NET tab in the previous release of IIS or directly in the web.config (see Figure 6.34).

Figure 6.34 Edit Forms Authentication Settings Dialog

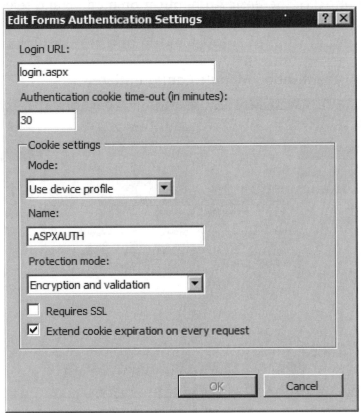

Considerations When Using Client Certificates

In Exercise 6.10, you may have noticed some options around whether or not to ignore, accept, or require client certificates. These options are contained within the

SSL Settings because the client certificate submission process is a part of the SSL module. This also means that you will need SSL enabled on sites and folders where you want to use client certificate mapping. When a client certificate is received it can be mapped back to a user account in one of three ways:

- **Active Directory Client Certificate Mapping** Looks to the local Active Directory domain to locate a match for the client certificate that was applied. Note that using this option requires that it be used across all sites on the server.

- **One-to-One Mapping** Allows you to specify through the configuration the identity to be used for the user with whom the certificate matches.

- **Many-to-One Mapping** Like one-to-one mapping it allows you to control through the configuration the user identity used when the certificate is matched. This method allows you to map multiple users to a single identity.

EXAM WARNING

Active Directory Client Certificate Mapping disables the ability to use one-to-one and many-to-one certificate mapping because it is able to resolve back to both users and groups within the directory, effectively doing the same thing as both one-to-one and many-to-one certificate mapping.

At the time of this writing there was no graphical interface to the one-to-one and many-to-one certificate mapping controls. Listing 6.6 shows an example of the configuration values for both of these mapping methods.

Listing 6.6 One-to-One and Many-to-One Certificate Mapping Configuration

```
<configuration>
  ...
  <system.webServer>
    ...
    <security>
      ...
      <authentication>
        <iisClientCertificateMappingAuthentication enabled="true">
          <manyToOneMappings>
            <add name="FinanceUsers" description="Finance Users"
```

```
                        enabled="true" permissionMode="Allow"
                        userName="CONTOSO\FinanceDelegate" password="DF923uD@#2">
                    <rules>
                      <add certificateField="Subject"
                           matchCriteria="john@contoso.com" />
                      <add certificateField="Subject"
                           matchCriteria="jane@contoso.com" />
                      <add certificateField="Subject"
                           matchCriteria="sam@contoso.com" />
                      <add certificateField="Subject"
                           matchCriteria="sally*@contoso.com" />
                    </rules>
                    </add>
                </manyToOneMappings>
                <oneToOneMappings>
                    <add enabled="true" certificate="—-BEGIN CERTIFICATE—-
MIIBqDCCARECAQAwaTELMAkGA1UEBhMCVVMx DjAMBgNVBAgTBVRleGFzMRMwEQYD
VQQHEwpMYXNDb2xpbmFzMRIwEAYDVQQKEwlNaWNyb3NvZnQx DjAMBgNVBAsTBU10
ZWFtMREwDwYDVQQDFAhOVFZPT0RPTzCBnjANBgkqhkiG9w0 BAQEFAAOBjAAwgYgC
gYBxmmAWKbLJHg5TuVyjgzWW0JsY5Shaqd7BDWtqhzy4HfR TW22f31rlm8NeSXHn
EhLiwsGgNzWHJ8no1QIYzAgpDR79oqxvgrY4WS3PXT7OLwI DAQABoAAwDQYJKoZI
hvcNAQEEBQADgYEAVcyI4jtnnV6kMiByiq4Xg99yL0U7bIp EwAf3MIZHS7wuNqfY
acfhbRj6VFHT8ObprKGPmqXJvwrBmPrEuCs4Ik6PidAAeEf oaa3naIbM73tTvKN+
WD30lAfGBr8SZixLep4pMIN/wO0eu6f30cBuoPtDnDulNT8AuQHjkJIc8Qc=
—-END CERTIFICATE—-"
                        userName="CONTOSO\FinanceDelegate" password="DF923uD@#2"
                    </oneToOneMappings>
                </iisClientCertificateMappingAuthentication>
            </authentication>
          ...
        </security>
      ...
    </system.webServer>
    ...
</configuration>
```

Unlike the other two methods, enabling Active Directory Client Certificate is exposed through the graphical interface. The option is exposed as the server node level and when it is set it disables the ability to use one-to-one and many-to-one mappings on the server. To learn how to associate a certificate with an Active Directory user account refer to the Windows Server 2008 documentation around public key infrastructure.

EXERCISE 6.12

ENABLING ACTIVE DIRECTORY CLIENT CERTIFICATE MAPPING

1. Open **Control Panel** and under **System and Maintenance | Administration Tools**, double-click the **Internet Information Services (IIS) Manager** shortcut,

2. In the **Internet Information Services (IIS) Manager** management console click the server node,

3. In the middle pane under **Features View** double-click **Authentication**.

4. Right-click the Active Directory Client Certificate Mapping module and select **Enable**.

Authorization

With the user's identity established the next step is to determine if the user can perform the action that is being requested. Authorization encompasses a set of rules that are evaluated based on a number of conditions, which could include the user's identity, to provide a decision as to whether or not to allow the user's request to be acted upon. IIS provides three core modules focused on authorization and supporting services—URL authorization, IP authorization, and request filtering.

URL Authorization

Originally brought into the IIS environment by ASP.NET, the URL Authorization module has been rewritten as a native IIS module to allow everyone to take advantage of an easy way of restricting access to specific folders and files. This module allows Web content managers the ability to control access in a manner similar to the use of NTFS permissions. Unlike NTFS permissions, you do not need file system access to the server to apply permissions since everything is managed through the web.config file stored at the root of the site or within a given folder. As well, this allows you to easily carry the permissions with the site as it moves environments.

EXERCISE 6.13

Restricting Access to a Folder

1. Open **Control Panel** and under **System and Maintenance | Administration Tools,** double-click the **Internet Information Services (IIS) Manager** shortcut.

2. In the **Internet Information Services (IIS) Manager** management console expand the server, site node, and locate a folder to secure (or choose the site as a whole) and click your selection.

3. In the middle pane under **Features View** double-click **Authentication**.

4. On the **Authentication** page ensure that the **Anonymous Authentication** module is **Disabled,** select one of the other authentication modules, and click **Enable** in the right-hand **Actions** pane.

5. Click the Back arrow in the top left-hand corner.

6. On the folder page in the middle pane under **Features View,** double-click **Authorization Rules.**

7. On the **Authorization Rules** page click the **Add Allow Rule** in the right-hand action page.

8. Select the **Specified Users** radio button, provide a username, and click **OK** (see Figure 6.35).

Figure 6.35 Add Allow Authorization Rule Dialog

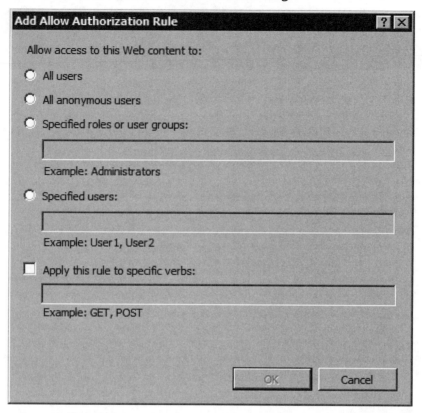

When users attempt to access a page to which they have been denied they will receive a 401.2 unauthorized error. With the addition of detailed error requests the server-side error message gives you a number of useful elements to help you troubleshoot access denied issues being caused by URL authorization. As shown in Figure 6.36, you can see that we are dealing with the URL Authorization Module, that the file is a static file, along with the logon method and user account being used to access the URL.

Figure 6.36 Server-Side Version of Unauthorized Page Access Error Message

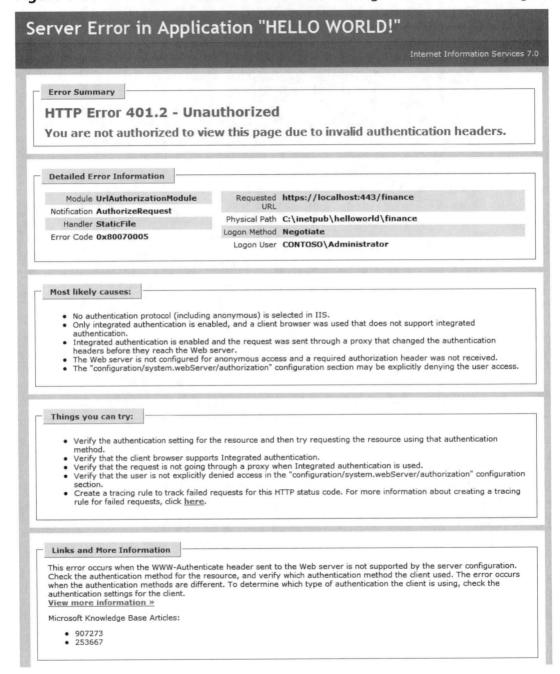

TEST DAY TIP

When faced with a troubleshooting situation, list the known facts for the situation and walk through the request process. As you walk through refer to the fact list to ask yourself how each relevant fact will affect that step in the request process.

IP Authorization

The ability to restrict access to specific IP addresses has existed for quite some time across both servers and networking devices such as firewalls. In the past this function, like file permissions, was available only through IIS Manager and was tough to replicate across to other servers as it was stored in the metabase. This setting, along with all other configuration options, has been moved to the new XML-based configuration files. This allows you to centralize, copy, and manipulate the settings using new programming interfaces and command-line tools as well as the traditional graphical user interface.

EXERCISE 6.14

RESTRICTING ACCESS TO USERS BASED ON THEIR IP ADDRESS

1. Open **Control Panel** and under **System and Maintenance | Administration Tools,** double-click the **Internet Information Services (IIS) Manager** shortcut.

2. In the **Internet Information Services (IIS) Manager** management console expand the server, site node, and locate a folder to secure (or choose the site as a whole) and click your selection.

3. In the middle pane under **Features View,** double-click **IPv4 Address and Domain Restrictions,**

4. In the right-hand actions pane click **Add Deny Entry**.

5. In the **Add Deny Restriction Rule** dialog, select the **Specific IPv4 Address** radio button, provide an IP address (e.g. 127.0.0.1 if you want to test http://localhost) and click **OK**.

When users attempt to access a page to which they have been denied, they will receive a 403.6 forbidden error. Another option is to restrict users based on their domain names (see Figure 6.37). You will need to enable this through the Edit Feature Settings link in the module page on IIS. Be aware that the added overhead of DNS resolution for each IP address could negatively affect the performance of your application.

Figure 6.37 Add Allow Restriction Rule Dialog with Domain Restrictions Enabled

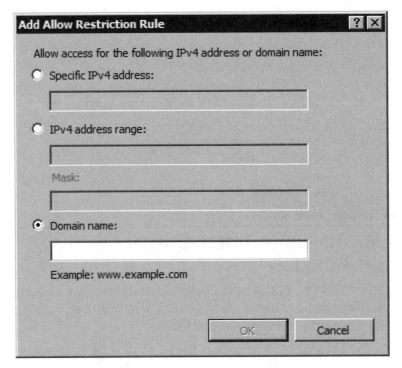

Request Filtering

Previously available through an add-on known as URLScan the request filtering features provide an additional layer of security by inspecting incoming requests for seven different characteristics that might indicate a malformed or malicious attack:

- **Double-Encoded Requests** Attackers may encode a request twice to get around a first layer of filtering. This filter will detect it, reject the request, and log a 404.11 error.

- **High Bit Characters** You may choose to not want to accept non–ASCII characters (e.g., Unicode characters) because your application has not been tested or does not support it. This filter will detect the non–ASCII characters, reject the request, and log a 404.12 error.

- **File Extensions** Your Web application may contain certain files that you do not want anyone to download in any case (e.g., a DLL file in an ASP.NET application). You can add a list of allowed and denied extensions, which will cause IIS to reject the request and log a 404.7 error.

- **Request Limits** This filter will look at how long the content is in the request, the length of the URL, and more specifically the length of the query string. If any of those measurements exceed the maximum values provided this filter will reject the request and log a 404.13, 404.14, or 404.15, respectively.

- **Verbs** There are different types of requests that are identified using verbs (e.g., PUT, GET, and POST). If your application uses only specific types you can tell IIS to reject the request for other types and log a 404.6 error.

- **URL Sequences** There are certain character sequences that you may wish to never have in your request (e.g., a double period ".." often signifies someone trying to relatively traverse your folder structure). This filter will reject requests that match the sequences and log a 404.5 error.

- **Hidden Segments** This filter will enable you to reject requests for content from certain segments. Listing 6.7 contains an example where the bin folder has been specified causing IIS to reject requests that contains the bin folder in the URL. Note that the filter is able to distinguish between a request for http://contoso.com/bin/somefile.dll and http://contoso.com/binary/somefile.zip. The latter request would be allowed through because the filter looks at the URL segment as a whole. It will reject the first request and log a 404.8 error.

Unfortunately IIS Manager does not expose these configuration values. If you want to enable request filtering and tune it to your environment you will need to do it directly in the configuration file or through one of the programmatic APIs. Listing 6.7 shows a sample excerpt of the configuration settings.

Listing 6.7 Request Filtering Configuration Example

```
<configuration>
  ...
  <system.webServer>
    ...
    <security>
      ...
      <requestFiltering allowDoubleEscaping="false"
                        allowHighBitCharacters="true"
                        maxAllowedContentLength="1024768"
                        maxQueryString="64"
                        maxUrl="260">
        <denyUrlSequences>
          <add sequence=".."/>
        </denyUrlSequences>
        <fileExtensions allowUnlisted="true" >
          <add fileExtension=".dll" allowed="false"/>
          <add fileExtension=".xml" allowed="false"/>
        </fileExtensions>
        <hiddenSegments>
          <add segment="BIN"/>
        </hiddenSegments>
        <verbs allowUnlisted="false">
          <add verb="GET" allowed="true" />
          <add verb="PUT" allowed="false" />
        </verbs>
      </requestFiltering>
      ...
    </security>
    ...
  </system.webServer>
  ...
</configuration>
```

Even though you may have to work with the application developer to gain
necessary input, this module in particular is extremely useful in reducing the attack

surface of your Web application. It is recommended that you take the time to take full advantage of the filters offered by this module.

.NET Trust Levels

With a number of new IIS features based around the .NET Framework it is important to understand how .NET Trust Levels impact your Web applications and IIS itself. A trust level conveys a policy of permissions that an application is allowed to perform. Each trust level has a different set of permissions applied. By default the policies build upon one another from Minimal, which can do very few things to Full, which can perform a number of things:

- **Full Trust** The application is able to execute anything with the security bounds granted to the process identity.

- **High Trust** Restricts applications from calling unmanaged code (e.g., Windows APIs, COM objects, etc.), writing to the event log, message queues, or databases.

- **Medium Trust** Restricts the application from navigating any part of the file system except its own application directory, accessing the registry, or making network and Web service calls.

- **Low Trust** Restricts the application from writing to the file system.

- **Minimal** Restricts the code to doing basic algorithmic work.

If the out-of-the-box trust levels do not suffice application developers can define a custom trust policy based on a series of intrinsic and custom permissions. For a complete list of permissions see the .NET Framework Developer's Guide at http://msdn2.microsoft.com/en-us/library/5ba4k1c5.aspx.

EXAM WARNING

The trust levels and permissions system, known as Code Access Security, is confusing to many developers as well as administrators. Think of the policies as another type of access control list (ACL) with individual access control entries (ACE) that allow or deny you from performing an action on a resource. The resources can vary from external services, such as databases and Web services, to internal Windows subsystems, such as the registry, event log, and file system.

The trust level that you chose for an application should be sufficient for it to function, but like all good security practices, not excessive beyond the needs of the application. In most environments application developers will communicate the level of trust their application needs. As IT professionals understanding what that means helps us understand the boundaries in which the application can function in the server environment. The trust levels can be set at the site and folder level. It is most practical, however, to set it at the level a Web application is defined or the root of the site.

Managing Internet Information Services

One of the big investments in this release of IIS is around management tools. There is both new functionality and existing hidden functionality exposed through the graphical interface, command-line, and programmatic interfaces. In this section we'll take a look at some of the key advancements in the management functionality including delegation, diagnostics tools, and scaling features.

Configuration and Delegation

As part of an overall effort to ease administration, this release saw the delivery of several features that focus around the delegation of administration. Whether you want to simply administer the server from a remote device or build levels of delegation for application owners or clients, IIS delivers a comprehensive system of permissions and services gives you the flexibility to define the scenario that best fits your needs.

The basis for delegation is a decision as to which features you want to delegate. Through IIS Manager, permissions to manage individual settings are controlled at the server, site, and folder level in that order. If you are familiar with ASP.NET's configuration hierarchy, then you will find this concept to be very similar.

All configuration files are defined in a series of schema files split into logical groups—IIS, .NET Framework, ASP.NET, and Runtime Status and Control. These files define the various elements that can be used in the configuration files (see Figure 6.38). Note that not all .NET Framework elements are defined in here, though, just those exposed through IIS configuration tools. All schema files are stored inside the WINDOWS\SYSTEM32\inetsrv\Config\Schema folder. Adding new schemas for custom modules or handlers is as simple as copying the new schema XML file into the folder. At the server level there are five configuration files, each with specific purposes. The first two are stored inside the .NET Framework configuration folder, by default WINDOWS\Microsoft.NET\Framework\<version>\CONFIG, or WINDOWS\Microsoft.NET\Framework64\<version>\CONFIG for the 64-bit runtime:

Figure 6.38 Configuration Files

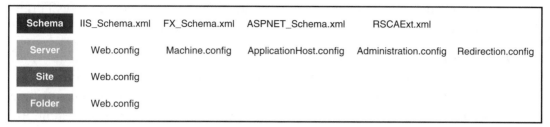

- **Machine.config** .NET Framework settings that will apply to all applications that run using the Common Language Runtime.

- **Web.config** Subordinate to machine.config, this file contains .NET Framework settings that will apply to all Web applications running under ASP.NET.

The other three server-level files reside in the WINDOWS\SYSTEM32\inetsrv\Config folder and are specific to the IIS configuration:

- **Redirection.config** Informs the server to look in an alternative location for server configuration (more on this in the Network Load Balancing section later).

- **Administration.config** Settings that control the modules loaded by IIS Manager to administer the server and its sites.

- **ApplicationHost.config** Configuration settings for the server that define sites, virtual directories, and application pools.

EXAM WARNING

Know the configuration files and what they do. This is a new feature in this release and a core tenant of a number of systems within the Web server. Make sure you understand how inheritance between the various configuration files works. When in doubt draw a picture for yourself.

Within each site resides a web.config, both at the root, and optionally in folders below. Each file is cumulative, meaning that a web.config in a folder can override certain settings from the root web.config if it is allowed. Inside each configuration file are a series of configuration sections defined in the configSections element. This defines the various groups and individual section containers contained within a configuration file. For each section you can define a scope of definition and delegation mode. This is done by the allowDefinition and overrideModeDefault attributes.

- In Listing 6.8 you can see that sections like system.webServer/cgi and system.webServer/security/access will not be allowed to be overridden in the site web.config because they have had the overrideModeDefault attribute set to Deny. As an administrator you can unlock these sections for definition at the site level and below by changing the attribute for a given section to Allow, as seen on the system.webServer/defaultDocument section. This technique can be applied at all levels in the configuration hierarchy. There are also times where certain configuration sections would either be ignored or have a system-wide impact when set at lower levels. The allowDefinition attribute allows you to control the location where the section should be defined. In Listing 6.8 the system.applicationHost values are all set to AppHostOnly because the application host is a server-level concept and doesn't apply to individual sites. Other values for this attribute include:

- **Everywhere** Section can be used in any configuration file (default)

- **MachineOnly** Section can be used only in the Machine.config file

- **MachineToApplication** Section can be used in the Machine.config file or in the Web site and Web application web.config files

- **MachineToWebRoot** Section can be used in the Machine.config file or in the Web site web.config file

Listing 6.8 Configuration Sections Snippet from ApplicationHost.config

```
<configuration>
  ...
  <configSections>
    <sectionGroup name="system.applicationHost">
      <section name="applicationPools" allowDefinition="AppHostOnly"
                  overrideModeDefault="Deny" />
      <section name="sites" allowDefinition="AppHostOnly"
                      overrideModeDefault="Deny" />
      ...
    </sectionGroup>
    <sectionGroup name="system.webServer">
      <section name="asp" overrideModeDefault="Deny" />
```

```
        <section name="caching" overrideModeDefault="Allow" />

        <section name="cgi" overrideModeDefault="Deny" />

        <section name="defaultDocument" overrideModeDefault="Allow" />

        <section name="directoryBrowse" overrideModeDefault="Allow" />

        ...

        <sectionGroup name="security">

          <section name="access" overrideModeDefault="Deny" />

          ...

        </sectionGroup>

        ...

      </sectionGroup>

      ...

    </sectionGroup>

  </configSections>

  ...

</configuration>
```

In addition to locking entire sections you can lock specific settings and combinations of settings across several configuration groups using location locking. This allows you to override values for specific folders and files in your Web site. For example, you could apply a different set of authorization rules to a section of your site to prevent anonymous users from accessing the content. When managing feature settings in IIS Manager on specific files or folders it is using this location element in the site's web. config to apply the changes you are specifying.

```
</configuration>
```

In Listing 6.9 the Web application and pages in the finance folder would not be able to use session state since it was both disabled and locked using the allowOverride attribute. The content in the marketing folder, however, would have session state disabled by default, but it could be overridden by a web.config in that folder. The configuration hierarchy plays a foundational role in the IIS feature delegation capabilities. The Feature Delegation user interface is modifying the configuration value with the allowOverride, allowDefinition, and overrideModeDefault attributes.

Listing 6.9 Example of Location Locking

```
<configuration>

  ...

  <location path="finance" allowOverride="false">
```

```
  <system.web>
    <sessionState enabled="false" />
  </system.web>
</location>
...
<location path="marketing" allowOverride="true">
  <system.web>
    <sessionState enabled="false" />
  </system.web>
</location>
```

In the Feature Delegation page (see Figure 6.39) you can enable sections to be overridden at lower levels (Read/Write), viewable by delegated users (Read Only), and set at the server-level only (Not Delegated).

Figure 6.39 Feature Delegation Module Configuration

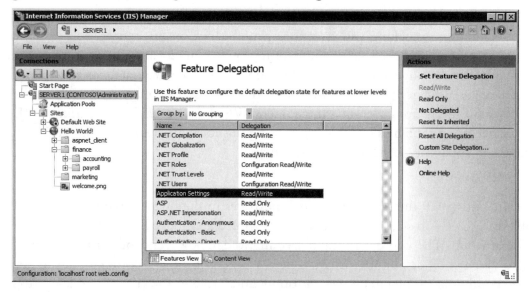

TEST DAY TIP

Notice that the features that can be delegated line up with the sections in the configuration file, and that any change in IIS Manager reflects to the file and section of the change on the status bar. The user interface in IIS 7 is always making some type of change in the configuration file.

Remote Administration

With specific features delegated to the site level you can set up IIS, under a full installation, to allow remote users to connect to the server using IIS Manager to administer one or more sites using the same rich interface that you access as a server administrator. The Management Service authenticates users using either a built-in user database or through Windows accounts. As with other modules the authentication module for the Management Service can also be replaced with a custom module if your scenario uses another user data store. Enabling the Management Service requires the check of a box. The service security options allow you to choose the source to look for user identities, the transport security certificate, and the ability to restrict access by IP address (see Figure 6.40).

Figure 6.40 Management Service Module Configuration

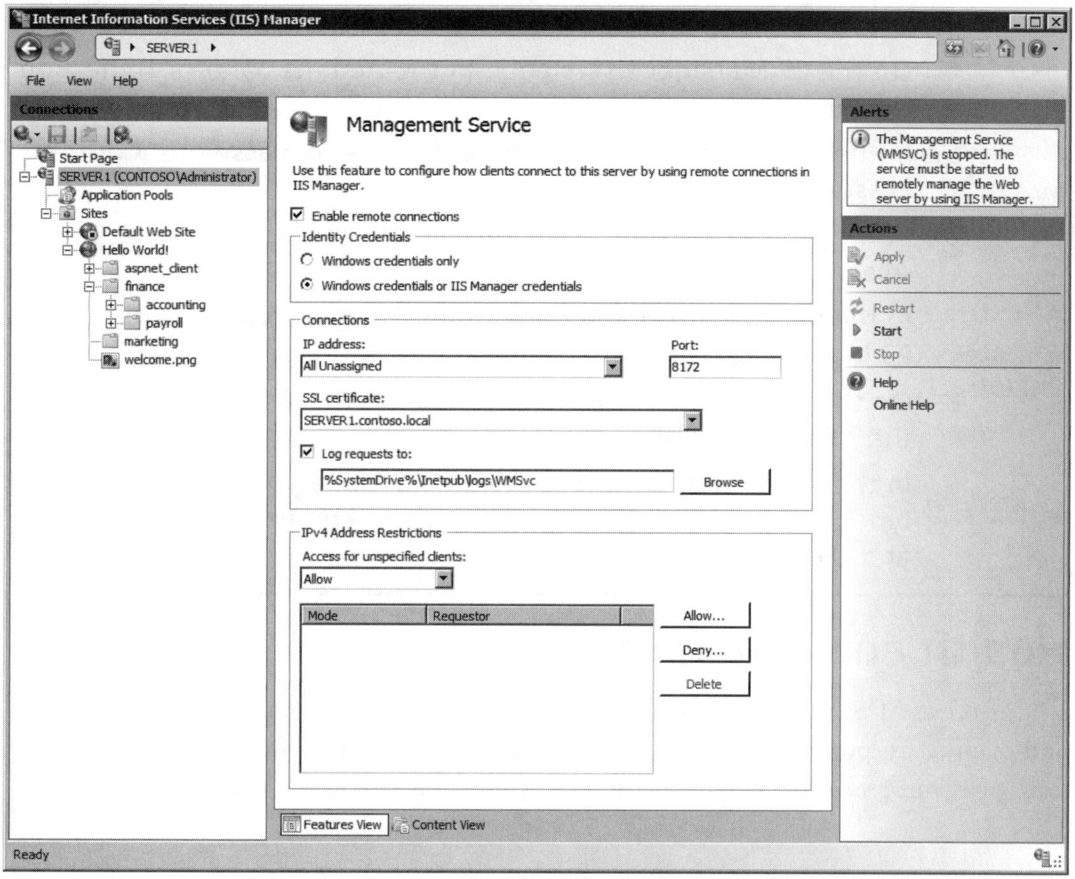

Once the Management Service is enabled you will need to grant users the ability to manage specific sites. Permissions to manage a site or application are granted at their respective level. At the server level the IIS Manager Permissions module will show you an aggregate view of the users and where they have been granted or denied management.

EXERCISE 6.15

ADDING IIS MANAGER USERS

1. Open **Control Panel** and under **System and Maintenance | Administration Tools**, double-click the **Internet Information Services (IIS) Manager** shortcut.

2. In the **Internet Information Services (IIS) Manager** management console click the server,

3. In the middle **Server Home** pane under **Features View**, double-click **IIS Manager Users**.

4. On the **IIS Manager Users** page in the **Actions** pane click the **Add User** link.

5. In the **Add User** dialog provide a **User name, Password, Confirm Password**, and click **OK**.

6. In the left **Connections** pane expand the server, sites node, and select your Web site.

7. In the middle **Site Home** pane under **Features View** double-click **IIS Manager Permissions**.

8. On the **IIS Manager Permissions** page in the **Actions** pane click the **Allow User** link.

9. In the **Allow User** dialog select the **IIS Manager** radio button, type in the username of the IIS user you created in previous steps, and click **OK**.

Health and Diagnostics

In this release IIS provides a rich set of new tools for use in maintaining the health and diagnosing problems that may arise. The tools give you different views into the state of IIS in real-time as well as capturing data when a request fails:

- **Runtime Status and Control Data Objects** Set of programmatic objects that enable you to query the state of application pools, Web sites, and Web applications at any given point in time.

- **Detailed Error Messages** Gives you deep insight into the state of the request that you would have had to use an HTTP debugging tool in the past to obtain.

- **Failed Request Tracing** Enables you to obtain snapshots of the request at the moment of failure, which will aid in the diagnosis and resolution of issues that arise.

- **Activity Logging** Historical logging of user requests and basic statistics on the response delivered.

Failed Request Tracing

When a request fails on the Web server, IIS has the ability to capture a snapshot of the request in an XML-formatted log file for later analysis (see Figure 6.41). This data helps administrators and developers understand the state of the request when it was made and provides valuable information that can be used to reproduce the issue. On a typical production server this may become overwhelming with the number of requests. The tracing facilities use a set of rules to determine the conditions under which it should capture data and the level of verbosity for the data it will capture.

Figure 6.41 Failed Request Trace Report

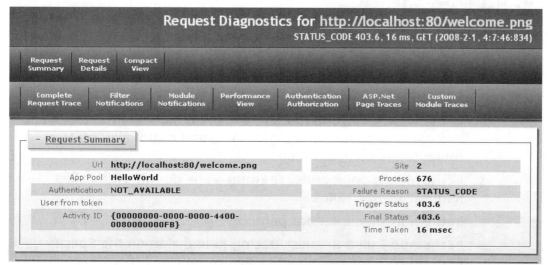

Before you add a rule you will need to enable failed request tracing. This can be done at the site level through IIS Manager. There are two settings that you can configure—the location of the output and the maximum number of traces (see Figure 6.42). The size of each trace will depend on the rules you create. Each component's verbosity level can be tuned or turned off to give you only what you need.

Figure 6.42 Edit Web Site Failed Request Settings Dialog

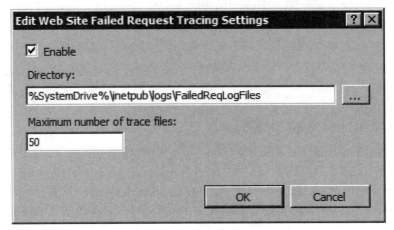

With tracing enabled, you can set up rules at all levels—server, site, folder, and file. Rules can be inherited and ordered to enable you to define the right combination for your needs.

EXERCISE 6.16

ADDING A FAILED REQUEST TRACING RULE

1. Open **Control Panel** and under **System and Maintenance | Administration Tools** double-click the **Internet Information Services (IIS) Manager** shortcut.

2. In the **Internet Information Services (IIS) Manager** management console expand the server, site node, and optionally locate a folder to enable tracing on.

3. In the middle pane under **Features View** double-click **Failed Request Tracing Rules**.

4. In the right-hand Actions pane click **Add**.

5. In the **Add Failed Request Tracing Rule** dialog on the **Specify Content to Trace** page choose **All Content** and click **Next**.

6. On the **Define Trace Conditions** page check **Status Code**, provide the status code (e.g., 404, 500) that you want to trigger a trace on, and click **Next** (see Figure 6.43).

Figure 6.43 Define Trace Conditions Page

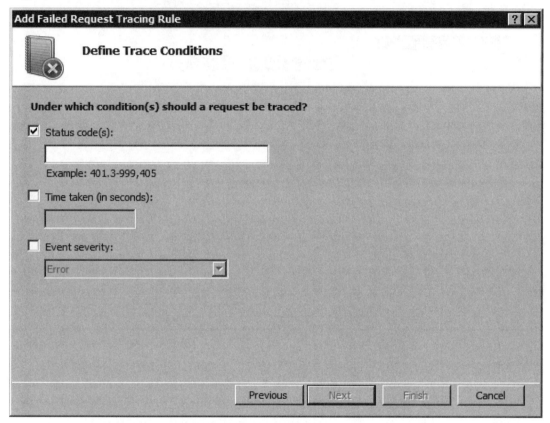

7. On the **Select Trace Provides** page select the appropriate trace providers, set the verbosity and areas to track for each, and click **Finish** (see Figure 6.44).

Figure 6.44 Select Trace Providers Page

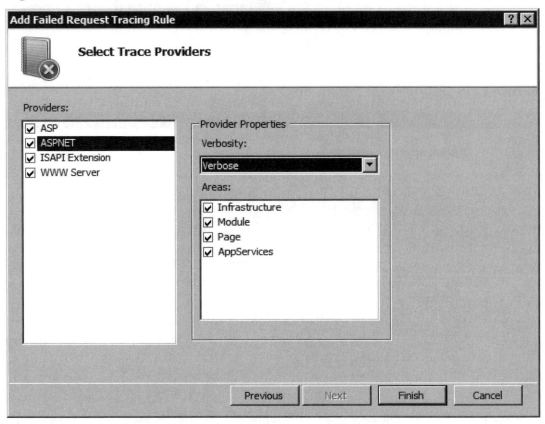

Logging

Activity logging is a standard feature in all Web servers today. For each request made to the server the log records particular properties of both the request and response for later analysis. Using Web log analysis tools you can review aggregate statistics to determine the number of people visiting your server, what they are doing, and when they are doing it. You can also use activity logs as a tool in troubleshooting. IIS ships with logging enabled by default, outputting them to the WINDOWS\ SYSTEM32\LogFiles folder. The logs can be written using IIS, NCSA, and W3C formats (see Figure 6.45). Alternatively, through the configuration files you can add logging to any ODBC-compliant database.

Figure 6.45 Logging Module Configuration

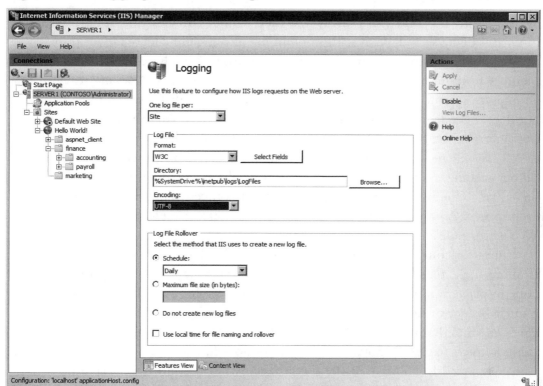

Scaling Your Web Farm

IIS provides the infrastructure necessary to get the most out of your Web applications and scale them out and up when the activity becomes too much for a single server to handle. Each mechanism addresses the scalability issue in a different manner and has a set of trade-offs. It will be up to you to experiment with each to determine to what degree you use caching, compressing, and load balancing for your scenario.

TEST DAY TIP

To help you recall the various methods of scaling a Web farm, classify them into scale up (doing more with the same hardware) and scaling out (doing more with more hardware).

Output Caching

When serving up content it is likely that there will be some degree of repetition in what is being served. With static content like images and client-side script files, caching provides a mechanism for storing the most frequently requested files in memory to minimize the disk I/O when servicing the request. Caching really makes an impact on semi-dynamic content. This means content that changes infrequently but does use a degree of assembly when creating the page. An example is a news page that queries a database for the list of headlines. If that list changes every few hours or few days there is no need to query the database every time a request is made. The output caching module will save a copy of the fully rendered page in memory and serve that to the user instead of consuming the resources to query the database for each request. As you can imagine, this can have a noticeable effect on not only the Web server utilization but the database server as well.

Output caching is applied using a set of policies. Each policy is based on one or more file extensions and a set of rules to govern how long to keep the cached copy in place, and if it should be varied based on a value in either the HTTP request header or query string. This gives you flexibility to deal with multilingual pages, or ones that render a different set of content based on the particular values in the request (e.g., Category.aspx?ID=Shoes does not serve up the same content as Category.aspx?Id=TShirts). At the server level you can control the maximum size of the cache and individual items in the cache as shown in Figure 6.46. The server level also allows you to disable caching for all sites on the server.

Figure 6.46 Output Caching Module Configuration

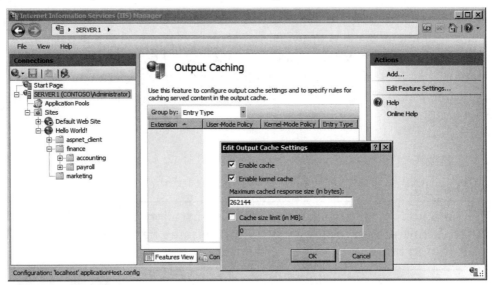

EXERCISE 6.17

CREATING A CACHING POLICY

1. Open **Control Panel** and under **System and Maintenance | Administration Tools** double-click the **Internet Information Services (IIS) Manager** shortcut.

2. In the **Internet Information Services (IIS) Manager** management console expand the server, site node, and optionally locate a folder to enable tracing on.

3. In the middle pane under **Features View** double-click **Output Caching**.

4. In the right-hand Actions pane click **Add**.

5. In the **Add Cache Rule** dialog provide a **file name extension**, select **User-mode caching**, and click **OK** (see Figure 6.47).

   ▪ Kernel-mode caching is faster but will not be able to consider any modules that need to run in user mode (e.g., authentication, authorization). It will not support variation by header or query string either. For more information on considerations when using Kernel-mode caching see KB817445 at http://support.microsoft.com/kb/817445.

Figure 6.47 Add Cache Rule Dialog

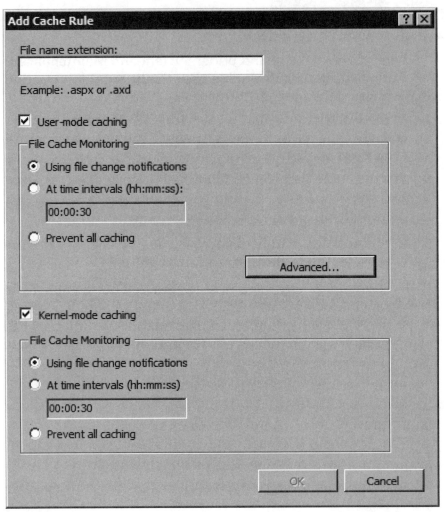

Compression

With the introduction of HTTP 1.1 in 1999, Web browsers gained the ability
to decompress content that was sent from a Web server. This was put in place to
help curb the exploding demand for bandwidth that was taking place at the time.
Through the middle part of this decade the explosion in rich applications using
AJAX technologies had another impact on the network bandwidth by causing a
lot of "chatter" between the client and the server. The compression standards went
a long way to cut the network bandwidth requirements for text-based content
such as Web pages and client-side script files by 80% or more depending on the

content's compression potential. IIS has shipped with compression capabilities since version 5.0.

Third-party software vendors shipped both companion products that exposed hidden configuration properties and replacements that added features such as the ability to back off on compression when the overall request load was high. Hardware vendors also got into the game by offering offloading devices to handle compression on behalf of the Web server. The hardware market, as of late, is evolving from single-purpose device to offering a suite of application optimization services such as caching and content substitution (which is particularly useful for ASP.NET pages that have a large client-side state field called View State).

Behind the scenes IIS 7 introduced changes to how caching is configured to give administrators more control over the behavior and to capture some of the compressible requests that were slipping through in previous release:

- **Compressed Content Cached by Application Pool** In previous releases all compressed content was cached in a single folder, which could be a potential security risk. In this release they separated out the cache folders by application pool and applied access control entries to ensure that only the application pool worker process can access the folders. In addition a per-application pool cache limit was introduced to provide more flexibility based on the type of application rather than the server as a whole.

- **Static Compression Enabled by Default** Since static content generally receives the biggest benefit for the least cost (no recompression with successive requests), it was turned on by default. After some research the default compression level was adjusted to 7 out of 10 to provide a degree of benefit without a lot of processing expense.

- **CPU Thresholds** Popular among third-party replacements was the ability to have compression back off when the request load was high. Due to popular demand this was introduced into the IIS compression module.

- **Deflate Removed by Default** With GZIP compression you typically get a better compression but under some circumstances like a high traffic Web server you may want to choose to add the Deflate compression scheme back in place. IIS ships with the module, just not configured by default.

- **Compress Based on Content Type** Probably the single biggest change, IIS now makes a decision on compression based on the content-type of the file. Instead of enumerating the various file extensions (e.g., htm, html, aspx, asp, php, etc.) you can classify the content based on their content type. This change will capture a number of requests that slipped through the cracks or were incorrectly classified from the previous file extension-based approach.

In IIS Manager the compression settings are split into server and site level compression. At the server level the settings are focused on enabling the service and setting size limits to control disk utilization (see Figure 6.48). On the site level it is a simple enable/disable setting.

Figure 6.48 Server-Level Compression Module Configuration

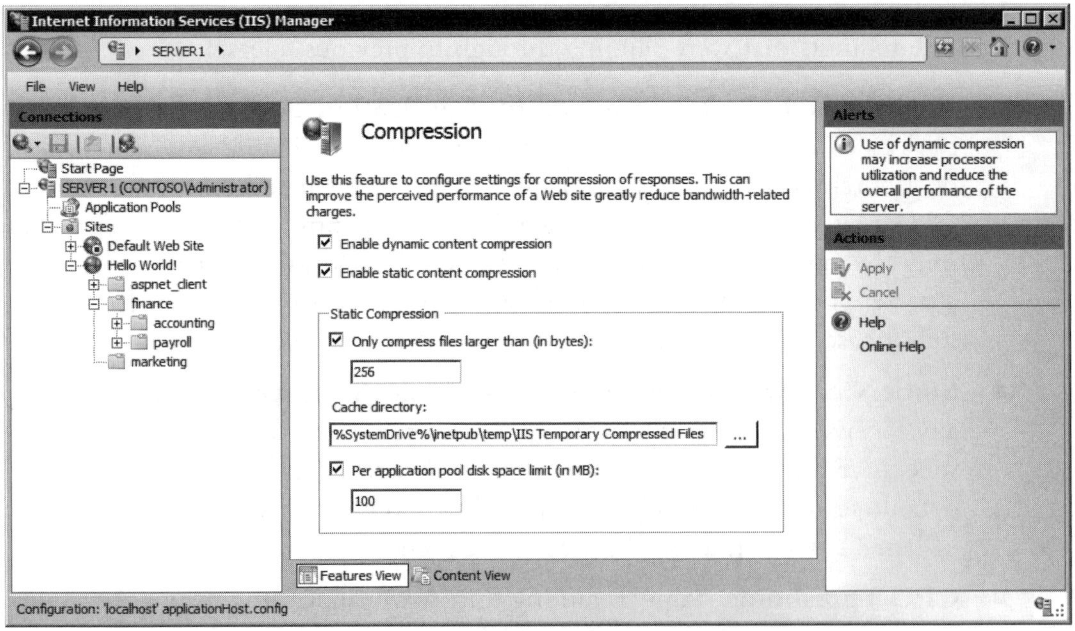

To fine-tune the compression settings you will need to open the ApplicationHost. config file and edit the properties there. Listing 6.10 is an example of what a typical section might look like.

Listing 6.10 HTTP Compression Settings in ApplicationHost.config

```
<configuration>
  ...
  <system.webServer>
    ...
```

```
<httpCompression directory="C:\inetpub\temp\IIS Temporary Compressed
Files">

    <scheme name="gzip" dll="%Windir%\system32\inetsrv\gzip.dll" />

    <dynamicTypes>

        <add mimeType="text/*" enabled="true" />

        <add mimeType="message/*" enabled="true" />

        <add mimeType="application/x-javascript" enabled="true" />

        <add mimeType="*/*" enabled="false" />

    </dynamicTypes>

    <staticTypes>

        <add mimeType="text/*" enabled="true" />

        <add mimeType="message/*" enabled="true" />

        <add mimeType="application/javascript" enabled="true" />

        <add mimeType="*/*" enabled="false" />

    </staticTypes>

</httpCompression>

...

<urlCompression doDynamicCompression="false"
                doStaticCompression="true" />

...

</system.webServer>

...

</configuration>
```

Refer to the IIS product documentation for a further explanation on the various attributes to tune IIS compression settings on your web server.

Network Load Balancing

As the number of requests to your Web site grows you will need to either scale up by using a more powerful server or look at scaling out with larger quantity of servers. IIS traditionally handles scaling out quite well, supporting load balancing through Windows Load Balancing Services and through dedicated hardware load balancing devices. If you are deploying IIS in a load balanced configuration there are two enhancements in this release that will make your job easier.

Shared Configuration

In a Web farm scenario often you are working to keep the configuration synchronized between nodes so they all respond in the same manner. In previous releases this was a challenging process that was enabled through scripts and other postrelease approaches to growing a Web farm. With this release and the move to break out the metabase into XML-based configuration files the ability to have shared configuration files among Web farm nodes was introduced. In this mode the Administration.config and ApplicationHost.config files are stored in a central location accessible by all nodes in the Web farm along with a configuration encryption key. You can specify a set of server-level credentials to ensure that only the server management process has access to the folder, especially since it stores shared encryption keys in this folder.

EXERCISE 6.18

ENABLING SHARED CONFIGURATION

1. Open **Control Panel** and under **System and Maintenance | Administration Tools** double-click the **Internet Information Services (IIS) Manager** shortcut.

2. In the **Internet Information Services (IIS) Manager** management console click the server node.

3. In the middle pane under **Features View** double-click **Shared Configuration**.

If this is the first server in the farm, perform the following actions, otherwise skip to step 6:

4. In the right-hand **Actions** pane click **Export Configuration**.

5. In the **Export Configuration** dialog provide a configuration location, a password for the encryption key, and click **OK**.

6. In the **Shared Configuration** page check the **Enable Shared Configuration** checkbox.

7. Provide the path to the configuration files along with the username and password required to access the files and in the **Actions** pane click **Apply**.

TCP and HTTP Service Unavailable Responses

Some hardware load balancing devices are capable only of detecting failures based on the inability to connect at the TCP level. When IIS is returning 503 Service Unavailable messages because of a security issue or the inability to respond to the request because of a high load, it is still alive at the TCP level. In this release of IIS the option to change how the server will communicate service unavailable messages was introduced. The default option remains the HTTP-based message, and a new option was added to refuse connections at the TCP level. In addition you can also trigger an executable to be run that can send an alert or reconfigure a load balancing device. These options are configured at the application pool level under the advanced settings as shown in Figure 6.49.

Figure 6.49 Application Pool Rapid-Fail Protection Settings

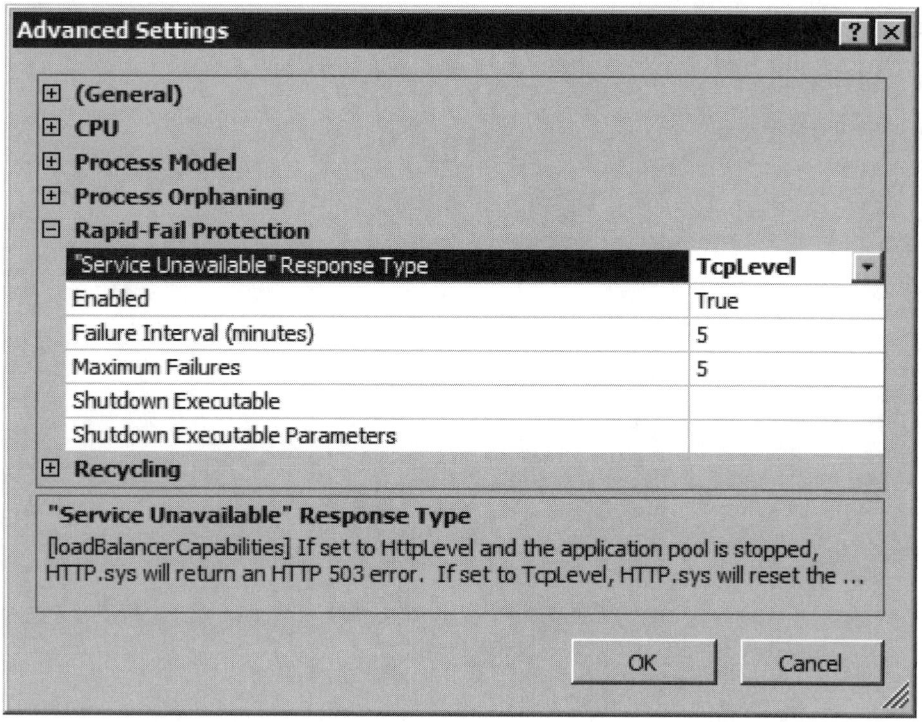

Backing Up and Restoring Server Configuration

In this release the backup and restore for the server configuration did not make it into the IIS Manager tool. There are three commands that can be used with the APPCMD command-line tool to view a list of backups, delete backups, backup, and restore the server-level configuration are as follows:

- AppCmd.exe Add Backup <description>
- AppCmd.exe Restore Backup <description>

- AppCmd.exe List Backup

- AppCmd.exe Delete Backup <description>

When you perform a backup it will copy the following files to the WINDOWS\SYSTEM32\inetsrv\Backup folder under a folder bearing the description provided in the command line:

- Administration.config

- ApplicationHost.config

- Redirection.config

- MBSchema.xml

- MetaBase.xml

Summary of Exam Objectives

This chapter focused on configuration of Internet Information Services and high-lighted the new features in this release that make it the first and best choice for Web applications on the Windows platform. In a world where the Web is having a bigger impact inside and outside of the corporate firewall having skills and knowledge around managing Web applications is an asset. We discussed the design goals of this release—a componentized, integrated, extensible, supportable, secure, compatible, and delegation-ready Web application platform. IIS ships across all Windows editions and installs on both the full and Server Core installations.

The componentized architecture allows you to selectively install components within the various role services. Administration can be done through graphical tools like IIS Manager, command-line tools like AppCmd.exe, Windows Management Instrumentation, COM, and .NET programmatic interfaces. Creating a Web site gives you a basic site for static content. Each site contains files, folders, and virtual directories. A site can be further enabled as a Web application to serve dynamic content. IIS ships with ASP and ASP.NET dynamic runtime environments along with support for Common Gateway Interface-based modules. Web applications execute in an application pool container named w3wp.exe. The container provides the security, resource, and process boundaries for the one or more Web applications that you choose to configure inside them. With ASP.NET applications in particular they support classic and integrated pipeline modes. Classic is mainly for backward compatibility in that the ASP.NET request life cycle is kept separate from the IIS request life cycle. In Integrated mode the two are merged into one empowering ASP.NET applications to more tightly integrate with IIS.

Your Web site can be secured using several tactics. Because Web applications flow over standard TCP-based communication the traffic can be wrapped inside a VPN tunnel or IPSec tunnel. It is more common, however, to see Web traffic privacy guarded by a Secure Socket Layers connection that is using a key-based encryption system. Authentication modules, used to identify who is accessing the site, are divided into IIS modules (Anonymous, Basic, Digest, Windows) and ASP.NET (Forms, Impersonation). With the integrated pipeline, however, you could integrate the ASP.NET Forms module with other dynamic runtime environments such as ASP and PHP. User actions are restricted by a new native URL authorization module, IP address and domain name restrictions, and request filtering. Web applications and modules can be controlled through a series of .NET trust levels powered by .NET's Code Access Security concepts. The levels (minimal, low, medium, high, and full) provide a building-blocks approach to permissions. You can also define your own custom level if none of the predefined ones suit your needs. Other enhancements to the IIS security infrastructure include the change of the default anonymous user account to a built-in system account and renaming the IIS_WPG to IIS_IUSRS.

Flexibility of management has been increased greatly in this release. The configuration system has been changed from a single XML Metabase file to a hierarchy of XML-based configuration files that draw heavily on the ASP.NET legacy. The schema defines the format of the configuration files. The server level configuration files (ApplicationHost.config, Administration.config, Redirection. config, Machine.config, and Web.config) provide you with ultimate control over sites and Web applications. Through a system of delegation using the allowOverride, overrideModeDefault, and allowDefinition attributes you can control at what level a setting can be changed. This allows you to open up administration of lower level sites, applications, folders, and files to other users through the new Management Service. This service allows you to connect to Full installations of Windows Server 2008 with IIS using IIS Manager. Users of this service can be either Windows users or internal IIS users. When an application crashes the new health and diagnostics tools go a long way to helping you get back online quickly. The runtime status and control data objects give you a set of programmatic objects to get a real-time picture of what is happening in the IIS server. Detailed server error messages give you much greater insight into the state of the request being made. Failed Request Tracking provides a forensic snapshot of the state when a defined failure condition occurs. To track user activity the Activity Logging provides the data necessary for Web analysis software to give you an aggregate view of activity on your server. Scaling out your Web farm has never been easier. With output caching to help you squeeze in a few more connections by caching frequently requested, semi-dynamic content and compression to minimize the network bandwidth you can get the most out of your server. When it is time to grow the enhancements to Web farm scenarios through support for a shared configuration and application pool failure to the TCP level you can easily grow your Web farm using either Windows Load Balancing Services or dedicated hardware devices that offload degrees of functionality.

Exam Objectives Fast Track

Installing and Configuring Internet Information Services

- ☑ IIS can be installed across all editions of Windows.

- ☑ On Server Core you will not be able to install role services that rely on the .NET Framework.

- ☑ You can manage your server through IIS Manager, AppCmd, Windows Management Instrumentation, and COM/.NET programmatic interfaces.

- ☑ Servers contain one or more Web sites that contain one or more Web applications, all of which are defined in the ApplicationHost.config file.

- ☑ Application pools are the security and process execution container for one or more Web applications.

- ☑ IIS ships with support for ASP, ASP.NET and CGI-based runtime environments (e.g., PHP, Python, Perl, Ruby on Rails).

- ☑ Migration from IIS 6 was a key focus with backward compatibility components such as the Admin Base Object (ABO) Mapper to help applications function under the architectural changes of IIS 7.

Securing Your Web Sites and Applications

- ☑ Transport Security is handled by Secure Socket Layer certificates that are bound to an IP address and port.

- ☑ SSL can be supported on multiple sites on a single IP address/port as long as the same certificate is used (wildcard, subjectAltName certificates).

- ☑ Certificates can be obtained from a third-party CA, Windows Certificate Services CA, or using a self-signed certificate (for testing purposes).

- ☑ Users are identified through IIS (Anonymous, Basic, Digest, Windows, Client Certificates) and ASP.NET (Forms, Impersonation) authentication modules.

- ☑ The anonymous user module now uses a built-in account called IUSR, whereas Digest encryption still requires passwords to be stored using reversible encryption, and Windows supporting NTLM and Kerberos authentication.

☑ Once identified, a user's request is evaluated based on a set of authorization rules including NTFS, URL, IP authorization, and request filtering.

☑ NTFS permissions typically are used for the application pool identity whereas URL authorization is defined in the web.config based on any of the given authentication modules.

☑ IP Address and Domain Name authorization allows you to include or exclude specific addresses.

☑ Request filtering inspects for potentially harmful requests by looking for double-encoded requests, high bit characters, particular file extensions, request limits being exceeded, HTTP verbs excluded, specific URL sequences, and special hidden segments being accessed.

☑ .NET trust levels (minimal, low, medium, high, and full) govern the execution of ASP.NET and when in integrated mode the entire IIS request pipeline.

☑ A trust level is a policy of allowable permissions that govern resource access such as the file system, database, network, and registry.

Managing Internet Information Services

☑ This release introduced a rich XML configuration hierarchy that allows for delegation of everything.

☑ The XML configuration is driven by a set of schema files.

☑ Configuration files exist at the server level (ApplicationHost.config, Administration.config, Redirection.config, Machine.config, and Web. config), at the site level (web.config), and applications/folder below that (web.config).

☑ The files have a cumulative effect on the end configuration for a particular request, however sections can be explicitly allowed or disallowed from having certain attributes or entire sections redefined.

☑ Once delegation has been configured you can enable remote administration of specific features and sites using the IIS Management Service (which is not supported on Server Core).

☑ When something goes wrong the detailed error messages provided by IIS give you a sense of the context of the request.

☑ If you are not sure how to reproduce an error you can use failed request tracking to take an automatic snapshot of the request state when an error that matches a specific rule occurs.

☑ You can get more out of your server using output caching, which can use both a user-mode (fast) and kernel-mode (faster, but restrictive) caching along with static and dynamic content compression.

☑ Both caching and compression have basic configuration exposed through IIS Manager with all advanced settings configurable through the configuration files.

☑ When expanding your environment you can take advantage of network load balancing to scale out your configuration.

☑ A shared configuration setup helps you to deploy a site across several servers without having to configure the site on each server manually.

☑ When a server in the farm fails you can have it stop responding at the TCP level or execute a program to tell the load balancer about the need to reconfigure.

Exam Objectives Frequently Asked Questions

Q: How do I administer IIS on Server Core?

A: You can administer the server through AppCmd, Windows Management Instrumentation, and the COM/.NET programmatic interfaces. You cannot use IIS Manager, even to connect to the server remotely.

Q: What is the difference between IIS on Windows Server 2008 and Windows Vista?

A: Beyond some minor bug fixes, and improved configuration interfaces in IIS Manager the major difference is the connection limit—on Windows Vista a maximum of 10 concurrent connections (three on Basic/Starter, three on Home Premium, and 10 on Ultimate/Business/Enterprise), and no limit on Windows Server 2008.

Q: What is an application pool?

A: It is a container for one or more Web sites and Web applications. It provides the context for the request to be processed and the security context under which the processing is completed.

Q: Can I use multiple SSL certificates and host headers?

A: It depends. SSL certificates are bound to an IP address and port. If the SSL certificate is a wildcard certificate or uses the subjectAltName property you can use it across multiple sites as long as the host name satisfies the wildcard value or subjectAltName list.

Q: I am trying to access an ASP page and I know that I have installed support for Active Server Pages, but IIS keeps giving me a 404 error How do I fix it?

A: When adding any new server extensions make sure to allow the ISAPI filter or CGI executable at the server level under ISAPI and CGI restrictions.

Q: My server is under a high load but I want to take advantage of compression. Can I have the best of both?

A: You can use the CPU throttling properties in the configuration files to set a percentage of processor utilization under which the compression will back off.

This will allow your server to focus on serving more requests until the number drops.

Q: I've configured an ASP.NET application, and when I run it I receive a SecurityPolicyException stating that I do not have enough permissions. I have checked the file system and the application pool worker process has enough rights to execute properly. Where should I look?

A: Check the .NET Trust Level for the Web application, it defines a policy as to which actions and resources the application can use and execute.

Q: I want to prevent users from accessing a specific folder on my server. I have set up URL authorization to allow only specific users but it never prompts me for a password. How do I get IIS to prompt for credentials?

A: Review the selected authentication modules. Chances are you have the Anonymous authentication module enabled. It will need to be disabled to force other authentication modules to prompt the user for credentials.

Q: I have two Web applications, one that uses Active Directory Certificate Mapping and one that uses many-to-one certificate mapping. I have configured the AD-based mapping application but I cannot find the many-to-one certificate mapping option. Where should I look?

A: When you enable Active Directory Certificate Mapping it will automatically disable many-to-one and one-to-one certificate mapping for all sites on the server.

Self Test

1. While starting to build a Web server for use by several business units, you have been asked to ensure that the Web applications running by different business units use separate security credentials for execution. At what level should you establish this separation to ensure each business unit is able to meet the security needs?

   A. Web Server

   B. Application Pool

   C. Web Site

   D. Web Application

2. You have been asked to build out a Web farm that can scale to handle thousands of concurrent users with maximum uptime to run a PHP application. Upon reviewing Windows Server 2008 you determine that IIS with FastCGI support will meet your requirements. What edition of Windows Server 2008 will you need to support PHP?

   A. Web Edition

   B. Standard Edition

   C. Enterprise or Datacenter Edition

   D. Any of them will work

3. After receiving a support request from one of your users you have determined that you need to adjust the URL authorization to allow users access to the /finance folder on the company intranet. In what configuration file should you make this modification?

   A. ApplicationHost.config

   B. Machine.config

   C. Server web.config

   D. Site web.config

4. A colleague has been trying to deploy an ASP.NET Web application to IIS on a Server Core installation of Windows Server 2008. They are unable to get the application to work telling you that when they try to access the default.aspx file that it keeps returning an HTTP 404 error. What should you do to help them?

A. Register the ASP.NET handler in the server configuration.

B. Inform them that they need a full installation of Windows Server 2008 for ASP.NET support.

C. Review the security permissions to ensure the IUSR account has access to the file and that anonymous authentication has been enabled.

D. Install the latest .NET Framework on the server.

5. After deploying the first ASP.NET application to a Web farm environment you have opened the application in a browser where ASP.NET has returned an exception: "[FileLoadException: Could not load file or assembly 'Contoso.Data.SQL, Version=1.0.0.0, Culture=neutral, PublicKeyToken=null' or one of its dependencies. Failed to grant minimum permission requests. (Exception from HRESULT: 0x80131417)]". What should you do to bring the application online?

A. Review the .NET Trust settings to ensure the required level has been set.

B. Run Process Monitor to see where IIS is trying to load the Conotos.Data.SQL.dll assembly from.

C. Grant the IIS_IUSRS group full control rights to the Contoso.Data.SQL.dll file.

D. Grant IUSR built-in account full control rights to the Contoso.Data.SQL.dll file.

6. You are about to migrate an older Web application from an IIS 6 server as part of your Windows Server 2008 migration project. The application uses custom metabase entries to store its configuration. IIS 7 introduced a new configuration API. Where will the entries be stored when the application is installed on IIS 7?

A. ApplicationHost.config

B. web.config

C. Administration.config

D. Redirection.config

7. IIS 7 introduced a number of new configuration tools to help you automate administrative tasks. Which of the following tools cannot be used to administer IIS 7 on Server Core?

A. Notepad

B. AppCmd

    C. Windows PowerShell

    D. IIS Manager

8. You have been asked by the security team to force the use of SSL on all Web applications. You want to configure this at the server level so that no one can modify it. What should you do to prevent people from changing this setting?

    A. Add an access section to the web.config files of each application and add a Deny file access control entry the file's access control list.

    B. Set the overrideModeDefault attribute on the access attribute in the ApplicationHost.config

    C. Create a location tag in each web.site config containing the access tag and set the allowOverride attribute

    D. Perform the administrative work on behalf of the users.

9. You have outgrown your single Web server and it is time to expand. You have installed IIS 7 on another Web server and moved your content to a network-attached storage device. The next step is to mirror the configuration on the second server. What feature will help you manage the configuration across both of your servers?

    A. AppCmd's Backup and Restore functions

    B. Configuration Inheritance

    C. Shared Configuration

    D. Windows PowerShell

10. The security team has alerted you to a large number of attempted SQL Injection Attacks coming from a specific host. What can you do to ensure that your Web server fends off the attacks without compromising your server's security?

    A. Add a request filter to minimize the length of the query string that will be accepted.

    B. Add the IP address to the server-level IP restriction list.

    C. Recycle the application pool.

    D. Disable the anonymous authentication module.

Self Test Quick Answer Key

1. **B**

2. **D**

3. **D**

4. **B**

5. **A**

6. **A**

7. **D**

8. **B**

9. **C**

10. **B**

Chapter 7

MCTS/MCITP
Exam 649

Configuring Web Infrastructure Services

Exam objectives in this chapter:

- **Installing and Configuring FTP Publishing Services**
- **Installing and Configuring SMTP Services**

Exam objectives review:

- ☑ **Summary of Exam Objectives**
- ☑ **Exam Objectives Fast Track**
- ☑ **Exam Objectives Frequently Asked Questions**
- ☑ **Self Test**
- ☑ **Self Test Quick Answer Key**

Introduction

It's easy to think of Internet Information Server (IIS) as a mechanism for hosting Web sites or Web applications. However, IIS provides several optional components that can either be used by themselves, or as a complement to an existing site. One such component is the File Transfer Publishing Service (FTP). FTP provides a mechanism for allowing users to upload and download files from your Web server.

Another optional component is the Simple Message Transfer Protocol (SMTP) service. You can use the SMTP service to turn your IIS server into an e-mail server, although the capabilities provided by the SMTP service are very crude when you compare them to those found in a full-blown mail server product, such as Microsoft Exchange. In this chapter, you will learn how to deploy, configure, and secure the FTP and the SMTP services.

Installing and Configuring FTP Publishing Services

File transfer services based on the File Transfer Protocol (FTP) have been around since 1971. As a protocol it has become a standard method for transferring files between remote systems running on various operating systems (see Figure 7.1). The protocol and surrounding services were designed to give the user a simple interface while handling the complexities of the differences among file systems under the covers. In addition to FTP you can use other protocols such as HTTP, WebDAV (based on HTTP), BITS, SMB/CIFS, and others. FTP delivers advantages when handling data exchange among remote systems and those with disparate system architectures.

Figure 7.1 FTP Service Model as Outlined in RFC 959

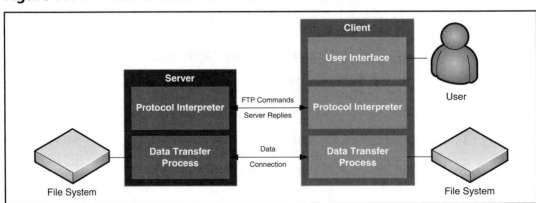

When you connect to an FTP server a control connection is established between the client and server's protocol interpreter. This process typically occurs on port 21 using TCP. Over this control connection the client sends commands and receives replies from the server acknowledging the commands in a fashion similar to a Telnet session. When a data transfer is requested, a data connection is established between the client and server. At this layer all of the translation occurs between the two file systems. Data transfer happens using either active or passive transfer modes. Each mode has a different method for establishing the data connection. In the active mode the server establishes the data connection with the client using a random TCP port 1024 and higher. In passive mode the client establishes the data connection with the server using a random TCP port 1024 and higher. For most security professionals the challenge of opening up ports 1024 and higher on either the client or the server is perplexing. Many firewalls deal with this scenario by listening to the control connection for the PORT command and dynamically opening the port needed to establish the data connection.

In 1997 an extension was proposed in the form of RFC 2228. This extension deals with the fact that FTP as defined back in 1971 uses an unencrypted control and data connection. Prior to RFC 2228 authentication credentials and files were transmitted without any privacy controls. The RFC describes the use of SSL to secure the control and data channels to address this problem and is known as FTPS. This release of IIS ships the FTP Publishing Service with support for SSL encryption. This provides a viable alternative to the recommendations for using WebDAV over HTTPS in past releases for secure file transfer.

Exam Warning

There is another variation of secure FTP transfer—SSH File Transfer Protocol (SFTP). This binary protocol based on RFC 4253 is not compatible with FTPS clients and servers. It does benefit from using a single connection as opposed to the split control and data connections; however it presents challenges such as the management of SSH keys and the changing standards and implementations.

In addition to security, this release also adds support for Unicode characters and IPv6 addressing, and taps into the rich architecture of IIS as part of a major rewrite. The tight integration allows you to leverage custom authentication modules, rich logging and tracing capabilities, and integration with the Web server for publishing scenarios.

Installing the FTP Publishing Service

With the amount of work undertaken by the IIS product group, the major enhancements to the FTP Publishing Service did not make it into this release. Microsoft
shipped the IIS 6 FTP Publishing Service with some compatibility fixes in its place. To
gain access to all of the new FTP Publishing Service features you will need to download the out-of-band release from the IIS Download Center (www.iis.net/downloads).

The Web release is a full installation; however it does require that the Web
Server (IIS) role be installed, as it integrates in with the IIS Management function-
ality. If you have previously installed the Web Server role with the FTP Publishing
Service you will need to uninstall it before using the Web release.

EXERCISE 7.1

INSTALLING FTP SERVER

1. From the Start Menu select **Server Manager.**

2. In Server Manager, scroll the right-hand pane to the **Roles
   Summary** section and click **Add Roles.**

3. In the Add Roles Wizard on the Before You Begin page, click **Next.**

4. On the Select Server Roles page, select the **Web Server (IIS)** role
   and click **Next** (see Figure 7.2).

Figure 7.2 Select Server Roles Page

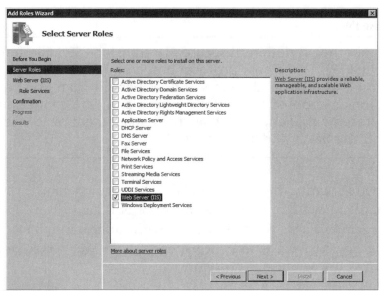

5. The Web Server (IIS) page gives you a brief description of the role along with some important notes and links to more information on the role (see Figure 7.3). Click **Next**.

   If this is your first time setting up the Web Server (IIS) role, you should read these notes, as they cover common issues that you will encounter.

Figure 7.3 Select Web Server (IIS) Role Services Page

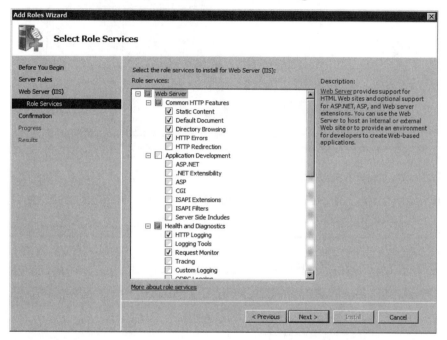

6. On the Role Services page you are prompted to install several groups of services to the role; leave the default values for the purposes of the upcoming exercises, and click **Next**.

7. On the Confirmation page review your choices and click **Install**.

8. On the Results page, review the success or failure of the installation and click **Close**.

9. Double-click the **FTP Server installation package**, follow the prompts for the update process to acknowledge the package, then read and accept the license agreement.

10. On the Custom Setup page, accept the defaults and click **Next** (see Figure 7.4).

Figure 7.4 Custom Setup Page

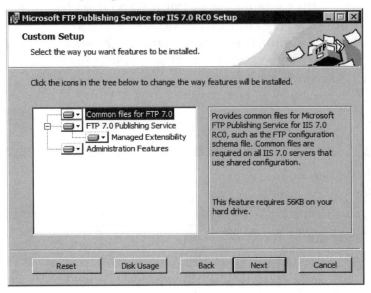

11. On the Ready to Install page click **Install.**

12. On the Completed page click **Finish.** Figure 7.5 shows the IIS Manager with the FTP server installed.

Figure 7.5 IIS Manager with the FTP Server Installed

With the installation complete you will see the Web Server role appear in Server Manager. From here you can get an overview of related event log entries, Windows services, and the Role Services you have chosen to install. In addition the Resources and Support section gives you at-your-fingertips access to resources that go in-depth on common issues and best practices to consider. The FTP Server will not appear in Server Manager. You will administer the FTP server through the IIS Manager.

Server Core installations of Windows Server 2008 allow you to install FTP Services in its entirety. The only functionality that will not be available is the graphical administrative interface and managed authentication modules.

EXERCISE 7.2

INSTALLING THE FTP SERVER ON SERVER CORE

1. Execute the following command to install the Web Server (IIS) role and the basic set of the role on a Server Core installation:

```
Start /W PkgMgr /IU:IIS-WebServerRole;IIS-WebServer;IIS-
CommonHttpFeatures;IIS-StaticContent;IIS-DefaultDocument;IIS-
DirectoryBrowsing;IIS-HttpErrors;IIS-HealthAndDiagnostics;IIS-
HttpLogging;IIS-RequestMonitor;IIS-Security;IIS-RequestFiltering; IIS-
Performance;IIS-HttpCompressionStatic;IIS-WebServerManagementTools;IIS-
IIS6ManagementCompatibility;IIS-Metabase;WAS-WindowsActivationService;WAS-
ProcessModel
```

2. Execute the following command to start installation of the FTP Server, follow the prompts for the update process to acknowledge the package, and read and accept the license agreement:

```
MSIEXEC /I FTP7_X86.msi
```

3. On the Custom Setup page, accept the defaults and click **Next.**

4. On the Ready to Install page click **Install.**

5. On the Completed page click **Finish.**

6. If you have enabled Windows Firewall and intend on using only non-secure FTP connections you will need to enable communication using the following commands:

```
NetSh AdvFirewall Set Global StatefulFTP Enable
NetSh AdvFirewall Firewall Add Rule Name="File Transfer Protocol (In)" Dir=In
Action=Allow Program="C:\WINDOWS\SYSTEM32\SvcHost.exe"
Protocol=TCP Service=ftpsvc
```

7. If you have enabled Windows Firewall and intend on using secure FTP (FTPS) connections you will need to disable stateful FTP inspection:

```
NetSh AdvFirewall Set Global StatefulFTP Disable
```

8. If you have enabled Windows Firewall and intend on using passive FTP connections, enable the FTP Publishing Service to communicate outwards as well:

```
NetSh AdvFirewall Firewall Add Rule Name="File Transfer Protocol (Out)"
Dir=Out Action=Allow Program="C:\WINDOWS\SYSTEM32\SvcHost.exe"
Protocol=TCP Service=ftpsvc
```

9. If you have enabled Windows Firewall on your server you will need to add the following exceptions:

Remote Administration Service Exception

```
NetSh Firewall Set Service Type=RemoteAdmin Mode=Enable
```

Windows Management Instrumentation Exception

```
NetSh AdvFirewall Firewall Set Rule Group="Windows Management
Instrumentation (WMI)" New Enable=Yes
```

Lockdown the AHAdmin DCOM Endpoint to Port 49494

```
Reg Add "HKCR\AppId\{9FA5C497-F46D-447F-8011-05D03D7D7DDC}" /v
Endpoints /t REG_MULTI_SZ /d "ncacn_ip_tcp,0,49494"
```

Remote Web Server Management Exception

```
NetSh AdvFirewall Firewall Add Rule Name="Remote Web Server Management
(RPC)" Dir=In Action=Allow
Program="C:\WINDOWS\SYSTEM32\dllhost.exe" Protocol=TCP LocalPort=49494

NetSh AdvFirewall Firewall Add Rule Name="Remote Web Server Management
(RPC-EPMap)" Dir=In Action=Allow
Program="C:\Windows\system32\svchost.exe" Service=RPCSS Protocol=TCP
LocalPort=RPC-EPMap
```

If your security policy requires a more strict security setting you can use port exceptions on all or specific interfaces.

10. If you want to use Windows Remote Shell you will need to enable it:

```
WinRM QuickConfig
```

A word of warning—the graphical tools cannot connect to a Server Core installation. This is because the graphical tools have a dependency on the IIS Management Service which is built on the .NET Framework and cannot be run on Server Core because of that. There are a few ways to remotely administer IIS on Server Core:

- **Command-line Tools** Using WinRS you can make calls to AppCmd.exe. Note that WinRM does not allow for interact sessions, instead outputting the results of your command.

```
WinRS.exe -Remote:FTPSERVER %SYSTEMROOT%\SYSTEM32\INETSRV\AppCmd.exe
LIST SITE
```

Test Day Tip

AppCmd uses a verb-noun combination. Open Command Prompt, type in AppCmd /? and get to know the list of objects which you can take an action upon. The verb list will generally follow a common sense approach (e.g., you Create Backup, not Add Backup).

- **Windows Management Instrumentation** Scripting, programming languages, Windows PowerShell, WMIC, WinRM, and WinRS can all administer IIS on Server Core through WMI.

```
WMIC.exe /Output:Sites.txt /Node:FTPSERVER
/Namespace:\root\WebAdministration Path Site Get
```

- **COM and .NET Programming Interfaces** In addition to WMI you can use the Microsoft.ApplicationHost.AdminManager DCOM object in VBScript/JScript or the Microsoft.Web.Administration assembly through Windows PowerShell scripts and .NET applications.

```
[Reflection.Assembly]::LoadFrom("C:\WINDOWS\SYSTEM32\inetsrv\Microsoft.
Web.Administration.dll");
$WebServer =
[Microsoft.Web.Administration.ServerManager]::OpenRemote("FTPSERVER");
$WebServer.Sites | Format-Table Id, Name;
```

With our server setup, you can now configure your server's features to fit your deployment scenario's needs. If you need to uninstall the FTP Publishing Service make sure that you remove it before removing the Web Server role. The following sections will take you through basic configuration steps for each of the functional areas.

> **EXAM WARNING**
>
> Know the differences between Server Core and full installations of Windows Server 2008 with Internet Information Services. There is a small subset of features that are not available on Server Core and they happen to be fairly important in the Microsoft Web application eco-system.

Provisioning FTP Sites

With the FTP Server installed the first step is to provision a new FTP site. You can setup independent FTP sites or bind them with a Web site on the server in this release. The latter is particularly useful in shared hosting environments to provide access to hosted sites.

EXERCISE 7.3

CREATING AN FTP SITE

1. Open **Control Panel** and under System and Maintenance | Administration Tools, double-click the **Internet Information Services (IIS) Manager** shortcut.

2. In the Internet Information Services (IIS) Manager management console, expand the server node in the left-hand pane, right-click **Sites**, and select **Add FTP Site.**

3. In the **Add FTP Site** dialog, provide a descriptive **FTP Site Name** and a **Physical Path** to the content and click **Next.**

4. On the Binding and SSL Settings page, select an **IP Address** and optionally an **SSL certificate** and click **Next** (see Figure 7.6).

Figure 7.6 Binding and SSL Settings Page

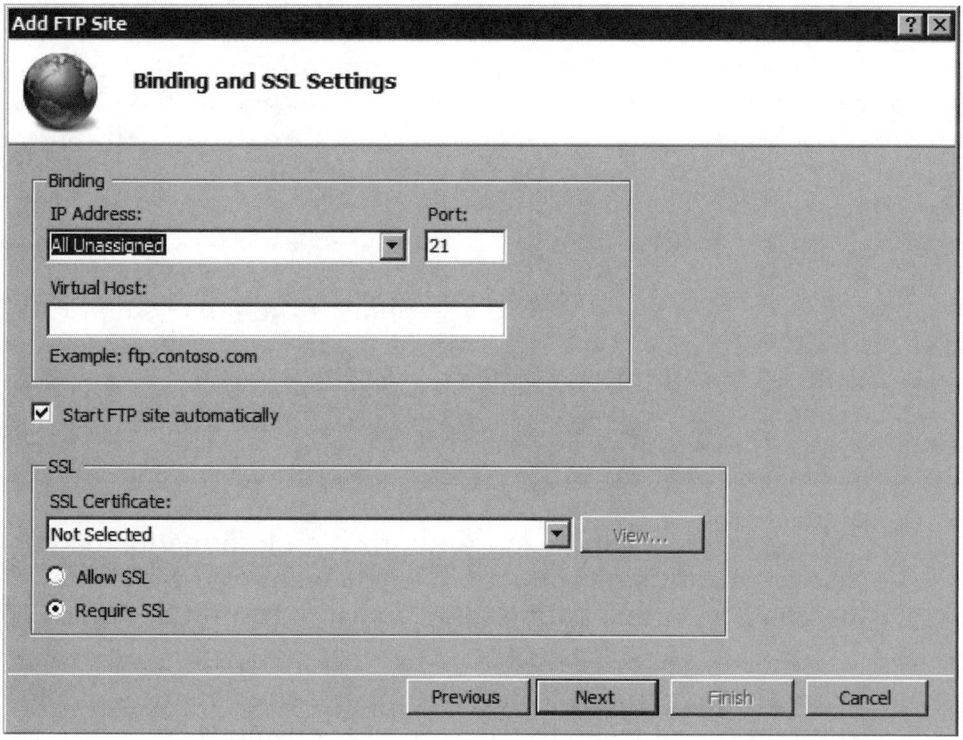

New & Noteworthy...

Host Headers and FTP

The ability to support virtual hosts is new to IIS 7. If you have used FTP in the past you may be asking yourself how exactly this works. It's a great question and one that deserves some investigation. FTP traditionally has worked without any reliance on DNS for resolution. You could just as easily FTP into an IP address as you could a host name. With this release of IIS the product group implemented two methods for supporting FTP virtual hosts: one is a band-aid solution, and another is part of a draft proposal from the Internet Engineering Task Force.

Continued

The band-aid approach is to prefix the username with the host name and a pipe symbol. The syntax for <hostname>|<username> means that if you want to login to the ftp.contoso.com virtual host as jsmith you would use ftp.contoso.com|jsmith as your username. This will tell the FTP server that the user is being authenticated in the context of the ftp.contoso.com virtual host. This approach allows you to use your favorite FTP client without worrying if it will support the proposed extensions.

The proposed draft outlines the addition of a new HOST command to be used by FTP clients and servers. Upon the connection to a site the FTP client sends a FEAT command to determine if the server supports the HOST command. If it does then it will send a HOST <hostname> command before the USER and PASS commands to authenticate the connection. The HOST command provides the necessary information for the server to determine which virtual host to connect to.

5. On the Authentication and Authorization Information page, select the **Authentication** module you want to use and the default site **Authorization** rules, and click **Finish** (see Figure 7.7).

    Unlike previous versions there is no site-wide Read / Write authorization. In this release you define a set of authorization rules that are applied to all users, all anonymous users, or a specific group of users or roles.

Figure 7.7 Authentication and Authorization Information Page

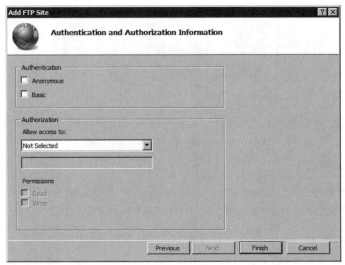

In addition to creating a standalone FTP site you can also enable an existing Web site with FTP access. This will allow users to work with their site content using the FTP protocol while keeping the configuration information tied to the Web site.

EXERCISE 7.4

CREATING A WEB SITE-BOUND FTP SITE

1. Open **Control Panel** and under System and Maintenance | Administration Tools double-click the **Internet Information Services (IIS) Manager** shortcut.

2. In the Internet Information Services (IIS) Manager management console, expand the server and sites node in the left-hand pane, right-click the Web site you wish to publish, and select **Add FTP Publishing.**

3. At the Add FTP Site Publishing screen, select an **IP Address** and optionally an **SSL certificate** and click **Next.**

4. On the Authentication and Authorization Information page, select the **Authentication** module you want to use and the default site **Authorization** rules, and click **Finish.**

With the site created there are a set of advanced settings available to help you fine tune the behavior of your FTP Site. They can be found by selecting the site from the left-hand pane, and in the right-hand Actions pane under Manage FTP site clicking **Advanced Settings** (see Figure 7.8).

Figure 7.8 FTP Site Advanced Settings

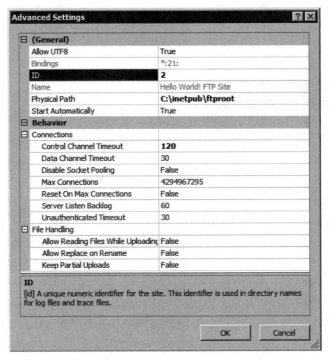

Directory Browsing

When using the FTP service clients will often browse the various folders to locate the content that they want to retrieve. You have the option of configuring several options that will affect how the items within a folder are listed, as shown in Figure 7.9.

Figure 7.9 FTP Directory Browsing Module Configuration

The first option group is a style preference between MS-DOS and UNIX directory listings:

- Listing 7.1 MS-DOS Directory Listings

```
02-01-08 08:33PM        0 default.txt
11-02-06 04:39AM        15821312 imageres.dll
```

- Listing 7.2 UNIX Directory Listings

```
-rwxrwxrwx 1 owner group          0 Feb    1    20:33      default.txt
-rwxrwxrwx 1 owner group    15821312 Nov    2    2006      imageres.dll
```

The second option group focuses on the information included within the directory listings. The first option enables or disables showing virtual directories in the listings. In previous releases this was disabled by default, creating the effect of "hidden" folders. With the industry shying away from the security-by-obscurity approach this option was exposed to give you the choice depending on your business needs. The second option determines if the remaining bytes are reflected in the directory listings. Typically this will show the remaining bytes left on the disk; however, if a folder-level quota has been enabled then it will reflect the remaining bytes based on the quota. The final option determines if the last modified date should reflect a two or four digit year.

Firewall Support

The Firewall Support feature allows you to facilitate passive connections to the FTP server when it is behind a firewall (see Figure 7.10). When the FTP server provides a port number for the client to establish a data connection, the IP address is embedded within the response. This feature allows you to both limit the port range and specify the appropriate external IP address. Once this feature is configured you will need to forward the specified port range from your firewall.

Figure 7.10 FTP Firewall Support Module Configuration

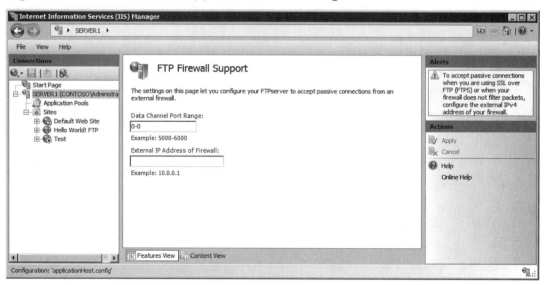

Configuring & Implementing...

Active versus Passive Mode

The key difference between active and passive FTP mode is the designation of who opens the port for the data connection. In active mode the client is responsible for opening the port. In passive mode it is the server which is responsible. In most deployments you will see passive mode as the preferred method because it represents the least amount of configuration and confusion across the spectrum of users that you will service. To enforce an even more secure approach look to add Windows Firewall with Advanced Security to your deployment using the service filtering options that ship with Windows Server 2008 to lock it down further to the FtpSvc service identifier.

Messages

When FTP sessions are established, authenticated, ended, or denied connection you can include a message for the user. The Messages feature gives you a chance to configure the default message at the server and specific site messages as shown in Figure 7.11. The first option group allows you to suppress the FTP service banner, enable the use of variables in the message, and show detailed error messages when connecting from the local machine. The variables available include:

- **%BytesReceived%** Total number of bytes sent to the client in the current session

- **%BytesSent%** Total number of bytes received from the client in the current session

- **%SessionID%** Unique identifier for the current session

- **%SiteName%** Site Name for the FTP Site being accessed

- **%UserName%** Username of the currently logged in user

The following is an example of the variables in action:

```
Thank you for visiting %SiteName%, during your session %SessionID% we
sent %BytesReceived% bytes to you and we received %BytesSent% from you.
We look forward to seeing you again %UserName%!
```

The preceding message would generate output similar to this:

```
Thank you for visiting Hello World! FTP Site, during your session 1 we
sent 5,729 bytes to you and we received 5,828,640 from you. We look
forward to seeing you again CONTOSO\Colin!
```

Figure 7.11 FTP Messages Module Configuration

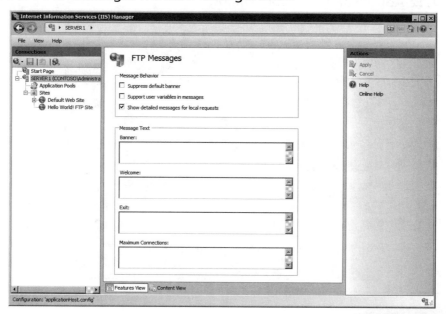

Virtual Directories

With FTP sites being used for more than managing Web content, it was quite common to see virtual directories being used to link to different folders within the system. A virtual directory works by creating a reference in the site configuration to where the content resides. The FTP service will parse the link and allow users to navigate to the folders as if they were another regular folder within the structure.

EXERCISE 7.5

CREATING A VIRTUAL DIRECTORY

1. Open **Control Panel** and under System and Maintenance | Administration Tools double-click the **Internet Information Services (IIS) Manager** shortcut.

2. In the Internet Information Services (IIS) Manager management console, expand the server and sites nodes in the left-hand pane, right-click your FTP site, and select **Add Virtual Directory.**

3. In the **Add Virtual Directory** dialog, provide the **Alias** of the virtual directory to be used by requests and a **Physical Path** to the content, and click **OK** (see Figure 7.12).

Figure 7.12 Add Virtual Directory Dialog

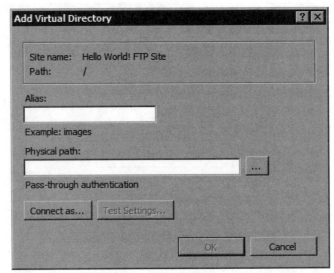

Application Pools

With the changes in architecture in this release, FTP sites have been shifted to use application pools for processing requests. This allows you to separate out the sites into individual worker processes and control their process identity and resource utilization as you would with a Web site.

EXERCISE 7.6

CONVERTING A FOLDER TO AN APPLICATION

1. Open **Control Panel** and under System and Maintenance | Administration Tools double-click the **Internet Information Services (IIS) Manager** shortcut.

2. In the Internet Information Services (IIS) Manager management console, expand the server and sites nodes in the left-hand pane, right-click a folder within a FTP site, and select **Convert to Application.**

3. In the **Add Application** dialog select the application pool you want your application to run under, if desired set a content access identity, and click **OK** (see Figure 7.13).

Figure 7.13 Add Application Dialog

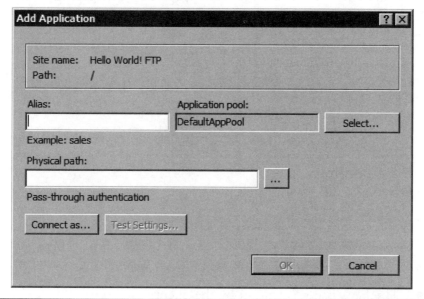

Securing Your FTP Site

Protecting your FTP site may require one or more tactics to ensure that the content is only accessed by authorized users:

- **Transport Security** Focused on privacy of data being transmitted between the user and the server

- **Authentication** Provides a method for determining the user's identity

- **Authorization** Evaluates a set of rules to determine if the user is allowed to make the request

This section will take you further into each tactic and the details behind them. The most notable changes in these sections for this release are the support of SSL and the ability to use custom authentication modules.

Transport Security

Protecting the privacy of the data being transmitted is the primary focus of transport security. There are a number of options within the Windows Server 2008 infrastructure to protect the privacy. You may want to wrap all data being transmitted, for example, through a virtual private network or IPSec tunnel. With this as the extreme at one end, IIS provides a more moderate and widely used method for protecting data using Secure Socket Layers (SSL). SSL uses digital certificates to encrypt the communication. There are two approaches to engaging SSL: implicit, where SSL is used for communication upon the initial connection, and explicit SSL, where SSL is enabled for the session after the initial connection is made. FTP Services was built to support explicit SSL, which is the method documented in RFC 2228. The implicit method has been documented in several drafts, but never formally adopted by the IETF. At a high level the explicit FTP SSL process works as follows:

1. The client connects to the server (typically through TCP port 21).

2. The client requests a secure session.

3. The server sends back its public encryption key.

4. The client checks the key to ensure:

   - The name of the host being requested matches the key,

   - The key is within the valid date range, and

   - The key's issuer is trusted by the client.

5. If the client determines that it can trust the server's public key, it will send its public key to the server.

6. The server will generate a password and encrypt it using both the client's public key and the server's private key and send it back to the client.

7. The client will decrypt the password as evidence that the server is the one who sent the password, thereby establishing that only the server and the client will be capable of reading the encrypted information.

8. The client will send the request to the server encrypted with the password that the server sent to it.

9. With the secure channel established, the FTP client continues on to authenticate the user and begin the session.

Before you can enable your FTP site for secure communication you will need to register a security certificate. IIS 7 introduces a new management interface for security certificates used by all protocols it handles. This new interface, as shown in Figure 7.14, gives you a single point to review all of the certificates installed on your server along with exposing the ability to generate a self-signed certificate from within the interface. Previously self-signed certificates were only available through the command-line SelfSSL tool that shipped with the IIS 6.0 Resource Kit tools.

Figure 7.14 Server Certificates Module Configuration

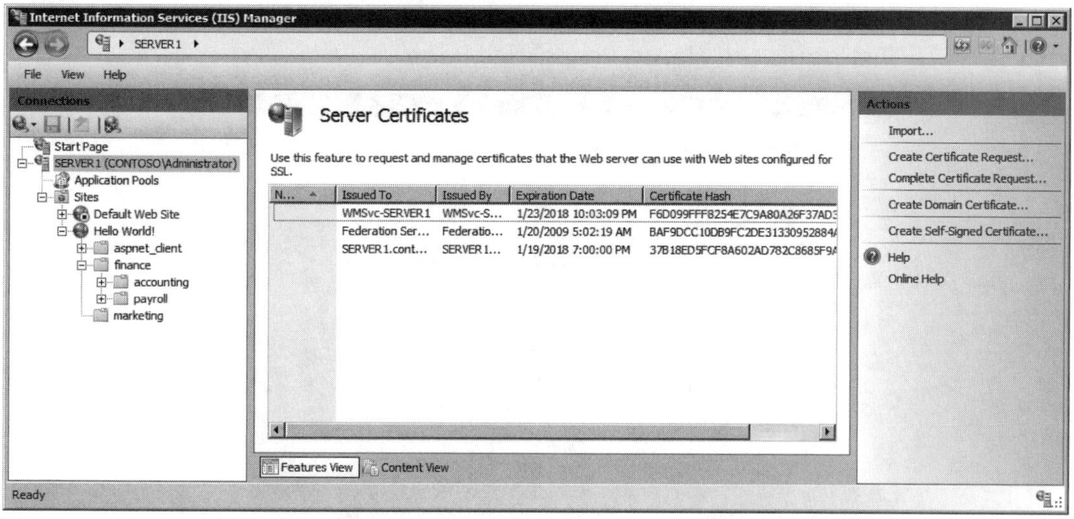

The first step to enabling a secure FTP site is to import or create a new certificate into the server. When creating a certificate you can create one from an online connected certificate authority (CA) like the Certificate Services role that ships with Windows Server 2008, a third-party CA (e.g., Comodo, Thwarte, Verisign), or generate a self-signed certificate. Whichever path you choose the one thing to remember is that the client will need to trust the certificate's issuer in order to trust the certificate. When using a self-signed certificate no one will trust it unless they take steps to specifically add it to their trusted certificates list.

EXERCISE 7.7

ADDING A NEW SECURITY CERTIFICATE

1. Open **Control Panel** and under System and Maintenance | Administration Tools double-click the **Internet Information Services (IIS) Manager** shortcut.

2. In the Internet Information Services (IIS) Manager management console, click the server node, and in the middle pane click **Server Certificates.**

3. In the right-hand actions pane click **Create Certificate Request.**

4. In the **Request Certificate** dialog on the Distinguished Name Properties page, provide the host name that will be used to access your site (e.g., ftp.contoso.com) along with your company information and click **Next** (see Figure 7.15).

Figure 7.15 Distinguished Name Properties Page

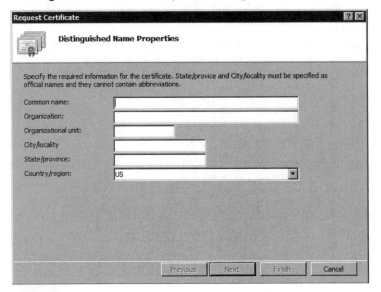

5. On the Cryptographic Service Provider Properties page, shown in Figure 7.16, choose a **Cryptographic Server Provider** and a minimum of 1,024 **Bit Length** for the key, and click **Next.**

    ■ **RSA SChannel Cryptographic Provider** Uses an MD5 hash with an SHA hash, signed with an RSA private key. It supports SSL2, PCT1, SSL3, and TLS1 protocols.

    ■ **DH SChannel Cryptographic Provider** Uses the Diffie-Hellman algorithm and supports SSL3 and TLS1 protocols. Use this algorithm when you must exchange a secret key over an insecure network without prior communication with the client.

    ■ **Bit Length** The default length supported by most browsers and certificate authorities is 1,024 bits. With processors becoming more powerful expect to see a move towards 2,048 bit length certificates past the year 2010. Be sure to check with your chosen certificate authority to ensure they will support bit lengths larger than 1,024 before increasing this value.

Figure 7.16 Cryptographic Service Provider Page

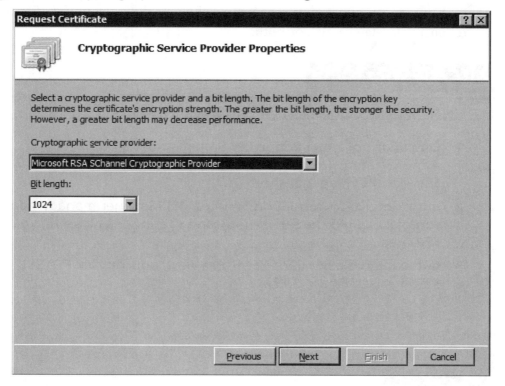

6. On the File Name page provide a path and name of a file for sorting the certificate request and click **Next**.

7. Contact your preferred certificate authority to obtain the response file for your request.

   If you are looking to test out the SSL functionality, there are a number of providers, such as Comodo and GeoTrust, that will give you a free trial SSL certificate that lasts anywhere from 15 to 60 days. This is handy because they have all of the trust features of regular certificates with no cost.

8. When you obtain the response file open IIS Manager and return to the Server Certificates section.

9. In the right-hand actions pane click **Complete Certificate Request.**

10. In the **Complete Certificate Request** dialog on the Specify Certificate Authority Response page, locate the **Certificate Authority's Response** file, provide a **Friendly Name** for the certificate, and click **Next** to complete the process.

With the certificate in place you can now bind the certificate to your FTP site. Once the certificate is bound you can choose to allow or force the use of SSL for the control channel, data channel, or both.

EXERCISE 7.8

ENABLING SECURE COMMUNICATIONS ON YOUR FTP SITE

1. Open **Control Panel** and under System and Maintenance | Administration Tools double-click the **Internet Information Services (IIS) Manager** shortcut.

2. In the Internet Information Services (IIS) Manager management console, expand the server node and sites node and select your FTP site.

3. In the middle pane under Features view, double-click **FTP SSL Settings** (see Figure 7.17).

Figure 7.17 FTP SSL Settings Module Configuration

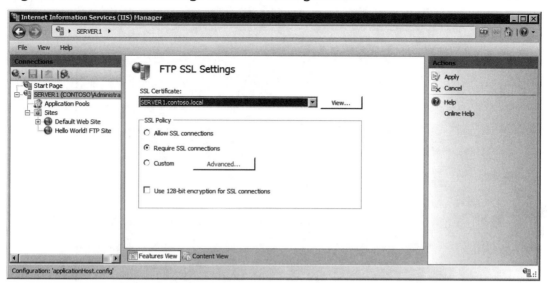

4. On the FTP SSL Settings page, select an **SSL Certificate**, choose whether to **Allow** or **Require SSL connections**, and in the actions pane click **Apply**.

As with\Web connections you can force a minimum of 128-bit encryption.

Any form of encryption will add overhead to the processing. If you have an FTP server that is heavily used or needs to coexist with other applications, you can also customize the behavior of SSL to protect one of the channels or just the login process. The choice will depend on your data privacy policies. At a minimum you will generally want to protect user credentials. If the FTP clients are unable to support FTP over SSL, you will need to leave these settings at *Allow*. Otherwise, you can use the "Require Only for Credentials" option to minimize overhead and protect what is traditionally a clear text exchange (see Figure 7.18). If you need to protect what the user is doing from anyone who may be monitoring the network traffic the encryption of the control channel as a whole is best. Finally if you are exchanging sensitive data such as customer information you may want to protect the data channel using the *Require* option. Specifically for the data channel, you can also deny the encryption which may be required for certain compliance monitoring scenarios.

Figure 7.18 Advanced SSL Policy Dialog

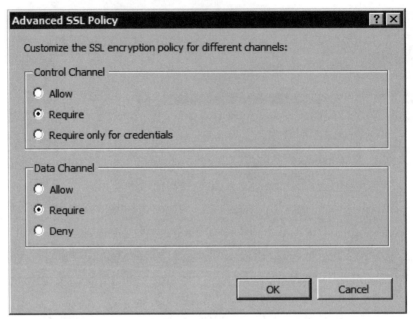

Authentication

Authentication is the process of asserting the identity of the user when they are establishing a session with the FTP site. With this identity we can track who is doing what and evaluate rules to determine if they are authorized to interact with content and folders. IIS ships with two types of authentication modules that can be used to determine a user's identity (see Figure 7.19):

- **Anonymous** Enabled by default to allow any user to access public content without a username and password. Anonymous connections use the username "anonymous" and prompt the user to enter their e-mail address as a password for logging purposes.

- **Basic** Requires the user to provide a username and password. This authentication protocol is a standard across all platforms. It does not perform any sort of encryption with the information provided by the user. As such you should use it with SSL to ensure that the credentials are sent over a secure connection.

Figure 7.19 FTP Authentication Module Configuration

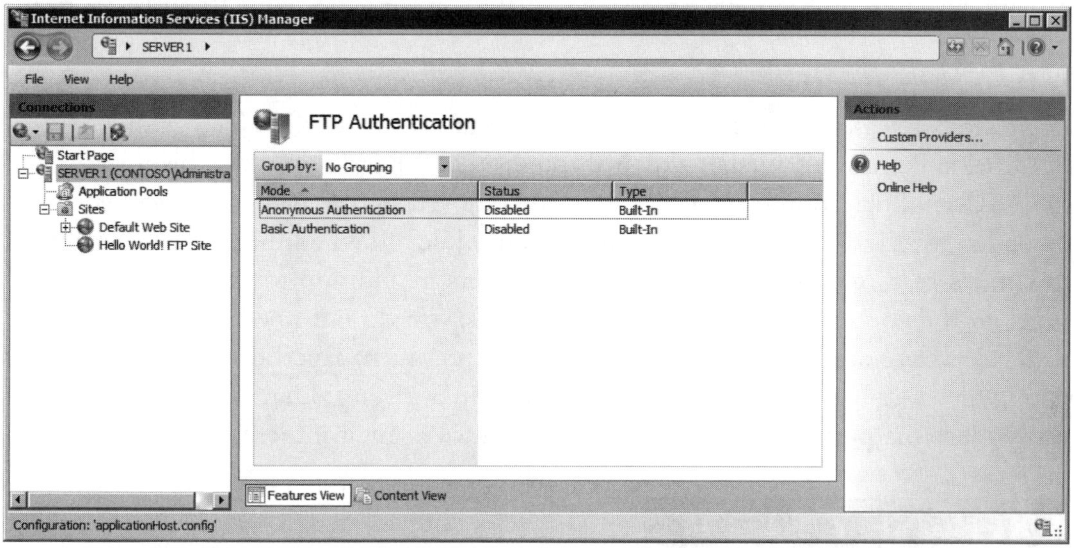

EXERCISE 7.9

ENABLING BASIC AUTHENTICATION

1. Open **Control Panel** and under System and Maintenance | Administration Tools double-click the **Internet Information Services (IIS) Manager** shortcut.

2. In the Internet Information Services (IIS) Manager management console, expand the server and select an FTP Site on which you want to enable authentication.

3. In the middle pane under Features view double-click **FTP Authentication.**

4. Right-click the **Basic Authentication** module and select **Enable.**

Authorization

With the user's identity established the next step is to determine if the user can perform the action that is being requested. Actions on an FTP site include downloading and uploading of content. They can also perform basic file management functions if authorized. The authorization module evaluates the action based on a set of rules that decide if the user should be allowed, based on the user's identity and if they are attempting to read or write data. IIS provides two modules focused on authorization and supporting services: URL authorization and IP authorization.

URL Authorization

In previous releases the authorization to perform actions was decided at the site level and enforced further down through NTFS permissions. In this release the URL authorization capabilities typically enjoyed by the Web site have been extended for the FTP server scenarios. This module allows administrators the ability to control read or write access to files and folders in addition to the NTFS permissions on the content. Unlike NTFS permissions, you do not need file system access to the server to apply permissions, since everything is managed through the web. config file stored at the root of the site or within a given folder. This allows you to easily carry the permissions with the site as it moves environments.

EXERCISE 7.10

RESTRICTING ACCESS TO A FOLDER

1. Open **Control Panel** and under System and Maintenance | Administration Tools double-click the **Internet Information Services (IIS) Manager** shortcut.

2. In the Internet Information Services (IIS) Manager management console, expand the server and site node, locate a folder to secure (or choose the site as a whole), and click your selection.

3. In the middle pane under Features View double-click **Authentication.**

4. On the Authentication page, ensure that the Anonymous Authentication module is **Disabled**, select one of the other authentication modules, and click **Enable** in the right-hand Actions pane.

5. Click the **Back** arrow in the top left-hand corner.

6. On the folder page in the middle pane under Features view, double-click **Authorization Rules.**

7. On the Authorization Rules page, click **Add Allow Rule** in the right-hand actions pane.

8. Select the **Specified Users** radio button, provide a username, and click **OK** (see Figure 7.20).

Figure 7.20 Add Allow Authorization Rule Dialog

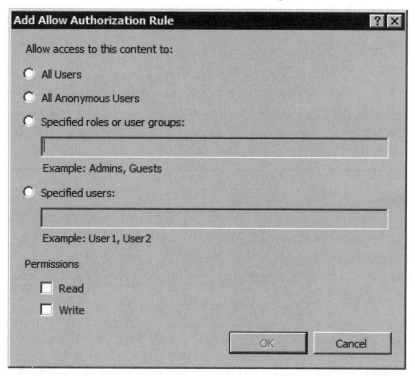

IP Authorization

The ability to restrict access to specific IP addresses has existed for quite some time across both servers and networking devices such as firewalls. In the past this function, like file permissions, was only available through IIS Manager and was tough to replicate across to other servers as it was stored in the metabase. This setting, along with all other configuration options, has been moved to the new XML-based configuration files. This allows you to centralize, copy, and manipulate the settings using new programming interfaces and command-line tools as well as the traditional graphical user interface.

EXERCISE 7.11

RESTRICTING ACCESS TO USERS BASED ON THEIR IP ADDRESS

1. Open **Control Panel** and under System and Maintenance | Administration Tools double-click the **Internet Information Services (IIS) Manager** shortcut.

2. In the Internet Information Services (IIS) Manager management console, expand the server and sites node, locate a folder to secure (or choose the site as a whole), and click your selection.

3. In the middle pane under Features view double-click **FTP IPv4 Address and Domain Restrictions.**

4. In the right-hand actions pane click **Add Deny Entry.**

5. In the **Add Deny Restriction Rule** dialog, select the **Specific IPv4 Address** radio button, provide an IP address (e.g., 127.0.0.1 if you want to test ftp access from the server), and click **OK.**

When users attempt to access a file or folder to which they have been denied they will receive a forbidden error. Another option is to restrict users based on their domain name. You will need to enable this through the *Edit Feature Settings* link in the module page on IIS. Be aware that the added overhead of DNS resolution for each IP address could negatively affect the performance of your FTP site. Just as you can restrict specific users, you can also deny all and only allow specific users. This process is similar to adding deny rules with the dialog, shown in Figure 7.21, looking very similar to that of adding deny restriction rules.

Figure 7.21 Add Allow Restriction Rule with Domain Restrictions Enabled

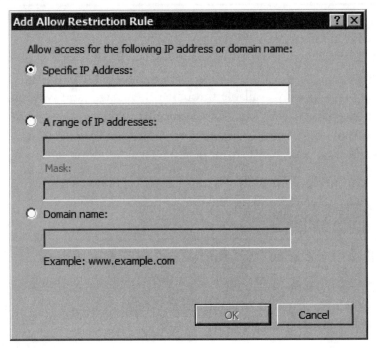

User Isolation

The User Isolation feature will place users into their own home folder when they login, while preventing them from viewing or overwriting other users' content (see Figure 7.22). This feature is most commonly used in shared hosting scenarios. Inside their home folder users can create, modify, and remove files and folders as they wish.

Figure 7.22 FTP User Isolation Module Configuration

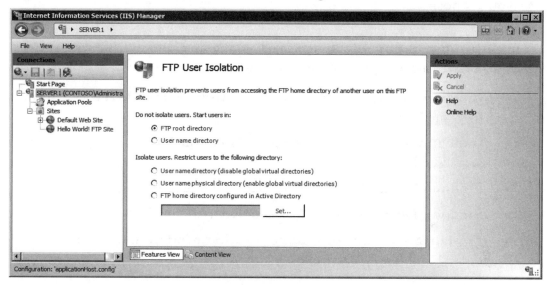

There are five isolation options to choose from:

- **Do Not Isolate Users: FTP Root Directory** This is the default option that places everyone in the FTP root folder upon logon.

- **Do Not Isolate Users: User Name Directory** Users will start in a folder that bears their username if it exists; otherwise they will be placed in the FTP root folder. The user can navigate to the root of the FTP site.

- **Isolate Users: User Name Directory** Isolate users to a physical or virtual directory that bears their username. The user cannot navigate to the root of the FTP site.

- **Isolate Users: User Name Physical Directory** Isolates users to the physical directory that bears their username. The user cannot navigate to the root of the FTP site.

■ **Isolate Users: FTP Home Directory Configured in Active Directory** Isolates users to the directory specified in their Active Directory account. The user cannot navigate to the root of the FTP site.

TEST DAY TIP

Study the different user isolation options carefully—the differences are slight, but they have a big impact on the security of the solution that you propose.

In all cases the folder needs to be created for the user before they login. The syntax for folder names depends on how the user account is stored:

■ **Anonymous Users for Non-Isolated User Name Directory Mode** (FTP Site Root)\Default

■ **Anonymous Users when using an Isolation Mode** (FTP Site Root)\ LocalUser\Public

■ **Windows Local Users** (FTP Site Root)\LocalUser\(Username)

■ **Windows Domain Users** (FTP Site Root)\(Domain Name)\(Username)

■ **IIS Manager or Custom Authentication Module Users** (FTP Site Root)\Local User\(Username)

To specify the starting directory for anonymous access, create a physical or virtual directory folder named *default* in the root directory of the FTP site.

Installing and Configuring SMTP Services

Many applications use e-mail delivery to support the functionality that they offer. The Simple Mail Transfer (SMTP) Service is a basic mail relay that ships with Windows Server 2008 and provides local and remote delivery of messages, as shown in Figure 7.23.

TEST DAY TIP

If you have used the IIS 6 SMTP Service you will find the differences in this release to be very minimal. Knowledge and skills attained through working with the previous release will apply to this release and as such to the exam.

Figure 7.23 SMTP Relay Process

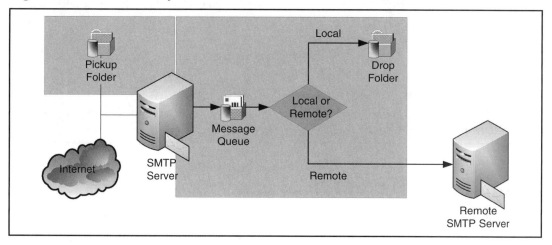

When you receive messages locally, they are received through the Drop folder. When you receive messages remotely, they are received through a TCP connection, by default port 25. Messages are placed into a message queue for processing. The SMTP server reviews the message destination and compares it with the list of domains that it maintains. If it contains explicit instructions on how to handle a message then it acts upon those. If the SMTP server is considered the local domain SMTP server, then it will place the message in a local Drop folder for another application to pickup and process. If it has explicit instructions to route to a remote SMTP server then it will follow those instructions. If it does not have any corresponding record for the domain and the caller has relay privileges then it will locate the remote SMTP server and send the message as well.

Configuring & Implementing...

Real-World Use of SMTP Server

Over the past few generations of Windows Server, the use of SMTP Server has started to dwindle. The major product group relying on SMTP Server was the Exchange Server team. With the recent Exchange Server 2007

Continued

> release, the Exchange Server team chose to write a new SMTP Server for use within the product. The SMTP Server today, as it exists in Windows Server 2008, now resides there primarily for backwards compatibility. This release saw very little development and no discussion of the future of the SMTP Server. To prepare your environment for future Windows Server releases, you should be aware of where the dependencies for this service exist (e.g., Windows SharePoint Services, third-party applications), and possible alternatives.

Installing SMTP Services

The Simple Mail Transfer Protocol (SMTP) Server is listed as a server-level Feature and not a part of any specific role. It has dependencies on the IIS 6 Management Compatibility and IIS 6 Management Console role server which is available in the Web Server role.

EXERCISE 7.12

INSTALLING SMTP SERVER

1. From the Start Menu select **Server Manager.**

2. In Server Manager, click the root node, scroll the right-hand pane to the **Features Summary** section, and click **Add Features.**

3. In the Add Features Wizard on the Before You Begin page, click **Next.**

4. On the Select Features page, select the **SMTP Server** role and click **Next**, as shown in Figure 7.24.

Figure 7.24 Select Features Page

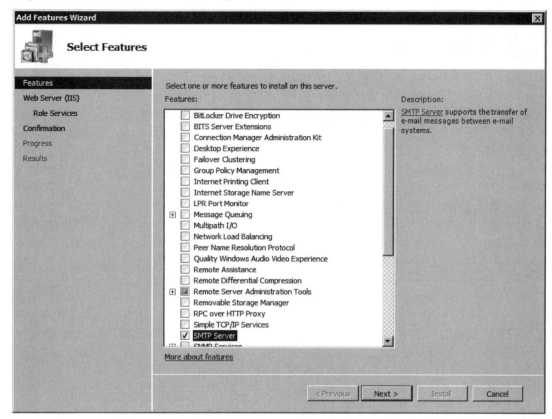

5. The Web Server (IIS) page gives you a brief description of the role along with some important notes and links to more information on the role. Click **Next**.

   If this is your first time setting up the Web Server (IIS) role, you should read these notes as they will cover common issues that you will encounter

6. On the Role Services page you are prompted to install several groups of services to the role (see Figure 7.25). Leave the default values and click **Next.**

Figure 7.25 Select Web Server (IIS) Role Services Page

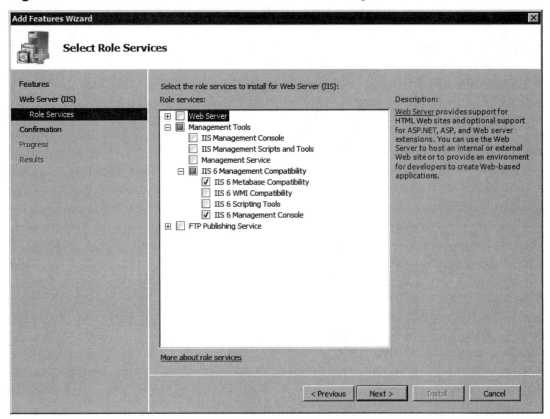

7. On the Confirmation page, review your choices and click **Install.**
8. On the Results page, review the success or failure of the installation, then click **Close.**

With the SMTP Server installed you can manage it through the Internet Information Services (IIS) 6.0 Manager console located in the Administrative Tools group on the server.

EXAM WARNING

With Windows Server 2008 there is a split installation of IIS 6 and IIS 7 components. Be sure to understand which services have a specific reliance on IIS 6 components as they are managed in two different interfaces.

Provisioning Virtual Servers

A virtual server is the container under which receive and delivery rules are configured. You can have multiple virtual servers on a server, but they cannot be bound to the same IP address and port combination.

EXERCISE 7.13

CREATING A NEW VIRTUAL SERVER

1. Open **Control Panel** and under System and Maintenance | Administration Tools double-click the **Internet Information Services (IIS) 6.0 Manager** shortcut.

2. In the Internet Information Services (IIS) 6.0 Manager management console, right-click the server node and select **New | SMTP Virtual Server.**

3. In the New SMTP Virtual Server Wizard on the Welcome page, provide a descriptive **Name** and click **Next.**

4. On the Select IP Address page, select an **IP Address** and click **Next.**

5. On the Select Home Directory page, set a root **Home Directory** for your virtual server working folders and click **Next.**

6. On the Default Domain page, provide a **Default Domain** for the virtual server (which serves as the local domain) and click **Finish.**

With your virtual server set up to receive mail, you will need to add a list of domains for which it can receive mail. By default, anonymous connections will only be able to send mail to the domains that you have configured. When you configure the domain using domain routing instructions you can choose whether mail should be delivered to the local drop folder or to a remote server.

EXERCISE 7.14

ADDING DOMAIN ROUTING INSTRUCTIONS

1. Open **Control Panel** and under System and Maintenance | Administration Tools double-click the **Internet Information Services (IIS) 6.0 Manager** shortcut.

2. In the Internet Information Services (IIS) 6.0 Manager management console, expand the server and virtual server node.

3. Right-click **Domains** and choose **New | Domain.**

4. In the New SMTP Domain Wizard on the Welcome page, select **Alias** or **Remote** depending on your needs.

5. On the Domain Name page enter a valid domain **Name** (e.g., contoso.com) and click **Finish.**

If you setup an alias domain there are no other properties available. The alias domains are an alternative name for the default local domain. The folder where the mail will be delivered is configured in the Properties of the default local domain, as shown in Figure 7.26.

Figure 7.26 Default Local Domain Properties Dialog

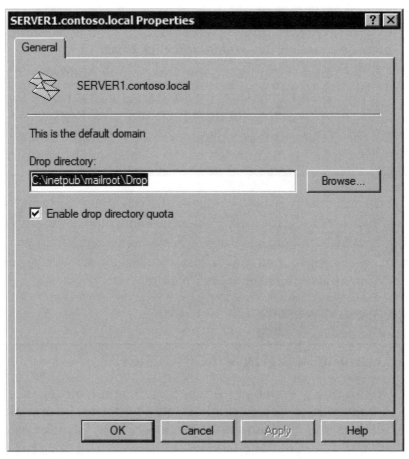

For remote domains you will need to select the **Allow incoming mail to be relayed to this domain** checkbox to enable the server to accept mail. This option is disabled by default. This was done specifically to force you to knowingly allow the SMTP to receive and process mail for this domain. Much of the early unsolicited email problems were due to "open relays." This meant the SMTP servers would accept mail for any domain and attempt to deliver the message. Spammers would take advantage of these open relays as a way to obscure the source of their annoyances.

The rest of the dialog box has domain-specific delivery instructions (see Figure 7.27). In the **General** tab you can tell the server to use HELO for older SMTP servers that do not support EHLO. The **Outbound Security** button allows you to specify a set of credentials to use when connecting to the remote server where the message will be delivered. The Route Domain group gives you the option of trying to look up the mail exchanger (MX) records for the domain or forward directly to a specific host (smart host).

Figure 7.27 Remote Domain Properties Dialog

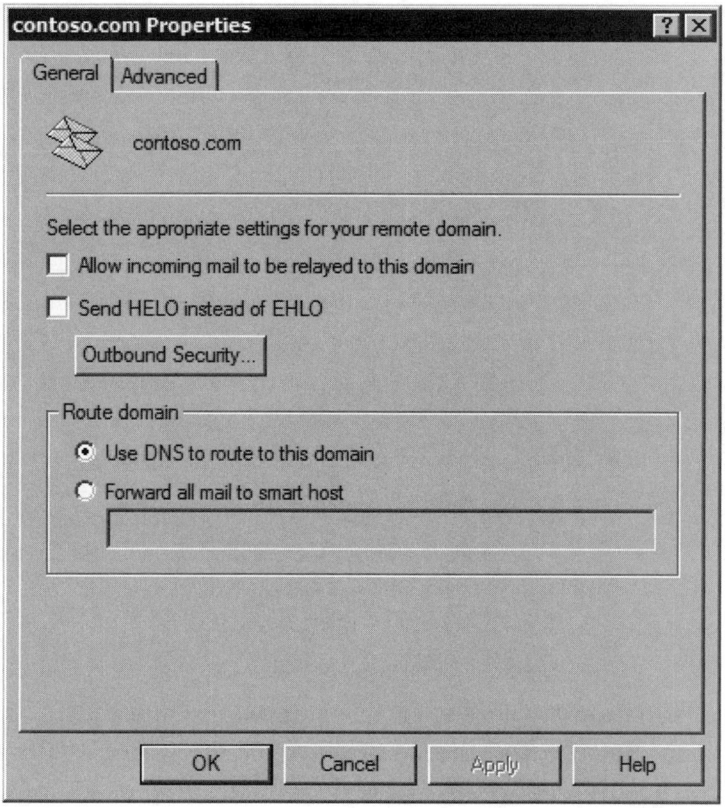

Under the **Advanced** tab, shown in Figure 7.28, you have the server queue the incoming messages until a client connects and issues the Authenticated TURN (ATRN) command. When this command is issued the messages will then be sent for delivery based on the configuration options specified under the **General** tab. If you need to secure this further you can specify that the ATRN command can only be executed by clients that connect and authenticate under specific accounts.

Figure 7.28 Advanced Tab

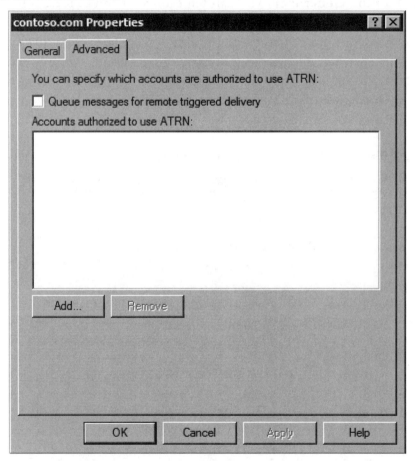

Configuring a Virtual Server

The default configuration for an SMTP virtual server requires little adjustment for most environments. Even so you should be aware of the various settings available (see Figure 7.29). In this section we will review each group of settings.

Figure 7.29 Virtual Server Properties Dialog

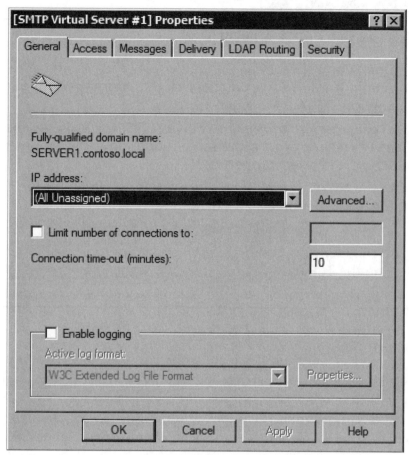

Server Bindings

By default the SMTP virtual server will look to bind to all IP addresses on the server using TCP port 25. There are scenarios where you might want to change this behavior to bind only to a specific network on a multi-homed server, or offer an alternative port for clients who are on a network that blocks port 25. If you are requiring users to use SSL/TLS (discussed later in this chapter) you will want to use port 465. In 1998 the Internet Engineering Task Force (IETF) published RFC 2476, which attempted to shift mail submission from port 25 to 587 for authenticated mail submission. In 2004 several major mail service providers echoed this push as part of the Anti-Spam Technical Alliance Technology and Policy Proposal (see www.microsoft.com/downloads/details.aspx?FamilyId=EF4A02D4-12AB-46A3-A4EC-9AADBED0ABB8 for a copy of the proposal).

EXERCISE 7.15

ADDING A NEW PORT BINDING

1. Open **Control Panel** and under System and Maintenance | Administration Tools double-click the **Internet Information Services (IIS) 6.0 Manager** shortcut.

2. In the Internet Information Services (IIS) 6.0 Manager management console expand the server node, right-click your virtual server, and select **Properties.**

3. In the **SMTP Virtual Server Properties** dialog under the **General** tab, click the **Advanced** button.

4. In the **Advanced** dialog click the **Add** button.

5. In the **Identification** dialog select the appropriate **IP Address**, provide the **TCP Port** number that you want to bind on, and click **OK** until all of the dialogs are closed.

Logging

Activity logging gives you a detailed picture of what your SMTP server is doing. For each request made to the server the log records particular properties of both the request and response for later analysis. Using log analysis tools you can review aggregate statistics to determine the number of messages passing through your server, where they are going, and when they are doing it (see Figure 7.30). You can also use activity logs as a tool in troubleshooting. IIS ships with logging disabled by default. You can enable logging by simply checking the **Enable Logging** checkbox in the **General** tab of the **Virtual Server Properties** dialog. The logs are written to the WINDOWS\SYSTEM32\LogFiles folder by default. The logs can be written using IIS, NCSA, and W3C formats. Alternatively you can log directly to any ODBC–compliant database.

Figure 7.30 W3C Extended Logging Options

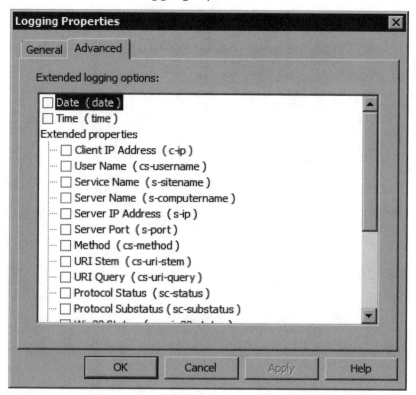

Message Limits

The message limits for a virtual server allow you to set various limits on incoming messages. This prevents people from overloading the server or downstream mail servers. If a message cannot be received or routed for any specific reason it will result in a non-delivery report being generated. You can specify to store a copy of the message in a local folder and send a copy of the non-delivery report to another address as well for troubleshooting purposes. The most common scenario for which you will visit this dialog is to adjust message size limits, as in Figure 7.31.

Figure 7.31 Messages Tab

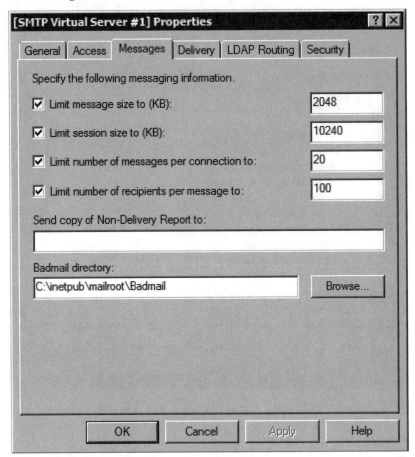

EXERCISE 7.16

INCREASING THE MESSAGE SIZE LIMIT

1. Open **Control Panel** and under System and Maintenance | Administration Tools double-click the **Internet Information Services (IIS) 6.0 Manager** shortcut.

2. In the Internet Information Services (IIS) 6.0 Manager management console expand the server node, right-click your virtual server, and select **Properties.**

3. In the **SMTP Virtual Server Properties** dialog select the **Messages** tab.

4. Set the value of **Limit Message Size** to the largest size of a message that you want to support and click **OK**.

Delivery Options

Once a message has been accepted the server needs to deliver the message. The SMTP protocol uses a store-and-forward approach to delivery, meaning that it does not require all mail servers to be online. The **Delivery** tab in the virtual server settings (see Figure 7.32) exposes the configuration options that control how long the server will wait to retry the delivery of a message. In most cases the default values are sufficient.

Figure 7.32 Delivery Tab

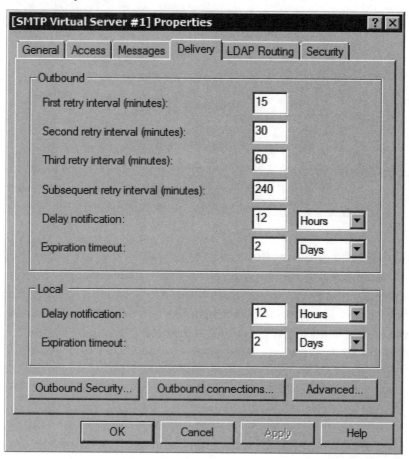

In the **Outbound Security** section you can specify the method and credentials used for delivery of messages, as shown in Figure 7.33. When set at the server level the selected method is used for delivery of all outbound messages.

Figure 7.33 Outbound Security Dialog

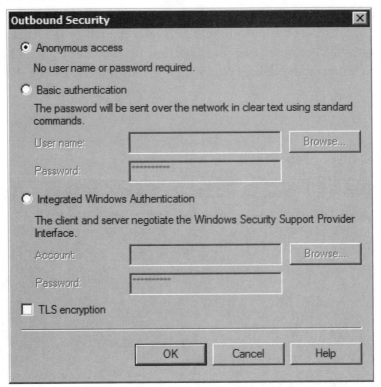

In the **Outbound Connections** section you can configure several options to throttle the number of concurrent outbound connections at the server and domain level, as shown in Figure 7.34. The TCP port can be changed for all outbound delivers. Unless you have a specific reason to change this port you should leave it at the default value since all Internet SMTP servers receive mail on port 25 by default.

Figure 7.34 Outbound Connections Dialog

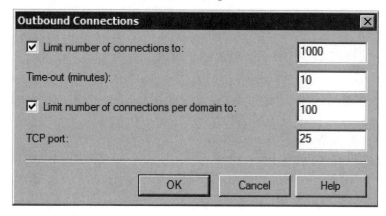

In the **Advanced** Delivery section you are presented with some advanced server behavior options (see Figure 7.35):

- **Maximum Hop Count** Stops messages from passing through this server if they have been through a certain number of servers already. This is useful to stop messages that may be stuck in a continuous loop.

- **Masquerade Domain** Replaces the domain name in the Mail From line with the specified value

- **Fully Qualified Domain Name** Server identifier added to message headers when a message passes through the SMTP gateway

- **Smart Host** Force all outbound messages to be routed to this server

- **Perform Reverse DNS Lookup on Incoming Messages** Will check all incoming messages to ensure that the domain that the server claims to be matches the reverse DNS record of the IP address. If no match can be made then an unverified message is added to the message header.

Figure 7.35 Advanced Delivery Dialog

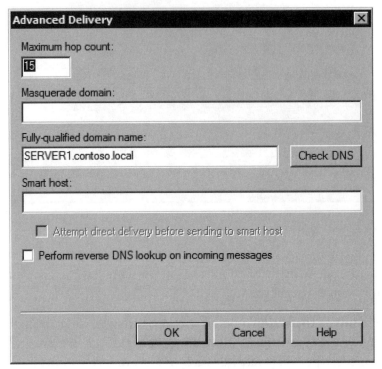

LDAP Routing

You can configure the SMTP Server to resolve recipients using Active Directory, Site Server Membership Directory (version 3.0 and earlier), and the Exchange LDAP Service (version 5.5 and earlier). When a message is received, SMTP will look up the email address in the directory and if it is a group it will send the message to all members in the group. The options in the **LDAP Routing** tab specify the name of the server and account to use for binding (see Figure 7.36). The account will require browse, read, and search permissions within the directory to function properly.

Figure 7.36 LDAP Routing Tab

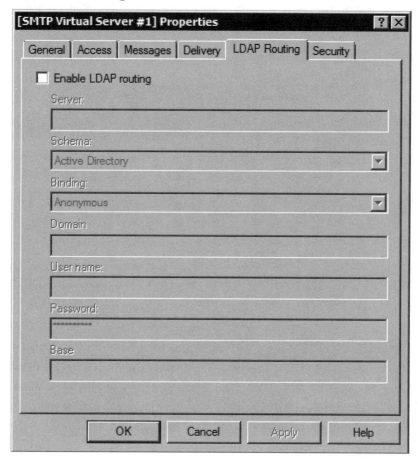

Securing Your SMTP Virtual Server

To secure your SMTP virtual server, you need to understand the Transport Layer Security (TLS) protocol, the three types of authentication that an SMTP Server supports for determining a user's identity, connection control, and relay restrictions. We'll now discuss each of these areas.

Transport Security

SMTP Server supports securing message communication using Transport Layer Security (TLS). The TLS protocol is known as the successor to Secure Socket Layers (SSL). It shares many of the same characteristics as SSL, including how the connection is set up, but it is not compatible. Under this release of the SMTP Server you cannot choose the server certificate that will be used for TLS encryption. The service will automatically look for a certificate that matches the full qualified domain name of the computer. The Access options tab is shown in Figure 7.37.

Figure 7.37 Access Tab

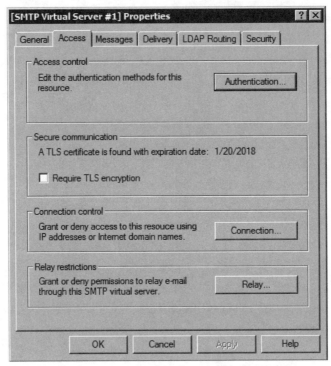

Certificate Creation Changes

If you have used the IIS 6 SMTP Server then you might notice that the Secure Communication section in the Windows Server 2008 release has changed. No longer do you have the ability to create and manage certificates from this interface. Instead that functionality has been moved over to the IIS 7 management tools. Another behavioral change to be aware of is the automatic choice of using a certificate that matches the machine's full qualified domain name.

Authentication

Authentication is the process of asserting the identity of the user or service that is sending a message through your virtual server. The SMTP Server supports three types of authentication to determine a user's identity:

- **Anonymous** Enabled by default to allow any user to send messages to authorized domains without a username and password

- **Basic** Requires the user to provide a username and password. This authentication protocol is standard across all platforms.

  Just as you can require TLS for the incoming communication as a whole, you can require TLS for any connection that tries to authenticate using Basic authentication. Using TLS will protect the otherwise clear text username and password.

- **Integrated Windows Authentication** Used mainly in intranet scenarios, it allows SMTP to use the current user's Windows domain credentials to authenticate the connection.

In public-facing scenarios where you are setting up SMTP Server to be an incoming mail relay, you will select **Anonymous access** authentication, as shown in Figure 7.38. For internal applications or to allow users to relay through the server to any domain, you will need to use either **Basic** or **Integrated Windows Authentication**.

Figure 7.38 Authentication Dialog

Connection Control

Connection Control allows you to limit the devices that can connect to the SMTP Server, as demonstrated in Figure 7.39. This can be useful if you are using the service as a relay for locally installed applications by restricting connections to that of the local host. You can alternatively prevent specific computers from connecting to the server. Connections can be evaluated based on a single IP address, a masked IP range, or a domain name. If you choose domain name the server will perform a reverse DNS lookup on all incoming connections, which may adversely affect performance.

Figure 7.39 Connection Control Dialog

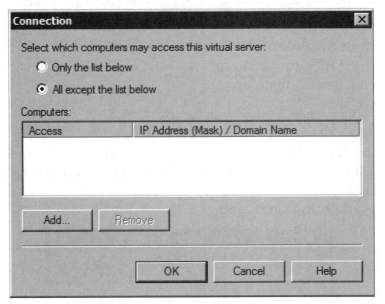

Relay Restrictions

By default the SMTP service will only allow users who authenticate to your server to relay. If you have applications that do not support SMTP authentication and need to relay you can add them to the relay restrictions list to allow them the ability to use the server as a relay (see Figure 7.40). This restriction provides you with another method to control who can relay through your SMTP server.

Figure 7.40 Relay Restrictions Dialog

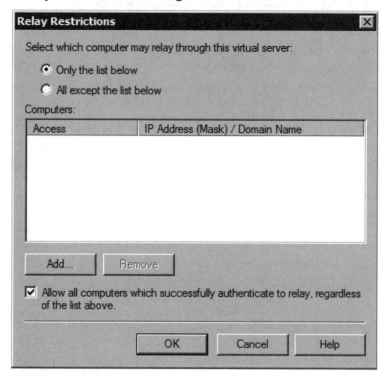

EXERCISE 7.17

ENABLING CLIENTS TO RELAY MAIL

1. Open **Control Panel** and under System and Maintenance | Administration Tools double-click the **Internet Information Services (IIS) 6.0 Manager** shortcut.

2. In the Internet Information Services (IIS) 6.0 Manager management console expand the server node, right-click your virtual server, and select **Properties.**

3. In the **SMTP Virtual Server Properties** dialog select the **Access** tab and click the **Relay** button.

4. In the **Relay Restrictions** dialog click **Add.**

5. In the **Computer** dialog select the **Single Computer** radio button, provide the **IP Address** of the client computer, and click **OK** until all of the dialogs are closed.

Summary of Exam Objectives

This chapter focused on configuration of the File Transfer (FTP) Publishing and Simple Mail Transfer (SMTP) Services. The major investments in this release focused on the FTP support by providing a re-written, integrated FTP service that takes advantage of the advancements brought forth in Internet Information Services. While Windows Server 2008 ships with the older IIS 6 FTP Publishing Service, you should use this new release, as it was the version intended to ship with Windows Server 2008, but missed the cutoff for inclusion. The SMTP Server, on the other hand, remains similar to the older IIS 6 SMTP Server with very little change.

With the FTP Server we discussed the installation of the service. It requires the Web Server role be installed and that the old IIS 6 FTP Publishing Service be removed. After installing the new FTP Publishing Service, you manage it through the wide array of tools provided by the IIS infrastructure, including IIS Manager, AppCmd, and the various programmatic interfaces (Windows Management Instrumentation, Microsoft.Web.Administration Assembly, and so on).

The new FTP Publishing Service supports both full and Server Core installations. When you are ready to create your first FTP site you can create a standalone or bound FTP site. The standalone version works much like a typical FTP site where you point it to a folder that may or may not contain content for users to download and upload. In the bound FTP site the functionality is tied into an existing Web site setup in IIS. This allows you to give users alternative means of managing the content and Web applications on their site. Combined with the IIS Management Service and the new XML-based configuration files this is a complete and powerful set of tools available to users.

When you have configured your FTP site, you will need to consider whether you want the user or your server to be responsible for opening up a port to receive the data connection. If you choose the server to be responsible for establishing a port for the data connection (active mode), then you can establish a pre-defined range for the security administrators to forward from the firewall. If you choose for the user to establish that port then no further configuration is required.

The new FTP Publishing Service shares a number of other concepts with the Web side, including virtual directories and hosting the request processing inside an application pool. Virtual directories allow you to link in content folders from several locations into a single easy-to-navigate tree for users. The application pool gives you added isolation and resiliency in that if your FTP site were to fail, it would not impact other sites within the server. In a standard configuration FTP will send your credentials and content over a clear text connection. Enabling FTP over SSL will give you the option to protect the authentication, control, and/or data conversations occurring. IIS implements an explicit SSL connection per RFC 2228 which means that the client connects over port 21 and explicitly asks the server for a secure conversation. With a secure connection in place you can further apply URL and IP restrictions to prevent groups of users from accessing the site as a whole or a specific section within. If you have users who need to access a personal home directory, user isolation gives you a chance to enforce the user's session to be isolated to that folder.

The SMTP Server enables you to receive mail from local Web applications or remote senders and forward them to other remote servers or keep them local for applications to process. Installation of the SMTP Server requires a full installation and depends on the IIS 6 backwards compatibility components of the Web Server role to function. After installing the SMTP Server it has a default virtual server created, however you can create others. A virtual server is a container for limits, authentication, authorization, and handling settings. It is bound to one or more IP address and port combinations. Each virtual server can be configured with specific instructions for handling mail destined to a particular domain, or with either authorization or being granted rights through the relay restrictions can relay mail to other mail exchangers (MX) in the network. If the SMTP server is being used as a local spool and you have an outbound SMTP gateway already in place through products like Exchange Server, you can configure the virtual server or specific domains to use that gateway as a default next point-of-contact (smart host). Incoming connections can be authenticated using Anonymous, Basic, or Integrated Windows Authentication modules. Likewise outbound connections can use the same three modules on a server or per-domain basis to ensure mail is transmitted in a secure manner. Privacy for mail is handled through TLS encryption. TLS draws upon the SSL family through the use of security certificates.

Exam Objectives Fast Track

Installing and Configuring FTP Publishing Service

- ☑ Windows Server 2008 ships with the older IIS 6 FTP Publishing Service. You should grab the Web release as it was the version that was meant to ship with Windows Server 2008 (but missed the deadline for inclusion by a few weeks).

- ☑ The new FTP Publishing Service is a major rewrite that adds a much tighter integration into the IIS 7 framework and several important security enhancements. It works on both full and Server Core installations.

☑ Sites can be either standalone or bound to a Web site to provide greater options for users who need to manage their Web site or Web application content.

☑ From a transport security perspective the support of Explicit SSL connections allows you to protect the control, authentication, and/or data conversations between the client and the server.

☑ The rules around security (SSL) certificates follow the same rules as the Web sites in terms of the types of certificates and how they are validated.

☑ Out-of-the-box authentication modules include anonymous and basic authentication. Building on the IIS Framework allows you to open that up to a number of custom authentication modules.

☑ The built-in authorization mechanisms include a URL and IP restriction based on a set of rules. Within the URL side you assign allow/deny access to one or more users (including user groups/roles). Alternatively you can control which devices can connect to the site through IP restrictions.

☑ Once into the site you can apply a set of user isolation policies to restrict users to their personal home directory, or you can let them navigate the structure you have created using a set of physical and virtual folders.

Installing and Configuring SMTP Services

☑ Windows Server 2008 ships with the older IIS 6 SMTP Server with a few minor compatibility fixes. It depends on the Web Server role for IIS 6 backwards compatibility components. It can only be installed on a full server installation.

☑ Virtual servers are bound to combination IP address and port to represent the container for authentication, limits, and domain handling instructions.

☑ Within the virtual server you can specify handling instructions for a domain including allowing the server to accept anonymous relays, the method of delivery (lookup via DNS or to a smart host), the outbound authentication method, and whether to queue the messages until triggered.

☑ Inbound and outbound communication can be protected using TLS, which is related to the SSL family of communication encryption protocols.

Exam Objectives
Frequently Asked Questions

Q: I need to set up an FTP site so our business partner can send us purchase orders. Where should I create their account so they can authenticate into the FTP site?

A: The new FTP Publishing Service supports basic authentication out-of-the-box, which looks to the IIS Users data store, local Windows security account manager, and, if a domain member, to Active Directory for authentication credentials. Using the IIS framework you can also implement a custom authentication module if needed.

Q: A user is trying to access the server using FTPS; however, they are being told that the certificate name does not match the host name. Where should I look?

A: The same rules for SSL on the Web apply to FTP—the certificate is bound to the IP address and port that the FTP site runs on. The certificate should reflect the name of the FTP site, use a wildcard sub-domain, or take advantage of the subjectAltName field to list several host names. If the client cannot match the host name, the user connected to it should show the warning about the certificate. In most clients the user can acknowledge the difference and continue to connect.

Q: We have set up the FTP Publishing Service in a shared hosting scenario. I need to isolate users to their own personal home directory in a way that they are unable to see others. Should I set up individual URL authorization rules to do this?

A: No, take a look at the user isolation feature in the FTP Publishing Service and choose between the three isolation modes to find one that matches your needs.

Q: I have set up an SMTP Server in our DMZ to receive mail from the Internet. I want it to forward to our internal mail server. What should I be doing to get it to forward the mail?

A: In the virtual server, set up a domain routing entry to allow it to receive mail for your domain and set it to forward to the specific IP address of your internal mail server (smart host) rather than look up how to deliver the messages.

Q: Our remote branch office has an unreliable connection. I have an Exchange Server there and I want to queue up the mail to be received by the remote server when it reconnects. What should I configure with SMTP Server to allow it to queue mail on behalf of this server?

A: You should set up your Exchange Server to issue an ATRN command to the SMTP server when it connects. This will cause the SMTP server to attempt to deliver all of the mail destined for that domain that resides in the queue.

Q: I think the SMTP server isn't processing mail it receives from the outside, but I'm not sure. Where can I look to determine that it is not working?

A: The first step is to send a message to the server. This can be done using a Telnet client and the steps outlined in Microsoft Support KB 323350 (http://support. microsoft.com/?id=323350). Once the message has been received you should check the Queue folder to see if you can see your message. The electronic mail (.eml file extension) files can be opened up with a text editor to view the contents of the message. From there you can turn on logging on the virtual server to see the outbound connection attempts to deliver the message. If all else fails use Network Monitor to ensure that SMTP is able to make an outbound connection.

Self Test

1. You have been asked to set up a secure FTP connection to receive confidential data from a business partner using FTP and SSL. After installing IIS with the FTP Publishing Service, you cannot find how to enable secure communications on the FTP site in IIS 6 Manager. What should you do?

    A. Obtain a new SSL certificate and add it using IIS Manager

    B. Ensure port 21 is not being used by another Web site or ftp site

    C. Install the Web version of the FTP Publishing Service

    D. You can't secure FTP communications

2. You need to set up several FTP sites on a single IP address. Using the FTP Publishing Service support for virtual hosts you have configured ftp.contoso.com, ftp.fabrikam.com, and ftp.woodgrove.com. When users attempt to log in, their account is not being recognized. How should you approach the problem?

    A. Reset the user's password

    B. Ask the users to try a different FTP client

    C. Ask the users to use the hostname|username format to ensure that they are connecting to the appropriate host

    D. Restart the application pool hosting each of the virtual hosts

3. You received a support call from a user trying to upload a file to the site. They are able to connect, authenticate using their network account, and browse the folder structure, but unable to upload a file. Where should you look?

    A. Ensure the FTP authorization rule includes Write permissions

    B. Ensure the anonymous module is disabled

    C. Change the port number the site is bound on

    D. Ensure that the passive data connection ports are accessible from the user's computer

4. You have recently set up an FTP site with a virtual directory that links to a network share where video journalists can upload their video. The authorization rules have been configured to allow only write access to this folder. When you logged in to the FTP site and attempted to change to the folder the server said that it was unable to change to the folder. How should you resolve the problem?

A. Remove and re-create the authorization rule

B. Write a batch file to copy the content to the network share on a regular basis

C. Configure the virtual directory to use a set of credentials to connect to the remote share

D. Turn on FTP Site logging and review the logs

5. An ISP has contacted you for guidance on enabling their Web hosting clients' access to their content using FTP. After reviewing their plans you have determined that they want an easy-to-maintain solution that minimizes the maintenance involved with maintaining the FTP access. What solution should you recommend?

A. Set up the FTP Site to use a User Name Directory

B. Set up User Isolation using Virtual Directories that link to the Web site

C. Bind the FTP Site to the Web Site in IIS Manager

D. Create a standalone FTP Site for each client that points to the location of the Web content

6. After setting up your new FTP site you need to enable FTP access to the server. The computer runs Windows Firewall and you are using the Passive FTP mode. What ports should you open up?

A. 21/tcp and 1024-65535/tcp

B. 21/udp and 1024-65535/tcp

C. 21/tcp and the range specified in the Firewall Settings module

D. Add a Program Exception for SvcHost.exe using FtpSvc as the service identified

7. Users accessing your FTP site have reported that they cannot see the virtual directory that you recently created. You can see that the virtual directory does exist and is set to the proper path through IIS Manager. What should you do to enable users to see the virtual directory?

A. Disable the Anonymous Authentication Module

B. Enable UNIX Directory Listing Style in the Directory Browsing module

C. Enable Virtual Directories in the Directory Browsing module

D. Change the incoming connections to require SSL

8. The new FTP Publishing Service introduces the ability to use SSL to protect the privacy of the connection. Where can SSL not be applied on an FTP session?

   A. SSL on the Control Channel

   B. SSL on the Control Channel during Authentication

   C. SSL on the Data Channel

   D. SSL on the Data Channel during Authentication

9. After a recent security audit you have been asked to disable anonymous authentication on your FTP site. What is the most secure option available using the authentication modules that are shipped with the FTP Publishing Service?

   A. Basic

   B. Windows

   C. Digest

   D. Client Certificate

10. You have installed SMTP Server to receive mail from outside users as well as let remote users authenticate and relay through. A user calls you telling you that their ISP has blocked port 25 and recommends using port 465 instead. What should you do to enable the user to connect?

   A. Create a new virtual server bound to port 465

   B. Add a port binding to the existing virtual server

   C. Add the user's IP address to the relay restrictions allow list

   D. Ask the user to use another SMTP Server

Self Test Quick Answer Key

1.	**C**	6.	**D**
2.	**C**	7.	**C**
3.	**A**	8.	**D**
4.	**C**	9.	**A**
5.	**C**	10.	**B**

Chapter 8

MCTS/MCITP
Exam 649

Deploying the Terminal Services

Exam objectives in this chapter:

- Deploying the Terminal Server Role Service
- Terminal Services Licensing
- Establishing Client Connections to a Terminal Server

Exam objectives review:

- ☑ Summary of Exam Objectives
- ☑ Exam Objectives Fast Track
- ☑ Exam Objectives Frequently Asked Questions
- ☑ Self Test
- ☑ Self Test Quick Answer Key

Introduction

Maintaining the applications that are running on each desktop can be a huge burden for administrators. As such, many organizations choose to run applications on terminal servers rather than installing them locally on each workstation. The advantage to doing so is that the application runs on the server, and only video images are sent to the workstations. This makes it much easier for an administrator to maintain the applications. The terminal services are good for security as well, because applications are much more resistant to user tampering since they do not actually reside on the user's workstations.

In this chapter, you will learn how to install the Terminal Server Role Service. One of the requirements associated with using the Terminal Services is that terminal servers must be licensed, and client access licenses are also required. Windows Server 2008 can be configured to act as a Terminal Service Licensing Server, and this chapter will show you how to do it. Finally, you will learn how to establish a client connection to a terminal server.

Head of the Class...

Where It All Began

The original components of terminal services were created by a company called Citrix Systems, Inc. Headed by a former IBM executive, Citrix became the only company ever to license the Windows NT source code from Microsoft for resale as a separate product. Their popular Windows NT 3.51-derived product was known as WinFrame. Prior to the release of a Windows NT 4.0 related version, Citrix and Microsoft struck a deal in which Microsoft licensed their MultiWin component.

This component lies at the heart of terminal services and enables multiple users to log on locally, as if they were sitting down at the actual server itself. It creates individual sessions for each user and keeps all of their session and application settings separate. The protocol Citrix created to access terminal services was not licensed by Microsoft. It supports a wide range of terminal services clients, load balancing, and application access methods that traditionally have not been supported by Microsoft's remote desktop protocol (RDP). However, with Windows Server 2008 Microsoft is catching up. For the first time, enterprise-level deployments of terminal services are considering going with Microsoft alone and not licensing the additional Citrix services.

Deploying the Terminal Server Role Service

The core component in the Terminal Services (TS) role is the Terminal Server role service. This is the actual component that clients connect to when establishing a TS session. In this section, we'll examine how to install the Terminal Services role and the Terminal Server role service. One key setting, the licensing mode, can be set during or after installation. We'll look at how to configure this component both during installation and after it.

TEST DAY TIP

Although not mentioned specifically in Microsoft's exam outline, be sure you are familiar with the basics of the Terminal Server role service and its requirements. This is a critical component of terminal services, and it can be used for remote administration in addition to application serving.

EXERCISE 8.1

INSTALLING THE TERMINAL SERVER ROLE SERVICE

To install the Terminal Services role and the Terminal Server role service, follow these steps:

1. Open Server Manager by clicking **Start | Server Manager**.

2. In the right pane, scroll down to the **Roles Summary** section and click **Add Roles**.

3. If the Before You Begin page of the Add Roles Wizard appears, click **Next**. If this screen does not appear, proceed to the next step.

4. On the Select Server Roles wizard page, select **Terminal Services** and click **Next**, as shown in Figure 8.1.

Figure 8.1 Selecting the Terminal Services Role

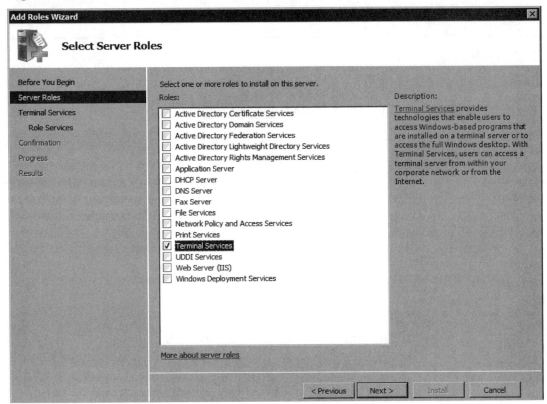

5. Read the introductory information on the Terminal Services wizard page, and click **Next**.

6. On the Select Role Services wizard page, select the components of Terminal Services you wish to install. Some may require additional roles. For example, if you select the **TS Web Access** component, you will be prompted to also install **Web Server (IIS)** and **Windows System Resource Manager (WSRM)**. In the **Role Services** box we will only select **Terminal Server** and click **Next**, as seen in Figure 8.2.

Figure 8.2 Selecting the Terminal Server Role Service

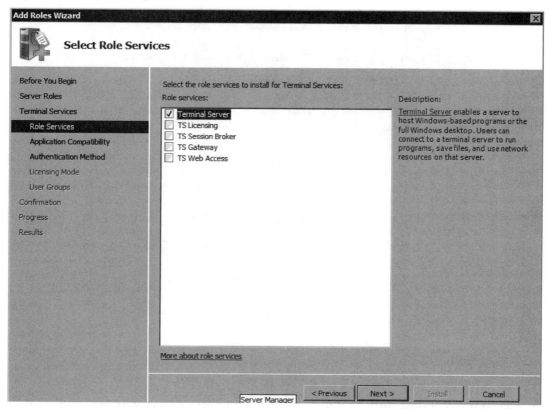

7. For security reasons, installing Terminal Services on a domain controller is not recommended. If you attempt it, a warning dialog will be displayed (see Figure 8.3). To proceed, select **Install Terminal Server anyway (not recommended)**. If you are not installing Terminal Server on a domain controller, skip to the next step.

Figure 8.3 The Terminal Server with Active Directory Warning Dialog

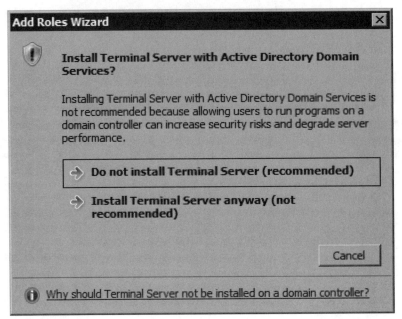

EXAM WARNING

When users establish a terminal services connection to a server, they are actually working remotely at that server just as if they were sitting down at it locally. Just as you would not want users to wander into the server room and physically sit down at domain controllers or other critical servers, you also don't want them to be able to establish terminal services connections to them. To minimize these security concerns, terminal servers are typically computers that are designed and configured only to host the Terminal Server role service.

8. Read the Uninstall and Reinstall Applications for Compatibility wizard screen, and click **Next**.

9. On the Specify Authentication Method for Terminal Server page, select either (see Figure 8.4):

- **Require Network Level Authentication**. Network Level Authentication (NLA) is a new, stronger form of authentication in Windows Server 2008 Terminal Services. In order to use it, users must connect from version 6 or higher of the Remote Desktop Connection (RDC) utility and be using a client operating system which supports the Credential Security Support Provider (CredSSP) protocol, such as Windows Vista or XP SP2. If your clients and connection application support this level of authentication, Microsoft recommends using it.

- **Do not require Network Level Authentication** If you have client computers and versions of RDC less than 6, or which cannot support CredSSP, select this option to allow users to connect to the Terminal Server.

Figure 8.4 Specifying the Terminal Server Authentication Method

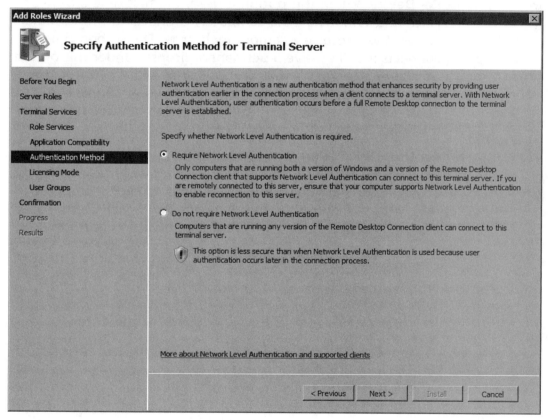

10. Click **Next**.

11. On the Specify Licensing Mode wizard page, select the appropriate option (see Figure 8.5):

- **Configure later** This option allows you to defer your licensing decision. Microsoft provides a 120-day grace period where temporary licensing can be used. The grace period begins the first time a client connects to the Terminal Server role service. After 120 days, if licensing is not configured, users will not be able to connect to the Terminal Server. If you select this option, each time you log on to the terminal server a message will appear in the lower right corner reminding you to configure the appropriate licensing mode.

  Note: Microsoft allows two administrators to simultaneously connect without requiring Terminal Services access licenses.

- **Per Device** When this option is used, the first time a device (such as a Windows Vista computer) connects to the Terminal Server it will receive a temporary license. The second time it connects it will receive a permanent license. Under this option, a fixed number of licenses are available, and if no more are available the computer will not be allowed to connect to Terminal Services. See the licensing section in this chapter for information on how to install and configure licensing.

- **Per User** This option assigns licenses to users rather than devices. This type of license provides a user with the right to access a terminal server from any number of client computers or devices. A major difference between Per Device Client Access Licenses (CALs) and Per User CALs is in how they are tracked. Per User CALs are not enforced by the terminal services licensing component, and as a result no user will be rejected because of license unavailability. Under this licensing scheme, the burden is on administrators to ensure they have purchased enough Per User CALs to meet Microsoft's licensing requirements.

Figure 8.5 Specifying the Terminal Services Licensing Mode

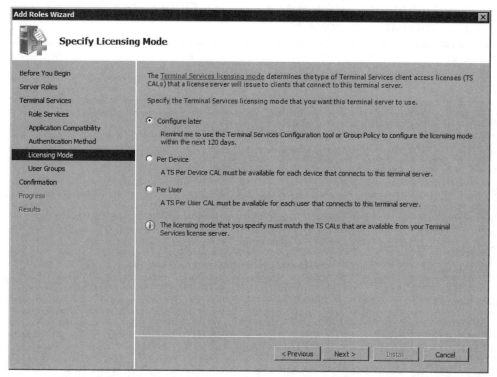

12. Click **Next**.

13. The Select User Groups Allowed Access To This Terminal Server wizard page is used to configure initial access to the Terminal Server. By default, only members of the **Administrators** group are allowed access. To add additional groups, click **Add** and enter or search for them in the standard **Select Users, Computers, or Groups** dialog that appears, then click **OK**.

14. Click **Next**.

15. Read over any warnings as well as the summary information provided on the Confirm Installation Selections wizard page. Click **Install** to begin the next phase of the installation.

16. The Installation Progress screen will provide information about the installation as it progresses. When it completes, you'll be asked to restart the computer. Click **Close**, and **Yes** to restart.

17. When the system restarts, log on.

18. The Resuming Configuration Wizard will open. It will progress through the Resuming Configuration and Installation Progress

pages and finish on the Installation Results page. Review the information on this page and click **Close** to complete the installation process.

Configuring & Implementing...

Proper Terminal Server Planning

The Terminal Server role service can use up considerable resources. When a user establishes a terminal server session, it's very similar to a workstation being created on the terminal server for them to use. Imagine what happens when a server has 20 or more of these workstations all running on it at the same time. If the server hardware and configuration is not adequately sized to the number of users, performance can degrade rapidly. The number one mistake made when installing terminal servers is failure to accurately estimate the amount of resources that will be needed to adequately serve users.

Another important consideration is security. Typically, users connect to servers as remote users. However, when users log on to a terminal server, they log on as a local user. There are substantial differences in user rights between local and remote users that administrators can easily overlook when configuring terminal services. Locking down the security on a terminal server is more art than science, and you should do everything possible to learn the best practices that are available from Microsoft regarding it.

Specifying the License Mode after Installation

If **Configure later** was selected on the Specify Licensing Mode wizard page during the installation of the Terminal Server role service, you must specify a license mode before the 120 day grace period expires. The following procedure shows how to specify a terminal server licensing mode:

1. Open the Terminal Services Configuration utility by clicking **Start | Administrative Tools | Terminal Services | Terminal Services Configuration**.

2. If Terminal Services Configuration is not pointing to the correct terminal server, follow steps 3–5. If it is, skip to step 6.

3. Connect to the correct server by selecting **Action | Connect to Terminal Server**.

4. In the **Select Computer** dialog box, choose one of the following:

   ■ Select the **Local computer** option if running Terminal Services Configuration on the terminal server you want to configure.

   ■ Select **Another computer** and click **Browse** if you are not running Terminal Services Configuration on the terminal server you want to configure. In the **Select Computer** dialog that appears, type the name of the server in the **Enter the object name to select (examples):** text area, click **Check Names**, verify the server name, and click **OK**.

5. Click **OK**.

6. In the center pane, right click **Terminal Services licensing mode** and click **Properties**. See Figure 8.6.

Figure 8.6 Opening Terminal Services Licensing Mode Properties

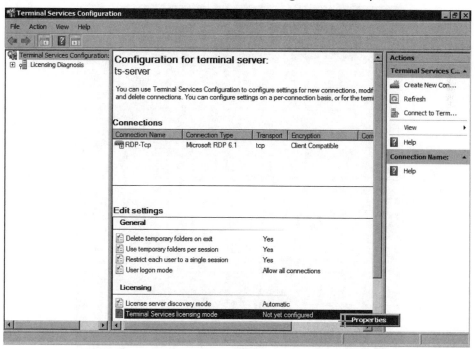

7. In the **Properties** dialog box, select either (see Figure 8.7):

   ■ **Per Device** When this option is used, the first time a device (such as a Windows Vista computer) connects to the Terminal Server it will receive a temporary license. The second time it connects it will receive a permanent license. Under this option, a fixed number of licenses are available, and if no more are available the computer will not be allowed to connect to Terminal Services. See the licensing section in this chapter for information on how to install and configure licensing.

- **Per User** This option assigns licenses to users rather than devices. This type of license provides a user with the right to access a terminal server from any number of client computers or devices. A major difference between Per Device CALs and Per User CALs is in how they are tracked. Per User CALs are not enforced by the terminal services licensing component, and as a result no user will be rejected because of license unavailability. Under this licensing scheme, the burden is on administrators to ensure they have purchased enough Per User CALs to meet Microsoft's licensing requirements.

Figure 8.7 The Properties Dialog

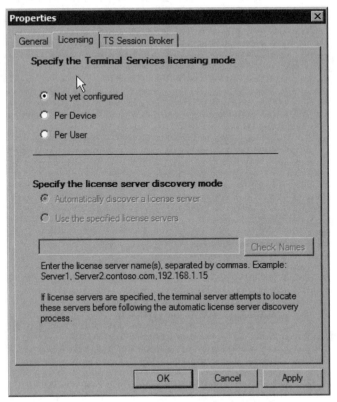

8. Click **OK** and close Terminal Services Configuration.

Terminal Services Licensing

To use terminal services beyond the 120 day grace period, at least one licensing server must be installed. Licensing servers handle the management and issuance of TS CALs. Typically, each user or device requires a CAL, as mentioned in step 11 under Installing the Terminal Services Role. When a client connects to a terminal server, the server determines if a TS CAL is needed. If one is required the terminal server requests it from a TS Licensing role service server, which issues the license to the client.

Small deployments may use a single license server, and may even combine the Terminal Server role service and the TS Licensing role service on the same server. The load exerted on terminal servers can be substantial, so these two role services are generally put on separate servers for mid to large size deployments. In addition to the required number of TS CALs, you must also have at least one server license. Environments might also run mixed versions of terminal services. If an environment runs Windows Server 2000, 2003, and/or 2008 terminal servers, it is best to move all license management to the Windows Server 2008 TS Licensing role service. This centralizes and simplifies management. Earlier versions of the terminal server licensing components are not compatible with Windows Server 2008 Terminal Services; however, Windows Server 2008's TS Licensing role service is backward compatible.

Installing a Terminal Service Licensing Server

There are three primary installation methods for the TS Licensing role service.

- If you are installing the Terminal Server and TS Licensing role services on the same server, you can install them at the same time.

- You can install the TS Licensing role service on an existing Terminal Server.

- You can install the TS Licensing role service on a separate server.

Microsoft will most likely test you on the separate installation steps, so we cover both ways of accomplishing this below. First we will install the TS Licensing role service on a server that the Terminal Server role service is already installed on. Next, we will install the role service on a separate server.

Installing the TS Licensing Role Service on an Existing Terminal Server

Follow the steps below to install the TS Licensing role service:

1. Open Server Manager by clicking **Start | Server Manager**.

2. Navigate to the **Terminal Services** role by either:

   ■ Scrolling down in the right pane to the Roles Summary section and clicking **Terminal Services**;

   ■ In the left pane, expanding the Roles node and clicking **Terminal Services**.

3. In the right pane, click **Add Role Services**.

4. The Add Role Services wizard appears. On the Select Role Services page, select **TS Licensing** and click **Next**. See Figure 8.8.

Figure 8.8 Selecting the TS Licensing Role Service

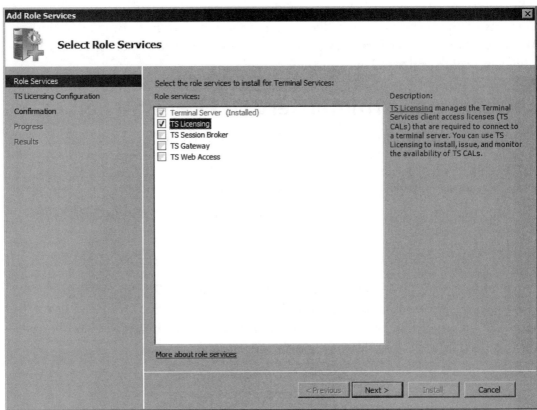

5. On the Configure Discovery Scope for TS Licensing wizard page, select the appropriate licensing option (see Figure 8.9):

-   **This workgroup** If the server you are installing the TS Licensing role service on is not a domain member, this option will be enabled. When used, terminal servers in the same workgroup can locate the license server without any additional configuration.

-   **This domain** This is the default setting for TS Licensing role service servers that are domain members. If the server is also a domain controller, terminal servers that are members of the same domain can locate the license server without any additional configuration. If the server is not a domain controller, the server must be published in Active Directory (AD) for terminal servers in its domain to locate it. See the *Publishing a TS Licensing Server* section in this chapter for more information. To select this option, you must be logged on as a domain administrator from the domain in which the server is a member.

-   **The forest** This is the recommended setting for TS Licensing role service servers that are domain members. When used, terminal servers that are members of any domain in the forest can locate the license server without any additional configuration. To select this option, you must be logged on as an enterprise administrator from the forest in which the server is a member.

Figure 8.9 Configuring the Discovery Scope for TS Licensing

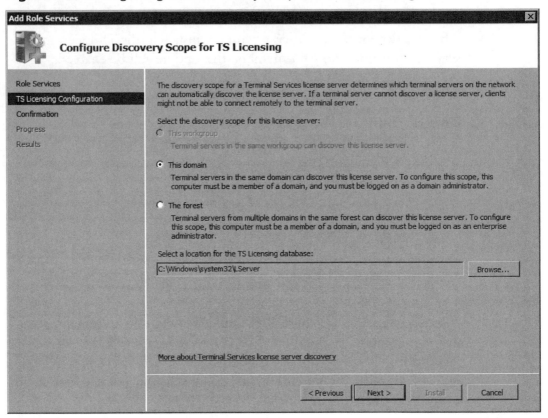

6. Select a new location for the TS Licensing database by clicking **Browse ...** or accept the default path, then click **Next**. The database location must be a local folder on the server on which TS Licensing is being installed.

7. On the Confirm Installation Selections wizard page, review the information you provided and click **Install**.

8. The Installation Progress screen will provide information about the installation as it progresses.

9. Review the information presented on the Installation Results wizard page, then click **Close.**

Installing the TS Licensing Role Service on a Separate Server

Follow the steps below to install the TS Licensing role service:

1. Open Server Manager by clicking **Start | Server Manager**.

2. In the right pane, scroll down to the Roles Summary section and click **Add Roles**.

3. If the Before You Begin page of the Add Roles Wizard appears, click **Next**. If this screen does not appear, proceed to the next step.

4. On the Select Server Roles wizard page, select **Terminal Services** and click **Next**.

5. Read the introductory information on the Terminal Services wizard page, and click **Next**.

6. On the Select Role Services wizard page, select **TS Licensing** and click **Next**.

7. On the Configure Discovery Scope for TS Licensing wizard page, select the appropriate licensing option (see Figure 8.9):

   - **This workgroup** If the server you are installing the TS Licensing role service on is not a domain member, this option will be enabled. When used, terminal servers in the same workgroup can locate the license server without any additional configuration.

   - **This domain** This is the default setting for TS Licensing role service servers that are domain members. If the server is also a domain controller, terminal servers that are members of the same domain can locate the license server without any additional configuration. If the server is not a domain controller, the server must be published in AD for terminal servers in its domain to locate it. See the *Publishing a TS Licensing Server* section in this chapter for more information. To select this option, you must be logged on as a domain administrator from the domain in which the server is a member.

   - **The forest** This is the recommended setting for TS Licensing role service servers that are domain members. When used, terminal servers that are members of any domain in the forest can locate the license server without any additional configuration. To select this option, you must be logged on as an enterprise administrator from the forest in which the server is a member.

TEST DAY TIP

Microsoft often uses default settings that are different than their recommended settings. The settings **This domain** and **This forest** are good examples. It's important for you to know not only what Microsoft recommends, but also what the default settings are when they differ.

8. Select a new location for the TS Licensing database by clicking **Browse...** or accept the default path, and click **Next**. The database location must be a local folder on the server on which TS Licensing is being installed.

9. On the Confirm Installation Selections wizard page, review the information you provided and click **Install**.

10. The Installation Progress screen will provide information about the installation as it progresses.

11. Review the information presented on the Installation Results wizard page, then click **Close.**

Activating a Terminal Service Licensing Server

After installing the TS Licensing role service, it must be activated. Microsoft provides a grace period of 90 days during which the license server can issue temporary TS CALs, but you should activate the server as soon as possible after installation. There are three methods of activation using the TS Licensing Manager utility:

- **Automatic connection (recommended)** This method uses TS Licensing Manager to connect directly to the Microsoft Clearinghouse using TCP port 443. The connection occurs from the computer running TS Licensing Manager, which can be a workstation or server. Microsoft also refers to this method as *Internet (automatic)*.

- **Web Browser** If the computer running TS Licensing Manager cannot access the Microsoft Clearinghouse via the Internet, you can complete the process through a standard Web browser from another computer.

- **Telephone** If you cannot use either of the previous methods, the process can also be completed by phone.

Let's examine how to use each method.

Activating a Terminal Service Licensing Server Using the Automatic Connection Method

Follow these steps to use the Automatic connection (recommended) installation method:

1. Open the TS Licensing Manager utility by clicking **Start | Administrative Tools | Terminal Services | TS Licensing Manager**.

2. When the utility opens, it will bring up the Finding Licensing Servers window, and search for all servers running the TS Licensing role service that it can find.

3. In the right pane, right click on the server you want to activate and select **Activate Server** from the context menu. See Figure 8.10.

Figure 8.10 The Activate Server Menu Option

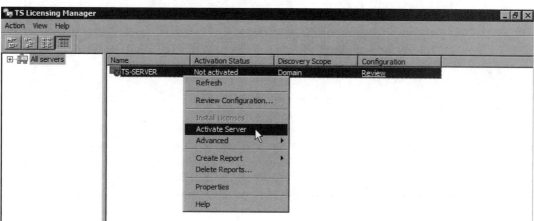

4. Read the Welcome to the Activate Server Wizard page of the Activate Server Wizard, and click **Next**.

5. On the Connection Method wizard page select **Automatic connection (recommended)** in the drop-down box, read the information presented, and click **Next**. See Figure 8.11.

Figure 8.11 The Connection Method Page

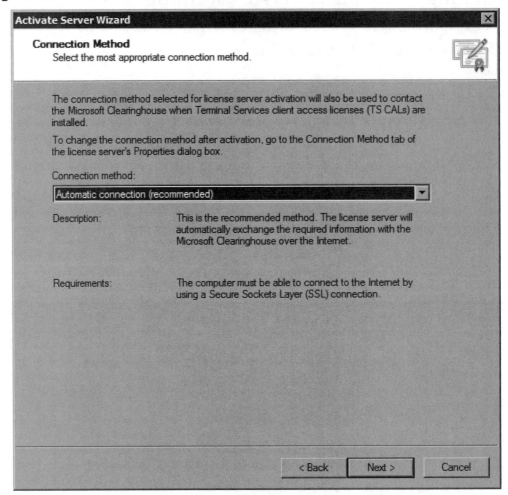

6. A brief dialog window appears while the wizard connects to the Internet and locates the Microsoft Clearinghouse.

7. On the Company Information wizard page, enter your: **First Name**, **Last Name**, **Company**, and **Region or Country**. See Figure 8.12.

Figure 8.12 The Required Company Information Dialog

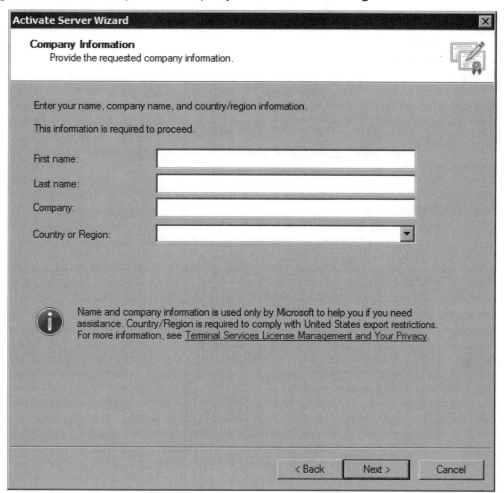

8. Click **Next**.

9. A second Company Information wizard page appears. The information asked for by this page is optional. The fields provided are: **E-mail**, **Organizational unit**, **Company address**, **City**, **State/province**, and **Postal code**. Once you have filled in the desired fields, click **Next**. See Figure 8.13.

Figure 8.13 The Optional Company Information Dialog

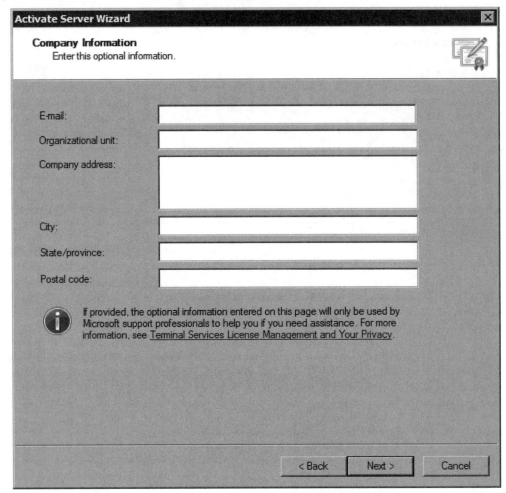

10. A brief **Activating the license server** dialog appears after which your license server is activated.

11. On the Completing the Activate Server Wizard page, do one of the following (see Figure 8.14):

   ■ Select **Start Install Licenses Wizard now** to proceed to installing TS CALs onto your license server. Click **Next** and follow the instructions. Installing TS CALs is covered in the *Managing Terminal Services Client Access Licenses (TS CALs)* section of this chapter.

- Deselect **Start Install Licenses Wizard now**, and click **Finish**. (Note: the button text changes between **Next** and **Finish** based on whether **Start Install Licenses Wizard now** is selected.)

Figure 8.14 The Completing the Activate Server Wizard Page

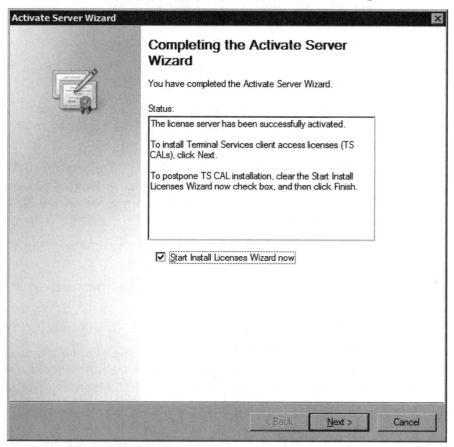

EXERCISE 8.2

INSTALLING AND ACTIVATING TS LICENSING ROLE SERVICE

In this exercise, we will install the TS Licensing role service on the same server that you installed the Terminal Server role service on during Exercise 8.1. You should complete Exercise 8.1 before completing this exercise. We will be using the Automatic connection (recommended) method, so your server will need access to the Internet. Follow the steps below to install and activate the TS Licensing role service:

1. Open Server Manager by clicking **Start | Server Manager**.

2. Navigate to the Terminal Services role by either:

   - Scrolling down in the right pane to the Roles Summary section and clicking **Terminal Services**;

   - In the left pane, expanding the **Roles** node and clicking on **Terminal Services**.

3. In the right pane, click **Add Role Services**.

4. The Add Role Services wizard appears. On the Select Role Services page, select **TS Licensing** and click **Next**.

5. On the Configure Discovery Scope for TS Licensing wizard page, select the appropriate licensing option: **This workgroup, This domain,** or **The forest**.

6. Select a new location for the TS Licensing database by clicking **Browse** or accept the default path, then click **Next**. The database location must be a local folder on the computer on which TS Licensing is being installed.

7. On the Confirm Installation Selections wizard page, review the information you provided and click **Install**.

8. The Installation Progress screen will provide information about the installation as it progresses.

9. Review the information presented on the Installation Results wizard page, then click **Close**.

10. Open the TS Licensing Manager utility by clicking **Start | Administrative Tools | Terminal Services | TS Licensing Manager**.

11. In the right pane, right click on the server you want to activate and select **Activate Server** from the context menu.

12. Read the Welcome to the Activate Server Wizard page of the Activate Server Wizard, and click **Next**.

13. On the Connection Method wizard page select **Automatic connection (recommended)** in the drop-down box, read the information presented, and click **Next**.

14. On the Company Information wizard page, enter your: **First Name, Last Name, Company,** and **Region or Country**.

15. Click **Next**.

16. On the second Company Information wizard page, optionally, enter information in the: **E-mail**, **Organizational unit**, **Company address**, **City**, **State/province**, and **Postal code**. Once you have filled in the desired fields, click **Next**.

17. A brief **Activating the license server** dialog appears after which your license server is activated.

18. On the Completing the Activate Server Wizard page, deselect **Start Install Licenses Wizard now**, and click **Finish**.

Activating a Terminal Service Licensing Server Using the Web Browser Method

The following steps can be used to activate the TS Licensing role service via Web browser:

1. Open the TS Licensing Manager utility by clicking **Start | Administrative Tools | Terminal Services | TS Licensing Manager**.

2. When the utility opens, it will bring up the Finding Licensing Servers window and search for all servers running the TS Licensing role service that it can find.

3. In the right pane, right click on the server you want to activate and select **Activate Server** from the context menu.

4. Read the Welcome to the Activate Server Wizard page of the Activate Server Wizard, and click **Next**.

5. On the Connection Method wizard page select **Web Browser** in the drop down box, read the information presented, and click **Next**.

6. The License Server Activation wizard page appears, which provides the Terminal Server Licensing Web site URL, as well as the Product ID which you will need to enter. Click on the hyperlink to visit the Web site or open a Web browser and type in the URL (https://activate.microsoft.com). See Figure 8.15.

Figure 8.15 The Web Browser-Based License Server Activation Page

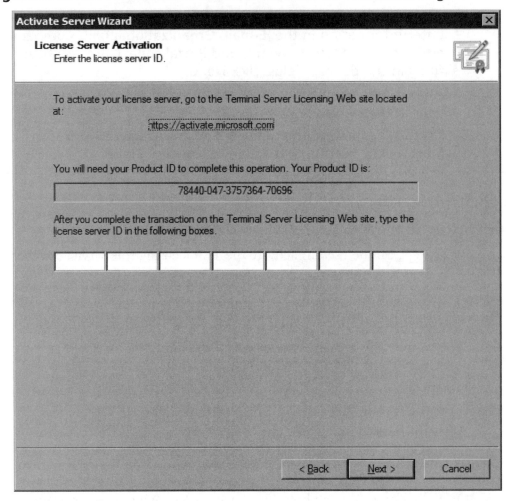

7. On the first page of the Terminal Server Licensing Web site, select **Activate a license server** and click **Next**.

8. Enter your **Product ID** as well as the following required fields: **Last/Surname**, **First/Given Name**, **Company**, and **Country/Region**. You can also choose to fill in several optional fields for your: **Organizational Unit**, **eMail Address**, **Phone Number**, **Company Address**, **City**, **State/Province**, and **Postal Code**.

9. Click **Next**.

10. Review and verify the information you provided, and click **Next**.

11. Write down the license server ID that is displayed and/or print the Web page.

12. Switch back to the License Server Activation page in TS Licensing Manager.

13. Enter the license server ID that you received, and click **Next**.

14. A brief **Activating the license server** dialog appears after which your license server is activated.

15. On the Completing the Activate Server Wizard page, do one of the following:

    ■ Select **Start Install Licenses Wizard now** to proceed to installing TS CALs onto your license server. Click **Next** and follow the instructions. Installing TS CALs is covered in the *Managing Terminal Services Client Access Licenses (TS CALs)* section of this chapter.

    ■ Deselect **Start Install Licenses Wizard now**, and click **Finish**. (Note: the button text changes between **Next** and **Finish** based on whether the **Start Install Licenses Wizard now** is selected.)

Activating a Terminal Service Licensing Server Using the Telephone Method

The following steps can be used to activate the TS Licensing role service via the telephone:

1. Open the TS Licensing Manager utility by clicking **Start | Administrative Tools | Terminal Services | TS Licensing Manager**.

2. When the utility opens, it will bring up the Finding Licensing Servers window, and search for all servers running the TS Licensing role service that it can find.

3. In the right pane, right click on the server you want to activate and select **Activate Server** from the context menu.

4. Read the Welcome to the Activate Server Wizard page of the Activate Server Wizard, and click **Next**.

5. On the Connection Method wizard page select **Telephone** in the drop down box, read the information presented, and click **Next**.

6. The Country or Region Selection wizard page appears. Click on your country or region in the **Country or Region:** selection box and click **Next**. See Figure 8.16.

Figure 8.16 The Telephone-Based License Server Activation Page

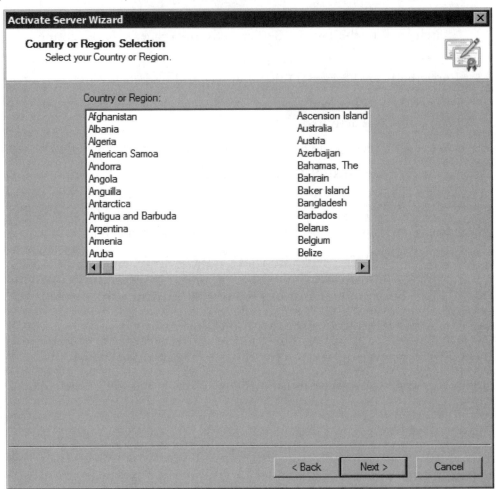

7. The License Server Activation wizard page appears that provides the telephone number to call, as well as the Product ID. See Figure 8.17.

Figure 8.17 The Phone-Based License Server Activation Page

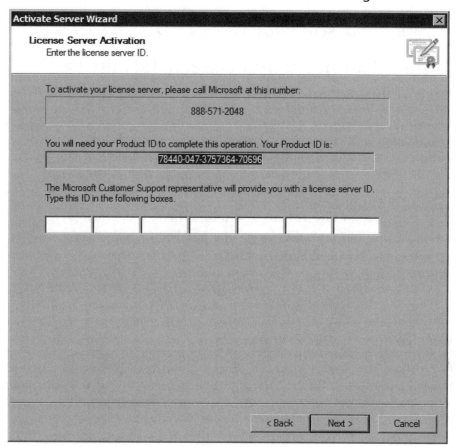

8. Call Microsoft at the number given, and provide all requested information. The Microsoft representative you speak to will process your request and provide your license server ID.

9. Switch back to the License Server Activation wizard page in TS Licensing Manager.

10. Enter the license server ID that you received from Microsoft, and click **Next**.

11. A brief **Activating the license server** dialog appears after which your license server is activated.

12. On the Completing the Activate Server Wizard page, do one of the following:

   ■ Select **Start Install Licenses Wizard now** to proceed to installing TS CALs onto your license server. Click **Next** and follow the instructions. Installing TS CALs is covered in the *Managing Terminal Services Client Access Licenses (TS CALs)* section of this chapter.

- Deselect **Start Install Licenses Wizard now**, and click **Finish**. (Note: the button text changes between **Next** and **Finish** based on whether the **Start Install Licenses Wizard now** is selected.)

Establishing Connectivity between Terminal Server and Terminal Services Licensing Server

As mentioned in the *Installing a Terminal Service Licensing Server* section of this chapter, the way you deploy a TS Licensing server relates directly to how a Terminal Server finds and uses it. There are three discovery scope configurations which can be specified during the installation of the TS Licensing role service: the Workgroup Discovery Scope **(This workgroup)**, the Domain Discovery Scope **(This domain)**, and the Forest Discovery Scope **(The forest)**. You must also decide which server will host the role. The TS Licensing role service can be installed on a domain controller, a server running the Terminal Server role service, or a separate server which is a workgroup or domain member.

TEST DAY TIP

Microsoft often changes the name of key items between releases, and then tests you on it. Be on the lookout for these types of exam tactics. For example, Forest Discovery Scope in Windows Server 2008 TS Licensing was referred to as the *Enterprise Scope* in Windows Server 2003. It's especially important to try to learn new terms as Microsoft adopts them. They expect their certified professionals to be able to accurately represent their products' features in the marketplace.

If the server you are installing the TS Licensing role service on is not a domain member, the **This workgroup** option will be enabled. When used, terminal servers in the same workgroup can locate the license server without any additional configuration. If you later join the server to a domain, the discovery scope will be automatically changed from **This Workgroup** to **This Domain**.

The default setting for a TS Licensing role service server that is a domain member is **This domain**. Although the wizard defaults to this option, Microsoft recommends using Forest Discovery Scope as the setting for all TS Licensing role service servers in a domain-based environment. When **This domain** is used and the server is also a domain controller, terminal servers that are members of the same domain can locate the license server without any additional configuration. If the server is not a domain controller, the server must be published in AD for terminal servers in its domain to locate it. See the *Publishing a TS Licensing Server* section in this chapter for more information. To select this option, you must be logged on as a domain administrator from the domain in which the computer is a member.

As mentioned, **The forest** wizard option is the recommended setting for TS Licensing role service servers that are domain members. When used, terminal servers that are members of any domain in the forest can locate the license server without any additional configuration. To select this option, you must be logged on as an enterprise administrator from the forest in which the server is a member. A terminal server in a Windows Server 2008 domain will attempt to locate and contact a license server in the following order:

1. License servers that are specified in the Terminal Services Configuration tool or by using Group Policy.

2. A license server that is installed on the same computer as the terminal server.

3. License servers that are published in Active Directory Domain Services.

4. License servers that are installed on domain controllers in the same domain as the terminal server.

Exam Warning

Just selecting the Forest Discovery Scope is not enough to enable a TS Licensing server to issue TS Per User CALs to users in multiple domains. To issue CALs to users of another domain, the server must be added to the Terminal Server License Servers group in that domain. It's also not necessary for a server to have its discovery scope set to **The Forest** in order to hand out TS CALs in multiple domains, as long as it is a member of this group in each domain it will service. However, by default only servers in its own domain will be able to automatically discover it.

Using the Terminal Services Configuration Tool to Specify a TS Licensing Server

Instead of using automatic discovery, a terminal server can be forced to use a specific TS Licensing server.

1. Open the Terminal Services Configuration utility by clicking **Start | Administrative Tools | Terminal Services | Terminal Services Configuration**.

2. If Terminal Services Configuration is not pointing to the correct terminal server, follow steps 3–5. If it is, skip to step 6.

3. Connect to the correct server by selecting **Action | Connect to Terminal Server**.

4. In the **Select Computer** dialog box, choose one of the following:

    ■ Select **Local computer** if running Terminal Services Configuration on the terminal server you want to configure.

    ■ Select **Another computer** and click **Browse** if you are not running Terminal Services Configuration on the terminal server you want to configure. In the **Select Computer** dialog which appears, type the name of the server in the **Enter the object name to select (examples):** text area, click **Check Names**, verify the server name, and click **OK**.

5. Click **OK**.

6. In the center pane, right click **License server discovery mode** and click **Properties**. See Figure 8.18.

Figure 8.18 Opening the License Server Discovery Mode Properties

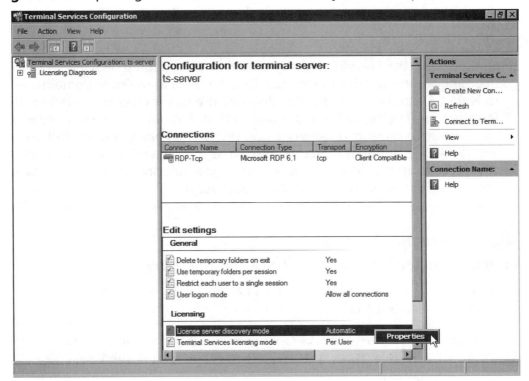

7. In the **Properties** dialog box, select the **Use the specified license servers** option.

8. Click the **Licensing** tab.

9. Enter one or more license servers into provided text box, and click **Check Names**. See Figure 8.19.

Figure 8.19 The Properties Dialog

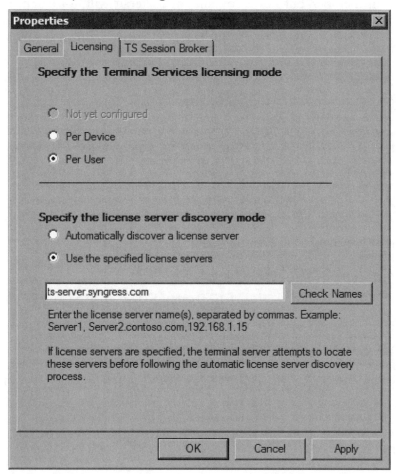

10. A **Terminal Services Configuration** dialog box briefly appears while the names you've entered are being checked.

11. A **Terminal Services Configuration** pop-up box appears that notifies you that the names have been successfully verified. Click **OK**.

12. In the **Properties** dialog, click **OK**.

13. In the center pane, verify that the **License server discovery mode** setting has changed to **As Specified,** and close Terminal Services Configuration.

Publishing a Terminal Services Licensing Server Using TS Licensing Manager

As mentioned previously, when the TS Licensing role service is installed on a server that is a domain member, but not a domain controller, it will not be automatically discovered by terminal servers in its domain. In order to make it discoverable, you must publish the server in AD. You must have membership in the local Administrators group on the license server and membership in the Enterprise Admins group in AD Directory Services (DS), or you must have been delegated the appropriate authority in order to complete the following procedure:

1. Open the TS Licensing Manager utility by clicking **Start | Administrative Tools | Terminal Services | TS Licensing Manager**.

2. In the right pane, right click on the server you want to publish and click on **Review Configuration . . .** .

3. In the **Configuration** dialog box, click on **Publish in AD DS**.

4. Click **Continue**, followed by **OK**.

Publishing a Terminal Server Licensing Server Using ADSI Edit and Active Directory Sites and Services

Sometimes it may be necessary for you to use ADSI Edit and Active Directory Sites and Services to publish a TS Licensing role service server in AD. There may be times when the server does not appear to be published in the TS Licensing Manager, and when it will not provide the **Publish in AD DS** button. To publish it, follow these steps:

1. Open ADSI Edit by clicking **Start | Administrative Tools | ADSI Edit**.

2. Right click on **ADSI Edit** in the left pane, and select **Connect to . . .**.

3. In the **Connection Settings** dialog, select the option **Select a well known Naming Context:** and specify **Configuration** in its drop-down box. Click **OK**.

4. In the left pane, double click on the **Configuration** node.

5. Double click on the node beneath Configuration that represents the domain of which the license server is a member.

6. Expand the **CN=Sites** node, right click the node which represents the site the license server is in, and select **New | Object...** as seen in Figure 8.20.

Figure 8.20 Selecting New Object in ADSI Edit

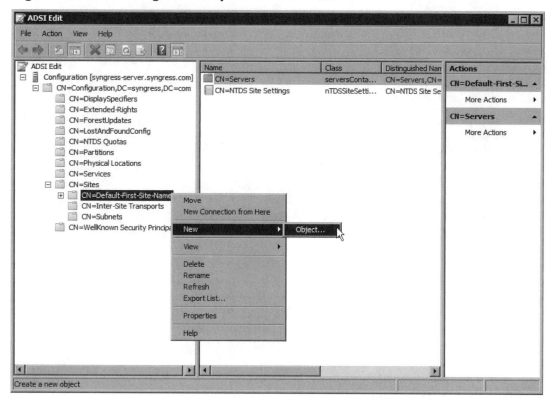

7. In the **Create Object** dialog, under **Select a class:** click **licensingSite-Settings**, followed by **Next**. See Figure 8.21.

Figure 8.21 The Create Object Dialog

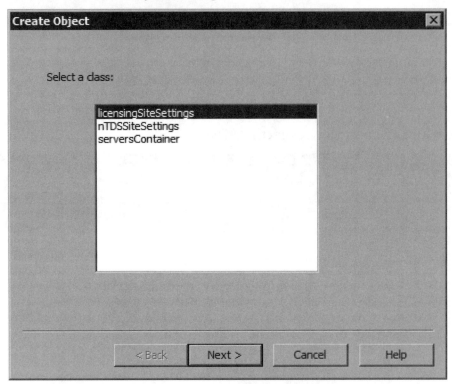

8. In the **Value** text box, enter **TS-Enterprise-License-Server** and click **Next**. See Figure 8.22.

Figure 8.22 The Value Text Box

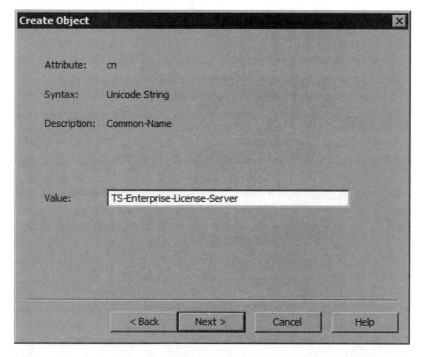

9. Click **Finish** and close ADSI Edit.

10. Open Active Directory Sites and Services by clicking **Start |
    Administrative Tools | Active Directory Sites and Services**.

11. In the left pane, expand the **Sites** node and click on the site containing
    the license server.

12. In the right pane, right click on **TS-Enterprise-License-Server** and
    click **Properties**. See Figure 8.23.

Figure 8.23 The AD Sites and Services Utility

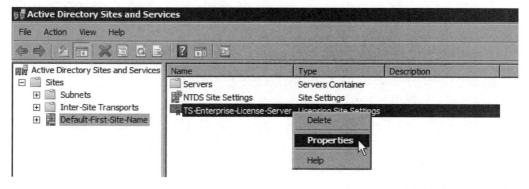

13. In the **Properties** dialog under Licensing Computer click **Change…**. See Figure 8.24.

Figure 8.24 The Properties Dialog

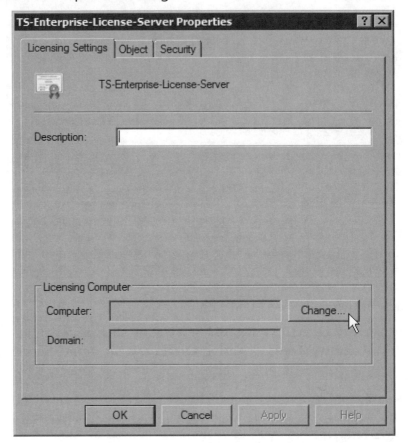

14. In the **Select Computer** dialog, type the server name in the **Enter the object name to select (examples):** text area, and click **Check Names**.

15. Verify the server name and click **OK**.

16. In the **Properties** dialog, verify that the proper server and domain are listed under Licensing Computer, and click **OK**.

17. Close Active Directory Sites and Services.

18. Even after performing the above steps, the TS Licensing utility may still display a warning on the license server's **Configuration** dialog. See Figure 8.25.

Figure 8.25 The Configuration Dialog on TS Licensing

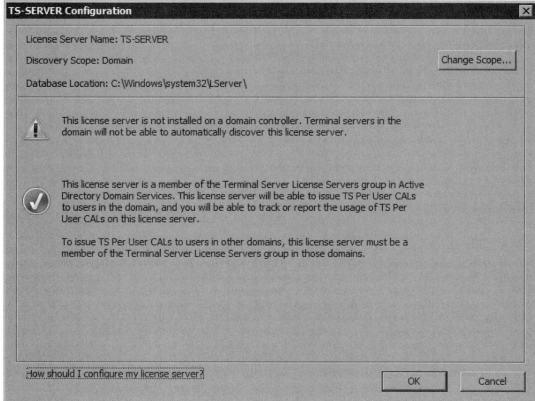

Installing and Managing Terminal Services Client Access Licenses (TS CALs)

Microsoft's Terminal Services licensing is among the most secure in its product line, and this extends all the way down to the TS CAL level. Administrators cannot simply enter a license code and have their CALs working. Just as with the TS Licensing role service itself, TS CALs must be activated. In fact, licenses can only be installed and activated on a TS Licensing server that has been successfully activated. There are three ways to activate TS CAL licenses:

- **Automatic connection (recommended)** This method uses TS Licensing Manager to connect directly to the Microsoft Clearinghouse using TCP port 443. The connection occurs from the computer running TS Licensing Manager, which can be a workstation or server. Microsoft also refers to this method as *Internet (automatic)*.

- ■ **Web Browser** If the computer running TS Licensing Manager cannot access the Microsoft Clearinghouse via the Internet, you can complete the process through a standard Web browser.

- ■ **Telephone** If you cannot use either of the previous methods, the process can also be completed by phone.

Let's examine how to use each method.

Installing and Activating Terminal Services Client Access Licenses Using the Automatic Connection Method

Follow these steps to use the Automatic connection (recommended) install method:

1. Open the TS Licensing Manager utility by clicking **Start | Administrative Tools | Terminal Services | TS Licensing Manager.**

2. When the utility opens, it will bring up the Finding Licensing Servers window, and search for all servers running the TS Licensing role service that it can find.

3. Verify that the TS Licensing server's installation method is set to **Automatic connection (recommended)**. In the tree on the left pane or in the right pane, right click on the desired server and click **Properties**. See Figure 8.26.

Figure 8.26 Opening the TS Licensing Server's Properties

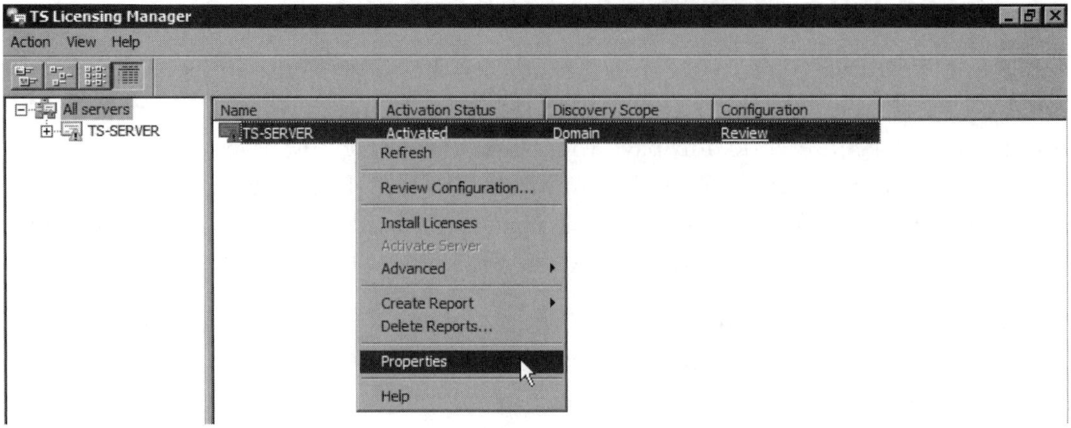

4. On the Connection Method tab in the **Properties** dialog box, make sure that the **Connection Method:** drop-down box is set to **Automatic connection (recommended)**. Change it if necessary. Click **OK**. See Figure 8.27.

Figure 8.27 Verifying the Connection Method

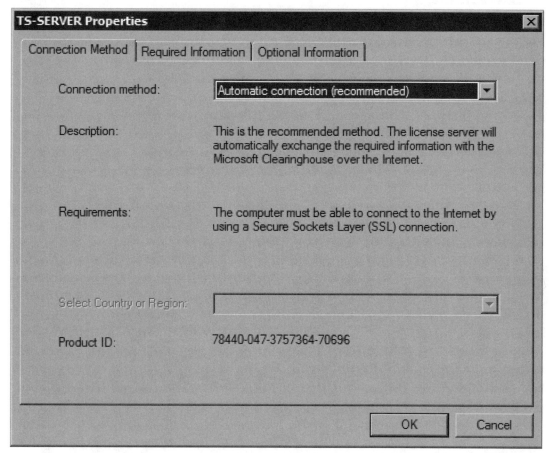

5. Right click on the server again, and select **Install Licenses**.

6. Review the information on the Welcome to the Install Licenses Wizard screen and click **Next**.

7. A **Locating the Microsoft activation server...** dialog opens briefly while the wizard connects to the Internet and locates the Microsoft Clearinghouse.

8. On the Licensing Program wizard page, select the appropriate license type in the **License program:** drop down box, and click **Next**. See Figure 8.28.

Figure 8.28 The Licensing Program Page

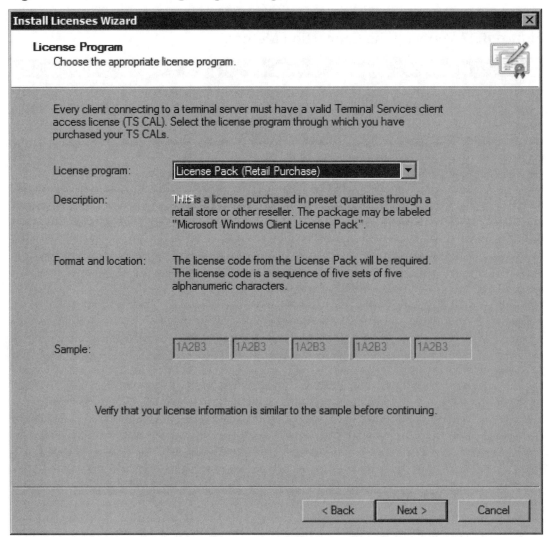

9. On the License Code wizard page, enter the codes you received from Microsoft when you purchased your TS CALs in the text boxes provided next to **License code:** and click **Add**. More than one code can be entered on this screen. When you have entered all licenses you'd like to activate, click **Next**. See Figure 8.29.

Figure 8.29 The License Code Page

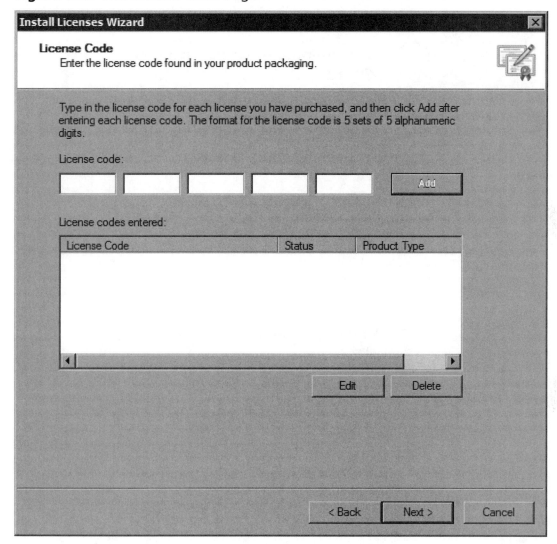

10. An **Installing Terminal Services client access licenses…** dialog appears while the licenses are activated and installed.

11. Review the information on the Completing the Install Licenses Wizard page and click **Finish**. See Figure 8.30.

Figure 8.30 Completing the Install Licenses Wizard

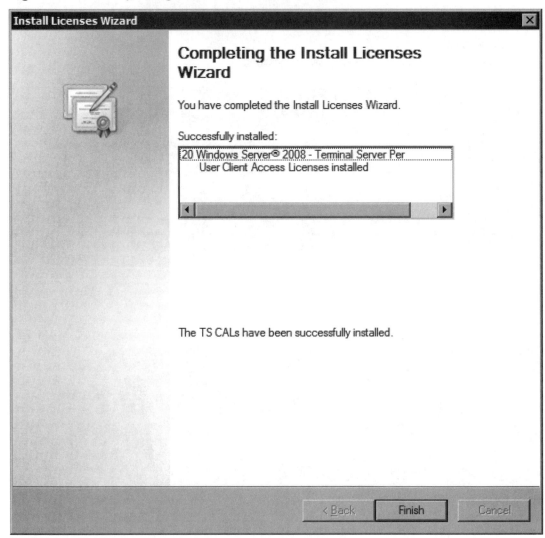

12. Select the server's node in the left pane of TS Licensing Manager. The licenses should now appear in the right pane along with the built-in grace period CALs. See Figure 8.31.

Figure 8.31 Verifying the Installed Licenses

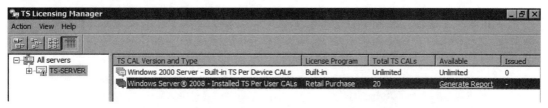

Installing and Activating Terminal Services Client Access Licenses Using the Web Browser Method

The following steps can be used to activate the TS Licensing role service via a Web browser:

1. Open the TS Licensing Manager utility by clicking **Start | Administrative Tools | Terminal Services | TS Licensing Manager**.

2. When the utility opens, it will bring up the Finding Licensing Servers window, and search for servers running the TS Licensing role service.

3. Verify that the TS Licensing server's installation method is set to **Web Browser**. In the tree in the left pane or in the right pane, right click on the desired server and click **Properties**.

4. On the Connection Method tab in the **Properties** dialog box, make sure that the **Connection Method:** drop-down box is set to **Web Browser**. Change it if necessary. Click **OK**.

5. Right click on the server again, and select **Install Licenses**.

6. Review the information on the Welcome to the Install Licenses Wizard screen and click **Next**.

7. The **Obtain Client License Key Pack** dialog appears, which provides the Terminal Services Licensing Web site URL, as well as the license server ID you will need to enter. You will also need the license code information received from Microsoft when you purchased your TS CALs. Click on the hyperlink to visit the Web site or open a Web browser and type in the URL (https://activate.microsoft.com). See Figure 8.32.

Figure 8.32 The Web Browser-Based Obtain Client License Key Pack Page

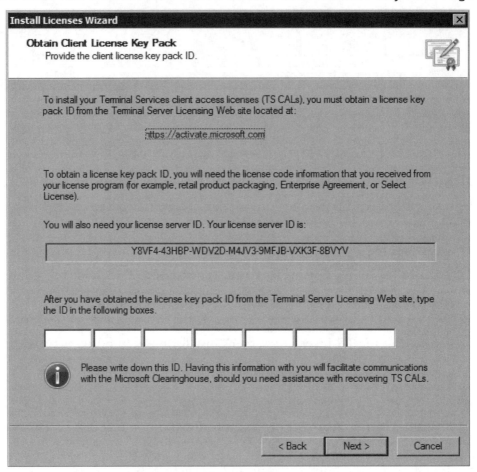

8. On the first page of the Terminal Services Licensing Web site, select **Install Client Access License tokens** and click **Next**.

9. Enter your **License Server ID** as well as the following required fields: **Last/Surname**, **First/Given Name**, **Company**, and **Country/ Region**. You can also choose to fill in several optional fields for your: **Organizational Unit**, **eMail Address**, **Phone Number**, **Company Address**, **City**, **State/Province**, and **Postal Code**.

10. Click **Next**.

11. In the text boxes provided next to **License Codes:** enter the codes you received from Microsoft when you purchased your TS CALs and click **Add**. More than one code can be entered on this screen. When you have entered all licenses you'd like to activate, click **Next**.

12. Review and verify the information you've entered. Use the **Back** button to make any necessary changes. When you are satisfied that all information is correct, click **Next**.

13. Your information is submitted to the Microsoft Clearinghouse, and a license key pack ID is returned. Record and/or print the ID and click **Finish**.

14. In the **VBScript: confirm** dialog, click **Yes** to verify that you have recorded the ID.

15. Return to the **Obtain client license key pack** dialog on TS Licensing Manager. Type the license key pack ID provided by the Web page where specified in the lower portion of the screen, and click **Next**.

16. A brief dialog appears as the server attempts to verify and activate the licenses.

17. Review the information on the Completing the Install Licenses Wizard page and click **Finish**.

18. Select the server's node in the left pane of TS Licensing Manager. The licenses should now appear in the right pane along with the built-in grace period CALs.

Installing and Activating Terminal Services Client Access Licenses Using the Telephone Method

The following steps can be used to activate the TS Licensing role service via telephone:

1. Open the TS Licensing Manager utility by clicking **Start | Administrative Tools | Terminal Services | TS Licensing Manager**.

2. When the utility opens, it will bring up the Finding Licensing Servers window, and search for all servers running the TS Licensing role service that it can find.

3. Verify that the TS Licensing server's installation method is set to **Telephone**. In the tree in the left pane or in the right pane, right click on the desired server and click **Properties**.

4. On the Connection Method tab in the **Properties** dialog box, make sure that the **Connection Method:** drop-down box is set to **Telephone**. Change it if necessary. Click **OK**.

5. Right click on the server again, and select **Install Licenses**.

6. Review the information on the Welcome to the Install Licenses Wizard screen and click **Next**.

7. The **Obtain client license key pack** dialog appears, which provides the telephone number to call, as well as the license server ID you will need to enter. You will also need the license code information received from Microsoft when you purchased your TS CALs.

8. Call Microsoft at the number given, and provide all requested information. The Microsoft representative you speak to will process your request and provide your license server ID.

9. Return to the **Obtain client license key pack** dialog on TS Licensing Manager. Type the license key pack ID provided by the Microsoft representative where specified in the lower portion of the screen, and click **Next**. See Figure 8.33.

Figure 8.33 The Telephone-Based Obtain Client License Key Pack Page

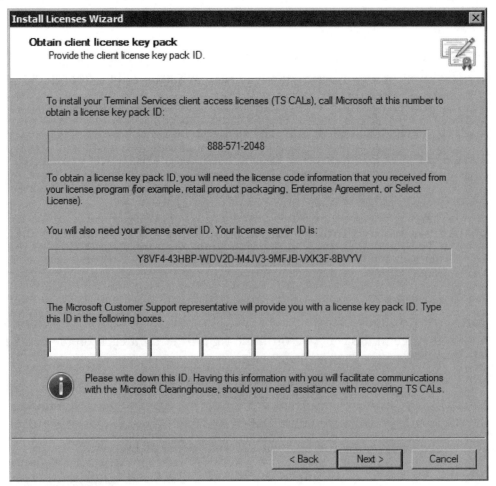

10. A brief dialog appears as the server attempts to verify and activate the licenses.

11. Review the information on the Completing the Install Licenses Wizard page and click **Finish**.

12. Select the server's node in the left pane of TS Licensing Manager. The licenses should now appear in the right pane along with the built-in grace period CALs.

Recovering a Terminal Service Licensing Server

Licensing servers are backed up and restored just like any other server on the network. You can use Microsoft's included Backup or a third party utility. Microsoft recommends that you perform regular, full backups of each license server in your organization. At a minimum, the following items should be backed up:

- The **System State** data, which contains activation and identity information for the license server.

- The **LServer** directory, to back up the licensing database (see below).

It's very important to ensure that your backup configuration includes the database that stores your TS CALs. By default, the database is located in the `%system-root%\system32\lserver` folder on the license server; however, administrators can specify an optional location. To verify the database's location follow this procedure:

1. Open the TS Licensing Manager utility by clicking **Start | Administrative Tools | Terminal Services | TS Licensing Manager**.

2. In the right pane, right click on the server you want to publish and click on **Review Configuration…**.

3. In the **Configuration** dialog, view information next to **Database Location:**.

EXAM WARNING

If a license server's licensing database is missing or corrupt and cannot be restored, you must reinstall the TS CALs. Previously installed and activated TS CALs can only be reinstalled and reactivated by calling Microsoft's Clearinghouse.

Establishing Client Connections to a Terminal Server

Connections to Windows Server 2008 terminal servers are established with the Remote Desktop Connection utility, the Remote Desktops Snap-in. Connections occur using Microsoft's Remote Desktop Protocol, which uses minimal bandwidth to exchange screen information and user data input over TCP/IP. In this section, we'll examine the Remote Desktop Connection utility and the Remote Desktops Snap-in.

TEST DAY TIP

Be sure to familiarize yourself with the properties available for configuration in each of the client tools prior to taking the exam.

Using the Remote Desktop Connection Utility

The Remote Desktop Connection utility (mstsc.exe) is the primary client for connecting to terminal services. It can be used for remote server administration or regular terminal server client use. RDC enables a user to connect to a single server running terminal services using the RDP protocol over TCP/IP. The utility is installed with the operating system in Windows XP SP2, Vista, Server 2003, and Server 2008. Version 6 is discussed in this chapter. The version on older systems such as Windows XP and Server 2003 will require upgrading to this version.

Launching and Using the Remote Desktop Connection Utility

In Windows Server 2008 the application can be opened by clicking **Start | All Programs | Accessories | Remote Desktop Connection**. RDC opens with most of its configuration options hidden. To proceed with the connection type the name or IP address of the terminal server you want to connect with in the **Computer:** drop-down box, select **Browse for more ...** from the drop down list, or select the server from the drop-down list if you have previously established a session to it; then click the **Connect** button. If you select **Browse for more ...** a **Browse for computers** dialog will appear which allows you to see available terminal servers.

EXAM WARNING

RDC can also be started from a command prompt by specifying its executable file **mstsc.exe**. In Windows Server 2008, the **/admin** option can be used when launching the utility to connect to the server's console session, instead of beginning a new user session. **/admin** replaces the **/console** option used in previous versions. Microsoft stresses this change quite heavily in their documentation. Be sure not to fall for any questions using the older **/console** option. The **/admin** option does not require a TS CAL for connection.

At this point, you might be automatically logged on. Your client may have cached credentials which automatically log you on, a group policy may exist that automatically logs you on with the credentials you logged on to your local computer with, or a similar option may automatically provide credentials for you. If that's the case, a Remote Desktop window will open. If not, the **Windows Security** dialog box will appear asking you to enter a valid username and password. You can also select the **Remember my credentials** box to save your log-on credentials for this server. Even if you do not select this box, RDC will remember the username used and automatically offer to use it for subsequent connection attempts. Once you are connected, by default the remote desktop will appear full screen on your system's display. You can move your cursor over, click on, and use any item in the remote desktop just as you would if using your local system. You can also copy and paste between the remote and local computers, using the standard methods of doing this.

Connecting is a simple process; however, terminating your session requires a bit more explanation. There are two methods that you can use to end your session: logging off and disconnecting. To log off click **Start | ▶ | Log Off**. When you do this, it will completely log you out of the remote system in much the same way as if you logged out on your local system. Registry entries are properly written, programs are elegantly closed, and so forth. The session is completely removed from the terminal services server, freeing up any system resources that were being used by your session. Make sure that you select **Log Off,** rather than **Shut Down**. If you select **Shut Down**, and are logged onto the remote session with rights that allow your account to shut down the server, it will power down. Obviously, this will affect everyone who is currently using it.

The second method of terminating your session is to use the process known as *disconnection*. When you disconnect from terminal services, your session remains on the server and is not removed. It continues to consume resources, although the video stream coming to your local computer and input stream going from your local computer to the terminal services system are terminated. When you launch RDC again and connect to the same server running terminal services, your session will still be there exactly as you left it and you can take up where you left off. This can be helpful in cases where an application is being run that requires lengthy processing. You do not have to remain connected for the application to run and you can check back later and obtain the result. You can disconnect from your session by clicking the close button (the **X**) in the top right corner of the Remote Desktop window, or in the full screen connection bar.

Configuring the Remote Desktop Connection Utility

In the previous section, we simply launched the Remote Desktop Connection utility and established a connection. When you initially launch the utility, most of its configuration information is hidden. To display it before you use it to establish a connection, click the **Options** button. This will reveal a series of tabs and many additional settings that can be configured. Let's take a look at each in the following sections.

The General tab

The General tab contains the **Computer:** drop-down box, which contains names and IP addresses of computers to which you have previously connected, along with an option to browse the network for computers not listed. This tab also contains the **User name:** text box. The **Allow me to save credentials** check box will ensure that the credentials you type in while logging on are saved for future sessions. This tab also allows you to save your connection settings. You might have several different terminal servers to which you connect using RDC. If so, it is helpful to not have to configure the utility each time you open it. When you click the **Save As ...** button, a **Save As** dialog box opens, asking you where you'd like to save the file that contains your configuration information. The file will be saved with an RDP extension, and can be double-clicked later to establish a terminal session. You can also use the **Open ...** button on this tab to specify that the settings from a previously saved RDP file be loaded into the utility.

EXAM WARNING

Asking RDC to remember your credentials doesn't work on all versions of Microsoft Windows Vista. The following versions of Windows Vista do not support this feature: Home Basic, Home Premium, and Starter.

The Display Tab

The display tab controls how the remote desktop appears on your client computer. The top portion contains a slider that controls the size of the remote desktop that will be displayed on your screen. The maximum resolution supported is 4096 × 2048, and the default setting is **Full Screen**. The next portion of this tab controls the color depth (in bits) of the remote desktop when it is displayed on your local computer. The drop-down list box contains the following options: **256 colors**, **High Color (15 bit)**, **High Color (16 bit)**, **True Color (24 bit)**. Higher color depths require more resources. Note that settings on the server may override your selection.

Finally, the bottom of the tab contains a check box entitled **Display the connection bar when in full screen mode**. When selected, this setting places a small bar at the top of a full screen remote desktop which makes it easier to size, minimize or maximize (to full screen), or close the Remote Desktop window.

The Local Resources Tab

The Local Resources tab allows you to control whether or not client resources are accessible in your remote session. When you are working in a session, you are actually working on the remote terminal server. This means that when you open Windows Explorer, the disk drives you see are the ones that are physically located on the terminal server, not the ones installed in your local computer. Selections on the Local Resources tab can be used to make your local drives, client-attached printers, and similar client side resources available for use within your remote desktop session.

The first setting on the tab deals with whether audio will be used in the session. The default setting, **Bring to this computer**, allows for any sounds played in the session to be transferred from the terminal server to the client. Audio transfer can be bandwidth intensive in a thin client environment, so Microsoft also gives you the opportunity to not transfer this audio. The **Leave at remote computer** setting plays the audio in the session on the terminal services computer but does not transfer it to the client. The **Do not play** setting prevents audio in the session altogether.

The next setting on the Local Resources tab relates to whether keyboard short-cut combinations are used by the local operating system or the Remote Desktop window. There are three possible settings for keyboard shortcut combinations:

- **In full screen mode only** In this mode (which is the default), when you use a shortcut combination, the system applies it to the local operating system, unless there is a full screen Remote Desktop window open.

- **On the local computer** This setting applies all shortcut combinations to the local operating system.

- **On the remote computer** This setting applies all shortcut combinations to the Remote Desktop window.

EXAM WARNING

You cannot redirect the **CTRL + ALT + DEL** keyboard combination. This combination only works on the local operating system. An equivalent that can be used in the Remote Desktop window is **CTRL + ALT + END**.

The final section of the tab deals with determining which devices from the client system are automatically made available to the user within the remote desktop session. By default, the following are selected: Printers, Clipboard, and Smart cards. The Smart cards option is available by clicking the **More...** button. Other options that clicking the **More...** button reveals include: Serial ports, Drives, and Supported Plug and Play devices. *Drives* can be expanded, which allows you to select the individual drive letters you'd like to have available from your local system. These will not be available with the same drive letters in your terminal session (the server most likely already has a drive C, for example), but will be clearly identified and easy to discern.

New & Noteworthy...

Plug and Play Device Support

Windows Server 2008 terminal servers include enhanced redirection support for plug and play devices that are physically plugged into your local computer but need to be available in your terminal services session. This includes media players that are based on the Media Transfer Protocol (MTP) and digital cameras that are based on the Picture Transfer Protocol (PTP). You cannot transfer digital rights management protected content from redirected media players to a terminal services session. To enable redirection, in the RDP utility click on the **Local Resources** tab, followed

Continued

by the **More...** button. Expand the **plus (+)** sign next to **Supported Plug and Play devices** to see all devices attached to your system which will work with this feature. If you have plug and play devices attached to your system that do not show up, they are not compatible with terminal services plug and play device support. Plug and play redirection only works for clients running Windows Vista Enterprise or Ultimate.

The nature of plug and play devices is that they are not always connected to your computer. You might be wondering how terminal services deals with devices that are plugged in during an active terminal services session. Microsoft considered this when designing this functionality and provides an option under **Supported Plug and Play devices** called **Devices that I plug in later**. By default neither **Supported Plug and Play devices** nor **Devices that I plug in later** are selected. By selecting these options, any compatible plug and play devices that you plug into your local system during an active terminal services session will be detected and made available not only on your local system but also in your terminal services session.

Test Day Tip

Make sure that you are familiar with new features such as plug and play device support. New components which relate directly to test objectives are likely to be featured in exam questions.

The Programs Tab

By default, when you connect to a terminal services session, you will receive a Windows desktop. The selections on this tab allow you to receive a specified application instead a desktop. If terminal services are being used to provide only a single application for each user, this setting can increase security by ensuring that users do not receive a full desktop upon connection. This will prevent them from performing tasks on the server other than running the specified application. If the check box next to **Start the following program on connection** is selected, only that application will be available in the session.

Selecting this check box enables the **Program path and file name:** text box. If the path to the application is already contained in one of the Windows path variables on the terminal services computer, you can just type the name of the application's executable file in this box. If not, you must include the full path and file name of the executable. The check box also enables the **Start in the following folder:** text box. If the application requires the specification of a working directory, enter it here. This is often the same directory in which the application is installed.

After the connection is made with a specified program starting, the traditional methods of ending your session (discussed previously) will not always be possible. Most programs have an **Exit** command on a menu, embedded in a button, or contained in a link. When you have specified an initial program, the **Exit** command is the equivalent of logging out. To disconnect, simply close the Remote Desktop window.

The Experience tab

The Experience tab allows you to customize several performance features that control the overall feel of your session. All of these settings except Bitmap Caching can generate substantial amounts of additional bandwidth and should be used sparingly in low bandwidth environments. Not all features are available for all client operating systems. The check boxes on this page include the following:

- **Desktop background** Allows the background image of the desktop (wallpaper) in the remote session to be transferred to and displayed in the Remote Desktop window on the client.

- **Font smoothing** Enables ClearType font support in a terminal services session.

- **Desktop composition** Enables the session to display the visually dynamic features, known as Windows Aero (such as translucent windows), implemented in Windows Vista. The client hardware must support this option, but the server does require compatible hardware.

- **Show contents of window while dragging** Rapidly refreshes a window so that its contents are visible as the user moves it around the screen in the Remote Desktop window.

- **Menu and window animation** Enables some sophisticated effects, such as the Windows Start menu fading in and out, to be displayed in the Remote Desktop window on the client computer.

- **Themes** Enables any themes used in the remote session to be enabled and transferred to the Remote Desktop window on the client.

- **Bitmap Caching** Enables bitmaps to be stored locally on the client system and called up from cache, rather than being transmitted multiple times across the network. Examples of bitmaps include desktop icons and icons on application toolbars.

At the top of this tabbed page, there is a drop-down box that contains several predefined combinations of these settings that Microsoft has optimized for different levels of available bandwidth. Table 8.1 shows which bandwidth level corresponds to which settings.

Table 8.1 Preconfigured Bandwidth Settings

Connection speed selection	Desktop Background	Font Smoothing	Desktop Composition	Show contents of window while dragging	Menu and window animation	Themes	Bitmap caching
Modem (28.8 Kbs)							X
Modem (56 Kbs) – default						X	X
Broadband (128 Kbps – 1.5 Mbps)			X	X	X	X	X
LAN (10 Mbps or higher)	X	X	X	X	X	X	X
Custom						X	X

The Experience tab also contains a check box entitled **Reconnect if connection is dropped,** which is selected by default. Windows Server 2003 and later versions of terminal services include the automatic reconnection feature. If dropped packets, network service interruptions, or other network errors cause your terminal services connection to disconnect, this feature will automatically attempt to reconnect to your session without requiring you to reenter your log-on credentials. By default, there will be a maximum of twenty reconnection attempts, which occur at five-second intervals. Generally, a notification message will pop up, informing you that the connection has been lost and counting down the remaining connection attempts.

The Advanced Tab

The top of this tab allows you to configure Server authentication options. Server authentication is an extra level of security that is used to verify that you are connecting to the intended terminal server. It contains three possible settings. The default, **Warn me**, notifies you if the authentication fails but still allows you to connect if desired. The option **Connect and don't warn me** will silently connect you to the terminal server even if RDC cannot verify the identity of the server. The final option, **Do not connect**, notifies you and will not allow the connection to proceed. Windows Server 2003 SP1 and earlier servers that cannot provide the type of authentication requested should be set to **Connect and don't warn me**. Later servers that can provide this authentication information should be set to one of the other options. The bottom of the Advanced tab, **Connect from anywhere**, allows you to configure TS Gateway connection settings.

Installing and Using the Remote Desktops Snap-in

The Remote Desktops (RD) Snap-in is another utility that can be used to establish terminal services connections to Windows Server 2008 terminal servers. The Remote Desktops Snap-in should be considered the primary terminal services client connection tool for administrators. Perhaps the most significant feature of the RD Snap-in is that a single instance of the utility can be used to simultaneously connect to multiple Windows Server 2008 terminal servers. An administrator can configure the RD Snap-in with connection information for multiple servers. These connections can be used to establish and switch between sessions. As an example, you could configure the snap-in with connections for each of your servers and have a single tool that allows for remote administration of them. With RDC, you must open a new instance of the utility for each server to which you want to connect simultaneously. You can use the RD Snap-in to quickly click between multiple terminal server sessions, as shown in Figure 8.34.

Figure 8.34 The Remote Desktops Snap-in

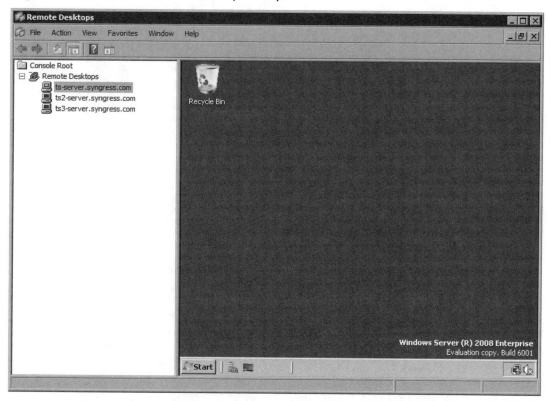

Adding a New Connection

In order to connect to a terminal server using Remote Desktops, you have to create a connection object for the terminal server. Right click the **Remote Desktops** node on the left side of the utility and click **Add new connection...**. This will open the Add New Connection window, as shown in Figure 8.35.

Figure 8.35 The Add New Connection Dialog Box in the Remote
Desktops Snap-in

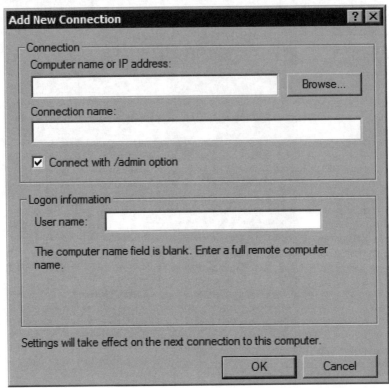

The top portion of the window contains the connection information. In the
Computer name or IP address: text box, enter the fully qualified domain name
(FQDN), NetBIOS name, or IP address of the server to which you wish to connect.
If you use a FQDN or NetBIOS name, you must make sure that you have the
necessary name resolution services running and properly configured on your network.
Next, enter a name to identify the connection in the **Connection name:** text box,
or accept the default (which will be the same as the server name or IP address you
entered in the previous field). This name will only be used to identify the connection
within the utility.

Finally, leave **Connect with /admin option** selected if you want to connect
to the server's console session. Because this snap-in is intended for remote administration, this is the default setting. If you deselect the check box, terminal services
will create a new session for you to use when you connect. If you leave this option
enabled, after you are authenticated, if someone else is logged on to and using the

console session (either locally or remotely), you will be notified and asked if you'd like to proceed. Only one user can be connected to and using the console session at any time. This means that if someone is using the console, whether remotely or locally, your new connection will force him or her out.

The lower half of the Add New Connection window allows you to store some log-on information to be used with the session. If you wish to do so, enter the desired log-on name in the **User name:** text box. When you are finished entering the information in the Add New Connection window, click the **OK** button to save the connection. The connection should now appear under the Remote Desktops node in the tree view on the left of the Remote Desktops window.

In the following exercise, you will practice creating a Remote Desktops connection.

EXERCISE 8.3

CONFIGURING A NEW CONNECTION IN THE REMOTE DESKTOPS SNAP-IN

1. Open Remote Desktops by clicking **Start | Administrative Tools | Terminal Services | Remote Desktops**.

2. In the left pane, right click on the **Remote Desktops** node and select **Add new connection…**.

3. In the **Computer name or IP address:** text box, enter the fully qualified domain name (FQDN), NetBIOS name, or IP address of the server to which you wish to connect.

4. Type an identifying name for the connection in the **Connection name:** text box, or accept the default.

5. Leave **Connect with /admin option** selected if you want to connect to the server's console. Deselect the check box if you want terminal services to create a new session for you to use.

6. To store your user credentials in the connection, enter your log-on name in the **User name:** text box, if desired.

7. Click **OK** to save the connection.

Configuring a Connection's Properties

You can configure several properties for saved connections. Right click the node in the left pane of the RD Snap-in that represents the connection you want to modify, and select **Properties**. The Properties window will appear with the General tab displayed. This tab is essentially the same as the Add New Connection window and contains the same fields for configuration. You can change any of the settings you made when you created the connection.

Click the **Screen Options** tab to bring it to the foreground. This tab allows you to choose the size of the remote desktop screen that will appear in the snap-in. The desktop will appear in the currently blank space on the right side of the Remote Desktops window. You can select the size of desktop that appears. The default, **Expand to fill MMC Result Pane**, fills all of the available space in the right pane of the MMC window with the remote session's desktop. You can change this by selecting one of the other choices on this tab. The second option, **Choose desktop size:**, enables a drop-down box containing two standard resolutions: **640×480** and **800×600**. The final option on the tab is **Enter custom desktop size:**. When selected, it enables two text boxes: **Width:** and **Height:**. If the other available options do not provide you with the desired desktop size, you can manually enter the size you want into these text boxes.

Note that the desktop size will be set at connection and will not change. If you start with Remote Desktops not maximized, connect to the remote server and then maximize the RD Snap-in window, the desktop will not fill the right side of the utility. If you change the properties to choose a specific desktop size or custom size while the session is running, you won't see any change. You can right click the connection name in the left pane, select **Disconnect,** then right click again and select **Connect** to see the size change.

Click the **Other** tab at the top of the window to view the final set of options. You will see some settings that are familiar from the RDC utility, such as the ability to start a program and/or redirect local drives. By default, you will receive a Windows desktop when you connect to a terminal session. The first selection on this tab allows you to receive only a specified application instead. If the check box next to **Start the following program on connection:** is selected, only that application will be available in the session. Selecting the box enables the **Program path and file name:** text box. If the path to the application is already contained in one of the Windows path variables, you can type the file name of the application's executable file in this box. If not, you must include the full path and file name of the executable. The check box also enables the **Working directory:** text box. If the application requires the specification of a working directory, enter it here. This is often the same directory in which the application is installed.

The middle portion of this tab is similar to RDC's Advanced tab settings for Server authentication. It contains three options. The default, **Always connect,**

even if authentication fails, will silently connect you to the terminal server even if Remote Desktops cannot verify the identity of the server. Windows 2003 SP1 and earlier servers cannot provide the type of authentication requested, so this is an appropriate option for those terminal servers. Later servers should be set to one of the other options. The second option, **Warn me if authentication fails**, notifies you if the authentication fails but still allows you to connect if desired. The final option, **Do not connect if authentication fails**, notifies you and will not allow the connection to proceed.

At the bottom of the Other tab is a check box entitled **Redirect local drives when logged on to the remote computer**. If selected, the drives on the computer running Remote Desktops will be visible from within the session. This provides you with access to those local drives from Windows Explorer, as well as Open and Save As dialog boxes within applications. If it is not necessary to allow access to these local drives, you should leave this option disabled for security purposes. Note that there is no option to redirect local printers, serial ports and smart cards as with the RDC utility.

Connecting and Disconnecting

When you have your connection added and configured, connecting is a snap. To connect, simply right click the node that represents your saved connection in the left pane and select **Connect**. If you did not save your log-on information in the properties of the connection, the information you provided was incorrect, or you want to log on with a different account, you will be required to enter a user name and password in the **Windows Security** dialog. Select the **Remember my credentials** box to have your log-on information stored for future connections. Disconnecting is just as simple. Right click the node that represents your saved connection in the left pane, and select **Disconnect**. Remember that disconnection leaves the session running on the server. If you are connecting to the console sessions, it is probably advisable to just disconnect. However, if you've connected to a new session, you should log off from it instead of disconnecting, unless you have processes running that you occasionally need to reconnect and check up on. To log off click **Start** | ▶ | **Log Off** in your terminal services session window (the right pane in Remote Desktops).

Summary of Exam Objectives

The Terminal Services role allows users and administrators to establish remote desktop and application connections to a terminal server from their workstation. Connections are established using the Remote Desktop Connection utility or the Remote Desktops Snap-in. The RDC utility is the primary connection utility for users. One instance of the utility is capable of establishing a session on a single terminal server. The Remote Desktops Snap-in is primarily used by administrators, because it allows them to establish simultaneous sessions on multiple terminal servers within a single application window. Both RDC and Remote Desktops can be used to connect to a terminal server's console session. This is the default in Remote Desktops. To access it using RDC, the utility must be launched from a command line by typing: **mstsc.exe /admin**.

When a terminal services connection is established, although an application window or desktop appears on the user's system, all processes are actually running on the terminal server. The Terminal Server role service is the key terminal services component, facilitating session creation, management, and destruction. For security reasons this role service should not be installed on a domain controller.

Within a 120-day grace period, the TS Licensing role service must be installed and activated on a Windows Server 2008 server. License servers can be activated by using **Automatic connection (recommended)**, **Web Browser**, and **Telephone** methods. Licensing servers manage Terminal Services Client Access Licenses, which make it possible for users and devices to establish connections to the server. There are two kinds of TS CALs: Per Device and Per User. Per Device TS CALs are issued and tracked by terminal services licensing. If not enough are available to service client demand, terminal services will not allow additional connections. Per User TS CALs are not tracked and will not block users from accessing terminal services, even if the organization has not purchased enough CALs for legal connections to occur. TS CALs must be activated using one of the three previously mentioned methods.

Terminal servers must be able to locate TS Licensing servers. Individual terminal servers can be configured to look for and use specific servers with the Terminal Services Configuration tool or through group policy. If configured, these license servers will be searched for and used first by a terminal server. If not configured or the license servers cannot be found, a terminal server will next check to see if it is installed on the same server as the TS Licensing role service. If it is, it will use the local license server. If not, it will check the Active Directory Directory Services database for published terminal servers, and finally seek a license server that is installed on a domain controller if one is available. When the TS Licensing role service is installed on a server in the domain that is not a domain controller, it must be manually published in Active Directory.

Exam Objectives Fast Track

Deploying the Terminal Server Role Service

☑ The Terminal Server role service is the core client connection service for the Terminal Services role.

☑ For security reasons, the Terminal Server role service should not be installed on a domain controller or any other server hosting critical applications.

☑ During the installation, the server can be configured to use the new, stronger Network Level Authentication method. This method is only compatible with newer clients running RDC 6 and later and CredSSP, such as Windows Server 2008, Windows Vista, and Windows XP SP2. Incompatible clients will not be able to connect to the terminal server with this option enabled.

☑ Either the **Per User** or **Per Device** licensing mode can be specified during the installation of the Terminal Server role service, or **Configure later** can be specified.

Terminal Services Licensing

☑ Valid terminal services licensing components must be installed and configured prior to the expiration of the 120-day grace period to ensure client service continuity.

☑ The TS Licensing role service is responsible for managing TS CALs.

☑ In addition to being installed on a Windows Server 2008 server, the TS Licensing role service must be activated. License servers can be activated via an Internet connection from within the TS Licensing Manager utility, through the Internet using a Web browser, or by phone.

☑ TS Licensing servers which are not installed on domain controllers must be published in Active Directory in order for terminal servers to automatically find them.

☑ Terminal servers can be configured to use specific license servers using the Terminal Server Configuration Utility.

☑ Per User or Per Device TS CALs must be installed and activated for users to connect after the 120-day grace period.

☑ TS CALs can only be installed on activated TS Licensing role service servers.

☑ TS CALs can be activated via an Internet connection from within the TS Licensing Manager utility, through the Internet using a Web browser, or by phone.

Establishing Client Connections to a Terminal Server

☑ The primary program users access a terminal server with is Remote Desktop Connection (RDC).

☑ The primary program administrators use to maintain a terminal server is the Remote Desktops Snap-in.

☑ A single running instance of Remote Desktops Snap-in can be used to quickly switch between terminal services connections to multiple terminal servers.

☑ Both RDC and Remote Desktops can be used to connect to the console session of a terminal server.

Exam Objectives
Frequently Asked Questions

Q: I'd like to install terminal services on an existing Windows Server 2008 server. Is this recommended?

A: It depends. For security and resource consumption issues, Microsoft recommends running terminal services on dedicated servers. If you have an unused server, or can free one up to dedicate to terminal services, that's fine. If not, however, you should acquire a new, dedicated server for terminal services.

Q: I'd like to begin testing terminal services right away, but am not sure which type of licensing I want to use and haven't purchased any TS CALs yet. Is there a way I can begin testing anyway?

A: Windows Server 2003 terminal services provide a 120-day grace period during which licensing doesn't need to be installed and configured. This provides time for administrators to test various options and determine their needs. The 120 days begins when the first temporary license is issued, not when terminal services is installed.

Q: Is it possible to configure licensing to block new user connections when the organization has run out of TS CALs?

A: Per Device TS CALs will block connections from new devices that have not been issued a license, unless one is available for issue. Per User TS CALs are not tracked by TS Licensing role service servers and will not prevent access if an organization exceeds its legal license count.

Q: The TS Licensing role service has been installed, why am I unable to add TS CALs?

A: In addition to installing the TS Licensing service, you must also activate it. License servers can be activated directly from within the TS Licensing Manager utility over the Internet, through the Internet using a Web browser, or by phone.

Q: I've installed the TS Licensing server on one of my company's Windows Server 2008 terminal servers. Why can that terminal server obtain licenses while the others in its domain cannot?

A: A terminal server that has the TS Licensing role service installed on it can automatically locate that license service and use it. However, when the TS Licensing role service is not installed on a domain controller or the terminal server itself, the license server must be manually published in AD DS, or the terminal servers that are not running the TS Licensing service must be manually configured to use the license server.

Q: Our company installs the Terminal Server and TS Licensing role services on the same computer. For security reasons, these computers are not allowed to access the Internet after they are configured in use. How can I add and activate additional licenses without Internet access?

A: When TS CALs cannot be activated directly over the Internet from the server, there are three options for activation. The TS Licensing Manager utility can be installed on a server or workstation that can access both the license server and the Internet, and used to install and activate the CALs; a Web browser can be used from a computer that is connected to the Internet; or you can call Microsoft and activate the licenses by phone.

Q: The TS Licensing Manager utility is warning me that my license server is not published in AD DS, but is not displaying the **Publish in AD DS** button. Is there another method I can use to publish this server in AD?

A: License servers can be published in AD DS using the TS Licensing Manager utility, and using ADSI Edit in conjunction with Active Directory Sites and Services. ADSI Edit is used to modify AD by adding a **licensingSiteSettings** with the value: **TS-Enterprise-License-Server**. This object is then displayed in Active Directory Sites and Services, and allows for the publication of the license server in AD DS.

Q: How can I use RDC to connect to the console session on a terminal server?

A: From the **Run** dialog box or a command prompt, run **mstsc.exe /admin**.

Q: I need to connect to multiple terminal servers' console sessions at the same time. What is the best utility to use for this?

A: The Remote Desktop Snap-in allows for this within a single running instance of the program. While RDC could be used, it would require opening an instance of the application for each terminal server you wanted to connect to.

Q: Every time I connect to a server using the Remote Desktop Snap-in, it displays the console session. How can I use the utility to access a regular terminal services session?

A: Remote Desktops connects to the console session by default. To change this, in the left pane of the utility, right click on the connection node and select **Properties**. On the General tab, deselect **Connect with /admin** option.

Q: Every time I use the RDC utility, it opens the Remote Desktop window full screen. I need to be able to easily use both my desktop and the remote desktop. Is there a way to change this setting?

A: By default, RDC connections open in full screen mode. To change this behavior, open RDC and before connecting click the **Options** button. Click on the **Display** tab to bring it to the foreground, and adjust the slider at the top of the screen to the desired window size.

Self Test

1. Several months ago, you installed the Terminal Server role service on one of the servers at your company. This morning, clients are having difficulty connecting to terminal services but are still able to use file and print services on the server. The error message says it is a licensing issue but you are sure that you properly licensed Windows Server 2008, as well as all of your client systems. What might be causing this? (Select all that apply.)

   A. The temporary evaluation period has expired

   B. You failed to properly configure TS CALs on the license server

   C. The server was installed with a temporary license code, which has expired

   D. You did not properly install a license server

2. You have several terminal servers and want to connect to each server's console session remotely, from within a single utility. Which graphical terminal services utility can you use to accomplish this?

   A. The Remote Desktop Connection version 6 utility

   B. The Remote Desktops Snap-in

   C. The Remote Desktop Connection Web utility

   D. The Terminal Services Client Configuration Manager utility

3. You've just installed your first Windows Server 2008 terminal server for your company, accepting all defaults in the wizard. The company currently has six Windows 2003 terminal servers, housed at a second facility across town. Clients connect via a private WAN from offices all over the country to each terminal server. While all clients are still able to log on to the Windows Server 2003 terminal servers, only Windows Vista and XP SP2 (and later) clients seem to be able to access the new Windows Server 2008 terminal server. None of the company's Windows 2000 workstations can log on to the server. Which one of the following is the most likely reason?

   A. The **Require Network Level Authentication** option was selected during server configuration.

   B. The **Do not require Network Level Authentication** option was selected by default during server configuration.

C. Only Windows XP and Vista clients can connect to Windows Server 2008 terminal services.

D. You did not update the RDC client on the Windows 2000 clients to version 6 or later.

4. Two months ago you installed the first Windows Server 2008 terminal server for your company, accepting all defaults in the Wizard. You recently finished the final testing, verified that Windows Server 2008 terminal services were a good solution for your company, and ordered the necessary licenses. You've installed and activated the TS Licensing role service on a domain controller in the same domain as the terminal server. You've also installed and activated Per Device TS CALs. Despite this, your users have not been able to obtain the CALs you installed, and temporary CALs are still being assigned. Which one of the following answers best explains the problem?

A. The **Per User** default setting was used during the terminal server installation, but Per Device CALs have been purchased and activated.

B. The **Configure later** default setting was used during the terminal server installation.

C. The TS Licensing server was not published in AD and the Terminal Server cannot find it.

D. The terminal server was not configured to manually use the TS Licensing server.

5. Your manager has heard that users can often connect to terminal services and obtain sessions, even if the company has not purchased enough licenses. She asks you to make sure this doesn't happen, and wants an automated solution. You're about to put in the first and only terminal server the company will install. Which one of the following is your best solution?

A. Use Per User CALs.

B. Use Per Device CALs.

C. Purchase a third party solution, such as Citrix.

D. Configure group policy to monitor the used licenses and disable logons when they are all in use.

6. Your manager insists that the company's only server will be more than adequate to install and use as a terminal server. The server currently hosts AD,

DNS, and several key applications such as e-mail and databases. What do you tell him? (Select one.)

A. You tell him that you agree, and will begin to plan and test the installation.

B. You tell him that you are concerned about the additional load that will be placed on such a critical server.

C. You tell him that you feel a second server is justified, and that installing it as a second domain controller in addition to a terminal server will provide needed fault tolerance for AD.

D. You tell him that security concerns dictate the purchase of a second server, which should be exclusively used as a terminal server.

7. You are the administrator for a small, single office company with 20 typical office users. The company currently has two Windows Server 2003 domain controllers, one of which also hosts Exchange Server. As part of your Windows Server 2008 upgrade plan, you've been asked to add a terminal server to facilitate greater remote access. The company plans to add additional terminal servers as the year progresses. Which one of the following do you recommend for the placement of the TS Licensing role service?

A. For security reasons, you do not recommend installing the TS Licensing role service on a domain controller after the upgrade.

B. You recommend a dedicated server for the TS Licensing role service.

C. You recommend that the License server be installed on a domain controller after the upgrade.

D. You recommend that the License server be installed on the new server which will be purchased for the Terminal Server role service.

8. Your manager stresses the incorporation of vendor best practices. She has asked you to ensure that the discovery scope used for the company's TS Licensing role service servers adheres to the best practices established by Microsoft. Which one of the following settings will you configure for your domain based computers?

A. **This workgroup**

B. **This domain**

C. **This forest**

D. **Configure later**

9. You are a server administrator for a large, multi-national company, and have just been sent the deployment documentation for Windows Server 2008 terminal services. One of the configuration line items calls for centralization of the TS Licensing databases on a single file server. What do you e-mail the deployment design team? (Select one.)

    A. You make them aware of the fact that the database has to be on the local TS Licensing servers.

    B. You ask which server to use, since it is not specified in the documentation.

    C. You make them aware of the fact that the database must use a mapped drive letter, and request specifics on how to configure it.

    D. You let them know that the database is stored in a fixed location which cannot be changed.

10. The terminal servers in your facility are used to deliver highly sensitive applications and data to users. No computers within the facility have Internet access. Which of the following is the best choice for activating your Windows Server 2008 TS Licensing role service server? (Select one.)

    A. The **Automatic connection (recommended)** method in TS Licensing Manager

    B. The **Web Browser** method in TS Licensing Manager

    C. The **Telephone** method in TS Licensing Manager

    D. Temporarily moving the server to a subnet with Internet access for activation

Self Test Quick Answer Key

1. **A, B, D**

2. **B**

3. **A**

4. **B**

5. **B**

6. **D**

7. **C**

8. **C**

9. **A**

10. **C**

Chapter 9

MCTS/MCITP
Exam 649

Configuring and Managing the Terminal Services

Exam objectives in this chapter:

- **Configuring and Monitoring Terminal Service Resources**
- **Load Balancing**
- **The Terminal Services Gateway**
- **Terminal Services RemoteApp**
- **Managing the Terminal Services**

Exam objectives review:

- ☑ **Summary of Exam Objectives**
- ☑ **Exam Objectives Fast Track**
- ☑ **Exam Objectives Frequently Asked Questions**
- ☑ **Self Test**
- ☑ **Self Test Quick Answer Key**

Introduction

Many organizations choose to run applications on terminal servers rather than installing them locally on each workstation. The advantage to doing so is that the application runs on the server, and only video images are sent to the workstations. This makes it much easier for an administrator to maintain the applications. The terminal services are good for security as well, because applications are much more resistant to user tampering since they do not actually reside on the user's workstations.

In this chapter, you will learn how to configure and monitor the Terminal Services Resources. Next, you'll learn about load balancing. You'll then learn about Terminal Services Gateway, which allows remote users to connect to internal resources securely. You'll then learn about configuring TS RemoteApp, which publishes the applications that can be accessed remotely. Finally, you will learn about managing Terminal Services.

Configuring and Monitoring Terminal Service Resources

Monitoring any network service is an important task of an IT administrator. Once Terminal Services are deployed, the job of regularly fine-tuning and monitoring them becomes essential to ensure network resources are optimally utilized and the users are getting what they want. Installation of specific server roles, installation of terminal server aware applications and publishing them to make it available to remote users, monitoring user sessions, and deploying load-balancing solutions when the network grows, are the important tasks. In this chapter, we'll discuss the Terminal Services management tools (snap-in/console in Microsoft terms).

Windows 2008 Terminal Services includes the following components:

- **Terminal Server** Provides the ability to publish Windows-based applications or provide access to the Windows desktop remotely. Users can run programs from remote clients and store data on the network. Users access local applications alongside the remote applications seamlessly.

- **Terminal Services Licensing** Manages the Terminal Services licensing including client access licenses (CALs). Every client requires a license to connect to a terminal server. You can install, assign, and monitor the CALs on your network.

- **Terminal Services Web Access** Provides a Web platform to access remote applications through a Web site. Remote applications appear as a Web link on the corporate Web site. When users click on the link the remote application opens up.

- **Terminal Services Gateway** Provides the ability to offer secure connection to your remote users without a need to establish a Virtual Private Network (VPN). Any Internet-connected device can initiate a Hypertext Transfer Protocol over SSL (HTTPS) connection. Remote Desktop Protocol (RDP) traffic is encapsulated into the HTTPS traffic until it reaches the TS Gateway server and then HTTPS is removed and only RDP traffic gets passed to the terminal servers.

- **Terminal Services Session Broker** Provides the session load balancing among the terminal servers in a farm. When a remote user session terminates for any reason, a reconnection is possible to resume the session from where it was left off.

For managing the sub-components of Terminal Services, various management and monitoring tools are provided by Microsoft. Figure 9.1 provides a pictorial view of the Windows 2008 Terminal Services components and management tools.

Figure 9.1 Microsoft Windows 2008 Terminal Service Components

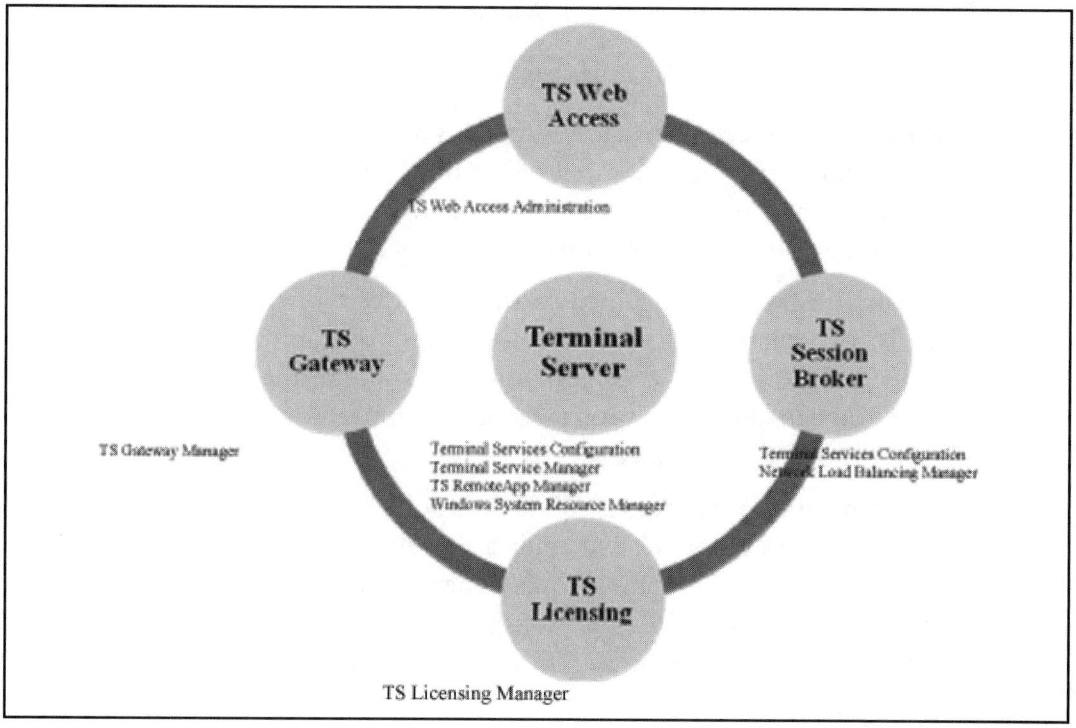

Terminal Server management tools include:

- Terminal Services Manager
- Terminal Services Configuration
- TS RemoteApp Manager
- Windows System Resource Manager

Terminal Services Licensing management tool includes:

- Terminal Services Licensing Manager

Terminal Services Web Access management tool includes:

- Terminal Services Web Access Administration

Terminal Services Gateway management tool includes:

- Terminal Services Gateway Manager

Terminal Services Session Broker management tools include:

- Terminal Services Configuration
- Network Load Balancing (NLB) Manager

The management and monitoring features offered by these management tools are:

- **Terminal Services Manager** With this tool, you can view and monitor users, sessions, and processes that are running on the terminal servers. Routine administration tasks such as sending a message, logging off users, or disconnecting them from a terminal service session are part of this tool.

- **Terminal Services Configuration** With this tool you can configure, modify, and delete RDP connection settings. You can configure on a per-connection basis or use configurations that apply to the whole terminal server. You can also configure farms; add members for a Terminal Services Session Broker load balancing.

- **TS RemoteApp Manager** With this tool you can provide access to Windows-based programs and applications for remote users. Remote users need only an Internet connection. Modern hand-held devices powered with the Windows Mobile operating system supports Remote Desktop Connection (RDC) client. Access to applications hosted centrally in the corporate networks is made available to these hand-held devices without consuming much of the network bandwidth. Only keyboard depressions, mouse clicks, and screen changes travel across the network. You can publish applications and manage it centrally in a scenario where branch offices may not have IT staff to install and configure applications.

- **Windows System Resource Manager** With this tool you can manage the resources by allocating memory and processing the terminal server on a per-user basis or per-session basis. Though this management tool is not specific to Terminal Services, you can configure resource allocation policies for Terminal Services.

- **Terminal Services Licensing Manager** With this tool you can manage Terminal Services CALs and you can install, allocate, and track the CALs. This is an important activity for a Terminal Services administrator.

- **TS Web Access Administration** With this tool you can access remote programs and desktops that are published by TS RemoteApp. You can also configure remote desktop parameters including devices and resources (printers, drives, serial ports, clipboard, and plug-and-play devices), sound, display resolution, and modem parameters.

- **TS Gateway Manager** With this tool you can configure secure remote sessions to access a resource on a corporate network. Resources include terminal servers, TS RemoteApp programs, or desktops with Remote Desktop enabled. RDP over HTTPS is used to create a secure connection without a need for a VPN.

- **NLB Manager** With this tool you can ensure servers' availability by load balancing between several identical roles. Load balancing can be extended to any service. However, in this context, NLB can be used to create terminal server clusters and efficiently load-balance the traffic. Dedicated hardware-based load balancers can also be considered for your network.

Allocating Resources by Using Windows System Resource Manager

Windows System Resource Manager (WSRM) allows you to allocate memory and processor resources to users, Terminal Service sessions, applications, and other services. Often, leaving the resources allocation to the applications or sessions will create a situation where some other services have to compromise their share of resources. Using WSRM you can ensure that the services offered by a server is allocated to all (applications, users, or services) on an equal basis or based on the prioritization of the organization.

WSRM gets into the act through policies and actively manages the resource allocation when the load of the server is greater than 70 percent. However, normal scenario WSRM policies do not play a role. This means contention of resources result in invoking the policies.

WSRM features include managing system resources through policies, calendar rules to define time-based policies, dynamically allocating resources based on server capability (such as powerful processor or higher memory), and accounting.

Resource allocation policies (RAP) specific to Terminal Service scenarios are *equal per session* and *equal per user* policies.

We'll briefly discuss the installation of WSRM and later configure resource allocation policies for Terminal Services.

Installing WSRM

Windows 2008 treats individual services as server roles. Some of the server roles are Domain Name System (DNS), Dynamic Host Configuration Protocol (DHCP), Fax, and ADS. Roles can be considered as logical software packages. Features are not directly part of any roles, but can enhance or support the functionality of a role in the Windows 2008 environment. Some of the features include Simple Transmission Control Protocol (TCP)/Internet Protocol (IP) services, .Net Framework 3.0, Failover Clustering, and Simple Network Management Protocol (SNMP) services. WSRM is also a feature. You need to access Server Manager to add WSRM to the server.

To install WSRM:

1. Click **Start | Administrative Tools | Server Manager** (see Figure 9.2).

Figure 9.2 Windows 2008 Server Manager

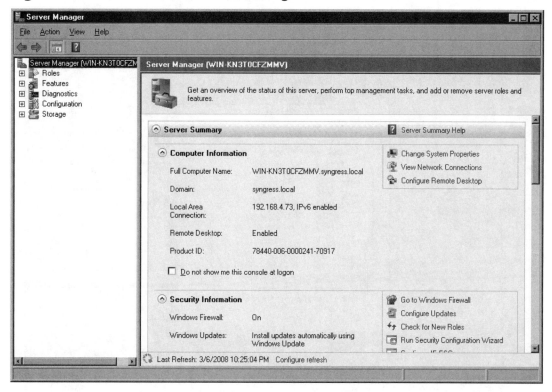

2. Select **Features** on the left pane, and click on **Add Features** on the right pane under the Features Summary.

3. Scroll-down to select **Windows System Resource Manager** under the "Select one or more features to install on this server" list (see Figure 9.3).

Figure 9.3 Adding Windows Resource Manager

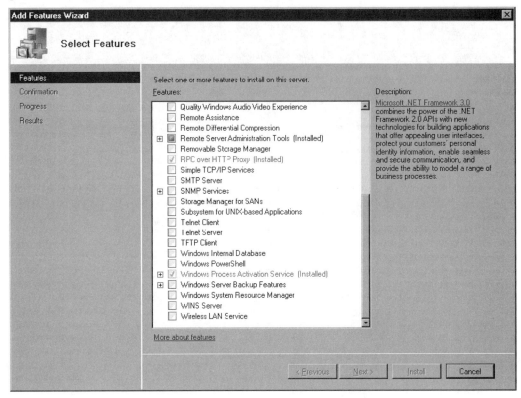

4. Click on the **Add Required Features** button in response to the prompt to add **Windows Internal Database**, a pre-requisite to install WSRM (see Figure 9.4).

Figure 9.4 Alert Message to Add Windows Internal Database Feature

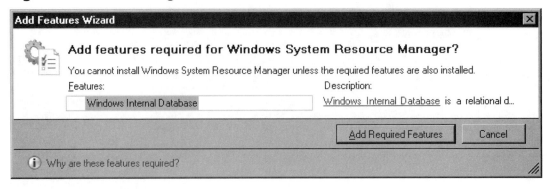

5. Click **Next**.

6. Click **Install**.

7. Click **Close** to complete the installation.

8. Click **Start | Administrative Tools | Services**, and check that the Windows System Resource Manager service is started.

To allocate resources for Terminal Services:

1. Click **Start | Administrative Tools | Windows System Resource Manager** (see Figure 9.5).

2. Click on **This Computer** and then click **Connect** in the "Connect to computer" dialog box.

3. Click on **Resource Allocation Policies** on the left pane (console tree).

4. Click on **Equal_Per_Session** policy.

Figure 9.5 WSRM Resource Allocation Policies

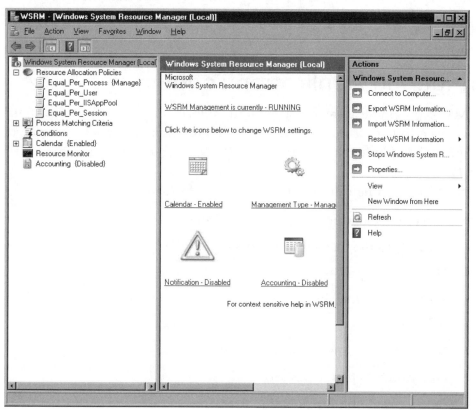

5. Click on **Set as Managing Policy** on the **Actions** pane (third window on your right).

6. Click **OK** on the warning dialog box, **The calendar will be disabled. Do you want to continue?**

Configuring & Implementing...

Allocating Resources: Resource Allocation Policy

Computer resources such as memory and central processing unit (CPU) are allocated to various processes running on the server. Resource allocation policy determines the usage of such resources. *Equal per user* or *Equal per session* can be configured as managing policy for Terminal Services. You may find more such resource allocation policies based on the services installed on your server. For example Internet Information Services (IIS) adds *Equal_Per_IISAppPool* policy. Default is the *Equal_Per_Process* policy.

Configuring Application Logging

WSRM's accounting feature logs accounting information of applications running on the server. To log accounting data, you need to ensure the policy is configured as managing policy (through *Set as Managing Policy*) or profiling policy (through *Set as Profile Policy*).

WSRM accounting captures the following information:

- Details on applications that exceeded the resources
- Changes to the managing policies
- Name of the process
- Name of the domain
- Name of the user
- Name of the resource allocation policy
- Policy time (when it was set)
- Process matching the policy criteria

- Program location

- Detailed information memory, disk, and processor operations

You have the option to store the data in the local WSRM database or on a Structured Query Language (SQL) database server. You also have the option to archive, export (*.txt* or *.csv* format), group similar items, sort items, and filter events for ease of viewing (through Filter View). Figure 9.6 shows the accounting screen of WSRM.

Figure 9.6 WSRM Accounting Data

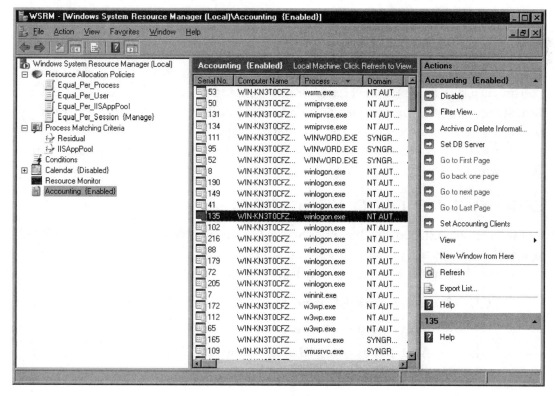

Load Balancing

Mission-critical servers require load-balancing techniques to ensure high availability and scalability. You may scale servers vertically by increasing memory and processors, or by adding additional network interfaces. Horizontal scaling means adding more identical servers, grouping them into one cluster, and then distributing the traffic evenly or based on certain algorithm between the member servers. It's a common practice in large enterprises to use network load balancers and have multiple mission-critical servers such as Web, File Transfer Protocol (FTP), Proxy, and other application servers. Terminal Services are no less mission-critical considering the fact that hundreds of remote users and branch offices may be accessing applications from a central location and also saving the data. In this topic, we'll discuss the Terminal Service Session Broker load balancing and NLB.

Terminal Service Load-Balancing Techniques

You can achieve load balancing in the Terminal Services environment using the TS Session Broker role service of Windows 2008. TS Session Broker maintains the track of a user session, and stores the session state information such as user names, name of the server, where the session is running, and the session IDs. This information is used to redirect a disconnected session back to the server where the user's session exists. TS Session Broker can also evenly distribute the load among the members of a terminal server farm. However, this requires an additional load-balancing mechanism such as a DNS round robin or a dedicated hardware-based load balancer to ensure the connection requests are distributed evenly.

Microsoft offers NLB to perform the distribution of connection requests. Apart from providing network-based load balancing, NLB also offers failed server detection.

Configuring Load Balancing

If you have not installed the Terminal Service Session Broker role service, you need to install the same to configure load balancing.

To install Terminal Service Session Broker role:

1. Click **Start | Administrative Tools | Server Manager**.
2. Click on **Roles** on the left pane.
3. Click on **Add Roles** under **Roles Summary**.
4. Click **Next** on the review page.
5. Select **Terminal Services** from the list of roles.
6. Select the **TS Session Broker** role and then click **Next**.
7. Click **Install**.
8. Click **Close** to complete the installation of TS Session Broker role service.

To configure TS Session Broker:

1. Click **Start | Administrative Tools | Terminal Services | Terminal Services Configuration** (see Figure 9.7).

Figure 9.7 Terminal Services Configuration

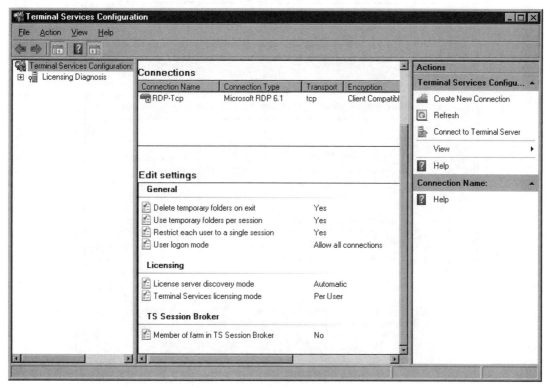

2. Double-click on **Member of farm** in the **TS Session Broker** option under **Edit Settings** in the center pane.

3. Select **Join a farm in TS Session Broker** (see Figure 9.8).

Figure 9.8 TS Session Broker Properties

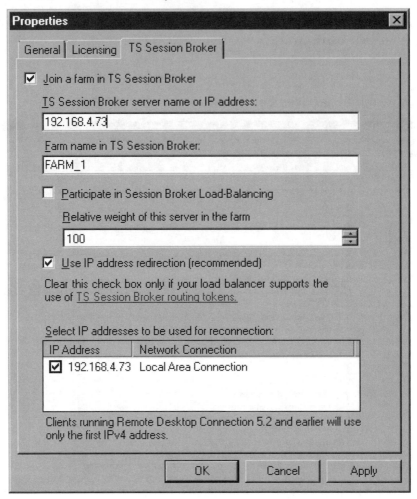

4. Provide the IP address of the server that is running TS Session Broker service in the **TS Session Broker Server name or IP address** text box.

5. Type a name of the server farm in the **Farm name in TS Session Broker** text box. This farm name will be used to add more servers to the farm. Ensure you use the same name so that all the new servers join the same farm correctly.

6. Select the check box **Participate in Session Broker Load-Balancing.**

7. Down-click from the pull-down list to select **Relative weight of this server in the farm.** The higher the number the more load the server will take.

You may use this relative weight number to assign weights to servers participating in this farm, to distribute load based on the server capabilities (memory, CPU, number of processors, and so forth).

8. Select the check box **Use IP address redirection**. Leaving it deselected will make the farm use token redirection.

9. Select the check box **IP address** of the server interface that will be used to participate in the farm. This is required when you have multiple interfaces and want the specific interface (network) to participate in the load balancing.

10. Click **OK** to complete the TS Session Broker configuration.

Adding Local Group On The TS Session Broker

The Session Directory Computers name for the local group has remained through the beta. This refers to the new TS Session Broker compared with the previous versions of Windows.

To add a terminal server to the Session Directory Computers local group:

1. Click **Start | Administrative Tools | Computer Management**.

2. Expand **Local Users and Groups**, and then click **Groups**.

3. Right-click on the **Session Directory Computers** groups, and then select properties (on the right pane).

4. Click **Add**.

5. Select the **Computers** option and then click **OK** from the **Select Users, Computers, or Groups** dialog box.

6. Add the computer account of the terminal server.

7. Click **OK**.

Installing NLB

To install NLB service:

1. Click **Start | Administrative Tools | Server Manager | Features**.

2. In the **Features Summary** on the right pane, click on **Add Features**.

3. Select **Windows Network Load Balancing** in the **Add Features** wizard.

4. Follow the prompts (**Next, Install, Close**) to complete the installation.

To create a NLB cluster:

1. Click **Start | Administrative Tools | Network Load Balancing Manager** (see Figure 9.9). The command prompt to open NLB manager is **nlbmgr**.

Figure 9.9 NLB Manager

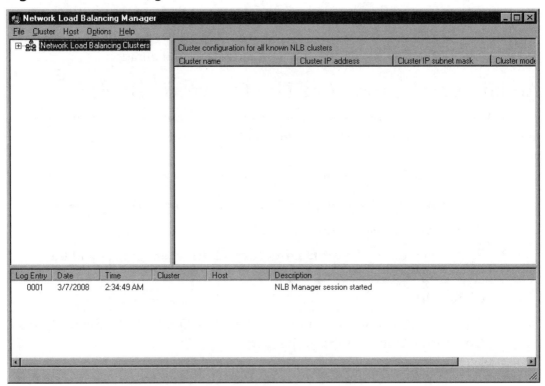

2. On the left pane, right-click on **Network Load Balancing Clusters** and select **New Cluster** (see Figure 9.10).

Figure 9.10 Configuring NLB Cluster Properties

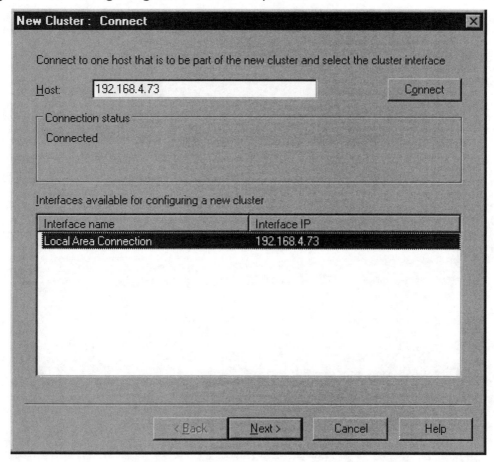

3. Type the IP address of the host and click **Connect**.

4. Click on the **Interface IP** to select a specific interface for the new cluster.

5. Click on the drop-down list to select the **Priority** (see Figure 9.11). Cluster traffic that is not handled by a port role will be handled by the server (host) that has low priority. Click **Next**.

Figure 9.11 NLB Cluster Host Parameters

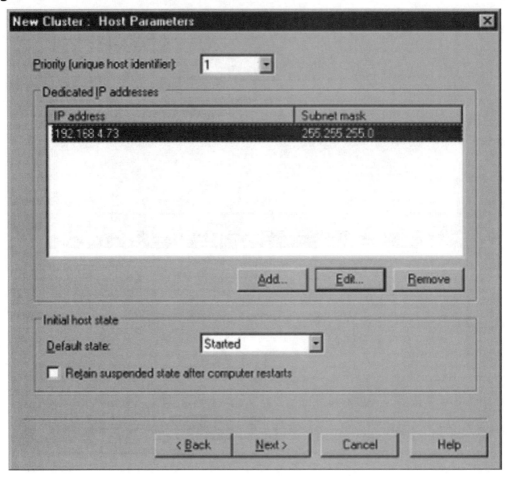

5. Click on **Add** and type the cluster IP address in the **Cluster IP Addresses** (see Figure 9.12) screen. Members of the cluster will share this cluster IP. Cluster heartbeats use the first listed IP address.

Figure 9.12 Configuring NLB Cluster IP Address

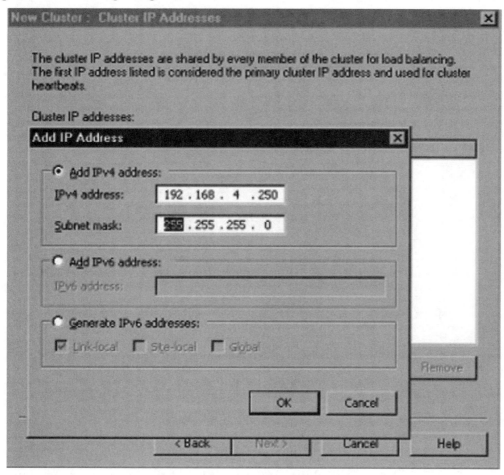

6. You may leave the Full Internet name blank as it's not required in the NLB with Terminal Services scenario (see Figure 9.13).

Figure 9.13 Configuring NLB Cluster Parameters

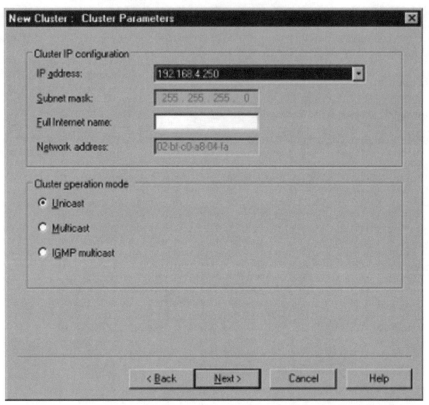

7. Select **Unicast** under **Cluster operation mode**. The media access control (MAC) address of the cluster is used instead of the server's network interface MAC when you select the Unicast option. This is the recommended cluster operation mode.

8. Select the **Cluster IP address** in the **Add/Edit Port rule** screen (see Figure 9.14).

9. Modify the port range to From (3389) and To (3389). This is the port number used by RDP.

10. Select **TCP** under **Protocols**.

11. Select **Multiple host** under **Filtering mode**. This means multiple hosts in the cluster will handle the traffic for this rule.

12. Select **Single** under **Affinity**. This is applicable only for **Multiple host mode**. If you are using TS Session broker, select none.

Figure 9.14 NLB Cluster Port Rule

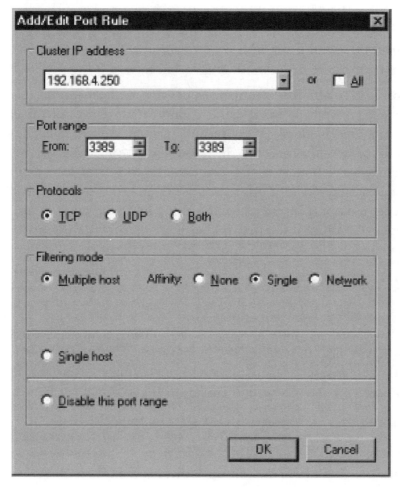

13.   Click **Finish** to complete the cluster creation.

Terminal Service
Session Broker Redirection Modes

TS Session Broker supports IP address and routing token redirection modes.
Redirecting a client to the terminal server where an active session exists for the
user is very important and is done by TS Session Broker.

■   **IP Address Redirection** This is the default redirection mode. First the
client queries the TS Session Broker. Then TS Session Broker redirects the

client to the appropriate server where an active session exists for the client using the IP address of the server. IP address-based connectivity between the client and server is the requirement to use this mode. In the scenarios using DNS round-robin NLB or a hardware balancer with no support for routing token redirection, IP address redirection is the preferred mode.

■ **Routing Token Redirection** To use this mode, the network balancer deployed in your network should support routing token redirection. Instead of using the IP address of the terminal server, a token embedded with the IP address is sent to the client. After a disconnection when the client attempts to reconnect to the server, the token is used to redirect the client to the appropriate terminal server where an active session exists for the client. Additional restrictions while using this redirection mode includes use of the IP address of the network adapter attached to the load balancer and configuration of the IP address as the terminal server IP address.

DNS Registration

The DNS round-robin feature along with the TS Session Broker service can be utilized to load-balance terminal service sessions in your network. You need to register the terminal servers first. To use the DNS round-robin feature you need to create host records for the terminal services and map it to the terminal server farm IP address.

To configure DNS for TS Session Broker load balancing:

1. Click **Start | Administrative Tools | DNS**.

2. Click on the **Server name** and expand.

3. Click on the **Forward Lookup Zones** and expand.

4. Right-click on the **domain name** (*syngress.local* in this exercise) and click on **New Host (A or AAA)...**

5. Type **FARM_1** (name of the farm we created earlier through NLB manager) in the **Name (uses parent domain name if blank)** text box (see Figure 9.15).

Figure 9.15 Configuring DNS for TS Session Broker Load Balancing

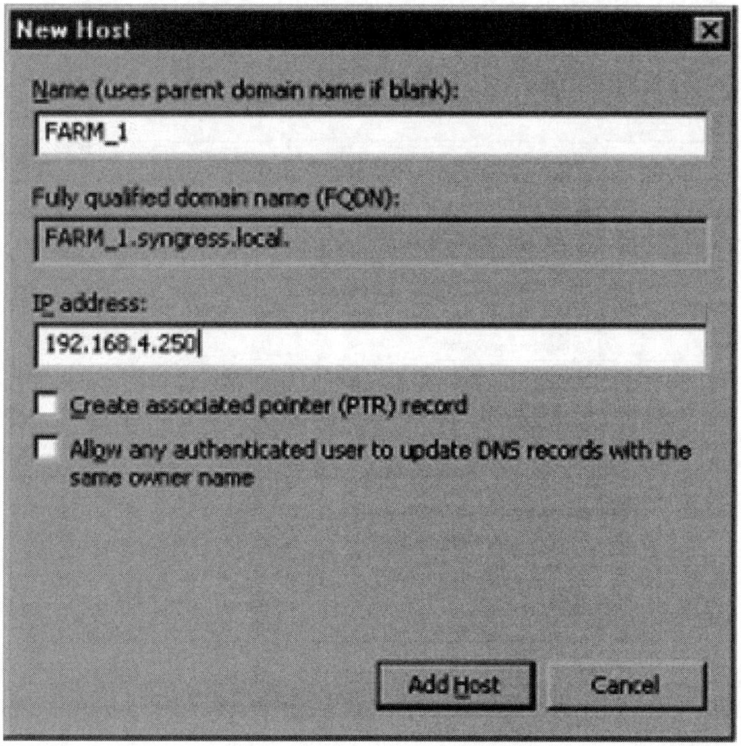

6. Type the **IP address** of the cluster (192.168.4.250).

7. Click on **Add Host**.

8. Right-click on the **domain name** and click on **New Host (A or AAA)...**

9. Type **FARM_1** in the **Name (uses parent domain if blank)** text box.

10. Type the **IP address** of the member server (192.168.4.73).

11. Repeat the steps to add another member server (192.168.4.51) with the same name (FARM_1).

12. Click **Done** to complete the DNS configuration for the cluster farm.

The new DNS zone information will look similar to the one shown in the Figure 9.16.

Figure 9.16 DNS Configuration of Cluster and Member Servers for TS Session Broker Load Balancing

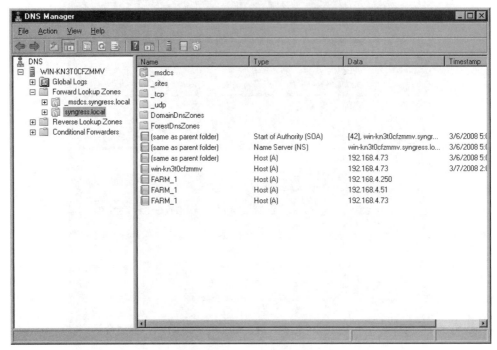

Configuring Load Balancing Through Group Policy

TS Session Broker load balancing can be configured through Active Directory (AD) Group Policy Object (GPO). You have to group terminal servers into an organizational unit (OU) and configure TS Session Broker parameters that apply on the GPO in the OU. It's preferred to have Terminal Server role service installed and configured for the TS Session Broker settings to be effective.

Add the Group Policy management console (**Start | Administrative Tools | Server Manager | Features | Add Features** and add **Group Policy Management Console**) before you create GPO and configure TS Session Broker settings.

To configure load balancing through group policy of Active Directory (AD):

1. Click **Start | Administrative Tools | Group Policy Management**.

2. Expand the forest and locate the domain name (syngress.local).

3. Right-click and select **Create a GPO in this domain, and Link it here.**

4. Type the name of the **Group Policy Object** (e.g., TerminalServices), in the **Name** text box and click **OK**.

5. Click on the new **GPO** created (TerminalServices).

6. On the right pane click the **Settings** tab.

7. Under **Computer Configuration**, right-click and select **Edit**.

8. Expand the **Policies** folder under **Computer Configuration**.

9. Expand **Administrative Templates**.

10. Expand **Windows components**.

11. Expand **Terminal Services**.

12. Expand **Terminal Server**.

13. Select **TS Session Broker** folder (as shown in the Figure 9.17).

Figure 9.17 Load Balancing Through Group Policy

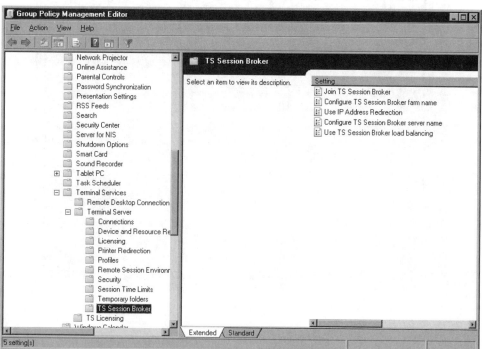

14. Double-click on **Configure TS Session Broker farm name** parameter on the right-pane.

15. Select **Enabled**.

16. Type **FARM_1** in the **TS Session Broker farm name** (FARM_1 was created earlier through NLB manager) as shown in the Figure 9.18.

Figure 9.18 TS Session Broker Parameter in Group Policy

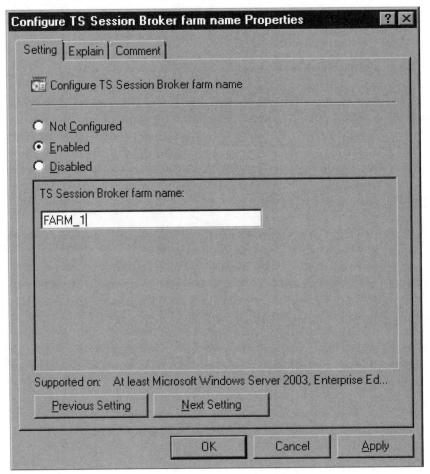

17. Click **OK**.

18. Double-click on **Use TS Session Broker load balancing**.

19. Select **Enabled** (see Figure 9.19).

Figure 9.19 TS Session Broker Load-Balancing Parameter in Group Policy

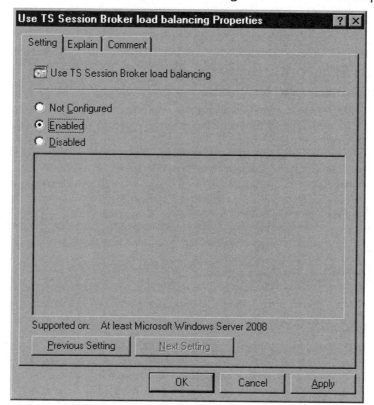

20. Click **OK**.

21. Double-click on **Use IP Address Redirection**. Click on **Enabled**. (This is required only when your setup has dedicated hardware-based load-balancing appliances. This hardware balancer should support token redirection mode).

The Terminal Services Gateway

Terminal Services Gateway helps administrators to enable remote users to access the corporate applications without a need to setup a VPN. Users with the RDC client can connect to internal network resources securely.

To achieve this, the RDP traffic is sent over a Secure Sockets Layer (SSL) Hypertext Transfer Protocol (HTTP) connection. Once the RDP-encapsulated traffic reaches the TS Gateway, TS Gateway strips the HTTPS headers and forwards the RDP traffic to terminal servers. Remote clients can access terminal servers or RemoteApp listed applications, or initiate a Remote Desktop session securely over the Internet.

In a conventional VPN network, the remote client runs an Internet Protocol Security (IPsec) VPN client. A secure IPSec session is established between the remote user terminating at the Firewall/VPN appliance or server. However, managing mobile user VPN for a large enterprise may be a cumbersome task due to managing and distributing security policies across the enterprise. Moreover, users are restricted to use the client with the VPN pre-installed and pre-configured. TS Gateway liberates users from device restrictions and can virtually access from any desktop, laptop from a trusted or untrusted network, and even from the mobile hand-held devices with RDP client. Apart from establishing a secure connection, administrators can granularly control which network resources need to be accessed by the remote users. HTTP and HTTPS are allowed by most corporate firewalls, therefore there is no need to open the RDP 3389 port on the firewall.

In addition to this, TS Gateway provides resource authorization policies for remote user terminal connections.

Figure 9.20 shows the scenario where different types of users establish a secure connection over HTTPS carrying RDP traffic.

Figure 9.20 TS Gateway Server Deployment Scenario

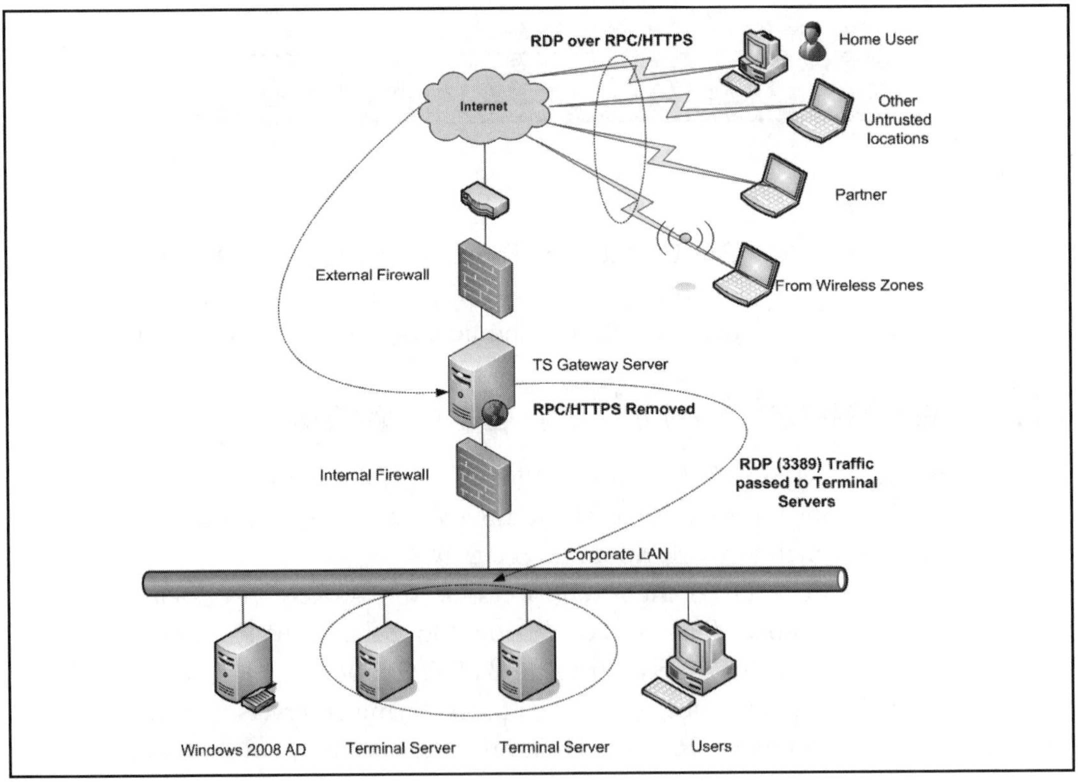

For large enterprises with a huge number of remote user sessions, TS Gateway can be deployed in a high-available load-balancing environment. Dedicated load-balances such as F5 FirePass controllers may be deployed with multiple TS Gateway servers to ensure continuous availability of remote user sessions. Figure 9.21 is an illustration of an environment with a dedicated hardware load balancer with two TS Gateway servers. HTTPS connections are load balanced between both of the TS Gateway servers. After HTTPS encapsulation is removed RDP traffic is passed to the terminal servers.

Figure 9.21 TS Gateway Server Deployment Scenario

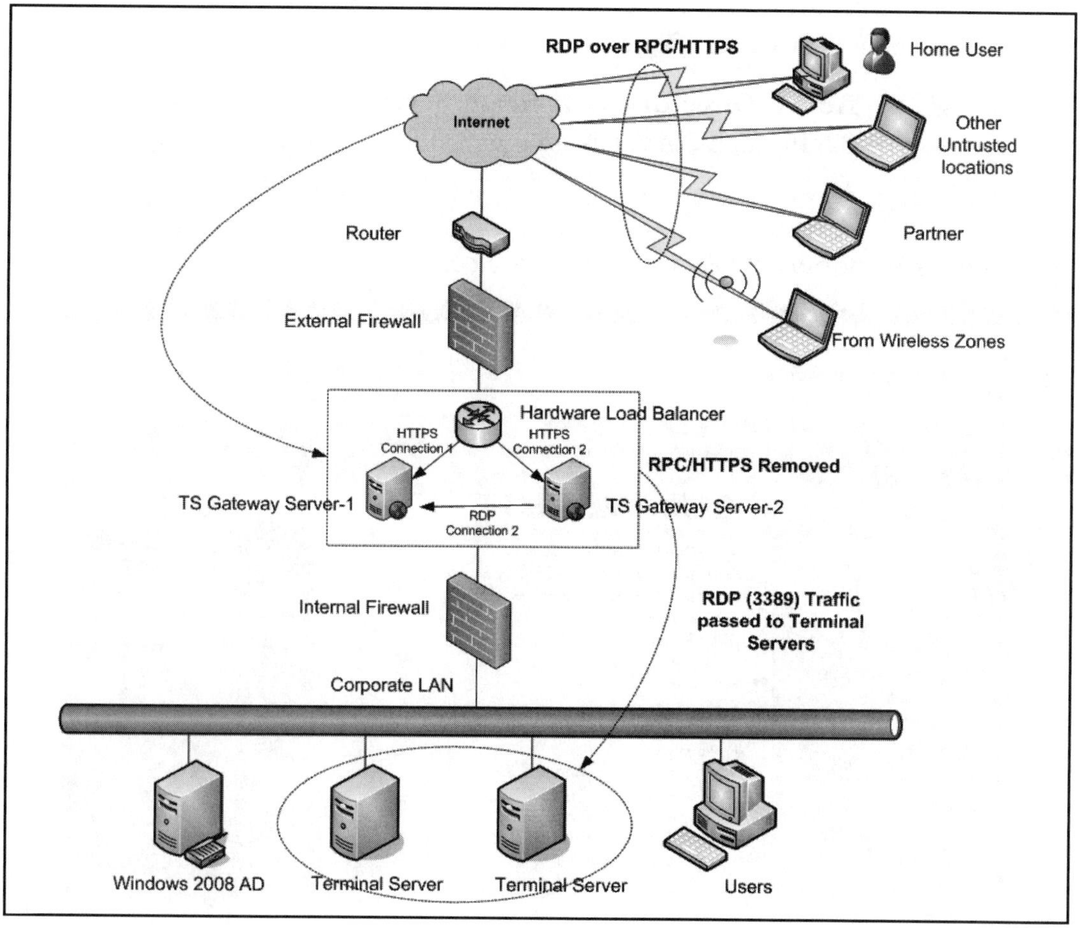

TS Gateway configuration involves the following procedure:

1. Install a SSL certificate (obtained through a trusted third party such as Verisign or create a self-signed certificate for the organization).

2. Map the SSL certificate to the TS Gateway Server.

3. Join the TS Gateway Server to an AD domain.

4. Create a Connection Authorization Policy (CAP)

5. Create a RAP.

Certificate Configuration

Configuring self-signed certificates involves two steps: installing and configuring the AD Certificate Services server role, and copying the certificate to the client computers (as the built-in Internet browsers only have trusted third-party certificates).

To create a self-signed certificate:

1. Add the **Active Directory Certificate Services** server role (see Figure 9.22) through **Server Manager** (adding roles were explained earlier).

Figure 9.22 Windows 2008 Certificate Services

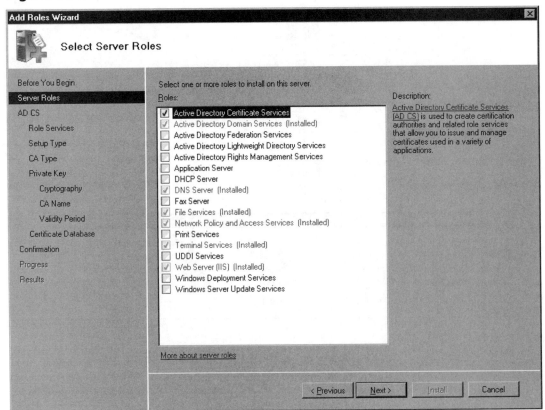

2. Follow the wizard to add Enterprise, stand-alone, Root CA. This will install a server certificate.

To map a certificate to the TS Gateway Server:

1. Click **Start | Administrative Tools | Terminal Services, | TS Gateway Manager**.

2. Select the **Server** on the left pane, right-click and select **Properties**.

3. Click on the **SSL Certificate** tab (see Figure 9.23).

Figure 9.23 Mapping a Certificate to TS Gateway Server

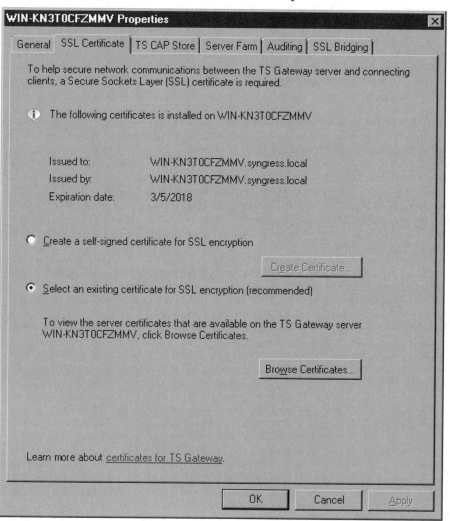

4. Click on **Select an existing certificate for SSL encryption (recommended)**, if not selected already by default.

5. Click on **Browse Certificates**.

6. Select the certificate on the **Install Certificate** screen and click **Install**.

7. Click **OK** to complete the certificate association with TS Gateway server.

Terminal Service (TS) Gateway Manager

TS Gateway Manager is the snap-in console that helps you manage TS Gateway server (see Figure 9.24). With the TS Gateway Manager you can perform the following tasks:

- Manage the TS Gateway Server

- Configure a SSL certificate

- Create CAPs

- Create RAPs

- Manage terminal services through CAP and RAP

- Create a TS Gateway server farm

- Add members to a TS Gateway server farm

- Limit the maximum number of simultaneously allowed connections

- Disable new connections

- Enable auditing

- Create a SSL bridge (HTTPS-HTTP bringing to terminate SSL requests and initiate new HTTP requests)

In the following pages we'll discuss resource allocation policies that can be configured through TS Gateway Manager.

Figure 9.24 TS Gateway Server Manager

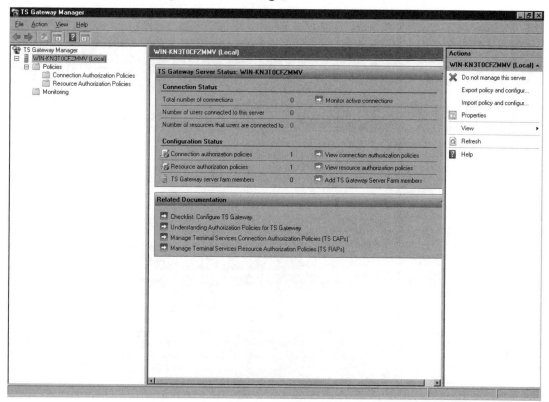

Accessing Resources through the TS Gateway Using TS CAP

TS Connection Authorization Policy (TS CAP) defines who can connect to a TS Gateway server. Unless clients meet these requirements, connection to the TS Gateway server is not allowed. CAP defines authentication methods (password or smart card, member of AD security groups) and device redirection parameters.

To create a new TS Connection Authorization Policy:

1. Click **Start | Administrative Tools | Terminal Services**, and then select the **TS Gateway Manager** (see Figure 9.25).

Figure 9.25 TS Gateway Server Manager Police Configuration

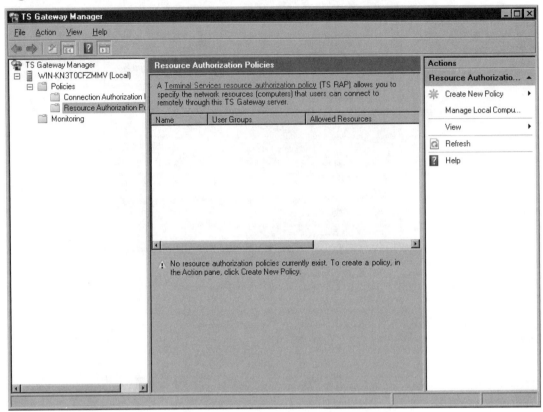

2. Click and expand the **Server**.

3. Click and expand the **Policies** folder. You will find **Connection Authorization Policies** and **Resource Authorization Policies** sub-folders.

4. Click on **Connection Authorization Policies**.

5. On the **Actions** pane, click on **Create New Policy** and select the wizard option. This will start the **Authorization Policies** wizard. The other option is **custom**, *which* will open up a New TS CAP window.

6. Select the **Create a TS CAP and a TS RAP (recommended)** option (see Figure 9.26). You have the option to create a CAP or a RAP. If you

select the first option (**Create a TS CAP and a TS RAP** (recommended)), the wizard will assist you in creating both the policies together. However, until you recreate both the options, you will not be able to access the network resources.

Figure 9.26 Policy Creation Wizard to Create TS CAP and TS RAP

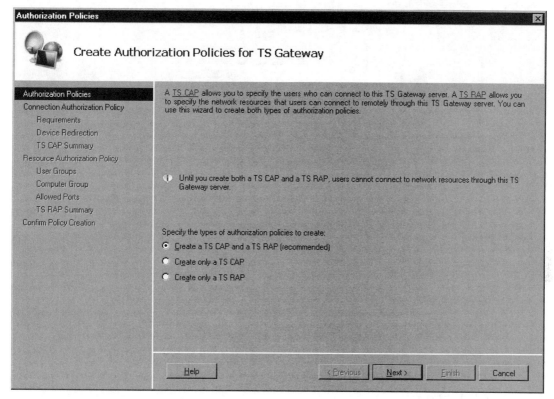

7. Type a name in the **Enter a name of TS CAP** text box and click **Next**.

8. Select the **Password** check box to select password as the authentication method. The other option is to use **Smart card** for user authentication (see Figure 9.27).

Figure 9.27 TS CAP Authentication Method and User Group Configuration

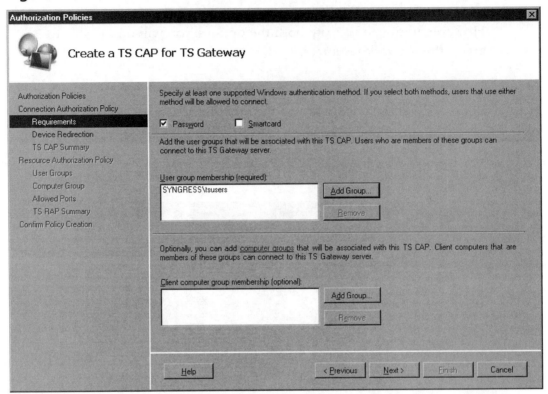

9. Click on **Add Group** and select the group created for Terminal Services. For this exercise, we have created **tsusers** group. You also have the option to add **Client computer group**.

10. Click **Next**.

11. Select **Enable device redirection for all client devices** (see Figure 9.28) and click **Next**. Device redirection includes disk drives, printers, clipboard, serial ports, and plug-and play-devices.

Figure 9.28 TS CAP Policy for Device Redirection

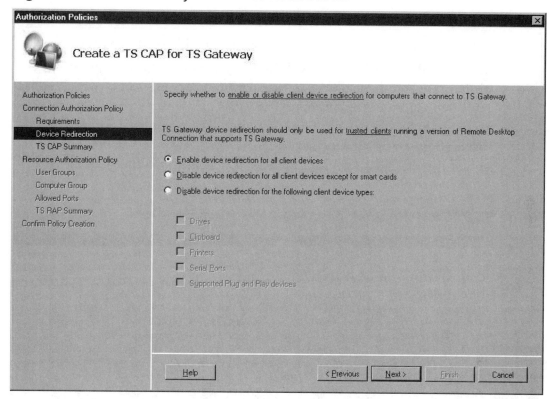

12. Review the **Summary of TS CAP settings** and click **Next**.

As we have chosen the option to create both the TSCAP and TSRAP policies, the wizard will continue with RSRAP creation. We'll discuss the same in the next section.

Accessing Resources through the TS Gateway Using TS RAP

TS Resource Authorization Policy (TS RAP) defines the type of network resources a remote user can connect through a TS Gateway server. RAP defines the AD security group and the port number the remote connections use (for example, RDP 3389). You can configure RAP to allow custom port numbers or connection through any port number (not recommended).

To configure TS RAP:

1. Continue with the wizard from the previous screen for creating **TS CAP**.

2. Type a name in the **Enter the name for the TS RAP** text box.

3. Select the **An existing Active Directory security group** option, click on **Browse** and then add the **tsusers** group that consists of terminal services users (see Figure 9.29). This option specifies the network resources users can access through TS Gateway. Other options include using a TS Gateway managed group or allowing any access to any network resources. The first option is preferred as you can integrate the security settings with the AD.

Figure 9.29 TS RAP Network Resource Access Configuration

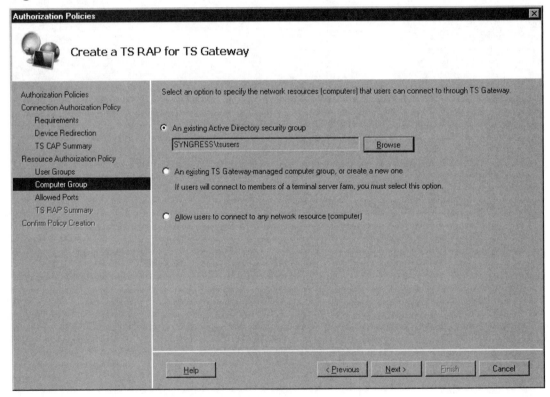

4. Select **Allow connections only through TCP port 3389** (see Figure 9.30). This is the RDP port. You have an option to provide custom ports. You need to exercise caution while choosing ports for the terminal services. It should not be from the well-known port range or ports that are

used by other applications in your network. The third option to allow connection through any port is not recommended.

Figure 9.30 TS RAP RDP Port Configuration

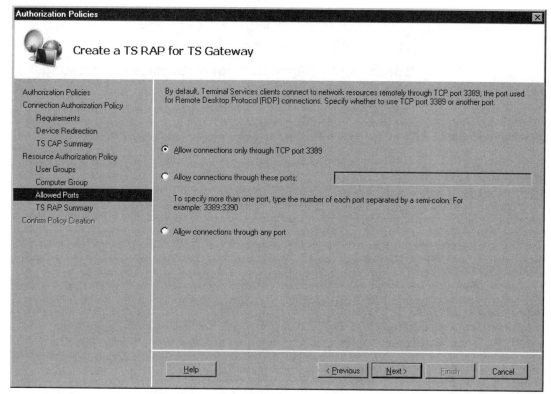

5. Review the settings on **Summary of TS RAP settings** screen and click **Next** to create the policy.

Terminal Service Group Policy Settings

Group Policy settings help you to define finer security settings, connection and session limits, resource management, and licensing. Table 9.1 summarizes the Group Policy settings available for Terminal Services. To configure these settings click **Start | Administrative Tools | Group Policy Management**, locate the **OU** and right click and select **Edit**. In the **Group Policy Management Editor** expand **Computer Configuration | Policies | Administrative Templates | Windows Components | Terminal Services**.

Table 9.1 Group Policy Parameters for Terminal Service Components

Category	Setting
Remote Desktop Connection Client	Allow .rdp files from valid publishers and use's default RDP settings
	Allow .rdp files from unknown publishers
	Do not allow passwords to be saved
	Specify SHA1 thumbprints of certificates representing trusted .rdp publishers
	Prompt for credentials on the client computer
	Configure server authentication for client
Terminal Server	
Connections	Automatic reconnection
	Allow users to connect remotely using Terminal Services
	Deny logoff of an administrator logged in to the console session
	Configure keep-alive connection interval
	Limit number of connections
	Set rules for remote control of Terminal Services user sessions
	Restrict Terminal Services users to a single remote session
	Allow remote start of unlisted program
Device and Resource Redirection	Allow audio redirection
	Do not allow clipboard redirection
	Do not allow COM port redirection
	Do not allow drive redirection
	Do not allow LPT port redirection
	Do not allow supported Plug-and-Play device redirection

Continued

Table 9.1 Continued. Group Policy Parameters for Terminal
Service Components

Category	Setting
	Do not allow smart card device redirection
	Allow time zone redirection
Licensing	Use the specified Terminal Services license servers
	Hide notification about TS Licensing problems that affect the terminal server
	Set the Terminal Services licensing mode
Printer Redirection	Do not set default client printer to be default printer in a session
	Do not allow client printer redirection
	Specify terminal server fallback printer driver behavior
	Use Terminal Services Easy Print printer driver first
	Redirect only the default client printer
Profiles	Set TS User Home Directory
	Use mandatory profiles on the terminal server
	Set path for TS Roaming User Profile
Remote Session Environment	Limit maximum color depth
	Enforce Removal of Remote Desktop Wallpaper
	Remove "Disconnect" option from Shut Down dialog
	Remove Windows Security item from Start menu
	Set compression algorithm for RDP data
	Start a program on connection
	Always show desktop on connection
Security	Server Authentication Certificate Template
	Set client connection encryption level
	Always prompt from password upon connection
	Require secure RPC connection

Continued

Table 9.1 Continued. Group Policy Parameters for Terminal Service Components

Category	Setting
	Require use of specific security layer for remote (RDP) connections
	Do not allow local administrators to customize permissions
	Require user authentication for remote connections by using Network Level Authentication
Session Time Limits	Set time limit for disconnected sessions
	Set time limit for active but idle Terminal Services sessions
	Terminate session when time limits are reached
	Set time limit for logoff of RemoteApp sessions
Temporary Folders	Do not delete temporary folder upon exit
	Do not use temporary folders per session
TS Session Broker	Join TS Session Broker
	Configure TS Session Broker farm name
	Use IP Address Redirection
	Configure TS Session Broker server name
	Use TS Session Broker load balancing
TS Licensing	License server security group
	Prevent License upgrade

Terminal Service RemoteApp

Terminal Service RemoteAPP (TS RemoteApp) can be considered a synonym to terminal service. TS RemoteApp publishes the network applications that can be remotely accessed through clients running RDC clients or through the Web. Only keyboard clicks, mouse movements, and display information is transmitted over the network. Users can see only their sessions. Remote applications can be executed along with local applications. Users get seamless access to the remote applications instead of accessing a remote desktop to open applications. Multiple remote applications can be run in a single terminal service session utilizing resources efficiently. While accessing remote applications through TS Web Access, remote applications appear as Web links. Remote Desktop Protocol (.rdp) files can be created by administrators and distributed over the network for remote users to install and access applications.

Benefits of TS RemoteApp include:

- Provide applications from a central location to remote offices

- Support branch offices with inadequate IT staff to offer system administration

- Install applications centrally and access from anywhere

- Manage frequently updated, difficult to manage, or infrequently used applications efficiently

- Improve performance even under limited network-bandwidth scenarios

- Offer applications through hand-held devices (such as Windows mobile powered phones/PDAs) with RDC Client

- Allow multiple versions of same applications to exist (in some scenarios that demand such co-existence)

Configuring TS RemoteApp

Configuring TS RemoteApp includes installing applications in a terminal-server aware mode (on the Terminal Server), enabling remote control configuration, configuring application parameters, adding users, and publishing it on TS Web for Web access.

To install an application in the Terminal Server mode:

1. Click **Start | Control Panel** and double-click on **Install Application on Terminal Server** (see Figure 9.31). It is recommended to install any new applications only after installing terminal services on the server. Microsoft applications (*.msi packages*) are terminal services aware and can be installed directly without going through the Install Application on Terminal Server option.

Figure 9.31 Windows 2008 Control Panel Option to Install Applications on Terminal Server

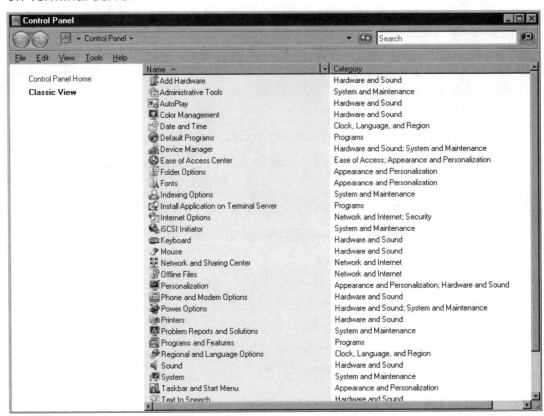

2. Click **Next** on the **Install program From Floppy Disk or CD–ROM** screen of the wizard (see Figure 9.32).

Figure 9.32 Installing Applications on Terminal Server

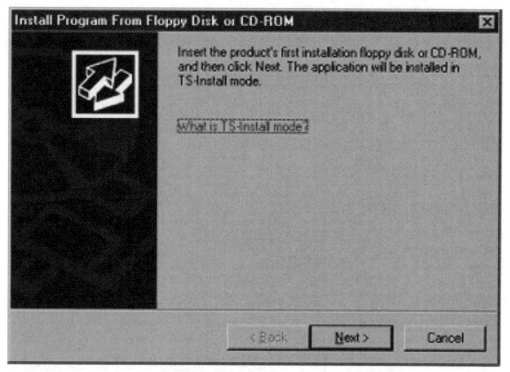

3. Type the location of the set-up file of the application (for example, *d:\setup. exe*) or click on **Browse** to locate the set-up file.

4. Wait until the installation of the software completes. The Finish button will turn gray until the application completes the installation. Do not close this screen until the Finish button becomes active (see Figure 9.33). Click **Finish** to complete the installation. Now you can use TS Remote App manager to publish the application you have installed.

Figure 9.33 Terminal Server Application Wizard Transferring
Control to Application

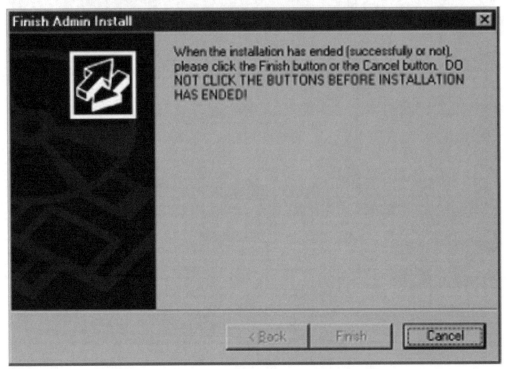

To verify the remote connection settings:

1. Click **Start** | **Run**, and then type **control system** into the **Open** box.
   This will open the **System** tool (see Figure 9.34).

Figure 9.34 Windows 2008 System Tool

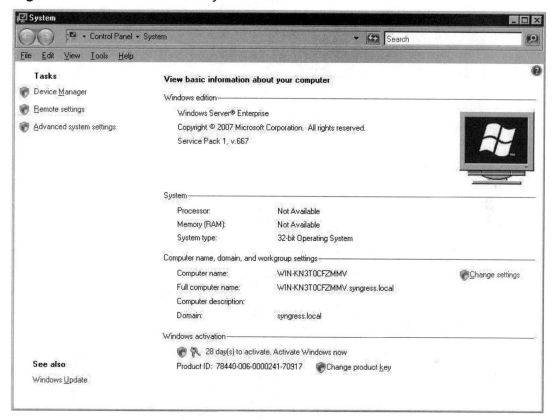

2. Click on **Remote Settings** under **Tasks**.

3. Click the **Remote** tab.

4. Select **Allow connections from computers running any version of Remote Desktop (less secure)** (see Figure 9.35). This will allow remote desktop connections from your present setup consisting of Windows XP clients. This option is also preferred when you are not sure about the RDP client versions that may connect to your network. If your network consists of Windows Vista and Windows 2008 or Windows XP with the latest RDP client, you can choose the more secure option, **Allow connections only from computers running Remote Desktop with Network Level Authentication (more secure)**.

Figure 9.35 Remote Desktop Configuration

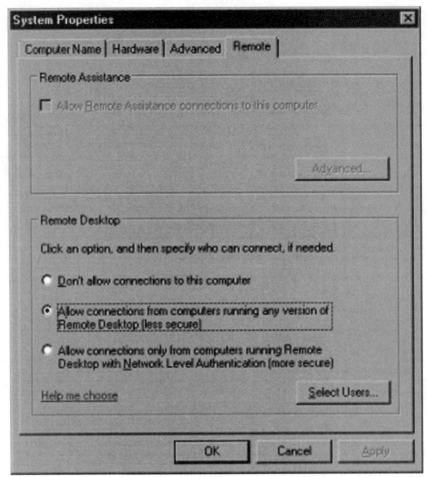

5. Click on **Select Users** and then click **Add**. Locate the Users or User groups (see Figure 9.36) and double-click to add.

Figure 9.36 RDP Users Configuration

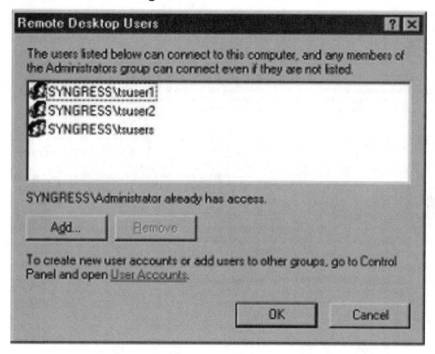

6. Click **OK** to complete the configuration.

To add an application to the RemoteApp Programs:

1. Click **Start | Administrative Tools | Terminal Services**, and then select **TS RemoteApp Manager** (see Figure 9.37).

Figure 9.37 TS RemoteApp Manager

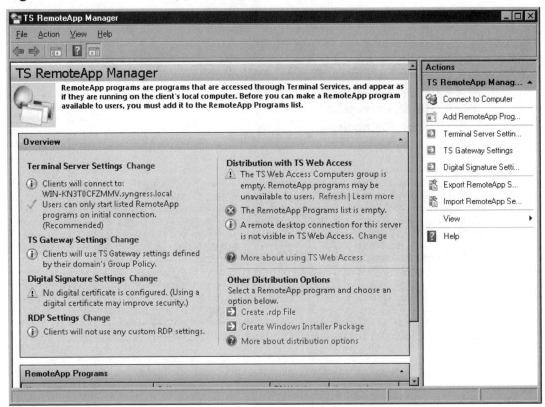

2. Click on **Add RemoteApp Programs** from the **Actions** pane (right). This will start the **RemoteApp wizard**.

3. Click **Next**.

4. Click on the check boxes on the left of the applications you want to publish for remote access. For this exercise we've installed Microsoft Word 2007 (see Figure 9.38).

Figure 9.38 Choosing Applications For Remote Access

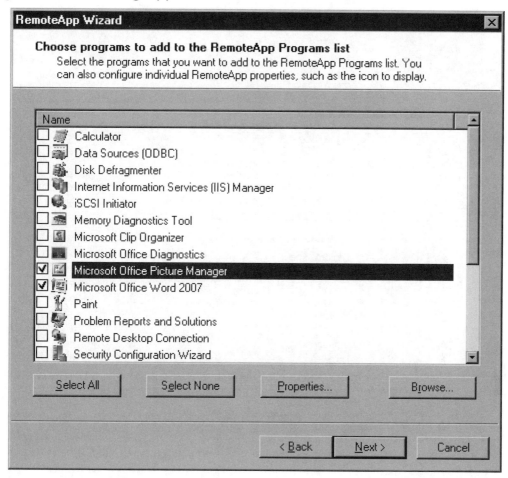

5. Click on **Properties** (see Figure 9.39).

Figure 9.39 Configuration Applications For Remote Access

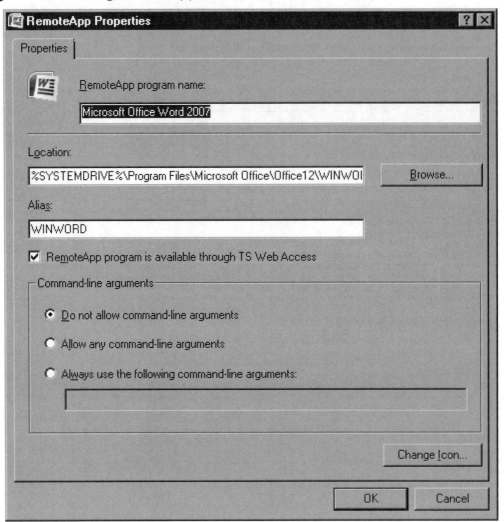

6. Select the **RemoteApp program is available through TS Web Access** check box. This will enable the application to be accessed by the users through Terminal Service Web Access (discussed later in this chapter).

7. You also have the option to **Change Icon** (if required).

8. Click **Finish** after you review the settings on the Review Settings screen. On the main screen of RemoteApp Manager now you can see Microsoft Office Word 2007 added to the RemoteApp Programs list. Repeat these steps to publish all the applications that require remote access.

Configuring TS Web Access

TS Web Access enables you to make RemoteApp programs appear as a link on the Web site and make them available to remote users. TS Web Access also provides direct access to remote access through the Web browsers.

Install the TS Web Access server role if you have not already done so. You can add the TS Web Access Web page as a Web Part to your corporate Web site. IIS is required by TS Web Access. All applications that need to be available through RemoteApp have to be installed only after installing Terminal Service.

If you have not installed TS Web Access role service, install it through Server Manager.

New & Noteworthy...

Remote Desktop Connection (RDC) Client 6.1

Client computers running RDC client 6.1 can access TS Web Access. RDC client 6.1 is included in Windows Server 2008, Windows Vista with SP1, and Windows XP with SP3 Beta or Windows XP with SP3 operating systems.

To configure TS Web Access:

1. Open the Internet Explorer browser.
2. Type **http://server_name/ts (In this exercise, win-kn3t0cfzmmv. syngress.local/ts)** (see Figure 9.40).
3. Click on the **Configuration** link.
4. Provide the name of the Terminal Server in the **Terminal server name** text box under **Editor Zone** and then click **Apply**.

Figure 9.40 TS Web Access Configuration

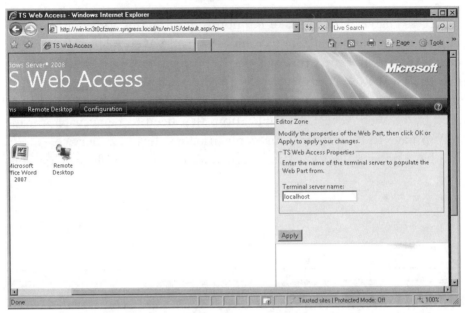

5. You will find the list of published applications in the **RemoteApp Programs** (see Figure 9.41) link.

Figure 9.41 Applications Through TS Web Access

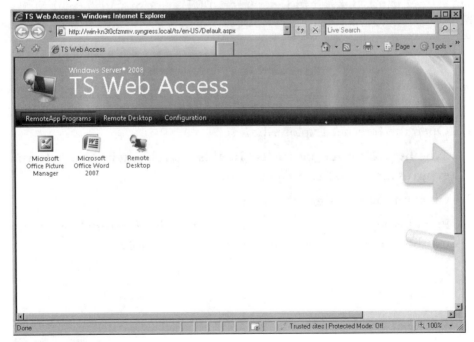

6. Click on the **Microsoft Office Word 2007** icon to start the remote application.

7. Provide the terminal server user name and password (*tsuser1*).

8. You may see a warning window (see Figure 9.42). Click on **Connect**.

Figure 9.42 RemoteApp Warning Message

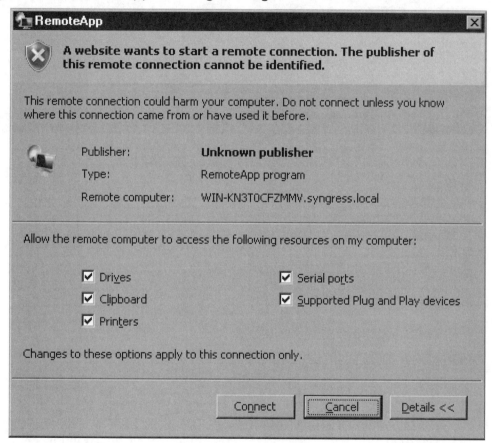

9. Microsoft Office Word 2007 should open with the look and feel of accessing a local application.

10. If you encounter an error message (**ActiveX control not installed or not enabled**) it's possibly due to the RDP client version running on your system (see Figure 9.43). RDP client version 6.1 is required to access TS Web service. Presently in the Windows 2008 RC1 version clicking on the visit

Web site link takes you to a blog suggesting some solution. You may click on Install ActiveX control without much success. Hopefully this will be resolved in the final release. To install the latest RDP client software, visit this link: http://support.microsoft.com/default.aspx/kb/925876.

Figure 9.43 ActiveX Error Message

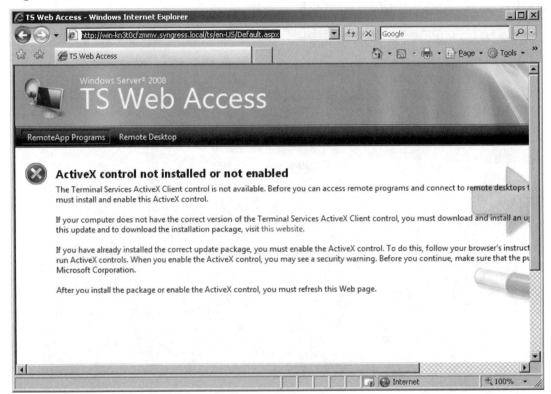

11. The RDP client (Terminal Services Client 6.0) is available for Windows Server 2003, Windows Server 2003, x64, Windows XP, and Windows XP, x64.

Configuring TS Remote Desktop Web Connection

TS Remote Desktop Web connection is a feature of TS Web Access that allows remote users to connect to a remote desktop, taking full control of the remote system instead of just accessing the remote applications (see Figure 9.44).

To configure TS Remote Desktop Web Access:

1. Open the Internet Explorer browser.

2. Type **http://server_name/ts** (in this exercise, **win-kn3t0cfzmmv. syngress.local/ts**).

3. Click on the **Remote Desktop** link.

4. Under the **Connection Options** provide the **Computer Name** or **IP address** of the Terminal Server.

Figure 9.44 Remote Desktop Configurations on TS Web Access

5. Choose from 800x600, 1024x768, 1280x1024, or 1600x1200 pixels for the **Remote desktop size**.

6. Click on **Options** to see other options available.

7. Choose the **Devices and resources** you want to use in the remote session (options are printers, clipboard, drives, supported plug-and-play devices and serial ports).

8. Choose **Additional Options** including **Remote Computer Sound** (Bring to this computer, Leave at remote computer, Do not play), **Apply keyboard shortcuts** (In full-screen mode only, On the local computer, On the remote computer), and **Performance** (Slow modem (28.8 Kbps), Fast modem (56 Kbps), Broadband (128 Kbps – 1.5 Mbps), and LAN (10 Mbps or higher).

9. Option for a legal disclaimer (**I am using a private computer that complies with my organization's security policy**) check box is available.

Managing the Terminal Services

Managing the terminal services includes various tasks such as assigning RDP permissions, configuring connection limits, session time limits, assigning session permissions, viewing process, monitoring sessions, logging off users, disconnect sessions, and resetting the terminal services. Terminal Services Manager is used to perform these administrative tasks. Ensure you have a thorough understanding of every task and the implications before you apply it on a production network. Improper configuration of permissions may result in assigning additional permissions to the users where not required and inadequate access where required.

RDP Permissions

Terminal Services Manager allows you to configure various RDP permissions. Permission sets such as Full Control, User Access, Guest Access, and Special Permissions can be assigned to users, clients, and groups. Each permission set has one or more permissions (see Tables 9.2 and 9.3). Figure 9.45 shows the RDP properties. Figure 9.46 shows the advanced security settings for RDP. Figure 9.47 shows RDP permissions.

Figure 9.45 RDP Properties

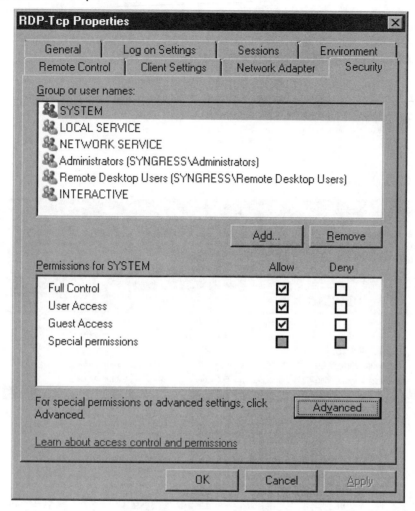

Table 9.2 Terminal Services Permissions

Permission[*]	Description
Full Control	Permission set providing Query Information, Set Information, Remote Control, Logon, Logoff, Message, Connect, Disconnect and Virtual Channels permissions
User Access	Permission set providing Query Information, Logon, and Connect permissions

Continued

Table 9.2 Continued. Terminal Services Permissions

Permission*	Description
Guest Access	Logon permission only
Logon	Logon to Terminal Server session

*Permissions are described more in the Table 9.3.

Figure 9.46 Advanced Security Settings for RDP

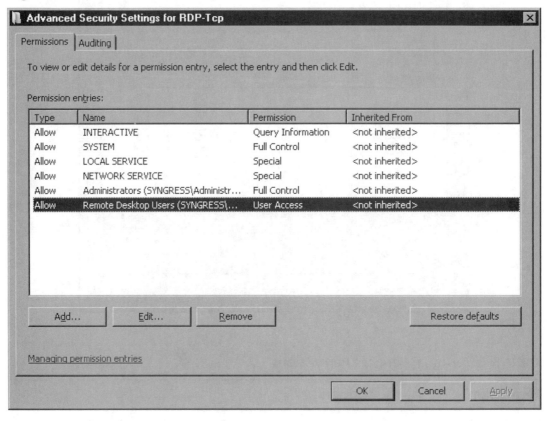

Figure 9.47 RDP Permissions

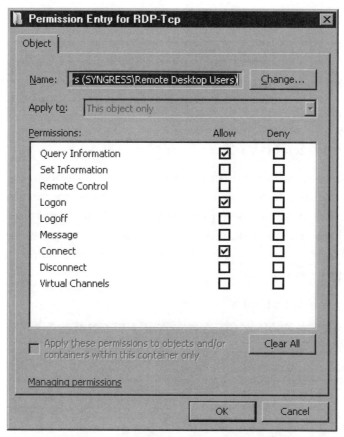

Table 9.3 Terminal Services Connection Permissions

Permission	Description
Query Information	Allows users to query for information from Terminal Servers and Sessions
Set Information	Allows users to configure properties of the connection
Remote Control	Allows users to view or control other users' sessions
Logon	Logon to Terminal Server session
Logoff	Log off a user from the Terminal Server session
Message	Allows users to send a message to a user session
Connect	Allows users to connect to another user's session

Continued

Table 9.3 Continued. Terminal Services Connection Permissions

Permission	Description
Disconnect	Disconnects a user session
Virtual Channels	Assigning this permission provides access to local (client computer's) device and redirects resources

Connection Limits

You can configure the number of simultaneous remote connections on a server. Administrators may decide to restrict remote connections to enhance the performance of the server or for security purposes. Figure 9.48 shows the connections limits. You have two options: unlimited connections and maximum connections. When Terminal Server is not installed, Windows 2008 server allows only two simultaneous remote connections.

Figure 9.48 Connection Limits

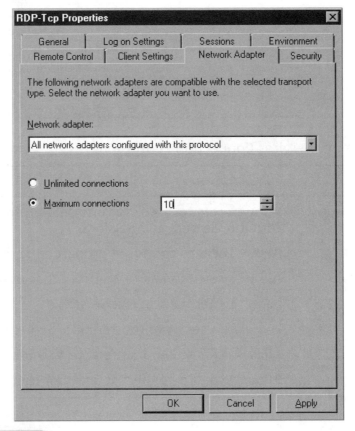

Session Time Limits

Session time limit (see Figure 9.49) configuration is an essential task due to the users' limited knowledge about running applications from their local computers, and the amount of resources a remote session may consume when running applications from the terminal server. Controlling active, idle, and disconnected sessions becomes important in such cases. Timeout and reconnection settings are configured on a per-user basis. This is done through the Active Directory Users and Computers. Table 9.4 explains the configuration options for controlling sessions.

Figure 9.49 Session Limits

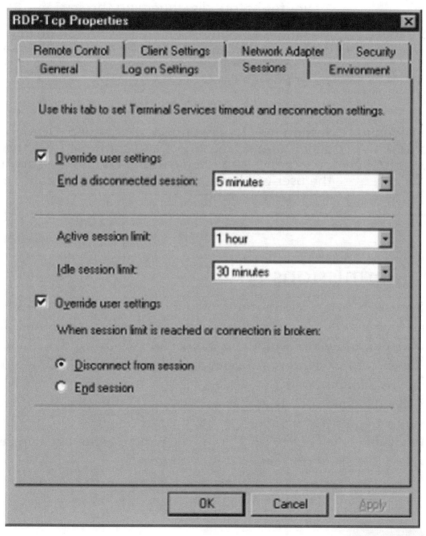

Table 9.4 Terminal Services Session Limits

Setting	Description
End a disconnected session	Maximum amount of time a disconnected session is active on the terminal server.
	Options: Minutes (1, 10, 15, 30), Hours (1, 2, 3, 6, 8, 12, 16, 18), Days (1, 2, 3, 4, 5). Never (session maintained for unlimited time). Not recommended.
Active session limit	Maximum amount of time a session can be active.
	Options: Minutes (1, 5, 10, 15, 30), Hours (1, 2, 3, 6, 8, 12, 16, 18), Days (1, 2, 3, 4, 5). A warning is sent 2 minutes before disconnecting the session.
Idle session limit	Maximum amount of time a session can be idle without receiving any input from the user. After this time the session is ended. Options: Minutes (1, 5, 10, 15, 30)
	Hours (1, 2, 3, 6, 8, 12, 16, 18), Days (1, 2, 3, 4, 5)
When a session limit is reached or connection is broken	Session may be disconnected or ended. Disconnected allows user to reconnect and continue from the previously established session. Ending a session means the user will have to establish a new session. This is a radio button option.

Session Permissions

Terminal Services Manager allows you to configure terminal service session permissions. Administrators can remotely connect and view user sessions. You may just view a session or interact with the session by actively using the mouse and keyboard. Often corporate privacy policies may require that for such sessions users should allow the administrators to remotely view or interact with their systems. You can enable the check box **Require user's permission** so that no remote control sessions are initiated without the user's permission. You can also disable remote control altogether. Figure 9.50 shows the remote control configuration options. Table 9.5 explains the remote control settings.

Figure 9.50 Remote Control Settings

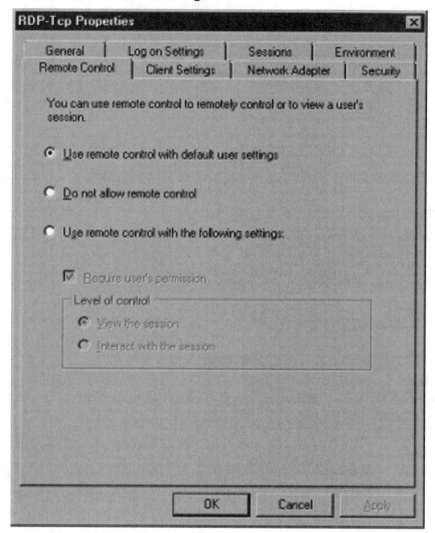

Table 9.5 Terminal Services Remote Control Configuration

Setting	Description
Use remote control with default user settings	If the user gives the permission you can establish a remote session with full control
Do not allow remote control	No remote control is possible

Continued

Table 9.5 Continued. Terminal Services Remote Control Configuration

Setting	Description
Use remote control with the following settings	User decides whether the remote user checks with him or her before establishing a remote control with his or her computer and decides the level of control. Options are: (checkbox) Require user's permission
	Level of control (view or interact with the session)

Viewing Processes

Terminal Services Manager also provides information on processes that are running on a terminal server. This information is available from the Processes tab of the right pane (see Figure 9.51). Table 9.6 summarizes the information gathered from the processes.

Table 9.6 Process Information

Column	Description
Server	Name of the terminal server the process is associated with.
User	User account associated with the process.
Session	Session on the terminal server associated with this process.
ID	Session identifier.
PID	Process identifier.
Image	Name of the executable associated with the process.

Figure 9.51 Viewing Users, Sessions, and Processes

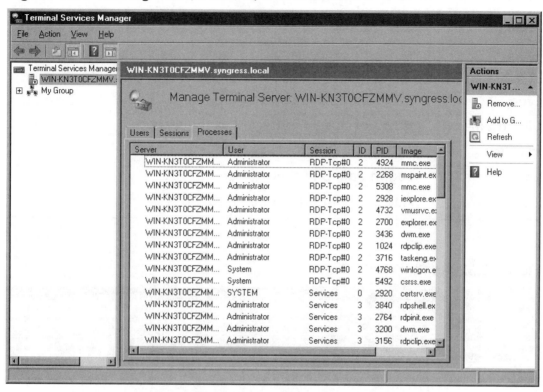

Monitoring Sessions

The Sessions tab of Terminal Services Manager provides you the information about terminal services sessions including services, listener, and console (see Figure 9.52). Table 9.7 summarizes the session monitoring information.

Table 9.7 Session Information

Column	Description
Server	Name of the terminal server the session is associated with.
Session	Current session running on the server.
User	User account of the session.
ID	Session identifier.

Continued

Table 9.7 Continued. Session Information

Column	Description
State	Session status such as active, connected, shadow, listen, disconnected, reset, idle, down, or init.
Type	Remote desktop client type.
ClientName	Name of the computer using the session.
IdleTime	Time elapsed since last input.
LogOnTime	Logon date and time.
Comment	Additional information, if available.

Figure 9.52 Monitoring Sessions

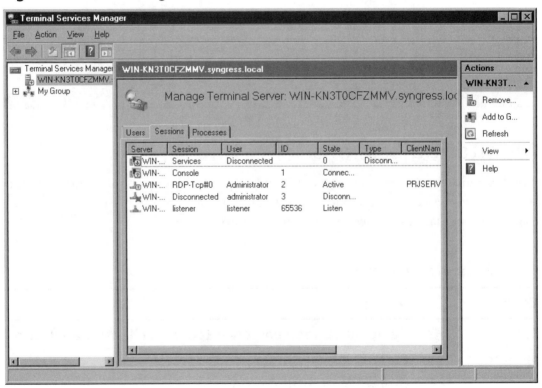

Displaying Data Prioritization

Printing and file transfer traffic are considered as *virtual channel* traffic. If such virtual channel traffic takes priority over the terminal service traffic such as display, keyboard, and mouse, it may adversely affect the performance as virtual channel traffic consumes a lot of bandwidth. Display and user input data is allocated 70 percent of the bandwidth in comparison to the rest of the traffic including clipboard, file, and print jobs, which get 30 percent of the bandwidth.

You can make some adjustments in the registry to control the allocation of bandwidth and ensure the display data gets the priority.

The registry keys under HKEY_LOCAL_MACHINE\SYSTEM\ CurrentControlSet\Services\TermDD (see Figure 9.53) need to be created and configured to control the prioritization. The parameters are:

- Flow Control Disable
- Flow Control Display Bandwidth
- Flow Control Channel Bandwidth
- Flow Control Charge Post Compression

You may have to create the keys if they do not exist in your registry. Create DWORD value keys (without spaces between the words) and assign the following values:

- **FlowControlDisable** To disable display data prioritization set to 1. All requests are handled on a First-In-First-Out (FIFO) basis. The default is 0.

- **FlowControlDisplayBandwidth** This is to control the relative bandwidth priority for display and input data. The default value is 70. The maximum value is 255.

- **FlowControlChannelBandwidth** This is to control the relative bandwidth priority for other virtual channels such as clipboard, file transfers, or print jobs). The default value is 30. The maximum value is 255.

- **FlowControlChargePostCompression** This is to control bandwidth allocation based on pre- and post-compression bytes. The default value is 0. This means the calculation will be based on pre-compression bytes.

Restart the terminal server for the registry changes to take effect.

Figure 9.53 Display Data Prioritization Registry Configuration

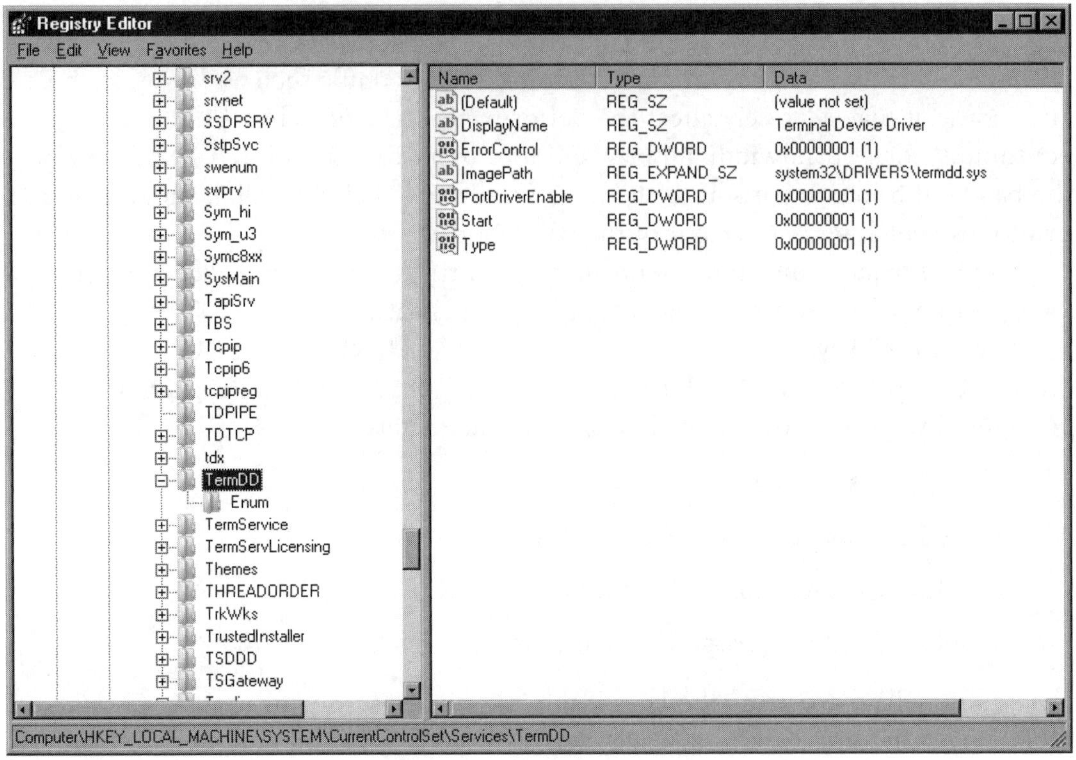

Logging Users Off

Terminal Services Manager allows you to log off a user from a terminal service session. To do this, right-click on the user and then click **Log Off** on the **Users** tab (see Figure 9.54). If you want to log off another user from a session, Full control permission is required. Ensure you send a message before you log off the user. This will prevent a loss of data while the user's session is active.

Figure 9.54 Disconnect, Reset and Log off Users

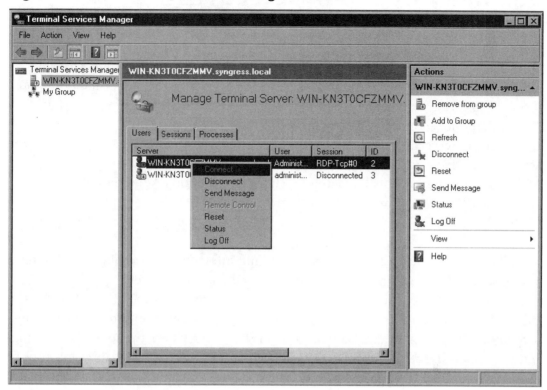

Disconnecting Sessions

Terminal Services Manager allows you to disconnect a user from a terminal service session. To do so, right-click on the user session and then click **Disconnect** on the **Users** tab. Similar to logging of another user, you need Full Control permission or Disconnect permission (Special Access) to disconnect a user or session. Figure 9.54 shows the options available when you right-click on a user name.

Resetting the Terminal Services

Terminal Services Manager allows you to reset a user session. To do so, right-click on the user session and then click **Reset**. If you reset a session without sending a warning message, it may result in a loss of data. To reset another user's session, Full Control access permission is required. You should choose to reset a session only when the session stops responding or when it encounters some error. Resetting a listener session will result in resetting all the sessions of a connection. Figure 9.54 shows the actions you can perform on a user session.

Summary of Exam Objectives

Monitoring any network service is an important task of an IT administrator. Fine-tuning and monitoring the Terminal Services ensures the network resources are utilized properly. In addition to that, users experience is enhanced while accessing remote applications. Installation of specific server roles, applications, enabling remote access, monitoring user sessions, and deploying load-balancing solutions are the Terminal Services administrator's tasks.

Terminal Server management tools include Terminal Services Manager, Terminal Services Configuration, TS RemoteApp Manager, TS Licensing Manager, TS Web Access Administration, and TS Gateway Manager. Additional Windows 2008 tools available are WSRM to manage the resources, and NLB Manager.

RAP's specific to Terminal Service scenarios are equal per session and equal per user policies.

WSRM's accounting feature logs accounting information of applications running on the server. You can configure the *managing* and *profiling* policies.

TS Session Broker role service of Windows 2008 performs the session load balancing. TS Session Broker maintains the track of a user session, and stores the session state information such as user names, name of the server where the session is running, and the session IDs. This information is used to redirect a disconnected session back to the server where the user's session exists. To evenly distribute the load between the servers of a terminal server farm requires load-balancing mechanisms such as the DNS round robin or network load balancers. TS Session Broker supports IP address and routing token redirection modes. The DNS round-robin feature along with the TS Session Broker service can be utilized to load-balance terminal service sessions in your network. TS Session Broker load balancing can be configured through AD GPO.

Managing IPSec mobile users VPN can become very tedious. IPSec VPNs are replaced with SSL-VPN appliances in large enterprises. Terminal Services Gateway removes the need to set up and manage VPNs for allowing access to applications. Users with RDC client can connect to internal network resources securely. To achieve the RDP traffic is sent over a SSL HTTP connection. CAP defines who can connect to a TS Gateway server. RAP defines the type of network resources a remote user can connect.

Group Policy settings help you to define finer security settings, connection and session limits, resource management, and licensing of the Terminal Services.

TS RemoteApp makes the network applications available for remote clients running RDC clients. Applications published through RemoteApp can also be accessed through the Web.

TS Web Access enables you to make RemoteApp programs appear as a link on the Web site and makes them available to remote users.

Managing Terminal Services includes configuring RDP permissions, session time limits, connection limits, monitoring users and sessions, perform ad hoc tasks such as disconnecting the users, log them off, or reset sessions. Display Data Prioritization enhances the remote desktop experience.

Exam Objectives Fast Track

Configuring and Monitoring Terminal Service Resources

- ☑ Configuring, monitoring, and fine-tuning are the routine tasks of the IT administrator responsible for Terminal Services.

- ☑ Windows 2008 offers TS Manager, TS Services Configuration, TS RemoteApp Manager, TS Licensing Manager, TS Gateway Manager, and TS Web Access Administration.

- ☑ In addition, resource allocation of memory and processors can be managed through WSRM.

Load Balancing

- ☑ Mission-critical services require high availability and scalability. Terminal Services deployed in large enterprises require careful planning in terms of high availability.

- ☑ The TS Session Broker service of Windows 2008 Terminal Services offers session-based load balancing. Disconnected user sessions are redirected back to the servers where the users' sessions exist. Additionally, load balancing can be configured through AD GPO features.

- ☑ The Network Load Balancing service of Windows 2008 ensures the front-end mechanism distributes the requests. NLB Manager is used to configure network load balancing and cluster parameters.

The Terminal Services Gateway

- ☑ Terminal Services Gateway helps administrators enable remote users to access the corporate applications without needing to set up a VPN.

☑ RDP traffic from the remote clients travel through a HTTPS encapsulation to reach TS Gateway, and later the HTTPS encapsulation is removed to pass only RDP traffic to the terminal servers.

☑ Configuration of TS Gateway servers includes installing SSL certificates and creating resource allocation policies CAP and RAP.

☑ Group Policy for Terminal Services defines finer security settings, connection and session limits, resource management, and licensing.

☑ RDC client parameters, connection, devices, and resource direction, licensing, printer redirection, user profiles, remote session environment, security, session time limits, temporary folders, and licensing are the options available for configuration.

☑ You need to group identical terminal servers into one GPO and place them under the OU to apply Group Policy settings.

Terminal Service RemoteApp

☑ TS RemoteApp makes the network programs available over the LAN and Internet that can be remotely accessed through clients running RDC clients or through Web.

☑ TS RemoteApp is an easier way to deploy applications once and manage it across the enterprise. Remote offices with limited IT staff greatly benefit from this feature.

☑ TS RemoteApp helps organizations manage frequently updated, difficult to manage, or infrequently used applications efficiently.

Managing the Terminal Services

☑ Managing Terminal Services includes configuring RDP permissions, session time limits, connection limits, monitoring users and sessions, perform ad hoc tasks such as disconnecting the users, log them off, or reset sessions.

☑ RDP Permission sets including Full Control, User Access, Guest Access, and Special permissions. These sets consist of more granular permissions.

Connection limits defines the number of concurrent connections. Session time limits define active, idle, and disconnected session restrictions. Session permissions define the remote control access.

☑ Viewing and monitoring sessions become part of the Terminal Services management tasks. You can log off users, send messages, reset a terminal session, disconnect, or check the status of a session. Desktop experience can be enhanced by configuring Display Data Prioritization.

Exam Objectives
Frequently Asked Questions

Q: What are the management tools available in Windows 2008 to manage Terminal Services environment?

A: Terminal Services Manager, TS RemoteApp Manager, TS Licensing Manager, TS Web Access Administration, and TS Gateway Manager. In addition to that, Windows System Resource Manager for managing system resources and NLB Manager for configuring load balancing are also available.

Q: What are the two RAP's available for Terminal Services in Windows 2008?

A: *Equal per session* and *Equal per user* are the two policies available. These are configured through WSRM.

Q: What information is available through WSRM accounting data?

A: Information about users, sessions, system resources, and events matching the policy criteria are available through the WSRM accounting.

Q: How to configure load balancing in Terminal Services?

A: Use TS Services Configuration to configure TS Session Broker and NLB Manager.

Q: What does Multiple host under Filtering mode of NLB clustering configuration mean?

A: Mutliple hosts mean several servers will handle the traffic for the specified port rule.

Q: What are the clustering modes supported by NLB?

A: Unicast, Multicast and Internet Group Management Protocol (IGMP) Multicast. IGMP is the Internet standard for Multicast.

Q: What are the TS Session Broker redirection modes available?

A: IP address and routing token are the two redirection modes supported by TS Session Broker.

Q: What is the function of TS Gateway in the Terminal Services environment?

A: Terminal Services Gateway helps administrators to enable remote users to access the corporate applications without a need to setup a VPN. This is done through encapsulating RDP within HTTPS.

Q: What are the TS CAP and TS RAP?

A: A TS CAP allows you to specify who can connect to the TS Gateway Server, while TS RAP allows you to specify the resources users can connect through the TS Gateway Server.

Q: What are the two authentication modes supported by TS CAP?

A: Password and Smart Card are the two authentication modes supported by TS CAP.

Q: I am unable to see Group Policy Management in the Administrative Tools.

A: You can add the Group Policy Management feature through the Server Manager, Add Features option.

Q: I have installed Terminal Services role service on my Windows 2008. What should I do next to publish the applications?

A: Install the applications through **Control Panel | Install Application** on a Terminal Server. Publish it through TS RemoteApp Manager.

Q: What are the different RDP connection options available?

A: Don't allow connections to this computer, Allow connections from computers running any version of Remote Desktop (less secure), and Allow connections only from computers running Remote Desktop with Network Level Authentication (more secure) are the available options.

Q: What are the tasks involved in managing Terminal Services?

A: Configuring RDP permissions, session limits, connection limits, monitoring sessions and processes, log off, disconnect, or reset terminal service sessions are the management tasks.

Self Test

1. Your nonprofit organization has an Active Directory forest with an Active Directory domain. There are 10 Windows XP clients in the domain with the Remote Desktop Client 6.1 installed. The organization also has a server named TSApp1 that runs the Terminal Server role for the main office. You want to deploy a new RemoteApp on the TSApp1 server. The application makes changes to the current user registry during installation. The program vendor has verified that the application can be deployed as a RemoteApp. However, you discover that running the provided *appsetup.exe* file does not install the application for multiuser usage. You need to modify the application installation process to install correctly as a RemoteApp. What do you need to do?

   A. Run the *mstsc /v:TSApp1 /admin* command from your workstation to log into the TSApp1 server. Install the application.

   B. Run the *chgusr /execute* command on the TSApp1 server. Install the application. Then, run the *chgusr /install* command on the TSApp1 server.

   C. Run the *chgusr /install* command on the TSApp1 server. Install the application. Then, run the *chgusr /execute* command on the TSApp1 server.

   D. Run the *chglogon /disable* command on the TSApp1 server. Install the application. Then, run the *chglogon /enable* command on the TSApp1 server.

2. Your company has two servers named TSApp1 and TSApp2 that have the Terminal Server role installed. The TSApp1 server also has the Terminal Server Web Access role installed. The applications on the TSApp2 server does not appear on the list of applications available from the Terminal Server Web Access Web page. You need to ensure that users are able to launch the applications on the TSApp2 server from the Terminal Server Web Access Web page. What do you need to do?

   A. Install the Terminal Server Gateway role on the TSApp2 server. Instruct users to use the TSApp2 server as their Terminal Server Gateway when they want to access the applications on the TSApp2 server.

   B. Publish all the applications on the TSApp1 server and the TSApp2 server by using Active Directory Domain Services (AD DS) as the repository. Publish the applications through a GPO for all the users that use the Terminal Server Web Access Web site.

C. Configure the applications on the TSApp2 server as Microsoft Windows Installer packages. Publish the applications using System Center Configuration Manager 2007 to the clients.

D. Publish the applications on the TSApp2 server as Microsoft Windows Installer packages. Initiate a group policy update on the TSApp1 server by using the *gpupdate /force* command.

3. Your government agency has a server named IntraNetTSApp1 that has the Terminal Server role installed. The government agency wants to deploy a new application named IntraNetApp on the IntraNetTSApp1 server. You publish the application on the IntraNetTSApp1 server by using a Microsoft RDP file. The clients are unable to pass parameters to the application. You need to ensure that the clients are able to launch the application on the IntraNetTSApp1 server by using any two parameters. What do you need to do?

A. Modify the Remote Program Properties setting for the IntraNetApp application. Activate the Allow any Command Line Arguments option in the Command Line Arguments dialog box.

B. Modify the Remote Program Properties setting for the IntraNetApp application. Activate the Always use the following Command Line Arguments option in the Command Line Arguments dialog box. Type %1 %2 in the Command Line Arguments field.

C. Modify the Alias setting for the IntraNetApp application from IntraNetApp to IntraNetApp %1 %2.

D. Publish the application on the Server2 server as a Microsoft Windows Installer package. Distribute the Microsoft Windows Installer package to the clients to replace the published RDP file.

4. Your company has a single AD forest that has an AD domain. The company has a server named TS1 that runs the Terminal Server role and the Terminal Server Web Access role. The company also has 150 client computers that run Microsoft Windows XP Service Pack 2 (SP2). You have an application named DBAExpress that you want to deploy on the TS1 server. You publish DBAExpress on the TS1 server. The clients are unable to access DBAExpress through the Terminal Server Web Access Web page. You verify that the Terminal Server Web Access role is using Active Directory Domain Services (ADDS) and that Network Level Authentication is enabled. You need to ensure

that the clients can launch DBAExpress on the TS1 server from the Terminal Server Web Access Web page. What do you need to do?

A. Install the Remote Desktop Client 6.0 application on the client computers that run Windows XP SP2.

B. Disable publishing to AD DS for the DBAExpress remote application.

C. Install the Terminal Services Gateway role on the TS1 server. Reconfigure the DBAExpress remote application publishing to reflect this change in the infrastructure.

D. Publish the DBAExpress application on the TS1 server as a Microsoft Windows Installer package. Distribute the Windows Installer package to the clients.

5. Your company has a server named TSWA that has the Terminal Services Web Access server role and the Terminal Services Gateway server role. The company has 25 Microsoft Windows XP SP2 remote client computers in the domain. You deploy a new application on the TSWA server. You make the new application available to users by publishing a Microsoft Windows Installer package that has a GPO. You discover that you can launch the new application from the TS2 server and the TSWA server by using the Terminal Services Web Access Web page. However, the users are unable to launch the application. You need to ensure that the users are able to launch the application. What do you need to do?

A. Install the RDP 6.1 client on the client computers.

B. Deactivate the Network Level Authentication option on the Server2 server and the Server3 server.

C. Install the Internet Explorer 7.0 browser application on the client computers.

D. Configure the Terminal Services Resource Access Policy (TSRAP) to include the Server3 server only.

6. The company has a server named Server2 that has the Terminal Server role. Applications on Server2 are published by using the RDP files. Users download the RDP files from the TSWeb virtual directory on Server2. You also have a new server named Server3 that has the Terminal Server role and the Terminal Server Gateway role. You reconfigure the applications on the Server2 server to use the Terminal Server Gateway role on the Server3 server. You export the Remote Program settings from the Server2 server and import them into the

Server3 server. Users report they are unable to access any of the remote applications on the Server3 server. Users are able to access the remote applications on the Server2 server through the Terminal Server Gateway role on Server3. You verify that the programs installed on the Server2 server are installed at identical locations on the Server3 server. You need to ensure that the users are able to access the applications on the Server3 server. What do you need to do?

A. Recreate the RDP files on the Server3 server and redistribute the files to the users.

B. Copy the RDP files from the Server2 server to a new TSWeb virtual directory on the Server3 server.

C. Configure and activate the Terminal Server Session Directory feature on the Server3 server. Configure the Server2 server and the Server3 server to use the Terminal Server Session Directory feature.

D. Deactivate the NLA feature on the Server3 server.

7. Your company has an AD domain. The company also has a server named Server1 that has the Terminal Server Gateway role. There are two more servers named Server2 and Server3 that have the Terminal Server role. Server2 and Server3 are configured in a load-balancing Terminal Server farm named TSLoad. The company deploys the Terminal Server Broker Service feature on a new server named Server4. The TSLoad farm is added to the Terminal Server Broker Service configuration on Server4. After configuring the published applications to use Terminal Server Broker Service, you observe that Terminal Server Broker Service does not accept connections from Server2 and Server3. You need to ensure that Terminal Server Broker Service can accept connections from Server2 and Server3. What do you need to do?

A. Recreate Add Server2 and Server3 to the Session Broker Computers local group on Server4.

B. Add Server2 and Server3 to a new Session Broker Computers group in the Active Directory domain.

C. Configure a group policy to set the Require secure RPC communications option in the Terminal Services Security section to True. Apply the policy to Server2 and Server3.

D. Configure a group policy to set the Allow reconnection from original client only option in the Terminal Services section to True. Apply the policy to all client computers.

8. Your company has an AD domain. The company also has a server named Server1 that has the Terminal Server Gateway role. There are two more servers named Server2 and Server3 that have the Terminal Server role. Server2 and Server3 are configured in a load-balancing Terminal Server farm named TSL. The company deploys the Terminal Server Broker Service feature on a new server named Server4. The TSL farm is added to the Terminal Server Broker Service configuration on Server4. After configuring the published applications to use the Terminal Server Broker Service feature, you observe that the Terminal Server Broker Service feature does not receive any server registrations. You need to ensure that the Terminal Server Broker Service feature receives server registrations. What do you need to do?

A. Create a new GPO that assigns Server4 to Server2 and Server3 as their session broker server. Apply the policy to Server2 and Server3.

B. Configure Server2 and Server3 to use the Terminal Server Gateway role to access the Terminal Server Broker Service feature.

C. Configure a group policy to set the Require secure RPC communications option in the Terminal Services Security section to False. Apply the policy to Server2 and Server3.

D. Configure a group policy to set the Set TS Gateway server address option in the Terminal Services section to Server1. Apply the policy to all client computers.

9. Your company has a server named Server1 that has the Terminal Server Gateway role. There are two more servers named Server2 and Server3 that have the Terminal Server role. Server2 and Server3 are configured in a load-balancing Terminal Server farm named TSLB. The company has a new server named Server4 that has the Terminal Server Broker Service feature. You deploy a hardware load-balancing device named F6 in front of the Terminal Server farm. The device has specialized support for terminal servers and routing tokens. The Terminal Server Broker Service feature stops working after you deploy F6 in front of the Terminal Server farm. You need to ensure that the Terminal Server Broker Service feature works. Which new GPO should you create and apply to the Terminal Server farm?

A. A GPO that deactivates the Use IP Address Redirection policy setting in the Terminal Server Broker section of the Terminal Server group policy template

B. A GPO that activates the Use IP Address Redirection policy setting in the Session Directory section of the Terminal Server group policy template

C. A GPO that activates the Use TS Session Broker Load Balancing policy setting in the Session Directory section of the Terminal Server group policy template

D. A GPO that deactivates the Use TS Session Broker Load Balancing policy setting in the Session Directory section of the Terminal Server group policy template

10. The company has a server named Server1 that has the Terminal Services server role and a new test server named TSL that has the Terminal Services Licensing role outside of the domain in a workgroup. You cannot enable the Terminal Services Per User Client Access License (CAL) mode in the Terminal Services Licensing role on TSL. You need to configure the Terminal Services environment so that you can use the Terminal Services Per User CAL mode on TSL. What should you do?

A. Join TSL to the domain. Enable the Terminal Services Per User CAL mode.

B. Configure Server1 to use TSL for the Terminal Services Licensing role. Reconfigure TSL for the Terminal Services Per User CAL mode when Server1 has registered with TSL.

C. Install the Terminal Server Gateway role on Server1. Configure a Group Policy Object that configures Server1 to use TSL for licensing. Apply the policy to Server1.

D. Call the Microsoft Clearinghouse with your Terminal Server license information. Obtain license keys to enter into the Licensing server.

Self Test Quick Answer Key

1.	**C**	6.	**A**
2.	**B**	7.	**A**
3.	**A**	8.	**A**
4.	**A**	9.	**A**
5.	**A**	10.	**A**

Chapter 10

MCTS/MCITP Exam 649

IP Addressing and Services

Exam objectives in this chapter:

- Configuring IPv4 and IPv6 Addressing
- Configuring Dynamic Host Configuration Protocol (DHCP)
- Configuring Network Authentication
- Configuring IP Security (IPsec)
- Windows Firewall with Advanced Security in Windows Server 2008

Exam objectives review:

- ☑ Summary of Exam Objectives
- ☑ Exam Objectives Fast Track
- ☑ Exam Objectives Frequently Asked Questions
- ☑ Self Test
- ☑ Self Test Quick Answer Key

Introduction

The Transmission Control Protocol/Internet Protocol (TCP/IP) is a suite of protocols used for communicating across a variety of networks. TCP/IP works well in part because it can send data across dissimilar network types. In this chapter, we'll look at how IP addressing is configured in the Windows Server 2008 environment and we'll also explore the related IP services. Much of the information in this chapter should be familiar to those of you who are already network administrators or who have experience with other Windows Server technologies.

We'll begin by reviewing IPv4 and IPv6 addressing fundamentals as they relate to setting up the network interface on a Windows Server 2008 computer. We'll walk through setting up DHCP as well as configuring network authentication, configuring IPsec, and configuring firewall settings. In each section, we'll cover the basics as well as highlight new features and new areas to focus on for the exam.

This chapter does assume you have a basic familiarity with IP addressing such as how to configure an IPv4 address using the dotted decimal notation and how to create a subnet using the subnet mask. If you're not familiar with these basics or if you're a bit rusty, we'll point you to some resources you can use to brush up on those much-needed networking skills.

Configuring IPv4 and IPv6 Addressing

Windows Server 2008 should install IPv4 and IPv6 by default so that you can configure them on the network interface card (NIC). If they're not already installed, you can install them from the Local Area Connection Properties dialog box. We'll briefly look at configuring IPv4 and IPv6 on the Windows Server 2008 NIC before heading into the DHCP configuration settings, where network IP settings are managed. Although we're assuming you're familiar with IPv4 and IPv6 to some extent, we've included Table 10.1 to give you a quick review of the differences between IPv4 and IPv6. If anything in this table is unfamiliar to you, please take some time out to revisit your IPv4 and IPv6 fundamentals.

TEST DAY TIP

The information in Table 10.1 is a great test day refresher. Even though the exam is not likely to quiz you on these specific details, expect to see a question or two on the exam that uses this information. Often you'll see several answers that are possibly correct and you'll need to have a solid understanding of the differences between IPv4 and IPv6 in order to determine the correct response.

Table 10.1 IPv4 and IPv6 Comparison

Category	IPv4	IPv6
Address length	32 bits	128 bits
Notation style	Four sets of three digits separated by a dot	Eight sets of four digits separated by a colon
Compression	If all three digits are zero, single zero is used	If all four digits are zero, a double colon is used
Types of addresses	Public, private, multicast	Global, local-use unicast, anycast
IPsec support	Optional	Required
Fragmentation	Done by hosts and routers	Done by hosts only
Error reporting and diagnostic	ICMP (for IPv4)	ICMPv6
Router discovery support	Optional	Required
Host configuration	DHCP or manual	Automatic, DHCP or manual
DNS record type for name resolution	A record	AAAA record
DNS record type and location for reverse name resolution	PTR records in IN-ADDR.ARPA domain	PTR records in IP6.ARPA domain

IPv4 Quick Review

You can skip this section if you're familiar with addressing in the IPv4 format. If not, this section will provide a very brief review. If it's not enough information for you, please refer to additional resources (some of which are mentioned throughout this chapter) to make sure you're comfortable with addressing in both schemas.

IPv4 typically uses three classes of network addresses—A, B, and C. A is for large networks (like the Internet), B is for medium networks, and C is for small networks. Each has a maximum number of network IDs and host IDs. In recent years as IP addresses became scarce, network address translation became popular. This method enables companies to use private IP addressing internally and then connect through an Internet Service Provider with a public IP address. This translation allows multiple companies to use the same internal IP addressing and it's only when traffic needs to cross the public network (the Internet) that addressing becomes important—so it gets translated to a unique public IP address for its trip to and from the Internet. Many smaller companies use the Class C 192.168.0.x range of private network addresses, though there are Class A and Class B private network addresses as well. Table 10.2 delineates the Class A, B, and C network ID boundaries along with network and host bits.

Table 10.2 IP Address Classes for IPv4 Networks

Class	Network Bits	Number of Networks	Host Bits	Maximum Number of Hosts
A	8	126	24	16,777,214
B	16	16,384	16	65,534
C	24	2,097,152	8	254

The subnet mask is used to indicate the network portion of an IP address. A subnet mask of 255.255.255.0 indicates that only the right-most eight bits (represented by the 0) are the host ID portion of the IP address, and the other 24 bits (represented by 255.255.255) are the network portion of the IP address. In this case, you have 1 through 254 as potential host IP addresses (i.e., 192.168.0.1 through 192.168.0.254). In many small companies, having 254 IP addresses for computers is more than enough. Many companies use the private network address space for addressing internal to their organization. This provides flexibility in addressing but requires the use of *network address translation*, so that the private IP addresses are translated into public IP addresses only when they cross your router to the Internet service provider's (ISP's) connection to the Internet. This network could be notated as 192.168.0.1/24, indicating the subnet mask or number of bits masked is 24. This style of notation, referred to as network/bits–masked notation is used in the Classless Inter–Domain Routing or CIDR. This same style of notation is used in IPv6 as well.

Configuring & Implementing...

Internet Protocol Basics

If you're not already familiar with IP addressing, you would do well to study this topic before taking the exam. IPv4 is the familiar IP addressing format with four octets. You've probably all seen 192.168.0.1, for example. IPv4 addresses require the use of a subnet mask and use four bytes (32 bits). IPv6 was developed because the world was running out of valid IP addresses under the IPv4 schema. IPv6 uses a different format than IPv4, but the underlying basics are similar, though there are significant differences between the two. IPv6 uses 16 bytes or 128 bits. There are a lot of great resources on IP addressing, but two of my favorites are www.learntosubnet.com and www.tcpipguide.com/free/t_toc.htm (this one unfortunately has a lot of pop up ads, but the information is solid). You can also get a quick refresher on the Microsoft Web site at http://support.microsoft.com/kb/164015. Of course, there are a lot of great books that discuss IP addressing if you really want to get in-depth knowledge in this area.

If you want to brush up on IPv6, you can read an overview article from Microsoft at http://technet2.microsoft.com/windowsserver/en/library/892c53fa-cf13-43d7-8086-11ab9ac1f0e81033.mspx or at http://download.microsoft.com/download/e/9/b/e9bd20d3-cc8d-4162-aa60-3aa3abc2b2e9/IPv6.doc. If you're brand new to IPv6, you might find this basic primer helpful, located on the Microsoft Web site at http://technet.microsoft.com/en-us/library/bb726944.aspx. There are a couple of others you might find helpful at www.windowsnetworking.com/articles tutorials/Crash-Course-IPv6-Part1.html and www.windowsnetworking.com/aritcles tutorials/Get-Ready-Run-IPv6.html to help you get up to speed on IPv6.

Keep in mind that because IPv6 is supported in Windows Server 2008, you can expect to see a lot of IPv6 types of questions. Even if your organization is not planning on going to IPv6 any time soon, you'll need to be familiar with the in's and out's of this protocol in order to successfully navigate the Windows Server 2008 exams.

Configuring Local IPv4 Settings

The Windows Server 2008 computer's network interface card can be configured with IPv4 and IPv6 addressing (see Exercise 10.1). As you know, you can access the computer's network settings in any one of several ways. Figure 10.1 shows the **Local Area Connection Properties** dialog box. IPv4 and IPv6 are both installed and enabled by default in Windows Server 2008 due to the implementation of **Next Generation TCP/IP stack**, which supports a dual IP stack sharing common transport and framing layers. If for some reason IPv6 is not installed and enabled on your Windows Server 2008 computer, you can install it by clicking the **Install** button and following the prompts.

Figure 10.1 Windows Server 2008 Local Area Connection Properties

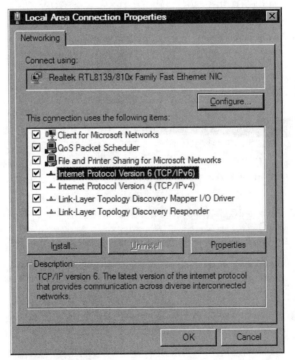

EXERCISE 10.1

CONFIGURING LOCAL IPV4 SETTINGS

To configure IPv4 settings, click to select **Internet Protocol Version 4 (TCP/IPv4)**, then click **Properties**. The **IPv4 Properties** dialog will open, as shown in Figure 10.2. For client computers, you'll typically select "Obtain an IP address automatically" so the client can utilize the DHCP server for dynamic addressing. In the case of a server, however, you typically choose a static IP address. We'll discuss creating a reservation within the DHCP server scope later in this chapter. You create a reservation on the DCHP server to ensure that the static IP address assigned to this server is not used by any other computer on the network. As you can see in this example, the server is manually configured to use 192.168.0.91 with a default gateway located at 192.168.0.2. The subnet mask for this network is 255.255.255.0, the standard subnet mask for a Class C private network address. You can also see that the primary and alternate DNS servers are located at 192.168.0.90 and 192.168.0.91, respectively. **Advanced** options allow you to configure additional DNS options as well as WINS servers, if needed. Click **OK** once you've configured your IPv4 settings.

Figure 10.2 IPv4 Configuration Settings

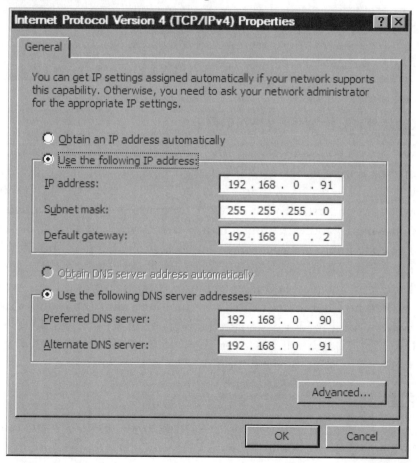

New & Noteworthy...

The Next Generation TCP/IP Stack

A full discussion of the changes to the TCP/IP implementation in Windows Server 2008 is outside the scope of this book but you might be interested in reading about this topic, especially if you plan on implementing IPv6 in your organization anytime soon. Microsoft's TechNet has an article located at www.microsoft.com/technet/community/columns/cableguy/cg0905.mspx that discusses the Next Generation TCP/IP Stack in Windows Vista and Windows Server 2008. There's also an article at www.microsoft.com/technet/community/columns/cableguy/cg1005.mspx that discusses the changes in TCP/IP in Windows Vista and Windows Server 2008. There are, of course, many other references on IPv6 but these are good to start with prior to the Windows Server 2008 exam.

Configuring IPv4 Options

In Windows Server 2008, you can use IPv4, IPv6, or a combination of the two. This is similar to Windows Server 2003, though in Windows Server 2008, IPv6 is enabled by default whereas in Windows Server 2003, you can add IPv6 if needed. Briefly, you should understand your network's physical and logical configuration if you're modifying IP address configurations, such as creating a new subnet. In addition, if you are implementing a new network altogether, you should take time to map out the physical and logical structure as well as create your IP addressing scheme. Planning in advance of implementation is crucial to avoid time-consuming errors. Each IPv4 host computer needs, at minimum, a host ID, a subnet mask, and a default gateway. You can also designate the preferred and alternate DNS server along with the WINS server, if used. Let's start with subnetting for IPv4 networks, since this is the most common IP option used.

Subnetting

IPv4 networks are divided into five types: A, B, C, D, and E though the commonly used are A, B, and C. This system is now referred to as *classful* networking because each range of IP addresses falls into one of these classes. Later implementations of

IPv4 and all implementations of IPv6 are considered *classless*, to distinguish them from this system. We'll discuss the classless system, known as *CIDR*, later in this chapter. Class A networks originally were intended for large organizations that had few networks but millions of hosts. Class C networks, on the other end of the spectrum, were designed for small companies that have perhaps a few hundred hosts. Class D networks are for IP multicast addresses and Class E addresses were not supported by Microsoft as late as Windows Server 2003. In Windows Server 2008, IPv4 and IPv6 are both supported; we'll discuss IPv6 later in this chapter.

Back to our discussion of classes. Class A addresses used 8 bits to define the network address and 24 bits to define host addresses. The left-most bit must be set to zero, so in practice, you can use only the right-most 7 bits of the left-most octet. If you're really good with binary and octal math, you know that there can be only 126 networks in the Class A category—total worldwide. A Class A network, however, can have 16,777,214 hosts in each network. Table 10.2, earlier in the chapter, shows the number of networks and hosts in each class of network.

As you can see, when you use 7 bits for the network ID in Class A, it yields only 126 possible network addresses, but millions of host IDs. When you use 8 bits for the *host* ID, it yields only 254 host IDs. If you recall, there are rules about the use of all ones or all zeros; it explains the discrepancy between the number of IDs and the number of bits used in the right-most and left-most segments of the IPv4 address. There are five rules you have to follow when enumerating IPv4 addresses:

- All bits in the host ID cannot be set to 1. That's reserved for broadcast addresses.

- All bits in the host ID cannot be set to 0. That's reserved for IP network IDs.

- Class A network IDs must have 0 as the left-most bit.

- Class B network IDs must have 10 as the two left-most bits.

- Class C network IDs must have 110 as the three left-most bits.

The host ID must be unique to the network. It makes sense that you can have two IP addresses that are the same only if they are on different networks that never talk to one another. Otherwise, there'd be no way to differentiate between two hosts.

With the increasing popularity of computer networking, at some point it became clear that the world would run out of valid IP addresses. As you can see from Table 10.2, there are only 16,384 possible Class B networks worldwide and there are only 2,097,152 Class C network IDs available. So, there are just over 2.1 million network IDs available and it's not hard to estimate there are far more networks than that in the world. As the number of available IP addresses decreased, private network addressing and network address translation grew in popularity and use.

Today many companies are using private IP addresses internally, then using Network Address Translation (NAT) when communicating across a public network (the Internet). The benefit of NAT is that you can use an internal addressing scheme that suits your company and network traffic cannot be routed outside the network unless it's translated into a public address. Internet service provider's routers will simply discard packets with private IP addresses. In our examples, we'll use the private IP range of 192.168.0.1 through 192.168.0.254 for illustration, but you can utilize any of the private address ranges, which are:

- 10.0.0.0 to 10.255.255.255

- 172.16.0.1 to 172.31.255.255

- 192.168.0.1 to 192.168.255.255

Private network addresses still come in Class A, B, and C flavors, but Company 1 can use a Class B private network address and so can Company 2, 3, 4....*n*. These addresses are not passed through routers heading out to the Internet; instead, they are translated into a public IP address, typically provided by the ISP. This provides a lot of flexibility in terms of addressing for companies and ISPs. In addition, CIDR was introduced, which was a step toward the classless system used in IPv6. More on CIDR later in this chapter.

If you choose to use private network addressing for your network, you will also need to have an ISP provide you with a public IP address and you'll need to utilize either a Proxy Server or NAT Router so that your private addressing can be routed out of the network to the Internet.

Head of the Class...

Subnetting and Active Directory
This chapter doesn't cover Active Directory (AD), but it's important to understand that subnets are assigned to sites through the AD interface. A subnet can belong to only one site; a site can contain more than

Continued

one subnet. Here's the quick way to create a subnet in Active Directory. Remember, though, that this is different than setting up DHCP options, which we'll discuss later in this chapter.

In Active Directory Sites and Services, shown in Figure 10.3, right-click the **Subnets** icon in the console tree and select **New Subnet** from the menu. The New Object Subnet dialog box is displayed. Enter the address prefix using network prefix notation (address/prefix length). You can enter either IPv4 or IPv6 subnet notation. The dialog box gives two examples—one of IPv4 and one of IPv6—along with a text box into which you can enter the prefix. For example, you might enter 192.168.7.0/24. Select the site with which the subnet should be associated, then click **OK** to apply the change and create a new subnet. When reading an exam question related to subnets, be sure to understand the context so you can decide whether you need to look at AD or DHCP for the answer.

Figure 10.3 Active Directory Sites and Services Console

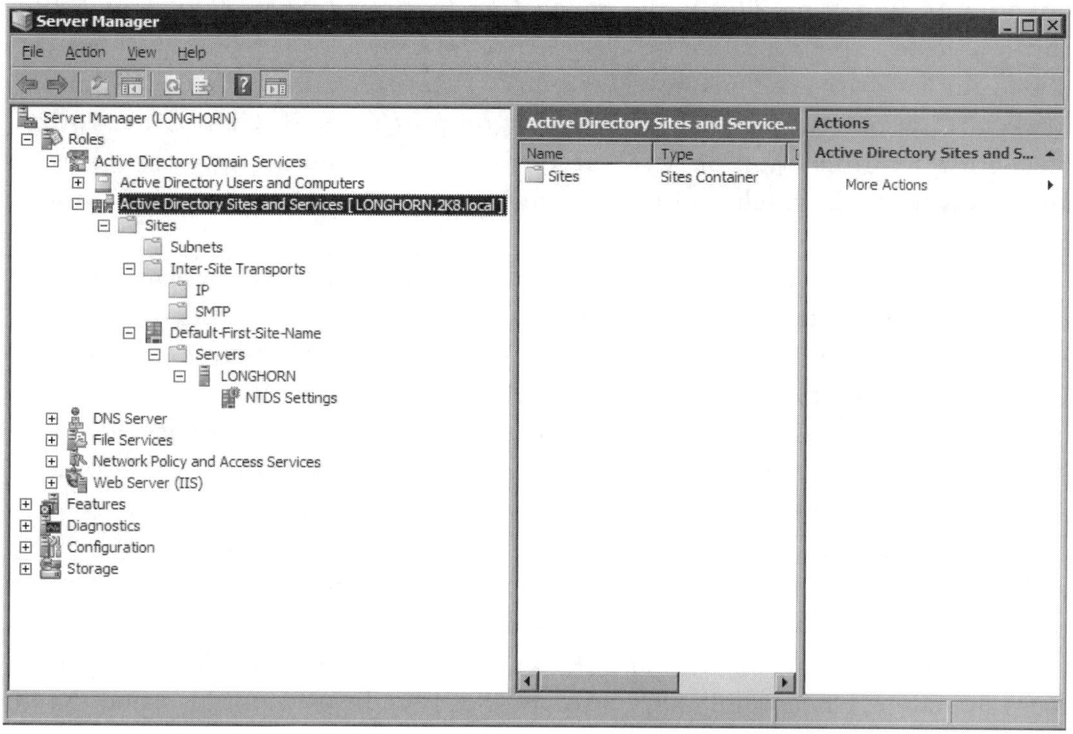

TEST DAY TIP

Remember that subnets are assigned to sites via Active Directory Sites and Services console whereas subnetting options are set up in the DHCP Server role. Also remember that subnets can easily be moved to different sites within the AD Sites and Services console simply by double-clicking the subnet in the Subnets folder and changing the site association in the Site selection list on the General tab. Changing the Site may impact other settings, so clearly you should have a plan in place before modifying these kinds of settings.

Supernetting

Another IP innovation that was developed prior to the implementation of IPv6 is supernetting. Supernetting is the combining of several smaller Class C networks into one larger network in order to accommodate the need for a network larger than Class C but not as large as a Class B. It is, in essence, the opposite of subnetting. This is also called *Classless Inter-Domain Routing* (CIDR) and is used to express a range of Class C networks at a single route. A super-netted subnet mask contains fewer network ID bits than a standard IPv4 subnet mask. CIDR sometimes is thought of as a group or range of Class C networks, but with the introduction of IPv6, CIDR is perhaps more fittingly viewed as an address space in which multiple classful networks are combined into a single, classless network.

If you consider a supernet as a range of Class C network IDs, you can easily understand supernetting. In order to create a supernet, you must have contiguous Class C network IDs (i.e., they must be sequential) and the number of Class C network IDs must be expressed as a power of 2 (due to the use of weighted binary in IPv4 addressing). Typically, a subnet mask for a Class C network would be 255.255.255.0 or it could be notated as the network ID with /24 indicating that 24 bits were used for the network ID.

Again, we're assuming you have a basic understanding of IP addressing including subnetting and supernetting—we're providing this information as a basic review for you. The Windows Server 2008 exam is likely to focus less on IPv4 than on the coexistence of IPv4 and IPv6 in the enterprise, so that's where your focus should be. Understanding the evolution of IPv4 helps you understand the new features of IPv6.

Alternative Configuration

Automatic alternate configuration is an enhancement to TCP/IP that allows for a valid static IP address configuration on DHCP configured machines. Without an alternate configuration defined, a computer that is unable to obtain an IP address lease from a DHCP server would automatically receive an Automatic Private IP Address (APIPA) from the 169.254.0.0/16 pool. If you're troubleshooting network connectivity (or answering a question about network connectivity on the exam) and you see that an address in this range has been assigned, it indicates the host was unable to obtain a valid IP lease. When answering questions about IP addressing on the exam, always think through the address provided and what the implications of that address might be.

Internet Protocol Version 6 (IPv6)

A discussion of IPv6 could take up an entire chapter and the focus of this chapter is configuring IPv6, so we're working on the assumption you have some familiarity with IPv6. That said, we'll spend just a bit of time here reviewing some of the basics to give you a quick refresher. If you're fully up to speed on IPv6, feel free to skip this section. If there are any concepts you're not familiar with, you should do additional research to fill in any gaps. Earlier in the chapter, we provided several links to resources you might want to look at it improve your IPv6 skills if you're not already conversant with the IPv6 addressing requirements.

IPv6 Address Format

As you know, IPv6 provides an alternative to the shortage of IPv4 addresses. As such, it uses 128 bits instead of the 32 bits used in IPv4. This enables 75 trillion trillion (yes, two *trillions* follow the number 75) potential unique IP addresses (or 2^{96}). Much of the newer hardware and software now supports IPv6 addressing (IPv6 has been around a while) but you can't simply plug in IPv6 equipment and expect everything to work. There are numerous transition technologies available, a full discussion of which is outside the scope of this chapter.

Typically, the IPv6 address is divided in half—64 bits for the network component and 64 bits for the host component. However, the IPv6 addressing format also used the CIDR notation, so that an address might look like this: 2424:DC8:4138::/48 indicating that the network is identified using 48 bits.

Each section of an IPv6 address is four digits, which are in hexadecimal format. That means that numbers can range from zero to F (0–F) in each place. F in hexadecimal is 15 and numbers 0 through F produces 16 numbers (hence the term hexadecimal).

There are eight groups of numbers and hypothetically, each can range from 0000 to FFFF (as with IPv4 addressing, there are rules about zeros and ones that we won't go into at the moment). Thus, an example of an IPv6 address is 4F5C:0000:0000:0000: BA59:093C:D102:4612. You can omit leading zeros and consecutive groups of zeros. When you omit groups of zeros, you use a double colon (::) notation. To determine how many groups of zeroes were omitted, you simply count the number of groups and subtract from eight. Thus, the address 4F5C:0000:0000:0000:BA59:093C:D102:4612 can be represented as 4F5C::BA59:93C:D102:4612.

IPv6 Address Types

Briefly, there are several types of IPv6 addresses. If you're not familiar with these, you'll need to do a bit of independent reading to fill in the gaps.

- **Local-link addresses**. Addresses that are accessible only on the local network segment.

- **Unique local IPv6 unicast addresses**. Routable on your network but not accessible from the Internet.

- **Global unicast addresses**. Addresses that can be routed on the IPv6 Internet (a portion of the Internet that uses IPv6).

- **Multicast addresses**. Single host can communicate with multiple recipients.

- **Anycast addresses**. Addresses that can be assigned to multiple interfaces, such as assigning a single IPv6 address to a multihomed computer.

- **Special addresses**. Includes special purpose addresses like loopback and others.

A **local link address** is used like a private address in IPv4. As such, it is not routable because the network prefix is always the same. In IPv6, the first left-most 10 digits are always 1111 1110 10. The next 54 bits are always 0. This comprises the 64-bit unroutable network ID. The right-most 64 bits are the host portion of the address. Thus, the local-link address is written as FE80::/64. If you run the **ipconfig /all** command from the command line on a Windows Server 2008 computer, you'll see the local link address listed.

Global addresses are like IPv4 public addresses and are routable across the Internet. The first three bits of a global address are 001, the next 45 bits are used for the global routing prefix, followed by 16 bits for the subnet ID. The remaining 64 bits identify the host segment of the address. This creates an address prefix notated in this way: 2000::/3.

A few of the **special addresses** include the following:

- **::1/128** (or just ::1). Local loopback address, refers to the local computer.

- **::FFFF:0:0/96**. Prefix used for IPv4 mapped addresses.

- **2002::/16**. Used for 6to4 addressing (discussed later in this section).

- **FE80::/64**. A local-link address. Seeing this address assigned to an interface indicates there was no DHCPv6 server available.

Note that almost all hosts can self-configure IPv6 local-link addresses themselves without contacting a DHCP server (or other infrastructure component), but additional configuration information is required for unique local addresses, global addresses, and other address types and that information typically does come from the DHCP server or other infrastructure component. IPv4 clients will look for a local DHCP server when they start up. By contrast, IPv6 clients will try to get address information from a router and perform a DHCP query only if instructed by the router to perform a stateful configuration.

IPv6 Autoconfiguration Options

Depending on how your IPv6 routers are set up, autoconfiguration of an IPv6 client can happen in three ways: stateless, stateful, and both. In *stateless* mode, an IPv6 client configures its own IPv6 address by using IPv6 Router Advertisements. In *stateful* mode, an IPv6 client will get its addressing information from a DHCPv6 server when it receives Router Advertisement messages with no prefix options (and when certain other conditions are met). This also occurs if no IPv6 routers are available. The *both* option uses stateful and stateless together. The most common example of this is an IPv6 client using stateless autoconfiguration to obtain an IPv6 address and using stateful autoconfiguration to get DNS and other IP configuration information from a DHCPv6 server.

In addition, addresses can be nontemporary (the equivalent of static IP addresses in IPv4) or temporary. Routers, gateways, and other devices may need these types of addresses and, just as with IPv4, you can allow a host to autoconfigure or you can manually set up the IPv6 addressing.

IPv6 Transition Technologies

Since the transition to IPv6 won't happen overnight (or even anytime soon), there are numerous ways companies can transition to IPv6. For more information, you can visit the Microsoft Web site and query the title "IPv6 Transition Technologies" for more information.

- **Dual IP Layer architecture**. Allows computers to communicate using both IPv6 and IPv4. This is required for ISATAP and Teredo hosts and for 6to4 routers.

- **IPv6 over IPv4 tunneling**. Places IPv6 packet data inside of an IPv4 header with an IP Protocol value of 41. This tunneling technique is used with ISATAP or 6to4.

- **Intra-Site Automatic Tunnel Addressing Protocol (ISATAP)**. Allows IPv6 hosts to use IPv6 over IPv4 tunneling to communicate on intranets.

- **6to4**. Allows IPv6 hosts to communicate with the IPv6 Internet. A 6to4 router with a public IPv4 address is required.

- **Teredo**. Allows IPv4/IPv6 hosts to communicate with the IPv6 Internet even if they are behind a network address translator (NAT).

Head of the Class…

Rolling Out IPv6

As you can imagine, it's a major job to roll out IPv6 in an organization. Windows Server 2008 and Windows Vista natively understand IPv6, but older operating systems, software programs, and hardware devices may not. Before you decide to run with IPv6, set up a test lab, configure it to use IPv6 and test your hardware, software, routers, and other network infrastructure in a closed environment. If you roll it out into a live environment, you are all but guaranteed that something will not work as expected. There are numerous tools available via the Microsoft Web site (and others) that will help you plan, assess, and manage your transition.

Configuring IPv6 Settings

When you access the local area connection properties of the Windows Server 2008 computer, you also have the option of configuring IPv6 settings if IPv6 is installed (it is installed by default in Windows Server 2008, so it should be there). You should be able to access IPv6 settings from the **Local Area Connection Properties** dialog box. If IPv6 is not shown, the protocol is not installed. Click the **Install** button and follow the on-screen prompts to install IPv6. Then, access the Local Area Connection Properties to configure the settings.

In the **Local Area Connection Properties** dialog box, shown in Figure 10.1 you can configure IPv6 addressing options by selecting Internet Protocol Version 6 (IPv6) and clicking **Properties**. The IPv6 Properties dialog box will open, as shown in Figure 10.4.

Figure 10.4 IPv6 Properties and Address Configuration

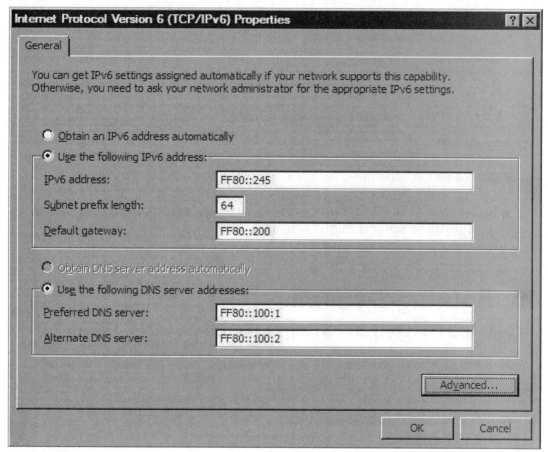

As with IPv4, you would typically allow host computers to obtain an IPv6 address automatically from the DHCP server. However, since this computer is a server, you may want to assign a *nontemporary* IP address to it (recall that nontemporary is the IPv6 equivalent of a static IP address in IPv4). If you choose to use a nontemporary address, you could click the radio button next to "Use the following IPv6 address:"

and enter the specifics. Also remember that if you set a nontemporary IP address here, you should create a reservation for this address in the DHCP server so that this address does not get assigned to another computer on the network. Best practices typically include creating your DHCP server scope and reservations before activating the DHCP server, then activating the DHCP server and assigning nontemporary (and static) IP addresses. This helps avoid potential problems with IP address assignments.

Let's look at how to configure IPv4 and IPv6 options in DHCP in Windows Server 2008. We're assuming you've enabled the DHCP Server role from within the Windows Server 2008 management console. If not, do so now but keep in mind that you want to do this on a test network or in a lab setting. As you know, activating more than one DHCP server on a network can cause the whole thing to crash, so be sure you're not connected in a way that will cause real-world problems.

EXAM WARNING

Be familiar with IP notation in both IPv4 and IPv6. You're likely to see more on IPv6 and transitioning to IPv6 than on standard IPv4 notation. If you're not up to speed on IPv6, you might want to take some time to thoroughly understand IPv6 and transition technologies before heading into the exam. The Microsoft exams pull questions from a pool of possible questions, so you might not see any questions in this topic area, but if you do, you'll be ready.

Configuring Dynamic Host Configuration Protocol (DHCP)

Dynamic Host Configuration Protocol (DHCP) allows DHCP servers to assign (lease) IP addresses to computers (hosts) and other devices on the network that are enabled as DHCP clients. We're assuming you have a solid foundation in DHCP, but we'll discuss some of the basics in this section as a quick review.

DHCP servers have pools of addresses defined, called scopes, which are handed out to (leased) DHCP clients on the network. The configuration information provided by the DHCP server to the DHCP client includes the IP address, subnet mask, default gateway, DNS server(s), WINS server(s) if any, and other options. The DHCP client will attempt to renew its IP address about halfway through the lease duration. If the DHCP server is online when that occurs, the renewal typically goes through and the lease period restarts. If the DHCP server is not online at the time of the lease renewal request, the client will continue to try to renew its lease periodically. If the lease is not renewed when 87.5% of the lease period has elapsed, the client will start looking for another DHCP server to provide the IP address. This may mean the client receives a new IP address or new configuration information based on the configuration of the new DHCP server it uses.

EXAM WARNING

Questions about DHCP on the exam will likely fall into one of three types—DHCP server questions, DHCP relay agent questions, and DHCP lease questions. DHCP servers should be highly available so you should have more than one on a network and you should try to avoid having clients get IP addresses from a DHCP server across a WAN link. Keep in mind that if you have more than one DHCP server per subnet, you must ensure the scopes are configured properly to avoid overlap and IP addressing issues. Look for questions with that type of scenario. DHCP relay agents should be configured on each network segment that does not have a DHCP server. This enables DHCP clients to contact DHCP servers on other network segments to obtain IP configuration data. Remember, the DHCP relay agent doesn't provide the lease, it simply forwards DHCP traffic to facilitate in the lease process. DHCP relay agents are typically routers on the network. Finally, lease duration questions might pop up and here's why. The longer the DHCP lease duration, the less DHCP traffic on the network. That's good. However, the longer the DHCP lease duration, the more likely it is that unused or inactive computers will hold onto IP addresses. That's bad. So, if your network is comprised largely of desktop computers, go for a longer lease period. If it's mostly mobile users with laptops coming on- and offline, set the duration lower to make better use of your IP addresses.

The short version of deploying DHCP is this: add the role, configure the scopes, options, and exclusions, then authorize the DHCP server. Configure routers as DHCP relay agents as needed. OK, now that we've got that all laid out, let's step through it in a bit more detail.

Adding the DHCP Server Role

DHCP is managed by the DHCP Server role in Windows Server 2008, as it was in Windows Server 2003. Once you've installed Windows Server 2008, you can select various roles to install on that computer, and DHCP is one. Install the role from the Server Manager interface (**Start | Server Manager**) or from the command line. We'll go over command line options later in this section. You can add the DHCP role to the server, but keep in mind that you should have a well thought out DHCP deployment plan before installing the DHCP server role on any computer. Scopes, reservations, and exclusions also should be planned out and set up on all DHCP servers before activating them so they don't overlap and accidentally assign identical IP addresses to different hosts on the network. You can see that the DHCP role in the Server Manager console, shown in Figure 10.5, includes both IPv4 and IPv6 configuration and options. Note that there are server options that can be configured at the DHCP Server level (click DHCP Server in the left pane and choose **Action** from the menu or **More Actions** from the right pane) or at the scope or reservation level. In Figure 10.5, we're looking at server-level options. We'll look at scope options in a moment.

Figure 10.5 DHCP Server Role with IPv4 and IPv6 Options

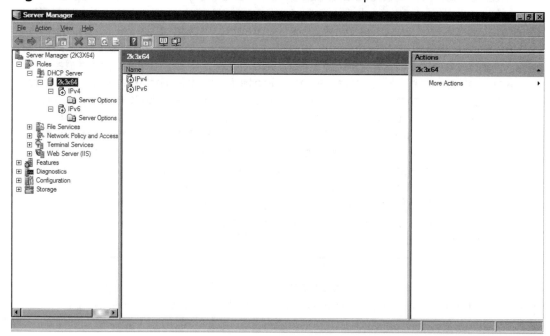

After you install the DHCP server role, you need to configure the DHCP settings. In the sections that follow, we'll look at:

- Scopes
- Scope options
- Creating new options
- Reservations

- Exclusions
- Authorizing the DHCP server

Notice that the server isn't authorized on the AD domain until it's been properly configured. Adding a DHCP server to the AD domain with improper configuration will likely cause massive problems on the network, so *configure*, *activate*, and *authorize*, in that order. We'll step through IPv4 first, then go back and step through IPv6 settings afterward. The reason for this is that when you're walking through the set up screens on the DHCP server, you set up all the IPv4 options at once. Of course, you can always go back in and modify settings but it will make more sense to walk through IPv4 completely and then step through IPv6.

Configuring DHCP Scopes

Scopes are groups of IPv4 or IPv6 addresses that can be dynamically assigned to hosts on the network. You can also assign *static* IPv4 addresses for servers, routers, and other network devices that require a permanent IP address, *nontemporary* addresses in IPv6 addressing space. Every subnet for which a DHCP server provides IP address configuration information, including remote subnets using a DHCP relay agent, must have a DHCP scope configured.

Scopes are created to specify IP address ranges available for lease by DHCP clients. For example, you could create a scope called Main Office and assign a range of addresses from 192.168.15.2 to 192.168.15.200. Any device on the Main Office network will contact the DHCP server and be assigned an IP address within that range. Note that scopes can use public or private IPv4 addresses.

A DHCP server can manage multiple scopes, which can be used for various purposes. In addition, there are three types of scopes with IPv4 addresses you can use:

- **Normal**. Normal scopes are ranges of IPv4 address pools from Class A, B or C networks.
- **Multicast**. Multicast IPv4 addresses are defined as Class D networks and are reserved for multicast traffic.
- **Superscopes**. Superscopes are essentially buckets into which you can put scopes to better manage groups of scopes.

Configuring IPv4 Scopes and Options

You're probably familiar with the basic configuration of IPv4 addressing in a DHCP server, so configuring DHCP IPv4 in Windows Server 2008 will be easy for you. Let's take a quick look at how to configure the scope and options in the IPv4 section of DHCP.

To configure IPv4 within DHCP, open the Server Manager console and click **DHCP Server**. Click **IPv4** in the left pane, then click **Action** from the menu and select **New Scope**. This initiates the New Scope Wizard. The first screen is the Welcome screen; click **Next**. The second step is to define the IP address range for the scope, as shown in Figure 10.6, where the private address range of 192.168.10.1 through 192.168.10.254 is shown. The subnet mask was calculated automatically for the range by the operating system and the suggested length of 24 bits with a subnet mask of 255.255.255.0 is the default and can be used. You can change this here or click **Next** to continue.

Figure 10.6 Creating a New DHCP IPv4 Scope

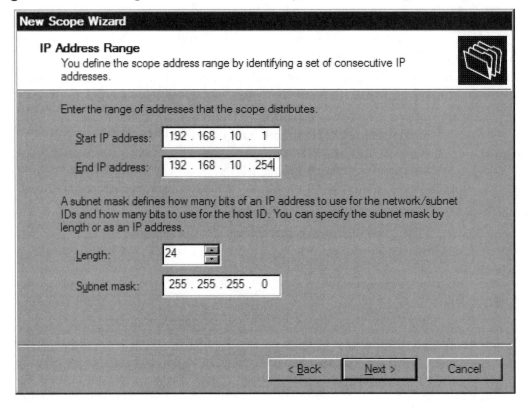

In the third screen, you can add exclusions. Ranges of IP addresses typically are excluded so that static IP addresses can be assigned to devices such as servers, routers, or printers that may require a static IP address. In Figure 10.7, you can see that two ranges have been excluded: 192.168.10.10 to 192.168.10.20 and 192.168.10.100 to

192.168.10.120. Addresses within these ranges will not be assigned automatically to dynamic DHCP clients. When you've completed entering any exclusions, click **Next**.

Figure 10.7 Excluded DHCP IPv4 Ranges

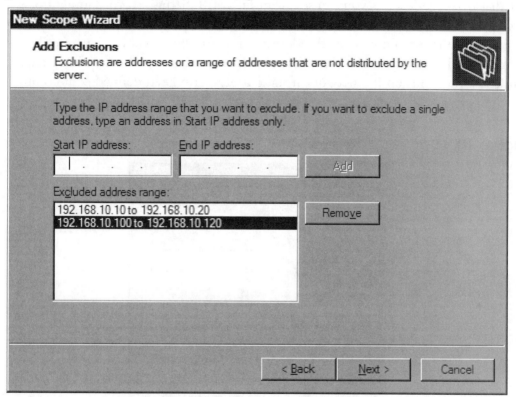

The next screen is the lease duration. This should be relatively short for networks that have a lot of mobile clients and relatively long for networks with mostly stable clients (desktops, etc.). If you have a mixture, a lease duration of two to four days might make the most sense. The default value is eight days and we'll leave it at the default for this example. The lease duration screen is self-explanatory and is not shown here.

After you've selected the lease duration, click **Next** to continue to the following screen where you can configure DHCP options. You can choose to set these now or later; we'll go through them later in the DHCP section. Click the radio button next to "No, I will configure these options later" then click **Next** and then **Finish**. Remember that before any clients can receive addresses from this DHCP server, you need to add any scope-specific options (which includes default gateway, among other things) and you need to activate the scope.

DHCP IPv4 Reservations

To reserve an address, you create a reservation and specify the Media Access Control (MAC) address of the host. This permanently reserves the designated IPv4 address for that MAC address. As you can see from Figure 10.8, this is a very straightforward process. Remember to set the IP address on the device to match this reservation. If the device is set to obtain an IP address automatically, it will be dynamically assigned an IP address that will not match the reservation. As you can imagine, this can cause problems on the network if static routes have been defined or if computers on the network are looking for a server at a specific IP address.

Figure 10.8 DHCP IPv4 Reservation

Configuring DHCP Scope Options

Before you can activate the scope, you need to set the scope options. Though we chose not to do this during the previous scope configuration, in the real world, you would most likely choose to set up the options at the same time you create the scope. We elected not to so that you can see how the scope options look in Server Manager. Keep in mind that there are three types of DHCP options—server, scope, and reservation, as shown in Figure 10.9.

Server Options

Server options are those set for the DHCP server. These options apply to all clients that use this DHCP server. Values set here apply to all scopes managed by this server.

These values can be overridden if those values are set at either a scope, options class, or reserved client level.

Scope Options

As the name implies, scope options are those set just for a particular defined scope on the DHCP server. Values set here can be overridden by values set at either an options class or reserved client level. We'll discuss scope options in more detail in a moment.

Reservation Options

Options set here are specific to a client reservation (reserved client level). Though it seems obvious, you must first add a reservation before you can configure options. Only properties manually configured at the client computer can override options assigned at this level.

When using any of the option configuration dialog boxes (Server Options, Scope Options, or Reservation Options), you can click the **Advanced** tab to set options for assignment to identifying member clients of a specified user class or vendor class. The available options are dependent upon whether you're configuring server, scope, or reservation options.

Figure 10.9 DHCP Server IPv4 Options

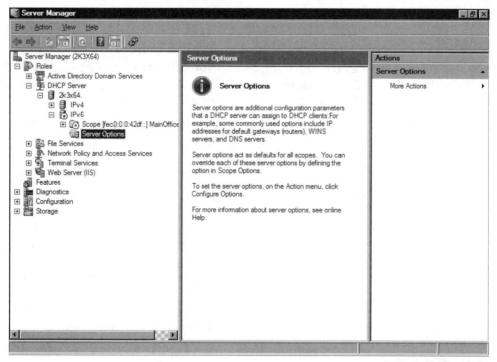

Setting Scope Options

To set up scope options, select the scope you want to configure, click **Scope Options** in the left pane, then click **Action | Scope Options** from the Server Manager menu.

To set an option, select it from the Available Options by clicking the checkbox to the left of the option. A brief description is shown to the right of each option. When you click an option, the data entry elements below are enabled and you can enter the server name and IP address. There is a long list of scope options that can be set here. A list and brief description of these is included in Table 10.3. You can also click the **Advanced** tab to select more advanced DHCP scope options. The Vendor class options include DHCP Standard Options, Microsoft Options, Microsoft Windows 2000 Options, and Microsoft Windows 98 Options. In addition to Vendor class options, you can select from among various user class options. These are Default BOOTP Class, Default Network Access Protection Class, Default Routing and Remote Access Class, and Default User Class. The data options beneath the Available Options section change depending on the option selected. These options should be modified only if you have a specific need to do so. In most cases, the default scope options are adequate.

Table 10.3 Scope Options List

Option Name	Settings	Notes
Router/Default Gateway	IP address	Identifies the default gateway for clients within this DHCP scope.
Domain Name and DNS Server	Parent domain, server name, IP address	Identifies the parent domain, the DNS server name, and IP address for clients within this DHCP scope.
WINS Node Type	Node type	The preferred NetBIOS name resolution method for the DHCP client to use such as b-mode for broadcast only or h-node for hybrid.
WINS Server(s)	Server name, IP address	If you have clients within the network that require the use of WINS name resolution, you should define your WINS server(s) here. This will be added to the DHCP option information provided to DHCP clients within this scope. A primary and secondary WINS server can be specified.

Most of the scope options available in Windows Server 2008 are the same as they were in Windows Server 2003. However, there are a lot of options available and if you're not familiar with these options, you can visit the Microsoft Web site to review details of each option to determine whether any of these more advanced options are appropriate for your network. Head up to http://technet2.microsoft.com/windowsserver/en/library/7f9261b1-92ef-40aa-a3b6-1dd9ab97c46e1033.mspx for more details.

Configuring IPv6 Scopes

As you know, IPv6 provides far more addresses than IPv4. Many firms use Network Address Translation so they can utilize private IP addressing on their local networks and then use public IP addresses to connect to the Internet. IPv6 can be used in a similar manner—it has both global and local IP addresses that correspond to public and private IP addresses. Site local addresses begin with FFE0, local link addresses begin with FE80. These can be used internally and are not routed by ISPs to the public domain.

Just as with IPv4 scopes in DHCP, the scope options for IPv6 are accessed through the Server Manager. Click **Server Manager | Roles | DHCP Server | IPv6** to configure IPv6 options. Click **IPv6** and then click **Action | New Scope** from the Server Manager menu. Like the IPv4 scope configuration process, this launches the New Scope Wizard. Click **Next** to continue from the Welcome screen. The next screen prompts you to type a name and description of the scope. Using a descriptive name and short description will help you keep your scopes organized. Click **Next** after entering the name and description. The following screen, shown in Figure 10.10, prompts you to enter the **Scope Prefix** as well as a **Preference** value for the scope. The CIDR notation is, by default, /64 and is provided by Windows automatically. In IPv6, note that /64 is a subnet identifier, /48 is a route identifier, and /8 is an address range.

Figure 10.10 DHCP IPv6 Scope Prefix Dialog Box

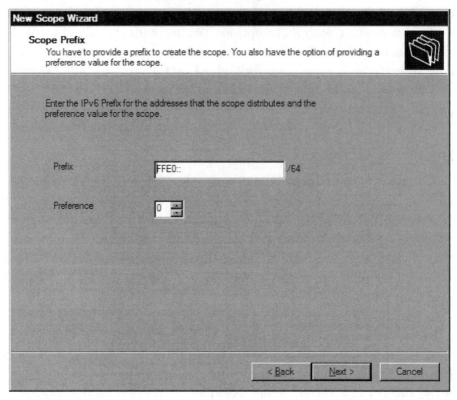

The preference value is optional and it sets the preference for a particular scope, meaning addresses will be assigned from the scope with the lowest preference first. This is an optional setting. Unless you're sure how to use this feature, leave the default value at 0.

When you've completed entering your scope data, click **Next** to access the **Add Exclusions** screen. As with the IPv4 wizard, you are prompted to enter the start and end IPv6 address for exclusions. When you've entered the range to exclude, click **Add** to add that range of addresses to the exclusions. If you want to remove an excluded range, select it and click **Remove**. When you're finished configuring exclusions, click **Next**. In the following screen, the **Scope Lease** screen, you're prompted to configure both temporary and nontemporary scope leases, as shown in Figure 10.11. As with IPv4 address leases, best practices include setting the lease duration equal to the average time a computer is connected to the same physical network. If you have a large number of mobile users, set the lease time to a shorter duration.

Figure 10.11 DHCP IPv6 Scope Lease Settings

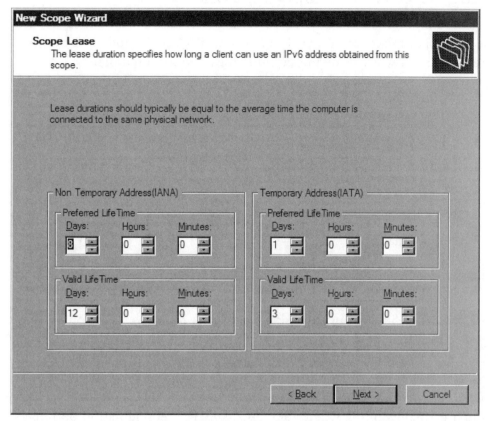

When you've completed setting the temporary and nontemporary lease duration settings, click **Next** to complete the scope configuration. The settings you've selected are recapped for you and if you've made a mistake, you can click **Back** to change them now. You can also choose to activate the scope at this point by selecting **Yes**. The scope is not available for leasing until the scope is activated, but if you want to configure all your scopes before activating, you can click **No** and come back and activate this scope later. We'll select **No** so you can see what it looks like when a scope is not yet activated. To activate the scope, click on the scope and choose **Action | Activate** from the Server Manager menu. The scope is activated and its status changes from inactive to active. You can deactivate the scope by clicking the scope and selecting **Action | Deactivate** from the menu. If you try to deactivate an active scope, you'll get a warning message reminding you that if you deactivate an active scope, clients will be unable to obtain a lease from that range of IP addresses.

Configuring IPv6 Scope Options

The options available in the IPv6 scope settings are different than those available in the IPv4 options section. When you select an IPv6 scope and click **Scope Options**, you can select from among numerous options listed here:

1. SIP Server Domain Name List
2. SIP Servers IPV6 Address List
3. DNS Recursive Name Server IPV6 Address List
4. Domain Search List
5. NIS IPV6 Address List
6. NIS+ IPV6 Address List
7. NIS Domain List
8. NIS+ Domain Name List
9. SNTP Servers IPv6 Address List

SIP stands for Session Initiation Protocol and a SIP server is an outbound proxy server. See the IEFT draft on SIP and DHCPv6 for more information (www3. tools.ietf.org/html/draft-ietf-sip-dhcpv6-01).

NIS stands for Network Information Service (and Network Information Service Plus, NIS+). You can read more about the NIS RFC specification at www. faqs.org/rfcs/rfc3898.html, where they discuss DHCP configuration options NIS, NIS+, NIS Domain List, and NIS+ Domain List.

As with the IPv4 options, you can configure individual options by clicking the checkbox to the left of the option in the Available Options section, then entering the specific data in the data entry section. The Advanced tab contains the same Vendor class and User class options as the IPv4 scope options dialog box and those options were previously described. Refer back to the section on Advanced IPv4 scope options for details on these options. When you're finished configuring scope options, click **OK**.

DHCP IPv6 Client Reservation Configuration

The client reservation configuration for IPv6 is very similar to the IPv4 configuration, though you have a few different options, as shown in Figure 10.12. The DUID is the device unique identifier, which in more common language is the device's MAC address. You can find the MAC address by opening a command prompt (**Start | Run | cmd**) on the client computer and typing in **ipconfig /all**.

The IAID is the *identity association identifier* that sets a unique identifier prefix for the client computer. This is typically a 9-digit value. The description is just a short description to help you identify the device. When you've configured the reservation, click **Add**.

Figure 10.12 DHCP IPv6 Client Reservation Configuration Options

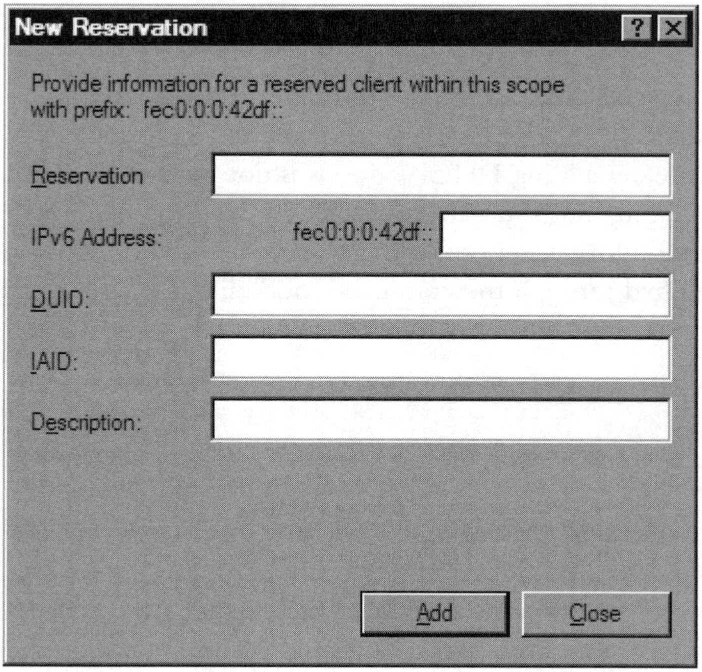

Creating New Options

You can create new options in DHCP through the interface or through the command line. Add or define new custom option types only if you have new software or applications that require a nonstandard DHCP option. There are vendor-defined classes, which are used to manage DHCP options assigned to clients by vendor type, and there are user-defined classes, which are used to manage DHCP options assigned to clients by a common need for similar DHCP configuration information. Note that after defining a new option class, you must configure your individual scopes with any class-related options that need to be provided to DHCP clients.

New Options Using the Windows Interface

Right-click the DHCP server in the left pane of Server Manager and select New User Class or New Vendor Class from the shortcut menu. Once you configure the new class, you can open the selected scope; right-click and choose **Scope Options** then **Configure Scope Options**. Click **Advanced** then click the check boxes next to the items you want to use with the new classes and click **OK** to accept changes, or **Cancel** to exit without accepting changes.

New Options Using the Command Line

You can add a new DHCP option type through the command line. This can be helpful if you want to use a batch file to add this option to multiple servers across the enterprise. Clearly, adding DHCP options is not for the faint of heart (or for the novice net admin), but the syntax is included here. You can query the Microsoft Web site for more information on adding DHCP options via the command line. This is accomplished through the command mode interface by typing **netsh dchp**. From the dhcp> prompt, you can enter this command to add a new option type:

```
add option defOptCode OptName{BYTE | WORD | DWORD | STRING | IPADDRESS}
[[IsArray=]{0 | 1}] [vendor=VendorClass] [comment=OptComment] [DefValue]
```

Exclusions

Exclusions are used to prevent a range of addresses from being handed out from within the scope. There are numerous reasons you might do this, but clearly you want to ensure your reservations are part of the excluded range of IP addresses. This helps manage static IP addresses for devices that should remain stable such as servers, routers, and other hardware devices that always need to be found. If an IP address is reserved but not excluded, the device using the static IP address will get the reserved IP address, but the DHCP server may also hand that same IP address out through normal DHCP activities. This would cause connectivity issues for one or both devices.

Exclusions are fairly straightforward and again, a bit of advanced planning goes a long way in making sure you set up your DHCP server right the first time. Typically, you'll set exclusions when you're setting up a new scope. From within the New Scope Wizard, you'll be prompted to set exclusions. If you have no ranges to exclude, you can skip this step by leaving the Start IP address and End IP address boxes blank and clicking **Next**. The New Scope Wizard in IPv4, shown in Figure 10.13, is similar in IPv6.

Figure 10.13 Setting DHCP Exclusions

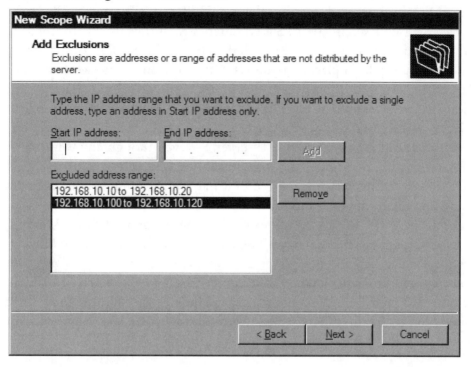

In this example, you can see that two ranges have been excluded. In this case, 192.168.10.10 through 192.168.10.20 is the first range excluded. The second range excluded is 192.168.10.100 through 192.168.10.120. The first range specifically excludes addresses (last octet) 10 through 20, providing 11 excluded addresses. The second range specifically excludes 100 through 120, providing 21 excluded addresses. These excluded addresses can be assigned as static IP addresses to servers, routers, printers and other devices requiring set IP addresses through setting reservations.

EXAM WARNING

All DHCP traffic uses the User Datagram Protocol (UDP). Messages from the client to the server use UDP port 68 as the source port and port 67 as the destination port. Messages from the server to the client use just the reverse—UDP port 67 as the source and UDP port 68 as the destination. If you see questions using UDP ports 67 or 68, think *DHCP*. Authorizing DHCP Server in Active Directory.

In order to help prevent the placement of rogue DHCP servers on the network, an Active Directory network requires that a DHCP server be specifically authorized to fill that role (see Exercise 10.2). Stated differently, in the AD environment, a Windows-based DHCP server will not start unless authorized. In older operating systems, it was possible to place a rogue DHCP server on the network and cause it to come to a crashing halt. This often was done erroneously but certainly there were intentional instances as well. Even in Windows Server 2008, it is possible to activate a non–Windows-based DHCP server (such as a Linux-based DHCP Server) on the network and introduce a rogue DHCP server. So, even though any Windows-based DHCP servers will not work without authorization, it is still possible to introduce a DHCP server on the network. Although it may be fairly unlikely to occur in your network environment, it's important to know it can happen and it's even more important to be aware of this for the exam. In order to prevent that, AD requires that the DHCP server be authorized. The steps for authorizing the DHCP server in AD are the same as in Windows Server 2003 and are provided in the *Configuring & Implementing* section that follows. DHCP servers should be authorized only after you've designed your DHCP configuration for the network and set up your scopes, exclusions, and reservations. Remember, too, that scopes can be configured but not activated, so you have three basic steps: *configure*, *activate*, and *authorize*.

EXERCISE 10.2

AUTHORIZE A DHCP SERVER

The following exercise will walk you through authorizing a new DHCP server on the domain. **CAUTION:** This should be done in a test environment or with a DHCP server that is properly configured to join the domain.

1. Log on as a member of the Domain Admins group.
2. Click **Start | Administrative Tools | DHCP**.
3. Under DHCP, right-click the server name and click **Authorize**.
4. Right-click the server name again and click **Refresh**.

A DHCP Server that is not yet authorized will have red arrows next to the IPv4 and IPv6 icons in the DHCP console. Figure 10.14 shows the red icon to the left of the specific IPv4 scope (the scope is in reversed type) and green icons to the left of the IPv4 and IPv6 DHCP server icons (although the color won't show up in this book, you can see where the icons are located). After you **Authorize** the DHCP server and click

Refresh, the red arrows should be gone, indicating the server has been authorized. The server will now begin handing out IP addresses for the scopes it manages. If you want to deauthorize a DHCP server, use the same steps, except in step three, the option will be **Unauthorize** instead.

Figure 10.14 DHCP Scopes—Activated and Not Activated

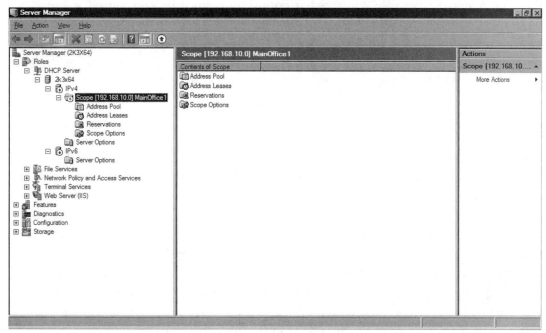

You can also authorize a DHCP server using a script. Run the following command with Domain Admin privileges: **netsh dhcp add server** *ServerName [ServerIPv4Address]*.

TEST DAY TIP

Only Windows-based DHCP servers must be authorized in an Active Directory domain. If someone wanted to install a non-Windows-based DHCP server (such as a Linux-based DHCP server) on the network, they could start it up and start handing out IP configuration data to unsuspecting DHCP clients. Check your answers on DHCP to ensure the server specified is (or is not) Windows-based.

DHCP Relay Agents

A DHCP relay agent is a network device configured specifically to relay DCHP traffic to a nearby DHCP server. Essentially, you must have a DHCP relay agent or a DHCP server on every network segment where DHCP client computers reside. In Windows Server 2008, the DHCP relay agent is enabled in the Routing and Remote Access Server role. Note that a computer cannot be configured as both a DHCP server and a DHCP relay agent. The DHCP relay agent is, essentially, a routing protocol that is installed on an appropriate device. Typically, a router is set up as a DHCP relay agent so that DHCP discovery traffic will be routed to the appropriate DHCP server.

PXE Boot

Let's begin by discussing the basics of the PXE Boot. The Pre-Boot Execution Environment, or PXE Boot, is a standard created by Intel to provide a consistent set of functionality prior to booting the operating system. These capabilities are stored in the boot firmware on the computer. The primary objective of the PXE Boot is to enable a client computer to boot up and receive a network boot program (NBP) from a server. PXE is used as part of the Windows Deployment Services feature because it enables remote computers without an operating system (new install or repair) to connect to the network and install the OS from a network share. If the OS is damaged, a computer can still be connected to the network to download repair tools. You can also use computers on the network that have no hard drive storage by booting to the network and downloading the software image needed to run a particular program.

Here's how PXE works. The computer's firmware contains the PXE Boot instructions, which allow the computer to boot and contact a DHCP server for an IP address using the normal DHCP discovery process. As part of the DHCP discovery process, the computer identifies itself as PXE Boot enabled so the PXE Server, which is a protocol extension of DHCP, knows it needs to service a PXE client. Any PXE server on the network can service the PXE client by providing the IP address of the PXE server to the PXE client. The initial communication also provides the name of a boot file the client should request if it wants service from that server.

After the PXE client has a valid IP address, it will attempt to connect to the PXE server and download the network boot program (NBP). The NBP is transmitted to the PXE client using the Trivial File Transfer Protocol (TFTP) from the PXE server and the client computer then executes the NBP file.

The PXE boot is able to obtain an IP address through the use of specific data fields (called options) in the DHCP packet. If you implement the Windows Deployment Services PXE Server (WDSPXE), you can place it on the same physical server as the DHCP Server though the default (and preferred) configuration is to place the PXE Server and the DHCP Server on different physical servers. If you're going to configure them to run on the same physical server, you need to make two changes:

1. You must configure WDSPXE not to listen to UDP Port 67, which is used by the DHCP Server.

2. You must add the DHCP option tag 60, set to the PXEclient string, and it has to be added to all active DHCP scopes. By doing so, you enable PXE booting clients to be notified of WDSPXE from the DHCP Server. However, setting DHCP option tag 60 has another effect you should know about—clients booting from the network will always be notified that WDSPXE is available, even if the server is out of service.

Head of the Class...

Network Boot Program Quick Facts

Windows Deployment Services uses the NBP feature extensively. Here are a few quick facts you should know. NBPs are both architecture- and firmware-specific. According to the PXE specification, on BIOS computers the NBP is a 16-bit real-mode application and can therefore be used both on the x86-based and x64-based operation system platforms. Windows Deployment Services provides a number of different NBP programs. For example, PXEboot.com, which is the default, requires users to press the F12 key to perform the PXE boot. PXEboot.n12 does not require the F12 key and will boot automatically. Windows Deployment Services is discussed later in this book, but since we were on the topic of DHCP, it was appropriate to introduce PXE Boot here. For very detailed information on PXE specification, see www.pix.net/software/pxeboot/archive/pxespec.pdf.

DHCP and Network Access Protection (NAP)

Network Access Protection (NAP) is a platform supported by over 100 independent software vendors (ISVs) and independent hardware vendors (IHVs). It is managed by Windows Server 2008 and works with Windows Vista clients natively. Support for NAP in Windows XP clients is part of Service Pack 3 (SP3). Network access protection is designed to prevent computers that are lacking appropriate security measures including service updates and service packs as well as up-to-date antivirus definition files. NAP is discussed in detail in Chapter 12, but since we're looking at DHCP, we'll take a quick detour to understand how DHCP and NAP interact (see Exercise 10.3). Keep in mind that NAP can be enforced in different ways but that using DHCP is one of the weaker forms since users with administrator-level access can override certain settings with respect to DHCP and NAP enforcement.

EXERCISE 10.3

CREATING A NAP AND DHCP INTEGRATION POLICY

If you haven't already, install the Network Policy Server (NPS) role on your DHCP server via the **Server Manager | Add Roles** function. In the left pane, select **NPS (Local)** then click **Configure NAP** in the main pane. This launches the **Configure NAP Wizard.**

1. In the **Network Connection Method** list, select Dynamic Host Configuration Protocol (DHCP) as the connection method you want to deploy for DHCP clients. The default policy name provided is NAP DHCP. You can accept this name or create another name. Click **Next** to continue.

2. The next screen is **Specify NAP Enforcement Servers Running DHCP**. Identify all the remote DHCP servers on your network by clicking **Add** and in the **Add New RADIUS client** box, type a friendly name of the remote server in the **Friendly Name** box. Enter the DNS name or IP address of the remote DHCP server in the **Address** box. Click **Verify** to validate the entered information before proceeding.

3. In the **Shared Secret** panel (of the **Specify NAP Enforcement Servers Running DHCP** dialog), select **Generate** then click **Generate** to create a long, shared secrete keyphrase. You'll use this same keyphrase in the NAP DHCP Policy on all remote DHCP

servers so be sure to make a note of it so you can locate it when needed. Click **OK**, then **Next** to continue.

4. In the **Specify DHCP Scope** page of the setup wizard, identify the scope(s) to which you want this policy to apply. If you do not specify any scopes, the policy is applied to all NAP-enabled scopes on the selected DHCP server(s). Click **Next**. On the next screen, you can **Configure Groups**. We'll skip this and click **Next** to continue.

5. The next screen is the **Specify NAP Remediation Server Group and URL** page, which allows you to specify where a client should go if it has problems with NAP. You can select a Remediation Server or click **New Group** to define a remediation group and select servers to handle the remediation. Note: Remediation Servers store software updates for NAP clients that need them. In the text box, provide a URL NAP clients can access with information on bringing their computers up to NAP health policy requirements. Click **Next** to continue.

6. The final screen of the wizard is the **Define NAP Health Policy** page. The default settings on this page are fine for most applications, but you can modify the defaults if you have reason to do so. Otherwise, accept the defaults and click **Next**, then **Finish**. These default settings essentially have the NAP-ineligible clients are denied network access, checked for compliance then automatically remediated by downloading and installing software updates from the remediation location you specified in Step 5.

In addition to enabling NAP, you can set NAP settings globally or on a per scope basis. To modify or view settings in Server Manager on the server you want to work with, right-click **IPv4** and select **Properties**. Click the **Network Access Protection** tab and either **Enable on all scopes** or **Disable on all scopes**. You can also specify how DHCP server should behave when if the NPS server is unavailable. You can choose from three options:

- **Full Access**. Allows DHCP clients full, unrestricted access to the network.

- **Restricted Access**. Allows DHCP clients restricted access to the network. Clients can work only with the server to which they are connected.

- **Drop Client Packet**. This is another way of saying No Access. When the server is instructed to drop client packets, all packets from the client will be dropped and the client will not be able to connect to a server or to the network.

When you've finished configuring these settings, click **OK** to accept changes or **Cancel** to exit without accepting changes.

Although integrating DHCP and NAP is the easiest method of enforcing NAP, it's also the weakest. To harden the implantation, you should combine DHCP enforcement with another form of enforcement such as 802.1x or IPsec.

EXAM WARNING

Microsoft exams are notorious for extensive testing on new features. In Windows Server 2008, there are two notable new features related to DHCP. The first is support for **Dynamic Host Configuration Protocol for IPv6 (DHCPv6)**, which is defined by the IETF's RFC 3315 specification. It provides stateful address configuration for IPv6 hosts on a native IPv6 network. In Windows Server 2008 and Windows Vista, the DHCP client service supports DHCPv6. A computer running either of these operating systems can perform *stateful* and *stateless* configuration of DHCPv6. *Stateful configuration* includes both addresses and configuration settings whereas *stateless configuration* is configuration settings only.

The second important change related to DHCP is the addition of Network Access Protection (NAP) enforcement support. DHCP enforcement in the NAP platform requires that the DHCP client prove it's healthy before it can receive an address configuration for unlimited access.

Network Access Protection in Windows Server 2008, Windows Vista, and Windows XP SP3 (with NAP Client for Windows XP) provides policy enforcement elements to ensure computers connecting to or communicating across a network are "healthy," meaning they comply with administrator-defined requirements for system health. One common example is that a computer must have the latest operating system updates and antivirus signature files installed before connecting to the network. This helps reduce the probability of a systemwide virus, for example, and helps isolate potential problems by preventing unhealthy computers from connecting.

DHCP Configuration via Server Core

You can enable and manage DHCP through the Server Core command-line interface. This can be helpful when remotely managing a DHCP server across a slower WAN link or when creating batch files to perform repetitive DHCP tasks. We'll include some of the commands you can use in Windows Server 2008 Core, but a more extensive listing of command line commands can be found in the Windows Server 2008 Help file or online at the Microsoft Windows Server 2008 Web site.

The **netsh** command can be implemented via the command line. Open a command window and type:

netsh dhcp (then press **Enter**)

to begin command line management of DHCP. Once you've done this, the command prompt line will show **dhcp>**. Commands include:

> Add Server (Adds a DHCP server to the domain)
>
> Syntax = **add server** DNSname IPaddress
>
> Example = **add server dhcpsrv1.example.microsoft.com 10.2.2.2**

Change Command Line focus to different DHCP Server

> Syntax = **server** IPaddress (or **server** \\path)
>
> Example = **server 10.0.0.1**

Add Scope

> Syntax = **add scope** ScopeAddress SubnetMask ScopeName [ScopeComment]
>
> Example = **add scope** 10.2.2.0 255.255.255.0 MainOfficeScope

You can manage the server scope from the netsh command as well. In the command line window, type:

netsh dhcp server scope (then press **Enter**)

This will result in a **dhcp server scope>** prompt. From there, you can utilize the following commands. You can get syntax assistance by using the ? variable.

- add excluderange
- add iprange
- add reservedip
- delete excluderange
- delete iprange
- delete lease

- delete optionvalue

- delete reservedip

- delete reservedoptionvalue

- dump

- initiate reconcile

- set comment

- set name

- set optionvalue

- set reservedoptionvalue

- set scope

- set state

- set superscope

- show clients

- show clientsv5

- show excluderange

- show iprange

- show optionvalue

- show reservedip

- show reservedoptionvalue

- show scope

- show state

TEST DAY TIP

Be sure to familiarize yourself with the command line options. Even though you won't have to memorize every command and all its syntax to pass the exam, you should expect to see a fair amount of emphasis on command line usage. Understanding the basics of how to use the command line window, which is the user interface for the Windows Server 2008 Core installation, will help you answer these types of questions, and they might be the difference between passing and just squeaking by (or not).

Configuring Network Authentication

Let's start with a quick review of the basics to set the foundation for this discussion of network access and authentication. Windows Server 2008 authentication is a two-part process involving authentication of the user (interactive login) and access control to network resources. When a user logs in, their identity is verified through Active Directory (AD) Domain Services and this provides controlled access to Active Directory objects. As the user attempts to access various network resources, their network authentication credentials are used to determine whether or not the user has permission to access those resources. Also part of AD are user accounts and groups that impact network access. Authentication can also occur through a public key infrastructure (PKI), which uses digital certificates and certification authorities to verify and authenticate entities including users, computers, and services. Group Policy is used to manage configuration settings for servers, clients, and users. Remote Authentication Dial-In User Service (RADIUS) is a protocol that originally was created for dial-in authentication and authorization service. Now, its role has expanded to include wireless access point access, authenticating Ethernet switches, virtual private network servers, and more. In Windows Server 2008, the RADIUS function is now handled by the Network Policy and Access Services role.

As you can see from Figure 10.15, the Network Policy and Access Services role installs Network Policy Server (NPS) and Routing and Remote Access (RRAS). Under the NPS node, you'll find RADIUS Clients and Servers, Policies, Network Access Protection (NAP) and Accounting. Under the Routing and Remote Access node, you'll find Network Interfaces, Remote Access Logging & Policies, IPv4 and IPv6.

Back to NPS: NPS allows you to configure and manage network policies from a centralized location. You can configure and manage RADIUS server, RADIUS proxy, and Network Access Protection (NAP) policy server from within this role. With NPS, you can authorize and authenticate network connections through different access servers such as 802.1x, wireless access points (WAP), virtual private network server (VPN), dial-up servers, and computers running Windows Server 2008 with Terminal Services Gateway (TS Gateway).

Network Policy Server creates and enforces organizationwide access policies for clients. These services include client health, connection request authentication, and connection request authorization. You can also use NPS as a RADIUS proxy to forward connection requests for authentication and authorization to NPS or other RADIUS servers. As part of NPS, routing and remote access services can also be installed. This provides users access to resources connecting remotely through VPN or dial–up connections. RRAS can also be used to provide routing services on small networks or to connect two private networks across the Internet.

To summarize, authentication in Windows Server 2008 is provided by numerous infrastructure components including Active Directory Domain Services, Group Policy, Public Key Infrastructure, and RADIUS. These interact with Network Policy Server (NPS). For example, in Active Directory, you can configure user or computer accounts to either *Allow Access* or *Control Access Through NPS Network Policy (recommended)*. In Windows Server 2008, the *Control Access Through NPS Network Policy (recommended)* is selected by default. When using groups to manage access, you can then use your existing groups and create network policies in NPS that either allow access (with or without restrictions) or deny access based on existing groups. For example, you can configure a policy in NPS that specifies the Marketing group have unrestricted VPN access. You might also configure another NPS policy that specifies that Vendors can never have VPN access.

Test Day Tip

Numerous authentication and communication-based protocols are no longer supported in Windows Server 2008 (and Windows Vista). We've listed a few here, but for the full list (and subject to change until the final version of Windows Server 2008 is released), refer to the Microsoft Web site. Support has been removed for:

- X.25
- SLIP-based connections (automatically updated to PPP-based connections)
- ATM
- NWLinkIPX/SPX/NetBIOS Compatible Transport Protocol
- Service for Macintosh
- OSPF
- SPAP, EAP-MD5-CHAP and MS-CHAPv1 authentication protocols

NTLMv2 and Kerberos Authentication

Starting with Windows 2000, Kerberos Version 5 (Kerberos) was supported as the default authentication protocol in Active Directory. The NT LAN Manager (NTLM) protocol is still supported for authentication with clients that required NTLM (i.e., for backward compatibility only). You can control how NTLM is used through

Group Policy. The default authentication level in most cases is "Send NTLMv2 Response Only." With this level of authentication, NTLMv2 is used with clients that use this authentication protocol and session security only if the server supports it.

You can configure Kerberos to utilize different methods of authentication, and these can be set via NPS for the network as well as in the IPsec Settings tab of the Windows Firewall with Advanced Security Properties, which we'll discuss a bit later in this chapter.

To begin, install this role on your Windows Server 2008 computer, if it's not already installed. To do so, open Server Manager, choose **Add Roles** from the interface option, then select **Network Policy and Access Services**. Follow the on-screen prompts to complete configuration, which are self-explanatory. In order to install *Health Registration Authority* (HRA) and *Host Credential Authorization Protocol* (HCAP), you also need to have web services (IIS) installed. For our purposes, we will disregard these two options and focus just on network access. Once Network Policy and Access Services are installed, you can access the services through the Server Manager interface. As shown in Figure 10.15, you can start, stop, or check the status of a service as well as set Preferences. Note that you can deploy NPS in a number of ways at various points in your forest or domain. It is beyond the scope of this chapter to discuss these options in detail.

Figure 10.15 Network Policy and Access Services Server Manager Interface

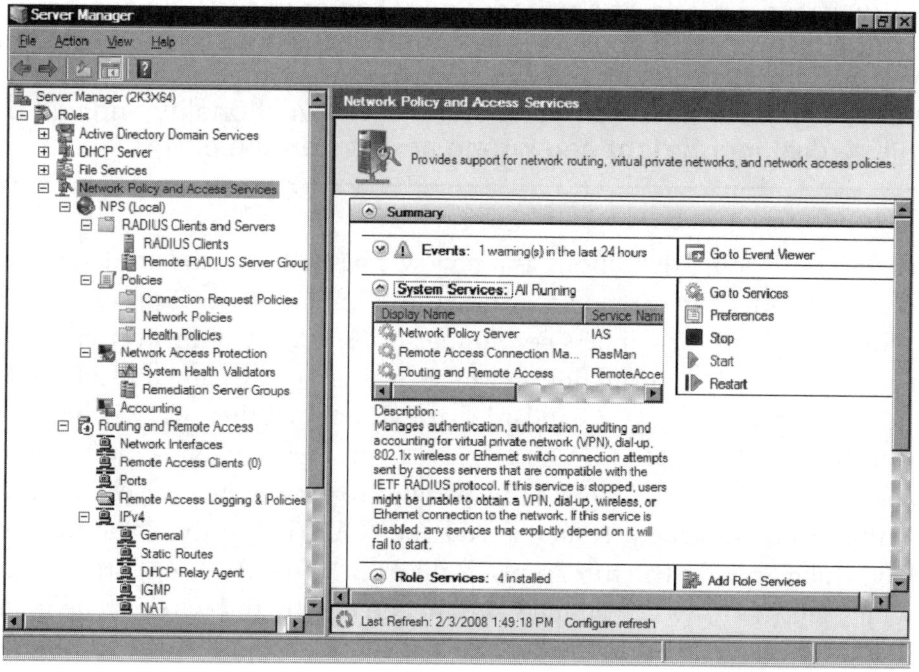

WLAN Authentication Using 802.1x and 802.3

NPS is responsible for network security and is used to provide secure wireless access through NPS. Windows Server 2008 also provides features that enable you to deploy 802.1x authenticated wired service for IEEE 802.3 Ethernet network clients. In conjunction with 802.1x capable switches and other Windows Server 2008 features, you can control network access through Wired Network Policies in Windows Server 2008 Group Policies. Recall that NPS is used to configure remote connections. The 802.3 wired network specification allows you to use the 802.1x specification to provide wired networking access. This is configured via NPS and uses Protected Extensible Authentication Protocol (PEAP) authentication. It is outside the scope of this book to discuss how to plan, configure, and deploy a WLAN authentication method, but we will discuss these concepts to the extent you need to understand the changes in the Windows Server 2008 environment.

TEST DAY TIP

Group Policy and Network Policy Server are two Windows Server 2008 areas with which you should be familiar. Understand the role of Group Policy versus the role of Network Policy Server in securing the network. Be able to explain in your own words what these two features do in Windows Server 2008. If you can describe them in your own words, there's a good chance you understand their functionality and will be able to distinguish right and wrong answers on the exam.

Let's start with some definitions as a review. The 802.11 standard defined the shared key authentication method for authentication and Wired Equivalent Privacy (WEP) for encryption for wireless communications. 802.11 ultimately ended up being a relatively weak standard and newer security standards are available and recommended for use. The 802.1x standard that existed for Ethernet switches was adapted to the 802.11 wireless LANs to provide stronger authentication than the original standard. 802.1x is designed for medium to large wireless LANs that have an authentication infrastructure, such as AD and RADIUS in the Windows environment. With such an infrastructure in place, the 802.1x standard supports dynamic WEP, which are mutually determined keys negotiated by the wireless client and the RADIUS server. However, the 802.1x standard also supports the stronger Wi-Fi

Protected Access (WPA) encryption method. The 802.11i standard formally replaces WEP with WPA2, an enhancement to the original WPA method.

Wireless and Wired Authentication Technologies

Windows Server 2008 supports several authentication methods for authenticating that a computer or user is attempting to connect via a protected wireless connection. These same technologies support 802.1x authenticated wired networks as well. These Extended Authentication Protocols (EAP) methods are:

- EAP–TLS
- PEAP–TLS
- PEAP–MS–CHAPv2

Extended Authentication Protocol–Transport Layer Security (EAP–TLS) and Protected Extended Authentication Protocol–Transport Layer Security (PEAP–TLS) are used in conjunction with Public Key Infrastructure (PKI) and computer certificates, user certificates, or smart cards. Using EAP–TLS, a wireless client sends its certificate (computer, user, or smart card) for authentication and the RADIUS server sends its computer certificate for authentication. By default, the wireless client authenticates the server's certificate. With PEAP–TLS, the server and client create an encrypted session before certificates are exchanged. Clearly, PEAP–TLS is a stronger authentication method because the authentication session data is encrypted.

If there are no computer, user, or smart card certificates available, you can use PEAP-Microsoft Challenge Handshake Authentication Protocol version 2 (PEAP-MS-CHAPv2). This is a password-based authentication method in which the exchange of the authentication traffic is encrypted (using TLS), making it difficult for hackers to intercept and use an offline dictionary attack to access authentication exchange data. That said, it's the weakest of these three options for authentication because it relies on the use of a password.

A Windows-based client running Windows Vista or Windows Server 2008 can be configured in the following ways:

- Group Policy
- Command line
- Wired XML profiles

Using Group Policy, you can configure the Wired Network (IEEE 802.3) Policies Group Policy extension, which is part of Computer configuration Group

Policy that can specify wired network settings in the AD environment. The Group Policy extension applies only to Windows Server 2008 and Windows Vista computers. The command line can be used within the **netsh** context using the **lan** command (**netsh lan**). You can explore the available comments by typing **netsh lan /?** at the command line prompt. Wired XML profiles are XML files that contain wired network settings. These can be imported and exported to Windows Server 2008 and Windows Vista clients using the **netsh** context as well. You can use **netsh lan export profile** or **netsh lan add profile** to export or import a wired profile using the command line.

For Windows XP SP2 or Windows Server 2003-basec computers, you can manually configure wired clients by configuring 802.1x authentication settings from the Authentication tab of the properties dialog box of a LAN connection in the Network Connections folder, as shown in Figure 10.16, which shows the Network Connections Properties dialog box from a Windows XP Pro SP2 computer.

Figure 10.16 802.1x Settings on Wired Windows XP SP2 Client

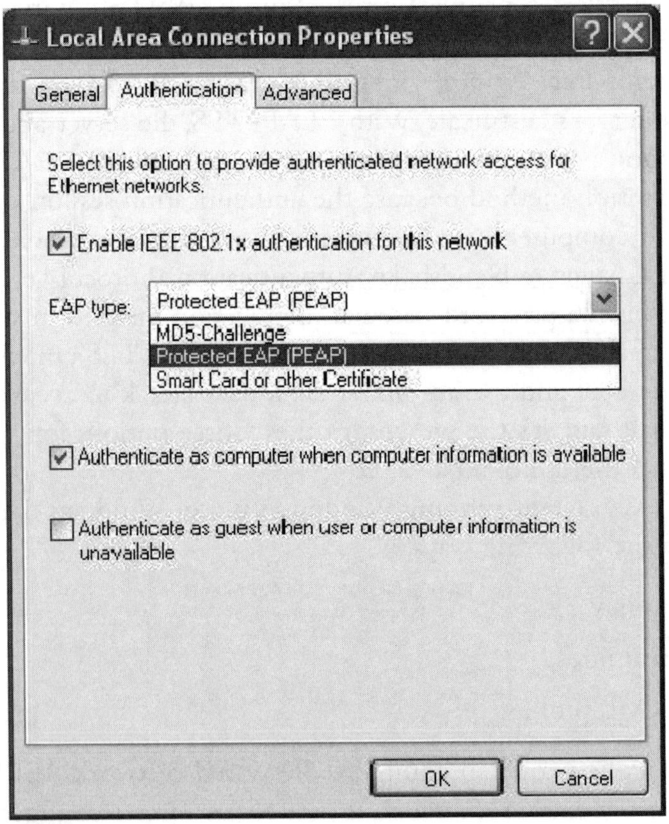

Implementing Secure
Network Access Authentication

Although it's outside the scope of this chapter to go into the details of PKI, it is useful to look at some of the ways PKI can be used as part of a Windows-based authentication infrastructure for secure network access using the protocols discussed in this section.

- When using PEAP–MS-CHAPv2 for network access authentication, configure Group Policy for autoenrollment of computer certificates to install computer certificates on the NPS servers.

- When using certificates for computer-level network access authentication, you should configure Group Policy for autoenrollment of computer certificates. This applies if you're using EAP–TLS or PEAP–TLS for computer-level wireless authentication.

- When using certificates for user-level network access authentication, configure a certificate template for user certificates and also configure Group Policy for autoenrollment of user certificates. As with computer-level certificates, this is needed when using EAP–TLS and PEAP–TLS.

Group Policy is also an important part of securing network access and authenticating computers and users. You can use Group Policy to deploy settings to install a root certificate on a domain member computer to validate computer certificates of the NPS servers. It can also be used to autoenroll user and computer certificates on domain member computers for user- and computer-level certificate-based authentication.

In addition to being useful in the deployment of certificate-based authentication, Group Policy is also useful in deploying configuration settings for:

- 802.11 wireless network profiles

- 802.1x wired network profiles

- Windows Firewall with Advanced Security connection security rules to protect traffic

- NAP client configuration

New & Noteworthy...

Changes to Authentication Protocols

PPP-based connections no longer support the SPAP, EAP-MD5-CHAP and MS-CHAPv1 authentication protocols. Remote access PPP-based connections now support the use of Protected EAP (PEAP) with PEAP-MS-CHAP v2 and PEAP-TLS. Keep this in mind as you plan out your new Windows Server 2008 remote access options.

EAPHost architecture in Windows Server 2008 and Windows Vista includes new features not supported in Windows Server 2003 and Windows XP including:

- Support for additional EAP methods
- Network discovery (as defined in RFC 4284)
- RFC 3748 compliance and support for expanded EAP types including vendor-specific EAP types
- Coexistence of multiple EAP types (Microsoft and Cisco, for example)

EXERCISE 10.4

CONFIGURING 802.1X SETTINGS IN WINDOWS SERVER 2008

You can configure wired policies form the **Computer Configuration | Policies | Windows Settings | Security Settings | Wired Network (IEEE 802.3) Policies** node in the **Group Policy Management Editor snap-in** via the MMC. By default, there are no wired policies in place. To create a new policy, use the following steps:

1. Right-click the **Wired Network (IEEE 802.3) Policies** in the console tree of the GP Editor snap-in.

2. Click **Create A New Windows Vista Wired Policy**.

3. The **New Windows Vista Wired Policy Properties** dialog is displayed, shown in Figure 10.17. It has two tabs: General and

Security. The **General** tab is selected by default. Enter the policy name and description and ensure the checkbox for "Use Windows Wired Auto Config service for clients" is checked.

Figure 10.17 New Vista Wired Network Policy Properties Security Tab

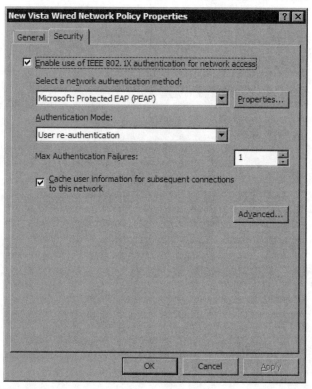

4. Click the **Security** tab to set security options. On this tab, click the checkbox next to "Enable use for IEEE 802.1X authentication for network access" then click the dropdown box to select a network authentication method (EAP, PEAP, MS-CHAPv2). Also select the "Authentication Mode" from the second dropdown box. The options are User re-authentication, computer only, user authentication, or guest authentication. Also select the number of times the authentication can fail before it is abandoned (1 is the default). The last setting in the Security tab is a checkbox whether to "Cache user information for subsequent connections to this network." If this checkbox is cleared, the credential data is removed when the user logs off. If the checkbox is checked, the credential data will be cached after user log off.

5. To access advanced settings, click the **Advanced** button on the Security tab. There are two Advanced segments: **IEEE 802.1X** and **Single Sign On**, shown in Figure 10.18.

Figure 10.18 Advanced Settings for new Vista Wired Network Policy Properties

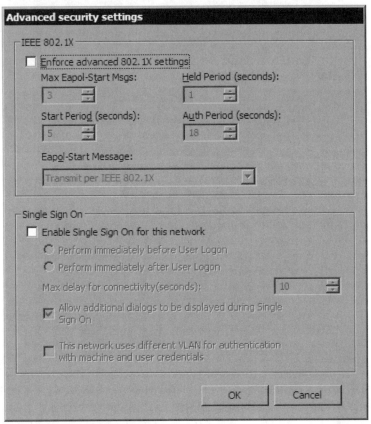

6. In the **IEEE 802.1X** section, click the checkbox to the left of "Enforce advanced 802.1X settings" to enable these options: Max Eapol-Start Msgs:, Held Period (seconds), Start Period (seconds), Auth Period (seconds), Eapol-Start Message. In most cases, the default settings are fine; it you believe you need these advanced settings, check the Microsoft documentation for details on how to set these.

7. In the **Single Sign On** section, click the checkbox next to "Enable Single Sign On for this network" to enable the following options: Perform immediately before User Logon, Perform immediately

after User Logon, Set Max. delay for connectivity (seconds), Allow additional dialogs to be displayed during Single Sign On, and This network uses different VLAN for authentication with machine and user credentials. Again, as with the IEEE 802.1X Advanced settings, these can be modified if you have a specific need to do so. Check Microsoft documentation for details on using these options within your network environment. A good starting place is www.microsoft.com/technet/technetmag/issues/2008/02/CableGuy/default.aspx.

8. Click **OK** to accept configuration; click **Cancel** to exit without saving changes.

Routing and Remote Access Services (RRAS) Authentication

Routing and Remote Access Services (RRAS), installed via the NPS, enables users to be authenticated and to connect to the network remotely. RRAS services are similar to those in Windows Server 2003, though there are a few updates to be aware of. For details of the Windows Server 2008 changes, read the New & Noteworthy section that precedes this section.

As we've mentioned, EAP-TLS and PEAP-TLS are supported in Windows Server 2008 and the less secure PEAP-MS-CHAPv2 is supported when certificates are not available. RRAS policies are configured here as well as via Group Policy in AD.

We're assuming you already have an understanding of a security infrastructure (AD, PKI, etc.), so we'll build on that knowledge. As you know, RRAS can be configured via Group Policy so you can control access based on group membership—whether that's a computer or user group. The most popular method of remote connection these days is through a Virtual Private Network (VPN) connection. You can secure that connection of a remote computer and the local network in different ways. The three methods in Windows Server 2008 are:

- Point-to-Point Tunneling Protocol (PPTP)

- Layer Two Tunneling Protocol with Internet Protocol security (L2TP/IPsec)

- Secure Socket Tunneling Protocol (SSTP)

Point-to-Point Tunneling Protocol (PPTP) uses PPP authentication methods for user-level authentication and it uses Microsoft Point-to-Point Encryption (MPPE) for data encryption. Layer Two Tunneling Protocol with Internet Protocol security (L2TP/IPsec), like PPTP, uses PPP for user-level authentication but it uses IPsec for computer-level security that includes peer authentication, data authentication, data integrity, and data encryption. Secure Socket Tunneling Protocol (SSTP) also uses PPP for user-level authentication and it uses Hypertext Transfer Protocol (HTTP) encapsulation over a Secure Sockets Layer (SSL) channel (Transport Layer Security) for data authentication, data integrity, and data encryption.

A remote client makes a remote connection via VPN to a private network through a VPN server, which provides access to the network to which that VPN server is connected. During the connection process, the VPN client authenticates itself to the VPN server. Depending on how VPN connections are configured, the VPN server may also authenticate itself to the client.

New & Noteworthy...

Changes to PPTP and L2TP/IPsec Protocols

Warning: This section refers to modifying the Windows registry file. Using Registry Editor incorrectly can cause serious problems that may make the system unstable or unusable and that may require you to reinstall the Windows operating system. There is no guarantee that problems resulting from the incorrect modification of the Registry file can be solved. Edit or modify the Registry at your own risk and do not do this on a live server unless you know exactly what you're doing and have a backup of the Registry. Always make a backup of the Windows Registry file before you modify any settings. You can back up the entire Registry or a single portion of the Registry using REGEDIT. For more information on backing up and restoring the Registry file, visit http://support.microsoft.com/kb/136393.

By default, Windows Server 2008 and Windows Vista have MPPE encryption with 40-bit and 56-bit keys disabled. Instead, the stronger 128-bit encryption is enabled. You can configure Windows Server 2008 to use 40-bit and 56-bit keys if you have a need to connect with Windows Server 2003 or Windows XP SP2-based computers. This can be enabled by setting the *HKEY_LOCAL_MACHINE\system\CurrentControlSet\Services\Rasman*

Continued

parameters\AllowPPTPWeakCrypto registry value to 1 and restarting the computer. Keep in mind, however, that this is a weaker encryption system and generally is not recommended.

As mentioned previously, support for the Message Digest (MD5) hash has been discontinued in L2TP/IPsec. Now, Windows Server 2008 supports only 3DES encryption and the Secure Hash Algorithm-1 (SHA1) hashed method authentication code (HMAC) by default. Support for the Advanced Encryption Standard (AES) using 128-bit or 256-bit keys has been added. As with MPPE encryption, you can enable MD5 support for interoperability, but this also is not recommended. If you have reason to enable this, you can access it via the following registry key and setting the value to 1: *HKEY_LOCAL_MACHINE\system\CurrentControlSet\Services\Rasman\parameters\AllowL2TPWeakCrypto.*

Any time you modify a registry key, you need to restart the computer before the setting takes place. Again, these changes are not recommended as they weaken security, but they can be modified if needed.

Configuring IP Security (IPsec)

The IP Security (IPsec) protocol is a standard that provides cryptographic security services for IP traffic. IPsec is an end-to-end security solution. The only two nodes aware of IPsec traffic on the network are the two peers communicating with each other. IPsec packets are forwarded by routers like any other packet on the network. As you probably recall, IPsec provides the following properties:

- **Peer authentication**. IPsec verifies the identity of a peer computer before data is sent.

- **Data origin authentication**. Each IPsec packet has an encrypted checksum in the form of a keyed hash. It ensures that only one computer could have sent the packet, preventing a malicious user from masquerading as the sender.

- **Data integrity**. The IPsec protocol protects the contents of the packet through the encrypted checksum. The receiver of the data can verify the data is unmodified by checking the checksum value. A malicious intruder would be unable to properly modify both the packet's data and it cryptographic checksum.

- **Data confidentiality**. IPsec uses secret key encryption techniques that protect the data being sent in the packet. If the packet is intercepted, only the packet's encrypted contents can be viewed.

- **Anitreplay**. Each protected packet has a sequence number that prevents an intruder from getting in the middle of the communications and modifying packet data.

- **Key management**. IPsec provides a secure way of deriving initial keying data and to periodically change the keys used for secure communications to prevent the key from being discovered through any other method than brute force.

IPsec does not provide nonrepudiation security service for data, meaning that the sender can later deny having sent the packet. IPsec uses a shared secret key, called a symmetric key, and since two peers share a key, nonrepudiation is not provided by IPsec.

IPsec can operate in either transport mode or tunnel mode. The transport mode protects communications between hosts and it encrypts the User Datagram Protocol/Transmission Control Protocol (UDP/TCP) protocol header and original data but not the IP header itself. In tunnel mode, IPsec protects host-to-network communications like that in virtual private networks (VPN). Since IPsec changes the IP packet, the original version of Network Address Translation did not support IPsec. However, the newer version, Network Address Translation–Traversal (NAT–T) is used. It allows IPsec traffic to pass through NAT–T compatible servers that are configured to allow traffic on UDP port 4500. All versions of Windows that support IPsec also support NAT–T.

IPsec supports numerous authentication and encryption standards, so two IPsec-capable computers might not support the same sets of standards. And, not all computers can support IPsec. So, before an IPsec connection can be made, whether in transport or tunnel mode, an IPsec negotiation is established to determine if the IPsec supported by the two end points (host-to-host or host-to-server) are supporting the same standards.

IPsec provides security by enveloping the data (the *IP payload*) in an additional header or trailer that provides data origin authentication, data integrity, data confidentiality, and antireplay protection. The IPsec protocol uses two elements, the authentication header (AH) and the encapsulating security payload (ESP) header and trailer. Applying the AH or ESP to an IP datagram transforms the packet into a secure datagram. As a result, AH and ESP sometimes are referred to as *transforms*.

ESP is widely supported and is therefore the preferred IPsec protocol, but AH is the fallback protocol if both hosts cannot support ESP. Let's look briefly at the AH and ESP protocols.

IPsec Authentication Header (AH)

The Authentication Header protocol provides data origin authentication, data integrity, and antireplay protection for the entire IP datagram. It does *not* provide data confidentiality (for that, use ESP, discussed in the next section). AH can be used in transport or tunnel mode. The packet format for both is shown in Figure 10.19. Notice that when AH is used in transport mode (Figure 10.19A), the AH header is added just after the IP header. The IP header is modified to indicate the presence of AH (the Protocol field is set to 51). This packet type is forwarded by routers just as any other standard IP packet would be. However, firewalls look for the modification of the IP header and might not allow this traffic through due to the modification of the Protocol field in the IP header. For that reason, some firewalls might need to be configured to forward data in which the IP header Protocol field is set to 51.

In Figure 10.19B, the tunnel mode for AH is shown. In this case, the IP packet is included without modification and the entire packet is authenticated, including the new IP header, the AH header, and the original IP header and payload. This added header allows the packet to pass through firewalls more easily but it does generate more network traffic by adding to the packet size.

Figure 10.19 AH in Transport and Tunnel Mode

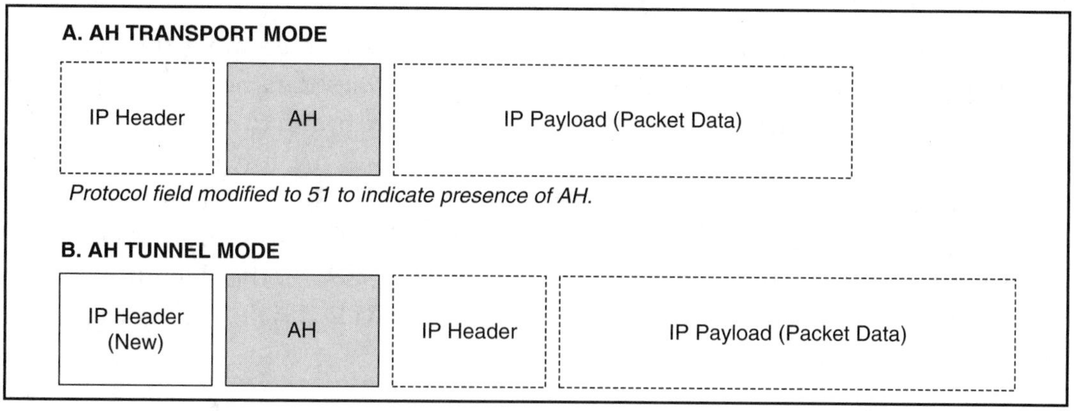

Head of the Class…

IPsec Headers and Footers

A security association (SA) is the combination of security services used by communicating peers. This typically includes security services, protection methods, and cryptographic keys. The SA contains the information needed to negotiate a secure communications between peers. Two types of SAs are created when IPsec peers communicate in a secure mode: ISAKMP SA and IPsec SA.

The Internet Security Association and Key Management Protocol (ISAKMP) SA also is known as the *main mode* SA and is used to protect IPsec security negotiations themselves. The IPsec SA also is known as the *quick mode* security association (SA). The IPsec SA cipher information is protected by the ISAKMP SA. In IPsec packets, no information about the type of traffic or the protection mechanisms is sent as plaintext. Recall that for a pair of IPsec peers, there are always two IPsec SAs—one for inbound and one for outbound traffic. The inbound SA for one IPsec peer is the outbound SA for the other IPsec peer.

IPsec Encapsulating Security Payload (ESP)

Encapsulating Security Payload (ESP) provides both a header and a trailer for an IP datagram that secures the packet. ESP provides data origin authentication, data integrity, antireplay, and data confidentiality protection for the ESP-encapsulated portion of the packet. Figure 10.20 shows the format of the ESP header in transport mode and Figure 10.21 shows the ESP header in tunnel mode. We've also included what the packet looks like if you use both AH and ESP, shown in Figure 10.22, though typically ESP is used as the default method of security the packet unless you have reason to use AH, which does not provide data confidentiality.

Figure 10.20 ESP in Transport Mode

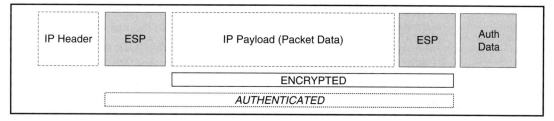

Figure 10.21 ESP in Tunnel Mode

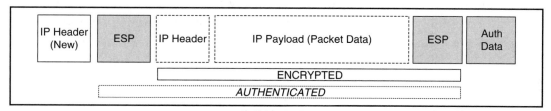

Figure 10.22 AH and ESP Packet Format

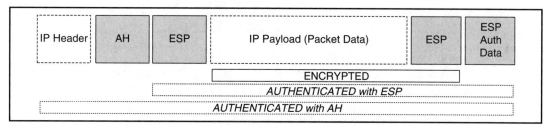

Now that we've refreshed your skills on the format of the IPsec AH and ESP data, let's get back to the practical IPsec skills needed to configure a Windows Server 2008 computer network.

Configuring IPsec in Windows Server 2008

IPsec is configured via Group Policy in Active Directory as well as through Windows Firewall with Advanced Security. In Windows Firewall with Advanced Security, IPsec inbound and outbound traffic rules can be configured along with connection security rules. In this section, we'll look briefly at IPsec in Group Policy and then we'll take a more detailed look at the integration of IPsec in Windows Firewall with Advanced Security since this is a new feature in Windows Server 2008.

In Windows Server 2003, configuring IPsec and configuring the Windows Firewall were configured separately and in two different places. This led to the possibility of conflicting settings. In Windows Server 2008, IPsec and the Windows Firewall functionality have been combined, removing the possibility of conflicting settings. IPsec and Windows Firewall are now configured via the Windows Firewall with Advanced Security snap-in. Note that the command line options, within the **netsh advfirewall** context, can be used for command line configuration of both firewall and IPsec behavior. Again, the command line options are helpful when setting up scripting, batch files, or when administering a remote server—so it's useful to make note of the commands you're most likely to need. You'll also see some of the more commonly used command line commands on the Windows Server 2008 exam, so we're including them when it seems likely you'll see it on the exam.

New & Noteworthy...

IPsec in Windows Server 2008

There are many new improvements to the IPsec implementation in Windows Server 2008. According to the Microsoft Web site, these are:

- Integrated firewall and IPsec configuration
- Simplified IPsec policy configuration
- Client-to-DC IPsec protection
- Improved load balancing and clustering server support
- Improved IPsec authentication
- New cryptographic support
- Integration with Network Access Protection
- Additional configuration options for protected communication
- Integrated IPv4 and IPv6 support
- Extended events and performance monitor counters
- Network Diagnostics Framework support

[Source: http://technet.microsoft.com/en-us/library/bb726965.aspx]

Continued

In the Window Server 2008 exam, expect to see questions that test your knowledge and understanding of the latest implementation of IPsec. Most notably, be familiar with how IPsec is integrated into and configured in the firewall. Also be aware of the Simplified IPsec policy configuration, which will likely show up on your exam in one form or another. Finally, be familiar with the integrated IPsec support with IPv4 and IPv6. Refer to the Microsoft Web site if you need to dig into the vast detail of IPsec in Windows Server 2008.

Creating IPsec Policy

IPsec policy is created either in Active Directory as a Group Policy or via the Windows Server 2008's Windows Firewall with Advanced Security. Clearly, IPsec settings in these two areas are related but are not interchangeable. Policy set in Active Directory is applied according to policies set at the domain level and will take precedence over local IPsec policy located on a member computer. IPsec policy will be applied according to AD and Windows Firewall with Advanced Security settings on a Windows Server 2008 computer.

We won't go into too much detail about AD IPsec policy here but we will discuss IPsec in Windows Firewall with Advanced Security in more detail later in this chapter. You can open the IP Security Policy Management console through the MMC snap-in. To open the MMC Console, click **Start | Run** and type **mmc**, then click **OK**. This opens the MMC console from which you can select the IPSecurity Management Snap-in. Right-click **IP Security Policies** in the left pane then choose **Create IP Security Policy** from the menu to launch the IPsec Security Policy Wizard.

IPsec Using the Command Line

As with many other functions in Windows Server 2008 management, you can configure IPsec policy via the command line. This section briefly outlines some of the more commonly used IPsec commands. However, you may want to explore the command line options for IPsec on your own so you're familiar with these options. You can configure static mode and dynamic mode options, as shown in Table 10.4. You can type **netsh ipsec /?** to get a full list of command line options related to IPsec.

Table 10.4 IPsec Command Line Options

IPsec Command	Details
netsh ipsec static add policy *name*	Creates an IPsec policy with the specified name.
netsh ipsec static delete *[option]*	Deletes the specific IPsec policy. Can be used with the switch *all* to remove all IPsec policies, filter lists, and filter actions.
netsh ipsec dynamic set policy *name*	Sets a policy name immediately.
netsh ipsec dynamic delete *name*	Removes a specific policy immediately.
netsh ipsec dynamic export policy *name*	Exports all IPsec policies to a specified file.
netsh ipsec dynamic show *all*	Used to view IPsec policy and statistics.
netsh ipsec dynamic set config ipsecdiagnostics 7	Enables IPsec driver logging of dropped inbound and outbound packets.
netsh ipsec dynamic set config ipsecloginterval 60	Used to change the default interval the IPsec log file writes entries to the log file. This example sets the interval to 60 seconds. This can be helpful in troubleshooting IPsec issues/.

Head of the Class…

Saving Command Line Output to a File

Sometimes the output of a command line command, such as a "show all" command, can be quite lengthy and can scroll off the screen making it hard to locate needed information. You can save the output to a file by using this sequence of commands. Although the example is used for the **netsh ipsec** context, this works anywhere in the command line context.

At the netsh command line context, type **set filename *filename.txt*** (where filename.txt is the file you want to create). Then, type **ipsec static**

Continued

show all. Finally, type **set file close**. The contents of the ipsec static show all command have been saved to the filename you specified.

Even faster is the command from the standard command line context (not within netsh): **netsh ipsec static show all >***filename.txt*. Saves time, saves your data.

If you want to see the entire output without dumping it to a file, you can use the |more switch so the command would be **netsh ipsec static show all |more**.

IPsec Isolation Policy

Server and domain isolation is accomplished through configuring IPsec computers to require protection for inbound traffic (or attempts at inbound traffic) and to request but not require protection for outbound traffic. Trusted computers in an isolation scenario use fallback to clear to initiate communication with hosts on their intranets that are not IPsec-enabled. However, beginning in Windows Server 2003 (and continued in Windows Server 2008), the Simple Policy Update changes the IPsec negotiation process. IPsec negotiation failures will still fallback to clear but because negotiation falls back to clear, it's possible for two peers using IPsec who cannot validate each others' credentials to allow unsecured communication with non–IPsec aware computers (if this setting is enabled) or to accept unsecured communication but always respond using IPsec (if the setting is enabled).

EXAM WARNING

A concept you should be familiar with is *defense-in-depth*. This refers to a network security strategy that uses layers of security methods to provide security at several different layers of the network. For example, on a server, you have various applications and services that are running and can be configured to require authentication for access or use. You also have a firewall application that filters traffic to and from the server based on configured settings. You can also use IPsec to protect traffic to and from that server (though there are some important considerations to review before implementing that) and you can use network access protection (NAP) at the network layer to protect the network (and servers) from computers that do not meet health requirements. On the client side, you use login credentials for access to the client, you may use a local firewall for filtering, and you also can use IPsec for IP security and tunneling or VPN for secure point-to-point communications. All these combined create a deep security framework that helps protect network resources. Though it's outside the scope of this chapter to discuss this in-depth, all the elements discussed in this chapter come into play with a defense-in-depth strategy and you are very likely to see these kinds of questions on the exam.

Windows Firewall with Advanced Security in Windows Server 2008

Firewalls can run on a network's perimeter to protect computers on the network via filtering both inbound and outbound traffic. Firewalls can also run on a host computer to protect that host. Let's look briefly at these two types of configurations.

Network Perimeter Firewalls

Network perimeter firewalls provide a variety of services to protect network traffic. They're typically either hardware- or software-based, some are both. Some perimeter firewalls also provide application proxy services as well. These perimeter firewalls typically provide the following services:

- Management and control of network traffic through stateful packet inspection, connection monitoring, and application-level filtering.

- Stateful connection analysis by inspecting the state of communications by computers on the network.

- Virtual private network (VPN) gateway functionality providing IPsec authentication and encryption services along with Network Address Translation-Transversal (NAT-T) to allow IPsec traffic to pass through the firewall between public and private IP addresses.

Host-based Firewalls

Although perimeter firewalls protect the network from traffic flowing into and out of the network itself, they cannot protect internal network traffic. Host-based firewalls are used to protect host computers from threats internal to the network itself. You can configure a firewall to block specific types of incoming and outgoing traffic to provide an extra layer of security for the host computer.

New Features in Windows Firewall with Advanced Security

Before we look at the specifics of Windows Firewall with Advanced Security, let's take a look at the new features. Be sure to explore these features fully on your

Windows Server 2008 computer since, as we've stated several times, the new features are the most likely to be tested on an exam.

1. IPsec Integration

2. Support for IPv6

3. Support for Active Directory user, computer, and groups

4. Location-aware profiles

5. Detailed rules

6. Expanded authenticated bypass

IPsec Integration

This is a pretty significant change from previous versions of Windows. In Windows Server 2008, IPsec is integrated into firewall functionality, as shown in Figure 10.23. In the Windows Firewall with Advanced Security snap-in, firewall filtering and IPsec rule configuration are integrated. Note, however, that if you want to configure IPsec for computers running an operating system prior to Windows Server 2008 or Windows Vista, you'll need to use the IPsec Policy Management snap-in instead.

Figure 10.23 Windows Firewall with Advanced Security Properties with IPsec Integration

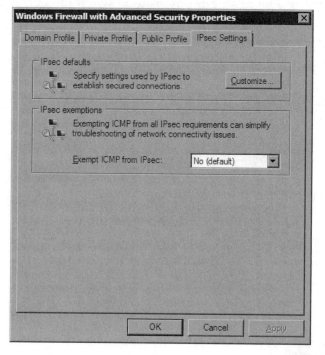

Support for IPv6

The firewall function in Windows Server 2008 provides native support for IPv6. Of course, it also still fully supports IPv4 as well as IPv6 to IPv4 (6 to 4) and the new NAT traversal for IPv6 called Teredo (discussed briefly in this chapter).

Support for Active Directory User, Computer, and Groups

You can create various firewall rules and these rules can filter connections by user, computer, or groups in Active Directory. These connections must be secured with IPsec using a credential that carries the AD account information. Kerberos V5 is the default for Windows Server 2008 and is an example of a credential that carries the AD account information.

Location-Aware Profiles

There are three built-in profiles in the firewall software that allow you to create location-aware profiles. The three profiles are domain, private, and public. If you enable all three of these profiles, the software will determine which profile to utilize based on your location (and connection). The domain profile is used when the computer is authenticated via AD and is active when all interfaces can authenticate to a domain controller. The private profile is used when the computer is connected to a private network behind a private gateway or router. The public profile is used when the computer is connected to a public network or unidentified connection, such as those found at airports and coffee shops. Clearly, you would likely never use the public profile on a server unless it happens to be in a DMZ on the network. Windows Vista and Windows Server 2008 are based on the same code, so the public profile is geared primarily toward Windows Vista-based computers rather than Windows Server 2008-based computers. You might choose to disable the public profile on your Windows Server 2008-based computers.

Detailed Rules

By default, Windows Firewall with Advanced Security is enabled for both inbound and outbound traffic. The default settings block most incoming traffic and allow outgoing traffic. This version of the firewall software enables you to configure detailed rules for filtering any Internet Assigned Numbers Authority

(IANA) protocol numbers. Previous versions supported only filtering UDP, TCP, and ICMP protocols. In addition, the firewall software in Windows Server 2008 supports configuration of AD domain service accounts and groups, application names, TCP, UDP, ICMPv4, ICMPv6, local and remote IP addresses, interface types and protocols, and ICMP type and code filtering. The good news, though, is that the default settings are a very good starting point and you now have the capability to be very detailed in configuring traffic rules if you have a need to do so.

Expanded Authenticated Bypass

Previous versions of the firewall software provided an "all or nothing" style of configuration. Either you could allow a computer full access to another computer if it was configured to use IPsec, but you couldn't specify ports or protocols, for example. In Windows Server 2008 (and Windows Vista), you can provide much more detailed authenticated bypass rules that will allow you to specify which ports or programs can have access and which computers or groups of computers can have access. This keeps computers protected while providing rule-based exceptions as needed.

Network Location–Aware Host Firewall

In Windows Server 2008, the Windows Firewall with Advanced Security can act both as a network location-aware host firewall and as part of a server and domain isolation strategy. Let's look at these two scenarios in detail to understand the considerations for these deployment options.

Windows Server 2008 (as well as Windows Vista) includes network awareness APIs that enable applications to sense changes to network configurations. What that means is that a corporate laptop that is placed into standby or hibernate and later fires up connected to a home network or a public hotspot will sense that it's on a new network and the firewall settings will be modified accordingly. The network awareness APIs handle that function. This function is clearly less useful on a Windows Server 2008 computer permanently connected to a corporate network. It's really intended for use on mobile computers (which could run Windows Server 2008, of course) that might be running Windows Vista as the client operating system. Although this functionality is included in Windows Vista, we'll refer to it within the Windows Server 2008 context. Windows Server 2008 identifies and remembers network connections and can apply settings according to these configurations. Applications can query for characteristics of networks including:

- **Connectivity**. Is the computer connected to a network, is it connected locally or to the Internet?

- **Connections**. Is the computer connected to the network by one or more connections?

- **Category**. What type of network is the computer connected to? Each network is assigned a category in Windows Server 2008 that helps identify the network type. Firewall settings can be applied based on the category assigned.

There are three network location types used in Windows Firewall with Advanced Security:

- **Domain**. A network on which the Windows Server 2008 (and Windows Vista) computer can authenticate via Active Directory.

- **Private**. A network is categorized as private if a user or application identifies it as such. Only networks behind a NAT device should be identified as private networks.

- **Public**. All other domain networks to which a computer connects. This includes public connections such as those found at airports, hotel lobbies and coffee shops (typically used for Windows Vista, not Windows Server 2008, though available in both operating systems).

Although all three profiles can be enabled simultaneously, only one profile is applied at a time and in this order:

1. If all connections (interfaces) are authenticated to the domain controller for the domain of which the computer is a member, then the **domain** profile is applied.

2. If all connections (interfaces) are authenticated to the domain controller or connected to networks identified as private, then the **private** profile is applied.

3. If either of the two previous scenarios does not apply, the **public** profile is applied.

Clearly, the public profile is the most restrictive and is applied in cases where the computer is not authenticated on its native domain or not connected to a private (and therefore somewhat protected) network. In all profiles, most incoming traffic is blocked by default with the exception of core networking traffic. With the private network profile applied, core networking traffic along with network discovery and remote assistance traffic is allowed. Default settings on all profiles also allow almost all out bound traffic; you must create specific rules to block outgoing traffic to suit your needs.

You might choose to configure specific rules for outbound traffic on your network. Although it's fairly clear why you'd block unsolicited incoming traffic, blocking outbound traffic can be extremely useful in preventing malware from "phoning home" and transmitting data back to a malicious source.

Server and Domain Isolation

As an experienced network administrator, you're probably familiar with the concept and practice of isolation. You know that you can physically and/or logically isolate network segments for a variety of reasons. You can use these segments to speed up the network by keeping local traffic local or you can use these segments as a way to increase network security. In a Windows Server-based network, you can isolate server and domain resources to limit access to authenticated and authorized computers to prevent unauthorized computers (and programs) from gaining access to resources. There are two primary types of isolation available in this regard: server and domain.

Server Isolation

A server can be configured to require secure authenticated communications only (IPsec). This means that the server will respond only to certain types of requests such as a database server that will respond only to a web application server. In this way, the only traffic allowed to the server is traffic coming from a specific computer or computers.

Domain Isolation

Domain isolation uses IPsec policy to provide protection for traffic sent between computers on a domain, including client (host) and server computers. Active Directory domain membership is used to ensure that computers that are members of the domain accept only secure, authenticated traffic (IPsec) from other members of the domain.

Configuring Windows Firewall with Advanced Security

Windows Firewall with Advanced Security is a *stateful* firewall and as such, it inspects all packets for all IP traffic (IPv4 and IPv6). The default setting is that all incoming traffic is blocked automatically unless it is a response to a host request (called *solicited traffic*) or unless it specifically has been allowed. Specific traffic can be allowed by configuring firewall rules to allow specific traffic by configuring the port number, application name, service name, and other settings.

Figure 10.24 shows the Windows Firewall with Advanced Security as viewed from within Server Manager. You can see the three profiles (Domain, Private, and Public) are all "on," but keep in mind that only one profile at a time is applied based on the connection type. The default settings for each profile are often adequate to start with. Notice in the right pane under Actions, you can import and export policies as well as restore defaults, a handy feature in the event you tweak your settings and create a problem that you can't pinpoint.

Notice also that you can access Inbound Rules, Outbound Rules, Connection Security Rules, as well as Monitoring (with additional options beneath Monitoring) from this screen. Keep in mind that the Windows Firewall with Advanced Security settings here are server-specific, meaning, these settings are applied to this server's connections. You can configure additional options by accessing the Windows Firewall with Advanced Security snap-in via the MMC console. We'll discuss that later in this chapter.

Figure 10.24 Windows Firewall with Advanced Security—
Server Manager View

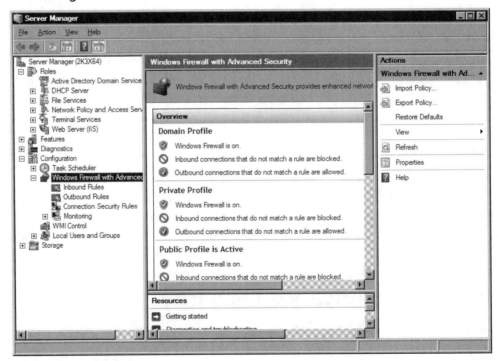

Incoming and Outgoing Traffic Filtering

Firewall rules are configured for incoming and outgoing traffic to determine which packets will be allowed and which will be blocked. When incoming traffic is blocked, an entry is made into the firewall log and the packet is discarded. The firewall options are numerous and we'll look briefly at these options.

In each profile (domain, private, and public), you can set rules regarding action taken for inbound and outbound connections. However, this is not the same thing as inbound and outbound rules for the firewall, though they certainly work together to provide security.

Firewall Rules

Rules can be configured for **inbound** or **outbound** traffic, for computers, users, programs, services, ports, and protocols. You can also specify which types of network adapters rules will apply to—local area connections, wireless, remote (VPN), and so on. You can also create a rule that is applied when a specific profile is used.

Inbound and outbound rules explicitly allow or block traffic that matches the criteria of the rule. For inbound traffic, you can configure rules that allow inbound traffic secured by IPsec, for example, but block traffic that is not secured by IPsec. You can also configure Windows Firewall with Advanced Security to take a specific action (to block or allow connections) when no inbound rules apply. Inbound traffic is blocked by default and must explicitly be allowed after installing Windows Firewall with Advanced Security.

Outbound rules can be used to block outbound traffic from a particular computer or group of computers, for example, or to block particular traffic types or through specific ports. Outbound traffic is allowed by default, so you must create an outbound rule to block any outgoing traffic.

By default, Windows Firewall with Advanced Security blocks all incoming unsolicited TCP/IP traffic. That's a good thing for security but usually creates connectivity problems of some sort in many networks. You may need to create rules for programs and services that act as servers, listeners, or peers. Program, port, and service rules have to be actively managed as server roles and configurations change. Therefore, less is more when creating rules. Create only the rules you need to get the job done and note which are likely to require on-going monitoring and maintenance versus those that you can set and forget.

The default behavior of Windows Firewall with Advanced Security is to dynamically open and close ports required by various programs. The recommended method, then, for allowing unsolicited incoming TCP/IP traffic through the firewall is to add programs to the rules list. That way, when a program is running, the needed traffic is allowed in. When the program is not running, traffic for that program is blocked. In Exercise 10.5, you can step through creating new inbound and outbound rules. Be sure to become familiar with setting up Windows Firewall with Advanced Security. Some of the new features are highly likely to end up as exam questions.

EXERCISE 10.5

CREATE NEW INBOUND AND OUTBOUND RULES

In this exercise, we'll walk through creating a new inbound and outbound rule. Begin by accessing the Windows Firewall with Advanced Security folder in the left pane of Server Manager (located under Configuration if the tree is collapsed). Expand the Windows Firewall node and right-click on Inbound Rules (or click New Rules in the Actions pane to the right) and select **New Rule**. The New Inbound Rule Wizard will launch.

1. The first screen gives you four options for a new rule: *Program*, *Port*, *Predefined*, and *Custom*. Select **Program** and click **Next**.

2. The Program screen prompts you to create a rule for all programs or for a particular program. If you want to set a rule for a particular program, click **This program path:** and the click **Browse** to locate the program file. We'll select **All programs** and click **Next**.

3. The next screen defines the Action to be taken. The choices are: Allow the connection; Allow the connection if it is secure (require the connection to be encrypted, override block rules), and Block the Connection. If you Allow the connection, all connections for

all programs will be allowed. If you Allow the connection if it is secure, you can require IPsec be used but you'll have to separately enable IPsec I the Connection Security rule node (more on that in a moment). You can require the connection be encrypted—this provides privacy along with data integrity and authentication. You can also specify that the rule override block rules. This can be helpful in using remote administration tools that might otherwise be blocked. However, to use this option, you must also specify an authorized computer or computer group. Select **Block the connection** (we're assuming your Windows Server 2008 is on a test network and not a live network for all exercises), then click **Next**.

4. In the Profile screen, you can apply this rule to any of the three profiles (domain, public, and private). The default setting selects all three profiles. Accept this setting by clicking **Next**.

5. The final screen of the New Inbound Rule Wizard is to create a name for the rule. Tip: Using a short descriptive name will help immensely if you want to manage the firewall rules via the command line netsh commands. For this rule, type **All Programs Blocked** in the Name: text box and leave the description blank. Click **Finish** to create this rule. Figure 10.25 shows the resulting new rule added to the Inbound Rules section. Notice that you can Disable Rule, Delete, check Properties, and get Help for the inbound rule you just created.

Figure 10.25 New Inbound Rule

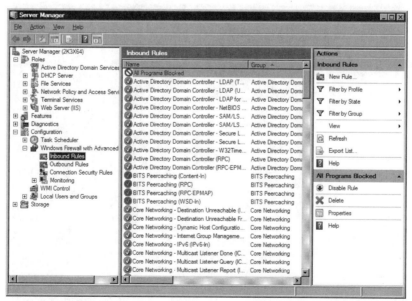

When you configure a new rule and select Port (instead of Program), you'll be prompted to create a rule for a specific TCP or UDP port. Once you select TCP or UDP, you can apply the rule to all local ports or just specific ports by entering port number(s). The Wizards for creating inbound and outbound rules have the same options and they're pretty straightforward. Keep in mind that you should start out with the default rules and add rules as you need them.

Connection Security Rules

Connection security rules are different than inbound and outbound traffic rules. Firewall rules allow traffic through the firewall based on rules you've configured, but they do not enforce connection security. To secure traffic with IPsec, you must create connection security rules. Note that the creation of connection security rules does not allow the traffic to pass through the firewall. These are two separate but interrelated concepts. Connection security rules are not applied to programs or services, they are applied only between the two computers trying to communicate.

Connection security rules work in conjunction with inbound and outbound rules. To create a new rule, click the **Connection security rules** node in the left pane and choose **New Rule** from the right pane (or click **Action** on the menu and select **New Rule** or right-click **Connection security rules** and select **New Rule** from the shortcut menu). When the New Connection Security Rule Wizard starts, you'll have several options. Figure 10.26 shows the Rule Type screen.

Figure 10.26 New Connection Security Rule Wizard

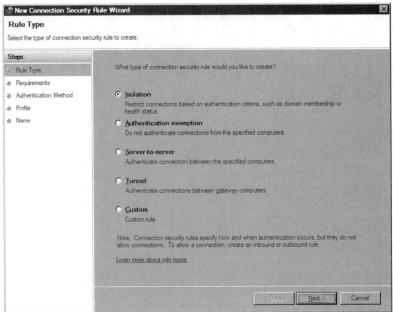

Your options on this screen are:

- **Isolation**. Restrict connections based on authentication criteria, such as domain membership or health status.

- **Authentication exemption**. Do not authenticate connections from specific computers.

- **Server-to-server**. Authenticate connections between the specified computers.

- **Tunnel**. Authenticate connections between gateway computers.

- **Custom**. Create a custom rule.

Remember, connection security rules specify how and when authentication and security occurs, but they do not allow or block connections; this is managed through inbound and outbound rules.

The options for the remaining screens of the wizard change depending on the option selected on the Rule Type screen. However, once you've made the Rule Type selection, the remaining configuration options are fairly straightforward (and vary depending on your Rule Type selection). If you choose to create a custom rule, you'll be prompted to provide Endpoint information for the computers creating the connection.

Firewall Profiles

You can configure different settings for different profiles. As mentioned earlier, there are three profiles: domain, private, and public. Figure 10.27 shows the Windows Firewall with Advanced Security Properties accessed by right-clicking Windows Firewall with Advanced Security and selecting **Properties** from the menu. You can see the three profiles in this dialog box: domain, private, and public. This is also where you can set IPsec Settings (not to be confused with AD IPsec policy).

Figure 10.27 Windows Firewall with Advanced Security Properties

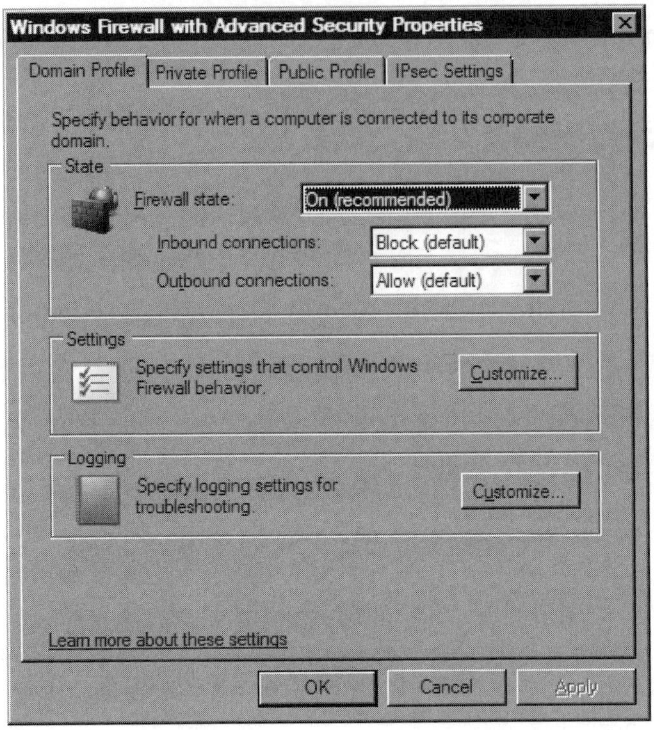

IPsec Settings

If you click the IPsec Settings tab in the Windows Firewall with Advanced Security Properties dialog box, you'll be able to access the IPsec settings, as shown in Figure 10.28. The key exchange (using ISAKMP if you recall the earlier discussion of IPsec basics) is the main mode. You can use the default settings or customize these settings by clicking the radio button to the left of **Advanced**, then clicking the **Customize** button, which will be enabled if you select Advanced. The quick mode (for data protection) also has Default and Advanced settings and advanced settings can be customized here. The Authentication Method can be configured to authenticate the computer, user, computer and user, computer certificate, or advanced. You can click the link at the bottom of the dialog box to learn more about your options or to understand what, exactly, the default settings are. In most cases, the default values are fine and you should start with these first. As you probably know, setting incorrect IPsec settings can interrupt communications. Also keep in mind that IPsec policy from Active Directory will also interact with these settings, so default settings is the best place to start unless you have a specific need to modify these settings.

Figure 10.28 IPsec Settings in Windows Firewall with Advanced Security

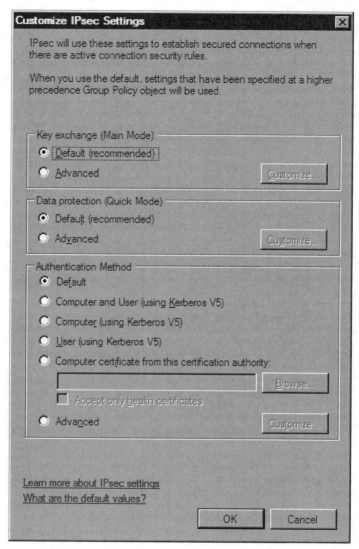

Though the default settings are fine in most cases, we've included a few screenshots of the advanced settings to give you an idea of just how much you can customize these settings. Be sure to scan these just so you're familiar with them. Although you probably won't see any questions on the exam testing your specific knowledge of the **Advanced** settings, it's good background knowledge to have in answering questions related to IPsec and firewall settings. Figure 10.29 shows the Advanced settings under the Main Mode (key exchange) section.

Figure 10.29 Main Mode Advanced Settings

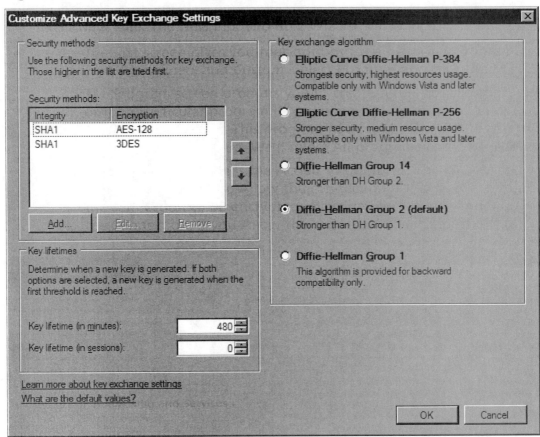

Figure 10.30 shows the Advanced settings for Quick Mode (data protection). As you can see, you can configure data integrity algorithms as well as data integrity and encryption algorithms in this area. You can add, remove, and edit these settings as well as move the algorithms up (or down) in the list. As stated in the dialog box, those algorithms higher in the list are tried first.

Figure 10.30 Quick Mode Advanced Settings

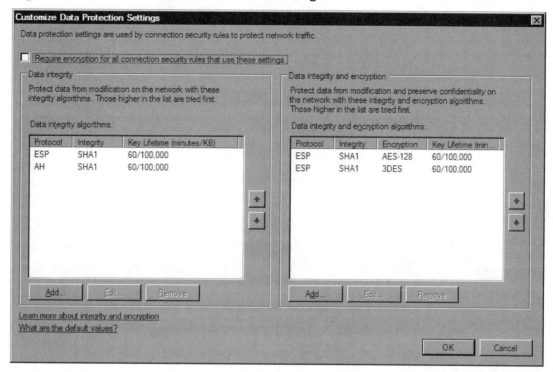

The third area of Advanced settings you can configure are the Authentication Method settings. If you click the **Advanced** radio button then click **Customize**, you'll see the settings shown in Figure 10.31. Notice that you can set a first and second authentication method but you cannot set a second authentication method if you specify a preshared key as the first authentication method. It doesn't matter where in the list the preshared key method is in the first authentication method list. If it's in the first authentication method list, you cannot specify a second authentication method.

Figure 10.31 Advanced Authentication Method Settings

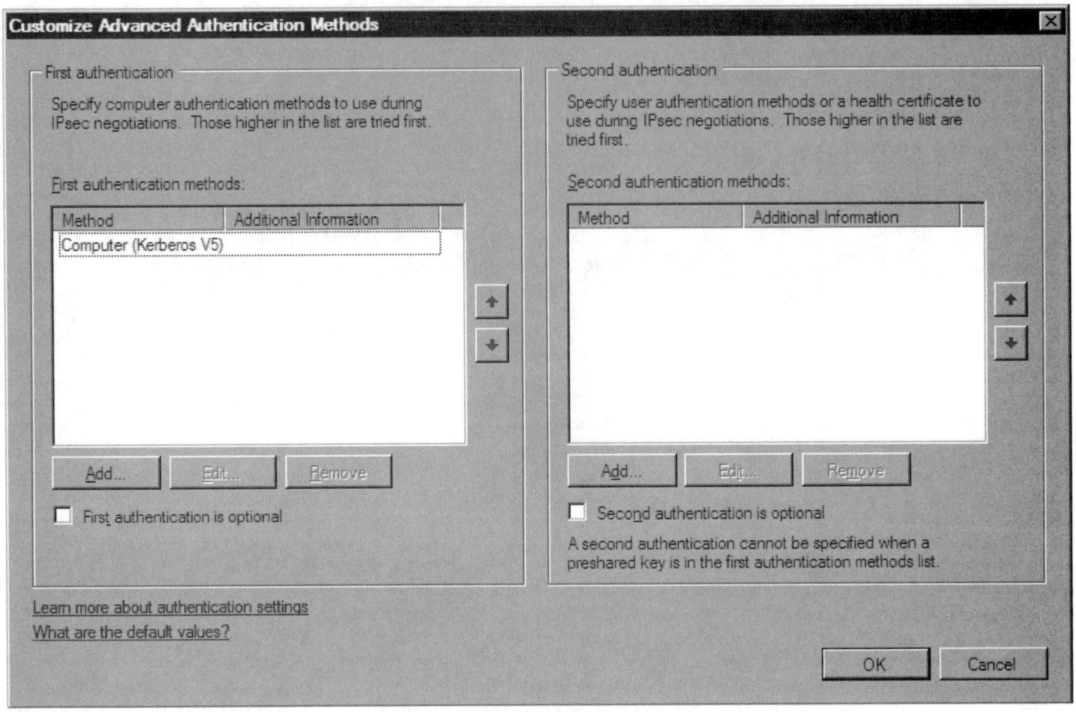

Monitoring

The monitoring folder under Windows Firewall with Advanced Security provides access to firewall, connection security rules and security associations monitoring features, shown in Figure 10.32. By default, when you select this folder in the left pane of Server Manager, you will see the three profiles in the center pane (domain, private, public). Each section can be collapsed and expanded as needed and the profile that is active will be shown as Active.

You can click **Firewall** in the left pane and see all the rules and traffic filtering in place. If you kept the All Programs Blocked rule we created earlier, you should see this rule in the list with a red circle with a line through it. Blocking rules show up with this red circle icon. Allow rules are displayed with a green circle and white checkmark so you can quickly locate Allow and Block rules.

Figure 10.32 Windows Firewall with Advanced Security Monitoring

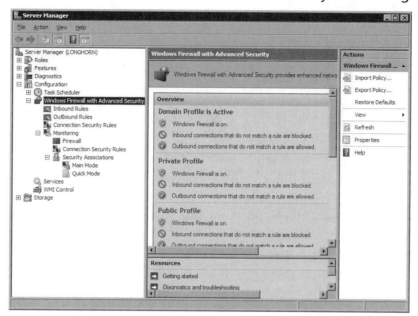

If you click **Connection Security Rules**, you can see all rules you created for connection security. If none are present, you are not requiring secure connections even if you allow or block secured traffic.

The last folder in the Monitoring tree is the Security Associations folder. It shows two modes: Main mode and Quick mode. Main mode lists all the Main mode security associations (SA) with detailed information about their settings and endpoints. You can view IP address of endpoints here. Quick mode lists all the Quick mode SAs with detailed information about them including IP addresses of endpoints. If you recall from our earlier discussion of IPsec, you have two SAs—Main mode (key exchange) and Quick mode (data protection).

Managing Windows Firewall with Advanced Security via Group Policy

In Microsoft operating systems prior to Windows Server 2008, local Group Policy was processed in the following order:

- Computer policies processed when the computer boots up.
- User policies processed when the user logs in.
- Computer and user policies refreshed at intervals.

Windows Server 2008 also provides the following:

- Computer and user policies processed when a computer establishes a VPN connection with a remote site.

- Computer and user policies processed when a computer comes out of hibernation or standby.

As you can see, these two additional processes are extremely helpful in maintaining a secure host through ensuring the computer has the most recent Group Policy settings related to the specific configuration of its connections.

To configure Windows Firewall with Advanced Security using Group Policy, access the Windows Firewall with Advanced Security snap-in from within the Group Policy Management Console. Note that if you deploy Windows Firewall with Advanced Security via Group Policy and block outbound connections, you'll have a problem unless you enable the Group Policy outbound rules. Otherwise, you might prevent all computers that receive the policy from updating the policy in the future, unless you manually update them, which defeats the purpose of using Group Policy to distribute settings.

Identifying Ports and Protocols

In some cases, you can't add the program or the service to the rules list. In these cases, you'll have to figure out which ports the program or service uses and add the port(s) to the rules list. When you add a port to the rules list, you have to specify the port number and protocol. You can specify ports only using TCP and UDP protocols.

EXAM WARNING

Here's a key take away for working with Windows Firewall with Advanced Security (and don't be surprised to see a question related to this on the exam). When you allow or block unsolicited traffic by creating a TCP or UDP port rule, that action will be taken any time Windows Firewall is running. This differs from creating a rule for a program in which the action is taken only when the program is running. So, if you create a rule to allow UDP 1443 traffic, that rule will be enabled when the firewall is enabled (which should be all the time). Contrast that to a program rule that specifies that it needs UDP 1443 traffic. In that case, the firewall will allow only UDP 1443 traffic when the program is running—a much more secure setting and the recommended method, whenever possible.

Command Line Tools for Windows Firewall with Advanced Security

As with just about any other server feature in Windows Server 2008, you can use the command line to adjust firewall settings. Once you've opened the command window (**Start | Run | cmd**), you use the **netsh** context with the **advfirewall** command. As with other commands, you can use the **netsh advfirewall /?** command to get a list of available options and switches. We've listed a few here for your convenience; all commands here begin with **netsh advfirewall** followed by the option shown.

- **Export**. Exports the current firewall policy to a file.
- **Import**. Imports a policy from a specified file.
- **Reset**. Restores Windows Firewall with Advanced Security to default settings.
- **Show**. Shows properties of a particular file including:
  - Show allprofiles
  - Show domainprofile
  - Show privateprofile
  - Show publicprofile
- **Help**. Displays a list of available commands.

In addition, you can use the subcontext commands as well. These are shown with their full syntax as an example of how they can be used:

- **netsh advfirewall consec /?** Shows the options available for the connection security settings within Windows Firewall with Advanced Security.
- **netsh advfirewall firewall /?** Shows the options available for configuring firewall rules.
- **netsh advfirewall monitor /?** Shows options available for configuring monitoring settings.

EXAM WARNING

Whenever you run server-type commands from the command line, you have must have Administrator-equivalent rights. Depending on the server and its roles, you may need Domain Administrator rights rather than local Administrator rights. That said, keep in mind that best practices suggest you log onto a server using a standard user account and log in using the Administrator account only by using the **Run As Administrator** option. This helps maintain tight security on your network. If you see questions on the exam that use the **Run As** option, chances are good it's a correct answer (or among possible correct answer candidates).

Windows Firewall with Advanced Security is a stateful host–based firewall that blocks incoming and outgoing traffic based on default profiles (domain, private, public) and based on connections using the Network Awareness API, which in Windows is called Network Location Awareness (NLA). You can configure the firewall on the local server via the Server Manger interface; advanced configuration must be done via the Microsoft Management Console (MMC) Windows Firewall with Advanced Security snap–in. IPsec is now integrated with firewall functions to help avoid conflicting settings between these two protective features.

Summary of Exam Objectives

Windows Server 2008 includes many of the IP features you're familiar with from Windows Server 2003, but there are important changes and additions as well. In order to score well on the exam, you'll need to have a solid foundation of IPv4 addressing and at least a basic understanding of IPv6. As with other Microsoft exams, the skills tested are not memorization of facts but the application of those facts in real world scenarios. In configuring IPv4 and IPv6, you're likely to see questions that test your knowledge and understanding of how you might transition to IPv6 or how you might incorporate IPv6 in an IPv4-based network. Knowing the length of IPv4 and IPv6 addresses along with how they are configured into network and host segments as well as how different network infrastructure components handle IP packets is important and will be tested. Concepts in IPv6 such as local-link addressing, global unicast, multicast, and anycast addressing and special addressing will likely show up in exam questions.

The role of DHCP server should be one that is familiar to you and as with IP in Windows Server 2008, many of the features and options are similar to Windows Server 2003. New features will be highlighted and you're likely to see questions regarding the implementation of DHCP in a mixed (IPv4 and IPv6) environment. Look for questions on configuring the DHCP server, especially in an IPv6 setting (scope, reservations, exclusions) and in a mixed environment. DHCP server, relay agent, and lease settings will be the most likely areas to be tested.

DHCP integrates with Network Access Protection (NAP), a new feature that enforces computer health through a variety of mechanisms. DHCP and NAP can be used to enforce client health through granting full access, restricted access, or no access (drop client packet) based on your network's unique needs.

With the release of the Windows Server 2008 Core, you're likely to see questions related to using the command line. Though you won't be expected to memorize every single command line command and all the options, you should be conversant with using the command line and with the general syntax of those commands. Also be prepared to answer questions that test your understanding of how command line commands can be utilized for security and efficiency such as using batch files that run various commands to configure and control remote devices.

Network authentication in Windows Server 2008 is managed through the familiar tools including Active Directory and Group Policy as well as through the latest addition, Network Policy and Access Services. Network Policy and Access services includes Network Policy Server (NPS), Routing and Remote Access (RRAS), Remote Authentication Dial In User Service (RADIUS) server,

RADIUS proxy, and Network Access Protection. This consolidation of network access services helps in managing network access and authentication. Just as with Windows Server 2003, Kerberos is the default authentication method through Active Directory. However, there are numerous settings for local, remote, wired, and wireless access to the network. Most of the changes involved upgrading authentication protocols and removing support for older, less secure protocols. In order to do well in the exam, you should be familiar with the basic mechanics of user and computer authentication as well as protocols used in various scenarios. The 802.11 and 802.1X standards are likely to be well-represented on the exam as will the 802.3 Wired Network Policies options. Familiarity with EAP, PEAP, MS-CHAPv2, PPTP, L2TP/IPsec, and SSTP will be needed in order to successfully navigate through network authentication questions.

Internet Protocol Security (IPsec) is being used by more and more organizations due to the ability to protect and encrypt network traffic through transport and tunnel modes. Your understanding of how to implement IPsec, especially through Active Directory Group Policy (as in Windows Server 2003 and prior) as well as through the Windows Firewall with Advanced Security, is likely to be highlighted. IPsec configuration for inbound and outbound traffic is now integrated in the firewall capabilities, and settings for domain, public, private, and IPsec can be configured through the firewall properties. A key takeaway is the understanding how IPsec Group Policy and IPsec settings in firewall interact to provide a secure framework for IP traffic. As with other technologies in Windows Server 2008, you can configure and check IPsec settings via the command line and you should have a solid understanding of the more commonly used IPsec command line options.

Another area highlighted in the exam is the Windows Firewall with Advanced Security. The addition of advanced security options provides new security methods that were not previously integrated into the firewall functionality. Understanding the new features, including how network perimeter firewall settings versus host-based firewall settings may differ; how to configure the firewall settings to enable IPsec, IPv6 and support for AD user, computer, and groups will be key to successfully navigating exam questions and answers. Again, the integration with IPsec settings will likely show up on your exam as well. Expect to see questions related to how you could configure the firewall to support various security scenarios such as preventing external users from pinging an internal server or how to limit DNS name resolution to internal computers only. This also includes the ability to configure inbound and outbound rules, set IP filtering, create connection security rules, and monitor results. Rule types are likely to be prominent in this section of your exam, so pay special attention to isolation, authentication exemption, server-to-server and tunnel rule types along with the associated authentication methods. Give some thought to various scenarios (especially based on your prior experience with the Microsoft exam style) to be sure you're comfortable with configuring firewall settings in Windows Firewall with Advanced Security.

If you're familiar with the Microsoft exam style, you know that questions are pulled from a pool of available questions, so no two exams are completely alike. However, Microsoft does have several reliable patterns and one is that questions typically focus more on new features, and questions test you on how you would use these in real-world scenarios. As you review material prior to the exam, keep that in mind and you should find yourself focusing on the highest priority topics.

Exam Objectives Fast Track

Configuring IPv4 and IPv6 Addressing

- ☑ IPv4 addressing uses 32-bits and a subnet mask to identify the network and host portions of the address.

- ☑ IPv6 addressing uses 128 bits and the network information is contained in the left-most 64 bits, host information in the right-most 64 bits. IPv6 uses hexadecimal notation.

- ☑ Supernetting uses the Classless Inter-Domain Routing (CIDR) notation, and this notation is also used in IPv6.

- ☑ IPv6 address types include local-link, unique local IPv6 unicast, global unicast, multicast, anycast, and special addressing. Local-link maps to IPv4 private addressing, global unicast maps to IPv4 public addressing.

- ☑ The local loopback address in IPv6 is ::1/128; FF80::/64 is used for local-link addressing.

- ☑ IP4 to IP6 transition technologies include dual IP layer architecture, IPv6 over IP4 tunneling, Intra-Site Automatic Tunneling Addressing Protocol (ISATAP), 6to4, and Teredo.

Configuring Dynamic Host Configuration Protocol (DHCP)

- ☑ The DHCP server role in Windows Server 2008 includes native support for IPv6 as DHCPv6.

☑ Scope, reservations, exceptions, and scope options are configured in IPv6 much the same as they are in IPv4.

☑ A DHCP server should have its scope and configuration data set, the scope should be activated, and the server should be authorized in the Active Directory domain in order to bring a new DHCP server online.

☑ DHCP and Network Access Protection (NAP) are integrated in Windows Server 2008, providing the ability to deny or limit access to network resources based on the client computer's health status. Health status includes having the latest operating system updates and antivirus signatures installed.

☑ DHCP can be configured using command line commands. This is helpful for managing DHCP servers remotely across the network.

Configuring Network Authentication

☑ Network authentication is managed through Active Directory and uses Kerberos as the default authentication protocol. NTLMv2 is supported for backward compatibility and should be used only if needed.

☑ Network Policy and Access Services is a role that can be installed on the Windows Server 2008 computer. It includes Network Policy Server (NPS), Routing and Remote Access Server (RRAS), Remote Authentication Dial In User Service (RADIUS), RADIUS proxy, and Network Access Protection (NAP).

☑ WLAN access and authentication follows 802.11, 802.1X, and 802.3 standards. Associated protocols include EAP-TLS, PEAP-TLS, PEAP-MS-CHAPv2, PPTP, and SSTP.

☑ Support for SPAP, EAP-MD5-CHAP, and MS-CHAPv1 has been removed in Windows Server 2008. EAPHost architecture includes new features not supported in earlier operating systems including support for additional EAP methods, network discovery, vendor-specific EAP types, and coexistence of multiple EAP types across vendors.

☑ Routing and remote access supports the use of IPsec through transport and tunnel modes. Point-to-point tunneling protocol (PPTP), Microsoft Point-to-Point Encryption (MPPE), Layer 2 Tunneling Protocol with IPsec (L2TP/IPsec), and Secure Socket Tunneling Protocol (SSTP) are supported for data authentication, integrity, encryption, and confidentiality.

Configuring IP Security (IPsec)

☑ Internet Protocol Security (IPsec) provides peer authentication, data origin authentication, data integrity, data confidentiality, antireplay, and key management. Due to increasing needs for network security, IPsec is being implemented with greater frequency.

☑ The AH and ESP protocols within IPsec provide different types of security. Data encryption is provided by ESP, not by AH, making it the preferred protocol.

☑ IPsec is integrated with Windows Firewall with Advanced Security and is also managed through Group Policy in the Active Directory context.

☑ IPsec can be configured via command line commands within the **netsh ipsec** context.

☑ IPsec can be used to provide server and domain isolation to ensure secure IP traffic remains secure.

Windows Firewall with Advanced Security in Windows Server 2008

☑ Windows Firewall with Advanced Security in Windows Server 2008 includes numerous new features to simplify and enhance both network perimeter and host security.

☑ New features include IPsec integration, support for IPv6, integration with Active Directory user, computer, and group settings, location aware profiles (for mobile computers), detailed rules, and expanded authenticated bypass capabilities.

☑ Inbound and outbound rules along with connection security rules provide the network administrator with the ability to create finely tuned rules to protect the network and the host.

☑ Connection security rules including isolation, authentication exemption, server-to-server, and tunnel rules can be configured with requirements, authentication methods, and profiles to manage and restrict connections on the network.

☑ IPsec settings, including Main Mode and Quick Mode (computer and user authentication, respectively), can be configured to use a variety of authentication methods.

☑ Customized IPsec data protection settings allow you to configure data protection to use the ESP and AH IPsec protocols. Advanced authentication methods, including the ability to provide primary and secondary authentication methods (Kerberos, certificates, NTLMv2, etc.), can also be configured within the IPsec settings of Windows Firewall with Advanced Security.

☑ Windows Firewall with Advanced Security can be configured using the snap-in from the Group Policy Management console.

☑ You can use command line options for configuring, managing, and monitoring Windows Firewall with Advanced Security.

Exam Objectives
Frequently Asked Questions

Q: I'm pretty solid with IP addressing in IPv4 but I'm not really well-versed in IPv6. How much do I need to know for the exam?

A: If you're familiar with Microsoft exams, you'll know that the questions are pulled from a pool of questions and that they'll progressively test you on various elements. So, the short answer is that there's no guarantee you'll see any questions about IPv6 on the exam, whether directly or indirectly, but there's a high likelihood you will need to be comfortable with IPv6 in order to navigate one or more questions on the exam. You should understand the basics such as the address format; how networks, hosts, and ranges are specified; as well as where you configure IPv6 settings. Also be clear about the terminology, such as temporary and nontemporary, specific to IPv6 and be sure to be familiar with site local, link local, and other IPv6 formats and naming conventions.

Q: I've been reading a bit about Windows Server 2008 online and there's a lot of discussion about the Core version. What do I need to know about this?

A: Throughout this chapter, we've included brief references to the Core installation and specifically to the command line commands available to you. Expect to see questions about using the command line on the exam. Command line options have always been available, but the release of the Core version of Window Server 2008 will certainly bring this to the forefront. Where applicable, we've included command line commands to demonstrate how these commands can be used. Don't expect the exam to test you on syntax necessarily, but do expect to see questions related to using the command line options for frequently used features.

Q: DHCP is pretty basic stuff, though the addition of IPv6 makes it a bit different. What should I expect in the way of DHCP questions on the exam?

A: Expect to see questions that test your understanding of DHCP configuration and settings as well as questions that test your understanding and knowledge of new DHCP features. Since IPv6 is just being rolled into organizations, you can expect to see some IPv6-based questions related to DHCP.

Q: There are tons of protocols—sometimes it's like alphabet soup—MS-CHAP, MS-CHAP v2, EAP, PEAP, PPP, Kerberos V5, and the list goes on. I'm having a hard time keep all these straight and remembering how they're used (or not) in Windows Server 2008. Any tips you can share?

A: It does seem like every new release from Microsoft comes with a lot of new acronyms to learn, so the ALC (acronym learning curve) can be a bit daunting. You're probably familiar with some of these protocols from previous versions of Windows. If not, you might want to brush up on those before heading in to Windows Server 2008. However, there are some basics that might help. First, divide protocols into those used to authentication users locally (Kerberos, etc.) and those used to authentication users remotely (PPP, EAP, PEAP). It can be helpful to divide the protocols according to these areas so you can better keep track of what they do and when they're used. Also, spend time in the Routing and Remote Access Server segment of Windows Server 2008 as well as in the Windows Firewall with Advanced Security section. The more you see the various protocols being used in the default screens, the more they should sink in. That said, there are a lot of acronyms and thankfully, Microsoft exams don't test you on acronyms. Most of the time, the item will be spelled out the first time you see it (as we do in this book). If it's not, then it's a pretty common acronym such as AD for Active Directory or IP, IPsec, or DHCP.

Q: I'm not sure I'm clear on the difference between IPsec settings in the Windows Firewall with Advanced Security and the IPsec settings in Active Directory Group Policy. I've reread the material in this chapter, but I am still a bit confused. Can you provide any additional information that might help?

A: Yes. Group Policy in AD is going to specify how computers, users, and groups much be configured or must interact with the network. If you specify IPsec within Group Policy for a set of computers, you are requiring that all computers to which that policy is applied must use IPsec to communicate with other computers (for example). Windows Firewall with Advanced Security, on the other hand, can be configured to require IPsec for inbound and/or outbound connections. So, the computers to which the IPsec Group Policy has been applied (we'll call them the GP computers for short here) can communicate with other GP computer or other computer using IPsec all day long and have no interaction with the IPsec rules in the Windows Firewall on the Windows Server 2008. Suppose, however, that one of those computers needs to access an application or service running on that Windows Server 2008 computer or access something on the other side of that server. Now the firewall rules come into play. Since the GP computer is already using IPsec, it's likely it will conform to the firewall rules and its communications will be conducted security. On the other hand, if the GP computer tried to communicate via the server to a computer elsewhere that was not IPsec compliant, either the GP policy or the firewall rules would prevent that (depending on configuration). GP will apply IPsec rules to computers and groups on your network. IPsec rules in Windows Firewall with Advance Security applies to inbound and outbound traffic on the server itself. Together, these can create a secure solution and unlike previous versions of Windows Firewall, the IPsec configuration is integrated to prevent unintentional gaps in IPsec settings.

Self Test

1. You need to set up a network in the lab for a training class. You want to isolate the lab network from the rest of the corporate network so students don't inadvertently do something that takes the entire network down. What IP addressing method would you use?

   A. Private network addressing

   B. Public network addressing

   C. Network Address Translation

   D. Subnet isolation through subnet mask

2. Your boss asked you to subnet a network in the lab for an upcoming class. He hands you a piece of paper while he's on the phone and it simply says "192.168.10.x/25. 4 subnets." What is the subnet mask and the first address in each subnet?

   A. 255.255.255.0/ 192.168.10.1, 192.168.10.32, 192.168.10.64, 192.168.10.128

   B. 255.255.255.252/ 192.168.10.0, 192.168.10.32, 192.168.10.64, 192.168.10.128

   C. 255.255.255.240/ 192.168.10.0, 192.168.16.0, 192.168.24.0, 192.168.32.0

   D. 255.255.255.128/ 192.168.10.1, 192.168.10.33, 192.168.10.65, 192.168.10.97

3. You have a growing network that originally was configured using the private Class C address space. However, you're now about to grow beyond the maximum number of devices and need to expand but you don't anticipate needing more than a total of 290 addresses. What action would you take to solve this problem that would create the least disruption to your network?

   A. Install a router. Create two new scopes on your DHCP Server and reassign IP addresses.

   B. Change the default subnet mask to 255.255.252.0.

   C. Change the IP addressing scheme from Class C to Class B.

   D. Assign new computers on the network IP addresses from the existing address pool.

4. Your company's president comes to you and says that he understands IPv6 is fully supported in Windows Server 2008. He will approve your IT budget if it includes plans to transition to Windows Server 2008 and IPv6. However, he wants to know how quickly you can transition to IPv6. What should you tell him?

A. There is no fast and easy way to transition to IPv6. Much of the Internet's backbone is running on IPv4, so transitional technologies will be required. You'd recommend setting up IPv6 segments and using a tunneling protocol for the transition to begin.

B. The transition to IPv6 on the Internet backbone has been completed and as soon as the company upgrades to Windows Server 2008 and replaces its routers, you're good to go.

C. There is no reasonable way to transition to IPv6 for this organization since all hardware and software would have to be replaced to run Windows Server 2008 or Windows Vista. The cost would be prohibitive and is therefore not recommended.

D. The transition to IPv6 requires the installation of new hardware and software on all subnets using IPv6 exclusively. In the meantime, IPv4 can be used on older subnets and IPv6 can be used on newer subnets and a specific IPv4 to IPv6 router can be installed to bridge the two.

5. You open Windows Server 2008 DHCP Server role and examine the scope settings one of your staff members created, shown in Figure 10.33. Based on this information, which statement is true?

Figure 10.33 Windows Server 2008 DHCP Configuration

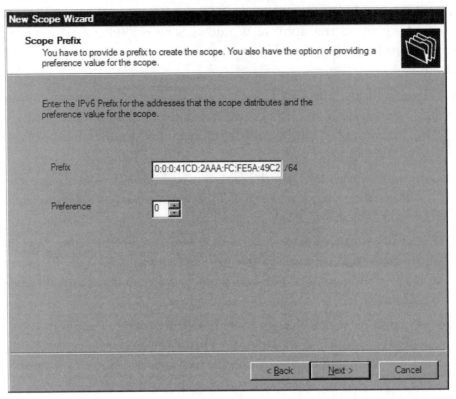

A. The Preference Value is incorrect. It must be set to 1 for all addresses that use the /64 option.

B. The Prefix Value is incorrect. It cannot begin with 0:0:0:.

C. The Prefix Value is too long. It should contain fewer digits.

D. Both B and C are correct.

E. The Prefix value and Preference values are correct.

6. You've asked Justin, a junior member of your IT staff, to install Windows Server 2008 on a spare computer in the lab and set up the DHCP role so you can teach a class on what's new in DHCP. Justin hesitates and asks how he should set the scope settings so it doesn't take the network down. What should you tell Justin?

A. DHCP in Windows Server 2008 cannot be installed on a computer attached to a network with a live DHCP server. Remove the server's network connection before installing DHCP.

B. Only one DHCP can exist on a network. He should configure the server as a DHCP relay agent instead.

C. A new DHCP server must be authorized in AD before it can perform the DHCP role.

D. Adding a new DHCP server could not take the network down.

7. You need to expand your network and create a new subnet for a new research project. You want the traffic for the research group to remain local to the subnet. None of the computers for the research project are installed yet. What's the fastest and easiest way to go about creating this subnet and keeping local traffic local?

A. Add the computers to the network, assign them a different subnet mask, enable IPsec through Group Policy, and assign it to the research project subnet.

B. Create a scope on the DHCP server that will provide addresses to just those computers, install a router, assign it a static IP address, and use that router as the default gateway for the computers on that subnet.

C. Install a new router and configure it as the DHCP Relay Agent for the existing scope using a static IP address. Then, connect the new computers to the network through the new router.

D. Modify the existing scope options on the DHCP server so that the subnet addresses for the new research subnet are excluded from the scope. Install a new router and configure it with a static IP address from the same range as the excluded IP addresses. Last, connect the new computers to the subnet and check that they are configured to automatically get IP configuration data.

8. The company has just leased a nearby building so it can expand operations. You've been asked to configure the network infrastructure in the new building. You configure the DHCP server that will go on this new network segment with the following options:

- Scope: 192.168.10.0 to 192.168.15.0
- Subnet mask: 255.255.252.0
- Default gateway: 192.168.10.1
- Exclusions: 192.168.12.0 to 192.168.12.20

■ Reservations: 192.168.10.1 DNS server, 192.168.12.2 DNS server, 192.168.12.5 WINS server, 192.168.12.6 Router8

You set Router 8 to have a static IP address of 192.168.12.6 and configure it to be a DHCP relay agent. What's wrong with your set up?

A. You can't have two DNS servers on one subnet, the scope and the subnet mask do not match, you can't set up a router as DHCP relay agent.

B. Your scope cannot have a zero in the last place, your subnet mask is wrong, your default gateway and your DNS server share the same IP address and may slow down the subnet, you don't need a WINS server.

C. Your default gateway and your DNS server use the same IP address. You cannot have a DHCP relay agent (your router) and a DHCP server on the same subnet. Your excluded range and your reservations settings are mutually exclusive.

D. The default gateway has the wrong IP address and all network traffic will be sent to the Router, causing all local traffic to be routed to the main network and back again, causing too much unneeded network traffic. You don't need a DHCP server on this subnet and should simply enable the server as a RRAS server to handle remote traffic to the main corporate site.

9. You've set up a new subnet with a DHCP server. After a few days, mobile users begin complaining they can't log onto the network when they're locally connected (at their desks, for example). What would you check in your DHCP settings?

A. Scope settings

B. Exclusions

C. Subnet mask or default gateway

D. Lease duration

10. A recent change to the network infrastructure configuration was completed over the weekend. Monday morning, users begin complaining that the network is terribly slow. The Help Desk phones are lit up and there's a rumble in the building as users start going to others' desks asking if they're having any luck using network resources and getting out to the Internet. The new configuration is shown in Figure 10.34. What would you change in order to best resolve this problem?

Figure 10.34 New Network Configuration

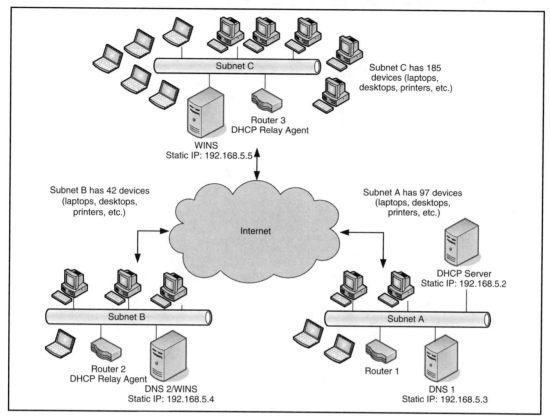

A. Add a DNS Server to Subnet C.

B. Remove the DHCP Relay Agent role from either Router 2 or Router 3.

C. Add a DHCP Server to Subnet C and remove Router 3.

D. Both A and C.

E. Add a DHCP Server to Subnet C.

Self Test Quick Answer Key

1.	**D**	6.	**C**	
2.	**D**	7.	**B**	
3.	**B**	8.	**C**	
4.	**A**	9.	**D**	
5.	**D**	10.	**E**	

Chapter 11

MCTS/MCITP
Exam 649

Configuring Network Access

Exam objectives in this chapter:

- **Configuring Routing**
- **Configuring Remote Access**
- **Configuring Wireless Access**

Exam objectives review:

- ☑ **Summary of Exam Objectives**
- ☑ **Exam Objectives Fast Track**
- ☑ **Exam Objectives Frequently Asked Questions**
- ☑ **Self Test**
- ☑ **Self Test Quick Answer Key**

Introduction

Organizations rely on networking and communications to meet the challenging requirements necessary to compete in the global marketplace. All members of these organizations need to have constant access to the files. This requires the ability to connect to the network wherever they may be and from any device that they have available to them at the time. In addition, those outside the vendor's network will require the ability to interact smoothly with the key resources they require. Partners and clients want to be able to also conduct quick and fluid transactions through the network. Security is more important than ever in networking, due to the constant threat of infiltration and exposure to the Internet. Successfully navigating all of these concerns relies on the knowledge of how to configure network access efficiently and provide the most secure yet accessible connection possible to your organization and its members.

As an administrator, you must accommodate these needs using the latest and most practical tools in your arsenal. To help accomplish this there have been a number of networking and communications enhancements made to Windows Server 2008 to address connectivity. This will help you to improve the ease of use, reliability, management, and security of your organization's assets. By applying what Windows Server 2008 has to offer with its latest features you will have more flexibility when managing your network infrastructure. Windows Server 2008 allows for a total system health by deploying settings for authenticated wireless and wired connections through Group Policy or scripts, and deploying protected traffic scenarios. In order to take on this task, a number of features from former versions of Windows Server have been improved upon or replaced with new updated features, which will allow you to provide the highest level of efficiency and security to your organization. For your exam, you will need to be familiar with the new and updated changes that Windows Server 2008 provides and how to best utilize these tools to manage and maintain your network.

The three main areas of focus or objectives for your exam will be configuring routing, remote access, and wireless access. This chapter will include a brief overview of the latest features available in Windows Server 2008 as well as detailed descriptions of the fundamental principals of these objectives and how to apply them to the newest version of Windows Server.

In this chapter, we will discuss the many new and powerful changes to Microsoft Windows Server 2008 that include innovative enhancements to networking technologies and network access configuration. We will go over the latest changes to protocols and core networking components, wireless and 802.1X-authenticated wired technologies. This will include network infrastructure components and services that can be applied when using Windows Server 2008. Before moving on in detail concerning the exam and what you will be required to know, let us take a more detailed overview of the latest features that Windows Server 2008 has to offer in terms of routing, remote access, and wireless access.

Windows Server 2008 and Routing

Routing is one element that helps to ensure successful network traffic flow. It has always been the framework for a functional logical network regardless of which version of Windows Server you may be working on. Because of this, Microsoft has taken some time to improve the overall ease of use for routing with this latest version. As you are probably aware, Windows Server 2003 used the Routing and Remote Access Service (RRAS) to handle many of the configuration needs for routing in the past. Windows Server 2008 also uses the RRAS, but features a number of changes to it when compared to older versions of Windows. Many former encapsulation protocols have been made obsolete or revised for Windows Server 2008. Here is a brief summarization of what changes and omissions to expect in this build.

- Bandwidth Allocation Protocol (BAP) is no longer supported by Windows Server 2008.

- X.25 is also no longer supported.

- Serial Line Internet Protocol (SLIP), an encapsulation of Internet Protocol (IP) meant for use over serial ports and modems, has also been excluded due to infrequency of use. All SLIP-based connections will automatically be updated to Point-to-Point Protocol (PPP)-based connections.

- Asynchronous Transfer Mode (ATM), which was used to encode data traffic into small fixed cells, has been discarded.

- IP over Institute of Electrical & Electronics Engineers (IEEE) 1394 is no longer supported.

- NWLink IPX/SPX/NetBIOS Compatible Transport Protocol has been omitted.

- Services for Macintosh (SFM).

- Open Shortest Path First (OSPF) routing protocol component in Routing and Remote Access is no longer present.

- Basic firewall in Routing and Remote Access has been replaced with a new Windows Firewall feature.

- Static IP filter application program interfaces (APIs) for Routing and Remote Access are no longer viable and have been replaced with Windows Filtering Platform APIs.

- SPAP, EAP-MD5-CHAP, and MS-CHAP authentication protocols for PPP-based connections are no longer used by Windows Server 2008.

EXAM WARNING

Some of the old familiar aspects of Windows Routing and Remote Access have changed since Windows Server 2003. Be sure to familiarize yourself with the improvements and discontinuations to these features before test day.

Don't get caught off guard by confusing old functionality with new functionality, such as the differences between Windows Firewall with Advanced Protection and the old Windows Firewall. Also be aware of technology that is no longer supported in this new build. This will help you to stay focused and result in better retention for the exam.

Window Server 2008 and Remote Access

As with past versions of RRAS, Windows Server 2008 offers exceptional ease of use and configuration for remote access. All features previously available are featured in this version of Windows Server. There is also the additional replacement of Internet Authentication Service (IAS) with Network Policy Server and Network Access Protection (NAP).

The change to Windows Server 2008 in regards to remote access is the addition of Secure Socket Tunneling Protocol (SSTP). SSTP is the latest form of VPN tunnel created for use with Windows Server 2008. It contains many new features that enable traffic to pass through firewalls that block Point-to-Point Tunneling Protocol (PPTP) and Layer 2 Tunneling Protocol (L2TP)/Internet Protocol Security (IPSec) traffic. In addition, SSTP uses the Secure Sockets Layer (SSL) channel of the Hypertext Transfer Protocol Secure (HTTPS) protocol by making use of a process that encapsulates PPP traffic. PPP is very versatile. It enables you to use strong authentication methods such as Extensible Authentication Protocol-Transport Layer Security (EAP-TLS), which were not possible in past versions of Windows for VPN. All traffic will be channeled through the TCP port 443, which is typically used for Web access, because of the use of HTTPS. Security features include transport level security with enhanced key negotiation, encryption, and integrity checking capabilities by using SSL.

Windows Server 2008 and Wireless Access

Windows Server 2008 includes the following changes and enhancements to IEEE 802.11 wireless support:

- Native Wi-Fi architecture
- User interface improvements for wireless connections
- Wireless Group Policy enhancements
- Changes in Wireless Auto Configuration
- WPA2 support
- Integration with Network Access Protection when using 802.1X authentication
- EAPHost infrastructure
- 802.11 wireless diagnostics
- Command-line support for configuring wireless settings
- Network Location Awareness and network profiles
- Next Generation Transmission Control Protocol (TCP)/IP stack enhancements for wireless environments
- Single Sign On

Configuring Routing

Routing is a sometimes-confused aspect of networking, which can be complicated due to lack of fundamental understanding and training. All information that travels through a network has two things in common: a device that sent it and a required routing decision. The decisions for these routes are conducted by comparing the destination address to a list of entries located on a routing table or stored in a remote location. The routing table is normally configured and built by the network administrator or from information gathered by the TCP/IP system. These configurations can take place in a number of ways to ensure the best and most secure transport of information. Windows Server 2008 has a number of features that previous versions of Windows Servers possessed as well as some new added updates. Before reviewing changes to the system let's take a better look at the fundamentals of routing.

Routing Fundamentals

When attempting to select a path in a network by which to send data or physical traffic, an administrator has many options available to him. There are a number of ways to send packets from one destination to another based on intermediary hardware or nodes. This can include a number of different hardware devices including bridges, gateways, routers, firewalls, and switches. Even computers with multiple network cards are capable of routing packets. There are different types of routing algorithms or protocols that can be used to organize the signal flow between these devices.

These algorithms rely on what is called a *routing metric*, a value used by a routing algorithm to determine whether one route should perform better than another. Metrics can include a number of different parameters to judge performance by, as configured by the administrator.

On the simplest level, the system will select an entry from the routing table and use the netmask from that entry (see Figure 11.1). The system then performs a comparison of this value and the destination address. The resulting value is cross-referenced to the network address in the table entry. If the two values match, the information can arrive at the destination through the gateway in that entry. If the two values do not match, the routing system continues along the routing table to the next entry and performs the same check again. If the "no matching entry" is found on the table, the routing system discards the packet and generates a message notifying the sender that the destination network cannot be reached.

Otherwise, when a routing table entry is found that matches the network value, the packet is sent based on the information in the table entry via the destination listed. If the destination exists on a portion of the network directly connected to the routing system, the packet is delivered to the destination system. If it does not exist on the same segment, the packet is sent to a gateway system for delivery. This is a very complicated way of describing what is referred to as *static routing*.

Figure 11.1 Routing Tables

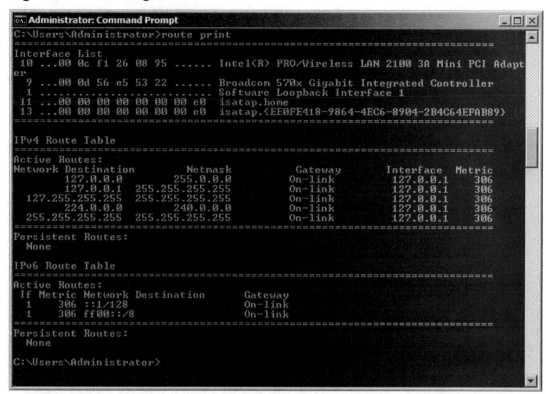

TEST DAY TIP

Take advantage of the fundamentals of routing by practicing with routing tables and configuring your traffic flow. Remember that even the most complicated networks can find a need for the use of static routing. Be aware of how static routing can affect a system as opposed to dynamic routing.

EXERCISE 11.1

WORKING WITH THE ROUTING TABLE ON WINDOWS SERVER 2008

When working with Windows Server 2008, you can configure the static routing table in many ways. With Internet Protocol version 4 (IPv4), you can configure the table with routes by removing or changing them. For example:

1. To display the entire contents of the IP routing table you can type **route print**.

2. To display the routes in the IP routing table that begin with 10. type **route print 10.**[*]

3. To add a default route with the default gateway address of 192.168.10.1, type **route add 0.0.0.0 mask 0.0.0.0 192.168.10.1**.

4. To add a route to the destination 10.40.0.0 with the subnet mask of 255.255.0.0 and the next hop address of 10.20.0.1, type **route add 10.41.0.0 mask 255.255.0.0 10.20.0.1**.

5. To add a persistent route to the destination 10.41.0.0 with the subnet mask of 255.255.0.0 and the next hop address of 10.20.0.1, type **route -p add 10.40.0.0 mask 255.255.0.0 10.27.0.1**.

6. To add a route to the destination 10.40.0.0 with the subnet mask of 255.255.0.0, the next hop address of 10.20.0.1, and the cost metric of 7, type **route add 10.40.0.0 mask 255.255.0.0 10.20.0.1 metric 7**.

7. To add a route to the destination 10.40.0.0 with the subnet mask of 255.255.0.0, the next hop address of 10.20.0.1, and using the interface index 0x3, type **route add 10.40.0.0 mask 255.255.0.0 10.20.0.1 if 0x3**.

8. To delete the route to the destination 10.40.0.0 with the subnet mask of 255.255.0.0, type **route delete 10.40.0.0 mask 255.255.0.0**.

9. To delete all routes in the IP routing table that begin with 10. type **route delete 10.**[*]

10. To change the next hop address of the route with the destination of 10.40.0.0 and the subnet mask of 255.255.0.0 from 10.20.0.1 to 10.20.0.25, type **route change 10.40.0.0 mask 255.255.0.0 10.20.0.25**.

If using IPv6, you can add a route just as easily. For example:

11. To display the entire contents of the IP routing table you can type **route print -6**.

12. To add a route, type **route add 3ffe::/32 3ffe::1**.

TEST DAY TIP

When using Windows Server 2008, remember that the output of the route command will now show IPv6 options by default. For the exam, make sure that you are familiar with the options of IPv6 and the route command.

Static Routing

Static routing describes a system that does not implement adaptive routing in its configuration. In these systems, routes through a network are defined by set paths referred to as *static routes*, which are inserted into the router manually by the system administrator. This is accomplished via the route command, which can be used to manipulate local routing tables. There is no fault tolerance in regards to static routing. Changes to the network or a failure between two statically defined nodes will cause any traffic between those points to not be rerouted. This means any packets that are awaiting transport between the affected paths will be forced to wait for repairs to the failure, or for an updated static route by the administrator. This also leaves open the issue of the request timing out before repairs can be made to the route.

Static routing is considered the simplest form of routing and requires excessive manual processes. It often is the least efficient way of routing in cases where information paths have to be changed frequently. This is also the case for configurations that require a large number of routing devices, because each one must be manually entered. Static routing is also the least preferred method of dealing with outages or down connections, because any route that is configured manually must be reconfigured manually to fix or repair any lost connectivity.

There may be many downsides to static routing, but there are many incidents where a static route is the most logical and efficient method for routing. Static routing is the opposite of dynamic routing, which is a system in which routers will automatically adjust to changes in network topology or traffic. *Dynamic routing* is used by most modern routers, but some amount of programming is still available for customizing routes if necessary.

As we mentioned earlier, you as an administrator will need to deal with clients and employees of your company attempting to access the network and Internet. The Internet and Local Area Networks (LANs) are referred to as *packet switching networks*.

The idea of packet switching networks is defined by the ability to optimize the use of the channel capacity available in a network. This helps to minimize transmission latency. This also requires the use of specific protocols for directing traffic through them. There are two major classes of routing protocols used in packet switch networking today:

- **Distance-vector Routing Protocol** A distance-vector routing protocol requires that a router contact and transmit to its neighbors of topology changes to the network. The frequency of this must be periodic and in most instances when a change is detected. Routing Internet Protocol (RIP) is the most popular example of this type of protocol.

- **Link State Protocol** The simplest explanation of link-state routing is that every node (router) is given a map of the topology of the network. This map is in graph form and shows the connectivity of nodes in the network. Then each individual node calculates the next best hop from every node in the network. This information then forms the routing table for each individual node based on its calculations. No other communication occurs between nodes. The most popular version of this is the OSPF.

Routing Internet Protocol (RIP)

The RIP was once the most commonly used Interior Gateway Protocol (IGP) on internal networks. It was also commonly used on networks connected to the Internet. RIP was used to help routers dynamically adapt to the variety of changes made to network connections. It accomplished this by relaying information about which networks each router had access to, and the distance those networks were from each other.

Although RIP is still actively used and has an important place in some networks, it is generally considered a dying protocol, which has been replaced by other routing protocols such as OSPF. RIP is a distance vector routing protocol that employs the hop count as a routing metric. RIP allows a maximum of 15 hops. The total hold down time for transfer is 180 seconds. Most traffic at the time RIP was commonly used was not significant, so each RIP router had an update time of 30 seconds by default, which was common practice. This proved to be a poor configuration and was later changed to randomized updates.

RIP is limited in a number of ways due to its lack of scalability. It prevents routing loops from continuing indefinitely, by implementing a limit on the number of hops allowed in a path from the source to a destination. It also limits the size of the network that RIP can support by design.

On the other hand, RIP is easier to configure than many other protocols, because it uses one of the smallest amounts of settings of any routing protocols. RIP does not require the use of any parameters on a router, and it can be ideal for small networks. RIP can be configured through the RRAS, which we will discuss later.

NOTE

Microsoft Windows Server 2008 supports RIP version 2 within RRAS.

Open Shortest Path First (OSPF)

OSPF was the natural successor to the RIP. OSPF protocol is a hierarchical IGP that uses a link state in the individual areas that make up the hierarchy. A link state database (LSDB) creates a tree-image of the network topology. It then sends copies of the LSDB periodically to update all routers in the area of the OSPF network.

OSPF is the most widely used IGP in regards to large enterprise networks. It has a much larger network size range than RIP. The OSPF protocol can determine the best path by communicating with other routers and then saving the routes in their LSDBs securely.

An OSPF network is divided into *areas*, which contain *area identifiers*. These identifiers are 32-bit and are usually written in the format of an IP address. Be aware that area identifiers are not IP addresses, and may often times duplicate any IP address without conflict occurring. These areas are logical groupings of routers whose information may be communicated to the rest of the network. There are several types of areas in an OPSPF network:

- **Backbone Area** The backbone area forms the central hub of an OSPF network. All other areas are connected to it, and inter-area routing happens via routers connected to the backbone area and to their own non-backbone areas. The backbone area distributes all routing information between the non-backbone areas. The backbone must be adjacent to all other areas, but does not need to be physically contiguous. Connectivity can be established and maintained through virtual links. All OSPF areas must connect to the backbone area. This connection, however, can be through a virtual link.

- **Stub Area** The stub area is an area that does not receive external routes except the default route, but does receive inter-area routes. All routers in the area need to agree they are stub, so that they do not generate types of LSA not appropriate to a stub area. Stub areas do not have the transit attribute and thus cannot be traversed by a virtual link.

- **Not-so-stubby area (NSSA)** The Not-so-stubby area (NSSA) is a type of stub area that can import autonomous system (AS) external routes and send them to the backbone, but cannot receive AS external routes from the backbone or other areas. The NSSA is a non-proprietary extension of the existing stub area feature, which allows the injection of external routes in a limited fashion into the stub area.

Exam Warning

As of this writing, the OSPF routing protocol component is no longer present in Windows Server 2008. Although this may not be covered in the exam extensively, knowledge regarding this protocol will help you better understand RIP and other routing protocols by comparison, and will help with real-world applications that may occur as a consequence of the removal of this element.

Configuring Remote Access

Remote access is commonly used by many companies today to allow access to a computer or a network from a remote location. Most corporations include people at branch offices, telecommuters, and people who are traveling that will need to be able to gain access to network resources. Even clients using your company's services from home need to gain access to the Internet through an Internet Service Provider (ISP). *Dial-up connection* through desktop, notebook, or handheld computer modem over regular telephone lines was a common method of remote access in the early years of its inception.

It is also possible to gain remote access using a dedicated line between a computer or a remote local area network and the central or main LAN. This tends to be a less flexible and more expensive method, but does offer faster data exchange rates and fewer configurations. Integrated Services Digital Network (ISDN) is a compromise between the two other common methods of remote access, since it combines dial-up access with faster data exchange rates. The most growing trends in remote access in recent years have included wireless, cable, and digital subscriber line (DSL) technologies, which offer more convenient and efficient methods for remote access.

A remote access server is comprised of a computer with a remote access application installed, which is configured to handle the authentication and authorization of clients seeking access to a network remotely. This can also be referred to as a *communication server*. A remote access server usually includes or is associated with a firewall server to ensure security, and a router that can forward the remote access request to another part of the network. A single remote access server may also be used as part of a much larger VPN.

Like past versions, Windows Server 2008 has included a wide array of options for configuring remote access for you company. You will be required to be familiar with the workings of how to set up a remote access server and all of the methods of connectivity available in a modern networking environment. Like its previous versions, Windows Server 2008 houses most of its remote access tools in the RRA role. This role is crucial to the successful deployment of remote access services for your company, and will be used heavily in the exam.

EXAM WARNING

Remote access is an important part of the exam, and will weigh heavily into the overall grade. Be sure to familiarize yourself with all of the aspects of the objective. Also be sure to familiarize yourself with usage of MMC, Network Policy Server (NPS), and NAP, which are additional tools that maybe be covered in a small portion of the exam. Remember, every question counts and a comprehensive knowledge of the subject matter will ensure total retention for usage in real-world environments.

Routing and Remote Access Services (RRAS)

Most of the major functions of network access and the objectives that you will be required to know for your examine, revolve around the RRAS role. This is not a new feature to Windows Server 2008, but has many omissions and additions since Windows Server 2003. From this role, you can access configuration tools for routing, connection manager, and remote access service all of which will be very helpful in setting up remote access on your machines and managing policies.

Let's install the RRAS role. This will help you to configure most of the remote access features available in Windows Server 2008 that we will be discussing. Be sure to start with a clean install of Windows Server 2008, and review all guidelines and requirements for the system you are using.

EXERCISE 11.2

INSTALLING RRAS

To begin installing RRAS, follow these steps:

1. Open the Server Manager by clicking on the **Administrative Tools** menu.

2. Scroll down to the **Roles Summary** section of the details pane.

3. Click **Add Roles** to launch the **Add Roles Wizard**, as seen in Figure 11.2.

Figure 11.2 Add Roles Wizard

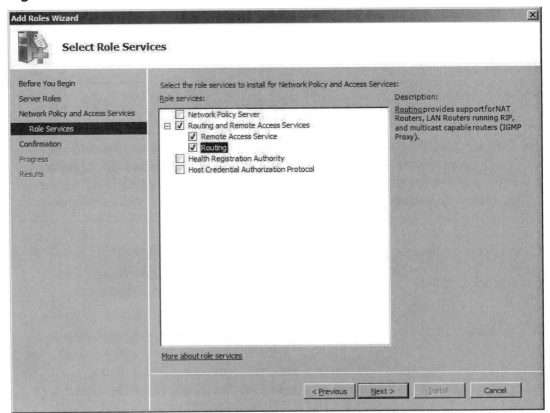

4. Click **Next** to bypass the Welcome screen.

5. Select the **Network Access Services** checkbox.

6. Click the **Next** button.

7. Click **Next** again to bypass the Network Access Service screen description.

8. Select the **Network Access Services** components that you want to install. Select the check boxes for **Network Policy Server (NPS)** and **Routing and Remote Access Services (RRAS)**.

9. When you select the Routing and Remote Access Services check box, the Remote Access Service, Routing, and Connection Manager Administration Kit check boxes will be selected automatically.

Network Policy Server and Network Access Protection

In the RRAS there are a number of snap-in roles that can be used in configuring and setting up your network access needs for Windows Server 2008. In previous incarnations of Windows Server 2003, Internet Authentication Service (IAS) snap-in was Microsoft's implementation of a Remote Authentication Dial-in User Service (RADIUS) server and proxy. It was capable of performing localized connection AAA Protocol for many types of network access, including wireless and VPN connections.

For Windows Server 2008, Microsoft has replaced IAS with a new snap-in called Network Policy Server (NPS). NPS is the Microsoft implementation of a RADIUS server and proxy in Windows Server 2008, and promises to be even simpler to use than IAS. For your exam, you will be required to be familiar with NPS.

NPS is not just a replacement for IAS; it does what IAS did but also offers another role called Network Access Protection (NAP). When you install NPS you will find that you have a lot of new functionality.

NPS does many of the same things that IAS did such as:

- Routing of LAN and WAN traffic.
- Allow access to local resources through VPN or dial-up connections.
- Creating and enforcing network access through VPN or dial-up connections.

For example, NPS can provide these functions:

- VPN services
- Dial-up services
- 802.11 protected access
- RRAS

- Offer authentication through Windows Active Directory

- Control network access with policies

What NPS does that is new, are all the functions related to NAP. NAP when used in unison with NPS creates a "total system health policy enforcement platform," which helps in the creation of health policies for your network, as shown in Figure 11.3.

Figure 11.3 NPS and NAP Health Policy Overview

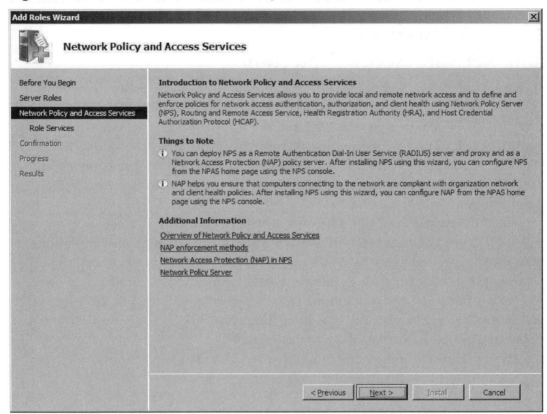

NAP is designed to enhance a corporate VPN. This is accomplished when clients establish a VPN session with a Windows Server 2008 system that is running the RRAS. Once a connection is made, a NPS will validate the remote system and determine the status of its health. The NPS collects information and compares the remote computer's configuration against a pre-determined network access policy that can be customized by the administrator. Policies can be configured to either monitor or isolate based on the administrators preference as, shown in Figure 11.4.

Figure 11.4 NPS Policy Configuration

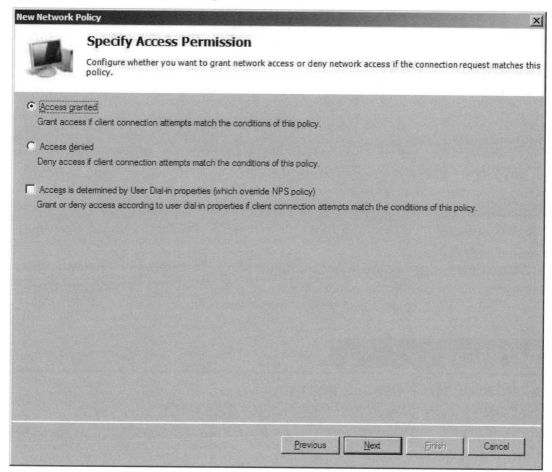

Although monitoring will not prevent any PCs from gaining access to your network, each PC logging on to the network will be recorded for compliance. Isolation will put non-compliant users onto an isolated segment of the network, where it cannot interfere with production or resources. Of course, the administrator is ultimately responsible for configuring what access non-compliant computers will be allowed.

If you are already familiar with Windows Server 2003 and the IAS snap-in, you will notice many changes to the NPS snap-in:

- Network policies have replaced remote access policies and have been moved to the policies node.

- RADIUS Clients and Servers node has replaced the RADIUS Client node.

- There is no Connection Request Processing node.

- Policies and the Remote RADIUS Server Groups node have been moved under RADIUS Clients and Servers.

- Remote access policy conditions and profile settings have been reorganized on the Overview, Conditions, Constraints, and Settings tabs for the properties of a network policy.

- The Remote Access Logging folder has been renamed the Accounting node, and no longer has the Local File or SQL Server nodes.

In addition, the System Health Validators node allows you to set up and adjust all NAP health requirements. The Remediation Server Groups node allows you to set up the group of servers that restricted NAP clients can access for the VPN and Dynamic Host Configuration Protocol (DHCP) NAP enforcement methods. Last, the Accounting node allows you to set up how NPS stores accounting information for the network.

The NAP wizard automatically configures all of the connection request policies, network policies, and health policies. Knowing how to set up and configure this feature will put you steps ahead of the competition.

EXERCISE 11.3

CONFIGURING POLICIES AND SETTINGS FOR NAP ENFORCEMENT METHODS IN NPS

To configure policies and settings for NAP enforcement methods in NPS:

1. Select **Network Access Protection** in the Standard Configuration drop-down box.

2. Click Configure NAP.

To configure policies and settings for VPN or dial-up network access:

3. Select RADIUS server for Dial-Up or VPN Connections from the drop-down box.

4. Click **Configure VPN** or **Dial-Up**.

    To configure policies and settings for 802.1X-authenticated wired or wireless access:

5. Select **RADIUS server for 802.1X Wireless** or **Wired Connections** from the drop-down box.

6. Click **Configure 802.1X**.

The wizard will guide you through the configuration process for your chosen scenario. The NAP wizard for VPN enforcement has a number of policy creation options, including ones for compliant NAP clients, noncompliant NAP clients, and non–NAP capable clients. It also includes two health policies for compliant and noncompliant NAP clients. The new NAP wizards and other wizards contained within will help you with creating RADIUS clients, remote RADIUS server groups, connection request policies, and network policies. Overall, this will make it that much easier to configure NPS for a variety of network access scenarios, and this will make your job and exam all the more simple.

Dial-Up

Dial-up by definition is the method used to connect a device to a network using a modem and a public telephone service. Dial-up access works in the same exact manner as a telephone connection does. The only true difference is that the two ends of the connections have computer devices communicating rather than people. Dial-up access utilizes normal telephone lines and because of this, the quality of the connection can suffer. Data rates are also limited. The maximum data rate with dial-up access for many years was 56Kbph. ISDN provides faster rates but are still limited compared to cable and DSL.

Dial-up networking using Windows Server 2008 include some of the following components:

- **Dial-up Networking Servers** You can configure a server running RRAS to provide dial-up networking access to an entire network, or restrict access to the shared resources of the remote access server only.

- **Dial-up Networking Clients** Remote access clients must be running Windows Server 2008, Windows Server 2003, Windows XP, Windows 2000, Windows NT to have access to the RRAS.

- **Remote Access Protocols** Remote access protocols are used to negotiate connections and provide framing for LAN protocol data that is sent over a wide area network (WAN) link. RRAS supports LAN protocols such as TCP/IP, which enable access to the Internet. RRAS supports remote access protocols such as PPP.

- **WAN Options** Clients can dial in by using standard telephone lines and a modem or modem pool. Faster links are possible by using ISDN. You can no longer connect remote access clients to remote access servers by using X.25 or ATM with Windows Server 2008.

- **Security Options** Windows Server 2008 provides logon and domain security, support for security hosts, data encryption, RADIUS, remote access account lockout, remote access policies, and callback for secure network access for dial-up clients.

Remote Access Policy

Remote access policies are an ordered set of rules that define how connections are either authorized or rejected. For each rule, there are one or more conditions, a set of profile settings, and a remote access permission setting. If a connection is authorized, the remote access policy profile specifies a set of connection restrictions. The dial-in properties of the user account also provide a set of restrictions. Where applicable, user account connection restrictions override the remote access policy profile connection restrictions.

For servers running the RRAS that are configured for the Windows authentication provider, remote access policies are administered from RRAS and apply only to the connections of the RRAS server. Centralized management of remote access policies is also used when you have remote access servers that are running RRAS. Remote access policies validate a number of connection settings before authorizing the connection, including the following:

- Remote access permission

- Group membership

- Type of connection

- Time of day

- Authentication methods

- Advanced conditions such as access server identity, access client phone number, or Media Access Control (MAC) address

- Whether user account dial-in properties are ignored

- Whether unauthenticated access is allowed

After the connection is authorized, remote access policies can also be used to specify connection restrictions, including the following:

- Idle timeout time
- Maximum session time
- Encryption strength
- IP packet filters

Advanced restrictions:

- IP address for PPP connections
- Static routes

Additionally, you can vary connection restrictions based on the following settings:

- Group membership
- Type of connection
- Time of day
- Authentication methods
- Identity of the access server
- Access client phone number or MAC address
- Whether unauthenticated access is allowed

For example, you can have policies that specify different maximum session times for different types of connections or groups. Additionally, you can also specify restricted access for business partners or unauthenticated connections. All of this can be configured using the RRAS panel on the client computer, as shown in Figure 11.5. This is accessible as follows:

1. Open **Server Manager** and expand the **Roles** tab.
2. Expand the **Network Policy and Access Service** tab, as seen in Figure 11.5.

Figure 11.5 Network Policy and Access Tab

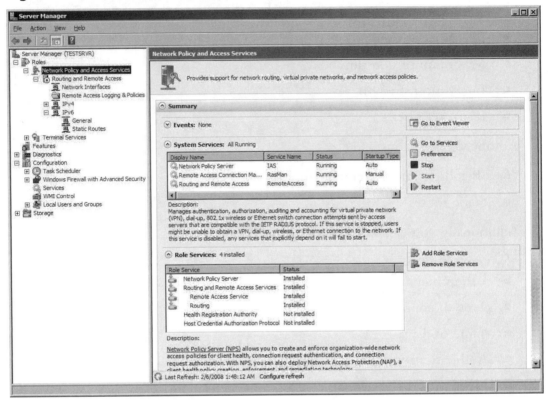

3. Expand the **Routing and Remote Access** panel and right click for **Properties**.

This will allow you to set up configurations for your remote access policies.

Network Address Translation (NAT)

Windows Server 2008 provides network address translation (NAT) functionality as part of the RRAS. NAT provides a method for translating the IPv4 addresses of computers on one network into IPv4 addresses of computers on a different network. A NAT-enabled IP router works as a translation service when deployed at the boundary where a private network meets a public network. This allows computers on the private network to access computers on the public network.

The whole reasoning behind the development of NAT technology was as a place holder solution for a greater issue that administrators faced. This problem was IPv4 address-depletion that plagued the Internet community. Due to a huge and continuing rise in computer usage, the number of available globally unique (public) IPv4 addresses was far too small to accommodate the need to access to the Internet. A long-term solution for the problem was well under way in the development of Internet Protocol version 6 (IPv6) addresses, which are supported by Windows Server 2008. Unfortunately, IPv6 is not yet widely adopted and would require extensive reconfiguring to deploy large scale in most organizations. The technology has been in use for more than a decade, but the practical deployment still remains an issue. This is why NAT is still in use, because it allows computers on any network to use reusable private addresses to connect to computers with globally unique public addresses on the Internet.

Small- to medium-sized organizations with private networks to access resources on the Internet or other public networks, use NAT for this reasoning. They configure reusable private IPv4 addresses while the computers on the public servers are set up with globally unique IPv4 addresses. The most useful deployment of NAT is in a small office or home office (SOHO) or a medium-sized business that uses RRAS. NAT technology enables computers on the internal corporate network to connect to resources on the Internet without having to deploy a proxy server.

NAT is a good solution for situations where ICS is not an option, such as when using a VPN or when the clients are using static IP addresses. A real benefit of NAT becomes apparent when dealing with Administration duties. For example, NAT makes it fairly simple to move your Web server or File Transfer Protocol (FTP) server to another host computer without having to worry about broken links. If you merely change the inbound mapping at the router, you can set it to reflect the new host. The same holds true of changes to your internal network. This is because the only external IP addresses either belong to the router or come from a pool of global addresses.

EXERCISE 11.4

ENABLING AND CONFIGURING NAT

Now that you understand how NAT works, let's look at how to enable and configure NAT:

1. In the left pane of the **Server Manager**, expand the **Routing and Remote Access** node, as shown in Figure 11.6.

2. Expand the **IPv4** node.

3. Click on the **NAT** node.

4. In the **NAT** node, right click on the external network server that you wish to enable NAT for on the middle pane of the console. For example, the external interface could be **Local Area Connection**.

5. Click **Properties** and select **NAT** and click **OK**, as shown in Figure 11.6.

Figure 11.6 Enabling NAT

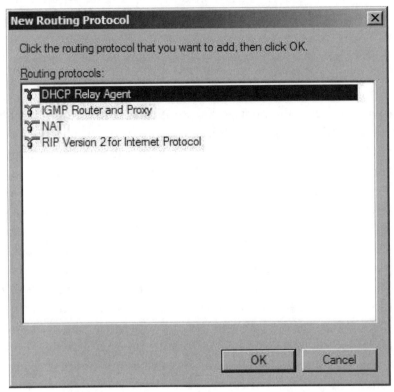

Internet Connection Sharing (ICS)

Internet Connection Sharing (ICS) is a feature that permits you to use Windows Server 2008 to connect a small office network or home network over the Internet. Not much has changed in this version of Windows Server 2008, and you may find that most of the features and set up procedures are very similar to that of Windows Server 2003. As it always has, ICS provides NAT, IP addressing, and name resolution services for all the computers on a small network. This method is best used for sharing an Internet connection among a small business network.

ICS routes TCP/IP packets that are present in a small LAN environment to the Internet. ICS will calculate and map individual IP addresses belonging to the clients of the LAN to unused port numbers in the TCP/IP stack. Because it uses NAT, IP addresses belonging to the local computer will not be visible on the Internet. All packets leaving or entering the LAN are sent from or to the IP address of the external adapter on the ICS host computer. This IP address is static and will always be 192.168.0.1, and will provide NAT services to the whole 192.168.0.x subnet.

ICS is not customizable in terms of which addresses are used for the internal subnet. It does not contain provisions for bandwidth limiting or other features common to more advanced systems. ICS is also not compatible and cannot be combined with Wi-Fi and dial-up mobile modems. ICS does offer limited configuration for other standard services and some configuration of NAT.

Configuring & Implementing...

Configuring ICS When Dealing with VPNs

Virtual private networks (VPNs), which we discuss later, are common in most companies today. When configuring an ICS, there are several things you should bear in mind concerning these types of connections and hazards that may occur if the proper precautions are not met.

Never create a VPN connection to a corporate network from the ICS computer. By doing so, you will cause the default setting for all traffic from the ICS computer to be forwarded over the VPN connection to the corporate network. This includes traffic from LAN clients. This will suspend Internet resources across the network and all the client computers will be sending data over the logical connection created with the credentials of the ICS computer user.

Never configure ICS on a computer that is a VPN server. If your Windows Server 2008-based computer is serving as a VPN server, you must use Windows Server 2008 NAT role.

These are very important configuration mistakes that, if avoided, can save wasted time and energy for you as an administrator.

Here is a list of required hardware and software for enabling ICS:

- A DSL or cable modem with an ISP connected to it and an active DSL or cable account.

- Two network adapters installed in the ICS machine.
- A network already configured with functioning TCP/IP.

Due to the nature of the way ISC works and its drawbacks, you should never install ICS on a machine that incorporates any of the following stipulations:

- Uses static IP addresses
- Has a domain controller
- Uses other DNS servers, gateways, or DHCP servers

ICS creates a static IP address for your network adapter and allocates IP addresses to other computers on your network. This means you will lose your connection to the rest of the network if other network computers already provide those services. If any of these conditions already exist in your network, you must use Windows Server 2008 NAT server instead of ICS.

Also bear in mind these other warnings:

- Do not create a VPN connection to a corporate network from the ICS computer. If you do, by default all traffic from the ICS computer, including traffic from local area network clients, will be forwarded over the VPN connection to the corporate network. This means that Internet resources will no longer be reachable, and all the client computers will be sending data over the logical connection created with the credentials of the ICS computer user.
- Do not configure ICS on a computer that is a VPN server. If your Windows Server 2008-based computer is serving as a VPN server, you must use Windows Server 2008 NAT role.

EXERCISE 11.5

Configuring ICS

The ICS host computer provides a connection through the second network adapter to the existing TCP/IP network. Log on as member of the Administrators group to set up the ICS host computer.

1. Click **Start**.
2. Click **Control Panel.**
3. Click **Network Connections**.

4. Right-click **Local Area Connection** (for the installed network card) and rename it "Internet Connection."

5. In the **Network and Dial-up Connections** dialog box, two connections are displayed (for different network adapters): the Internet Connection and Local Area Connection.

6. Right-click **Internet Connection** and then click **Properties**.

7. Click the **General** tab, and then verify that **Client for Microsoft Networks** and **Internet Protocol** (TCP/IP) are displayed.

8. Click the **Advanced** tab, and then click to select the **Enable Internet Connection Sharing for this Connection** check box.

NOTE

Make sure that firewall software or other Internet-sharing software from any third-party manufacturer has been removed.

---

9. Click **OK**

Remote Access Protocols

Setting up remote access servers and connections in Windows Server can be somewhat overwhelming and confusing if you don't understand the protocol configuration options available to you. You have a number of remote access protocol options to choose from, and deciding which ones to use will be based on the exact task and functionality you seek to accomplish. This will depend on your system configurations, your hardware, you're your communications capabilities.

You must try to organize and make sense of all these options. To start, let's take a look at the categories of protocols and the advantages and disadvantages of the various protocols within each one.

Microsoft's PPTP is most commonly used for voluntary authenticated and encrypted tunneling between dial-up clients and a PPTP Network Server located just inside the customer's network.

The PPTP Network Server authenticates the tunnel user with Challenge-Handshake Authentication Protocol (CHAP) and negotiates data compression and encryption as dictated by security policies. PPTP offers payload privacy, but does not encrypt session control traffic.

The L2TP consolidates the best of other protocols within a single standard. L2TP Access Concentrators terminate PPP Link Control Protocol (LCP) and carry out dial session authentication. L2TP can be used with a separate LAC at the ISP NAS, or with a LAC Client on the end-user's PC. L2TP Network Servers terminate PPP NCP, provide routing and bridging for the PPP session, and make the user appear directly connected to the "home" network.

L2TP is transparent in compulsory mode, multiprotocol support, and leaving authentication, authorization, and addressing responsibility within the customer's network. L2TP is a tunneling protocol, not an encryption protocol. If customers require data confidentiality, you'll need to run L2TP over IPSec.

Features have been added to the IP protocol to provide greater security for IP packets that transit public networks. The Encapsulating Security Payload (ESP) encrypts packets, usually by encapsulating a private IP packet inside an outer public IP packet. Another standard known as Internet Security Association and Key Management Protocol (ISAKMP) can be used for strong authentication of tunnel endpoints and key management. Collectively, these extensions are called IPSec.

IPSec supports Site-to-Site VPNs by building security associations between gateways at the edge of customer networks. Every packet that enters or leaves each network will be tunneled according to customer-defined policy, with filtering down to the individual host and port level. IPSec-compatible encryption and packet authentication algorithms support a wide variety of security policies, allowing customers to strike their own balance between security and performance.

IPSec can also be used to support Remote Access VPNs, by tunneling from an individual host to a security gateway, topologically similar to voluntary PPTP tunnels. IP packets sent by an IPSec host to a protected network are encrypted and delivered to the security gateway for that network. IP packets to public destinations are sent without the addition of IPSec protocols.

Windows Server 2008 has offered many new upgrades. Their newest to the realm of VPNs is the addition of SSTP, which is the latest alternative form of VPN tunnel. SSTP is an application-layer protocol. It uses a synchronous communication, which works in unilateral motion between two programs allowing a constant exchange and comparison of data. By doing this, it allows for many application endpoints over a single network connection. This allows for a very efficient usage of the communication resources that are available to that network. SSTP is based on SSL as opposed to IPSec or PPTP, and thereby uses port 443 for traffic.

New & Noteworthy...

Microsoft's Development Direction of SSL

When developing SSTP to be a viable and improved VPN tunneling protocol, Microsoft had many available resources to build upon. Two of the most commonly used were IPSec and SSL. Both had benefits, but it took much consideration to determine which would provide the better ground work to allow the most benefits. At the conclusion of their decision-making process, SSL was chosen as the basis for the SSTP, which is used in Windows Server 2008.

There are many obvious reasons for this choice. Most become apparent when you examine the downsides of IPSec. IPSec main function is supporting site-to-site VPN connectivity and no roaming. SSL was obviously a better base for SSTP development, as it supports roaming. Besides the obvious, there are several other reasons for not basing SSTP on IPSec:

- Strong authentication is not required.

- User Clients must be present.

- No sense of conformity in regards to support and coding from one vendor to the next.

- No Default non-IP protocols.

- Remote users attempting to connect via a site with limited IP addresses would cause problems due to the inherent site-to-site secure connections design.

With SSL, VPN static IP addresses are not required, clients are unnecessary in most cases, and since connections are made via a browser over the Internet, the default connection protocol is TCP/IP. This makes connections transparent to the user. Microsoft hopes that this sort of forethought in their development will ensure more user friendly interactions when using SSTP in Windows Server2008.

SSTP allows for the passage of traffic through firewalls that would normally inhibit PPTP and L2TP/IPSec traffic. SSTP is able to incorporate PPP traffic over the SSL channel of the HTTPS protocol. By using PPP, SSTP can utilize well-protected authentication methods such as EAP-TLS. By involving HTTPS, traffic is directed and flows through TCP port 443. This port is commonly used for Web access, which is why the SSTP is so versatile compared to past VPN protocols. Key negotiation, integrity checking, and encryption are handled via SSL VPN. This also allows for transport-level security when dealing with these functions.

TEST DAY TIP

As you can see there are many similarities between the new features available in Windows Server 2008 and previous versions of Windows Server. Try to be certain of the distinguishing elements that separate the two. Although two features may have similar uses and applications, their exact functionality may be very different.

For example, you should remember that although STTP may be closely related to SSL, no cross comparison can be made between the two. You should be sure not to confuse the two, as SSTP is only a tunneling protocol, unlike SSL.

SSL uses a cryptographic system. This system uses two encrypted keys to secure data. One is the public key and the other is the private key. The public key is recognizable to everyone and the private key can only be identified by the recipient. A secure connection between a client and a server is created by this method of encryption. You can thereby establish secure remote access from almost any Internet connected to a Web browser, which was not possible using traditional VPN. Thanks to this new method, there are not issues with instability in connection and loss of service due to connectivity issues for the client. The added bonus is that with SSL VPN, the session is completely secured.

Remember that while SSTP is a strong method for client-to-site VPN connections, it is not designed for site-to-site VPN connections. Let's review the assets that SSTP can provide to you and your organization:

- SSTP takes advantage of HTTPS to establish a secure and stable connection.

- The SSTP (VPN) tunnel will function over Secure-HTTP. This means that Web proxies, firewalls, and NAT routers present on the path between clients and servers will no longer block VPN connections.

- Port blocking is greatly decreased.

- Clients will be able to connect from anywhere on the Internet.

- SSTP is built into Windows Server 2008, providing higher compatibility.

- SSTP allows simpler training procedures, because the end-user VPN controls are identical to previous versions.

- The SSTP-based VPN tunnel will directly plug into the current interfaces for Microsoft VPN client and server software.

- IPv6 is fully supported.

- It takes advantage of the new integrated network access protection support for client health-check.

- MS RRAS client and server are strongly supported, allowing for two-factor authentication capabilities.

- VPN coverage is expanded from limited points of access to almost any Internet connection.

- The use of port 443 for SSL encapsulation.

- Acts as a full network VPN solution over all applications.

- NAP integration.

- SSL tunnel is created in s single session.

- Stronger forced authentication process than other methods like IPSec.

- Supports non-IP protocols.

- No additional costs or hard-to-configure hardware firewalls that do not support Active Directory integration and integrated two-factor authentication.

Now that we know the benefits of using Secure Socket Protocol, lets examine the data flow for an SSTP-based VPN connection in action:

If a user on a computer running Windows Server 2008 initiates an SSTP-based VPN connection, the following occurs:

1. A TCP connection between the STTP client and the SSTP server is made. This happens between a dynamically allocated TCP port on the SSTP client. The same connection occurs on the TCP port 443 on the SSTP server.

2. An SSL Client-Hello message is sent by the SSTP client. This Client-Hello Message acts as an invitation from the SSTP client to create an SSL session with the SSTP server.

3. The SSTP server responds by providing and sending its computer certificate to the SSTP client.

4. The computer certificate is validated by the STTP client.

5. Next, the STTP determines the encryption method for the SSL session.

6. Then the SSTP Client creates an SSL session key.

7. This SSL session key is then encrypted with the public key of the SSTP server's certificate.

EXAM WARNING

SSL uses a cryptographic system, which uses two encrypted keys to secure data. One is the public key and the other is the private key. The public key is recognizable to everyone and the private can only be identified by the recipient. A secure connection between a client and a server is created by this method of encryption. You can thereby establish secure remote access from almost any Internet-connected Web browser, which was not possible using traditional VPN.

Please remember that while SSTP is a strong method for client-to-site VPN connection, it is not designed for site-to-site VPN connections. If you need a site-to-site VPN connection, you should use a traditional VPN.

---

8. The SSL session key is then sent as the encrypted form of the SSL session key to the SSTP server.

9. The SSTP server decrypts the encrypted SSL session key with the private key of its computer certificate. Now any further communication between the SSTP client and the SSTP server will be encrypted with the negotiated encryption method and SSL session key.

10. The SSTP client sends an HTTP over SSL request message to the SSTP server.

11. The SSTP client attempts to negotiate for an SSTP tunnel with the SSTP server.

12. The SSTP client attempts to negotiate a PPP connection with the SSTP server. All user credentials are negotiated at this time with a PPP authentication method. Also during the negotiation they configure settings for IPv4 or IPv6 traffic.

13. Once negotiation is completed, the SSTP client begins sending IPv4 or IPv6 traffic over the PPP link.

Configuring & Implementing...

Taking Advantage of Virtual Networking

Microsoft Windows 2008 has a variety of new networking options available to you, but it also offers other peripheral roles that can helpful in a variety. One huge trend in today's networking is virtual networking. This allows you to more efficiently economize and consolidate the number of physical machines by replacing them with virtual ones. While testing out different aspects of networking in this chapter such as creating a VPN using SSTP protocol, it will be helpful to you to work in real-world testing environments. Normally, in previous editions of Windows, this would require many physical computers to create an accurate test case or a program like Virtual PC 2007 to simulate this.

Using the Hyper V role of Windows Server 2008, you can create the same test scenario with only one or two physical computers and still accurately test your deployment cases. This will allow you to more effectively test a variety of VPN configurations using only a limited number of physical machines. It will also familiarize you with other aspects of the Windows Server 2008 roles that are available to you as an administrator, and also gain more proficiency with the operating system (OS).

By utilizing all of the new features of Windows Server 2008 in unison, you can take advantage of the full power of real-world networking benefits that Windows Server 2008 has to offer your organization. This will also present the option of virtualization and the benefits it can bring to your organization.

EXERCISE 11.6

CONFIGURING SSTP ON WINDOWS SERVER 2008

Now that we understand how STTP using the SSL VPN works, let's go over the steps required to set up an SSTP connection in Windows Server 2008.

1. On **SSTP client**, click on **Network and Sharing Center**.
2. Click **Manage network connections**.

3. Double-click the **VPN Connection**, and then click on **Properties.**

4. Click on the **Networking** tab and find the **Type of VPN** drop-down list.

5. Select **Secure Socket Tunneling Protocol** (SSTP) from the **Type of VPN** drop-down list.

6. Click **OK.**

7. Click **Connect** on the **Connect VPN Connection** dialog box. The Client will then connect to the VPN server using the SSTP connection.

Virtual Private Networks

VPNs use public wires to join nodes to create a network. This network allows the user to create their own private networks for the transfer of data. There are a large number of security systems at play within the VPN, such as encryption and other security measures. This makes certain that no data is intercepted by unauthorized users. VPN has been used successfully for several years, but has recently encountered problems. Many organizations have widely increased the number of roaming users that have access to their networks. Because of this, other methods have been in development to accomplish this same type of access. IPSec and SSL VPN are two such methods commonly in use by many organizations.

VPNs typically use an encrypted tunnel that keeps data confidential within the tunnel. By doing this, when the tunnel routes through typical NAT paths, the VPN tunnel fails to remain active and stops working completely. VPNs will most often connect a node directly to an endpoint. If the node and the endpoint have the same internal LAN address and NAT is involved, many problems and complications will arise causing a lack of service to your end client.

TEST DAY TIP

Be familiar with all of the tools available to you in Server Manager. Windows Server 2008 provides a number of roles and snap-in features that help immensely with your job as an administrator. When you are prepping the day of the exam, make sure you can identify and locate roles like RRAS and Network protection and Access roles. This will help you gain a better understanding of the design structure for Windows Server 2008, and help you to apply what you know on your exam.

Installing and Configuring a SSL VPN Server

Now that you have an idea of how SSTP and new SSL VPNs work, we will explain how to use the RRAS panel to install and configure a VPN. Before beginning, be sure that you have a clean version of Windows Server 2008 installed. Also, you must not have RRAS installed yet to set up the SSL VPN. Before installing RRAS, you must request a machine certificate server.

The VPN server needs a machine certificate to create the SSL VPN connection with the SSL VPN client computer. The name on the certificate should match the name that the VPN client will use to connect to the SSL VPN gateway computer. This means that you will need to create a public DNS entry for the name on the certificate, so that it will resolve to the external IP address on the VPN server or the IP address of a NAT device in front of the VPN server, as described earlier in this chapter. This will forward the connection to the SSL VPN server.

EXERCISE 11.7

REQUESTING AND INSTALLING THE MACHINE CERTIFICATE ON THE SSL VPN SERVER

Perform the following steps to request and install the machine certificate on the SSL VPN server:

1. Open **Server Manager**. Expand the **Roles** node in the left pane.

2. Expand the **Web Server** (IIS) node. Click on **Internet Information Services (IIS) Manager**.

3. Locate the **Internet Information Services Manager** console and find the pane to the right of the left pane, and click on the **name** of the server you are using.

4. Click on the **Server Certificates** icon in the right pane of the IIS console.

5. In the right pane of the console, click the **Create Domain Certificate** link.

6. Fill out the information on the **Distinguished Name Properties** page. Remember to correctly enter the **Common Name** entry as mentioned previously. This name is the name that VPN clients will use to connect to the VPN server. You will need a public Domain Name Server (DNS) entry for this name, so that it resolves either to the external interface of the VPN server, or the public address

of a NAT device in front of the VPN server (e.g., the common name *sstp.msexamfirewall.org*). The VPN client computer should have Host files created so that it can resolve this name later.

7. When finished click **Next**.

8. On the **Online Certification Authority** page, find and click the **Select** button.

9. In the **Select Certification Authority** dialog box, click the name of the **Enterprise CA** and click **OK**.

10. Enter a name for the certificate in the Friendly name text box (e.g., the name SSLVPN).

11. Click **Finish** on the Online Certification Authority page.

When the Wizard completes its work, you will see the certificate appear in the IIS console:

12. Double click on the **certificate** and you can see the common name in the "Issued to" section, and that we have a private key that corresponds to the certificate.

13. Click **OK** to close the Certificate dialog box.

Once you have a certificate, you can then install the RRAS Server Role as described earlier in this chapter. It is critical that you install the certificate first, before you install the RRAS Server Role. If you do not, you will have to use a fairly complex command-line routine to bind the certificate to the SSL VPN listener.

To set up a VPN, proceed with the following steps. Once RRAS is installed, you must first enable RRAS.

Perform the following steps to enable the RRAS service:

1. Open Server Manager and expand the **Roles** node in the left pane of the console.

2. Expand the **Network Policy and Access Services** node and click on the **Routing and Remote Access** node. Right-click on the **Routing and Remote Access** node and click **Configure and Enable Routing and Remote Access**, as shown in Figure 11.7.

Figure 11.7 Configure and Enable Routing and Remote Access

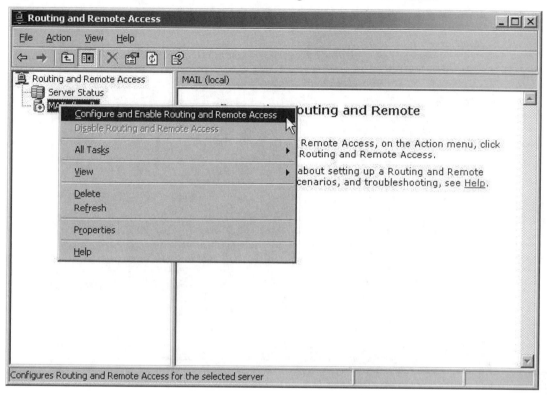

3. Click **Next** on the **Welcome to the Routing and Remote Access Server Setup** Wizard page.

4. On the **Configuration** page shown in Figure 11.8, select the **Virtual private network (VPN) access and NAT** option.

5. Click **Next**.

Figure 11.8 Routing and Remote Access Server Setup Wizard

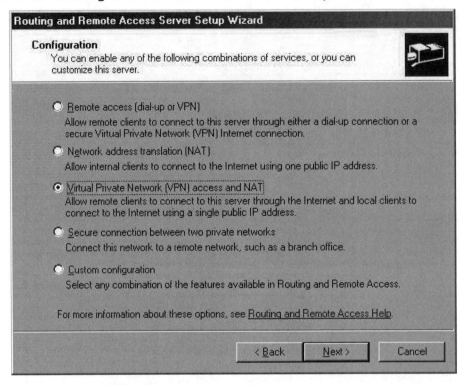

6. On the **VPN Connection** page, select the **NIC** in the **Network interfaces** section that represents the external interface of the VPN server.

7. Click **Next**.

8. On the **IP Address Assignment** page, select the **Automatically** option if you have a DHCP server. If you do not have a DHCP server, select the **From a specified range of addresses** option and provide a list of addresses that VPN clients would use when connecting to the network through the VPN gateway.

9. Click **Next**.

10. On the **Managing Multiple Remote Access Servers** page, select **No, use Routing and Remote Access to authenticate connection requests**. Use this option when there is no NPS or RADIUS server available. If the VPN server is a member of the domain, you can authenticate users using domain accounts. If the VPN server is not a member of the domain, then only local accounts on the VPN server can be used.

11. Click **Next**.

12. Review the summary information on the **Completing the Routing and Remote Access Server Setup** Wizard page for accuracy and click **Finish**.

13. Click **OK** in the Routing and Remote Access dialog box telling you that relaying of DHCP messages requires a DHCP relay agent.

14. Expand the **Routing and Remote Access node** and then click on the **Ports** node. In the middle pane you will see that WAN Miniport connections for SSTP are now available.

EXAM WARNING

There are a number of server types that can be set up in a given real-world situation. It is up to you to determine which suits your clients' needs the best. For the exam, however, you must be aware of what type of information concerning what type of access is being asked of you. Remember that RRAS and NPS are two different means of setting up many of the available services. Be sure to double check the type of server information the question is calling for.

Inbound/Outbound Filters

Windows Server 2008 features a variety of inbound and outbound features that you will need to be able to implement for your exam. The old version of Windows Firewall has been upgraded and is now called Windows Firewall with Advanced Security (WFAS).

This new version of WFAS has a number of advanced components that will help with you security needs.

- **New GUI Interface** MMC is a snap-in that is available to help configure the advanced firewall.

- **Bi-directional Filters** Unlike past versions of Windows Firewall, WFAS filters both outbound traffic as well as inbound traffic.

- **Better IPSec Compatibility** WFAS rules and IPSec encryption configurations are both integrated into the same singular interface.

- **Enhanced Rules Generation** Using WFAS, you can create firewall rules for Windows Active Directory service accounts and groups. This includes source/destination IP addresses, protocol numbers, source and destination TCP/User Datagram Protocol (UDP) ports, Internet Control Message Protocol (ICMP), IPv6 traffic, and interface all on the Windows Server.

With the addition to having inbound and outbound filters, the WFAS has advanced rules configuration.

The first concern of any server administrator in using a host-based firewall is "What if it prevents critical server infrastructure applications from functioning? While that is always a possibility with any security measure, WFAS will automatically configure new rules for any new server roles that are added to the server. However, if you run any non-Microsoft applications on your server that need inbound network connectivity, you will have to create a new rule for that type of traffic.

By using the advanced windows firewall, you can better secure your servers from attack and secure your servers from attacking others, and really nail down what traffic is going in and out of your servers.

Configuring Remote Authentication Dial-In User Service (RADIUS) Server

RADIUS is protocol used for controlling access to network resources by authenticating, authorizing, and accounting for access, and is referred to as an AAA protocol. RADIUS is the unofficial industry standard for this type of access. It is more common today than ever before, being employed by ISPs, large corporations that need to manage access to the Internet, and also internal networks that operate across a large variety of access providing technologies such as modems, DSL, wireless and VPNs. To better understand what RADIUS does, let's try to understand each of its required functions as an AAA protocol.

- **Authentication** The server seeking access sends a request to NAS. The NAS then creates and sends a RADIUS Access Request to the RADIUS Server. This request acts as an authorization to grant access. Typically, a user name and password or some other means of establishing identity is requested for this process, which must then be provided by the user seeking access. The request will also contain other means of verification that the NAS collected, such as physical location of the user and/or the phone number or network address of the user.

- **Authorization** Upon receipt of the request, the RADIUS server processes the new request for access. Most times, the RADIUS server will have access to a list of accounts or be able to query an external database to cross reference the provided information on the user. RADIUS will verify the user information and, if configured to do so, other information such as the user's network address or phone number that it has access to against the information it has stored. Based on the result of the check, the RADIUS server will respond with one of three responses to the NAS responsible for enforcing the access decision of the RADIUS server:

- **Access Accept** This result indicates that the user is granted access. The terms of access are based on the information the RADIUS server has on file, and is conveyed to the NAS, which allows the conditional access based on these terms. A variety of terms could be stipulated, such as time restrictions, bandwidth restrictions, security access control restrictions, and others.

- **Access Challenge** This requests further verification from the user before access will be granted. These types of verification can include a secondary password, PIN, or token card challenge response.

- **Access Reject** This indicates that there has been a failure to prove the user's identity or that their account is inactive or unusable. This means that the user has been completely denied access to all network resources requested.

- **Accounting** If network access is granted to the user by the NAS based on the authentication and authorization phases, NAS then sends an *Accounting Start* request to the RADIUS Server to indicate that the user has begun accessing the network. These types of records will contain a variety of information concerning the identity, point of attachment, and unique session ID for the user. Active session may have periodic updates sent out called *Interim Accounting* records. These records may update the session duration and information on current data usage. When the user exits the network and the access point (AP) is again closed, the NAS will send a final *Accounting Stop* record to the RADIUS server. This informs it of the final information related to the user's network access.

NAS devices communicate with the RADIUS via the link-layer protocol, using PPP for example. The RADIUS server responds using the RADIUS protocol. The RADIUS server authenticates using security schemes such as PAP, CHAP or EAP.

Remember that just because the user is authenticated, it does not give him or her total access to all resources the network has to offer, so the RADIUS server will often check that the user is authorized to use the network service requested. There are a number of specifications that access can be based on once authenticated. These include:

- The specific IP Address that will be assigned to the user.

- The total amount of time that the user is permitted to remain connected.

- Limited access or priority based access to certain resources.

- L2TP parameters.

- Virtual Local Area Network (VLAN) parameters.

- Other Quality of Service (QoS) parameters.

In previous incarnations of Windows Server 2003, Internet Authentication Service (IAS) was Microsoft's implementation of a RADIUS server and proxy. IAS performed centralized connection AAA Protocol for many types of network access, including wireless and VPN connections.

For Windows Server 2008, Microsoft has replaced IAS with a new feature called NPS. NPS is the Microsoft implementation of a RADIUS server and proxy in Windows Server 2008, and promises to be even simpler to use than IAS. You will need to know how to set up a RADIUS server using NPS. Begin by installing NPS and setting up your RADIUS Server.

EXERCISE 11.8

INSTALLING NPS AND SETTING UP YOUR RADIUS SERVER

1. Open **Server Manager** and click on the **Add Roles.**

2. Choose the **Network Policy and Access Services** shown in Figure 11.9, and review the overview screen (see Figure 11.10).

Figure 11.9 Choosing the NPS Role

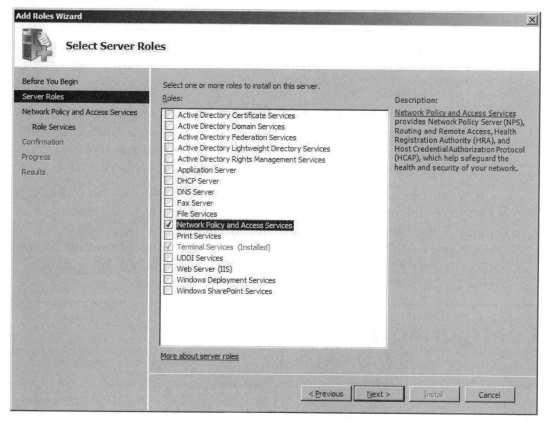

Figure 11.10 Overview Screen on NPS

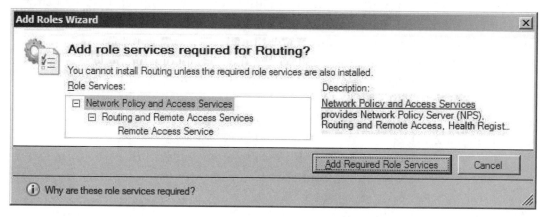

3. Select the **Network Policy Service** role. You may notice that the Network Policy Service is actually the RADIUS server that you are used to seeing with previous versions of Windows Server in IAS.

4. Click **Next**. You will see a final confirmation screen, as seen in Figure 11.10.

5. Click **Install**.

6. Once the software has been loaded, click on **Network Policy Server** under administrator tools. You will see that the RADIUS Client and Server Tabs are available and can be configured according to your needs by right-clicking on them and selecting **Properties**.

NPS can be used as a RADIUS proxy to provide the routing of RADIUS messages between RADIUS clients (access servers) and RADIUS servers that perform user AAA for the connection attempt. When used as a RADIUS proxy, NPS is a central switching or routing point through which RADIUS access and accounting messages flow. NPS records information about forwarded messages in an accounting log.

Configuring Wireless Access

Increased use of laptop computers and other wireless access devices within an enterprise along with an increase in worker mobility, have fuelled the demand for wireless networks in recent years. Up until recently, wireless technology was plagued with incompatibility issues and vendor-specific products. The technology was slow, expensive, and reserved for mobile situations or hostile environments where cabling was impractical or impossible. In recent years, the maturing of industry standards has caused a leveling point. This is thanks to industry-enforced compatibility standards and the deployment of lightweight wireless networking hardware. All of these factors have allowed wireless technology to come of age in the modern company.

Wireless networking hardware requires the use of technology that deals with radio frequencies as well as data transmission. The most widely used standard is 802.11 produced by the IEEE. This is a standard defining all aspects of radio frequency wireless networking. There have been several amendments to the 802.11 standard, the most recent being 802.11i.

Many Wireless networks use an AP to gain connectivity. In this type of network, the AP acts like a hub, providing connectivity for the wireless computers. It can connect the wireless LAN to a wired LAN, allowing wireless computer access to LAN resources. This includes such resources as file servers or existing internet connectivity. This type of wireless network is said to run in infrastructure mode.

An ad hoc or peer-to-peer wireless network is one in which a number of computers each equipped with a wireless networking interface card, can connect without the use of an AP. Each computer communicates with all of the other wireless-enabled computers directly. This allows for the sharing of files and printer services, but may not be able to access wired LAN resources. The exception to this is if one of the computers acts as a bridge or AP to the wired LAN using special software.

As you might be familiar with in Windows Server 2003, Wireless Auto Configuration will attempt to pair up configured preferred wireless networks with the wireless networks that are broadcasting their network name. If no such available networks exist that match a preferred wireless network, Wireless Auto Configuration will then send a number of probe requests to attempt to find a match. These are to try and determine if the preferred networks in the ordered list are non-broadcast networks. The end result of this total process should be that broadcast networks are connected to before non-broadcast networks. This even includes situations where a non-broadcast network is higher in the preferred list than a broadcast network. A big downside of this method, however, is that a Windows XP or Windows Server 2003 wireless client has to advertise its list of preferred wireless networks when sending probe requests. This leaves clients vulnerable while sending these probe requests.

Windows Server 2008 presents a better option. By configuring the wireless networks as broadcast, the wireless network names will be included in the Beacon frames sent by the wireless AP. If you set the wireless network as non-broadcast, the Beacon frame contains a wireless network name. This name is set to NULL, which results in Wireless Auto Configuration attempting connection to the wireless networks in the preferred network list order. This is regardless of whether they are broadcast or non-broadcast. By explicitly marking wireless networks as broadcast or non-broadcast, Windows Server 2008 wireless clients only send probe requests for non-broadcast wireless networks. This reduces wireless client side vulnerability and enhances security.

Previously, if a preferred wireless network could not be connected to and the wireless client was configured in a way that prevented automatic connections not in the preferred list by default, then Wireless Auto Configuration would create a random wireless network name. Then it would place the wireless network adapter in infrastructure mode. The random wireless network does not have a security configuration, making it possible for all kinds of malicious users to connect to the wireless client, thereby using the random wireless network name.

For computers running Windows Server 2008 that use updated wireless drivers designed for Windows Vista, Wireless Auto Configuration will remove this vulnerability by parking the wireless network adapter in a passive listening mode. A parked wireless device does not send probe request frames for a random wireless network name. It also does not allow for any other names, so malicious users cannot connect to the wireless client.

If you are using a wireless network adapter driver that was designed for Windows XP, computers running Windows Vista or Windows Server 2008 will use the behavior of the Wireless Client Update for Windows XP with Service Pack 2 (a random wireless network name with a security configuration).

Windows Server 2008 troubleshooting wireless connections is made much easier through the following features:

- **Network Diagnostics Framework** The Network Diagnostics Framework is an extensible architecture that provides users with a means to recover from and troubleshoot problems with network connections. In the case of a failed wireless connection, Network Diagnostics Framework will give the user the option to identify and correct the problem. Wireless support for the Network Diagnostics Framework tries to discover the source of the failed connection and will automatically fix the problem. Also based on your security considerations, it can be made to prompt the user to make the appropriate configuration change themselves.

- For a failed wireless connection attempt, the wireless components of Windows Server 2008 now records detailed information about the connection attempt in the Windows event log. Support professionals can now access and use these records to perform troubleshooting tasks, and attempt to resolve the problem quickly if the wireless diagnostics either could not resolve the problem or when it could resolve the problem, but the problem cannot be fixed by changing wireless client settings. This will cut down on the time needed to resolve wireless connection support problems. These can also be automatically collected by network administrators using Microsoft Operations Manager, to be analyzed for patterns and wireless infrastructure design changes.

- You can now gain access to in-depth information about the computer's state and wireless components in Windows, and their interaction when the problem occurred. This can be done using information from *wireless diagnostics tracing* in Windows Server 2008. To use wireless diagnostics tracing, you must start tracing, reproduce the problem, stop tracing, and then collect the tracing report. To view the tracing report, in the console tree of the Reliability and Performance Monitor snap-in open **Reports | System | Wireless Diagnostics**.

Windows Server 2003 and Windows XP do not have a command-line interface that allows you to configure the wireless settings that are available from the wireless dialog boxes in the Network Connections folder, or through the Wireless Network (IEEE 802.11) Policies Group Policy settings. Command-line configuration of wireless settings can help deployment of wireless networks in the following situations:

- **Automated script support for wireless settings without using Group Policy Wireless Network (IEEE 802.11) Policies Group Policy settings only apply in an Active Directory domain.** For an environment without Active Directory or a Group Policy infrastructure, a script that automates the configuration of wireless connections can be run either manually or automatically, such as part of the login script.

- **Bootstrapping of a wireless client onto the protected organization's wireless network.** A wireless client computer that is not a member of the domain cannot connect to the organization's protected wireless network. Furthermore, computers are not able to join the domain until a successful connection has occurred to the organization's secure wireless network. A command-line script provides a method to connect to the organization's secure wireless network to join the domain.

In Windows Server 2008, you can use **Netsh** commands in the **netsh wlan** context to do the following:

- Save all wireless client settings in a named profile including general settings (the types of wireless networks to access), 802.11 settings (SSID, type of authentication, type of data encryption), and 802.1X authentication settings (EAP types and their configuration).

- Specify the list of allowed and denied wireless network names.

- Specify the order of preferred wireless networks.

- Display a wireless client's configuration.

- Remove the wireless configuration from a wireless client.

- Migrate a wireless configuration setting between wireless clients.

Many applications are not network aware, resulting in customer confusion and developer overhead. For example, an application cannot automatically adjust its behavior based on the currently attached network and conditions. Users might have to reconfigure application settings depending on the network to which they are attached (their employer's private network, the user's home network, the Internet).

To remove the configuration burden, application developers can use low–level Windows APIs, data constructs, and perhaps even probing the network themselves to determine the current network and adjust their application's behavior accordingly.

To provide an operating system infrastructure to allow application developers to more easily reconfigure application behavior based on the currently attached network, the Network Awareness APIs in Windows Server 2008 make network information available to applications and enables them to easily and effectively adapt to these changing environments. The Network Awareness APIs allow applications to obtain up-to-date network information and location change notification.

Let's take a look at how to deal with the variety of elements available with Windows Server 2008 in regards to wireless network access and how they will be applied to your exam.

Set Service Identifier (SSID)

The Service Set Identifier (SSID) is a 32-character unique identifier attached to the header of packets that are sent over a Wireless Local Area Network (WLAN). The SSID acts as a password when a mobile device tries to connect to the BSS. The SSID differentiates one WLAN from another. This way all APs and all devices attempting to connect to a specific WLAN must use the same SSID in order to succeed. No device will be permitted to join the BSS unless it can provide the unique SSID. SSID is not a security measure, because it can very easily be sniffed due to being stored in plain text.

In Windows Server 2008, an additional wireless network configuration setting has been added that can indicate whether a wireless network is broadcast or non-broadcast. This setting can be configured locally through the "Manually connect to a wireless network" dialog box, the properties of the wireless network, or through Group Policy. The "Connect even if the network is not broadcasting" check box determines whether the wireless network broadcasts or does not broadcast its SSID. Once selected, Wireless Auto Configuration sends probe requests to discover if the non-broadcast network is in range.

Configured wireless networks are now openly marked as broadcast or non-broadcast. Windows Server 2008-based wireless clients only send probe requests for wireless networks that are configured for automatic connection and as non-broadcast.

This method allows Windows Server 2008-based wireless clients to detect non-broadcast networks when they are in range. Therefore, even though they are not broadcasting the name of their wireless network, they will appear in the list of available wireless networks when they are in range. The wireless client detects whether the automatically connected, non-broadcast networks are in range based on the probe request responses. Then Wireless Auto Configuration attempts to connect to the wireless network in the preferred networks list order. This is regardless of whether they are configured as broadcast or non-broadcast. By only sending probe requests for automatically connected, non-broadcast networks, Windows Server 2008-based wireless clients reduce the number of situations in which they disclose their wireless network configuration.

You can also configure manually connected, non-broadcast wireless networks. In doing so, you can control exactly when to send probe requests. Manually connected, non-broadcast wireless networks are always displayed in the list of available networks, allowing users to initiate connections as needed.

Despite the improvements in non-broadcast network support in Windows Server 2008, Microsoft recommends against using non-broadcast wireless networks.

Wi-Fi Protected Access (WPA)

Wi-Fi Protected Access (WPA) was designed to provide a much higher level of security for wireless users than existing WEP standards provide. The WPA specification makes allowances both for network-based authentication for corporate networks, and for a special home mode for use in a SOHO or home-user environment. WPA is capable of interoperating with WEP devices, although in cases of interoperability, the default security for the entire wireless infrastructure reverts to the WEP standard. WPA's network-based authentication can make use of existing authentication technologies such as RADIUS servers, so adding the secure technology that WPA represents won't disrupt existing network infrastructures too much. Windows Server 2008 offers full support and configuration for WPA through the Wireless Group Policy settings.

TEST DAY TIP

Remember to know your hardware. The installed wireless network adapter must be able to support the wireless LAN or wireless security standards that you require. For example, Windows Server supports configuration options for the Wi-Fi Protected Access (WPA) and Wi-Fi Protected Access 2 (WPA2) security standards. However, if the wireless network adapter does not support WPA2, you cannot enable or configure WPA2 security options.

Wi-Fi Protected Access 2 (WPA2)

Windows Server 2008 includes built-in support to configure WPA2 authentication options with both the standard profile (locally configured preferred wireless networks), and the domain profile with Group Policy settings. WPA2 is a product certification available through the Wi-Fi Alliance that certifies wireless equipment as being compatible with the IEEE 802.11i standard. WPA2 in Windows Server 2008 supports both WPA2-Enterprise (IEEE 802.1X authentication) and WPA2-Personal (pre-shared key authentication) modes of operation.

Windows Server 2008 also includes full support for WPA2 for an ad hoc mode wireless network including the *Fast Roaming* settings. Fast roaming is an advanced capability of WPA2 wireless networks that allow wireless clients to more quickly roam from one wireless AP to another by using pre-authentication and pair wise master key (PMK) caching in infrastructure mode. With Windows Server 2008, you can configure this feature using the Wireless Group Policy settings.

Ad Hoc vs. Infrastructure Mode

To set up an ad hoc wireless network, each wireless adapter must be configured for ad hoc mode versus the alternative infrastructure mode. In addition, all wireless adapters on the ad hoc network must use the same SSID and the same channel number.

An ad hoc network tends to feature a small group of devices all in very close proximity to each other.

Performance suffers as the number of devices grows, and a large ad hoc network quickly becomes difficult to manage. Ad hoc networks cannot bridge to wired LANs or to the Internet without installing a special-purpose gateway.

Ad hoc networks make sense when needing to build a small, all-wireless LAN quickly and spend the minimum amount of money on equipment. Ad hoc networks also work well as a temporary fallback mechanism if normally available infrastructure mode gear (APs or routers) stop functioning.

Most installed wireless LANs today utilize infrastructure mode that requires the use of one or more APs. With this configuration, the AP provides an interface to a distribution system (e.g., Ethernet), which enables wireless users to utilize corporate servers and Internet applications.

As an optional feature, however, the 802.11 standard specifies ad-hoc mode, which allows the radio network interface card (NIC) to operate in what the standard refers to as an independent basic service set (IBSS) network configuration. With an IBSS, APs are not required. User devices communicate directly with each other in a peer-to-peer manner.

Ad hoc mode allows users to form a wireless LAN with no assistance or preparation. This allows clients to share documents such as presentation charts and spreadsheets by switching their NICs to ad hoc mode to form a small wireless LAN within their meeting room. Through ad hoc mode, you can easily transfer the file from one laptop to another. With any of these applications, there's no need to install an AP and run cables.

The ad hoc form of communications is especially useful in public-safety and search-and-rescue applications. Medical teams require fast, effective communications when attempting to find victims. They can't afford the time to run cabling and install networking hardware.

Before making the decision to use ad hoc mode, you should consider the following:

- **Cost Efficiency** Without the need to purchase or install an AP, you'll save a considerable amount of money when deploying ad hoc wireless LANs.

- **Rapid Setup Time** Ad hoc mode only requires the installation of radio NICs in the user devices. As a result, the time to set up the wireless LAN is much less than installing an infrastructure wireless LAN.

- **Better Performance Possible** The question of performance with ad hoc mode is very debatable. Performance can be higher with ad hoc mode because there is no need for packets to travel through an AP. This only applies to a small number of users, however. If you have many users, then you will have better performance by using multiple APs to separate users onto non-overlapping channels. This will help to reduce medium access contention and collisions. Also, because of a need for sleeping stations to wake up during each beacon interval, performance can be lower with ad hoc mode due to additional packet transmissions if you implement power management.

- **Limited Network Access** There is no distribution system with ad hoc wireless LANs. Because of this, users have limited effective access to the Internet and other wired network services. Ad hoc is not a good solution for larger enterprise wireless LANs where there's a strong need to access applications and servers on a wired network.

- **Difficult Network Management** Network management can become a nightmare with ad hoc networks, because of the fluidity of the network topology and lack of centralized devices. The lack of an AP makes it difficult for network managers to monitor performance, perform security audits, and manage their network. Effective network management with ad hoc wireless LANs requires network management at the user device level. This requires a significant amount of overhead packet transmission over the wireless LAN. This again disqualifies ad hoc mode away from larger, enterprise wireless LAN applications.

Infrastructure mode requires a wireless AP for wireless networking. To join the WLAN, the AP and all wireless clients must be configured to use the same SSID. The AP is then cabled to the wired network to allow wireless clients access to, for example, Internet connections or printers. Additional APs can be added to the WLAN to increase the reach of the infrastructure and support any number of wireless clients.

Compared to the alternative, ad hoc wireless networks, infrastructure mode networks offer the advantage of scalability, centralized security management, and improved reach.

The disadvantage of infrastructure wireless networks is simply the additional cost to purchase AP hardware.

Wireless Group Policy

New technology makes it easier for mobile workers to connect to hotspots or corporate LANS, by eliminating the need for manual configuration of the network connection. Enterprises can better manage guest access on their network and provide payment plans such as pay-per-use or monthly Internet access to customers, but in order to do so a strict wireless group, policy must be maintained to better control access.

Wireless network settings can be configured locally by users on client computers, or centrally. To enhance the deployment and administration of wireless networks, you need to take advantage of Group Policy. In doing so, you can create, modify, and assign wireless network policies for Active Directory clients and members of the wireless network. When you use Group Policy to define wireless network policies, you can configure wireless network connection settings, enable IEEE 802.1X authentication for wireless network connections, and specify the preferred wireless networks that clients can connect to. By default, there are no Wireless Network (IEEE 802.11) policies.

EXERCISE 11.9

CREATING A NEW POLICY

To create a new policy:

1. Right-click **Wireless Network (IEEE 802.11) Policies** in the console tree of the **Group Policy** snap-in.

2. Click **Create Wireless Network Policy**.

3. The Create Wireless Network Policy Wizard is started, from which you can configure a name and description for the new wireless network policy. You can create only a single wireless network policy for each Group Policy object.

4. To modify the settings of a **Wireless Network Policy**, double-click its name in the details pane.

5. Locate the **General** tab for the **Wireless Network Policy** you wish to update.

6. Click on the **General** tab and configure the following:

   ■ **Name** Specifies a friendly name for the wireless network policy.

   ■ **Description** Provides a description for the wireless network policy.

   ■ **Check for Policy Changes Every…** Specifies a time period in minutes, after which wireless clients that are domain members will check for changes in the wireless network policy.

   ■ **Networks to Access** Specifies the types of wireless networks with which the wireless client is allowed to create connections to. Select either **Any available network** (AP preferred), **Access point** (infrastructure) networks only, or **Computer-to-computer** (ad hoc) networks only.

7. Select the **Windows to configure wireless network settings for clients** check box if you wish to enable the Wireless Auto Configuration.

8. Click the **Automatically connect to non-preferred networks** check box if you wish to allow automatic connections to wireless networks that are not configured as preferred networks.

9. Click the **Preferred** tab of the **Wireless Network Policy** pane to configure these options:

   ■ **Networks** Displays the list of preferred wireless networks.

   ■ **Add/Edit/Remove** Creates, deletes, or modifies the settings of a preferred wireless network.

   ■ **Move Up/Move Down** Moves preferred wireless network up or down in the Networks list.

10. Click on a **Preferred Wireless Network** to open up advanced configuration options.

Summary of Exam Objectives

The main objectives covered in this chapter deal with the routing and configuration of network access in a windows Server 2008 environment. It includes all of the new features that have been introduced, as well as old technology no longer supported in this build.

This also includes the routing of network topography using static and dynamic routing, and the differences between the two. You should now be familiar with the fundamentals of routing and the protocols used in its practice. This will also include RIP and OSPF protocols. Windows Server 2008 has chosen not to support OSPF for this build.

You should be aware of the need for remote access in the business environment. This includes what features of remote access are supported such as dial up, VPNs, NAT, and RADIUS, and how each of these aspects can be configured and installed. You should also be aware of the newest VPN protocol for Windows Server 2008, SSTP, and how it compares to other VPN protocols. You should now be able to set up a SSL VPN network from start to finish using the RRAS, NPS, and NAP. Additionally, you should be aware of all of the necessary installation methods for these snap-in features.

Lastly you should have a good grasp of wireless access methods such as infrastructure mode and ad hoc mode, and be able to distinguish which of these options is best for the situation you are presented with. This also includes the security methods that are supported for wireless access in Windows Server 2008, such as WEP, WPA, and WPA2. You should be confident in how to distinguish the advantages and disadvantages of each of these methods and also be able to Group Policy for each of them.

Exam Objectives Fast Track

Configuring Routing

- ☑ **Static Routing** Describes a system that does not implement adaptive routing in its configuration. In these systems, routes through a network are defined by set paths referred to as static routes. These types of routes are inserted into the router manually by the system administrator. This is accomplished via the route command, which can be used to manipulate local routing tables.

- ☑ **Distance-vector Routing Protocol** A distance-vector routing protocol requires that a router contact and transmit to its neighbors any topology changes to the network. The frequency of this must be periodic and in most instances when a change is detected. RIP is the most popular example of this type of protocol.

☑ **Link State Protocol** The simplest explanation of link-state routing is that every node (router) is given a map of the topology of the network. This map is in graph form, and shows the connectivity of all the nodes in the network. Then each individual node calculates the next best hop from every node in the network. This information then forms the routing table for each individual node based on its calculations. No other communications occur between nodes. The most popular version of this is the OSPF.

☑ OSPF routing protocol component in Routing and Remote Access is no longer present.

Configuring Remote Access

☑ Remote access is commonly used by many companies today to allow access to a computer or a network from a remote location. Most corporations include people at branch offices, telecommuters, and people who are traveling that will need to be able to gain access to network resources. Even clients using your companies services from home need to gain access to the Internet through an ISP.

☑ Most of the major functions of Network Access and the objectives that you will be required to know for your examine, revolve around the RRAS role.

☑ Remote access policies validate a number of connection settings before authorizing the connection, including the following: Remote access permission, Group membership, Type of connection, Time of day, and Authentication methods.

☑ Small- to medium-sized organizations with private networks to access resources on the Internet or other public network, use NAT for this reasoning. They configure reusable private IPv4 addresses while the computers on the public servers are set up with globally unique IPv4 addresses. The most useful deployment of NAT is in a SOHO or a medium-sized business that uses RRAS.

☑ SSTP is the latest alternative form of VPN tunnel. SSTP is an application-layer protocol. It uses a synchronous communication, which works in unilateral motion between two programs, allowing a constant exchange and comparison of data. It allows for a very efficient usage of the communication resources available to a network. SSTP is based on SSL as opposed to IPSec or PPTP, and thereby uses port 443 for traffic.

☑ VPN uses public wires to join nodes to create a network. This network allows the user to create their own private networks for the transfer of data. There are a large number of security systems at play within the VPN, such as encryption and other security measures. This makes certain that no data is intercepted by unauthorized users.

☑ RADIUS is protocol used for controlling access to network resources by authenticating, authorizing, and accounting for access, referred to as an AAA protocol. RADIUS is the unofficial industry standard for this type of access.

☑ Windows Server 2008 Microsoft has replaced IAS with a new feature called NPS. NPS is the Microsoft implementation of a RADIUS server and proxy in Windows Server 2008, and promises to be even simpler and more secure to use than IAS.

☑ NAP, when used in unison with NPS, creates a "total system health policy enforcement platform." NAP is designed to enhance a corporate VPN. This is accomplished when clients establish a VPN session with a Windows Server 2008 system that is running the RRAS. Once a connection is made, a NPS will validate the remote system and determine the status of its health.

Configuring Wireless Access

☑ The SSID is a 32-character unique identifier attached to the header of packets that are sent over a WLAN. The SSID acts as a password when a mobile device tries to connect to the BSS. The SSID differentiates one WLAN from another. This way all access points and all devices attempting to connect to a specific WLAN must use the same SSID in order to succeed. No device will be permitted to join the BSS, unless it can provide the unique SSID. SSID is not a security measure, because it can very easily be sniffed due to being stored in plain text.

☑ In Windows Server 2008, an additional wireless network configuration setting has been added that can indicate whether a wireless network is broadcast or non-broadcast. This allows Windows Server 2008-based wireless clients to detect non-broadcast networks when they are in range. Even though they are not broadcasting the name of their wireless network, they will appear in the list of available wireless networks when they are in range.

☑ Windows Server 2003 and Windows XP do not have a command-line interface that allows you to configure the wireless settings that are available from the wireless dialog boxes in the Network Connections folder, or through the Wireless Network (IEEE 802.11) Policies Group Policy settings. Windows Server 2008 has a command-line configuration of wireless settings that can help deployment of wireless networks.

☑ WPA was designed to provide a much higher level of security for wireless users than existing WEP standards provide. The WPA specification makes allowances both for network-based authentication for corporate networks, and for a special home mode for use in a SOHO or home-user environment. WPA is capable of interoperating with WEP devices.

☑ Windows Server 2008 includes full support for WPA2 for an ad hoc mode wireless network, including the Fast Roaming settings. Fast roaming is an advanced capability of WPA2 wireless networks, that allows wireless clients to more quickly roam from one wireless AP to another by using pre-authentication and PMK caching.

☑ On wireless computer networks, ad hoc mode is a method for wireless devices to directly communicate with each other. Operating in ad hoc mode allows all wireless devices within range of each other to discover and communicate in peer-to-peer fashion without involving central access points (including those built in to broadband wireless routers).

☑ Infrastructure mode requires a wireless AP for wireless networking. To join the WLAN, the AP and all wireless clients must be configured to use the same SSID. The AP is then cabled to the wired network to allow wireless clients access to, for example, Internet connections or printers. Additional APs can be added to the WLAN to increase the reach of the infrastructure and support any number of wireless clients.

Exam Objectives
Frequently Asked Questions

Q: What is Static Routing?

A: Static routing describes a system that does not implement adaptive routing in its configuration. In these systems, routes through a network are defined by set paths referred to as static routes.

Q: What changes have been made to Windows Server 2008 in regards to routing?

A: These are the major changes present in Windows Server 2008 in regards to routing:

- BAP is no longer supported by Windows Server 2008.

- X.25 is also no longer supported.

- SLIP, an encapsulation of IP meant for use over serial ports and modems, has also been excluded due to infrequency of use. All SLIP-based connections will automatically be updated to PPP-based connections.

- ATM, which was used to encode data traffic into small fixed cells, has been discarded.

- IP over IEEE 1394 is no longer supported.

- NWLink IPX/SPX/NetBIOS Compatible Transport Protocol has been omitted.

- Services for Macintosh (SFM).

- OSPF routing protocol component in Routing and Remote Access is no longer present.

- Basic Firewall in Routing and Remote Access has been replaced with the new Windows Firewall feature.

- Static IP filter APIs for Routing and Remote Access are no longer viable, and have been replaced with Windows Filtering Platform APIs.

- SPAP, EAP-MD5-CHAP, and MS-CHAP authentication protocols for PPP-based connections are no longer used by Windows Server 2008.

Q: Is IAS still a feature of Windows Server 2008 and if not, what has replaced it?

A: In previous incarnations of Windows Server 2003 IAS snap-in was Microsoft's implementation of a RADIUS server and proxy. It was capable of performing localized connection AAA Protocol for many types of network access, including wireless and VPN connections. For Windows Server 2008, Microsoft has replaced IAS with a new snap in called NPS. NPS is the Microsoft implementation of a RADIUS server and proxy in Windows Server 2008, and promises to be even simpler to use than IAS.

Q: What is an SSL VPN?

A: An SSL VPH is a VPN that uses SSTP as its tunneling protocol. With SSLVPN, static IP addresses are not required, clients are unnecessary in most cases, and since connections are made via a browser over the Internet, the default connection protocol is TCP/IP. This makes connections transparent to the user.

Q: How is Windows Firewall with Advanced Security better than previous versions?

A: This new version of WFAS has a number of advanced components that will help with your security needs.

- **New GUI Interface** MMC is a snap-in that is available to help configure the advanced firewall.

- **Bi-directional Filters** Unlike past versions of Windows Firewall, WFAS filters both outbound traffic and inbound traffic.

- **Better IPSec Compatibility** WFAS rules and IPSec encryption configurations are both integrated into the same singular interface.

- **Enhanced Rules Generation** Using WFAS, you can create firewall rules for Windows Active Directory service accounts and groups. This includes source/destination IP addresses, protocol numbers, source and destination TCP/UDP ports, ICMP, IPv6 traffic, and interface all on the Windows Server.

Q: When does ad hoc mode work best for wireless access?

A: Ad hoc networks work best when building a small, all-wireless LAN quickly, with the lowest cost possible for equipment. Ad hoc networks also work well as a temporary fallback mechanism if normally available infrastructure mode gear (APs or routers) fail to function.

Self Test

1. You are asked by your employer to set up a LAN using Windows 2008 Server RRAS. Which of these types of routing algorithms or protocols cannot be used to organize the signal flow between the devices in the network, according to the supported Windows Server 2008 features?

   A. RIP

   B. RIP2

   C. OSPF

   D. None of the Above

2. You are asked to configure a routing table based on information gathered to optimize the network. You find that a static route with the IP destination 10.40.0.0 and the subnet mask of 255.255.0.0 requires deleting. Which of the following commands would successfully accomplish this routing change?

   A. route delete 10.40.0.0 mask 255.255.0.0

   B. route delete 10.*

   C. route change 10.40.0.0 mask 255.255.0.0 10.20.0.25

   D. route add 10.41.0.0 mask 255.255.0.0 10.20.0.1

3. You are troubleshooting a network system that has applied a number of static routes. After reviewing the information used to make these routes, you determine that an error was made while entering the routes into one of the gateways. Which of the following choices best defines your actions as a result of this error?

   A. No effect because the Static Routes act the same way dynamic ones do, and will auto correct itself.

   B. An immediate change must be made because there is no fault tolerance in regards to static routing.

   C. A system reboot should be performed to clear all persistent routes.

   D. None of the above.

4. You are responsible for upgrading and configuring a large enterprise's LAN network to Windows Server 2008. It will include a high number of physical machines and will need to be scalable for aggressive growth over the next year

as the company expands. Which of the following answers best describes why you should not use a Distance Vector Routing protocol like RIP for this task?

A. Distance Vector Routing Protocols like RIP are not scalable for large networks.

B. Distance Vector Routing Protocols like RIP are not usable for LAN configurations.

C. RIP does not understand VLSM.

D. All of the Above.

5. You are about to set up and configure a VPN for your client's communications server using Windows Server 2008. Before going through the set up and configuration process, which of the following steps need to be taken before you can configure the connection on the machine to ensure the best possible outcome?

A. Ensure a clean install of Windows Server 2008 has been installed.

B. Enter Add Roles Wizard and ensure that the RRAS role has been installed.

C. Both A and B.

D. Configure the SSTP protocols for the VPN.

6. You are working with a server running the RRAS that is configured for the Windows authentication provider. You have administered several policies from RRAS to the server. Which of the following connection settings cannot be validated before authorization occurs by the policies you set up?

A. Advanced conditions such as access server identity, access client phone number, or MAC address.

B. Remote access permission.

C. Whether user account dial-in properties are ignored.

D. None of the above.

7. Your company has begun a migration from Windows Server 2003 to Windows Server 2008 throughout their network. The RADIUS configurations for the old build were configured through IAS for Windows Server 2003. The new build for Windows Server 2008 will be using NPS. Which of the following statements would be true in regards to NPS?

A. The Connection Request Processing node still exists.

B. The Remote Access Logging folder still contains the Local File or SQL Server nodes.

C. The Network policies have replaced Remote Access policies and have been moved to the Policies node.

D. All of the Above.

8. You are the administrator of a network employing the Network Access Protection snap-in in conjunction with NAP. You have configured a set of monitoring policies in NAP for use on the network. Which of the following options will the new NAP monitor policies of Windows Server 2008 be able to accomplish?

A. Recording for compliance of each PC logging in to the system.

B. Isolation of non-compliant users.

C. Restricting access of non-compliant users.

D. None of the above.

9. You are asked to reconfigure a cheap and efficient access solution using the newly installed Windows Server 2008's RRAS role for your company. The access solution must have medium data transfer rates and reliable connection stability. The company's existing method of connection is ISDN and is utilizing the X.25 protocols for transfer. Which of the following changes in regards to Windows Server 2008 would need to be made to the existing system to make these adjustments?

A. The connection type should be downgraded, because the data transfer rate for ISDN is very unstable.

B. The connection type should be improved to Cable or DSL, because ISDN has the slowest data transfer rate.

C. The X.25 protocol needs to be changed because it is not supported by Windows Server 2008.

D. None of the above.

10. You are setting up a communications server for your small- to medium-sized organization with private networks to handle their need to access resources on the Internet and other public networks. You have installed Windows Server 2008 and are using IPv4 currently. You need more globally unique (public) IPv4 addresses to accommodate the need to access to the Internet. Which of the following solutions is the most simple and cost effective?

A. Plan a conversion of the existing setup to accommodate IPv6, because it is supported by Windows Server 2008.

B. Enable the NAT technology on the computers of the corporate network.

C. Deploy a Proxy server.

D. None of the Above.

Self Test Quick Answer Key

1. **C**   6. **D**

2. **A**   7. **C**

3. **A**   8. **A**

4. **A**   9. **C**

5. **C**   10. **B**

MCTS/MCITP
Exam 649

Network Access Protection

Exam objectives in this chapter:

■ Working with NAP

Exam objectives review:

☑ Summary of Exam Objectives

☑ Exam Objectives Fast Track

☑ Exam Objectives Frequently Asked Questions

☑ Self Test

☑ Self Test Quick Answer Key

Introduction

Microsoft for some time has been making security its main priority with the Microsoft Trustworthy Computing initiative. Starting with Microsoft Windows 2003 Server we were introduced to Network Access Quarantine Control. This feature enabled administrators to control remote access to a private network until the remote computer was validated by a script. The components necessary to deploy this solution included Microsoft Windows 2003 remote access servers, the Connection Manager Administration Kit, and Internet Authentication Service.

The most obvious problem with Network Access Quarantine Control was that it worked with only remote computers connecting to the network using Routing and Remote Access Services (RRAS). This solution left a wide gap throughout the network infrastructure for other types of clients to cause issues and management problems for network administrators.

With Microsoft Windows 2008 Server, Windows Vista, and Windows XP Service Pack 3, Microsoft has introduced Network Access Protection (NAP). NAP can control virtual private network (VPN) connections better than Network Access Quarantine Control, but NAP can also enforce policy compliance through the following types of network access or communications:

- Internet Protocol security (IPSec) protected traffic
- IEEE 802.1x authenticated network connections
- Dynamic Host Configuration Protocol (DHCP) address configurations
- Remote access VPN connections

The key word to keep in mind when discussing NAP and its features is "compliance." With the introduction of NAP into our network, we can force Windows Server 2008, Windows Vista, and Windows XP Service Pack 3 to comply with standards set forth on our network. If for some reason a client does not comply with standards set forth by an administrator, the client could be directed to a separate network segment. On the separate network segment, a Remedial Server could update the client to the company's standards and then allow the client access to the network. Examples of these standards include but are not limited to:

- Windows update files
- Virus definitions
- Windows firewall settings

In addition, Microsoft has provided an application program interface (API) so that Network Access Protection Partners can write their own piece of software to add to the functionality of NAP. Some of the Access Protection Partners already providing add-ons include AppSense, Citrix, Intel, and Symantec. For a complete list of Access Protection Partners, go to the following Web site: www.microsoft. com/windowsserver2008/en/us/nap-partners.aspx.

In the following section, we are going to first look at all of the components of implementing NAP on a network. Once we gain a broad understanding of the components needed to build a NAP-supported network, we will look at different scenarios and implementation steps through the exercises throughout this chapter.

New & Noteworthy...

Network Access Quarantine Control vs. Network Access Protection

For the examination this text prepares you for, you will not need to know anything about the Windows 2003 Server feature Network Access Quarantine Control. We discussed it here to give you a way to associate NAP with a feature from Windows 2003 Server.

For the test objectives in this chapter, you will need to understand what each component of NAP does and how it fits into the overall design of the NAP network solution. Keep this in mind—understand the terminology of the components. Also, the management interface has been totally redesigned for Windows 2008 Server. Do not rely on your hands-on experience with Windows 2003 Server. The best advice we can give you is to perform the exercises as presented in this chapter and on the links we will provide to other step-by-step exercises that Microsoft makes available to the public. Some questions on this exam will have you demonstrating that you understand a feature by simulation and not by a multiple choice question. That is why it is imperative to actually gain hands-on experience for this exam.

As a side note: we would recommend that you download the free version of Microsoft Virtual PC 2007, get a 180-day trial copy of Windows Server 2008, build a network with Microsoft Virtual PC 2007, and practice the exercises presented not only in this chapter but throughout the whole book.

Working with NAP

The NAP platform main objective is to validate the state of a client computer before connecting to the private network and offer a source of remediation. To validate access to a network based on system health, NAP provides the following areas of functionality:

- Health state validation
- Network access limitation
- Automatic remediation
- Ongoing compliance

Network Layer Protection

All the components of NAP reside at the network layer. It is very important to understand where each component can reside and what the function of each component does. We are first going to look at a very general Microsoft Visio drawing and then point out each component and its function as related to NAP. Like a lot of Microsoft network designs, some servers can play multiple Windows Server 2008 roles within the NAP-enabled network architecture. Later in this chapter we will point out during the hands-on exercises where these servers with multiple Windows 2008 Server roles can reside, but for now we will concentrate on each individual function of the components and server roles (see Figure 12.1).

Figure 12.1 NAP Network Design

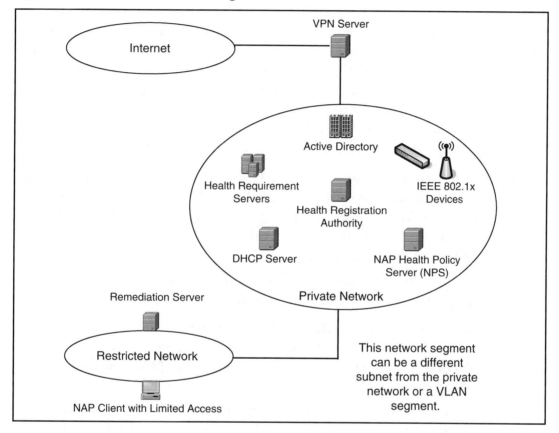

NAP Clients

NAP clients can be Windows Vista, Windows 2008 Server, or Windows XP Service Pack 3 clients. At the time of this writing these are the only operating systems that support the NAP platform for system health validated network access or communication. Microsoft does plan on supporting other operating systems through third-party software providers—independent software providers (ISVs). Microsoft is also planning to provide support to the Microsoft Windows Mobile platform, including support for handheld devices and Microsoft Windows Mobile phones.

The NAP API is really important for the adoption of NAP-based networks. The API that Microsoft is releasing for developers allows them to write code to support various other clients that are not Microsoft based. Expect to see these devices become more popular as more and more enterprises adopt Microsoft Windows Server 2008.

NAP Enforcement Points

NAP enforcement points are parts of the NAP infrastructure that determines the health and compliance of a NAP client before allowing network access. To determine if the NAP client is in compliance by the policies set forth by the administrator, the NAP Health Policy Server (NPS) evaluates the health and compliance of the NAP client. The NPS also decides the remediation process that is going to be applied to the NAP client. For instance, the client can be forwarded to restricted network where a remediation server will offer the updates or settings needed to enforce the compliance policy. NAP enforcement points include the following:

- Health Registration Authority (HRA) The HRA is a Windows 2008 Server with the roles of Internet Information Server 7.0 (IIS) and Certificate Authority (CA) role installed. This enforcement point is used primarily with IPSec Enforcement policies. The CA uses health certificates to enforce NAP compliance to the NAP client.

- Windows 2008 VPN Server A server running Windows 2008 Server Network Policy Server can enforce NAP compliance to a NAP client.

- DHCP Server Servers installed into the NAP network infrastructure running Windows 2008 Server with the DHCP server role providing Internet Protocol version 4 (IPv4) addresses to NAP clients can enforce NAP compliance to a NAP client.

- Network access devices Network hardware, such as switches and wireless access points that support IEEE 802.1 x authentication, can be used to support NAP compliance to a NAP client. Types of protocols supported include Extensible Authentication Protocol (EAP), Lightweight Extensible Authentication Protocol (LEAP), and Protected Extensible Authentication Protocol (PEAP).

EXAM WARNING

During the examination, Microsoft sometimes like to give you a scenario questions and ask what it is wrong with the provided solution. One of the multiple choice answers could be none—meaning the solution is correct on its own merit. At face value this may be correct. For example, a scenario question may include the addition of a DHCP server running Internet Protocol version 6 (IPv6) in a NAP client. Windows Server 2008 does support IPv6; however, NAP does not support IPv6, only IPv4. Make sure you read the scenario in its entirety and pay close attention to detail.

Active Directory Domain Services

As you already know, Active Directory Services store account and group policy information for an Active Directory Domain. NAP does not necessarily rely on Windows 2008 Server Active Directory Domain Services or Windows 2003 Server Active Directory Domain Services. NAP definitely does not need Active Directory Services to determine if a client is compliant, but other services and roles depend on Active Directory Services.

Active Directory Domain Services is needed for Network Policy Server VPN enforcement, IEEE 802.1x network device enforcement or IPSec-based enforcement. Also, as you will see later in this chapter, using group policy objects is a good way to set compliance and enforcement settings to NAP clients on your network.

NAP Health Policy Server

The NAP Health Policy Server is the heart of the NAP-supported network infra-structure. The NAP Health Policy Server runs Windows 2008 Server and has the NPS server role installed. The NPS server role is responsible for storing health requirement policies and provides health state validation for NAP.

Interestingly, the NPS server role replaces Internet Authentication Service (IAS), Remote Authentication Dial-In User Service (RADIUS), and proxy server provided by Windows 2003 Server. So NPS not only supports the NAP infrastructure but also acts as the authentication, authorization, and access (AAA) server in Windows 2008 Server. The NPS role can act as the RADIUS proxy to exchange RADIUS data packets with another NAP health policy server.

Health Requirement Server

Health requirement servers contain the data that NAP NPS servers check for current system health state for NAP NPS servers. Examples of the data that health require-ment servers may provide are the latest virus DAT information files for third-party antivirus packages or updates for other software packages that the ISVs use the NAP API to develop.

Restricted Network

A restricted network is where NAP sends a computer that needs remediation services or to block access to the private network until remediation can take place. The restricted network can be a different subnet that has no routes to the private network or a different logical network in the form of a virtual local area network (VLAN). A good NAP design would place remediation servers located within the restricted network. Placing remediation servers inside the restricted network, enables NAP clients to get updated and then be allowed access to the private network.

The remediation server could be in the form of a Windows 2008 Server or Windows 2003 Server running Windows Server Update Services (WSUS). WSUS provides an easy way to update the NAP client system files using Microsoft Update Services. You could also place virus update files and other third-party critical update files on the remediation server.

Test Day Tip

A good review on the test date is to go through this book and look over the diagrams and understand different network designs. Glancing over these network diagrams is a good refresher right before entering the testing center.

Head of the Class...

Understanding VLANs

When you are working with NAP, one of the best technologies to take advantage of is working with virtual local area networks. Microsoft does not go into great detail about how VLANs work, but for any student or a well-seasoned network administrator, understanding this technology is vital.

VLANs are basically multiple networks on the same switch. The switching management software allows us to take ports from the switch and build many virtual local area networks. These virtual networks are

Continued

independent networks of each other. Newer switches actually allow us to configure routing between these VLANs. This makes setting up the restricted network in NAP easy and more efficient. To read more about VLAN technology, go to this Web address: http://www.cisco.com/univercd/ cc/td/doc/cisintwk/idg4/nd2023.htm#wp3280.

Software Policy Validation

Before you actually start doing some exercises, it is important to understand what actually goes on during system-compliant testing and validation. NPS uses System Health Validators (SHVs) to analyze the compliance of a client computer. SHVs determine whether a computer is getting full access to the private network or if it will be isolated to the restricted network. The client has a piece of software installed called a System Health Agent (SHA) to monitor its system health. NPS uses SHVs and SHAs to determine the health of a client computer and to monitor, enforce, and remediate the client computer.

Built into Windows Server 2008 and Windows Vista are the Windows Security Health Agent (WSHA) and Windows Security Health Validator (WSHV). These agents are used to enforce the most basic compliance settings in a NAP infrastructure. The settings provided by WSHA and WSHV are:

- The client computer has firewall software installed and enabled.

- The client computer has antivirus software installed and enabled.

- The client computer has current antivirus updates installed.

- The client computer has antispyware software installed and enabled.

- The client computer has current antispyware updates installed.

- Microsoft Update Services is enabled on the client computer.

Even without third-party SHVs and SHAs, Microsoft has built very powerful tools into Windows Server 2008, Windows Vista, and Windows XP Service Pack 3 to validate the compliance and health of computers.

DHCP Enforcement

DHCP enforcement is probably the easiest NAP infrastructure design to implement. In Exercise 12.1, we are going to show you how to implement NAP DHCP enforcement.

EXERCISE 12.1

IMPLEMENTING DHCP ENFORCEMENT

In this exercise we are going to implement the DHCP and NPS server roles on the server NPS1. We will then configure NAP with the wizard and also configure the SHVs that will force any connecting client using DHCP to be network compliant. The domain name is CONTOSO.COM, Keeping with the Microsoft tradition. Figure 12.2 depicts this simple network. We are going to imply that both servers are Windows Server 2008 and Active Directory Domain Services have already been set up for the CONTOSO.COM domain.

Figure 12.2 Network Diagram for Exercise 12.1

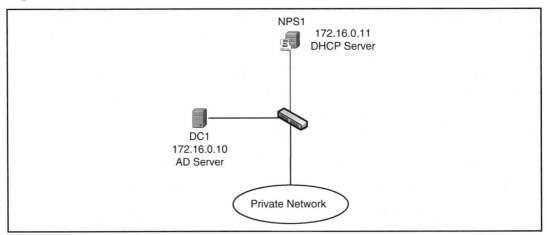

1. First we will install the NPS and DHCP server roles on NPS1. Click **Start** and then click **Server Manager**.

2. Under **Roles Summary**, click **Add Roles** and then click **Next**.

3. On the Select Server Roles page, select the **DHCP Server** and **Network Policy and Access Services** check boxes and then click **Next** twice (see Figure 12.3).

Figure 12.3 Server Roles Page

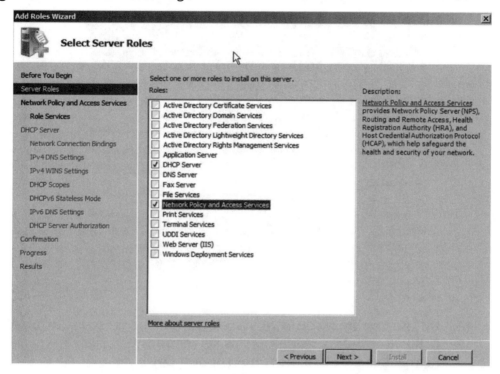

4. On the **Select Server Roles** page, select the **Network Policy Server** check box and then click **Next** twice.

5. On the **Select Network Connection Bindings** page, verify that **172.16.0.11** is selected and click **Next**.

6. On the **Specify IPv4 DNS Server Settings** page, verify that **contoso.com** is listed under **Parent Domain**.

7. Type **172.16.0.10** under the **Preferred DNS server IP address** and click **Validate**. Verify that the server was able to validate the DNS server.

8. On the **Specify WINS Server Settings**, click **Next,** accepting the default settings.

9. On the **Add or Edit DHCP Scopes** page, click **Add**.

10. In the **Add Scope** dialog box, type **NAP SCOPE** next to **Scope Name**. Add **172.16.0.20** as the **Starting IP Address** and **172.16.0.30** as the **Ending IP Address**. For the **Subnet Mask** use **255.255.255.0**. Select the **Activate this scope** check box. Notice in Figure 12.4 that we do not specify a **Default Gateway**.

Figure 12.4 Add Scope Dialog Box

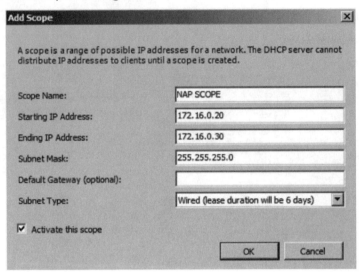

11. On the **Configure DHCPv6 Stateless Mode** page, select **Disable DHCPv6 stateless mode for this server** and then click **Next**. Remember that NAP does not support DHCPv6.

12. On the **Authorize DHCP Server** page, select **Specify,** enter **Administrator information**, and then click **Next**.

13. On the **Confirm Installation Selections** page, click **Install**.

14. Verify the installation completed with no errors and then click **Close**.

At this point, we now have our DHCP Server and NPS installed. The DHCP Server is configured and authorized for the domain CONTOSO. COM. Now we need to configure NPS as a NAP health policy server so that it can validate the clients connecting to our domain via DHCP. To do this, we will use the NAP configuration wizard.

1. Click **Start**, click **Run**, type **nps.msc** and press **Enter**.

2. Make sure that in the Network Policy Server console tree, that **NPS (Local)** is selected.

3. Under **Standard Configuration**, click **Configure NAP**. The NAP configuration wizard will start. See Figure 12.5.

Figure 12.5 NAP Configuration Wizard

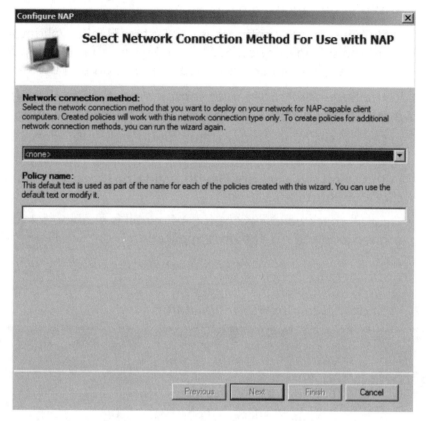

4. On the **Select Network Connection Method for Use with NAP** page, under **Network connection method**, select **Dynamic Host Configuration Protocol (DHPC)**, and then click **Next**.

5. On the **Specify NAP Enforcement Servers Running DHCP** page, click **Next**.

6. On the **Specify DHCP Scopes** page, click **Next**.

7. On the **Configure User Groups and Machine Groups** page, click **Next**.

8. On the **Specify a NAP Remediation Server Group and URL** page, click **Next**.

9. On the **Define NAP Health Policy** page, verify that **Windows Security Health Validator** and **Enable auto-remediation of client computers** check boxes are selected, click **Next**.

10. Click **Finish** on the Completing NAP **Enforcement Policy and RADIUS Configuration** page.

The only thing left to configure is our System Health Validators (SHVs). We are going to set up our new SHV to make sure that the Windows Firewall is enabled, and an antivirus application is on and up-to-date.

1. In the Network Policy Server console tree, double-click **Network Access Protection**, and then click **System Health Validators**.

2. In the details pane, under **Name**, double-click **Windows Security Health Validator**.

3. In the **Windows Security Health Validator Properties** dialog box, click **Configure**.

4. Clear all check boxes except for **A firewall is enabled for all network connections** and **An antivirus application is on**. See Figure 12.6.

Figure 12.6 Windows Security Health Validator

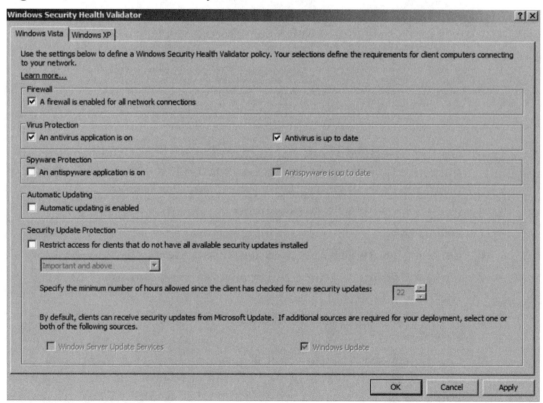

5. Click **OK** to close the **Windows Security Health Validator** dialog box, and then click **OK** to close the **Windows Security Health Validator Properties** dialog box.

6. Close the Network Policy Server console.

This was a long exercise, but it is very important to see this process from start to finish—it helps facilitate your understanding of all concepts dealing with implementing DHCP enforcement.

EXAM WARNING

Microsoft new exams test whether or not you understand the location of certain properties and how to implement a process—these are simulation type questions. Be sure that when you practice exercises, to take the time to notice the layout and where items are located.

VPN Enforcement

Windows Server 2008 and Network Policy Server (NPS) can facilitate NAP connections—allowing remote VPN clients to be checked for compliance and be remediated.

Communication Process with VPN Client and NAP

When a Windows Vista or Windows XP Service Pack 3 computer connects to a NPS server that is NAP enabled, the communication process is a little different than a normal VPN connection. The NAP client in this case becomes the VPN client and uses simple Point-to-Point Protocol (PPP) messages to establish a remote access VPN connection. While this is going on, Protected Extensible Authentication Protocol (PEAP) messages are sent over the PPP connection to indicate the client system current health state to the NAP health policy server. If the connecting client is not compliant, the NAP health policy server uses PEAP to send remediation instructions to the VPN client. If the client is compliant, the NAP health policy server will use PEAP messages to tell the client that it has access to the private network. Because all

PEAP messages between the VPN client and NAP health policy server are routed through the VPN server, this process is encrypted.

If the VPN client is noncompliant, the Windows 2008 Server NPS will use a set of remote access IP filters to limit the traffic of the VPN client so that it can reach only the restricted network. Once directed to the restricted network, the client can become compliant through the remediation resources provided. While the system is noncompliant, the VPN server will continue to apply the IP packet filters to the IP traffic that is received from the VPN client and silently discard all packets that do not correspond to a configured packet filter.

EXERCISE 12.2

CONFIGURE NPS FOR REMOTE VPN CONNECTIONS

In this exercise, we are going to configure NPS for use with remote VPN connections. This exercise assumes that RRAS is already configured on the server DC1 (172.16.0.10). This exercise also assumes that DC1 is an Enterprise Certification Authority (CA) for the domain CONTOSO.COM.

EXAM WARNING

Configuring an Enterprise Certification Authority is beyond the scope of this chapter, but is explained in more detail in Chapter 3. It is important to understand implementing an Enterprise CA—especially with RRAS and IPSec NAP enforcement.

1. Click **Start**, click **Run**, type **nps.msc**, and then press **Enter**.
2. In the Network Policy Server console tree, click **NPS (Local)**.
3. In the details pane, under **Standard Configuration**, click **Configure NAP**. The NAP configuration wizard will start.
4. On the **Select Network Connection Method for Use with NAP page**, under **Network connection method**, select **Virtual Private Network (VPN)** and click **Next**. See Figure 12.7.

Figure 12.7 Select Network Connection Method for Use with NAP

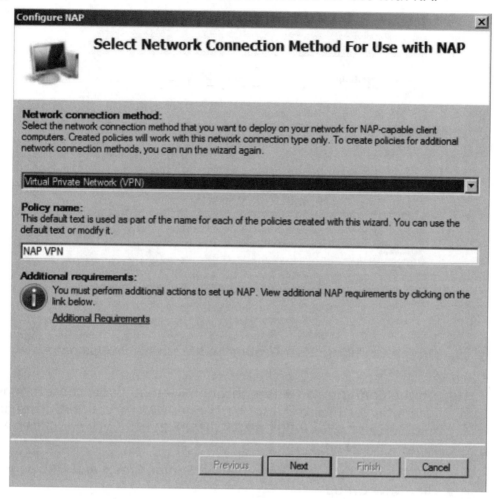

5. On the **Specify NAP Enforcement Servers Running VPN Server page**, under **RADIUS clients**, click **Add**.

6. In **the New RADIUS Client** dialog box, under **Friendly Name**, type **NAP VPN Server**. Under **Address (IP or DNS)**, type **DC1**.

7. Under **Shared secret**, type **secret**.

8. nder **Confirm shared secret**, type **secret**, click **OK** and then click **Next**. See Figure 12.8.

Figure 12.8 New RADIUS Client

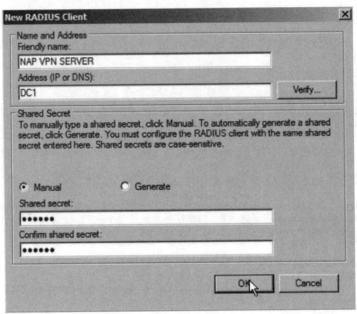

9. On the **Configure User Groups and Machine Groups** page, click **Next**.

10. On the **Configure an Authentication Method** page, confirm that a computer certificate is displayed under **NPS Server Certificate** and that **Secure Password (PEAP-MSCHAP-v2)** is selected under **EAP types**. Click **Next**.

11. On the **Specify a NAP Remediation Server Group and URL** page, click **New Group**.

12. In the **New Remediation Server Group** dialog box, under **Group Name**, type **Domain Services** and then click **Add**.

13. In the **Add New Server** dialog box, under **Friendly name**, type **DC1**.

14. Under **IP address or DNS name**, type **172.16.0.10** and then click **OK** twice.

15. Under **Remediation Server Group**, verify that the newly created remediation server group is selected and then click **Next**.

16. On the **Define NAP Health Policy** page, verify that **Windows Security Health Validator** and **Enable auto-remediation of client computers** check boxes are selected and then click **Next**.

17. On the **Completing NAP Enforcement Policy and RADIUS Client Configuration** page, click **Finish**.

18. Close the NPS console.

EXAM WARNING

Whenever you add a remediation server group to NAP—noncompliant computers are automatically granted access to the group. To deny access to a remediation group, at least one IP filter is required.

Configuring NAP Health Policies

NAP Health Policies are a combination of settings for health determination and enforcement of infrastructure compliance. Health requirement policies on the NAP health policy server determine whether a NAP client is compliant or noncompliant, how to treat noncompliant NAP clients and whether they should automatically remediate their health state, and how to treat clients that are not NAP capable for different NAP enforcement methods. The following settings make up the NAP Health Policies:

- Connection Request Policies

- Network Policies

- Health Policies

- Network Access Protection Settings

All the NAP Health Policies are configured within the Network Policy Server console, as shown in Figure 12.9. Interestingly, Microsoft recommends starting with the Configure NAP Wizard to build your initial settings for your NAP installation. To access the Configure NAP Wizard, click the **NPS (LOCAL)** node of the configuration tree and then click **Configure NAP** under the Standard Configuration in the right window. In Figure 12.9, we can see where you can access the Configure NAP Wizard within the Network Policy Server console.

Figure 12.9 The Network Policy Server Console

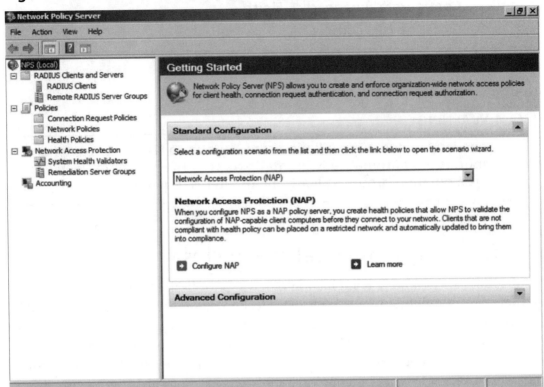

Connection Request Policies

As we discussed earlier, NPS replaces IAS in Windows Server 2003. NPS handles all RADIUS activities in Windows 2008 Server—RADIUS can be configured to handle the authentication and logging locally. Also, RADIUS in Windows 2008 can be configured as a RADIUS proxy and forward all authentication request to another RADIUS server.

Connection Request Policies are a set of rules that can be processed in a set order. Connection Request Policies determine whether RADIUS request should be processed locally or forward the requests to another RADIUS server. Connection Request Policies are configured and ordered in the NPC console under the Policies node (see Figure 12.10). When the NPS server is configured for NAP health compliance and enforcement, the local server is acting as a RADIUS server locally.

Figure 12.10 Connection Request Policies

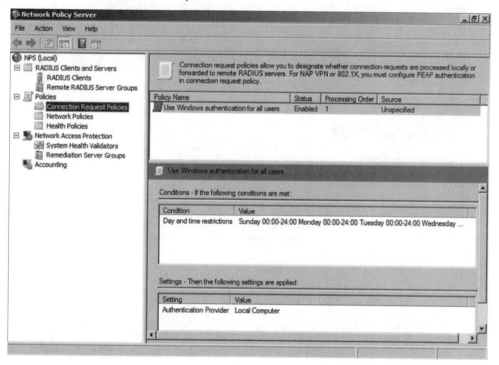

Network Policies

Network Policies either deny or grant access to network connection attempts. These policies, like Connection Request Policies, are an ordered group of rules. For each rule, there are a set of conditions, constraints, an access permission that either grants or denies access and network policy settings. For NAP, network policies specify the conditions to check for health requirements and, for computers that are not capable of NAP—the enforcement behavior.

When setting the Network Policies, you have four options for NAP Enforcement settings—these settings specify the type of network access the client will have. The four options include (also see Figure 12.11):

1. Allow full network access
2. Allow full network access for a limited time
3. Allow limited access
4. Enable auto-remediation of client computers

Figure 12.11 Compliant Properties

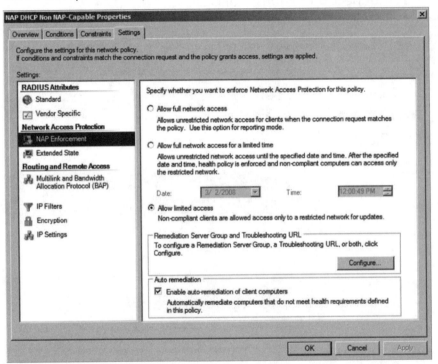

Health Policies

Health Policies check the client for compliance via the system health validators (SHVs). If you recall from earlier in this chapter, we discussed Windows Security Health Validator (WSHV). These SHVs are the ones provided with Windows 2008 Server, Windows Vista or Windows XP Service Pack 3. Other SHVs can be created by independent software vendors (ISVs) via the application programming interface provided by Microsoft. By default, the WSHV is always listed in the health policies.

EXERCISE 12.3

CREATE A HEALTH POLICY

In this short exercise, we are going to create a Health Policy on NPS1 server. Pay close attention to all of the options available to you in the exercise.

1. Click **Start**, click **Run**, type **nps.msc**, and then press **Enter**.
2. In the Network Policy Server console tree, click **Policies**.
3. In the details pane, under **Health Policies**, click **Configure Health Policies**.
4. **Right-click** the **Health Policies** node and click **New**.
5. For the **Policy Name** enter **CONTOSO Policy 1**.
6. In the **Client SHV checks** drop down menu select Client **fails one or more SHV checks**.
7. Make sure under **SHVs used in this health policy** that **Windows Security Health Validator** is **Checked**. See Figure 12.12.

Figure 12.12 Configure Health Policy Settings

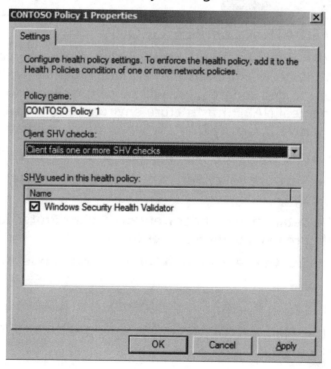

8. Click **OK**.

9. Close the NPS console.

Network Access Protection Settings

Network Access Protection (NAP) settings consist of two components. The components that make up NAP settings include:

- System Health Validators
- Remediation Server Groups

System Health Validators (SHVs) specify the configuration of installed SHVs for health requirements and error conditions. By default, Windows Server 2008, Windows Vista, and Windows XP Service Pack 3 include the Window Security Health Validator (WSHV).

Remediation Server Groups specifies the set of servers that are accessible to computers that are not NAP compliant with limited network access. If you recall Figure 12.1, these servers would be located on the restricted network.

EXERCISE 12.4

CREATE REMEDIATION SERVER GROUP

In this exercise, we are going to create a remediation server group on server NPS1 to allow computers that are not compliant with the NAP infrastructure to get updated. We will point the clients to DC1 to get updates—in a real NAP infrastructure environment, we would never point to an Active Directory Domain Server as a remediation server.

1. Click **Start**, click **Run**, type **nps.msc**, and then press **Enter**.

2. In the Network Policy Server console tree, click **Network Access Protection**.

3. In the details pane, under **Network Access Protection**, click **Configure Remediation Server Groups**.

4. **Right-click** the **Remediation Server Groups** node and click **New**.

5. Click **Add**.

6. For the **Friendly name** enter **CONTOSO Remediation Server Group**.

7. For the IP address or DNS name enter **172.16.0.10** (DC1). See Figure 12.13.

Figure 12.13 Remediation Server Groups

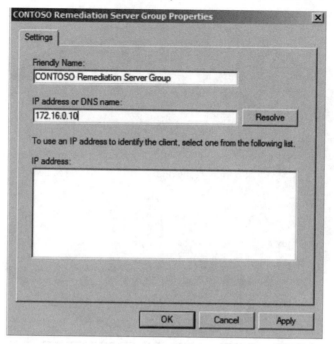

8. Click **OK** twice.

9. Close the NPS console.

IPsec Enforcement

IPsec enforcement breaks a network down to three different logical networks by using health certificates provided by the Health Certificate Server (HCS). Any computer can be a member of only one of the three networks at any given time—membership to the network is determined by the status of the computers health certificate. The logical networks are defined by which computers have valid health certificates and which computers require IPSec authentication for incoming access connections. Computers requiring IPSec authentication would normally be servers on the private network. Figure 12.14 shows a basic diagram of what an IPSec-based NAP infrastructure would look like. As you can see, there are three distinct networks:

1. Secure network

2. Boundary network

3. Restricted network

Figure 12.14 IPSec-Based NAP Network

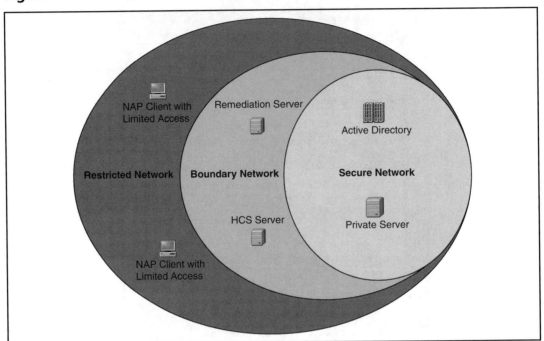

Secure Network

The secure network is where all computers have health certificates and require IPsec authentication to communicate with any other computer. If a computer tries to communicate with a computer in the secure network without a health certificate, the computer in the secure network will ignore the client's request. In a NAP infrastructure, computers in the secure network would be members of the Active Directory domain.

Boundary Network

Boundary networks are where computers that are not NAP compliant can access a remediation server and become compliant. Once compliant, they can access an HCS Server and acquire a health certificate to participate in the secure network. Computers on the boundary network will accept communication requests from computers with a health certificate or without—this is how remediation occurs. Both the restricted network and the secure network have access to the boundary network.

Restricted Network

All the computers in the restricted network do not have a health certificate. The only network they can communicate with is the boundary network—for the purpose of remediation and acquiring the appropriate health certificate to access the secure network.

Flexible Host Isolation

Flexible Host Isolation refers to the ease of network isolation provided with the IPSec method of NAP enforcement. Isolation can be performed easily on the network with no infrastructure upgrade by using NAP and health certificates. This type of isolation cannot be easily circumvented by reconfiguring the client or using hardware like hubs. Basically, healthy systems can connect to anything, as long as the NAP policy allows it, whereas quarantined systems are isolated to the restricted network.

EXAM WARNING

For this exam, it is very important to understand the communication between the three different types of networks in an IPSec NAP infrastructure. The secure network can communicate with any of the other networks via IPSec authentication and without it. The boundary network can communicate with the secure network via IPSec authentication and also allow nonsecured traffic with the restricted network. The restricted network can communicate with the boundary network only via an unsecured means.

EXERCISE 12.5

INSTALL THE NPS, HRA AND CA SERVER ROLES

In this exercise, we are going to install the NPS, HRA and CA server roles on NPS1 server.

1. Click **Start** and then **Server Manager**. Under **Roles Summary**, click **Add Roles** and then click **Next**.

2. On the **Select Server Roles** page, select the **Active Directory Certificate Services** and **Network Policy and Access Services** check boxes and then click **Next** twice.

3. On the **Select Role Services** page, select the **Health Registration Authority** check box, click **Add Required Role Services** in the **Add Roles Wizard** window and then click **Next**.

4. On the **Choose the Certification Authority to use with the Health Registration Authority** page, choose **Install a local CA to issue health certificates for this HRA server** and then click **Next**. See Figure 12.15.

Figure 12.15 Choose the Certification Authority to use with the Health Registration Authority

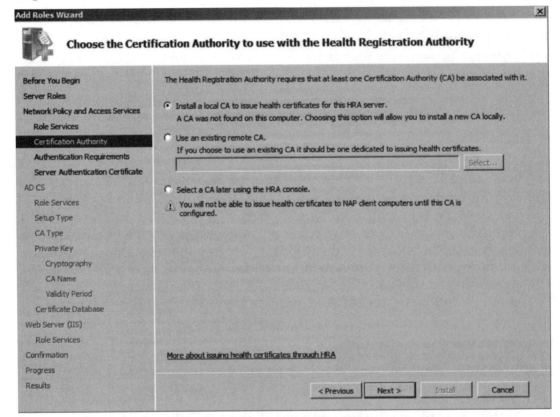

5. On the **Choose Authentication Requirements for the Health Registration Authority** page, choose **No, allow anonymous requests for health certificates** and then click **Next**. This choice allows computers to be enrolled with health certificates in a workgroup environment.

6. On the **Choose a Server Authentication Certificate for SSL Encryption** page, choose **Create a self-signed certificate for SSL encryption** and then click **Next**.

7. On the **Introduction to Active Directory Certificate Services** page, click **Next**.

8. On the **Select Role Services** page, verify that the **Certification Authority** check box is selected and then click **Next**.

9. On the **Specify Setup Type** page, click **Standalone** and then click **Next**.

10. On the **Specify CA Type** page, click **Subordinate CA** and then click **Next**.

11. On the **Set Up Private Key** page, click **Create a new private key** and then click **Next**.

12. On the **Configure Cryptography for CA** page, click **Next**.

13. On the **Configure CA Name** page, under **Common name for this CA**, type **contoso-NPS1-SubCA** and then click **Next**.

14. On the **Request Certificate from a Parent CA** page, choose **Send a certificate request to a parent CA** and then click **Browse**.

15. In the **Select Certification Authority** window, click **Contoso-DC1-CA** and then click **OK**. See Figure 12.16.

Figure 12.16 Select Certification Authority

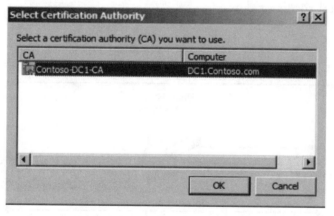

16. Verify that **DC1.Contoso.com\Contoso-DC1-CA** is displayed next to **Parent CA** and then click **Next**.

17. Click **Next** three times to accept the default database, Web server, and role services settings and then click **Install**.

18. Verify that all installations were successful and then click **Close**.

19. Exit the Server Manager.

802.1x Enforcement

IEEE 802.1x standards define an effective framework for controlling and authenticating clients to a wired or wireless protected network—in this case a NAP infrastructure. These standards define port-based authentication on supported devices. These devices could be switches or wireless access points that support the IEEE 802.1x standard. The IEEE standard is significant it has been accepted by hardware and software vendors—their products will be designed with the standards in mind. What does this mean for you and me? All hardware that is 802.1x based should work with RADIUS and NAP.

An 802.1x deployment consists of three major components that allow for the authentication process to work correctly (see Figure 12.17).

- **Supplicant** a device that requests access to our network and is connected via a pass-through authenticator.

- **Pass-through authenticator** a switch or access point that is 802.1x compliant.

- **Authentication server** when the supplicant connects to the pass-through authenticator, the request is passed to the authentication server by the pass-through authenticator. The authentication server decides whether the client is granted access or denied.

Figure 12.17 Components of 802.1x

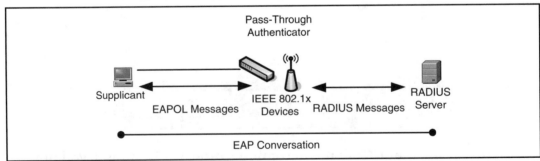

Authentication is handled using the Extensible Authentication Protocol (EAP). EAP messages used in the authentication process are transmitted between the supplicant and pass-through authenticator using EAP over LAN (EAPoL). The pass-through authenticator talks to the RADIUS using RADIUS messages and EAP.

When NAP uses IEEE 802.1x, the authenticating pass-through authenticator uses the RADIUS protocol. NPS instructs the pass-through authenticator (wireless access-point or switch) to place supplicants that are not in compliance with NPS into a restricted network. The restricted network could be a separate VLAN or a network with IP filters in place to isolate it from the secured network.

TEST DAY TIP

While studying for this exam, keep a list of new terms written down somewhere. This step will make for a great review tool on test day. Also, notice in the last section we used terminology like supplicant instead of computer or device. Always use the Microsoft terminology when studying—it will benefit you later!

EXERCISE 12.6

CONFIGURE NAP CLIENT AUTHENTICATION METHODS

In this exercise, we are going to configure a Windows Vista client authentication method.

1. Click **Start**, right-click **Network** and then **Properties**.
2. Click **Manage network connections**.
3. Right-click **Local Area Connection** and then click **Properties**. See Figure 12.18.

Figure 12.18 Windows Vista Network Properties

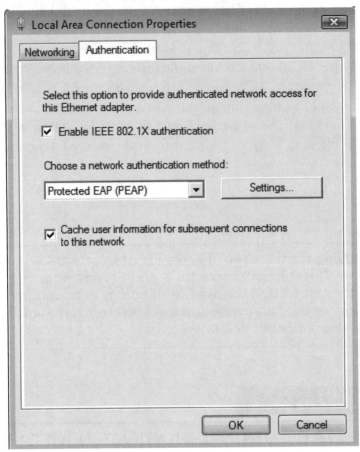

4. Click the **Authentication** tab and verify that Enable **IEEE 802.1x authentication** is selected.

5. Click **Setting**. See Figure 12.19.

Figure 12.19 Protected EAP Properties

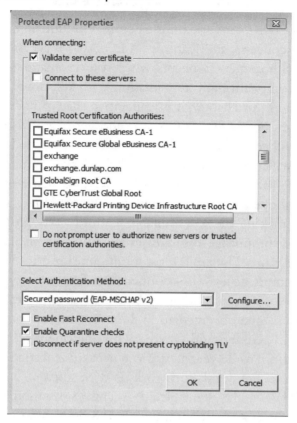

6. In the **Protected EAP Properties** dialog box, clear the **Enable Fast Reconnect** check box and verify that only the following check box is selected—**Enable Quarantine checks**.

7. Close all property sheets.

TEST DAY TIP

When you get to the test center and check in, you will be taken to your workstation and given an erasable board or paper. Use this to your advantage. Before you begin the examination, write down any network designs or acronyms you are afraid that you may forget.

Summary of Exam Objectives

The Window Server 2008 Network Infrastructure, Configuring Exam is going to contain a lot of new concepts and features—and network access protection (NAP) is going to be one of those new concepts. Microsoft has made great strides in network infrastructure compliance and remediation with Windows 2008 Server. As mentioned earlier in this chapter, it is imperative that you actually sit down and play with the Network Policy Server Console and get to know the interface. Most questions on NAP will come directly from the interface of the console.

Microsoft NAP will work with Windows 2008 Server, Windows Vista, and Windows XP Service Pack 3 at the time of this writing. More operating systems (including third-party operating systems) will be supported in the future—mostly because Microsoft is making the API available to third-party programmers.

NAP can enforce compliance through protected traffic, IEEE 802.1x authenticated network connections, Dynamic Host Configuration Protocol (DHCP) address configurations and remote access VPN connections. The main objective of NAP is to validate the state of a client computer before connecting to the private network and offer some source of remediation. It is very important to understand the drawing in Figure 12.1. Understand where each component of NAP is located—Microsoft newer exams have fewer questions but more realistic scenario questions.

The way software policy validation works is with software agents called System Health Validators (SHVs) and System Health Agents (SHAs). NPS uses SHVs to analyze the compliance of a client computer. SHVs determine whether a computer is getting full access to the private network or will it be isolated to the restricted network. The client has a piece of software installed called a SHA to monitor its system health. NPS uses SHVs and SHAs to determine the health of a client computer and to monitor, enforce and remediate the client computer. The main Microsoft SHA and SHV are—Windows Security Health Agent (WSHA) and Windows Security Health Validator (WSHV). The Microsoft agent and validator basically monitor the Microsoft Security Center.

Understand the different NAP Health Policies and where they are configured. NAP Health Policies include: Connection Request Policies, Network Policies, Health Policies and Network Access Protection Settings. All of the policies are configured with the Network Policy Server Console.

When working with NAP, understand the concept of Secure Network, Boundary Network and Restricted Network. The secure network is where all domain members should be located. The boundary network contains the remediation server and offers the client a way to become compliant. The restricted network is for clients with limited access.

802.1x enforcement relies on the access connection hardware. It is made up of three components—the supplicant, pass-through authenticator and the RADIUS server. The supplicant would be the client trying to connect to the network. The pass-through authenticator is the 802.1x device that is relaying authentication information back to the RADIUS server. The RADIUS server authenticates the network connections.

Exam Objectives Fast Track

Working with Network Access Protection

☑ The Network Access Protection (NAP) platform main objective is to validate the state of a client computer before connecting to a private network and offer a source of remediation.

☑ NAP clients include Windows Vista, Windows Server 2008 and Windows XP Service Pack 3.

☑ The NAP API will allow other ISVs to write software to be enforced by NAP.

☑ NAP provides the following areas of functionality: Health State Validation, Network Access Limitation, Automatic Remediation and Ongoing Compliance.

☑ DHCP NAP enforcement is the easiest enforcement implementation of NAP available.

☑ IPv6 is not supported with DHCP enforcement implementation.

☑ The DHCP server and NPS server can be supported on the same server by installing the 2 server roles.

☑ During the VPN connection—NPS uses PEAP messages to send NAP information to the client.

☑ All PEAP messages between the VPN client and NAP are routed through the NPS server.

☑ If the VPN client is noncompliant—the client will be directed to the restricted network with IP filters.

☑ NAP Health Policies are a combination of settings for health determination and enforcement of infrastructure compliance.

☑ The following sets of settings make up NAP Health Policies: Connection Request Policies, Network Policies, Health Policies and NAP Settings.

☑ NAP Health Policies are configured using the Network Policy Server console.

☑ NPS in Windows 2008 Server replaces IAS in Windows 2003 Server.

☑ Network Policies have four options for NAP enforcement: Allow full network access, Allow full network access for a limited time, Allow limited access and Enable auto-remediation of client computers.

☑ IPsec NAP enforcement breaks the network down to three logical networks by using health certificates provided by the Health Certificate Server (HCS).

☑ The three distinct networks are: secure network, boundary network and restricted network.

☑ Flexible Host Isolation refers to the ease of network isolation provided with the IPsec method of NAP enforcement.

☑ IEEE 802.1x standards define an effective framework for controlling and authenticating clients to a wired or wireless protected network.

☑ An 802.1x deployment consists of three major components: Supplicant, Pass-Through Authenticator and Authentication Server.

☑ Authentication is handled using the Extensible Authentication Protocol (EAP).

☑ NPS instructs the pass-through authenticator (wireless access-points or switch) to place supplicants that are not in compliance with NPS into a restricted network.

Exam Objectives
Frequently Asked Questions

Q: I have worked with Windows 2003 Server Network Access Quarantine Control extensively. Will this help me better work with Network Access Protection?

A: The short answer is no. Microsoft has totally changed the way network access is controlled in Windows Server 2008. For instance, there is no longer an Internet Authentication Service and Routing and Remote Access Service—these have been wrapped up into the Network Access Protection.

Q: You mentioned VLANs in this chapter. I am not very familiar with this technology. Should I seek other sources to help me understand this new subject?

A: Definitely! Microsoft probably does not give VLAN technology the time it deserves in its courseware or exams. In the workplace, it is almost a must to understand how VLANs work—especially if you are wanting to work (or already do work) in an enterprise environment. Earlier in this chapter, I gave you a link to a Cisco article that explains VLANs in detail. It would probably be a good idea to go out and give this article a once over.

Q: My employer has not installed or migrated to Windows Server 2008 yet. Should I get hands on experience before sitting this exam?

A: Yes! The best advice for any Microsoft exam is to actually sit down and work with the product. Go out and download the free copy of Microsoft Virtual PC 2007 and register for a 180 day trial of Windows Server 2008 Enterprise Edition. With Microsoft Virtual PC 2007, you can use multiple virtual machines to build virtual networks. This way you can setup just about any scenario in a test environment.

Q: I noticed in this chapter a lot of new acronyms that I never had heard before. This is kind of makes me nervous. Is there a way to cover them all?

A: There are a lot of new services and server roles with Windows 2008 Server. The best way to learn new acronyms and their meanings are good old fashion flash cards. Also, keeping a list with any new terms and definitions is always a good study habit.

Q: What is the technology in this material the hangs up students the most?

A: The technology that seems to always get a lot of questions has to usually deal with IP Security enforcement and 802.1x. IP Security normally causes students problems with Certificate Authorities and learning how to manage certificates. There are a lot of good whitepapers on Microsoft TechNet Web site to help you with this topic. Also, 802.1x causes some issues because the student does not understand VLANs and RADIUS. It gets a lot of attention on tests and course-ware—but a lot of students have never really got to play with this type of technology.

Q: I am having some problems understanding a specific topic in this chapter. Is there any place I can go for more help?

A: The best place to go would be the Network Access Protection Web site on TechNet. There are Web casts, whitepapers and labs out there for download. The Web site is http://technet.microsoft.com/en-us/network/bb545879.aspx. You will find an answer to just about any question concerning NAP on this site.

Self Test

1. Network Access Protection (NAP) will only work with certain operating systems at the time of Windows 2008 Server release. What operating systems will NAP support?

   A. Window XP

   B. Windows XP Service Pack 3

   C. Windows Vista

   D. Windows Server 2008

2. Network Access Protection (NAP) can provide network protection to various types of network communications. Which of the following will not support NAP?

   A. RRAS Connections

   B. DHCP Supported Network

   C. WINS Supported Network

   D. IEEE 802.11B Wireless Network

3. Network Access Protection (NAP) was designed for third-party vendors to take advantage of the infrastructure. This is really important for NAP to become popular throughout the IT community. What is the name of the item that allows third-party developers to write programs that can take advantage of the NAP infrastructure?

   A. ISV

   B. HRA

   C. API

   D. CA

4. NAP enforcement points are what determine if a client wanting to connect to a restricted network is healthy and compliant. What are the valid enforcement points listed below?

   A. Windows 2008 VPN Server

   B. HUB

   C. DHCP Server

   D. IEEE 802.1x Network Access Device

5. The NAP Health Policy Server is responsible for storing health requirement policies and provides health state validation for the NAP Infrastructure. What Windows Server 2008 roles have to be installed for the NAP Health Policy Server to be configured?

   A. Active Directory Domain Role

   B. NPS Server Role

   C. NAP Server Role

   D. DHCP Server Role

6. You have decided to implement NAP into your existing network. During the design, you need to make a decision as to how the Restricted Network will be secured from the Remediation Network. Given the options below, which one(s) would work in this scenario?

   A. Use IPsec with Health Certificates

   B. Use a secondary switch to split the networks

   C. Use IP packet filters

   D. Use VLANs

7. Using Figure 12.20 as a reference point, where would the Remediation Server be located on this network?

Figure 12.20 Network Design

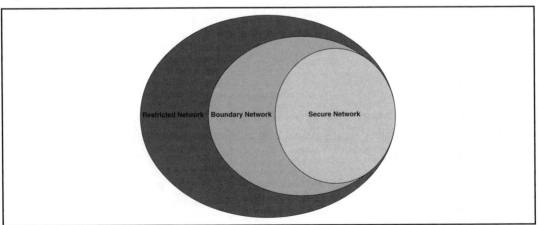

A. Secure Network

B. Boundary Network

C. Restricted Network

D. Location Does Not Matter

8. The remediation server could run Windows 2008 Server or Windows 2003 Server software. To remediate Windows Vista, Windows 2008 Server or Windows XP Service Pack 3—what other software would the remediation server need to run?

A. Windows Server Update Services (WSUS)

B. Network Protection Services (NPS)

C. Routing and Remote Access Services (RRAS)

D. Windows Security Health Validator (WSHV)

9. You instruct your junior network administrator Roger to setup a NAP enforcement point using a DHCP server. After his installation, he comes to you complaining that DHCP is working fine—but he cannot get NAP to work with Windows Vista clients. You go through the installation with him— using 802.1x certified switches, he setup a Windows 2008 Server with both the DHCP and Network Policy and Access Services server roles. Once configured successfully, he set the DHCP settings for DHCPv6 Stateless Mode. Once configured—he set up the NPS policies with the NAP wizard. What is the problem with this scenario?

A. The equipment needs to support 802.11 certified devices.

B. Roger did not install Routing and Remote Access Services (RRAS) on the Windows 2008 Server.

C. NAP does not support IPv6.

D. Windows Vista needs to be updated to Service Pack 1 to work in this network.

10. NAP Health Policies are a combination of settings for health determination and enforcement of infrastructure compliance. What are the sets of settings that make up the NAP Health Policies?

A. Connection Request Policies

B. Network Policies

    C. Health Policies

    D. Network Access Protection Settings

Self Test Quick Answer Key

1. **B, C, D**
2. **C**
3. **C**
4. **A, C, D**
5. **B**

6. **A, C, D**
7. **B**
8. **A**
9. **C**
10. **A, B, C, D**

MCTS/MCITP
Exam 649

Self Test Appendix

Chapter 1: Deploying Servers

1. Your company has recently increased in size, after acquiring another company twice the size. You have been given the task to set up a cluster in the main datacenter. You have been given the scope of the project and decided that the cluster will have to consist of eight nodes for high availability. Which editions of Windows Server 2008 will not be suitable for the eight nodes in the cluster? (Choose all that apply.)

   A. Windows Server 2008 Standard Edition

   B. Windows Server 2008 Enterprise Edition

   C. Windows Server 2008 Datacenter Edition

   D. Windows Web Server 2008

   Correct Answer & Explanation: **A, D**. Both the Standard and Web editions of Windows Server 2008 do not come with the failover clustering feature.

   Incorrect Answers & Explanations: **B, C**. Answers **B** and **C** are incorrect, because failover clustering is a feature in both of these editions.

2. You have been asked to install the first Windows Server 2008 server in the domain. This server will be for testing purposes, so you will use older hardware with minimum hardware requirements for Windows Server 2008. You have decided to install a 32-bit edition of Server 2008 Standard Edition. What is the minimum amount of disk space required to install the Standard Edition of Server 2008?

   A. 8 GB

   B. 10 GB

   C. 12 GB

   D. 40 GB

   Correct Answer & Explanation: **B**. The minimum amount of hard drive space required to install Server 2008 is 10 GB. Note that servers with more than 16 GB of RAM will require more disk space for paging, hibernation, and dump files.

   Incorrect Answers & Explanations: **A, C, D**. Answers **A** and **C** are incorrect, because 8 GB and 12 GB are not the minimum requirements, although it is recommended that you have more than the minimum requirements. Answer **D** is incorrect, because 40 GB is the recommended size to install a Server 2008 operating system.

3. You have been running Windows Server 2003 Enterprise Edition with Service Pack 2 (SP2) on all five of the current Exchange Servers in the organization's datacenter, which serves e-mail for the company on a global basis. You have now been asked to upgrade all the Exchange Servers to Windows Server 2008. Which of the following options do you have as an upgrade path for the Exchange Servers?

A. Full installation of Windows Server 2008 Standard Edition

B. Full installation of Windows Server 2008 Standard Edition R2

C. Full installation of Windows Server 2008 Enterprise Edition

D. Full installation of Windows Server 2008 Datacenter Edition

E. Full installation of Windows Server 2008 for Itanium-based systems

Correct Answer & Explanation: **C.** The only supported upgrade path from Server 2003 Enterprise Edition is to a full installation of the Enterprise Edition of Windows Server 2008.

Incorrect Answers & Explanations: **A, B, D, E.** Answer **A** is incorrect, because an Enterprise Edition cannot be upgraded to a Standard Edition. Answer **B** is incorrect, because there is no such edition as Server 2008 R2. Answer **D** is incorrect, because only a Datacenter edition can be upgraded to a Datacenter edition. Answer **E** is incorrect, because no upgrade path exists for Windows Server 2008 for Itanium-based systems..

4. You have been running earlier releases of Windows Server 2008 on test servers to see whether your organization will be able to make good productive use of Server 2008. You have been running the RC0 release of Windows Server 2008 Standard Edition and have now been asked to upgrade the current RC0 release. Which of the following options do you have as an upgrade path? (Choose all that apply.)

A. Full installation of Windows Server 2008 Standard Edition

B. Full installation of Windows Server 2008 Standard Edition R2

C. Full installation of Windows Server 2008 Enterprise Edition

D. Full installation of Windows Server 2008 Datacenter Edition

E. Full installation of Windows Server 2008 for Itanium-based systems

Correct Answer & Explanation: **A, C.** The only supported upgrade paths from the RC0 release to a full installation are to the Standard and Enterprise editions of Windows Server 2008.

Incorrect Answers & Explanations: **B**, **D**, **E**. Answer **B** is incorrect, because there is no such edition as Server 2008 R2. Answer **D** is incorrect, because only Enterprise editions of 2003 Server and 2008 Server can be upgraded to the Datacenter edition. Answer **E** is incorrect, because no upgrade path exists for Windows Server 2008 Itanium-based systems.

5. You have been asked to upgrade the 28 domain controllers in the organization to Windows Server 2008. Upgrading a server with Active Directory installed requires you to make provisions for the extra hard drive space needed when upgrading the operating system. What size requirements does Active Directory have during an OS upgrade?

A. 5% of the current database size or 200 MB, whichever is greater

B. 10% of the current database size or 250 MB, whichever is greater

C. 25% of the current database size or 550 MB, whichever is greater

D. 50% of the current database size or 1 GB, whichever is greater

Correct Answer & Explanation: **B**. Upgrading a domain controller requires 10% of the current database size or 250 MB, whichever is greater.

Incorrect Answers & Explanations: **A**, **C**, **D**. Answers **A**, **C**, and **D** are incorrect, because the default installation of the Active Directory database and log file is temporarily copied to the quarantine location, and for this only 10% of the size of the database is required.

6. Installing Active Directory Domain Services on a newly installed Windows Server 2008 computer gives you three new additional options to install during the installation of Active Directory. Which of the following is not one of them? (Choose all that apply.)

A. DNS Server

B. Global Catalog

C. DHCP

D. Server Core

E. RODC

Correct Answer & Explanation: **C**, **D**. DHCP is not necessarily needed by a DC, and Server Core is a new operating system installation option for Windows Server 2008.

Incorrect Answers & Explanations: **A**, **B**, **E**. Answers **A**, **C**, and **D** are incorrect, because these are the three new AD DS installation options. DNS is one of the needed options and is selected by default. Global Catalog and RODC are available depending on the plan for this DC.

7. You have five member servers, each with its own role. Before you upgraded all five member servers to Windows Server 2008 Standard Edition, you had Windows Server 2003 Standard Edition SP2 on all the member servers. The decision has now been made to create an Active Directory domain and have these five member servers all take the domain controller role. You need to install Active Directory on all five member servers. What should you do?

A. Install the Active Directory Federation Services role on one of the five member servers

B. Install the Active Directory Rights Management Services role on one of the five member servers

C. Install the Active Directory Lightweight Directory Services role on all five of the member servers

D. Run the Dcpromo utility on one of the five member servers

E. Run the Dcpromo utility on all five of the member servers

Correct Answer & Explanation: **E**. Running Dcpromo on all five of the member servers will start the installation of Active Directory. To make each of the five member servers domain controllers, you have to run Dcpromo on each and make them part of the same new forest.

Incorrect Answers & Explanations: **A**, **B**, **C**, **D**. Answers **A**, **B**, **C**, and **D** are incorrect, because these options will not install Active Directory, which is what makes a server a domain controller.

8. When installing the very first domain controller in a new forest, which one of the following must be installed during the Active Directory installation?

A. DHCP

B. DNS

C. WINS

D. Global Catalog

E. RODC

Correct Answer & Explanation: **D.** The Global Catalog holds account and schema information which will be replicated to other Global Catalog servers.

Incorrect Answers & Explanations: **A, B, C, E.** Answers **A, B, C,** and **E** are incorrect, because none of these is compulsory.

9. One of the domain controllers in one of the remote sites has crashed. You have instructed the local resource to install Server 2008 Standard Edition on a new server. You have created a recent backup of the Active Directory database and made this database available to the local resource as a restore database on DVD. What feature will you now use to restore Active Directory to the new server?

   A. AD Recovery Tool

   B. ADSI Edit

   C. Install from Media

   D. Server Core Installation from Media

   E. Recover from Media

   Correct Answer & Explanation: **C.** Install from Media (IFM) is used to recover a corrupt or damaged domain controller.

   Incorrect Answers & Explanations: **A, B, D, E.** Answers **A, B, D,** and **E** are incorrect, because these options will not restore Active Directory to a server.

10. The new Server Core installation option for Windows Server 2008 has the benefit of reduced management and maintenance and a reduced attack surface. Also, the Server Core has a smaller hardware requirement than a full installation of the operating system. What is the minimum amount of hard disk space required to install Server Core?

    A. 1 GB

    B. 4 GB

    C. 8 GB

    D. 10 GB

    Correct Answer & Explanation: **A.** 1 GB of hard disk space is required to install Server Core and 2 GB of hard disk space is required to run more operations on Server Core.

    Incorrect Answers & Explanations: **B, C, D.** Answers **B, C,** and **D** are incorrect, as only 1 GB of hard drive space is required for the installation of Server Core.

Chapter 2: Configuring Server Roles in Windows 2008

1. You are the administrator for a nationwide company with over 5,000 employees. Your main office has approximately 4,500 employees, while the company's ten remote offices have 50 users residing in each. You are often unaware of the physical security in place at these offices. However, since there is a fairly sizable amount of users at each office, you must provide them with directory services. What is the BEST option to use for directory services when security is often an unknown?

A. Lightweight Directory Services

B. Read-only domain controllers

C. Active Directory Federation Services

D. Active Director Rights Management Services

Correct Answer & Explanation: **B.** This is essentially the ideal scenario for the use of a read-only domain controller, since only the accounts of users authenticating from the remote office will be cached on the server.

Incorrect Answers & Explanations: **A, C,** and **D.** Answer **A** is incorrect because LDS is used in situations when all of the features of a full Active Directory are not required. Answers **C** and **D** are incorrect because these are used for authentication between domains and document security, respectively.

2. _____ is a format and application-agnostic technology, which provides services to enable the creation of information-protection solutions.

A. Lightweight Directory Services

B. Read-only domain controllers

C. Active Directory Federation Services

D. Active Director Rights Management Services

Correct Answer & Explanation: **D.** Active Directory Rights Management Services, or AD RMS, is a technology now available as part of Windows Server 2008 that protects documents (such as e-mails and spreadsheets) by assigning Active Directory–based credentials to the documents.

Incorrect Answers & Explanations: **A, B,** and **C.** Answer **A** is incorrect because LDS is used in situations when all of the features of a full Active Directory are not required. Answer **B** is incorrect because RODCs are used as a secure

Directory Services solution in remote offices, and **C** is incorrect because AD FS is used for synchronizing external Active Directory domains for authentication purposes.

3. You are the administrator for a nationwide company with over 5,000 employees. Your director tells you your company has just signed into a partnership with another organization, and that you will be responsible for ensuring that authentication can occur between both organizations without the need for additional sign-on accounts. Your boss mentions that the partner has a variety of Directory Services installed throughout their organizations. Which of the following can Active Directory Federation Services NOT connect to?

    A. Lightweight Directory Services

    B. Windows Server 2003 Directory Services

    C. Windows Server 2003 R2 Directory Services

    D. All of the above

    Correct Answer & Explanation: **B**. Active Directory Federation Services was not introduced until the R2 release of Windows Server 2003.

    Incorrect Answers & Explanations: **A**, **C**, and **D**. Answers **A** and **C** are incorrect because AD FS can connect to both LDS and Windows Server 2003 DS. Answer **D** is incorrect because AD FS can connect to both LDS and Windows Server 2003 R2.

4. You are the administrator for a nationwide company with over 5,000 employees. Your main office has approximately 4,500 employees, while your company's ten remote offices have 50 users each residing in them. You are often unaware of the physical security in place at these offices. However, since there is a fairly sizable amount of users at each office, you need to provide them with directory services. What is the BEST option to use for directory services when security is often an unknown?

    A. Lightweight Directory Services

    B. Read-only domain controllers

    C. Active Directory Federation Services

    D. Active Director Rights Management Services

    Correct Answer & Explanation: **B**. This is essentially the ideal scenario for the use of a read-only domain controller since only the accounts of users authenticating from the remote office will be cached on the server.

Incorrect Answers & Explanations: **A**, **C**, and **D**. Answer **A** is incorrect because LDS is used in situations when all of the features of a full Active Directory are not required. Answers **C** and **D** are incorrect because these are used for authentication between domains and document security, respectively.

5. The Web development team has requested that you implement a new Web server in a DMZ that will be used for presenting Web sites to customers. Which of the following is NOT a reason for using Windows Server 2008 Core Server?

   A. A Core installation does not require a Windows Server 2008 license.

   B. A Core installation does not provide GUIs, which limits console access.

   C. Core Server installs fewer services than a full installation of Windows Server 2008.

   D. Core Server uses fewer resources than a full installation of Windows Server 2008.

   Correct Answer & Explanation: **A**. Although Core Server looks nothing like the full installation, it still requires the appropriate server license

   Incorrect Answers & Explanations: **B**, **C**, and **D**. Answer **B** is incorrect because Core Server offers absolutely no GUIs by default. Answers **C** and **D** are incorrect because there are both fewer services and fewer hardware resources (memory, CPU, and disk space) than a full installation.

6. You have a Windows Server 2003 R2 domain currently running in your organization. You would like to install a read-only domain controller into your Directory Services structure, but you do not want to completely upgrade your domain to Windows Server 2008 Directory Services just yet. What do you need to do in order to add an RODC?

   A. Change the domain functional level to Windows Server 2008 mixed mode.

   B. Change the forest functional level to Windows Server 2008 mixed mode.

   C. Run *adprep* on a Windows Server 2003 R2 domain controller.

   D. An RODC cannot be added until the entire domain is a Windows Server 2008 Directory Services domain.

   Correct Answer & Explanation: **C**. *adprep* must be run on a Windows Server 2003 R2 domain controller using Windows Server 2008 media.

   Incorrect Answers & Explanations: **A**, **B**, and **D**. Answers **A** and **B** are incorrect because a Windows 2003 R2 domain and forest would not have an option to raise the functional levels to 2008. Answer **D** is incorrect because an RODC can be added to a Windows Server 2003 R2 domain.

7. You are looking to upgrade your environment to Windows Server 2008, and you are explaining the new Server Manager console to your boss. Which *three* of the following answers correctly describe ways that Server Manager can be used?

   A. Server Manager can be used to add new server roles.

   B. Server Manager can be used to add new server features.

   C. Server Manager can be used to configure server failover.

   D. Server Manager can be used for scripting commands.

   Correct Answers & Explanation: **A**, **B**, and **C**. These three are functions available via Server Manager. For a more complete list, see Table 1.1

   Incorrect Answer & Explanations: **D**. Answer **D** is incorrect because scripting is done through command lines and PowerShell.

8. You are attempting to install Directory Services on a Windows Server 2008 Server Core installation. You type *dcpromo* at the command prompt, but the server fails to install Directory Services. What is the MOST LIKELY reason for this?

   A. Directory Services are not supported on a Server Core installation, only read-only domain controllers.

   B. You must use an unattended file to complete the Directory Services installation.

   C. You must use the Server Manager from another Windows Server 2008 system to complete the installation.

   D. Your server's chipset does not support Directory Services in a Server Core installation.

   Correct Answer & Explanation: **B**. An unattended file (a text file with information about the planned installation) must be referenced during the installation procedure.

   Incorrect Answers & Explanations: **A**, **C**, and **D**. Answer **A** is incorrect. Directory Services can be installed on a Server Core installation. Answer **C** is incorrect because Directory Services cannot be installed from another server. Answer **D** is incorrect because the chipset would not cause Directory Services to fail during installation.

9. Which of the following Directory Services administration tools can be used in a Windows Server 2008 Lightweight Directory Services installation?

   A. Active Directory Users and Computers

   B. Active Directory Sites and Services

   C. Active Directory Domains and Trusts

   D. Active Directory Licensing Manager

   Correct Answer & Explanation: **B**. Active Directory Sites and Services can be used for configuring sites, which is particularly useful in configuring geographically disbursed LDS implementations.

   Incorrect Answers & Explanations: **A**, **C**, and **D**. Answers **A** and **C** are incorrect because these tools are not supported in an LDS implementation. Answer **D** is incorrect because no such tool exists.

10. BitLocker is a new technology that is available in Windows Server 2008 as well as Windows Vista. Which is NOT an advantage of using BitLocker?

    A. BitLocker can be used to prevent a hacker from detecting my password.

    B. BitLocker prevents someone from removing a hard drive from a system and reading it by installing it on another system.

    C. BitLocker prevents someone from loading another operating system onto the server and reading the contents of the disk using this additional operating system.

    D. All of the above selections are an advantage of using BitLocker.

    Correct Answer & Explanation: **A**. BitLocker does not prevent someone from booting your system normally and cracking your password using brute force.

    Incorrect Answers & Explanations: **B**, **C**, and **D**. Answer **B** is incorrect because BitLocker prevents someone from reading an encrypted hard drive on another system. Answer **C** is incorrect because even if another operating system is loaded onto the server, the encrypted drive can still not be read.

Chapter 3: Configuring Certificate Services and PKI

1. You have been asked to provide an additional security system for your company's internet activity. This system should act as an underlying cryptography system. It should enable users or computers that have never been

in trusted communication before to validate themselves by referencing an association to a trusted third party (TTP). The method of security the above example is referencing is?

A. Certificate Authority (CA)

B. Nonrepudiation

C. Cryptanalysis

D. Public Key Infrastructure (PKI)

Correct Answer & Explanation: **D**. Answer **D** is correct because an underlying cryptography system that enables users or computers that have never been in trusted communication before to validate themselves by referencing an association to a trusted third party (TTP) is called a Public Key Infrastructure (PKI).

Incorrect Answers & Explanations: **A, B, C**. Answer **A** is incorrect, because Certificate Authority (CA) is a term that refers to the TTP in the PKI transaction. Answer B is incorrect, because it describes only one single goal of PKI. Answer **C** is incorrect; it refers to the process of decrypting or cracking data, not securing it.

2. You are engaged in an exercise that is meant to demonstrate the Public-Key Cryptography Standards (PKCS). You arrive at a portion of the exercise dealing with encrypting a string with a secret key based on a password. Which of the following PKCS does this exercise address?

A. PKCS #5

B. PKCS #1

C. PKCS #8

D. PKCS #9

Correct Answer & Explanation: **A**. PKCS #5 is correct because it is a Password-based Cryptography Standard that deals with the method for encrypting a string with a secret key that is derived from a password. The result of the method is an octet string (a sequence of 8-bit values).

Incorrect Answers & Explanations: **B, C, D**. Answer **B** is incorrect, because PKCS #1deals with RSA Cryptography Standards and outlines the encryption of data using the RSA algorithm. The purpose of the RSA Cryptography Standard is in the development of digital signatures and digital envelopes. Answer **C** is incorrect, because PKCS #8 is the Private-key Information Syntax Standard and describes a method of communication for private-key information that includes the use of public-key algorithm and additional attributes (similar to PKCS #6). Answer **C** is incorrect, because PKCS #9 deals with Selected Attribute Types and defines the types of attributes for use in extended certificates (PKCS #6), digitally signed messages (PKCS #7), and private-key information (PKCS #8).

3. You are working in a Windows Server 2008 PKI and going over various user profiles that are subject to deletion due to company policy. The public keys for these users are stored under Documents and Settings\Administrator\System Certificates\My\Certificates and the private keys would be under Documents and Settings\Administrator\Crypto\RSA. You possess copies of the public keys in the registry, and in Active Directory. What effect will the deletion of the user profile have on the private key?

   A. It will have no effect.

   B. It will be replaced by the public key that is stored.

   C. The Private Key will be lost.

   D. None of the above.

   Correct Answer & Explanation: **C**. The private key will be lost if the user profile is deleted. The private keys are vulnerable to deletion and are stored under the user's profile.

   Incorrect Answers & Explanations: **A, B, D**. Answer **A** is incorrect, because the private keys are vulnerable to deletion and are stored under the user's profile, so deletion of the user profile will effect the private key. Answer **B** is incorrect, because the public key can not be used to replace the private key in any instance. Answer **D** is incorrect, because answer **C** is the correct answer.

4. Two users, Dave and Dixine, wish to communicate privately. Dave and Dixine each own a key pair consisting of a public key and a private key. If Dave wants Dixine to send him an encrypted message, which of the following security measures occurs first?

   A. Dave transmits his public key to Dixine.

   B. Dixine uses Dave's public key to encrypt the message.

   C. Nothing occurs the message is simply sent.

   D. Dixine requests a access to Dave's private key.

   Correct Answer & Explanation: **A**. Dave transmits his public key to Dixine is the correct answer because Dixine must receive Dave's public key to be able to encrypt the message so that Dave can use his private key to decrypt it.

Incorrect Answers & Explanations: **B**, **C**, **D**. Answer **B** is incorrect, because Dave must transmit his public key for Dixine to have access to it. This is the second step in the process not the first. Answer **C** is incorrect, because the encryption process is not automatic and an exchange of public and private keys must occur for communication to be encrypted. Answer **D** is incorrect because private keys are never transmitted or shared and are used only to decode message encrypted with a matching public key pair.

5. You are browsing your company's e-commerce site using Internet Explorer 7 and have added a number of products to the shopping cart. You notice that there is a padlock symbol in the browser. By right clicking this symbol you will be able to view information concerning the site's:

A. Private Key.

B. Public Key.

C. Information Architecture.

D. Certificates.

Correct Answer & Explanation: **C**. Certificates is the correct answer because by clicking on the padlock you access the view Certificate information tab. This allows you to verify certain aspects of the certificate.

Incorrect Answers & Explanations: **A**, **B**, **C**. Answer **A** is incorrect, because you can never access another party's private key. Answer **B** is incorrect, because the public key has already been transmitted and is not accessible in this manner. Answer **C** is incorrect because information architecture (IA) of the site has nothing to do with the encryption process or PKI.

6. You are engaged in an exercise that is meant to demonstrate the Public-Key Cryptography Standards (PKCS) used in modern encryption. You arrive at a portion of the exercise which outlines the encryption of data using the RSA algorithm. Which of the following PKCS does this exercise address?

A. PKCS #5

B. PKCS #1

C. PKCS #8

D. PKCS #9

Correct Answer & Explanation: **B**. Answer **B** is correct, because PKCS #1 deals with RSA Cryptography Standards and outlines the encryption of data using the RSA algorithm. The purpose of the RSA Cryptography Standard is in the development of digital signatures and digital envelopes.

Incorrect Answers & Explanations: **A, C, D.** Answer **A** is incorrect; PKCS #5 is a Password-based Cryptography Standard that deals with the method for encrypting a string with a secret key that is derived from a password. The result of the method is an octet string (a sequence of 8-bit values). Answer **C** is incorrect, because PKCS #8 is the Private-key Information Syntax Standard and describes a method of communication for private-key information that includes the use of public-key algorithm and additional attributes (similar to PKCS #6). Answer **D** is incorrect, because PKCS #9 deals with Selected Attribute Types and defines the types of attributes for use in extended certificates (PKCS #6), digitally signed messages (PKCS #7), and private-key information (PKCS #8).

7. You are the administrator of your company's Windows Server 2008-based network and are attempting to enroll a smart card and configure it at an enrollment station. Which of the following certificates must be requested in order to accomplish this action?

A. A machine certificate.

B. An application certificate.

C. A user certificate.

D. All of the above.

Correct Answer & Explanation: **C.** Answer **C** is correct because user certificates are certificates that enable the user to do something that would not be otherwise allowed. The Enrollment Agent certificate is one example of a user certificate. Without it, even an administrator is not able to enroll smart cards and configure them properly at an enrollment station.

Incorrect Answers & Explanations: **A, B, D.** Answer **A** is incorrect, because machine certificates (as the name implies) give the system—instead of the user—the ability to do something out of the ordinary. The main purpose for machine certificates is authentication, both client-side and server-side. Answer **B** is incorrect, because the term application certificate refers to any certificate that is used with a specific PKI-enabled application. Examples include IPSec and S/MIME encryption for e-mail. Applications that need certificates are generally configured to automatically request them, and are then placed in a waiting status until the required certificate arrives. Answer **D** is incorrect because it is generally never required to for all of the listed certificates to be requested from a single action.

8. Dave and Dixine each own a key pair consisting of a public and private key. A public key was used to encrypt a message and the corresponding private key was used to decrypt. Dave wants Dixine to know that a document he is responding with was really written by him. How is this possible using the given scenario?

   A. Dave's private key can encrypt the document and the matching public key can be used to decrypt it.

   B. Dave can send Dixine his private key as proof.

   C. Dixine can allow Dave access to her private key to encrypt the document.

   D. None of the above.

   Correct Answer & Explanation: **A**. Dave's private key can be used to encrypt the document and the matching public key can be used to decrypt is the correct answer because if a user uses your public key to read the document and they are successful, they can be certain that it was "signed" by your private key and is therefore authentic.

   Incorrect Answers & Explanations: **B**, **C**, **D**. Answer **B** and **C** are incorrect, because private keys should never be shared with other users. Answer **D** is incorrect, as stated a private key can be used to encrypt a document so that the matching public key can be used to decrypt it.

9. You are administrating a large hierarchal government environment in which a trust model needs to be established. The company does not want external CA's involved in the verification process. Which of the following is the best trust model deployment for this scenario?

   A. A hierarchal first party trust model.

   B. A third party single CA trust model.

   C. A first party single CA trust Model.

   D. None of these will meet the needs of the company.

   Correct Answer & Explanation: **A**. Choice **A** is correct because Hierarchical models work well in larger hierarchical environments, such as large government organizations or corporate environments and use multiple levels of subordinate CA's that are governed by a root CA. First party CA's are internal and adminis-tered by the company deploying them.

Incorrect Answers & Explanations: **B**, **C**, **D**. Answer **B** and **C** are incorrect, because hierarchal models are better suited for larger hierarchal environments because they offer more layers of verification. Answer **D** is incorrect, because as stated choice A will meet the needs of this example.

10. Two users, Dave and Dixine, wish to communicate privately. Dave and Dixine each own a key pair consisting of a public key and a private key. A public key was used to encrypt a message and the corresponding private key was used to decrypt. What is the major security issue with this scenario?

A. Private keys are revealed during the initial transaction.

B. Information encrypted with a public key can be decrypted too easily with out the private key.

C. An attacker can intercept the data mid-stream, and replace the original signature with his or her own, using his private key.

D. None of the Above

Correct Answer & Explanation: **C**. Answer **C** is correct because there is nothing to prevent an attacker from intercepting the data mid-stream, and replacing the original signature with his or her own, using his private key. The solution to this problem in Windows PKI is the certificate.

Incorrect Answers & Explanations: **A**, **B**, **D**. Answer **A** is incorrect, because private keys arte never accessible to other users. Answer **B** is incorrect, because while the encryption process is not completely impervious to cracking with out the private key to decrypt the data an attacker would have an incredibly hard time decrypting the transmission. Answer **D** is incorrect because as stated an attacker can intercept the data mid-stream, and replace the original signature with his or her own, using his private key.

Chapter 4: Maintaining an Active Directory Environment

1. You've just finished installing a new Windows Server 2008 DC. It is the policy of the IT department to perform a full backup of newly installed DCs. You click on **Start | Administrative Tools | Windows Server Backup**. When Windows Server Backup loads you see the following screen.

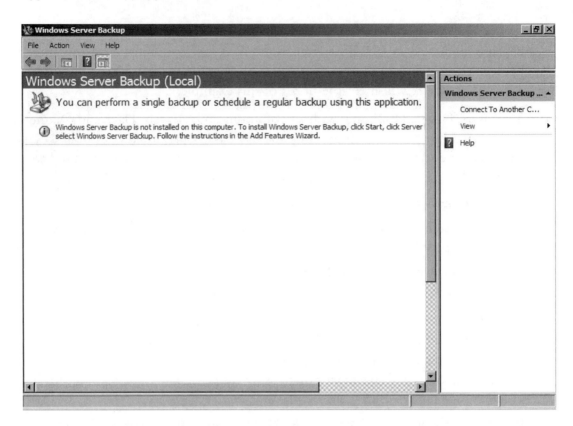

What do you need to do to ensure that the backup takes place?

A. Run DCPROMO

B. Install the Windows Server Backup feature

C. Go to a command prompt and run wbadmin.exe

D. Boot into DSRM and conduct the backup from there

Correct Answer & Explanation: **B**. Even though Windows Server Backup appears in the list of Administrative Tools doesn't mean it's been installed. Install the feature via Server Manager.

Incorrect Answers & Explanations: **A**, **C**, **D**. Answer **A** is incorrect, because DCPROMO is used to convert a server into a DC; it has nothing to do with the backup software. Answer **C** is incorrect, because wbadmin.exe is a part of the Windows Server Backup feature. Simply running it will provide you with the same message popping up. Answer **D** is incorrect, because with the backup software not being installed you cannot conduct the backup regardless of what mode you've booted in on the DC.

2. You are responsible for performing backups on the DCs on your network. Your boss has requested that you conduct system state backups to DVD. How do you accomplish this?

   A. Run the **Windows Server Backup Wizard**, select **System State Backup**, and set your target to the DVD drive

   B. Run the **Windows Server Backup Wizard**, select a local drive as the target, and then copy the system state backup to the DVD drive

   C. Run the *wbadmin.exe* command with the *start systemstatebackup* command and target it to the DVD drive

   D. Run the *wbadmin.exe* command with the *start systemstatebackup* command, set the target to a local fixed drive, and then copy the system state backup to a DVD

   Correct Answer & Explanation: **D**. System state backups are done using the wbadmin.exe command and must have local drives as targets. To back up to DVD, you must manually copy the system state backup to the DVD drive and burn the backup onto disk.

   Incorrect Answers & Explanations: **A, B, C**. Answers **A** and **B** are incorrect, because Windows Server Backup cannot specifically back up the system state. You must use the wbadmin.exe command. Answer **C** is incorrect, because system state backups must have a local drive as the target.

3. You are the network administrator for your company. Last night you successfully performed a system state backup of one of your DCs. Do to an unforeseen issue, you now need to perform a system state restore. What do you need to do to conduct a system state restore on a DC?

   A. Reboot the DC, go into DSRM, and run wbadmin.exe to perform the system state restore

   B. Log on to the DC as usual and run wbadmin.exe to restore the system state

   C. Stop Active Directory Domain Services and then run the *wbadmin.exe* command to restore the system state

   D. Just restore the system state via the Windows Server Backup Wizard

   Correct Answer & Explanation: **A**. To recover the system state for a DC, you must be in DSRM and then run the *wbadmin.exe* command.

Incorrect Answers & Explanations: **B, C, D**. Answer **B** is incorrect, because you cannot restore the system state of a DC in normal mode. Answer **C** is incorrect, because stopping Active Directory Domain Services will not allow you to restore the system state on a DC. Answer **D** is incorrect, because the Windows Server Backup Wizard does not restore the system state specifically.

4. You are the network administrator for your company. You have a scheduled backup job run three times a day: 10:00 A.M., 4:00 P.M., and 11:00 P.M. At 4:50 P.M., you get a call that user Janet Harrell has deleted the company budget on the server. There are no previous versions available. What should you do to restore the company budget?

   A. Run **ntbackup**, select the company budget from the list of files backed up, and choose **Restore**

   B. Run **Windows Server Backup**, select **Recover** from the **Actions** pane, choose **Files and Folders** as the recovery type. Select the company budget from the **Available items** list. Choose **Original location** for recovery destination, create copies so that you have both versions of the file or folder under **When the wizard find files and folders in the recovery destination**, and choose **Restore security settings**.

   C. Go into **DSRM**, run **wbadmin.exe**, and conduct a system state recovery

   D. Stop Active Directory Domain Services, load ntbackup, select the company budget, and choose Restore

   Correct Answer & Explanation: **B**. You would run through the restore wizard in Windows Server Backup, choose the budget file, and restore to the original location along with the original security settings. Windows Server Backup provides the ability to individually choose which files and/or directories to restore.

   Incorrect Answers & Explanations: **A, C, D**. Answers **A** and **D** are incorrect, because ntbackup is no longer the backup and restore software that comes with Windows Server 2008. The ntbackup version for Windows Server 2008 that you can download can recover only .bkf files and not the .vhd files that Windows Server Backup creates. Answer **C** is incorrect, because you do not have to go into DSRM to recover key files.

5. You are the network administrator at your company. The Active Directory database file on one of your DCs is corrupt. You decide to perform a nonauthoritative restore on the DC. You reboot the server into DSRM and try to

log on as the domain administrator but you cannot. You need to get this DC back up and functioning as soon as possible. What can you do to achieve this?

A. Log on to the server with another domain administrator's account

B. Log on to the server using the local administrator's account

C. Change the domain administrator's password from another DC and then log on using the account with the new password

D. Log on using the DSRM administrator's account and password

Correct Answer & Explanation: **D.** You must log on using the DSRM administrator's account and password which you created during the DCPROMO wizard while converting this server into a DC.

Incorrect Answers & Explanations: **A, B, C.** Answer **A** is incorrect, because you must log on using the DSRM account. A domain admin account cannot log on to the server in DSRM mode. Answer **B** is incorrect, because you must log on using the DSRM administrator's account and there are no local administrator accounts on a DC. Answer **C** is incorrect for the same reasons as answer **A**.

6. You are the domain admin for your company. You have tasked Susan, a member of the Account Operators group, to delete Amber Chambers' user account because she quit yesterday. Susan accidentally deletes Andy Chambers' account. Before she realizes what's happened the change is replicated to the other DCs. What can you do to bring back Andy Chambers' user account?

A. Reboot the DC into DSRM, restore the system state, and conduct a nonauthoritative restore on Andy Chambers' user account from the most recent backup using wbadmin.exe

B. Reboot the DC into DSRM, restore the system state, and conduct an authoritative restore on Andy Chambers' user account from the most recent backup using wbadmin.exe

C. Log on to the DC in normal mode, stop Active Directory Domain Services, load Windows Server Backup, restore the system state, and perform an authoritative restore of Andy Chambers' user account

D. Log on to the DC in normal mode, stop Active Directory Domain Services, load Windows Server Backup, restore the system state, and perform a nonauthoritative restore of Andy Chambers' user account

Correct Answer & Explanation: **B.** Only an authoritative restore can restore the user account and prevent it from being overwritten by directory replication.

To perform an authoritative restore you must boot up into the DSRM, run wbadmin.exe to restore the system state, and then perform an authoritative restore.

Incorrect Answers & Explanations: A, C, D. Answer **A** is incorrect, because a nonauthoritative restore would bring the user account back but it would be deleted once directory replication took place. Answers **C** and **D** are incorrect, because you must be in DSRM to restore the user account. Windows Server Backup has no way of performing an authoritative restore via the GUI.

7. You are the domain administrator for your company. Examining one of the DCs, you notice that the file ntds.dit is almost 6 GB in size. You decide that to save disk space and increase performance you will defrag Active Directory Domain Services. How would you accomplish this?

   A. Log on to the server as an administrator. Perform a system state backup of the DC. Create a new directory on the system drive called C:\defrag. Stop Active Directory Domain Services. Start an instance of ntdsutil and activate Instance ntds. At the ntdsutil prompt pull up the file maintenance prompt and type **compact to c:\defrag**. Go to the %systemdrive%\Windows\ NTDS directory and delete the old ntds.dit file as well as any .log files. Copy the ntds.dit file in the C:\defrag folder to %systemroot%\Windows\ NTDS, and then restart Active Directory Domain Services.

   B. Log on to the server as an administrator. Perform a system state backup of the DC. Create a new directory on the system drive called C:\defrag. Start an instance of ntdsutil and activate Instance ntds. At the ntdsutil prompt, pull up the file maintenance prompt and type **compact to c:\defrag**. Go to the %systemdrive%\Windows\NTDS directory and delete the old ntds.dit file as well as any .log files. Copy the ntds.dit file in the C:\defrag folder to the %systemroot%\Windows\NTDS.

   C. Log on to the server as an administrator in DSRM. Perform a system state backup of the DC. Create a new directory on the system drive called C:\defrag. Stop Active Directory Domain Services. Start an instance of ntdsutil and activate Instance ntds. At the ntdsutil prompt, pull up the file maintenance prompt and type **compact to c:\defrag**. Go to the %systemdrive%\Windows\NTDS directory and delete the old ntds.dit file as well as any .log files. Copy the ntds.dit file in the C:\defrag folder to the %systemroot%\Windows\NTDS, and then restart Active Directory Domain Services.

D. Log on to the server as an administrator. Perform a system state backup of the DC. Create a new directory on the system drive called C:\defrag. Stop Active Directory Domain Services. Start an instance of ntdsutil and activate Instance ntds. At the ntdsutil prompt, pull up the file maintenance prompt and type **compact to c:\defrag**. Go to the %systemdrive%\ Windows\NTDS directory and delete the old ntds.dit file as well as any .log files. Copy the ntds.dit file in the C:\defrag folder to %systemdrive%\ Windows\NTDS.

Correct Answer & Explanation: **A**. These are the steps in performing a defrag/ compact of the Active Directory Domain Services database file. Although the system state backup is not required, it is highly recommended.

Incorrect Answers & Explanations: **B, C, D**. Answer **B** is incorrect, because you never stopped Active Directory Domain Services. Answer **C** is incorrect, because you no longer need to boot into DSRM to defrag the database. Answer **D** is incorrect, because you never restarted Active Directory Domain Services.

8. You are the domain administrator for your company. Your network consists of three DCs, each running Windows Server 2008. Two are at site A, and the third is located at site B. There seems to be a replication problem between the DCs at site A and the DC at site B. What is the best tool to use in troubleshooting directory replication?

A. Network Monitor

B. Task Manager

C. RepAdmin

D. Event Viewer

Correct Answer & Explanation: **C**. RepAdmin can be used for monitoring Active Directory replication, topology, and even force replication.

Incorrect Answers & Explanation: **A, B, D**. Answer **A** is incorrect, because it doesn't show what's actually being replicated. It can show that the DCs are communicating, but it cannot truly tell whether replication is taking place. Answer **B** is incorrect, because the Task Manager is more for administrators to get a real-time view of the performance of the server and not that of directory replication. Answer **D** is incorrect, because it doesn't show the topology, nor can it initiate replication. It is probably the best place to start, but not to finish.

9. You are the domain administrator for your company. Your network consists of multiple DCs at multiple sites. A DC at your local site is having problems with replicating. You need to know when this DC last attempted to perform an inbound replication on the Active Directory partitions. How would you accomplish this?

A. Open a command prompt on the DC and run *ntdsutil*

B. Open a command prompt on the DC and run *repadmin /replicate*

C. Open a command prompt on the DC and run *repadmin /rodcpwdrepl*

D. Open a command prompt on the DC and run *repadmin /showrepl*

Correct Answer & Explanation: **D**. Running *repadmin /showrepl* displays the replication status when a specified DC has last attempted to perform inbound replication on Active Directory partitions.

Incorrect Answers & Explanations: **A, B, C**. Answer **A** is incorrect, because ntdsutil does not provide information about directory replication. Answer **B** is incorrect, because the */replicate* switch triggers immediate replication and does not provide information about when a particular DC last attempted to perform an inbound replication. Answer **C** is incorrect, because the */rodcpwdrepl* switch triggers the replication of passwords for specified users from a source DC to one or more RODCs.

10. You are the domain administrator for your company. At your site you have a single DC that also acts as an application server. From 10:00 A.M. to 4:00 P.M., users complain about slow logons to the network and that accessing resources from this DC is incredibly slow during most of the workday. You log on to the DC, pull up the Task Manager, and notice that a process called CustApp.exe is using just more than 90% of the CPU cycles. The application must remain running during the day, but you also need to resolve the slow logon issues. There is no money in the budget for additional hardware. What is the best way to handle this situation?

A. Go into the Windows System Resource Manager on the DC, and create a new recurring calendar event to start at 8:00 A.M. and end at 5:00 P.M., daily. Associate the event with the Equal_Per_Process policy.

B. Go into the Task Manager and into the Processes tab. Find CustApp.exe and set the priority to Below Normal.

C. Go into the Task Manager and into the Process tab. Find CustApp.exe and end the process.

D. Purchase a second server to run only the CustApp.exe application

Correct Answer & Explanation: **A**. The Windows System Resource Manager (WSRM) allows administrators to set policies and thresholds on applications and processes on the number of CPU cycles they can max out at and the amount of memory they are allowed to consume. Setting a calendar policy allows the administrator to allow the application to run at high CPU levels if needed after hours; that way, it doesn't affect the end-users at work.

Incorrect Answers & Explanations: **B, C, D**. Answer **B** is incorrect, because by setting the priority level to below normal it is possible that the threads within the CustApp.exe will never execute depending on whether there are a large number of threads with higher-priority numbers in the queue. Answer **C** is incorrect, because it completely stops the CustApp.exe process which may belong to a mission-critical application, thereby affecting productivity in a highly negative manner. Answer **D** is incorrect, because the scenario clearly states that there is no money in the budget for additional hardware.

Chapter 5: Configuring the Active Directory Infrastructure

1. A large company has just merged with yours. This organization has recently converted its internal network from IPv4 addressing to IPv6 to support a number of new network applications that required it. You must now begin to plan for IPv6 support on your own internal network. You are creating training materials for your junior networking staff. Which of the following features is built into IPv6 that was not required in IPv4?

    A. Classless Inter-Domain Routing (CIDR)

    B. IP Security through the use of IPSec

    C. Network address translator (NAT)

    D. Loopback IP addressing

    Correct Answer & Explanation: **B**. Answer **B** is correct because IPSec is a mandatory component of IPv6, whereas its use is optional in IPv4.

    Incorrect Answers & Explanations: **A, C**, and **D**. Answer **A** is incorrect because CIDR notation is used to express IP addresses for both IPv4 and IPv6 TCP/IP addresses. Answer **C** is incorrect because NAT is not a mandatory component of IPv6. Answer **D** is incorrect because the loopback IP address is available in both IPv4 and IPv6. In IPv4, the loopback address is 127.0.0.1; in IPv6 the loopback address is ::1.

2. Your IT manager wants you to link four divisions of the company through a ring of eight unidirectional cross-forest trusts. He uses this reasoning: If multiple forest trusts are established, authentication requests made in any domain of any forest can pass through multiple forest trusts, hence multiple Kerberos domains, on their way to their destination. Why is he wrong?

   A. Although each cross-forest trust is transitive at the forest level, where all domains in both forests can authenticate, they are not transitive at the federated forest level as he suggests. The trust path cannot include more than one cross-forest trust.

   B. Cross-forest trusts are not transitive, and will not allow pass-through authentication.

   C. To create a mesh trust relationship between four forests, you need only four cross-forest trusts.

   D. Cross-forest trusts are bidirectional, so only three trusts are needed to link all four forests. Completing the "ring" is not necessary.

   Correct Answer & Explanation: **A.** Answer **A** is correct because cross-forest trusts are transitive only between the source and destination forests. This means that every domain in Forest A will automatically trust every domain in Forest B. This transitivity does not extend to multiple forests: If a cross-forest trust exists between Forest A and Forest B, and a second cross-forest trust exists between Forest B and Forest C, this does not automatically create a trust relationship between Forest A and Forest C.

   Incorrect Answers & Explanations: **B**, **C**, and **D**. Answer **B** is incorrect because cross-forest trusts are transitive between the source and domain forests, and will allow pass-through authentication between them. Answer **C** is incorrect because in order to create a mesh trust relationship between four forests, you would need to create a total of six cross-forest trusts: between Forest A and Forest B, Forest A and Forest C, Forest B and Forest D, Forest C and Forest D, Forest A and Forest D, and Forest B and Forest C. Answer **D** is incorrect because in order to create a mesh trust relationship between four forests, you would need to create a total of six cross-forest trusts: between Forest A and Forest B, Forest A and Forest C, Forest B and Forest D, Forest C and Forest D, Forest A and Forest D, and Forest B and Forest C.

3. What FSMO roles should exist in a child domain in a Windows Server 2008 forest? (Choose all that apply.)

A. Schema Master

B. Domain Naming Master

C. PDC Emulator

D. RID Master

E. GC

F. Infrastructure Master

Correct Answers & Explanations: **C, D**, and **F**. Answer **C** is correct because the PDC Emulator FSMO role exists in each domain in an Active Directory forest. Answer **D** is correct because the RID Master FSMO role exists in each domain in an Active Directory forest. Answer F is correct because the Infrastructure Master FSMO role exists in each domain in an Active Directory forest.

Incorrect Answers & Explanations: **A, B**, and **E**. Answer **A** is incorrect because the Schema Master FSMO role exists only in the forest root domain. Answer **B** is incorrect because the Domain Naming Master FSMO role exists only in the forest root domain. Answer E is incorrect because the Global Catalog is not a FSMO role.

4. Your network operations center has identified excessive bandwidth utilization caused by authentication traffic in the root domain subnet, especially between Calico.cats.com and Labs.dogs.com. Your logical network is set up as shown in the diagram. What type of trust or trusts would you set up to alleviate the situation?

Question #4 Diagram

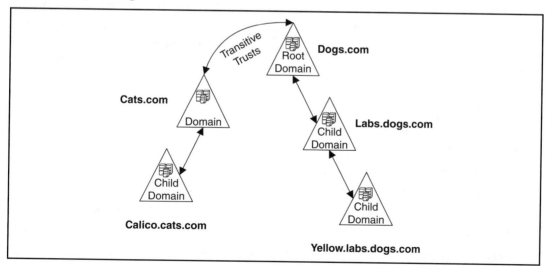

A. Set up a bidirectional transitive parent and child trust between Calico.cats.com and Labs.dogs.com.

B. Set up a shortcut trust between Calico.cats.com and the forest root, and set up a second shortcut trust between Labs.dogs.com and the forest root.

C. Set up a shortcut trust between Calico.cats.com and Labs.dogs.com.

D. Set up two shortcut trusts between Calico.cats.com and Labs.dogs.com.

E. Set up a realm trust between Calico.cats.com and Labs.dogs.com.

Correct Answer & Explanation: C. Answer **C** is correct because this solution will allow authentication traffic to pass directly between Calico.cats.com and Labs.dogs.com rather than "walking the tree" through the forest root domain.

Incorrect Answers & Explanations: A, B, D, and **E.** Answer **A** is incorrect because parent-child trust relationships are created automatically by Active Directory; you cannot manually create one between domains that do not already exist in a parent-child relationship. Answer **B** is incorrect because this solution will not improve how authentication traffic is transmitted on your network in this situation. Answer **D** is incorrect because in this scenario, only a single shortcut trust relationship is required, as all authentication requests are being sent in a single direction. Answer **E** is incorrect because realm trusts are configured between an Active Directory domain and an MIT Kerberos realm, not between two Active Directory domains within a single forest as described in this scenario.

5. Your company, mycompany.com, is merging with the yourcompany.com company. The details of the merger are not yet complete. You need to gain access to the resources in the yourcompany.com company before the merger is completed. What type of trust relationship should you create?

A. Forest trust

B. Shortcut trust

C. External trust

D. Tree Root trust

Correct Answer & Explanation: C. Answer **C** is correct because an external trust is a one-way, nontransitive trust that can be configured between separate Active Directory forests, especially if the two-way transitivity of a cross-forest trust relationship is not desired for a particular scenario.

Incorrect Answers & Explanations: A, B, and **D.** Answer **A** is incorrect because a forest trust is a two-way transitive trust and will likely create more access between the two domains than is desired before the merger is completed. Answer **B** is incorrect because a shortcut trust is configured between two domains within the same Active Directory forest and is not appropriate for this scenario. Answer **D** is incorrect. There is no such thing as a tree root trust within Active Directory.

6. Your boss just informed you that your company will be participating in a joint venture with a partner company. He is very concerned about the fact that a trust relationship needs to be established with the partner company. He fears that an administrator in the other company might be able to masquerade as one of your administrators and grant himself privileges to resources. You assure him that your network and its resources can be protected from an elevated privilege attack. Along with the other security precautions that you will take, what will you tell your boss that will help him rest easy about the upcoming scenario?

A. The permissions set on the Security Account Manager (SAM) database will prevent the other administrators from being able to make changes.

B. The *SIDHistory* attribute tracks all access from other domains. Their activities can be tracked in the System Monitor.

C. The *SIDHistory* attribute from the partner's domain attaches the domain SID for identification. If an account from the other domain tries to elevate its own or another user's privilege, the SID filtering removes the SID in question.

D. SID filtering tracks the domain of every user who accesses resources. The *SIDHistory* records this information and reports the attempts to the Security log in the Event Viewer.

Correct Answer & Explanation: **C**. Answer **C** is correct because SID filtering can be configured on an Active Directory trust relationship to prevent administrators from one domain from maliciously elevating their privileges within another domain.

Incorrect Answers & Explanations: **A**, **B**, and **D**. Answer **A** is incorrect because without SID filtering, an Active Directory trust relationship is susceptible to elevation of privilege attacks. Answer **B** is incorrect because SID filtering prevents elevation of privilege attacks between domains, but is not an attribute that can be monitored using System Monitor. Answer **D** is incorrect because SID filtering prevents elevation of privilege attacks between domains, but does not track user access to resources.

7. You recently completed a merger with yourcompany.com. Corporate decisions have been made to keep the integrity of both of the original companies;

however, management has decided to centralize the IT departments. You are now responsible for ensuring that users in both companies have access to the resources in the other company. What type of trust should you create to solve the requirements?

A. Forest trust

B. Shortcut trust

C. External trust

D. Tree root trust

Correct Answer & Explanation: **A**. Answer **A** is correct because a forest trust is a two-way transitive trust, which will allow users in each company to access resources in the other company.

Incorrect Answers & Explanations: **B**, **C**, and **D**. Answer **B** is incorrect because a shortcut trust is used to shorten the authentication path between domains within a single Active Directory forest. Answer **C** is incorrect because an external trust is a one-way nontransitive trust that can only be configured between a single domain in each direction; it will not allow transitive access to all resources in both forests. Answer **D** is incorrect because this term does not describe a type of trust relationship that can be configured within Active Directory.

8. Robin is managing an Active Directory environment of a medium-size company. He is troubleshooting a problem with the Active Directory. One of the administrators made an update to a user object and another reported that he had not seen the changes appear on another DC. It was more than a week since the change was made. Robin checks the problem by making a change to another Active Directory object. Within a few hours, the change appears on a few DCs, but not on all of them. Which of the following is a possible cause for this problem?

A. Connection objects are not properly configured.

B. Robin has configured one of the DCs for manual updates.

C. There might be different DCs for different domains.

D. Creation of multiple site links between the sites.

Correct Answer & Explanation: **A**. Answer **A** is correct because if Active Directory connection objects are not configured between DCs, changes on one DC will not be reflected on one or more other DCs in your environment.

Incorrect Answers & Explanations: **B**, **C**, and **D**. Answer **B** is incorrect because Active Directory DCs cannot be configured for manual updates;

connection objects must be created to allow DCs to be automatically updated with changes from other DCs. Answer C is incorrect because Active Directory replication can take place between DCs belonging to different domains. Answer **D** is incorrect because creating multiple site links between sites will not prevent Active Directory replication from taking place.

9. James is a systems administrator for an Active Directory environment that consists of two dozen sites. The physical network environment is not fully routed, and James has disabled automatic site link transitivity. He now wants to set up three site links to be transitive, as they are physically connected to one another. Which of the following Active Directory objects is responsible for representing a transitive relationship between sites?

  A. Additional sites

  B. Additional site links

  C. Bridgehead servers

  D. Site link bridges

  Correct Answer & Explanation: **D**. Answer **D** is correct because configuring site link bridges will allow specific site links to be considered transitive when automatic site link bridging has been disabled.

  Incorrect Answers & Explanations: **A**, **B**, and **C**. Answer **A** is incorrect because configuring additional sites does not affect site link transitivity in a network that is not fully routed. Answer **B** is incorrect because configuring additional site links does not affect site link transitivity in a network that is not fully routed. Answer **C** is incorrect because configuring bridgehead servers does not affect site link transitivity in a network that is not fully routed.

10. Steffi is an administrator of a medium-size organization responsible for managing Active Directory replication traffic. She finds an error in the replication configuration. How can she look for specific error messages related to replication?

  A. Use the Active Directory Sites and Services administrative tool

  B. Use the Disk Management tool

  C. View the System log option in the Event Viewer

  D. View the Directory Service log option in the Event Viewer

  Correct Answer & Explanation: **D**. Answer **D** is correct because error messages related to Active Directory replication appear in the Directory Services log in the Windows Event Viewer.

Incorrect Answers & Explanations: **A**, **B**, and **C**. Answer **A** is incorrect because the Active Directory Sites and Services MMC snap-in does not provide any visibility into any error messages related to Active Directory replication. Answer **B** is incorrect because the Disk Management MMC snap-in does not provide any visibility into any error messages related to Active Directory replication. Answer **C** is incorrect because error messages related to Active Directory replication do not appear in the System log in the Windows Event Viewer.

Chapter 6: Configuring Web Application Services

1. While starting to build a web server for use by several business units you have been asked to ensure that the web applications running by different business units use separate security credentials for execution. At what level should you establish this separation to ensure each business unit is able to meet the security needs?

    A. Web Server

    B. Application Pool

    C. Web Site

    D. Web Application

    Correct Answer & Explanation: **B**. The application pool is the container for the web site and web application where the worker process is defined and subsequently the security context. An application pool is configured with a process identity that governs what resources the application is able to access.

    Incorrect Answers & Explanations: **A**, **C**, and **D**. Answer **A** is incorrect because separating out at the web server level is not a cost-effective solution considering hardware, software, and management costs. Answer **C** is incorrect because two web sites can share the same application pool, and thus the same process identity. Answer **D** is incorrect because two web applications can also share the same application pool.

2. You have been asked to build out a web farm that can scale to handle thousands of concurrent users with maximum uptime to run a PHP application. Upon reviewing Windows Server 2008 you determine that IIS with FastCGI support will meet your requirements. What edition of Windows Server 2008 will you need to support PHP?

A. Web Edition

B. Standard Edition

C. Enterprise or Datacenter Edition

D. Any of them will work

Correct Answer & Explanation: D. IIS supports Common Gateway Interface as a standard component across all editions of Windows. In fact there are no differences in the feature set across the various editions.

Incorrect Answers & Explanations: A, B, and **C.** Individually these answers are incorrect because all of them support CGI-based runtime environments like PHP.

3. After receiving a support request from one of your users you have determined that you need to adjust the URL authorization to allow users access to the /finance folder on the company intranet. In what configuration file should you make this modification?

A. ApplicationHost.config

B. Machine.config

C. Sever web.config

D. Site web.config

Correct Answer & Explanation: D. The change should be made in the web. config within the web site to ensure that if the site were to move that the authorization rules moved with it.

Incorrect Answers & Explanations: A, B, and **C.** Answer **A** is incorrect because the ApplicationHost.config has server-level configuration settings dealing with the definition of application pools, sites, and web applications, not individual files and folders within each. Answer **B** is incorrect because it deals with configuration for all .NET applications. Answer **C** is incorrect because the settings in the file apply to all .NET web applications and could impact others that may have a folder named /finance.

4. A colleague has been trying to deploy an ASP.NET web application to IIS on a Server Core installation of Windows Server 2008. They are unable to get the application to work telling you that when they try to access the default.aspx file that it keeps returning an HTTP 404 error. What should you do to help them?

A. Register the ASP.NET handler in the server configuration.

B. Inform them that they need a full installation of Windows Server 2008 for ASP.NET support.

C. Review the security permissions to ensure the IUSR account has access to the file and that anonymous authentication has been enabled.

D. Install the latest .NET Framework on the server.

Correct Answer & Explanation: **B.** You require a full installation of Windows Server 2008 to support .NET-based functionality.

Incorrect Answers & Explanations: **A**, **C**, and **D**. Answer **A** is incorrect because the supporting modules for the handler are not available in Server Core installations. Answer **C** is incorrect because pages with an ASPX extension do not have an associated handler in Server Core installations. Answer **D** is incorrect because Server Core does not support the .NET Framework.

5. After deploying the first ASP.NET application to a web farm environment you have opened the application in a browser where ASP.NET has returned an exception: "[FileLoadException: Could not load file or assembly 'Contoso. Data.SQL, Version=1.0.0.0, Culture=neutral, PublicKeyToken=null' or one of its dependencies. Failed to grant minimum permission requests. (Exception from HRESULT: 0x80131417)]". What should you do to bring the application online?

A. Review the .NET Trust settings to ensure the required level has been set.

B. Run Process Monitor to see where IIS is trying to load the Conotos.Data. SQL.dll assembly from.

C. Grant the IIS_IUSRS group full control rights to the Contoso.Data.SQL. dll file.

D. Grant IUSR built-in account full control rights to the Contoso.Data.SQL. dll file.

Correct Answer & Explanation: **A.** The message tells you that the problem is a permissions issue. Since it does not indicate which permissions you need to have it at you will need to review the .NET trust settings and consult with the application developer.

Incorrect Answers & Explanations: **B**, **C**, and **D**. Answer **B** is incorrect because Process Monitor will not show you any load issues as the worker process is able to find and load the file, but not execute it because of trust settings. Answer **C** is incorrect because the worker process has sufficient permissions to the file to load it, just not execute it. There is also no reason for IIS_IUSRS to have anything more than Read & Execute rights on a .NET assembly. Answer **D** is incorrect because the IUSR account is not involved in the execution of ASP.NET applications. The application pool worker process provides the identity under which the application is executed. In fact, you should never allow anonymous user access to the ASP.NET /bin folder and should be using request filtering to deny all requests to that folder.

6. You are about to migrate an older web application from an IIS 6 server as part of your Windows Server 2008 migration project. The application uses custom metabase entries to store its configuration. IIS 7 introduced a new configuration API. Where will the entries be stored when the application is installed on IIS 7?

   A. ApplicationHost.config

   B. web.config

   C. Administration.config

   D. Redirection.config

   Correct Answer & Explanation: **A**. The Admin Base Object (ABO) Mapper translates calls to the older metabase APIs and stores the resulting values in the ApplicationHost.config.

   Incorrect Answers & Explanations: **B, C**, and **D**. Answer **B** is incorrect because it stores configuration settings specific to the web site and web application features native to IIS 7. Answer **C** is incorrect because it contains IIS Manager module settings. Answer **D** is incorrect because it is used to direct the server to the location of a shared configuration.

7. IIS 7 introduced a number of new configuration tools to help you automate administrative tasks. Which of the following tools cannot be used to administer IIS 7 on Server Core?

   A. Notepad

   B. AppCmd

   C. Windows PowerShell

   D. IIS Manager

   Correct Answer & Explanation: **D**. IIS Manager does not run on Server Core because it is a graphical tool, nor can it connect remotely because the Management Service requires the .NET Framework, which cannot be installed on Server Core.

Incorrect Answers & Explanations: **A**, **B**, and **C**. Answer **A** is incorrect because you can use Notepad to edit the configuration files. Answer **B** is incorrect because AppCmd is the primary command-line tool used for administering IIS on Server Core. Answer **C** is incorrect because PowerShell can use the Microsoft. Web.Administration assembly or Windows Management Instrumentation to manage a Server Core installation.

8. You have been asked by the security team to force the use of SSL on all web applications. You want to configure this at the server level so that no one can modify it. What should you do to prevent people from changing this setting?

   A. Add an access section to the web.config files of each application and add a Deny file access control entry the file's access control list.

   B. Set the overrideModeDefault attribute on the access attribute in the ApplicationHost.config.

   C. Create a location tag in each web.site config containing the access tag and set the allowOverride attribute.

   D. Perform the administrative work on behalf of the users.

   Correct Answer & Explanation: **B**. The ApplicationHost.config provides the configuration for each of the containers along with server-level defaults.

   Incorrect Answers & Explanations: **A**, **C**, and **D**. Answer **A** is incorrect because adding the file permission will prevent the users from administering other settings in their application. Answer **C** is incorrect because the user can easily remove the value from the web.config. Answer **D** is incorrect because it creates extra work for you.

9. You have outgrown your single web server and it is time to expand. You have installed IIS 7 on another web server and moved your content to a network-attached storage device. The next step is to mirror the configuration on the second server. What feature will help you manage the configuration across both of your servers?

   A. AppCmd's Backup and Restore functions

   B. Configuration Inheritance

   C. Shared Configuration

   D. Windows PowerShell

   Correct Answer & Explanation: **C**. Shared configuration enables both servers to operate off the same web site and application configuration enabling you to make a change once and have it take effect on two or more servers.

Incorrect Answers & Explanations: **A**, **B**, and **D**. Answer **A** is incorrect because it introduces a large manual maintenance effort and could inadvertently expose your users to unexpected behavior as you try to back up and restore changes across several servers. Answer **B** is incorrect because it focuses on enabling configuration sharing through the hierarchy of a web site, not across servers. Answer **D** is incorrect because it provides an administration interface, not a configuration sharing solution.

10. The security team has alerted you to a large number of attempted SQL Injection Attacks coming from a specific host. What can you do to ensure that your web server fends off the attacks without compromising your server's security?

    A. Add a request filter to minimize the length of the query string that will be accepted.

    B. Add the IP address to the server-level IP restriction list.

    C. Recycle the application pool.

    D. Disable the anonymous authentication module.

    Correct Answer & Explanation: **B**. By adding the host to the IP restriction list they will not be allowed to connect to the server, effectively blocking the attack from that host.

    Incorrect Answers & Explanations: **A**, **C**, and **D**. Answer **A** is incorrect because a SQL Injection Attack can be made through a number of attack vectors including form submission, query string, or an HTTP request depending on the web application. Answer **C** is incorrect because it will do nothing to prevent someone from attacking your web application. Answer **D** is incorrect because a poorly written module that that is early in the page request cycle could be exposed as an attack vector.

Chapter 7: Configuring Web Infrastructure Services

1. You have been asked to set up a secure FTP connection to receive confidential data from a business partner using FTP and SSL. After installing IIS with the FTP Publishing Service, you cannot find how to enable secure communications on the FTP site in IIS 6 Manager. What should you do?

    A. Obtain a new SSL certificate and add it using IIS Manager

    B. Ensure port 21 is not being used by another Web site or ftp site

C. Install the Web version of the FTP Publishing Service

D. You can't secure FTP communications

Correct Answer & Explanation: **C.** The security features shipped in the Web release of the FTP Publishing Service.

Incorrect Answers & Explanations: **A**, **B**, and **D.** Answer **A** is incorrect because the FTP Publishing Service that ships with Windows Server 2008 does not have the security features for enabling SSL. Answer **B** is incorrect because the port has no bearing on whether or not SSL is enabled. Answer **D** is incorrect because you can secure the connection with SSL using the Web release of the FTP Publishing Service.

2. You need to set up several FTP sites on a single IP address. Using the FTP Publishing Service support for virtual hosts you have configured ftp.contoso. com, ftp.fabrikam.com, and ftp.woodgrove.com. When users attempt to log in, their account is not being recognized. How should you approach the problem?

A. Reset the user's password

B. Ask the users to try a different FTP client

C. Ask the users to use the hostname|username format to ensure that they are connecting to the appropriate host

D. Restart the application pool hosting each of the virtual hosts

Correct Answer & Explanation: **C.** Virtual hosts require that the host name be passed in the username since the FTP protocol doesn't have a host name header value in the currently adopted specification.

Incorrect Answers & Explanations: **A**, **B**, and **D.** Answer **A** is incorrect because the account is not being recognized, not the password. Answer **B** is incorrect because the FTP client has no bearing on virtual host support under current protocol specifications. Answer **D** is incorrect because restarting the application pool will not resolve the issue.

3. You received a support call from a user trying to upload a file to the site. They are able to connect, authenticate using their network account, and browse the folder structure, but unable to upload a file. Where should you look?

A. Ensure the FTP authorization rule includes Write permissions

B. Ensure the anonymous module is disabled

C. Change the port number the site is bound on

D. Ensure that the passive data connection ports are accessible from the user's computer

Correct Answer & Explanation: **A**. If the user is able to connect, authenticate, and browse the network, then connectivity is not in question. The problem will be an authorization one and the rules include the ability to allow people to read and/or write.

Incorrect Answers & Explanations: **B**, **C**, and **D**. Answer **B** is incorrect because the user was able to connect and so authentication is not in question. Answer **C** is incorrect because the port has no bearing on the authorization process. Answer **D** is incorrect because the user was able to browse the directory which engaged the data connection successfully.

4. You have recently set up an FTP site with a virtual directory that links to a network share where video journalists can upload their video. The authorization rules have been configured to allow only write access to this folder. When you logged in to the FTP site and attempted to change to the folder the server said that it was unable to change to the folder. How should you resolve the problem?

A. Remove and re-create the authorization rule

B. Write a batch file to copy the content to the network share on a regular basis

C. Configure the virtual directory to use a set of credentials to connect to the remote share

D. Turn on FTP Site logging and review the logs

Correct Answer & Explanation: **C**. In order to access a remote share the credentials must support delegation or have a set user account in order to access the site. The easiest way to manage the remote virtual directory access is to provide a set of credentials used to access the folder contents.

Incorrect Answers & Explanations: **A**, **B**, and **D**. Answer **A** is incorrect because the authorization rule is already configured to meet the requirements. Answer **B** is incorrect because a copy situation introduces a challenge to manage duplicate uploads. Answer **D** is incorrect because the FTP logging won't indicate that the site was inaccessible because of network connectivity issues.

5. An ISP has contacted you for guidance on enabling their Web hosting clients' access to their content using FTP. After reviewing their plans you have determined

that they want an easy-to-maintain solution that minimizes the maintenance involved with maintaining the FTP access. What solution should you recommend?

A. Set up the FTP Site to use a User Name Directory

B. Set up User Isolation using Virtual Directories that link to the Web site

C. Bind the FTP Site to the Web Site in IIS Manager

D. Create a standalone FTP Site for each client that points to the location of the Web content

Correct Answer & Explanation: **C.** The ability to bind an FTP site to a Web site is new in IIS 7. It greatly simplifies maintenance by keeping both access methods tied together for each management of the functionality.

Incorrect Answers & Explanations: **A, B,** and **D.** Answer **A** is incorrect because without user isolation the user will be able to navigate to the root of the FTP site and view the list of clients. Answer **B** is incorrect because the virtual directories will need to be configured with each new Web site. This is an extra step that does not need to be done with the ability to bind directly to the Web site available. Answer **D** is incorrect because it creates two separate entities that need to be managed.

6. After setting up your new FTP site you need to enable FTP access to the server. The computer runs Windows Firewall and you are using the Passive FTP mode. What ports should you open up?

A. 21/tcp and 1024-65535/tcp

B. 21/udp and 1024-65535/tcp

C. 21/tcp and the range specified in the Firewall Settings module

D. Add a Program Exception for SvcHost.exe using FtpSvc as the service identified

Correct Answer & Explanation: **D.** Adding the program exception will allow the FTP Server to open the ports necessary without inadvertently exposing entire ranges of ports to programs that another program might set up a listener on and unknowingly expose a security risk.

Incorrect Answers & Explanations: **A, B,** and **C.** Answer **A** is incorrect because it exposes a number of services that might not be safe for general external access. Answer **B** is incorrect because FTP requires port 21/tcp and the effects of Answer **A** apply. Answer **C** is incorrect because the port range exposes a number of ports that another program might set up a listener on and unknow-ingly expose a security risk.

7. Users accessing your FTP site have reported that they cannot see the virtual directory that you recently created. You can see that the virtual directory does exist and is set to the proper path through IIS Manager. What should you do to enable users to see the virtual directory?

   A. Disable the Anonymous Authentication Module

   B. Enable UNIX Directory Listing Style in the Directory Browsing module

   C. Enable Virtual Directories in the Directory Browsing module

   D. Change the incoming connections to require SSL

   Correct Answer & Explanation: **C**. Virtual directories are not visible by default.

   Incorrect Answers & Explanations: **A**, **B**, and **D**. Answer **A** is incorrect because it has nothing to do with the visibility of virtual directories. Answer **B** is incorrect because it only affects how the directory listing appears, not what appears in the directory listings. Answer **D** is incorrect because it will have no bearing on which folders are listed.

8. The new FTP Publishing Service introduces the ability to use SSL to protect the privacy of the connection. Where can SSL not be applied on an FTP session?

   A. SSL on the Control Channel

   B. SSL on the Control Channel during Authentication

   C. SSL on the Data Channel

   D. SSL on the Data Channel during Authentication

   Correct Answer & Explanation: **D**. Authentication doesn't happen through the Data Channel

   Incorrect Answers & Explanations: **A**, **B**, and **C** are incorrect because they can all have SSL applied.

9. After a recent security audit you have been asked to disable anonymous authentication on your FTP site. What is the most secure option available using the authentication modules that are shipped with the FTP Publishing Service?

   A. Basic

   B. Windows

   C. Digest

   D. Client Certificate

Correct Answer & Explanation: **A**. Basic authentication is the only other authentication module that ships with the FTP Publishing Service.

Incorrect Answers & Explanations: **B**, **C**, and **D** are incorrect because they are only available for HTTP and HTTPS-based traffic accessing Web sites.

10. You have installed SMTP Server to receive mail from outside users as well as let remote users authenticate and relay through. A user calls you telling you that their ISP has blocked port 25 and recommends using port 465 instead. What should you do to enable the user to connect?

   A. Create a new virtual server bound to port 465

   B. Add a port binding to the existing virtual server

   C. Add the user's IP address to the relay restrictions allow list

   D. Ask the user to use another SMTP Server

Correct Answer & Explanation: **B**. With everything else remaining the same, the easiest configuration change is to add a new IP address and port binding combination to the existing virtual server.

Incorrect Answers & Explanations: **A**, **C**, and **D**. Answer **A** is incorrect because it creates additional management burden because the two virtual servers will not share the same configuration properties yet need to satisfy the same set of users. Answer **C** is incorrect because the user being on the relay list does not affect which port the SMTP Server listens on. Answer **D** is incorrect because current Internet standards are asking domain owners to apply Sender ID records which state which SMTP servers can originate email for the domain. If the user is sending from a random server then it prevents you from using Sender ID.

Chapter 8: Deploying the Terminal Services

1. Several months ago, you installed the Terminal Server role service on one of the servers at your company. This morning, clients are having difficulty connecting to terminal services but are still able to use file and print services on the server. The error message says it is a licensing issue but you are sure that you properly licensed Windows Server 2008, as well as all of your client systems. What might be causing this? (Select all that apply.)

   A. The temporary evaluation period has expired

   B. You failed to properly configure TS CALs on the license server

C. The server was installed with a temporary license code, which has expired

D. You did not properly install a license server

Correct Answer & Explanation: **A, B, D**. Answers **A, B**, and **D** are correct. In addition to installing the Terminal Server role service, you must also install the TS Licensing role service and TS CALs on it. These are different from the CALs for the operating systems on your client computers. If you fail to complete any of these steps, your terminal services clients will be unable to connect when the evaluation period expires, which is 120 days after the first terminal services client connection occurs.

Incorrect Answers & Explanations: **C**. Because clients can still connect to file and print services on the Windows Server 2008 server hosting the Terminal Server role service, it is clear that the server itself is licensed and functioning properly. Therefore, Answer **C** is incorrect.

2. You have several terminal servers and want to connect to each server's console session remotely, from within a single utility. Which graphical terminal services utility can you use to accomplish this?

A. The Remote Desktop Connection version 6 utility

B. The Remote Desktops Snap-in

C. The Remote Desktop Connection Web utility

D. The Terminal Services Client Configuration Manager utility

Correct Answer & Explanation: **B**. The Remote Desktops Snap-in can be used to connect to the console sessions on multiple terminal servers from within a single instance of the utility. On the Add New Connection window, select **Connect with /admin option**. It is important to note that a console connection can also be established from Remote Desktop Connection version 6 utility using the command line by entering the **mstsc.exe /admin** command; however, only one session can be established within a single instance of this utility.

Incorrect Answers & Explanations: **A, C, D**. Answers **A, C**, and **D** are incorrect, because each of these utilities are primarily designed to allow users to establish a single connection to a terminal services computer. By contrast, the Remote Desktop MMC Snap-in is a tool that is intended for administrators to use in establishing connections to one or more terminal services sessions within a single interface.

3. You've just installed your first Windows Server 2008 terminal server for your company, accepting all defaults in the wizard. The company currently has six

Windows 2003 terminal servers, housed at a second facility across town. Clients connect via a private WAN from offices all over the country to each terminal server. While all clients are still able to log on to the Windows Server 2003 terminal servers, only Windows Vista and XP SP2 (and later) clients seem to be able to access the new Windows Server 2008 terminal server. None of the company's Windows 2000 workstations can log on to the server. Which one of the following is the most likely reason?

A. The **Require Network Level Authentication** option was selected during server configuration.

B. The **Do not require Network Level Authentication** option was selected by default during server configuration.

C. Only Windows XP and Vista clients can connect to Windows Server 2008 terminal services.

D. You did not update the RDC client on the Windows 2000 clients to version 6 or later.

Correct Answer & Explanation: **A.** When the **Require Network Level Authentication** option is enabled during the installation of the Terminal Server role service it enables a level of security not all clients can accommodate. This option requires RDC 6 or later, and client support for the Credential Security Support Provider (CredSSP) protocol. Pre-Windows XP SP2 clients, such as Windows 2000, do not support the level of security required to connect.

Incorrect Answers & Explanations: **B, C, D.** Answer **B** is incorrect because it is used to support earlier non-CredSSP client systems. Answer **C** is also incorrect. Pre-Windows XP SP2 clients can connect to Windows Server 2008; however, different clients support different levels of features during and after connection. Answer **D** is incorrect because Windows 2000 does not have CredSSP support.

4. Two months ago you installed the first Windows Server 2008 terminal server for your company, accepting all defaults in the Wizard. You recently finished the final testing, verified that Windows Server 2008 terminal services was a good solution for your company, and ordered the necessary licenses. You've installed and activated the TS Licensing role service on a domain controller in the same domain as the terminal server. You've also installed and activated Per Device TS CALs. Despite this, your users have not been able to obtain the CALs you installed, and temporary CALs are still being assigned. Which one of the following answers best explains the problem?

A. The **Per User** default setting was used during the terminal server installation, but Per Device CALs have been purchased and activated.

B. The **Configure later** default setting was used during the terminal server installation.

C. The TS Licensing server was not published in AD and the Terminal Server cannot find it.

D. The terminal server was not configured to manually use the TS Licensing server.

Correct Answer & Explanation: **B**. By default, the **Configure later** licensing mode option is selected during the installation of the Terminal Server role service. Prior to handing out full TS CALs, the server must have its license mode set to **Per Device** using the Terminal Services Configuration utility.

Incorrect Answers & Explanations: **A, C, D**. Answer **A** is incorrect because **Per User** is not the default setting during terminal server installation. Answers **C** and **D** are incorrect because a license server that is installed on a domain controller in the same domain as the terminal server does not need to be manually published in AD and will be automatically discovered by all terminal servers in the domain.

5. Your manager has heard that users can often connect to terminal services and obtain sessions, even if the company has not purchased enough licenses. She asks you to make sure this doesn't happen, and wants an automated solution. You're about to put in the first and only terminal server the company will install. Which one of the following is your best solution?

A. Use Per User CALs.

B. Use Per Device CALs.

C. Purchase a third party solution, such as Citrix.

D. Configure group policy to monitor the used licenses and disable logons when they are all in use.

Correct Answer & Explanation: **B**. When Per Device CALs are used, terminal services licensing keeps track of the number of licenses available. When all licenses have been assigned, sessions from devices that have not yet received a license cannot connect.

Incorrect Answers & Explanations: **A, C, D**. Answer **A** is incorrect. Per User CALs are not tracked by terminal services licensing. Answer **C** is also not the best option. A third party solution is not necessary because Per Device CALs solve the problem. Answer **D** is incorrect because group policy is not capable of performing this task.

6. Your manager insists that the company's only server will be more than adequate to install and use as a terminal server. The server currently hosts AD, DNS, and several key applications such as e-mail and databases. What do you tell him? (Select one.)

   A. You tell him that you agree, and will begin to plan and test the installation.

   B. You tell him that you are concerned about the additional load that will be placed on such a critical server.

   C. You tell him that you feel a second server is justified, and that installing it as a second domain controller in addition to a terminal server will provide needed fault tolerance for AD.

   D. You tell him that security concerns dictate the purchase of a second server, which should be exclusively used as a terminal server.

   Correct Answer & Explanation: **D**. Allowing users to establish terminal server sessions to key servers is unwise for security reasons. Users often find ways to install additional software, can run local applications on the computer, and so forth. Even if the users do nothing damaging themselves, their use opens the system to much greater virus, trojan, and similar risks.

   Incorrect Answers & Explanations: **A**, **B**, **C**. Answers **A**, **B**, and **C** are incorrect because of the security concerns. No reason provided can justify allowing users to, in effect, log on locally to the company's only server; especially given the critical applications it runs.

7. You are the administrator for a small, single office company with 20 typical office users. The company currently has two Windows Server 2003 domain controllers, one of which also hosts Exchange Server. As part of your Windows Server 2008 upgrade plan, you've been asked to add a terminal server to facilitate greater remote access. The company plans to add additional terminal servers as the year progresses. Which one of the following do you recommend for the placement of the TS Licensing role service?

   A. For security reasons, you do not recommend installing the TS Licensing role service on a domain controller after the upgrade.

   B. You recommend a dedicated server for the TS Licensing role service.

   C. You recommend that the License server be installed on a domain controller after the upgrade.

D. You recommend that the License server be installed on the new server which will be purchased for the Terminal Server role service.

Correct Answer & Explanation: **C**. Installing the TS Licensing role service on a domain controller will ensure that it can be automatically discovered by all terminal servers in the domain. When additional terminal servers are added, no additional configuration will be required.

Incorrect Answers & Explanations: **A, B, D**. Answer **A** is incorrect. There are no security reasons which prevent the installation of the TS Licensing role service on Windows Server 2008 domain controllers. Answer **B** is also incorrect. The TS Licensing role service uses minimal resources and does not require its own server. Finally, answer **D** is a possible answer but not the best one. If the company was only going to have one terminal server this option would be acceptable. However, because the question states that additional servers will be added, future configuration can be minimized by ensuring that the TS Licensing role service is automatically discoverable. To achieve this from a server that is not a domain controller requires considerable additional configuration.

8. Your manager stresses the incorporation of vendor best practices. She has asked you to ensure that the discovery scope used for the company's TS Licensing role service servers adheres to the best practices established by Microsoft. Which one of the following settings will you configure for your domain based computers?

A. **This workgroup**

B. **This domain**

C. **This forest**

D. **Configure later**

Correct Answer & Explanation: **C**. Microsoft recommends the **This forest** license discovery scope for all TS Licensing role service servers that are domain members.

Incorrect Answers & Explanations: **A, C, D**. Answer **A** is incorrect because it cannot be used in a domain. Although answer **B** is the default selection for a TS Licensing server that is a domain member, it is not the recommended setting. Answer **D** is an option for setting the type of licensing used by a Terminal Server role service server, not a TS Licensing role service server.

9. You are a server administrator for a large, multi-national company, and have just been sent the deployment documentation for Windows Server 2008

terminal services. One of the configuration line items calls for centralization of the TS Licensing databases on a single file server. What do you e-mail the deployment design team? (Select one.)

A. You make them aware of the fact that the database has to be on the local TS Licensing servers.

B. You ask which server to use, since it is not specified in the documentation.

C. You make them aware of the fact that the database must use a mapped drive letter, and request specifics on how to configure it.

D. You let them know that the database is stored in a fixed location which cannot be changed.

Correct Answer & Explanation: **A.** A TS Licensing database must be contained in a local folder on the TS Licensing role service server.

Incorrect Answers & Explanations: **B, C, D.** Answers **B** and **C** are incorrect because the database must use a local folder on the TS Licensing server. Answer **D** is also incorrect; a location other than the default can be configured.

10. The terminal servers in your facility are used to deliver highly sensitive applications and data to users. No computers within the facility have Internet access. Which of the following is the best choice for activating your Windows Server 2008 TS Licensing role service server? (Select one.)

A. The **Automatic connection (recommended)** method in TS Licensing Manager

B. The **Web Browser** method in TS Licensing Manager

C. The **Telephone** method in TS Licensing Manager

D. Temporarily moving the server to a subnet with Internet access for activation

Correct Answer & Explanation: **C.** Telephone activation is the best option when no Internet access is available.

Incorrect Answers & Explanations: **A, B, D.** Answer **A** is not possible without Internet access from a computer that can connect to both the server and the Internet. While you could use a Web browser that is outside of the facility, this is not the best option, making **B** also incorrect. Finally, answer **D** presents an unacceptable security risk and is not correct.

Chapter 9: Configuring and Managing the Terminal Services

1. Your nonprofit organization has an Active Directory forest with an Active Directory domain. There are 10 Windows XP clients in the domain with the Remote Desktop Client 6.1 installed. The organization also has a server named TSApp1 that runs the Terminal Server role for the main office. You want to deploy a new RemoteApp on the TSApp1 server. The application makes changes to the current user registry during installation. The program vendor has verified that the application can be deployed as a RemoteApp. However, you discover that running the provided *appsetup.exe* file does not install the application for multiuser usage. You need to modify the application installation process to install correctly as a RemoteApp. What do you need to do?

    A. Run the *mstsc /v:TSApp1 /admin* command from your workstation to log into the TSApp1 server. Install the application.

    B. Run the *chgusr /execute* command on the TSApp1 server. Install the application. Then, run the *chgusr /install* command on the TSApp1 server.

    C. Run the *chgusr /install* command on the TSApp1 server. Install the application. Then, run the *chgusr /execute* command on the TSApp1 server.

    D. Run the *chglogon /disable* command on the TSApp1 server. Install the application. Then, run the *chglogon /enable* command on the TSApp1 server.

Correct answer and explanation: **C.** TSApp1 will be placed into install mode, which is required for set-up programs that are not auto-detected or do not use Windows Installer packages.

Incorrect answers and explanations: **A**, **B**, and **D**. **A** is incorrect because this will not install the program properly. Due to changes in "Session 0" functionality, the console switch behaves differently than in Server 2000 and 2003. **B** is incorrect because TSApp1 needs to be in install mode while the installation program is running. It is the exact opposite of the correct answer. **D** is incorrect because this will disable terminal server logins on TSApp1 but will not install the program correctly.

2. Your company has two servers named TSApp1 and TSApp2 that have the Terminal Server role installed. The TSApp1 server also has the Terminal Server Web Access role installed. The applications on the TSApp2 server does not appear on the list of applications available from the Terminal Server Web Access Web page. You need to ensure that users are able to launch the applications on the TSApp2 server from the Terminal Server Web Access Web page. What do you need to do?

   A. Install the Terminal Server Gateway role on the TSApp2 server. Instruct users to use the TSApp2 server as their Terminal Server Gateway when they want to access the applications on the TSApp2 server.

   B. Publish all the applications on the TSApp1 server and the TSApp2 server by using Active Directory Domain Services (AD DS) as the repository. Publish the applications through a GPO for all the users that use the Terminal Server Web Access Web site.

   C. Configure the applications on the TSApp2 server as Microsoft Windows Installer packages. Publish the applications using System Center Configuration Manager 2007 to the clients.

   D. Publish the applications on the TSApp2 server as Microsoft Windows Installer packages. Initiate a group policy update on the TSApp1 server by using the *gpupdate /force* command.

   Correct answer and explanation: **B**. This will change TSApp1 from displaying all the applications installed locally on it, to populating the list from AD DS. This allows applications from TSApp1 and TSApp2 to be listed on TSApp1.

   Incorrect answers and explanations: **A**, **C**, and **D**. **A** is incorrect because this will provide access to the applications on TSApp2, but you want users to access the applications through TSApp1. **C** is incorrect because this will not list the applications properly on TSApp1. **D** is incorrect because this will publish the applications on TSApp2, but will not publish anything on TSApp1. Forcing a group policy refresh will not help anything related to listing the application.

3. Your government agency has a server named IntraNetTSApp1 that has the Terminal Server role installed. The government agency wants to deploy a new application named IntraNetApp on the IntraNetTSApp1 server. You publish the application on the IntraNetTSApp1 server by using a Microsoft RDP file. The clients are unable to pass parameters to the application. You need to ensure that the clients are able to launch the application on the IntraNetTSApp1 server by using any two parameters. What do you need to do?

A. Modify the Remote Program Properties setting for the IntraNetApp application. Activate the Allow any Command Line Arguments option in the Command Line Arguments dialog box.

B. Modify the Remote Program Properties setting for the IntraNetApp application. Activate the Always use the following Command Line Arguments option in the Command Line Arguments dialog box. Type %1 %2 in the Command Line Arguments field.

C. Modify the Alias setting for the IntraNetApp application from IntraNetApp to IntraNetApp %1 %2.

D. Publish the application on the Server2 server as a Microsoft Windows Installer package. Distribute the Microsoft Windows Installer package to the clients to replace the published RDP file.

Correct answer and explanation: **A**. It will provide access to the program on IntraNetTSApp1 and allow users to pass parameters.

Incorrect answers and explanations: **B**, **C**, and **D**. **B** is incorrect because this will provide access to the program on IntraNetTSApp1, but it will always pass %1 %2 to the program. It will not pass the parameters the users provide. **C** is incorrect because this will change the alias of the program and will not pass additional parameters to the program. **D** is incorrect because this will not change the default behavior of published applications to not pass command-line parameters. Although you could change the publishing type from RDP to MSI, it will not help solve the problem overall.

4. Your company has a single AD forest that has an AD domain. The company has a server named TS1 that runs the Terminal Server role and the Terminal Server Web Access role. The company also has 150 client computers that run Microsoft Windows XP Service Pack 2 (SP2). You have an application named DBAExpress that you want to deploy on the TS1 server. You publish DBAExpress on the TS1 server. The clients are unable to access DBAExpress through the Terminal Server Web Access Web page. You verify that the Terminal Server Web Access role is using Active Directory Domain Services (ADDS) and that Network Level Authentication is enabled. You need to ensure that the clients can launch DBAExpress on the TS1 server from the Terminal Server Web Access Web page. What do you need to do?

A. Install the Remote Desktop Client 6.0 application on the client computers that run Windows XP SP2.

B. Disable publishing to AD DS for the DBAExpress remote application.

C. Install the Terminal Services Gateway role on the TS1 server. Reconfigure the DBAExpress remote application publishing to reflect this change in the infrastructure.

D. Publish the DBAExpress application on the TS1 server as a Microsoft Windows Installer package. Distribute the Windows Installer package to the clients.

Correct answer and explanation: **A**. It will provide access to the program on the TS1 server and allow users to access the program. The default client in Windows XP SP2 does not support Network Level Authentication (NLA).

Incorrect answers and explanations: **B**, **C**, and **D**. **B** is incorrect because this will leave NLA enabled, which is the root cause of the problem. **C** is incorrect because this will leave NLA enabled and it will install a feature that the default RDP client for XP does not support. **D** is incorrect because the Windows XP clients would still need the updated RDP client.

5. Your company has a server named TSWA that has the Terminal Services Web Access server role and the Terminal Services Gateway server role. The company has 25 Microsoft Windows XP SP2 remote client computers in the domain. You deploy a new application on the TSWA server. You make the new application available to users by publishing a Microsoft Windows Installer package that has a GPO. You discover that you can launch the new application from the TS2 server and the TSWA server by using the Terminal Services Web Access Web page. However, the users are unable to launch the application. You need to ensure that the users are able to launch the application. What do you need to do?

A. Install the RDP 6.1 client on the client computers.

B. Deactivate the Network Level Authentication option on the Server2 server and the Server3 server.

C. Install the Internet Explorer 7.0 browser application on the client computers.

D. Configure the Terminal Services Resource Access Policy (TSRAP) to include the Server3 server only.

Correct answer and explanation: **A**. It will provide access to the program on Server2 from XP clients.

Incorrect answers and explanations: **B**, **C**, and **D**. **B** is incorrect because the Windows XP clients would still need the updated RDP client. **C** is incorrect because IE 6 or IE 7 will work with the Web Access Web page. The clients need the RDP 6.0 client. **D** is incorrect because this will break all access to the new application for remote users.

6. The company has a server named Server2 that has the Terminal Server role. Applications on Server2 are published by using the RDP files. Users download the RDP files from the TSWeb virtual directory on Server2. You also have a new server named Server3 that has the Terminal Server role and the Terminal Server Gateway role. You reconfigure the applications on the Server2 server to use the Terminal Server Gateway role on the Server3 server. You export the Remote Program settings from the Server2 server and import them into the Server3 server. Users report they are unable to access any of the remote applications on the Server3 server. Users are able to access the remote applications on the Server2 server through the Terminal Server Gateway role on Server3. You verify that the programs installed on the Server2 server are installed at identical locations on the Server3 server. You need to ensure that the users are able to access the applications on the Server3 server. What do you need to do?

A. Recreate the RDP files on the Server3 server and redistribute the files to the users.

B. Copy the RDP files from the Server2 server to a new TSWeb virtual directory on the Server3 server.

C. Configure and activate the Terminal Server Session Directory feature on the Server3 server. Configure the Server2 server and the Server3 server to use the Terminal Server Session Directory feature.

D. Deactivate the NLA feature on the Server3 server.

Correct answer and explanation: **A.** You need to create RDP files specific to Server3 so that it uses the Gateway and points to Server3. Exporting the Remote Program list does not export the RDP files. The RDP files on Server2 will still point to Server2 instead of Server3. The Windows XP clients would still need the updated RDP client.

Incorrect answers and explanations: **B, C,** and **D. B** is incorrect because the RDP files will still point to Server2 internally. **C** is incorrect because the Session directory will not help in this situation. **D** is incorrect because NLA is not preventing Server3 from working properly.

7. Your company has an AD domain. The company also has a server named Server1 that has the Terminal Server Gateway role. There are two more servers named Server2 and Server3 that have the Terminal Server role. Server2 and

Server3 are configured in a load-balancing Terminal Server farm named TSLoad. The company deploys the Terminal Server Broker Service feature on a new server named Server4. The TSLoad farm is added to the Terminal Server Broker Service configuration on Server4. After configuring the published applications to use Terminal Server Broker Service, you observe that Terminal Server Broker Service does not accept connections from Server2 and Server3. You need to ensure that Terminal Server Broker Service can accept connections from Server2 and Server3. What do you need to do?

A. Recreate Add Server2 and Server3 to the Session Broker Computers local group on Server4.

B. Add Server2 and Server3 to a new Session Broker Computers group in the Active Directory domain.

C. Configure a group policy to set the Require secure RPC communications option in the Terminal Services Security section to True. Apply the policy to Server2 and Server3.

D. Configure a group policy to set the Allow reconnection from original client only option in the Terminal Services section to True. Apply the policy to all client computers.

Correct answer and explanation: **A.** The servers that will be using the broker service need to be in the local Session Broker Computers group on the Session Broker server.

Incorrect answers and explanations: **B, C,** and **D. B** is incorrect because the Session Broker Computers group needs to be a local group on the actual Session Broker server, not a domain group. **C** is incorrect because this is unrelated to the problem with the Session Broker service configuration. **D** is incorrect because this is unrelated to the problem with the Session Broker service configuration.

8. Your company has an AD domain. The company also has a server named Server1 that has the Terminal Server Gateway role. There are two more servers named Server2 and Server3 that have the Terminal Server role. Server2 and Server3 are configured in a load-balancing Terminal Server farm named TSL. The company deploys the Terminal Server Broker Service feature on a new server named Server4. The TSL farm is added to the Terminal Server Broker Service configuration on Server4. After configuring the published applications to use the Terminal Server Broker Service feature, you observe that the Terminal Server Broker Service feature does not receive any server registrations. You need

to ensure that the Terminal Server Broker Service feature receives server registrations. What do you need to do?

A. Create a new GPO that assigns Server4 to Server2 and Server3 as their session broker server. Apply the policy to Server2 and Server3.

B. Configure Server2 and Server3 to use the Terminal Server Gateway role to access the Terminal Server Broker Service feature.

C. Configure a group policy to set the Require secure RPC communications option in the Terminal Services Security section to False. Apply the policy to Server2 and Server3.

D. Configure a group policy to set the Set TS Gateway server address option in the Terminal Services section to Server1. Apply the policy to all client computers.

Correct answer and explanation: **A**. The servers that will be using the broker service need to be configured to use the Session Broker server.

Incorrect answers and explanations: **B**, **C**, and **D**. **B** is incorrect because the Gateway does not need to be involved and would not fix the problem. **C** is incorrect because this is unrelated to the problem with the Session Broker service configuration. **D** is incorrect because this is unrelated to the problem with the Session Broker service configuration.

9. Your company has a server named Server1 that has the Terminal Server Gateway role. There are two more servers named Server2 and Server3 that have the Terminal Server role. Server2 and Server3 are configured in a load balancing Terminal Server farm named TSLB. The company has a new server named Server4 that has the Terminal Server Broker Service feature. You deploy a hardware load-balancing device named F6 in front of the Terminal Server farm. The device has specialized support for terminal servers and routing tokens. The Terminal Server Broker Service feature stops working after you deploy F6 in front of the Terminal Server farm. You need to ensure that the Terminal Server Broker Service feature works. Which new GPO should you create and apply to the Terminal Server farm?

A. A GPO that deactivates the Use IP Address Redirection policy setting in the Terminal Server Broker section of the Terminal Server group policy template

B. A GPO that activates the Use IP Address Redirection policy setting in the Session Directory section of the Terminal Server group policy template

C. A GPO that activates the Use TS Session Broker Load Balancing policy setting in the Session Directory section of the Terminal Server group policy template

D. A GPO that deactivates the Use TS Session Broker Load Balancing policy setting in the Session Directory section of the Terminal Server group policy template

Correct answer and explanation: **A.** The Session Broker needs to be configured to not send clients to servers directly by IP.

Incorrect answers and explanations: **B, C,** and **D. B** is incorrect because this would not allow the Session Broker to operate properly. **C** is incorrect because this is unrelated to the problem with the Session Broker load balancing configuration. The Session Broker needs to be configured so that it does not send clients directly to the terminal servers by IP address. Enabling or disabling the Session Broker Load Balancing will not change the end result. **D** is incorrect because this is unrelated to the problem with the Session Broker load balancing configuration. The Session Broker needs to be configured so that it does not send clients directly to the terminal servers by IP address. Enabling or disabling the Session Broker Load Balancing will not change the end result.

10. The company has a server named Server1 that has the Terminal Services server role and a new test server named TSL that has the Terminal Services Licensing role outside of the domain in a workgroup. You cannot enable the Terminal Services Per User Client Access License (CAL) mode in the Terminal Services Licensing role on TSL. You need to configure the Terminal Services environment so that you can use the Terminal Services Per User CAL mode on TSL. What should you do?

A. Join TSL to the domain. Enable the Terminal Services Per User CAL mode.

B. Configure Server1 to use TSL for the Terminal Services Licensing role. Reconfigure TSL for the Terminal Services Per User CAL mode when Server1 has registered with TSL.

C. Install the Terminal Server Gateway role on Server1. Configure a Group Policy Object that configures Server1 to use TSL for licensing. Apply the policy to Server1.

D. Call the Microsoft Clearinghouse with your Terminal Server license information. Obtain license keys to enter into the Licensing server.

Correct answer and explanation: **A.** Terminal Services Per User CAL mode requires Active Directory Domain Services.

Incorrect answers and explanations: **B, C,** and **D. B** is incorrect because Terminal Services Per User CAL mode will still be unavailable. **C** is incorrect because Terminal Services Per User CAL mode will still be unavailable. **D** is incorrect because they can validate your client licenses but the TS CAL mode you want will still be unavailable.

Chapter 10: IP Addressing and Services

1. You need to set up a network in the lab for a training class. You want to isolate the lab network from the rest of the corporate network so students don't inadvertently do something that takes the entire network down. What IP addressing method would you use?

    A. Private network addressing

    B. Public network addressing

    C. Network Address Translation

    D. Subnet isolation through subnet mask

    Correct Answer & Explanation: **D.** If you install a router or switch and use a different subnet mask, you can isolate the subnet in the lab so that the local traffic isn't routed to the network.

    Incorrect Answers & Explanations: **A, B, C.** Answer **A** is incorrect, because your corporate network may already be using private network addresses. Without more specificity, this answer is incorrect. Answer **B** is incorrect, because a public network addressing scheme is inappropriate for a lab environment, especially one that has no need to connect to the Internet. Even if Internet connectivity was needed, a private address scheme with a router using NAT would make more sense. Answer **C** is incorrect, because network address translation is used when private IP addresses need to head out to the Internet. No mention of Internet connectivity is made and it does not solve the subnet isolation issue.

2. Your boss asked you to subnet a network in the lab for an upcoming class. He hands you a piece of paper while he's on the phone and it simply says "192.168.10.x/25. 4 subnets." What is the subnet mask and the first address in each subnet?

    A. 255.255.255.0/ 192.168.10.1, 192.168.10.32, 192.168.10.64, 192.168.10.128

B. 255.255.255.252/ 192.168.10.0, 192.168.10.32, 192.168.10.64, 192.168.10.128

C. 255.255.255.240/ 192.168.10.0, 192.168.16.0, 192.168.24.0, 192.168.32.0

D. 255.255.255.128/ 192.168.10.1, 192.168.10.33, 192.168.10.65, 192.168.10.97

Correct Answer & Explanation: **D**. Using the network notation /25 indicates you need to use 25 network bits. 255.255.255.0 typically is used for the default subnet mask for Class C networks and uses 24 bits (often notated /24). Therefore, if you add one bit, you change the left-most bit in the right-most octet to 1. This equals 128, creating a subnet mask of 255.255.255.128. The starting addresses (the first assignable IP address) in each subnet would have the right-most octet set to 1, 33, 65, and 97. The network addresses themselves would be 192.168.10.0, 192.168.10.32, 192.168.10.64, and 192.168.10.96.

Incorrect Answers & Explanations: **A, B, C**. Answer **A** is incorrect, because the subnet mask is incorrect (as are the starting IP addresses). The subnet mask with zero as the last octet is the default subnet mask for a Class C network and uses only 24 bits. The network would have been notated as 192.168.10.x/24 if you were to use this subnet mask.. Answer **B** is incorrect, because the bits in the last octet of the subnet mask 255.255.255.252 are set to 1111 1100 and would have to be notated as 192.168.10.x/30. Answer **C** is incorrect, because 255.255.255.240 would be notated as 192.168.10.x/28 so that the last octet would be set to 1111 0000.

3. You have a growing network that originally was configured using the private Class C address space. However, you're now about to grow beyond the maximum number of devices and need to expand but you don't anticipate needing more than a total of 290 addresses. What action would you take to solve this problem that would create the least disruption to your network?

A. Install a router. Create two new scopes on your DHCP Server and reassign IP addresses.

B. Change the default subnet mask to 255.255.252.0.

C. Change the IP addressing scheme from Class C to Class B.

D. Assign new computers on the network IP addresses from the existing address pool.

Correct Answer & Explanation: **B**. Changing the subnet mask from the default 255.255.255.0 to 255.255.252.0 would increase your address space and allow existing computers to continue to use their IP addresses (as long as they got the new subnet mask). Your IP address space then would span from 192.168.0.x through 192.168.3.x. This potentially could slow down network traffic because these added IP addresses would be on the network as the existing ones. However, if you don't plan on expanding much beyond about 300 devices, this would be the fastest and easiest way to go.

Incorrect Answers & Explanations: **A, C, D**. Answer **A** is incorrect, because although you could install a router to create a new subnet, the creation of a new subnet mask is probably easier. In addition, you would not need to create two new scopes on your DHCP server, and reassigning addresses could take some work if you have static IP addresses assigned. Answer **C** is incorrect, because although you could change your addressing scheme to a Class B network, that would yield far more host addresses than needed and would take more configuration than just changing the subnet mask. Answer **D** is incorrect, because if you were to allow the new computers to try to lease an IP address from the existing address pool, you would have overlapping IP addresses (depending on configuration) or a computer that could not get a lease. Either scenario would degrade the network service and availability and is the worst option of all.

4. Your company's president comes to you and says that he understands IPv6 is fully supported in Windows Server 2008. He will approve your IT budget if it includes plans to transition to Windows Server 2008 and IPv6. However, he wants to know how quickly you can transition to IPv6. What should you tell him?

A. There is no fast and easy way to transition to IPv6. Much of the Internet's backbone is running on IPv4, so transitional technologies will be required. You'd recommend setting up IPv6 segments and using a tunneling protocol for the transition to begin.

B. The transition to IPv6 on the Internet backbone has been completed and as soon as the company upgrades to Windows Server 2008 and replaces its routers, you're good to go.

C. There is no reasonable way to transition to IPv6 for this organization since all hardware and software would have to be replaced to run Windows Server 2008 or Windows Vista. The cost would be prohibitive and is therefore not recommended.

D. The transition to IPv6 requires the installation of new hardware and software on all subnets using IPv6 exclusively. In the meantime, IPv4 can be used on older subnets and IPv6 can be used on newer subnets and a specific IPv4 to IPv6 router can be installed to bridge the two.

Correct Answer & Explanation: **A**. The eventual transition to IPv6 will be gradual and will require a lot of planning at each stage. There are various transition strategies that can be employed, one of which is to create IPv6 subnets that can talk directly using IPv6 via a tunnel and then employ other transitional methods to enable IPv4 and IPv6 traffic to coexist on the network.

Incorrect Answers & Explanations: **B, C, D**. Answer **B** is incorrect, because although agencies and organizations are interested in transitioning quickly to IPv6, it is not a simple task. The transition to Ipv6 is not complete and simply replacing routers will not address the issue. Answer **C** is incorrect, because many hardware and software systems currently support IPv4 and IPv6. Not all hardware and software would have to be replaced, though it's possible some new equipment will be needed to aid in the transition to IPv6. Answer **D** is incorrect, because the transition to IPv6 does not necessarily require new hardware or software—much of the newer equipment (such as Windows Server 2003 and Windows XP) can accept IPv6 addressing. The key is planning the infrastructure transition. Though a router might be needed to help bridge mixed network traffic, this is not the best answer.

5. You open Windows Server 2008 DHCP Server role and examine the scope settings one of your staff members created, as shown in Figure 10.33. Based on this information, which statement is true?

Figure 10.33 Windows Server 2008 DHCP Configuration

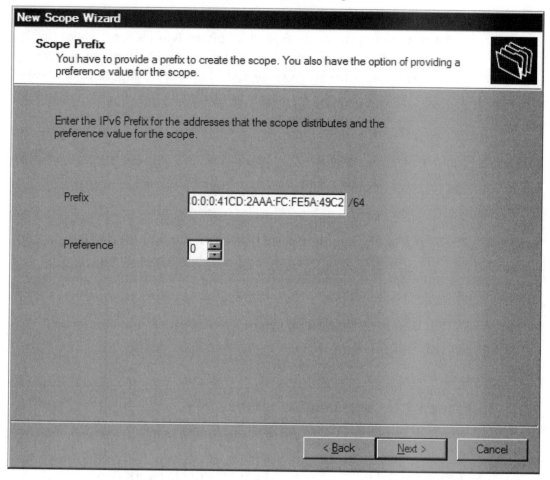

A. The Preference Value is incorrect. It must be set to 1 for all addresses that use the /64 option.

B. The Prefix Value is incorrect. It cannot begin with 0:0:0.

C. The Prefix Value is too long. It should contain fewer digits.

D. Both B and C are correct.

E. The Prefix value and Preference values are correct.

Correct Answer & Explanation: **D.** The Prefix Value should contain the prefix for the addresses the scope distributes. The /64 indicates that there are 64 bits used for the network address. In IPv6, each digit represents 16, so /64 indicates that the prefix should be four digits. For example, FEC8: uses four 16-bit digits (hexadecimal notation).

Incorrect Answers & Explanations: **A**, **B**, **C**. Answer **A** is incorrect, because The Preference Value can be set to 0, the default value. The Preference determines the preferred order in which these addresses will be allocated to hosts. Preference 0 addresses will be handed out before Preference 1 addresses. Answer **B** is incorrect, because that would indicate a network address of 0. The issue is not with the second two zeroes, the address cannot begin with zero. Answer **C** is incorrect, because the Prefix box should contain the Prefix not a full IPv6 address as appears to be the case in this figure. Answer **E** is incorrect because the Prefix value is incorrect. The Preference value is fine as is.

6. You've asked Justin, a junior member of your IT staff, to install Windows Server 2008 on a spare computer in the lab and set up the DHCP role so you can teach a class on what's new in DHCP. Justin hesitates and asks how he should set the scope settings so it doesn't take the network down. What should you tell Justin?

A. DHCP in Windows Server 2008 cannot be installed on a computer attached to a network with a live DHCP server. Remove the server's network connection before installing DHCP.

B. Only one DHCP can exist on a network. He should configure the server as a DHCP relay agent instead.

C. A new DHCP server must be authorized in AD before it can perform the DHCP role.

D. Adding a new DHCP server could not take the network down.

Correct Answer & Explanation: **C**. You can install the DHCP server role and configure scope, reservations, and exclusions without activating the server. In addition, you must authorize the DHCP server via AD before it will be allowed to function as a DHCP server on the network. This helps prevent rogue DHCP servers from popping up, intentionally or otherwise.

Incorrect Answers & Explanations: **A**, **B**, **D**. Answer **A** is incorrect, because you can install the DHCP server role on a server attached to a network with a live DHCP server. The role can be installed and not activated, which is the default setting. Once activated, it still must be authorized in AD. Answer **B** is incorrect, because you can have more than one DHCP server on a network, though you typically have only one per subnet. DHCP relay agents are typically routers and switches designed to forward DHCP traffic. Answer **D** is incorrect, because although a new DHCP server on the network could take the network down, it could do so only if the scope settings were incorrect and it was authorized in AD. As long as Justin doesn't activate the DHCP server role or authorize it in AD, there should be no problem.

7. You need to expand your network and create a new subnet for a new research project. You want the traffic for the research group to remain local to the subnet. None of the computers for the research project are installed yet. What's the fastest and easiest way to go about creating this subnet and keeping local traffic local?

A. Add the computers to the network, assign them a different subnet mask, enable IPSec through Group Policy, and assign it to the research project subnet.

B. Create a scope on the DHCP server that will provide addresses to just those computers, install a router, assign it a static IP address, and use that router as the default gateway for the computers on that subnet.

C. Install a new router and configure it as the DHCP Relay Agent for the existing scope using a static IP address. Then, connect the new computers to the network through the new router.

D. Modify the existing scope options on the DHCP server so that the subnet addresses for the new research subnet are excluded from the scope. Install a new router and configure it with a static IP address from the same range as the excluded IP addresses. Last, connect the new computers to the subnet and check that they are configured to automatically get IP configuration data.

Correct Answer & Explanation: **B.** Creating a new scope for those computers allows you to create a distinct subnet through the use of a new subnet mask in the IP configuration data with the DHCP scope data. A router is used to physically separate the segments, keeping local traffic local to the research group, meeting the stated requirements.

Incorrect Answers & Explanations: **A, C, D.** Answer **A** is incorrect, because if you add computers to the network before you've set up the subnet isolation, they'll simply be added to the regular network and receive their IP addresses from the scope that is currently defined on your DHCP server. Answer **C** is incorrect, because assigning IP addresses from the existing scope essentially defines these new computers as part of the larger network. Although they may be separated by a router, they are still part of the network at large if they're using the same DCHP IP settings. Answer **D** is incorrect, because excluding addresses from the scope simply makes them unavailable to computers configured to get IP configuration data from that server. If those excluded addresses are not included in a scope, they are simply unavailable.

8. The company has just leased a nearby building so it can expand operations. You've been asked to configure the network infrastructure in the new building. You configure the DHCP server that will go on this new network segment with the following options:

   A. Scope: 192.168.10.0 to 192.168.15.0

   B. Subnet mask: 255.255.252.0

   C. Default gateway: 192.168.10.1

   D. Exclusions: 192.168.12.0 to 192.168.12.20

   E. Reservations: 192.168.10.1 DNS server, 192.168.12.2 DNS server, 192.168.12.5 WINS server, 192.168.12.6 Router8

You set Router 8 to have a static IP address of 192.168.12.6 and configure it to be a DHCP relay agent. What's wrong with your set up?

A. You can't have two DNS servers on one subnet, the scope and the subnet mask do not match, you can't set up a router as DHCP relay agent.

B. Your scope cannot have a zero in the last place, your subnet mask is wrong, your default gateway and your DNS server share the same IP address and may slow down the subnet, you don't need a WINS server.

C. Your default gateway and your DNS server use the same IP address. You cannot have a DHCP relay agent (your router) and a DHCP server on the same subnet. Your excluded range and your reservations settings are mutually exclusive.

D. The default gateway has the wrong IP address and all network traffic will be sent to the Router, causing all local traffic to be routed to the main network and back again, causing too much unneeded network traffic. You don't need a DHCP server on this subnet and should simply enable the server as a RRAS server to handle remote traffic to the main corporate site.

Correct Answer & Explanation: **C.** Your default gateway and DNS server use the same IP address. If these two functions reside on different machines, the network will not find one or the other of these devices. You should set up either a DHCP server or a DHCP relay agent, not both. If you want to isolate DHCP traffic, you need a DHCP server. If you want to have all computers from this subnet get their IP address configuration data from the main site's DHCP server, you need a DHCP relay agent. Excluded ranges are ranges of

IP addresses the DHCP server cannot hand out, thus the reservations should be from within the excluded range to prevent the DHCP server from dynamically assigning those reserved IP addresses.

Incorrect Answers & Explanations: **A**, **B**, **D**. Answer **A** is incorrect, because you can have more than one DNS server on a subnet, the scope and the subnet mask could be used together, and you can have a router as a DHCP relay agent. In fact, that is the most common device for DHCP relay agents. Answer **B** is incorrect, because your network ID should end with a zero, devices cannot have a zero address, the subnet mask is correct, you probably don't want the same computer to act as default gateway and DNS server (though it is physically possible), and you don't have enough information to know if you need a WINS server or not. WINS is used for backward compatibility with older Microsoft operating systems, no data was provided on this so including or omitting a WINS server is irrelevant to this question. Answer **D** is incorrect, because the default gateway address is not wrong though it is the same as the DNS server, which may not be the best set up. Though you may not need a DHCP server on the network (you would then rely on a DHCP relay agent), you don't necessarily need to enable the server as a RRAS server. Your connection to the main corporate network is not specified.

9. You've set up a new subnet with a DHCP server. After a few days, mobile users begin complaining they can't log onto the network when they're locally connected (at their desks, for example). What would you check in your DHCP settings?

   A. Scope settings

   B. Exclusions

   C. Subnet mask or default gateway

   D. Lease duration

   Correct Answer & Explanation: **D**. If mobile users are the only ones complaining about getting onto the network, you would limit your search for things related to mobile users. A long lease duration could cause IP addresses to be unavailable for mobile users. If a mobile user connects to the network and receives an IP address then disconnects from the network, it may keep the IP address even if it's disconnected from the network for an extended period of time. When mobile users log back into the network and attempt to get IP configuration settings, there may be no available IP addresses to give them. Shorter lease durations are typically better where there are many mobile users on a network or subnet.

Incorrect Answers & Explanations: **A, B, C.** Answer **A** is incorrect, because your scope settings are not necessarily incorrect. If your scope was incorrect, there would be problems with other users as well. However, if your scope did not include enough IP addresses for stationary and mobile users, you could have a problem with your scope. This would most likely be experienced by mobile users first. Although this is a possibility, this is not the best answer. Answer **B** is incorrect, because exclusions would not impact just mobile users and would essentially have no impact on users at all. Answer **C** is incorrect, because if the subnet mask or default gateway settings were wrong, all users would experience problems.

10. A recent change to the network infrastructure configuration was completed over the weekend. Monday morning, users begin complaining that the network is terribly slow. The Help Desk phones are lit up and there's a rumble in the building as users start going to others' desks asking if they're having any luck using network resources and getting out to the Internet. The new configuration is shown in Figure 10.34. What would you change in order to best resolve this problem?

Figure 10.34 New Network Configuration

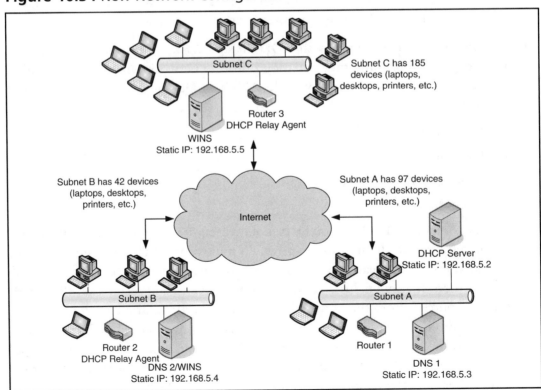

A. Add a DNS Server to Subnet C.

B. Remove the DHCP Relay Agent role from either Router 2 or Router 3.

C. Add a DHCP Server to Subnet C and remove Router 3.

D. Both A and C.

E. Add a DHCP Server to Subnet C.

Correct Answer & Explanation: **E**. If host computers have to cross a WAN link for DHCP configuration information, the link and the network can get pretty slow. If users are complaining about the response time on a subnet like C, which is the largest subnet in the company, the best solution (other than ensuring there is nothing wrong with the WAN link) is to install a DHCP server on Subnet C.

Incorrect Answers & Explanations: **A**, **B**, **C**, **D**. Answer **A** is incorrect, because DNS typically affects users trying to resolve domain names. It's not likely this would slow things down on the subnet. Though this is a possible answer, it's not the most likely cause. Answer **B** is incorrect, because if you remove the DHCP Relay Agent role from either router, the host computers on that subnet won't be able to get DHCP configuration settings. Answer **C** is incorrect, because although you do want to add a DHCP server to Subnet C, you should not remove the router. You should, however, remove the DHCP Relay Agent role from the router once the DHCP server is installed and authorized. Answer **D** is incorrect, because Answer **A** is not the best answer and Answer **C** is incorrect.

Chapter 11: Configuring Network Access

1. You are asked by your employer to set up a LAN using Windows 2008 Server RRAS. Which of these types of routing algorithms or protocols cannot be used to organize the signal flow between the devices in the network, according to the supported Windows Server 2008 features?

A. RIP

B. RIP2

C. OSPF

D. None of the Above

Correct Answer & Explanation: **C**. The correct answer is **C**, because it is no longer supported in the RRAS of Windows Server 2008. RIP and RIP2 are both supported by Windows Server 2008.

2. You are asked to configure a routing table based on information gathered to optimize the network. You find that a static route with the IP destination 10.40.0.0 and the subnet mask of 255.255.0.0 requires deleting. Which of the following commands would successfully accomplish this routing change?

A. route delete 10.40.0.0 mask 255.255.0.0

B. route delete 10.*

C. route change 10.40.0.0 mask 255.255.0.0 10.20.0.25

D. route add 10.41.0.0 mask 255.255.0.0 10.20.0.1

Correct Answer & Explanation: **A**. The correct answer is **A**, because it is the only correct command that will delete the aforementioned route. The other commands perform actions that would not accomplish the proper activity required.

3. You are troubleshooting a network system that has applied a number of static routes. After reviewing the information used to make these routes, you determine that an error was made while entering the routes into one of the gateways. Which of the following choices best defines your actions as a result of this error?

A. No effect because the Static Routes act the same way dynamic ones do, and will auto correct itself.

B. An immediate change must be made because there is no fault tolerance in regards to static routing.

C. A system reboot should be performed to clear all persistent routes.

D. None of the above.

Correct Answer & Explanation: **A**. The correct answer is **A**, because changes to the network or a failure between two statically defined nodes will cause any traffic between those points to not be rerouted. This means any packets that are awaiting transport between the affected paths will be forced to wait for repairs to the failure or for an updated static route by the administrator.

4. You are responsible for upgrading and configuring a large enterprise's LAN network to Windows Server 2008. It will include a high number of physical machines and will need to be scalable for aggressive growth over the next year as the company expands. Which of the following answers best describes why you should not use a Distance Vector Routing protocol like RIP for this task?

A. Distance Vector Routing Protocols like RIP are not scalable for large networks.

B. Distance Vector Routing Protocols like RIP are not usable for LAN configurations.

C. RIP does not understand VLSM.

D. All of the Above.

Correct Answer & Explanation: **A**. The correct answer is **A**, because RIP is limited in a number of ways due to its lack of scalability. It prevents routing loops from continuing indefinitely by implementing a limit on the number of hops allowed in a path from the source to a destination. It also limits the size of the network that RIP can support by design.

5. You are about to set up and configure a VPN for your client's communications server using Windows Server 2008. Before going through the set up and configuration process, which of the following steps need to be taken before you can configure the connection on the machine to ensure the best possible outcome?

A. Ensure a clean install of Windows Server 2008 has been installed.

B. Enter Add Roles Wizard and ensure that the RRAS role has been installed.

C. Both A and B.

D. Configure the SSTP protocols for the VPN.

Correct Answer & Explanation: **C**. The correct answer is **C**, because Microsoft recommends that a clean install of Windows Server 2008 be installed before configuring the RRAS role. Both of these choices are pre-requisites to setting up a VPN, and with RRAS installed you cannot proceed with the VPN configuration.

6. You are working with a server running the RRAS that is configured for the Windows authentication provider. You have administered several policies from RRAS to the server. Which of the following connection settings cannot be validated before authorization occurs by the policies you set up?

A. Advanced conditions such as access server identity, access client phone number, or MAC address.

B. Remote access permission.

C. Whether user account dial-in properties are ignored.

D. None of the above

Correct Answer & Explanation: **D**. The correct answer is **D**, None of the above. All of the listed conditions can be validated before authorization with Remote Access Policies. Advanced conditions such as access server identity access phone number or MAC address are easily accessible with Windows Server 2008.

7. Your company has begun a migration from Windows Server 2003 to Windows Server 2008 throughout their network. The RADIUS configurations for the old build were configured through IAS for Windows Server 2003. The new build for Windows Server 2008 will be using NPS. Which of the following statements would be true in regards to NPS?

A. The Connection Request Processing node still exists.

B. The Remote Access Logging folder still contains the Local File or SQL Server nodes.

C. The Network policies have replaced Remote Access policies and have been moved to the Policies node.

D. All of the Above.

Correct Answer & Explanation: **C.** The correct answer is **C**, because while those familiar with IAS may find much of the functionality the same, there have still been a significant number of changes to the interface that should be noted. There is no Connection Request Processing node and the Accounting node has replaced the Remote Access logging folder and no longer has the Local File or SQL Server nodes.

8. You are the administrator of a network employing the Network Access Protection snap-in in conjunction with NAP. You have configured a set of monitoring policies in NAP for use on the network. Which of the following options will the new NAP monitor policies of Windows Server 2008 be able to accomplish?

A. Recording for compliance of each PC logging in to the system.

B. Isolation of non-compliant users.

C. Restricting access of non-compliant users.

D. None of the above.

Correct Answer & Explanation: **A.** The correct answer is **A**, because NAP offers both Monitor and Isolate policies. Isolate policies would be able to accomplish choices **B** and **C**, but monitor policies would only be able to record the compliance of the PC's logging on to the network.

9. You are asked to reconfigure a cheap and efficient access solution using the newly installed Windows Server 2008's RRAS role for your company. The access solution must have medium data transfer rates and reliable

connection stability. The company's existing method of connection is ISDN and is utilizing the X.25 protocols for transfer. Which of the following changes in regards to Windows Server 2008 would need to be made to the existing system to make these adjustments?

A. The connection type should be downgraded, because the data transfer rate for ISDN is very unstable.

B. The connection type should be improved to Cable or DSL, because ISDN has the slowest data transfer rate.

C. The X.25 protocol needs to be changed because it is not supported by Windows Server 2008.

D. None of the above.

Correct Answer & Explanation: **C**. The correct answer is **C**, because Windows Server 2008 no longer supports X.25 protocol. The other options are not correct. The downgrade of the connection type would result in extremely slow data transfer rates. Improving the connection type would increase data transfer rates, but does not account for the lack of support of the X.25 protocol in Windows Server 2008.

10. You are setting up a communications server for your small- to medium-sized organization with private networks to handle their need to access resources on the Internet and other public networks. You have installed Windows Server 2008 and are using IPv4 currently. You need more globally unique (public) IPv4 addresses to accommodate the need to access to the Internet. Which of the following solutions is the most simple and cost effective?

A. Plan a conversion of the existing setup to accommodate IPv6, because it is supported by Windows Server 2008.

B. Enable the NAT technology on the computers of the corporate network.

C. Deploy a Proxy server.

D. None of the Above.

Correct Answer & Explanation: **B**. The correct answer is **B**, because NAT was designed to be the solution to for SOHO networking situations involving IPv4. It is much simpler to set up than setting up a proxy server. Although choice A is feasible with Windows Server 2008, due to its support of IPv6, it is an extremely complicated transition and not cost effective either.

Chapter 12: Network Access Protection

1. Network Access Protection (NAP) will only work with certain operating systems at the time of Windows 2008 Server release. What operating systems will NAP support?

   A. Windows XP

   B. Windows XP Service Pack 3

   C. Windows Vista

   D. Windows Server 2008

   Correct Answer & Explanation: **B,C,D**. At the time of this writing, the only operating systems that are supported by NAP are Windows XP Service Pack 3, Windows Vista and Windows Server 2008. Look for future operating system support via Independent Software Providers. Answer **A** is incorrect— Windows XP will need Service Pack 3 to support NAP.

2. Network Access Protection (NAP) can provide network protection to various types of network communications. Which of the following will not support NAP?

   A. NPS Connections

   B. DHCP Supported Network

   C. WINS Supported Network

   D. IEEE 802.11B Wireless Network

   Correct Answer & Explanation: **C**. NAP can provide network protection to the following network types: **A,B,D**. Internet Protocol security (IPsec) protected traffic, IEEE 802.1x authenticated networks, Dynamic Host Configuration Protocol (DHCP) address configurations and NPS VPN connections. All of the listed networks are supported except for the WINS Supported Network. WINS is not required on a Windows 2008 Server infrastructure unless old operating systems are in use.

3. Network Access Protection (NAP) was designed for third party vendors to take advantage of the infrastructure. This is really important for NAP to become popular throughout the IT community. What is the name of the item that allows third party developers to write programs that can take advantage of the NAP infrastructure?

   A. ISV

   B. HRA

C. API

D. CA

Correct Answer & Explanation: **C**. API stands for Application Programming Interface—this is what allows ISVs (Independent Software Vendors) tie their products in to other programs. Microsoft has provided an extensive API for NAP. Answer's **B** and **D** are acronyms that are dependant on each other— but do not help third party vendors; HRA stands for Health Registration Authority which requires a Certificate Authority (CA) to work. Answer **A** is an acronym that stands for Independent Software Vendor.

4. NAP enforcement points are what determine if a client wanting to connect to a restricted network is healthy and compliant. What are the valid enforcement points listed below?

A. Windows 2008 VPN Server

B. HUB

C. DHCP Server

D. IEEE 802.1x Network Access Device

Correct Answer & Explanation: **A,C,D**. All of the devices listed can be a network enforcement point except for a hub. Answer **B** is not correct because hubs are a physical layer device and is not 802.1x compliant like most switches.

5. The NAP Health Policy Server is responsible for storing health requirement policies and provides health state validation for the NAP Infrastructure. What Windows Server 2008 roles have to be installed for the NAP Health Policy Server to be configured?

A. Active Directory Domain Role

B. NPS Server Role

C. NAP Server Role

D. DHCP Server Role

Correct Answer & Explanation: **B**. The only Windows 2008 Server Role that needs to be installed to support a NAP Health Policy Server is the Network Policy Server Role. Other Windows 2008 Server roles can be installed along with the NPS Server Role—but, NPS is the primary role that needs to be installed. So, **A,C,D** are incorrect because they are not needed to install the NPS role on the Windows 2008 Server with the NPS Server Role.

6. You have decided to implement NAP into your existing network. During the design, you need to make a decision as to how the Restricted Network will be secured from the Remediation Network. Given the options below, which one(s) would work in this scenario?

   A. Use IPsec with Health Certificates

   B. Use a secondary switch to split the networks

   C. Use IP packet filters

   D. Use VLANs

   Correct Answer & Explanation: **A,C,D.** You have a couple of options to split the secured network from the remediation network. Using IPsec and Health Certification provides an excellent way to split the network. Any client connecting to the restricted network would have to present a valid Health Certificate to authenticate to the network. IP packet filters would work—especially if you where using a RRAS VPN as an enforcement point for the restricted network. Optionally, VLANs would suffice also—a VLAN would work fine, but adding secondary switches would not help secure the restricted network from the secured network. Answer **B** is incorrect because adding a second switch would not split the networks as needed for the infrastructure.

7. Using Figure 12.20 as a reference point, where would the Remediation Server be located on this network?

Figure 12.20 Network Design

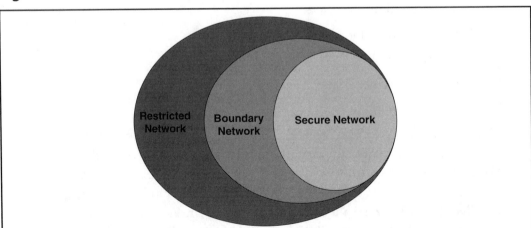

A. Secure Network

B. Boundary Network

C. Restricted Network

D. Location Does Not Matter

Correct Answer & Explanation: **B.** This network diagram represents an IPsec NAP enforcement design. The network is separated using Health Certificates. In this design, the Remediation Server would be located in the Boundary Network. This location would allow both the Secure Network to connect to the device via IPsec authentication and also allow the restricted network to connect so the clients can be remediated—then they would have access to the Secure Network. Answer **A** is incorrect because if the Remediation Server was located on the Secure Network, it would not be able to remediate noncompliant computers. Answer **C** is not correct because the Remediation Server needs to be accessible by both the Secured Network and Restricted Network. Location of the Remediation Server does matter so answer **D** is incorrect.

8. The remediation server could run Windows 2008 Server or Windows 2003 Server software. To remediate Windows Vista, Windows 2008 Server or Windows XP Service Pack 3—what other software would the remediation server need to run?

A. Windows Server Update Services (WSUS)

B. Network Protection Services (NPS)

C. Routing and Remote Access Services (RRAS)

D. Windows Security Health Validator (WSHV)

Correct Answer & Explanation: **A.** The remediation server would need to have some kind of software in place to correct clients and make them compliant to access the secured network. The Windows Security Health Validator is installed by default on clients. When these clients need to update Microsoft software—the will need Windows 2003 Server or Windows 2008 Server running Windows Server Update Services (WSUS). Answers **B** and **C** are incorrect because either service or role does not remediate an incompliant computer. The Windows Security Health Validator (WSHV) is the server side software that checks to see if the computer is compliant—it does not remediate the server; so answer **D** is incorrect.

9. You instruct your junior network administrator Heather to setup a NAP enforcement point using a DHCP server. After his installation, he comes to you complaining that DHCP is working fine—but he cannot get NAP to work with Windows Vista clients. You go through the installation with him—using 802.1x certified switches, he setup a Windows 2008 Server with both the DHCP and Network Policy and Access Services server roles. Once configured successfully, he set the DHCP settings for DHCPv6 Stateless Mode. Once configured—he set up the NPS policies with the NAP wizard. What is the problem with this scenario?

   A. The equipment needs to support 802.11 certified devices.

   B. Heather did not install Routing and Remote Access Services (RRAS) on the Windows 2008 Server.

   C. NAP does not support IPv6.

   D. Windows Vista needs to be updated to Service Pack 1 to work in this network.

   Correct Answer & Explanation: **C.** All of the information in this scenario is fine and should work except that NAP does not support IPv6. NAP only supports IPv4. Also answer **B** is incorrect, Windows 2008 Server does not have Routing and Remote Access Service or Internet Authentication Services—these services have been replaced by the Network Policy and Access Services Role. Answer **A** is incorrect because with a DHCP implementation, you do not need to have 802.1x certified devices. Answer **D** is incorrect—at the time of this writing, there is now Windows Vista Service Pack 1.

10. NAP Health Policies are a combination of settings for health determination and enforcement of infrastructure compliance. What are the sets of settings that make up the NAP Health Policies?

    A. Connection Request Policies

    B. Network Policies

    C. Health Policies

    D. Network Access Protection Settings

    Correct Answer & Explanation: **A, B, C, D.** All of the multiple choice answers are correct. NAP Health Policies are configured within the Network Policy Server console. NAP Health Policies are made up of all of the above choices.

Index

Syngress: *The Definition of a Serious Security Library*

Syn·gress (sin-gres): *noun, sing.* Freedom from risk or danger; safety. See *security*.

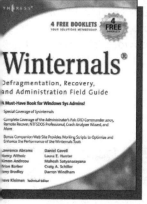

Winternals Defragmentation, Recovery, and Administration Field Guide

Dave Kleiman, Laura E. Hunter, Tony Bradley, Brian Barber, Nancy Altholz, Lawrence Abrams, Mahesh Satyanarayana, Darren Windham, Craig Schiller

As a system administrator for a Microsoft network, you know doubt spend too much of your life backing up data and restoring data, hunting down and removing malware and spyware, defragmenting disks, and improving the overall performance and reliability of your network. The Winternals® Defragmentation, Recovery, and Administration Field Guide and companion Web site provide you with all the information necessary to take full advantage of Winternals comprehensive and reliable tools suite for system administrators.

ISBN: 1-59749-079-2

Price: $49.95 US $64.95 CAN

Video Conferencing over IP: Configure, Secure, and Troubleshoot

Michael Gough

Until recently, the reality of videoconferencing didn't live up to the marketing hype. That's all changed. The network infrastructure and broadband capacity are now in place to deliver clear, real-time video and voice feeds between multiple points of contacts, with market leaders such as Cisco and Microsoft continuing to invest heavily in development. In addition, newcomers Skype and Google are poised to launch services and products targeting this market. *Video Conferencing over IP* is the perfect guide to getting up and running with video teleconferencing for small to medium-sized enterprises.

ISBN: 1-59749-063-6

Price: $49.95 U.S. $64.95 CAN

SYNGRESS®

Syngress: *The Definition of a Serious Security Library*

Syn·gress (sin–gres): *noun, sing.* Freedom from risk or danger; safety. See *security*.

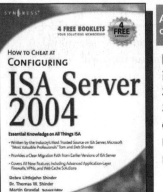

Syngress: *The Definition of a Serious Security Library*

Syn·gress (sin-gres): *noun, sing.* Freedom from risk or danger; safety. See *security.*

SYNGRESS®